Fourth Edition

UNDERSTANDING HUMAN EVOLUTION

Frank E. Poirier
The Ohio State University

Jeffrey K. McKee
The Ohio State University

Prentice Hall, Upper Saddle River, New Jersey 07458

Library of Congress Cataloging-in-Publication Data

Poirier, Frank E.
 Understanding human evolution / Frank E. Poirier and Jeffrey K.
McKee. — 4th ed.
  p. cm.
 Rev. ed. of: Understanding human evolution / Frank E. Poirier, 3rd
ed. c1993.
 Includes bibliographical references (p.) and index.
 ISBN 0–13–096152–3
 1. Fossil hominids. 2. Human evolution. 3. Prehistoric peoples.
I. McKee, Jeffrey Kevin. II. Title.
GN282.R35 1998
599.93'8—dc21   98–27730
                  CIP

Editorial director: *Charlyce Jones Owen*
Editor-in-chief: *Nancy Roberts*
Editorial assistant: *Maureen Diana*
Managing editor: *Ann Marie McCarthy*
Production liaison: *Fran Russello*
Editorial/production supervision and
 interior design: *P. M. Gordon Associates, Inc.*

Prepress and manufacturing buyer: *Lynn
 Pearlman*
Art director: *Jayne Conte*
Cover design: *Bruce Kenselaar*
Electronic art creation: *Asterisk Group, Inc.*
Marketing manager: *Christopher DeJohn*

This book was set in 10/12 New Baskerville by Pub-Set, Inc.
and was printed and bound by RR Donnelley & Sons Company.
The cover was printed by Phoenix Color Corp.

 © 1999, 1993, 1990, 1987 by Prentice-Hall, Inc.
Simon & Schuster/A Viacom Company
Upper Saddle River, New Jersey 07458

Printed in the United States of America
10 9 8 7 6 5 4 3 2 1

ISBN 0-13-096152-3

Prentice-Hall International (UK) Limited, *London*
Prentice-Hall of Australia Pty. Limited, *Sydney*
Prentice-Hall Canada Inc., *Toronto*
Prentice-Hall Hispanoamericana, S.A., *Mexico*
Prentice-Hall of India Private Limited, *New Delhi*
Prentice-Hall of Japan, Inc., *Tokyo*
Simon & Schuster Asia Pte. Ltd., *Singapore*
Editoria Prentice-Hall do Brasil, Ltda., *Rio de Janeiro*

As always, dedicated to my family,
Darlene, Alyson, and Sevanne—FEP

And dedicated to the McKees:
my parents, Jeannine and Bill;
my brothers and their families;
and especially to Jean, Nathan, and Aaron—JKM

And to our extended family,
the hominids

Contents

4

Reconstructing Ancient Human Behavior and Social Organizations: Use of the Comparative Approach   55

5

Early Primate Evolution   80

6

The Transition to Apes   94

7

Trends in Human Evolution   123

8

The Earliest Hominids   149

9

10

11

12

Neandertals and Their Immediate Predecessors   263

13

The Appearance of *Homo sapiens sapiens*   295

14

Preface

This book—an outgrowth of a desire to present an up-to-date picture of primate evolution in a relatively nontechnical manner that can be appreciated by the general reader—presents an overview of the field of paleoanthropology.

A major feature of this presentation is its approach to the study of the primate fossil record. Skeletal remains are viewed in light of what they can reveal about the populations they represent: their anatomy, behavior, and social organization. The primate fossil record is presented as an evolutionary theater and not merely as isolated bones uncovered by tireless investigators.

The text is written primarily for the uninitiated, and there are a number of features to aid the reader's comprehension and allow further research on the topics discussed. A glossary of many of the technical terms is appended as a reference. A number of theoretical possibilities provide the reader with alternative views.

Because our knowledge is changing rapidly, who knows what theory now in vogue or disrepute will be ignored or championed a few years hence? It would be a gross misreading of the material and a disservice to many working in the field if one were to close the book feeling that all the work has been done and that all questions have been settled. Few other fields of scientific endeavor leave so much unanswered and have so much work yet to be done. Perhaps some who read this book will rise to the challenge.

Until fairly recently, the discovery of evidence for primate evolution and earlier stages of human cultural development was largely the result of accident. Now, however, sufficient material exists for planned research to proceed. New technologies have provided new insights. Within recent times the following changes in fossil studies have occurred: (1) Paleoanthropology has become more concerned with framing questions than with simply collecting more evidence such as tools and fossils; (2) the successful application of newer dating techniques and the refinement of others have allowed a more accurate time scale to be established; and (3) the understanding of human evolution has expanded as its study has become interdisciplinary. The rapid development of the field of paleoanthropology and the remarkable success (as a result of both field and laboratory studies) obtained in understanding primate evolution are all the more dramatic given the limited funding available.

The scientific approach attempts to understand the universe through direct observation. Science searches for knowledge and understanding through the formulation of theories of nature. Scientific theories are first forwarded as hypotheses, which scientists utilize to explain phenomena. Together with certain initial data, a hypothesis entails the facts of observation. The hypothesis considers a supposition as if it were true, without actually accepting it as true. The researcher needs to have some clue as to what facts will help solve a problem. The best guide is a tentative hypothesis, which concurs with existing knowledge and is so framed that with its help the researcher can deduce that under certain conditions certain other facts will be found if the hypothesis is valid. The initial conditions of the hypothesis should be observable or experimentally produced, and the deduced facts should be observed. When assessing the strength or predictability of a hypothesis, stress is laid on the range and variety of facts that can be brought under its explanatory umbrella. Each hypothesis is tested against new information, and it can and should be modified to reflect new data or be rejected in favor of another.

Scientific theories are explanatory principles that stand the test of time. A theory may signify any hypothesis, whether confirmed or not, or it may be restricted to hypotheses that have been so strongly confirmed as to have become part of accepted scientific doctrine. A theory generally signifies a systematic account of some field of endeavor, derived from a set of general propositions. There may be rival theories, and scientists must jettison one theory for another if circumstances dictate. The scientific attitude is scientific only to the extent that its practitioners are prepared to admit that a favored theory is no longer functioning.

Science is about the systematic search for answers to questions. For paleoanthropology the main question is, **Who are we and how did we get here?** Paleoanthropologists are not the only ones seeking to answer the query. This is either **the** or **a** fundamental question for anthropology, philosophy, and theology, for example. This book records scientific endeavors to explain who we are and how we got here. We try to explain human evolution and try to place humans into the context of geological and biological change on planet Earth.

Scientists often work in steps, first asking limited questions to get at a broader question. One discovery may lead to another; one question may be the basis of another question; one answer may lead to another question. Major scientific breakthroughs are usually the result of the work of many people building upon one another's work.

Knowledge advances through seeking answers to questions. The following questions were asked and answered in the process of formulating the modern theory of evolution. Geologists provided hypotheses (often competing at first) to explain geological change and the appearance of fossils. First Jean-Baptiste de Lamarck and then Charles Darwin and Alfred R. Wallace asked why there was variation in life and how such variation was produced and maintained. Having provided the answer as to why variation exists, Darwin attempted to explain how such variation was passed generationally. His explanation was incorrect. Gregor Mendel asked the same question, and provided the correct answer. The synthesis of Mendel's theories with the Darwin/Wallace hypothesis led to new insights and a more comprehensive theory of evolution.

Observing phenomena is only one part of the scientific endeavor. The phenomena need to be explained, measured, and described. Sometimes a problem cannot be approached directly because of the nature of the available evidence. For example, the knowledge we seek about the behavior and social organization of extinct human and nonhuman primates is only partially attainable through analysis of their fossilized remains. We use models such as living monkeys and apes to overcome this obstacle (Chapter 4). Monkeys, apes, and humans share an evolutionary history (Chapter 3).

New technologies developed in geology, chemistry, and molecular genetics provide data greatly enhancing the work of anthropologists. The fruits of some of these technologies are discussed in Chapter 3, where we describe the genetic evidence that reveals the closeness of the human-ape relationship, and in Chapter 1, where we discuss how new dating techniques have provided new insights into the evolutionary relationships of our primate ancestors.

Neither the scientific method nor its practitioners are infallible. Because the scientific method requires replicability, wrong answers and misplaced emphases eventually save time because they represent an avenue of investigation that was tried and proved fruitless. Science thus becomes a self-correcting process, working toward the realization of objective truths about nature. The evolutionary origin of the diversity of life on earth today appears to be one of those objective truths.

Many authors have a particular theoretical perspective they wish to champion. This statement is especially true of the scholarship in paleoanthropology. A conscious effort is made here to prevent our views from becoming the focal point of this presentation. Students do not need to be told that one viewpoint is gospel; they need a wide spectrum of explanations, which we have attempted to provide by describing feasible alternatives. In a true learning situation, students should be helped to form opinions based on current evidence. Hopefully, enough evidence for conflicting viewpoints is presented here so that students can begin this opinion-making process.

Discoveries occurred as this book was being published. This is the frustrating, yet fascinating, aspect of this work. New frameworks appear as the fossils themselves emerge from their long entombment beneath centuries of sedimentary deposition. Explanations based on earlier materials are constantly being revised, and in this sense, the text must always be somewhat dated. However, the revision process must not be taken to mean that all that appears is mere guesswork. To reach this conclusion precludes discovery and reveals a bias against the scientific method. The scientific method demands revision, the testing and retesting of hypotheses, and only in this manner can scientific understanding inch forward.

The following acknowledgments are particularly important because this book would have been impossible without the help of many persons. First and foremost, we offer thanks to the hundreds of tireless scholars whose work is noted herein. Their efforts have provided many wonderful hours of reading and teaching. We have quoted and referred to so many individuals that we can only trust we have portrayed their ideas accurately and have given them credit where appropriate. We acknowledge the help and insight of numerous graduate and undergraduate students whose probing questions and keen interest forced us to rethink, reread, and rephrase much of what follows. We thank Nancy Roberts and Robert Thoresen of Prentice Hall for their help. We also thank Kristin Ossa and John Seyler for their assistance.

Frank E. Poirier
Jeffrey K. McKee

1

Fossils, Fossilization, and Dating Methods

The Fossilization Process
Dating Fossil Materials
Determining Past Environments
Summary
Suggested Readings

Fossilization is a rare event affected by the nature of the material being fossilized, climate, and geology. Different body parts fossilize at different rates and incidences. Large bones, such as leg bones, and materials with high mineral contents, such as teeth, are the most likely to fossilize.

The scientific value of an artifact or fossil depends heavily on accurate dating of either the specimen or the deposit in which it is found. Methods used to date remains or geological deposits fall into the category of either relative or chronometric dating techniques. The former technique provides a chronological sequence of youngest to oldest. Chronometric dating methods provide an actual numerical date. Most contemporary evolutionary schemes rely upon chronometric dating.

THE FOSSILIZATION PROCESS

Fossilization rarely occurs, and fossil finds are a rare event. **Fossils** (boldfaced words appear in the Glossary) are either the remains or the imprints left in soil or rock of plants or animals that once existed. The word *fossil*, from a Latin word that means "dug from the earth," was once applied to rocks and minerals, as well as to organic materials. Eventually it became apparent that rocks, minerals, and "fossils" had a different origin and nature. The word *fossil* is now reserved for the remains or indications of the remains of ancient organisms. The most common process in the formation of fossils involves the preservation of specific parts of an organism. Most commonly in fossilization the organic components of the organism are replaced by minerals. For example, when bone is deposited and exposed to soils, its original components begin a series of gradual chemical reactions with the materials surrounding it. As water seeps through soil, minerals contained in the water often fill gaps left by decomposing organic substances, and the bone fossilizes.

A dead organism is quickly destroyed by bacteria and fungi, which cause decay. Many organisms are also scavenged upon death—the scavengers destroy and disperse the dead organism. Destruction can be prevented or minimized if the organism is protected by burial in a stream or lake, in a cave, in mud, or in volcanic ash. Even if this fortuitous event occurs, most parts of the organism may be destroyed before burial and fossilization.

Organisms living in or near water have a far better chance of leaving a trace of their existence than do those inhabiting humid jungles, where fossilization conditions are very poor (however, Peterhaus et al., 1993, provide an exception). Fortunately for *paleoanthropology*, one of the scientific specialties that study primate fossils, primates tend to live close to water sources and thereby increase their chances of fossilization.

Caves are good sources for fossilized remains because cave deposits are often protected from the ravages of weather and time. Although early humans do not seem to have inhabited caves, their bones were often dragged into caves for consumption by predators or scavengers. Because caves are relatively sheltered environments, remains found there are sometimes quite complete and in a relatively good state of preservation—as we will learn in later chapters. Caves have been occupied or used by humans over long time periods. The accumulated dirt and debris in the cave may reveal a long and often startlingly clear history of occupation.

Usually the older the geological deposits, the less chance there is of uncovering fossil remains, because of the process of decomposition. This and the fact that earlier life forms are often found more rarely are two reasons why the human fossil record of 2 to 5 million years ago is rather scanty when compared to the record of human evolution 50,000 years ago. Not only were humans more numerous 50,000 years ago, but they also inhabited a wider geographical area. In later stages of human evolution the practice of deliberate burials contributed to preservation and fossilization.

Different body parts fossilize at different rates. The so-called hard tissues (the bones and teeth) are partially composed of inorganic minerals and are more likely to fossilize because of their high mineral content. Soft tissues, that is, skin, muscles, and cartilage, are unlikely to fossilize. Usually, the higher the bone's mineral content, the greater the chance of fossilization. Teeth, which contain over 90 percent mineral content, are the most commonly fossilized body parts. The harder and larger bones, such as the upper leg bone (the **femur**) and the upper arm bone (the **humerus**), are much more commonly fossilized than lighter bones such as the ribs. The fossilization event is also influenced by the type of soil in which the material comes to rest.

Taphonomy, the study of the fossilization process, has revealed a wealth of useful information about fossilization (Andrews, 1991; Behrensmeyer, 1984). Taphonomic analysis can tell whether bones or debris was disturbed pre- or post-mortem, for example, by a predator or scavenger. Taphonomic analysis can also reveal much about the environmental context through demonstrating how materials were deposited. Deposits disturbed by water will contain a higher proportion of heavier bones and a lesser proportion of lighter bones—which are more likely to have been washed away.

Taphonomic studies consider the geological and biological processes that have helped to accumulate, modify, and bury remains. The goal of taphonomic analysis is to assess the contribution of geological events, carnivore and human activity, and other factors to the formation of clusters of animal bone and stone artifacts. Taphonomic analysis helps to assess if and what kind of human activity was responsible for the pattern of distribution of the debris that is excavated. If humans deposited at least some of the remains at the **site**, it is then necessary to assess the kinds of activities that occurred there. In archaeological studies, *sites* are locations, often of varying sizes, where traces of occupation or activity are found.

Even bones that fossilize can be destroyed or become distorted during the fossilization process. Many fossilized skulls, for example, were distorted during fossilization by the weight of the earth pressing down on them. Sometimes soft tissue such as the brain, which is cradled by bone, may be destroyed; but the space left by the brain may be filled by mud or other material, which then hardens and provides a mold or cast of the tissue. In the case of the brain, such a mold is called an **endocranial cast** or *endocast*. The endocranial cast, an impression of the interior of the braincase, can provide an impression of the gross structure and size of the brain, but little else. For example, the endocast can tell little about structures and functions buried deep in the brain's interior.

The fossilization process is dependent on local conditions, occurring quite rapidly in some areas and quite slowly in others. Despite the many variables influencing fossilization, and despite the rarity of fossils, fossil remains continue to be a prime form of evidence for interpreting evolutionary history.

DATING FOSSIL MATERIALS

Although the recovery of new and important fossils often makes the headlines, it is only one part of paleoanthropological studies. The importance of any fossil is directly associated with whether the fossil itself or the deposit from which it is derived can be dated (Table 1-1).

TABLE 1-1   Some Major Methods for Determining Chronometric Ages

Time Period	Dating Method
Modern period to 2500 B.C.	Historical documents, tree ring (dendrochronology), glacial varve
Recent times to ca. 50,000 years	Carbon 14, amino acid racemization (amino acids other than aspartic acid can be used to obtain dates older than 50,000 years), thermoluminescence (TL), electron-spin resonance (ESR)
50,000 to 500,000 years	Various means utilized, but there is no good accuracy here; many of these dates are assessed through relative dating, TL, ESR
500,000 years to 3 billion years ago	Potassium-argon, fission track

Fossil remains are put within a time sequence so that the **osteological** (bone) evidence can be placed within an evolutionary sequence and so that environmental information for a site can be correlated with fossil or cultural remains. Rigorous dating also eliminates questionable materials. Answers to two questions are sought when the age of a fossil or cultural specimen is considered: (1) What is the relationship of the specimen to the geological, floral, faunal, and archaeological sequence at the site? and (2) What is the chronological age of the specimen in years **B.P.** (before present, that is, before 1950)? The first query asks if the fossilized remains are contemporaneous with the deposit in which they lie, and, therefore, whether the site's faunal, floral, climatic, and archaeological information can be properly associated with the find. The answer to the second query provides a figure—the chronometric age of the fossil.

Determining the chronological order of fossil remains is fundamental to understanding their evolutionary relationships. To establish the contemporaneity of osteological or cultural material with the enclosing deposit, it must be demonstrated that the deposit has not been unnaturally disturbed and that there is no possibility of an intrusive derivation from younger to older deposits. Unless these conditions are met, all dates are suspect. A poorly excavated site is largely devoid of scientific value; an undated site is of questionable value and continually open to speculation.

There are two categories of dating techniques: **relative dating** and **chronometric dating**. Both are necessary because they are applicable to different situations. Relative dating establishes that one object is older or younger than something else; thus it is possible to arrange objects in chronological order, although the total time span and interval between the items being compared are unknown. Relative dating establishes a sequence; chronometric dating determines the actual chronological age of a specimen or source deposit.

Cross-dating establishes relationships between assemblages, or significant elements therein, from various geographic locales. Cross-dating ties sites into a preexisting scheme; sites must be cross-dated with other sites to establish temporal relationships.

Relative Dating

It is important to determine if the archaeological and bone evidence is contemporaneous with the deposit in which it lies and to determine the **stratigraphy** at the site, that is, the relative vertical position of the objects in the soil. In an undisturbed site, materials in the lowest levels should be the oldest. In a disturbed site, other dating methods may be useful, but these yield far less conclusive evidence than in an undisturbed site. One of these methods is relative dating by typology, which is based on the fact that objects and organisms undergo changes that reflect general cultural change or, in the case of organisms, evolutionary change. It may be possible on this basis to arrange objects or organisms of different ages in a time sequence.

When an object is not associated with organic material useful in age determination, or when a fossil is found out of stratigraphic context, it can sometimes be dated by its **morphology** (its form or structure). Morphological dating should be attempted only if there is a large well-known fossil series with a well-documented evolutionary history. If such a history is available, bone remains often can be dated according to the tool types with which they are associated. This, however, leads to problems, because archaic human fossils have been found with what are considered to be more advanced tool types and vice versa.

Faunal analysis is an important means of establishing a relative chronological framework for fossil sites. There is a continual emergence and spreading of new faunal forms and extinction of older types, and animals often migrate in response to climatic oscillations. Some genera and species are more useful than others as age indicators. For example, the most useful mammalian groups for correlating Pleistocene deposits include the elephant, rhinoceros, bear, hyena, deer, and antelope. Major limitations for worldwide or even continental correlation of faunal remains are the facts that some forms do not migrate far and that most widespread species fail to cross certain barriers.

Elephants are useful markers of Pleistocene subdivisions. Although there is a temporal overlap of elephant species, the time of the first appearance of each species serves to demarcate the base of a Pleistocene subdivision. The dating of European human fossil sites relies on the contiguous evidence of associated fossil elephant remains.

Hyenas, especially *Crocuta crocuta,* have proved useful for purposes of relative dating. *C. crocuta* evolved from the Indian species and spread rapidly throughout other parts of Asia and Africa, replacing *C. brevirostris* around the time of the Mindel glaciation. The presence or absence of each species serves as a temporal marker.

Some mammalian fossils indicate a climatic stage rather than a restricted time period. It may be inferred, for example, that a deposit containing hippopotamus is of a different climatic period than one containing musk ox. Fossil invertebrates are also used for correlating Pleistocene deposits; freshwater and land mollusks (e.g., snails), as well as insects, are valuable climatic indicators. Some of these have restricted time ranges, making them additionally valuable as time indicators.

Faunal dating has been particularly important for establishing the temporal context of early hominid fossils from South Africa. These fossils are mostly found in cave deposits that are not conducive to chronometric dating techniques. By comparing the presence of extinct species with the well-dated sites of East Africa, the cave sites can be bracketed within a likely time frame.

A major problem with faunal dating is the existence of what are commonly called *relic faunas.* Species or genera survive in some areas after dying out in others, making it dangerous to infer contemporaneity of deposits over long distances simply on the basis of shared faunal assemblages. Many members of the African fauna survived, whereas their relatives died out in Europe, a situation complicating cross-dating. A similar problem arises from biogeographic differences between East and South Africa. It is thus valuable to establish a relative chronological sequence, known as a *seriation,* within a particular region. Sites can be seriated on the proportion and types of extinct species found relative to extant species of the fossil assemblages. Used cautiously and with a suitably reliable paleontological history, faunal dating and climatic inferences can be quite useful.

A major means of relative dating involves testing bone to establish its contemporaneity with other bones in a deposit or with the soil deposit itself. Three major analytical methods of bone dating include fluorine, nitrogen, and uranium dating (Oakley, 1970). These methods are especially important in disturbed sites, where it is necessary to determine the contemporaneity of the materials. The relative age of fossil bone is determined by comparing its chemical composition with other fossil bone of known ages from the same site or the same area if they are preserved under comparable conditions. When buried, bone composition is subject to chemical changes. The organic matter of bone is mainly fat and protein (collagen); the fatty matter disappears soon after burial, but the protein disappears at a much slower rate.

Fluorine dating depends on groundwater seepage through the bones. Fluorine in the water combines with the bone's calcium to form a compound known as fluorapatite, the measurement of which from various bones in a site determines their contemporaneity or lack thereof. Fluorine dating allows bones of an assemblage to be tested for stratigraphical equivalence because contemporaneous bones should contain roughly the same amount of fluorapatite.

Nitrogen dating of bone is often coupled with fluorine dating because the results complement one another. Bones that have accumulated little fluorine retain much nitrogen and vice versa. Nitrogen tests are most useful for assaying whether enough collagen degradation has occurred to attempt to date the bone directly by the radiocarbon method (pages 7–9), which often entails destroying part of what may already be a small sample.

Uranium circulates in the bloodstream and is fixed in the mineral matter of bone, probably through calcium ion replacement. The same replacement process occurs in buried bones through percolation of groundwater containing traces of uranium. The longer a bone lies in a deposit, the more uranium it absorbs. Uranium is radioactive, and its content within bone can be measured by determining the amount of radioactive deterioration. Although the amount of radioactivity varies in bones from different sites, its progressive buildup with increasing age has been established. Uranium analysis can sometimes serve to distinguish between specimens that for various reasons are younger or older than the containing deposit. It has a clear advantage over fluorine dating because it does not involve bone destruction.

These three relative dating methods are useful only in circumscribed situations. The major drawback is that they do not permit cross-dating; that is, the information at one site cannot be compared with the information at a different site. The prime value of relative dating lies in determining the relative ages of bone or bone objects from the same deposit. Because of the variables involved, it is usually impossible to use fluorine, nitrogen, or radioactive content as more than a rough guide to the geological age of an isolated specimen. The major problem with all three methods lies in the fact that ground soils vary, permitting differing amounts of percolating water. Fluorine cross-dating is especially hampered by the fact that the amount of fluorine permeating through a bone depends on the amount present in the groundwater, which varies from place to place. Therefore, bones of the same age from different areas might have very different fluorine contents.

Paleomagnetic dating is based on the facts that the Earth's magnetic field periodically change in direction and intensity, and that these changes can leave natural records. The magnetic pole is now oriented in a northerly direction, but this statement was not always true. Paleomagnetic dating involves taking samples of sediments that contain magnetically charged particles. Such particles retain the magnetic orientation they had when becoming consolidated into rock. Such changes take 5,000 years to occur.

Geomagnetic polarity epochs that last between 0.5 and 1 million years have been established. Polarity was reversed between 0.5 and 2.5 million years ago (mya) and before 3.4 mya. Over the past 4 million years or so, it has been possible to determine the history of polarity changes with some precision and to construct what is called *reversal chronology*. Throughout this time, there has been no period longer than about 600,000 years that has not witnessed a paleomagnetic change unique in terms of its frequency and duration. Reversal chronology has been used successfully at a number of human fossil sites in East Africa, for example, at Olduvai Gorge, Tanzania; Lake Turkana, Kenya; and Omo, Ethiopia. Kappelman (1993) provides a good review of paleomagnetic dating.

Chronometric Dating

Of the various chronometric dating methods, radiocarbon (carbon 14) is most useful for dating from 500 years ago to 70,000 to 50,000 years ago. Radiocarbon dating has been greatly improved and the time span extended since it was first devised by the physicist W. F. Libby (Aitken, 1961; Libby, 1955). Although all organic materials are theoretically susceptible to radiocarbon dating, some are more readily datable and require far smaller samples. The best substance is charcoal, a common organic remain in archaeological sites (sites showing human alteration or occupation). A sample of 1 gram of charcoal is adequate. Radiocarbon dating is fairly reliable provided that proper precautions are taken in selecting samples and ensuring that they have not been contaminated by additional radiocarbon from more recent materials.

There have been great improvements in C^{14} (also written as ^{14}C) dating in the last decade—through the use of high-energy accelerators, for example, which allow a direct reading of the decay of C^{14} to C^{12} atoms. This contrasts with the less accurate, indirect approach of measuring radioactive emissions and inferring the number of carbon atoms from that signal. The new technique allows the use of smaller samples, and the process is faster.

Although wood charcoal is best for radiocarbon dating, burned and unburned bone can be used. A fairly large sample, from 20 to 100+ grams, of unburned bone is required because it does not contain much carbon. It does, however, contain collagen, which is rich in carbon, and the carbon can be extracted and dated. A few finds have been directly radiocarbon dated. Most skeletal finds are incomplete, and researchers are hesitant to destroy the amount necessary for the C^{14} dating procedure; they rely instead on radiocarbon dates of associated but more expendable materials.

The basic principle behind the method is that cosmic radiation produces a small amount of the radiocarbon isotope C^{14} in the atmosphere. A more or less constant level of C^{14} is present in Earth's atmosphere. Assimilation of carbon, in the form of carbon dioxide, includes a certain amount of the C^{14} isotope. Carbon 14 is present in the cellular structure of all plants and animals. Water also absorbs carbon dioxide, which is exchanged between the atmosphere and hydrosphere, so that inorganic as well as organic sedimentation of carbonates includes a ratio of C^{12} to C^{14}.

Plants maintain their C^{14} level during oxygen exchange with the atmosphere; animals maintain their level from eating plants or other animals that have eaten plants. Organisms lose C^{14} at a steady rate, but they also take it in, so the equilibrium is maintained throughout life. Intake promptly ceases upon death, and the C^{14} present begins to disintegrate radioactively into nitrogen. Because disintegration occurs at a known rate (based on C^{14}'s half-life of 5,730 or 5,568 years), by measuring the amount of C^{14} in a dead organism one can calculate the length of time in "radioactive years" that has elapsed since the organism lived. **Half-life** refers to the length of time during which half the original atoms have disintegrated. After one half-life, the amount of radioactive isotope is halved. After a span of another half-life, half of the remaining atoms, or one-quarter of the original atoms, remain. This process of halving the rate of radioactive decay allows dating.

Radiocarbon dates indicate a time interval within which there is a 66 percent chance that the actual age of the dated material most probably lies. This age is expressed in terms of a date midway between two points, representing a margin of error of one standard deviation. The limits are indicated by plus (+) and minus (−) signs; a typical C^{14} date reads 40,000 ± 1,000 years. The older the sample, usually the higher the plus or minus figure. Generally speaking, the lack of absolute precision in these dates is not a serious problem given the material and the time spans involved.

Three major types of radiocarbon dating errors reduce the value of the technique (Butzer, 1964): (1) statistical errors as indicated by the plus or minus dates; (2) errors pertaining to the C^{14} level of the sample itself; and (3) errors related to laboratory storage, preparation, and management. Errors relating to the C^{14} level of the sample itself result from past fluctuations of C^{14} intake and unequal C^{14} concentration in different materials, as well as from contamination. Some dates diverge from the true age of the sample more than others. Contamination of a C^{14} sample by ancient organic materials, such as coal, can lead to a misrepresentation of age. Corrections also must be made for past fluctuations in the amount of atmospheric C^{14}. Volcanoes can sometimes add other forms of carbon to the atmosphere, temporarily lowering the proportion of C^{14} and resulting in a sample dated older than it actually is.

When reading a radiocarbon date, one must ask what is being dated. Various dates have different reliability and are not strictly comparable because of differences in technique and basic assumptions on the part of the laboratory running the test. A series of dates from any one laboratory is needed. One single date from one sample from one laboratory compared with one single date from one sample from a different laboratory is of limited value.

Electron-spin resonance (ESR) and thermoluminescence (TL) both test for minute, radiation-induced changes in crystal. Both methods have been key in providing dates for the earliest recognizable members of modern *Homo sapiens* in the Middle East and Africa (Chapter 13). ESR and TL date a time period reaching beyond the normal range of C^{14} and prior to approximately 500,000 years ago.

Both ESR and TL measure radiation damage sites by examining the behavior of electrons trapped in the sites. The number of sites increases with age, because ionizing radiation from such natural sources as uranium and thorium penetrates crystal and punches "holes" in the structure. Both ESR and TL measure radiation damage. In addition, both ESR and TL share the weakness of assuming that present-day estimates of radiation dose rates can be applied retroactively. In reality, however, rates change (Marshall, 1990) and must be corrected for.

Doubts have been expressed about the results yielded in TL dating (Gibbons, 1997). Luminescence dating relies on a clock set to natural radiation in common minerals like quartz and feldspar. Radiation bumps electrons from their normal positions in the mineral's crystal lattice into traps, or defects, at a roughly constant rate over time. Exposure to sunlight or heat from a fire at a human occupation site empties many of the traps, setting the clock back to zero. When the site is abandoned, the clock begins anew. As long as the mineral grains remain in the dark, the traps refill with electrons at a regular rate.

Because of their extraordinary antiquity, TL dates at some recently discovered sites have raised concerns. For example, the Jinmium site in Australia (Chapter 13) may be much more recent than originally reported. The same can be said of the Katanda site in Africa (Chapter 13) and of the Diring Yuriakh site in Siberia (Chapter 10).

Radiocarbon dating encompasses the most recent periods of human evolution, but it leaves a large percentage of human history beyond reach. This period is dated with other techniques, one of which is **potassium-argon, or K/Ar, dating**. This method ascertains the age of volcanic materials and other igneous rocks (rocks of volcanic origin) as well as tektites, which are glasslike objects thought to have been formed during the impact of large meteorites on Earth's surface and diffused over large areas. Potassium-argon dates the age of the deposits in which the materials are found and not the object itself. The principles of K/Ar dating are analogous to those of radiocarbon dating, whereby the ratio of $^{40}K/^{40}Ar$ indicates the degree of decay and hence age. Potassium-argon's half-life is 1,330 million years. The lower datable range is 500,000 years, with an upper range of 3 billion years.

Potassium-argon dating measures the accretion of daughter atoms. The radioactive potassium isotope potassium-40 (^{40}K) occurs in all natural potassium. Part of this minute amount decays to stable argon-40 (^{40}Ar) atoms. If a sample of potassium-containing rock is melted in a vacuum, these atoms can be counted. The age of the sample can be measured by comparing this amount to the known isotopic abundance of ^{40}K in natural potassium and applying the decay constant derived from its half-life. However, if argon gas gets trapped in a sample and if such argon is measured along with that derived from the decay of radioactive potassium, the resultant date will be too old. Because volcanic rocks crystallize at temperatures at which no mineral can retain argon, they are the favored samples for K/Ar dating.

Potassium-argon dating has been of exceptional value in the case of East African volcanic deposits. It has also been used to help determine the age of *Homo erectus* (an early human group; see Chapter 10) from the Trinil faunal beds in central Java.

Potassium-argon dating has limitations. The main problem is selection of suitable datable material because this dating method is used primarily in volcanic areas. The datable sample need not come from the fossiliferous deposit but can come from a different deposit containing datable material. The problem then is to relate the dated sample to the sample one is trying to date. Although K/Ar dating is promising, datable volcanic deposits are lacking in many situations badly needing dating. Because one source of potential error is statistical, K/Ar dates are given within plus or minus ranges. Contamination must be avoided, and duplication of dates is important.

Fission-track dating was originally devised to date manufactured glass. Many volcanic ashes contain zircons, which are crystals of zirconium silicate, a mineral that always contains trace amounts of the radioactive isotope uranium 238. Because it is radioactive, uranium 238 atoms decay at a precisely known rate. When the uranium 238 atom explodes, it tears its nucleus into two halves, each of which is propelled in an opposite direction through the crystal. Each time a uranium 238 atom fissions, a tiny tunnel is bored out through the crystal. In fission-track dating the number of such fission tracks within the zircon crystal is counted: the greater the number of tracks, the older the specimen. Each volcanic eruption provides a new set of tracks. A good review is found in Wagner (1996).

The material used to fission-track date an early hominid site at Bed I at Olduvai Gorge, Tanzania, was obtained from the same deposit that yielded the sample for the K/Ar date. The fission-track date of 2.0 ± 0.28 million years compared well with the average K/Ar date of 1.8 mya. Fission-track dating is extremely important because possible sources of error differ from those of K/Ar dating. If dates from both methods agree, a fairly accurate age determination is assured. A major problem with fission-track dating is that too much heat destroys the tracks, leading to a low age estimate. By dating obsidian (volcanic glass) flows from various sources, fission-track dating can prove useful for identifying the geographical locations of obsidian used in artifact manufacture.

Amino acid racemization is another chronometric dating technique. All living organisms have L-amino acids in their proteins, but after death and over long time periods all L-amino acids except glycine undergo a change called *racemization* and become nonprotein D-amino acids. The proportion of D-amino acids to L-amino acids increases with time, and the age of skeletal material can be estimated by determining the amount of change, racemization, that has occurred. The racemization process is the conversion of an optically active substance into a racemic or optically inactive substance. Amino acids do not racemize at the same rate; for skeletal material in the age range of 5,000 to 100,000 years, aspartic acid provides the best results. This method has advantages over radiocarbon dating; much smaller bone quantities are needed, and the practical dating range of aspartic amino acid racemization of 100,000 years is appreciably longer than the 50,000-plus year range of radiocarbon dating (Bada et al., 1974). Heat, soil pH, and climate all affect the accuracy of amino acid dating.

Amino acid racemization dating can be valuable for dating mollusks and ostrich eggs, as well as eggshells generally (Brooks et al., 1990). This fact is potentially important because many human paleontological sites contain eggshell remnants. Amino acid racemization dating of ostrich eggshells seems to provide a new tool to date the period from 40,000 to 180,000 years ago, the time when anatomically modern humans were appearing. Many such human specimens come from sites in Africa and the Middle East, sites rich with ostrich eggshell remains.

Amino acid racemization dates of ostrich eggshells from the very important Middle Eastern site of Qafzeh cave (Chapter 12) suggest that early anatomically modern human populations intermittently occupied the cave at least 20,000 to 30,000 years ago. The ostrich eggshell dates at a South African cave called Boomplaas indicate that an unusually sophisticated stone tool complex was being manufactured as early as 80,000 years ago. The same technology is dated to approximately the same time at the South African cave sites of Border Cave and Klasies River Mouth, both of which may yield examples of anatomically modern *H. sapiens* (see Chapter 13).

DETERMINING PAST ENVIRONMENTS

Human evolution can only be understood within an ecological context. We must look beyond a series of fossils with particular morphological traits, for the fossils represent living beings that were trying to survive in a sometimes hostile world.

Many features of the **hominids** (past and present members of the taxonomic family of humans) resulted from adaptations to their ecological **niche** (the role they played in the community of plants and animals) within a particular **habitat** (the local environment in which they lived). The hominid course of evolution was shaped by the foods they could find, the shelter they secured, and the predators they tried to avoid. The study of prehistoric environments and ecological relationships is known as **paleoecology**.

The relevant features of the environment that may have affected human evolution range from climate and geology down to the local animal communities in which ancestral humans lived, including members of their own families. The amount and type of vegetative cover, even the microbes in the environment, all played a part in the evolutionary process. It is worth taking a generalized look at how each of these components may have been relevant, as well as at trends that are evident.

Climate and Geology

Global climatic changes accompanied the stages of primate evolution, including that of humans. At the time of primate origins in the Eocene epoch (Chapters 3 and 4, Table 3-2), 55 million years ago, the world was considerably warmer and wetter. Once the first higher primates evolved in the Oligocene (beginning around 34 mya), a slow trend of cooling and drying began, and antarctic ice began to build. By about 6 mya, enough polar ice had accumulated to lower sea levels considerably, possibly affecting hominid origins in Africa (Chapter 8). The Mediterranean Sea became isolated from the other oceans and began to dry into a barren land, an event known as the **Messinian salinity crisis**. Although the sea basin was not an inviting environment, it did allow an exchange of mammals between Europe and Africa, thus shaping the mammalian community with which the earliest hominids had to live and compete for resources.

By about 3.3 mya, after hominids had established themselves in Africa for up to 2 million years, a further decline in temperatures began. This culminated about 2.5 mya, with 41,000-year cycles of temperature fluctuations above and below present values. With these fluctuations came greater seasonality across the African continent and a gradual drying trend that affected the patterns of vegetation; in particular, the African forests dwindled at the expense of savanna grasslands and desert.

Another significant climatic change occurred about 900,000 ya, during the Pleistocene epoch, challenging the members of our genus *Homo* who by that time had spread from Africa to other parts of the Old World. Temperature fluctuations shifted to cycles lasting about 100,000 years each, and temperature declines left many high-latitude regions under ice. These **glaciations** determined the movements and adaptations of a variety of plants and animals, including humans. The major European glaciations were originally named Günz, Mindel, Riss, and Würm, after Alpine valleys (Table 1-2). These glacial periods were subdivided into two or more cold phases, or *stadials*, and separated by the warmer

TABLE 1-2 European and North American Glaciations

Dating (years ago)	Scandinavian	Alpine	North American
75,000–10,000	Weichsel	Würm	Wisconsin
125,000–75,000	Eem Interglacial	Riss-Würm Interglacial	Sangamon Inter.
265,000–125,000	Saale	Riss	Illinoian
300,000–265,000	Holstein Interglacial	Mindel-Riss Interglacial	
435,000–300,000	Elster	Mindel	
500,000–435,000	Cromerian Interglacial	Günz-Mindel Interglacial	
before 500,000	Menapian	Günz	

Note: Except for the Würm glaciation, the exact dates for the glacial and interglacial periods are unsettled.

interstadials. The glaciations themselves were not all unrelentingly cold; temperatures fluctuated as the ice sheets advanced and retreated. The glaciations alternated with warmer periods known as *interglacials*. At lower elevations and lower latitudes, sea levels rose during the warmer interglacials because of melting of portions of the ice sheets.

Pleistocene glaciations most drastically affected the higher latitudes in North America and Europe. The ice sheets covered up to three times as much land area as they do today. In the more tropical latitudes, less conspicuous and very complex climatic shifts also occurred. The shifts in climatic zones depended on the extent of the arctic zones. For example, during colder periods the dry Sahara supported some grasslands, and the Mediterranean became a temperate sea. Snow lines were sometimes lowered on tropical mountain ranges, and rain forests expanded and contracted, depending on the amount of rainfall.

The vast ice sheets held enormous amounts of water, lowering sea levels far below their present position. Land bridges were formed as the sea level dropped and exposed the continental shelf. It was across one of these land bridges, called Beringia, that human migrants crossed out of what is now Siberia and into what is today called Alaska and Canada and moved south to colonize the New World. These immigrants were the ancestors of today's Native Americans (Chapter 13).

Throughout the course of primate evolution, the tectonic forces that moved continents and shaped their geological structure also affected the distributions and adaptations of plant and animal species. For example, the separation of Africa from South America divided the early monkeys, allowing completely separate evolutionary pathways on the respective continents (Chapter 5). Likewise, the uplift of the African continent (Partridge, Wood, & de Menocal, 1995) coupled with global climatic trends to determine the local landscapes inhabited by early hominids. This was accompanied by considerable volcanism, leaving parts of East Africa covered in volcanic ash—a fortunate consequence for paleontologists, for rocks of volcanic origin are datable by radiometric techniques (as described on pages 7–11) and provide a temporal context for the fossils found there.

Plant Communities

The vegetation that covers an area is a strong determinant of the life forms that live there. Vegetation is the primary source of food for most mammals, and it may also provide shelter. More heavily vegetated areas, such as tropical rain forests, can support a large number of species—they have high species **biodiversity** (richness and variability of species). The species biodiversity of primates and other mammals is much less in grasslands, and even more diminished in desert environments that support little vegetation.

Paleoecologists have many clues to the vegetative cover of past environments. **Palynology**, the study of fossil pollen, is a valuable tool. Throughout the year pollen fills the air; when these nearly indestructible granules settle, they become incorporated in deposits and can be almost indefinitely preserved. Pollens of various floral species are quite individualistic; in many cases, they can be readily identified at the generic level. Pollen analysis is useful for reconstructing past local vegetation, for establishing regional pollen maps, for indicating climatic changes, and for indicating prehistoric settlement. Palynology has been used to suggest that one of the human skeletons from Shanidar cave in Iraq was buried on or covered over by a bed of flowers (Chapter 12), thus giving insight into past human behavior.

Other direct methods of assessing past vegetation include the analysis of seeds and **phytoliths** (fossil wood or plant remains). Some woody plants can be identified by their cellular structure, as preserved in phytoliths; in other cases phytoliths of plants are found on fossilized teeth, giving clues to diets (see Chapter 6). Different kinds of plants have different photosynthetic pathways, using different carbon isotopes. The analysis of carbon isotopes in fossil soils can thus give a general idea of the types of vegetation growing in a region.

Mammalian fossils provide an indirect method of determining past plant communities. For example, in a wooded environment one finds more browsers (animals that eat leaves). Grass-eating animals, the grazers, are more prevalent in areas with less tree cover. Thus the relative proportions of mammal types, as well as the morphology of mammals adapted to specific types of environments, can contribute greatly to our understanding of past ecological conditions. Likewise, if modern ecological rules apply to the past, then high species biodiversity of fossil mammals at a specific site should be indicative of a lush habitat capable of supporting those species.

Mammal Communities

The vast majority of our evidence for past environments during the periods of primate evolution comes from the variety of mammal species found in fossil deposits. Once paleontologists have a clear understanding of the taphonomic processes leading to the deposition of fossils, past mammalian communities can be partially reconstructed. These reconstructions provide information about former vegetative cover, as mentioned before, and about climatic conditions (as some animals are adapted to cold, some to warm environments). The animals of the past acted as competitors, predators of our ancestors, and eventually as human prey and even companions. An understanding of changes in the human niche relies on assessments of the position humans held in the mammalian community.

One of the most unique aspects of human evolution is that early members of our genus *Homo* began to take control of the environment and shape it to their own needs and desires. This process started simply with stone tools, and later with the use of fire (Chapters 9 and 10). Eventually humans made their own environments in the form of clothing and shelters, and they domesticated plants and animals to create a community uniquely suited for human life. The fossil and archeological records give us insight into these ecological transitions. The change was not without consequence, and thus we see evidence of increases in the rates of mammalian extinction as humans take over the varied habitats of the world. Paleoecologists must consider not only the environmental factors that shaped or drove human evolution, but also the effects that human evolution had on communities of plants and animals, and perhaps even on climate.

SUMMARY

Fossils provide a glimpse of past life and are the primary source of data for studies of human evolution. Without reference to a documented time span and an interpretive framework, fossil remains are of limited value. Taphonomy, the study of the fossilization process, can reveal a wealth of information useful in helping reconstruct the condition of a site. Paleoecology derives information about past environments and climates to provide a context for human evolution. Sites providing the most useful data are usually chronometrically dated by such means as potassium-argon for early sites and radiocarbon for more recent sites. Chronometric dating techniques are restricted to areas of volcanic activity or to organic materials. The first requirement leaves many important human fossil sites such as those in limestone deposits in South Africa without solid dates. In such cases relative dating based on geomorphology or analysis of extinct fossil fauna helps to establish a general time frame.

SUGGESTED READINGS

Behrensmeyer, A. 1984. Taphonomy and the fossil record. *American Scientist* 72:558–567.
Brothwell, D., and E. Higgs, eds. 1970. *Science in Archaeology.* New York: Praeger.
Deino, A., P. Renne, and C. Swisher III. 1998. ^{40}Ar/^{39}Ar dating in paleoanthropology and archaeology. *Evolutionary Anthropology* 6:63–74.
Gibbons, A. 1997. Doubts over spectacular dates. *Science* 278:220–222.
Kappelman, J. 1993. The attraction of paleomagnetism. *Evolutionary Anthropology* 2:89–99.
Libby, W. 1955. *Radiocarbon Dating.* Chicago: University of Chicago Press.
Marshall, E. 1990. Paleoanthropology gets physical. *Science* 247:798–801.

Oakley, K. 1966. *Frameworks for Dating Fossil Man.* Chicago: Aldine-Atherton.

Partridge, W., B. Wood, and P. de Menocal. 1995. The influence of global climatic change and regional uplift on large-mammalian evolution in East and Southern Africa. In *Paleoclimate and Evolution, with an Emphasis on Human Origins.* E. Vrba, G. Denton, T. Partridge, and L. Burckle (eds.). New Haven: Yale University Press.

Wagner, G. 1996. Fisson-track dating in paleoanthropology. *Evolutionary Anthropology* 5:165–171.

2

Determining Evolutionary Relationships

Understanding the diversity of the world's plants and animals requires a universal reference system. That system was devised by C. Linnaeus. Once discovered, a plant or animal is provided with a name as a universally recognized reference point. The scientific study of the types and diversity of living organisms and of the interrelationships among them is called systematics. *Classification is a formal system that is used to relate organisms to one another. Assigning names to related groups of organisms is called* nomenclature.

Two basic taxonomic units, the genus *and the* species, *are important in the fossil record. A* species *is a group of interbreeding individuals that can produce fertile offspring. Under normal conditions members of one species cannot breed with members of another species. Groups of species sharing similar traits are placed into a* genus. *The scientific name of an organism contains both a genus and a species referent, a* binomial, *which for modern humans is* Homo sapiens.

LINNAEAN CLASSIFICATION SCHEME

Eighteenth-century scientific inquiry was characterized by a concept known as *naturalism* whereby humans were viewed as a natural phenomenon, as part of the universe and governed by its laws. There was considerable activity in the disciplines of comparative anatomy and systematics during the eighteenth century. As early as 1732, the Swedish naturalist Carolus Linnaeus discussed the relationship between human and nonhuman primates (the monkeys and apes, for instance). In the tenth edition of his book entitled *Systema Naturae*, Linnaeus included humans in the category of "Anthropomorpha," a group that included all other known primates (Figure 2-1).

The Linnaean classification scheme, the cataloging system for all life forms, is hierarchical; categories are based on inclusive traits. Those at the top (kingdoms) are the most inclusive; and those at the bottom (species) are the least inclusive. Each category includes a group or groups of related organisms whose members share common traits.

The Linnaean system is nonevolutionarily oriented. It was intended to represent the "real world" as it was thought to have been created by a Supreme Being, and all species represented were thought to be permanent and immutable results of a special creation. The Linnaean system is a stable two-dimensional framework that can represent only discontinuous relationships, whereas evolution is a dynamic and multidimensional process that involves change through time. However, since the work of Darwin, the zoological classification system has been slowly overhauled to incorporate the view that the living world is constantly changing, evolving new life from preexisting life.

Although various rules are used to establish categories within the classification scheme, the system is arbitrary and names are imposed on the natural order of life only for convenience. The **taxon** (plural *taxa*) is a group within the classificatory scheme containing members that are related to one another by descent from a common ancestor. Each taxon is distinct enough to be given a name to differentiate it from other taxa.

RULES OF NOMENCLATURE

Naming a taxon is based on a set of arbitrarily agreed-upon rules embodied in the "codes" of nomenclature. These rules have been established over generations and work to ensure clarity and usefulness. Used correctly, nomenclature eliminates confusion and ensures a common language in biological classification. **Taxonomy** is the science of classifying organisms according to their degree of relatedness. Taxonomy includes the principles, procedures, and rules of classification.

The rules of nomenclature follow a number of precedents. The law of priority applies to all names used as of January 1, 1758, the publication date accepted by convention of Linnaeus's authoritative edition of *Systema Naturae*.

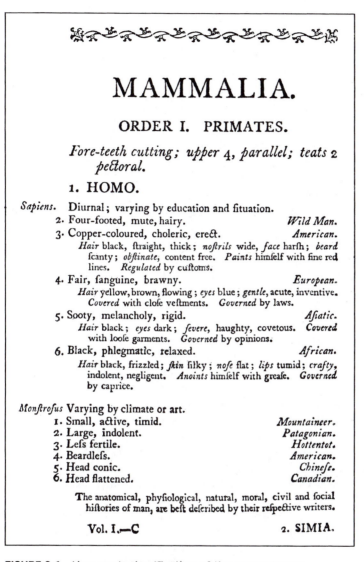

FIGURE 2-1 Linnaeus's classification of the genus *Homo*.
(Courtesy American Museum of Natural History.)

This law was instituted to bring order out of the confusion caused by an unsystematic use of Latin names. The first name validly used after the 1758 date has priority if the material was properly interpreted and proposed and published according to rules established in the *International Code of Zoological Nomenclature*. There are provisions for ignoring this rule under extenuating circumstances. Certain conventions are followed in forming the names of some higher categories (Table 2-1).

TABLE 2-1   Names of Higher Categories

Category	Suffix	Stem	Name of Higher Category
Superfamily	-oidea	Homin	Hominoidea
Family	-idae	Homin	Hominidae
Subfamily	-inae	Homin	Homininae

The smallest group regularly used in the classification scheme is the **species**. Species which are more similar to one another than like other species are grouped into a **genus**. Likewise, many *genera* (the plural of genus) are grouped into families, families into orders, orders into classes, and classes into phyla. Most living organisms also belong to either the animal or the plant kingdom, the highest classificatory unit.

All taxonomic groups of any one kind, like the family, are supposed to differ from related forms belonging to the same taxonomic group by a roughly equal degree. In the modern taxonomic system, biological classification is usually intended to reflect degrees of evolutionary relationship. The system is not rigid and is always subject to modification as more is learned about an organism contained within the system.

The two categories within the classification system to which we continually refer are the genus and the species. The species, also discussed elsewhere in this book, is the group whose members have the greatest genetic resemblance. The term *species* usually refers to a group of individuals that can interbreed and produce fertile offspring but normally cannot breed with members of another species. When different species can interbreed, the offspring are usually sterile.

A species is a group of organisms whose ecologic and physiologic functions are the same and whose offspring are similar and capable of reproducing the same line. When the elements of time and evolution are superimposed, we find that in those cases where complete lineages are known, there is morphological and reproductive overlap through many populations.

Species are usually reproductively isolated units. The problem with the species concept, however, is that the degree of reproductive isolation may be unknown. It may be unknown, in fact, especially with species from the fossil record and separated over time, whether two kinds of organisms were able to breed under natural conditions. Furthermore, organisms meeting the criteria for separate species under natural conditions may breed in artificial conditions such as zoos or laboratories. Taxonomists thus often recognize species on the basis of differences that are assumed to reflect the consequences of reproductive isolation.

Local differences can occur among members of the same species. These small differences, maintained by partial reproductive isolation, are recognized in classification as **subspecies**. Subspeciation can be the first step to the formation of new species.

Groups of species sharing similar traits are placed into a single genus. Species belonging to one genus usually share the same broad adaptive zone. This represents a general ecological lifestyle more basic than the more specialized niches characteristic of a species.

The ecological definition of a genus is very important to understanding the evolutionary relationships among fossil remains. For example, limb bones are often a good indication of the type of locomotion practiced, and locomotion is strongly tied to the habitat. Likewise, dental remains are often a good indication of diet, and diet is strongly tied to the habitat. If there are indications in the fossil record that a creature inhabited a different ecological zone than previously described creatures, then we are justified in supposing more than one genus.

An organism's scientific name contains a number of parts, its genus and species, as well as subspecies if such is applicable. Providing a genus and species name follows the Linnaean practice of establishing a **binomial** (a two-term name). A binomial must be applied to each newly described species; however, ascription of a subspecies designation is optional. For modern humans, the binomial reference is *Homo* (the genus) and *sapiens* (the species): We are referred to the scientific category of *Homo sapiens*. To distinguish modern humans from our ancestors, we add a third name, the subspecific designation; thus we have *Homo sapiens sapiens*. The genus designation always begins with a capital letter and the species and subspecies designations with lowercase letters. Each binomial is unique and must not be given to another form. The binomial always appears in italics or is underlined.

You might ask, why use the binomial? Why not refer to animals and plants by a common name such as "horse" or "rose"? We cannot do so because there are many millions of different species of plants and animals living today. In the past the figure may have been many millions more. Common names are ambiguous and differ in different languages. Scientific names are a universally understood language.

A **type specimen** is designated whenever a new species is described. The type specimen is a particular specimen, a single designated skull, for example, that establishes the criteria for a certain classification and is the form with which all subsequent discoveries are compared. Type specimens are established at the species, genus, and family levels. The type of a species is an individual specimen; for a genus the type is a species; and for a family the type is established on a genus. The concept of a type specimen poses a unique dilemma because a single specimen may not be typical of the species it is supposed to represent. The species to which the type specimen belongs will probably exhibit a range of variation in physical appearance that no single member of the species can adequately manifest. Although type specimens of species are the real entities to which the species name is applied, they cannot represent or typify the variation found within the group they represent. The concept of a type specimen has often been badly misunderstood and has led to the unjustified idealization of an individual as a representative of the entire species.

PARALLEL AND CONVERGENT EVOLUTION

Similar structures, adaptive relationships, or behaviors can occur in different groups as a result of similar evolutionary opportunities. Structural similarities traceable to a common descent are called **homologies** (Figure 2-2). For example, the forelimb bones of frogs, lizards, birds, and humans are so similar in arrangement and number that the simplest explanation for the resemblances is that all four vertebrates ultimately derived their forelimbs from a common ancestor. Functionally similar structures in nonrelated animals, animals without a common ancestor, are called **analogous** structures. The wings of butterflies and birds perform similar functions but belong to unrelated animals. Therefore, the wings are analogous structures.

A fundamental principle of evolutionary biology is that if two organisms are similar in appearance, they are related. Evolutionary relationships are deduced from the fossil record on this basis. There is a problem, however, because similarity may be due to parallelism or convergence, neither of which necessarily implies a close evolutionary relationship. **Parallelisms** are structural developments

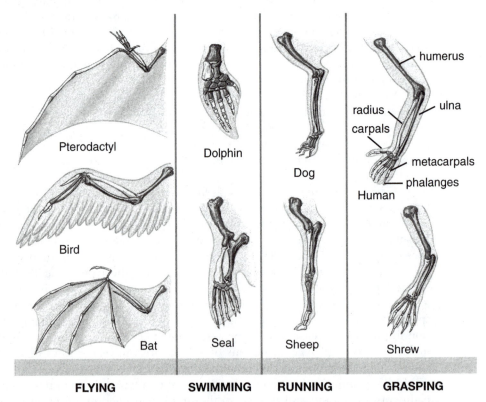

FIGURE 2-2 Homologous structures. The bones in the forelimbs of these animals are similar despite considerable differences in function. (*From* LIFE ON EARTH by Audesirk/ Audesirk, © 1997. Reprinted by permission of Prentice-Hall, Inc., Upper Saddle River, NJ.)

within a related group that occur independently in more than one segment of that group and are probably due to similar evolutionary conditions. For instance, among primates, which are basically arboreal (tree living), long forearms have evolved a number of times, as adaptations for hanging and feeding. **Convergence** occurs when structures of remotely related forms come to resemble each other, for example, flipperlike fins in whales, seals, and sea cows. When two animals or groups that are not closely related develop similarities in adaptive relationships or structures, the two groups are said to have converged.

ESTABLISHING EVOLUTIONARY RELATIONSHIPS

The recovery and collection of fossils is preceded by extensive planning, geological surveys, the solution of problems special to the locales, and so on. A relatively complete account of any group should await the collection of a fairly large sample. Then follows the demanding task of comparing the material with other possibly related forms to establish its evolutionary relationships. A taxonomic designation (for example, naming the form) must address the problems of geographical and temporal variation of related samples of other localities of known stratigraphical relationship, as well as problems of variation within the study sample.

Taxonomic or evolutionary relationships are often used to express two different concepts. First, there is a relationship based on similarity between forms that can be attributed to their sharing a common ancestor. The more similar two forms are in their **plesiomorphies (ancestral characteristics)**, that is, inherited adaptations from their ancestors, the more closely they are related. Second, a relationship can be expressed in the genealogical sense of the number of generations separating forms from their common ancestry. The more recently two forms shared a common ancestry, the more closely they are related.

In evolutionary taxonomy or systematics, observed similarities or differences are evaluated in terms of their presumed line of evolutionary descent. Because some traits (or characters) have more relevance than others (see page 26), these traits or characters are weighted in importance. In an effort to avoid the inherent subjectivity of weighting of traits, practitioners of *phenetic taxonomy* or *numerical taxonomy* classify organisms solely on the basis of overall morphological similarity. In the phenetic approach, every character is considered coequal and is assigned some numerical value (Sneath & Sokal, 1973).

Numerical taxonomy or phenetics uses the largest number of traits possible, thereby avoiding the bias of choosing only a few traits. In this way minor evolutionary changes do not greatly influence the final endeavor, as might be true if only a few traits are used. Phenetics does not recognize the distinction between ancestral and derived traits.

There are several difficulties with the phenetic approach. Convergence and parallelism can lead to similarity, and the indiscriminate use of total morphological similarity may indicate evolutionary relationships where none exist. Phenetics cannot account for the sometimes mosaic nature of evolutionary change, when different body parts evolve at different rates. When only a few traits have changed compared to the ancestral state, the largest contribution to phenetic similarity will be based on **symplesiomorphy**, the sharing of ancestral traits. The few derived traits indicating the correct evolutionary relationship will be swamped, resulting in an incorrect assessment of evolutionary relatedness.

Another approach to classification is called *cladistics, cladism,* or *phylogenetic systematics* (Ashlock, 1974). Cladistics is concerned only with the branching patterns of phylogeny, which reflect the distribution of traits within a clade. A **clade** is a group of related organisms. Members of a clade possess shared **derived characters**, that is, traits in common with each other but not with earlier ancestors. It must be shown, however, that shared derived traits related to function are not the result of parallel or convergent evolution. Cladistic analysis is graphically represented by a branching diagram known as a *cladogram.* In the cladistic approach the parent taxon splits into daughter or sister groups.

Table 2-2 compares the three classification schemes we have discussed. Until recently species were usually grouped according to the number of shared anatomical traits, sometimes with different traits receiving more attention than others. The cladistic approach argues that this method is imprecise. It holds that evolutionary relatedness should be based only on shared derived traits that arise as new features in a group of organisms. Primitive or generalized traits (plesiomorphies or symplesiomorphies) arise early in the evolutionary history of a group. These are widespread traits and are not of much help in determining evolutionary relationships.

As a group evolves, features particular to that evolutionary line are shared only by its members. These advanced derived traits, termed **apomorphies**, identify forms sharing one common ancestor. Derived characters can be further subdivided into (1) shared derived traits or **synapomorphic features**, which demonstrate a special evolutionary relationship among taxa that share their traits and (2) unique, derived characters (*autapomorphies*) or novelties, which distinguish a taxon from all others. Unique, derived traits are not useful for inferring evolutionary connections, though they may ultimately eliminate one taxon from ancestry to another that lacks such traits.

There are problems with the cladistic approach (Brace, 1981). First, it has difficulty dealing with the time component—a fact that is often offered as a virtue. Second, there is the problem of differing rates and times of change for different traits within a single line or between related lines. And finally, cladistics

TABLE 2-2   Classification Methods and Their Emphasis on Different Kinds of Data

Classification Method	Data Emphasis
Phenetics	Adaptation
Evolutionary taxonomy	Combines adaptation and relatedness
Cladistics	Relatedness

Adapted from R. Lewin, *Principles of Human Evolution,* 1997, Malden, MA: Blackwell Science.

ignores the distinction between parallelisms and convergence. Those who follow the cladistic approach favor the punctuated equilibrium model of evolution, discussed later in this chapter.

GUIDELINES FOR EVALUATING FOSSIL MATERIALS

The basic problem confronting the researcher is that of evaluating evolutionary change in the fossil sample. The researcher tries to establish which of many possible and sometimes conflicting relationships is most consistent with the known pattern of evolution. Some criteria utilized in evaluating fossil samples follow.

There should always be an economy of hypotheses. Whenever possible, all available reliable material and its affinities should be embraced by a single coherent scheme. The fraudulent nature of the Piltdown material, a combination of human and orangutan bones, which until the early 1950s confounded human evolutionists, was first suggested by the fact that the remains would not fit into any unitary evolutionary scheme embracing the rest of the then known human fossils.

On December 18, 1912, the Piltdown finds were introduced to the Geological Society of Great Britain. France and Belgium long boasted of Neandertal and other human fossils. Germany had Neandertal and *Homo erectus* finds, but Great Britain had nothing until Piltdown. The Piltdown finds put Great Britain on the fossil map with a stupendous find that had all the look of the oldest human yet found. The hoax, uncovered in 1953, was remarkable because its unveiling took so long, and it was sinister because it long stalled human evolutionary studies.

Tobias (1992, 1994), working with the ideas of the historian Ian Langham, thinks the hoaxer was Sir Arthur Keith, who helped announce the discovery and perhaps profited from the hoax. For example, he profited by the establishment of a particular concept of human evolution (his own), and his career profited when he was elected a Fellow of the Royal Society after having twice been rejected. However, the final identification of the hoaxer(s) may never be known (Spencer, 1990).

The economy principle should be extended to naming new fossil materials. The number of discarded primate taxa attests to the fact that an individual fossil has not always been viewed as only one member of a larger and variable group. There has been a tendency to multiply taxonomic categories among primate fossil remains because these remains are frequently few and fragmentary. It may be best to withhold judgment of fragmentary remains. When taxonomic categories become outmoded, or when the record shows that the names are incorrectly applied, the names must be dropped.

The assessment of an evolutionary relationship must be based on a well-authenticated and fairly complete fossil sample. This requirement is often difficult to meet because we are extremely fortunate when we find a fairly complete and datable assemblage. If a new specimen is recovered, and if the interpretation of the form is inconsistent with present schemes, it may be best to wait until further material is recovered. Such patience has not always been characteristic of primate fossil research.

The concept of specialization has frequently been invoked to exclude some fossil forms from the ancestry of later forms. Although the term **specialization** is often used to indicate some rather strikingly distinctive feature, it refers to a trait, or group of traits, that cannot be lost and thus restricts the evolutionary opportunities of its owner. Attribution of specialization is primarily a post hoc process; if a lineage becomes extinct, it may be argued that it was too specialized to meet changing environmental pressures. However, one is on tenuous grounds when making the subjective judgment about whether or not a character was too specialized and ultimately led to extinction (Gould, 1974).

Some traits have more taxonomic "value" than others; they are more important for determining an organism's status in relation to others. Although of great importance, the principle of taxonomic relevance (Clark, 1967) is frequently overlooked. The distinction between relevant and irrelevant traits is based on the fact that each living group is defined by a pattern of morphological traits found to be useful in distinguishing it from other groups. In primate evolution, for example, the taxonomically relevant traits for distinguishing early humans from the common human-ape ancestral stock are found in the lower limbs and pelvis, skeletal parts important in the evolution of bipedal locomotion (walking on the hind legs).

Failure to understand the principle of morphological equivalence is another serious source of error when making skeletal comparisons. To compare, for example, the skull height of the modern human genus *Homo* and the gorilla, one would measure from the auditory aperture (ear hole) to the highest point on the top of the skull. However, this measurement is misleading because in male gorillas skull height is often considerably extended by the development of a **sagittal crest** (a strut of bone across the top of the skull to which the temporalis muscle attaches).[1] A comparison of the height of the human braincase with the height of the braincase *plus* the sagittal crest in male gorillas would be a morphologically meaningless measurement.

The material being compared must be compatible in terms of age, sex, and size. Age is a main cause of skeletal variability. As among most mammals, mature primates are inevitably more robust than the young. Sex is another variable to be considered; most primate males are more robust (heavier and larger) than females. A third cause of variability is geographical distribution. Populations of widely ranging species show specific adaptations to differing habitat conditions. Time is a fourth factor. Because most specimens are isolated in time, it must be remembered that there is some likelihood of genetic change between descendants and their ancestors. Other genetic factors probably contributing to the variability seen in the fossil record result from genetic drift, that is, random genetic changes within a small, relatively isolated population; gene flow, or the transmission of genetic material between populations that are not reproductively isolated; and mutation.

---

[1]The temporalis muscle is the largest of the muscles that function to close the jaw. Large temporalis muscles are usually associated with large jaws and heavy molar and premolar teeth designed for crushing and grinding. Because bone is plastic and changes shape according to the stresses imposed by muscles attached to it, a large temporalis muscle often results in the development of a crest or ridge of bone atop the skull, the site where the temporalis muscle has its origin.

Age changes often lead to considerable modifications in structural details and skeletal proportions. Age changes in the skull are so marked that it would be fallacious to compare a few measurements of the adult skull of a human with those of a young ape and thus to infer that the former is not markedly different from apes in general. There are significant changes in the ape's skull as it matures, erasing many of the similarities that exist between the young ape and the adult human skull.

Morphological differences between males and females, termed **sexual dimorphism**, are an important consideration in interpreting fossil materials (Figure 2-3). One must make every effort to compare male with male and female with female skeletons. Many factors influence sexual dimorphism: overall body size of the species; group size; group composition; breeding system or sex ratio; and habitat. The weight of the brain is related to overall body size and weight. As we will see in Chapter 8, tooth and brain size differences between species of our earliest African ancestors, the australopithecines, may be related to overall body

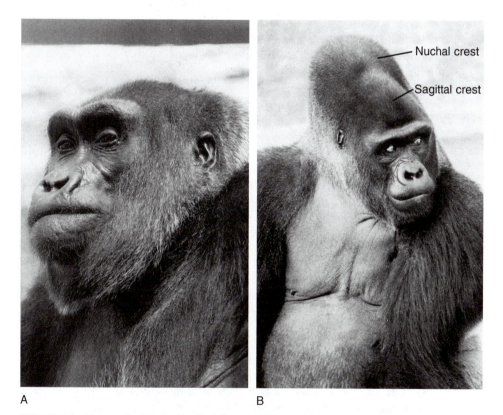

A   B

FIGURE 2-3 These photographs depict sexual dimorphism in the appearance of the sagittal crest in modern lowland gorillas (*Gorilla gorilla gorilla*): *A*, Adult female gorilla without a sagittal crest; *B*, Young adult male with both a sagittal and nuchal crest. (Photos courtesy of Rick Prebeg taken at the Columbus Zoo.)

size differences. Tooth size and brain size differences may be of only minimal taxonomic value because they may be reflecting nothing more than body size differences—which are probably related to dietary differences.

At each stage in the evolutionary history of a group, different morphological traits will be of differing evolutionary significance. One factor hindering the correct assessment of such early human fossils as the African australopithecines and the later *Homo erectus* was the failure to understand this situation (see Chapters 8 and 10). The femur (upper leg bone) of *H. erectus* was quite similar to that of modern humans, whereas the skull and face looked very different. Many originally assumed that the femur and skull could not belong to the same individual. The major selection pressure during early stages of human evolution was on the lower limb and pelvic structure. We should expect to find, therefore, individuals with more modern-looking lower limb structures and more archaic skull and facial features. This is indeed the case. Early scientists cannot be faulted for their failure to recognize that different traits evolve at different rates—**mosaic evolution**—because it was only after a number of skeletons were recovered that this pattern became apparent. At different points in its evolutionary history, a group faces different problems of adaptation. One of the first adaptive changes made by early humans was bipedalism. We should therefore expect features differentiating early humans and apes to be found primarily in the lower limbs.

THE EVOLUTIONARY PROCESS

The process of evolution was not fully understood when Darwin proposed the theory of natural selection, because genetics and the origin of variability were unknown. Since the 1920s, when evolution through natural selection was tied to genetic concepts, evolution has been understood as the combined effect of four "forces": **natural selection, gene mutation, gene flow**, and **genetic drift**. Here we present a brief overview of these evolutionary forces.

The logic of natural selection, conceived by Charles Darwin and Alfred Russel Wallace, is fairly simple. The first assumption is that more offspring are produced within a species than can possibly survive. Species are variable, and some variants of morphology and physiology afford a plant or animal a better chance to survive and reproduce than those with other variants. The more beneficial variants or set of variants are more likely to be passed to subsequent generations than other variants that are eventually lost. This selective process thus decreases variability within a population and drives the population toward what is best for survival and reproduction in a particular place and time.

The type of selection that leads to adaptive changes within a species is called **directional selection**. In this case, variants such as a larger brain or a more agile hand may provide advantages to an individual and may spread throughout the population at the expense of other variants. But there are other forms of natural selection as well. **Stabilizing selection** acts to maintain the norm of a population and leads to evolutionary stasis; for example, the four-chambered heart is a mammalian feature that works better than the variants, often seen as anomalies, that constantly appear in newborn mammals (including humans). It thus takes stabilizing natural selection to maintain a feature, for new variants are always appearing. A third type of selection is less intuitive, and is known as **disruptive selection**. In this process the average individual (for a particular trait) may be at a disadvantage, leading to selection for the extremes of variation. Disruptive selection may lead to sexual dimorphism, such as that seen among gorillas (Figure 2-3), in which males and females maintain disparate traits.

Gene mutations provide the ultimate source of variability upon which natural selection can operate. Mutations are chance mistakes in the copying of the genetic code that result in novel **alleles** (or different forms of a gene). If these mutations affect the physiology or morphology of an individual in a population, then natural selection may tend to favor or disfavor the new variant. Mutations are uncommon; among humans, on the average, there may be between one in a million and one in 100,000 new mutations per gene per generation. These figures may mean that each person carries one or two new mutations. Many of these are selectively neutral; that is, they neither enhance nor detract from one's ability to survive and reproduce. Few mutations are beneficial enough to be subject to directional selection and bring novel adaptations to a species, thus rendering evolution a normally slow and opportunistic process.

A further source of genetic variation is known as gene flow. Gene flow is simply hybridization between populations. As populations tend to vary from each other, reproduction between members of different populations may introduce new gene alleles into one group or the other. Gene flow helps maintain the cohesiveness of a species. In Chapter 13 we will investigate the question of whether or not the characteristics that defined modern *Homo sapiens* spread throughout the Old World by gene flow and if gene flow occurred between the Neandertals and the ancestors of modern *H. sapiens*.

Genetic drift is a chance effect occurring in very small populations. For example, if a boatload of people colonized an island, there is very little chance that they would carry a representative sample of all the variation from a larger continental population. Furthermore, from generation to generation, some variants would become lost as a result of chance alone; alternative variants may become *fixed* in the population (i.e., reach 100% frequency). The island population would then carry its own peculiar set of characteristics (which may or may not provide adaptive advantages). Whereas genetic drift is nothing more than a sampling error, it has a directional effect. Some researchers suspect that genetic drift may be important in the production of new species, as the isolated populations take on their own evolutionary course.

The four forces of evolution are summarized in Figure 2-4. Gene mutation and gene flow provide the raw materials, the genetic variation, for evolutionary change. Natural selection and genetic drift are then the conservative forces that limit variation and guide the direction of evolution.

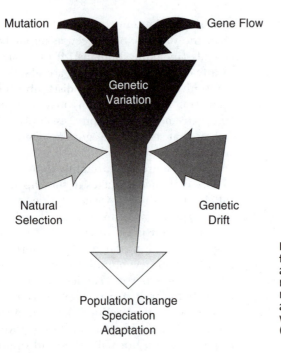

Mutation

Gene Flow

Genetic
Variation

Natural
Selection

Genetic
Drift

Population Change
Speciation
Adaptation

FIGURE 2-4   Interaction of the four forces of evolution. Mutation and gene flow are the sources of novelty in the gene pool, whereas natural selection and genetic drift are conservative forces removing variation from a population. (Courtesy Jeffrey K. McKee.)

SPECIATION

The species concept is of key importance in modern evolutionary biology. (A useful review of the nature and origin of primate species appears in Godfrey & Marks, 1991.) Reproductive isolation, the principal criterion for defining a genetic species, is often synonymous with geographical isolation, one of the most important means of speciation. A population that moves into different habitats, each with its own peculiarities, must adapt to these local conditions. Such adaptation, molded by natural selection, may eventually result in genetic differences between populations in local areas. Such differences will eventually magnify into speciation, with its concomitant reproductive isolation. Although geographical isolation is a major source of speciation, behavioral isolating mechanisms, such as differences in mating patterns, and other factors, can also lead to speciation.

Because most of the material dealt with in this book is fossil material, *species* usually means evolutionary species—an ancestral-descendant sequence of populations evolving from others. Such species are difficult to distinguish because of the incomplete fossil record. Because species often change slowly, the evidence would show slight gradual changes in the organisms, such that it would be difficult to make distinctions.

Although speciation is often considered to have occurred when one can distinguish closely related forms, a consistent relationship between speciation and morphological change is absent. The appearance of a new species might be accompanied by striking anatomical change, which is seen in the fossils, or by little or no change, which cannot be identified in fossils. The absence of marked anatomical change between two individuals does not necessarily indicate that they belong to the same species. In terms of the primate fossil record, for example, morphological differences between closely related species are small and restricted to only one or a few traits.

The gradual evolution of one species from another of the same lineage is called **anagenesis** or **phyletic evolution** (Figure 2-5). Although phyletic evolution is a real phenomenon, the division of a lineage into temporal species is somewhat arbitrary. Phyletic evolution is not associated with any particular event but is a matter of definition and convenience. When enough change has occurred, it is convenient to divide the lineage into time segments and give them different species names. This practice leads to some of the problems associated with primate taxonomy because there is often room for disagreement about the designation of "enough" change.

Cladogenesis occurs when one ancestral species becomes two or more descendant species. The splitting of one species into two or more species takes time and only happens when populations are geographically and genetically isolated from one another. Cladogenesis is most likely to occur in narrowly ranging populations. Because humans are now a widely ranging species, many think that cladogenesis has rarely if ever characterized later stages of human evolution.

The pace at which evolution occurs is a source of contention among evolutionary biologists. Since the 1940s evolutionary theory has been dominated by the *modern synthesis*, a term coined by Julian Huxley. According to the modern synthesis, mutations are the source of all variability, and evolutionary change results from shifting gene frequencies within a population. Within the framework of

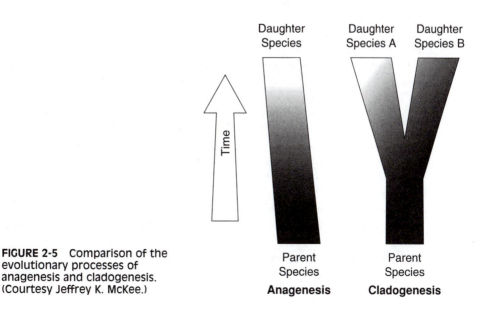

FIGURE 2-5 Comparison of the evolutionary processes of anagenesis and cladogenesis. (Courtesy Jeffrey K. McKee.)

modern evolutionary theory, the origin of species and trends within evolving groups of species are the result of the gradual accumulation of these small genetic changes. This slow change is called **microevolution**. As visualized in the modern synthesis, the rate of evolutionary change is slow. Also, the direction of evolutionary change is determined through the process of natural selection working on small variations within a population. Because of their higher reproductive rates, and most importantly their higher survival rates, surviving variants are those that are said to be the best adapted, the most reproductively fit.

According to the modern synthesis, evolution occurs at a slow pace as small genetic changes accumulate over time. These changes result in steadily advancing lineages as revealed in the fossil record. Many paleontologists, however, have noted an inconsistency in this process because the principal feature of individual species in the fossil record is an apparent lack of continual change over time.

There is no questioning that, overall, the fossil record reflects a steady increase in diversity and complexity of species, with the origin of new species and the extinction of others. For the most part, however, fossils do not document a smooth transition from old morphologies to new ones. According to one of the most articulate of the so-called new evolutionists, Stephen Jay Gould, "For millions of years species remain unchanged in the fossil record, and they then abruptly disappear, to be replaced by something that is substantially different but clearly related" (quoted in Lewin, 1980:883).

The absence of transitional forms between established species has been traditionally explained as a fault of an imperfect fossil record, an argument first advanced by Charles Darwin in *The Origin of Species*. Darwin favored an evolutionary pattern characterized by slow, gradual change. It has been assumed that with more research, coupled with finding geological strata with the necessary fossils, a complete record of fossil prehistory would be forthcoming. Although G. G. Simpson (1951) has shown this theory to be true in the evolutionary history of the horse, it has not always been the case. Gould has long argued that gaps exist in the fossil record and that "the jerkiness you see . . . is the consequence of the jerky mode of evolutionary change" (quoted in Lewin, 1980:884).

Problems with the modern synthesis have resulted in new interpretations of the fossil record and new theoretical stances. For some researchers, the picture of evolutionary change is one of long periods during which individual species remain virtually unchanged, punctuated by abrupt events of change when a descendant species arises. This model of evolutionary change is called **punctuated equilibrium** (Figure 2-6), which refers to the fact that in the evolutionary history of some groups long periods of stasis (relative stability) are broken or punctuated by short bursts of evolutionary change stimulated by speciation. It is currently being argued that such a process may be responsible for the divergence of humans and apes from a common ancestor.

There are five major points to the punctuated equilibrium model (Levinton & Simon, 1980):

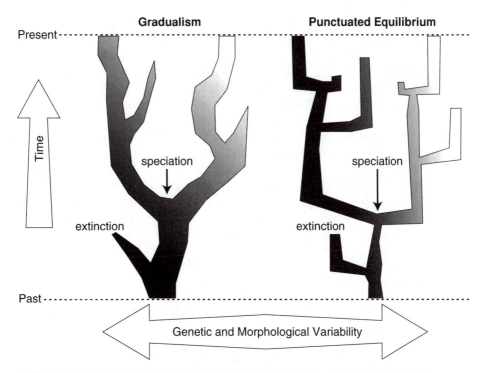

FIGURE 2-6 Two conceptions of the evolutionary process. Gradualism involves continuous evolution of variation leading to divergence of new species; punctuated equilibrium involves little evolutionary change except at the points of speciation or extinction. (Courtesy Jeffrey K. McKee.)

1. New species result from the splitting of existing lineages.
2. New species develop rapidly.
3. New species arise from a small subpopulation of the ancestral species.
4. The new species (or daughter species) arises in a small and isolated part of the geographical range of the ancestral species.
5. Species change little throughout much of their evolutionary history.

Trends in the fossil record have always been cited as the best fossil evidence for Darwinian gradualism, that is, anagenesis or phyletic evolution. However, Eldredge and Tattersall (1982), two major proponents of punctuated equilibrium, argued that the trends are *between* species and not *within* species.

Although punctuated equilibrium allows for some transitional forms, it does not demand the existence of a long series of very finely graded intermediates in the fossil record, as does phyletic gradualism. Anatomical change would be complete in ten or one hundred generations, depending on a particular species' generation time. This transitional phase would be very short compared with the species' total life on Earth—a fact which explains the failure to find fossils of intermediate forms.

As envisaged by the punctuated equilibrium model, the origin of a new species always occurs in small groups geographically isolated from the main population of the species. Later the new, or daughter, species usurps the territory of the main, or parent, species' population and appears in the fossil record in its fully developed form. According to this model, the incompleteness of the fossil record is accepted; fossilization is a rare event, and there is never a complete record of year-by-year changes. The so-called jerkiness (change and stability) of the record is accepted as being a true reflection of how evolution occurs.

In the punctuationists' model, much of the "work" of adaptation results from interspecific rather than intraspecific factors. Using as an example the evolution of the horse, changes occur through the preferential survival of the species rather than through selection of individual traits within the species. Punctuationists argue that a number of relatively unchanging species exist at any one time, with evolutionary novelties arising as new species from preexisting stocks. Better-adapted species have longer durations and are, therefore, more likely to produce daughter species, thereby promoting the adaptive success of the entire group. Although we are still dealing with selection, it is not the within-species selection that Darwin proposed. The punctuation model downgrades the role of traditional natural selection in speciation. It postulates macroevolution, the rise and divergence of discontinuous groups, as a distinct process, operating above the species level.

Although there is considerable disagreement among paleontologists, evidence for both gradual evolutionary change and for the punctuated equilibrium model can be gleaned from the fossil record. There is very heated debate on this point. It should not surprise us, however, that evidence seems to exist for both evolutionary models, and we shall encounter this problem at other points in this book.

SUMMARY

In this chapter we have reviewed some principles involved in formulating evolutionary relationships, which are organized by the Linnaean classification scheme. This scheme was proposed prior to the acceptance of the theory of evolution, and that fact has resulted in a number of problems. The rules of nomenclature were formulated to prevent sloppy taxonomic procedures. Whenever a new organism is described, it must be given a genus and species designation, the so-called binomial reference. A type specimen is designated whenever a new species is described. Phylogenetic trees, branching diagrams representing the evolutionary history of a group, are used to depict an evolutionary history. There are various approaches for constructing evolutionary histories, among them are phenetics and cladistics. A number of problems complicate assessing evolutionary relationships.

A significant problem facing modern evolutionary biologists is the tempo and mode of speciation. Was change slow and gradual, as Darwin suggested, or is a period of stability abruptly broken by rapid change—punctuated equilibrium—

the most likely model? Although there appears to be evidence supporting both positions, not all researchers accept the evidence proposed by the other side.

SUGGESTED READINGS

Clark, W. L. G. 1967. *The Fossil Evidence for Human Evolution: An Introduction to the Study of Paleoanthropology.* Chicago: University of Chicago Press.

Cronin, J., N. Boaz, C. Stringer, and Y. Rak. 1981. Tempo and mode in hominid evolution. *Nature* 292:113–122.

Eldredge, N., and I. Tattersall. 1982. *The Myths of Human Evolution.* New York: Columbia University Press.

Gould, S. 1984. Smooth curve of evolutionary rate: A psychological and mathematical artifact. *Science* 226:994–995.

Gould, S., and N. Eldredge. 1993. Punctuated equilibrium comes of age. *Nature* 366:223–227.

Henning, W. 1966. *Phylogenetic Systematics.* Urbana: University of Illinois Press.

Simpson, G. 1951. *The Meaning of Evolution.* New York: New American Library.

Simpson, G. 1961. *Principles of Animal Taxonomy.* New York: Columbia University Press.

Stanley, S. 1979. *Macroevolution: Pattern and Process.* San Francisco: W. H. Freeman.

3

Our Place in the Animal Kingdom

Geologic Time Scale
Vertebrate Evolution
Mammal-like Reptiles and Mammalian Evolution
The Insectivora
The Primates
The Human Primate
Summary
Suggested Readings

When I view all beings not as special creations, but as the lineal descendants of some few beings which lived long before the first bed of the Cambrian system was deposited, they seem to me to become ennobled.

(Charles Darwin, *The Origin of Species*)

Within the classification system modern humans, scientifically called Homo sapiens sapiens, *occupy such categories as kingdom Animalia, class Mammalia, order Primates, suborder Anthropoidea, and family Hominidae (Table 3-1). Our mammalian heritage is briefly discussed by tracing the evolutionary history of mammalian groups, especially placentals. Although we trace our primate origins back to about 55 mya, we differ from such nonhuman primates as the monkeys and apes in a number of anatomical and behavioral traits. This chapter highlights our commonalities and differences with other members of the animal kingdom. Humans have an especially close evolutionary relationship with the African chimpanzee.*

TABLE 3-1 Humans in the Animal Kingdom

Category		Traits and Representatives
Kingdom	Animalia	Multicelled animals; representatives that are mobile, ingesting, and have sense organs
Phylum	Chordata	Animals with notochords and gill slits
Subphylum	Vertebrata	Fish, amphibians, reptiles, birds, mammals
Class	Mammalia	Monotremes (egg-laying mammals), placental mammals (Eutheria), and others
Subclass	Eutheria	Rodents, carnivores, primates, and others
Order	Primates	All representatives of the order Primates
Suborder	Anthropoidea	Old and New World monkeys and the Hominoidea (apes and humans)
Superfamily	Hominoidea	Lesser apes (gibbons), great apes (orangutans, chimpanzees, gorillas), and the Hominidae (humans)
Family	Hominidae	Fossil and modern representatives of humans (i.e., *Australopithecus, Ardipithecus,* and *Homo*)
Genus	*Homo*	Fossil and modern representatives (i.e., *Homo habilis, Homo erectus,* and *Homo sapiens*)
Species	*sapiens*	Fossil and modern representatives
Subspecies	*sapiens*	Modern representatives and their ancestors dating back to the Late Pleistocene

GEOLOGIC TIME SCALE

A brief review of geologic history (Table 3-2) should prove useful before a fuller discussion of the evolution of the major classes of animal life. Geologic history is divided into four *eras*. The three later eras, the Paleozoic, Mesozoic, and Cenozoic, are subdivided into *periods*—six for the Paleozoic, three for the Mesozoic, and two for the Cenozoic. Periods are further subdivided into *epochs*.

The earliest evidence of life seems to come from sedimentary rocks in Greenland, dating to perhaps 3.8 billion years ago. Fossil evidence of organisms called *stromatolites* that appeared shortly thereafter has been found in Australia. This fossil material belongs to the earliest geologic sequence called the Pre-cambrian era, which dates from the beginning of life to the beginning of the Paleozoic era. Fossil evidence is scant during the Precambrian, but toward the end of the era there is evidence of plants and wormlike animals.

Fossils become more abundant during the Paleozoic era. Land plants occur toward the middle and land animals toward the end of that era. Invertebrates appear in the first period of the Paleozoic, the Cambrian period, and become a dominant life form. Vertebrates appear rather early in the Paleozoic, during the Ordovician period about 500 mya. Toward the end of the Paleozoic, in the Devonian period, we find fossils of amphibians, and during the Carboniferous period, the first fossil evidence of reptiles appears. These are discussed in more detail later in this chapter.

New findings reveal a fossil history of animals at least 10 million years older than previously assumed (Kerr, 1998). Microscopic fossils of animals and their

TABLE 3-2   Vertebrate Evolution during the Mesozoic and Cenozoic Eras

Era (and Duration)	Period	Estimated Time since Beginning of Each Period (in millions of years)[a]	Epoch	Life
Cenozoic, age of mammals (about 65 million years)	Quaternary	0.01	Holocene (Recent)	*Homo sapiens sapiens*, the modern species of humans
		1.8	Pleistocene	Modern species of mammals and their forerunners; extinction of many species of large mammals; the great glaciations
	Tertiary	5.2	Pliocene (beginning date of this epoch is debated)	Appearance of many of today's genera of mammals
		25	Miocene	Rise of modern subfamilies of mammals; spread of grassy plains; evolution of grazing animals
		37 to 38	Oligocene	Rise of modern families of mammals
		53 to 54	Eocene	Rise of modern orders and suborders of mammals, including primates
		65	Paleocene	Dominance of archaic mammals
Mesozoic, age of reptiles (about 185 million years)	Cretaceous	145		Extinction of large reptiles
	Jurassic	200+		Dominance of reptiles; appearance of birds, archaic mammals
	Triassic	225		Appearance of dinosaurs, turtles, ichthyosaurs, plesiosaurs
Paleozoic (about 300 million years)		580		Invertebrates first appear

(Neogene spans Pleistocene, Pliocene, and Miocene epochs; Paleogene spans Oligocene, Eocene, and Paleocene epochs.)

[a]These times vary a few million years with different investigators.

embryos are preserved in rocks at least 570 million years old in southern China. This record suggests that the ancestors of modern kinds of animals were diverse and abundant much earlier than assumed. The complexity of the recently found fossils suggests that they must have had even earlier, unknown ancestors, perhaps stretching the animal record back to at least 600 mya.

During the Paleozoic era, South America, Africa, Antarctica, Australia, and India were merged in a land mass known as *Gondwanaland.* North America, Greenland, Europe, and Asia were known as *Laurasia.* These two land masses united during the Carboniferous and Permian periods, 345–225 mya, to form a huge land mass, *Pangea.*

The Mesozoic era did not experience the climatic extremes of the preceding Paleozoic era. However, by the termination of the Mesozoic, Pangea had pulled apart and the continents were approximately in their present-day positions. Reptiles had risen to dominance during the Permian period; that is, the last part of the Paleozoic era. The later Jurassic period is often called the Age of the Dinosaurs. Dinosaurs reached their peak during the Cretaceous period. After approximately 150 million years, dinosaurs met their demise—the cause is still hotly debated. Climatic changes, perhaps the result of extraterrestrial events, are most often cited.

Mammals first appear as small animals during the Mesozoic era. The earliest mammals were probably dwarfed by the dinosaurs; however, they survived in what were probably wooded areas. Mammals are discussed in more detail later in this chapter.

Earth assumed its present geological and geographical character during the Cenozoic. Major continental drifting slowed considerably, and the extent of many interior seas was greatly reduced. Weather conditions changed in association with these alterations.

The Cenozoic era has two periods, the Tertiary, when primates first appear, and the Quaternary, when humans come to play a major role in the primate world. Although first thought to appear during the Paleocene epoch of the Tertiary period, primates are now thought to have appeared somewhat later during the Eocene epoch, about 55 mya (Chapter 5). Ancestral apes appear during the late Eocene and the Oligocene epochs (Chapter 6). Ancestral humans, the earliest of whom are referred to as *hominids,* first appear during the Pliocene epoch in Africa about 5.5 mya. During the Quaternary period of the Cenozoic era, humans eventually leave Africa and move to other parts of the world. By the later Upper Pleistocene epoch, humans had moved into the New World and the Greater Australian region (Chapter 13). The Holocene (Recent) epoch, the geological epoch in which we now reside, began about 10,000 years ago.

VERTEBRATE EVOLUTION

Humans are vertebrates; that is, we have a spinal column. The earliest vertebrates evolved hundreds of millions of years before humans first made their appearance. Vertebrates may have evolved 520 to 435 mya. The first vertebrates may have resembled the modern-day sea lancelet (*Amphioxus*), a small animal presently inhabiting coastal regions around the world. The sea lancelet has a notochord and a dorsal nerve cord. Vertebrates, such as the jawless fishes, the ostracoderms, dating to 435 mya, had a true spinal column enclosing the nerve cord and an internal skeleton composed of soft cartilage rather than bone.

There are five large categories of vertebrates: fish, amphibians, reptiles, birds, and mammals. There is a relatively complete fossil record for most of these groups, and the evolutionary relationships between major categories are apparent. The Early and Middle Paleozoic (beginning 520 mya) can be regarded as the age of fishes, the Upper Paleozoic–Mesozoic (280–145 mya), the age of reptiles, and the Cenozoic (beginning 75 mya), the age of mammals (Table 3-2).

Many vertebrates are land-dwelling (terrestrial) creatures. All animals that successfully adjusted to terrestrial life had to solve two problems: respiration and reproduction. Solutions to these problems varied as animal groups responded with different physiological and anatomical adaptations. The immediate problem to be solved if vertebrates were to survive on land was obtaining oxygen. Fish gills, for example, cannot function in air. Fish lack a protective covering to prevent water loss; they soon dehydrate when placed in the relative dryness of the atmosphere.

Among the many fish species populating the seas hundreds of millions of years ago were the lobefins. Lobefins made a successful transition from an aquatic to a terrestrial habitat because of the unique sturdy structure of their fins and the presence of primitive lungs. The lobefin's fin structure permitted it to "walk" for short distances. This was important, for example, when it needed to move from a pool that was drying or becoming stagnant (low in oxygen) to a more favorable location. The ability to move short distances on land meant the difference between survival and extinction.

While in the water the lobefin obtained oxygen by breathing through its gills; on land it obtained oxygen by breathing with its primitive lungs. With gradual modification of the lungs into specialized organs capable of breathing air, lobefins greatly extended the time they could spend on land.

Lobefins had other traits aiding their survival out of water: (1) Thick skin helped to reduce water loss; (2) strengthening and modification of the spine, shoulder girdle, and limbs occurred, which provided more limb mobility and aided movement on land; (3) changes in the skull and teeth allowed feeding on land plants; and (4) their sense of smell and hearing were improved. These changes accumulated and appear in the first terrestrial vertebrates, the amphibians, a group intermediate between fish and reptiles that today contains such forms as frogs, toads, and salamanders.

Amphibians, appearing about 280 to 225 mya, retain the external reproductive system of their ancestors and must return to water to reproduce. Amphibian females lay their eggs in or near water, and the eggs are externally fertilized by the male. Water is essential in amphibian reproduction because the eggs lack a hard shell, and when exposed to air, they dry quickly. This method of reproduction cannot take place on land.

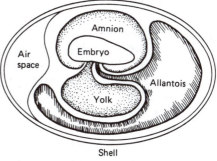

FIGURE 3-1 Amniotic egg. (*From INTRODUCTION TO EVOLUTION by F. Racle, © 1979, p. 104. Reprinted by permission of Prentice-Hall, Inc., Upper Saddle River, NJ.)*

Between 225 and 200 mya, a new group of vertebrates, reptiles, rose to dominance. Reptiles were the first completely terrestrial vertebrates. With the evolution of internal fertilization, reptiles were no longer required to return to water to reproduce. The first reptiles were the primitive cotylosaurs.

Reptiles show several evolutionary changes when compared to their amphibian ancestors, the most important being the development of the amniotic egg (Figure 3-1). Reptiles evolved an internal reproductive system in which sperm is introduced into the female's body and fertilization occurs in the moist environment of the female's reproductive tract. After fertilization, the embryo (the early stage of development) is enveloped by a membranous sac, the amnion, which maintains a moist environment for the developing embryo. A second sac, the allantois, surrounds the amnion and receives and stores the waste products of respiration. In mammals, the allantois contributes to the formation of the placenta (discussed later). The entire structure is surrounded by a thick leathery shell, which prevents water loss and dehydration.

The amniotic egg permits the embryo to develop in its original environment by enclosing it in the liquid-filled sac, the amnion. The egg contains a food supply, the yolk, and membranous structures that allow exchange of oxygen and carbon dioxide through the shell and storing of waste materials from the embryo. These structures allow the reptile to develop into a nearly fully formed miniature adult at the time of hatching. This development eliminates the larval stage of the amphibian life cycle and the necessity to return to a water environment. The amniotic egg is a major adaptation to a terrestrial lifestyle.

MAMMAL-LIKE REPTILES AND MAMMALIAN EVOLUTION

The earliest mammal-like reptiles belonged to the order Pelycosauria, animals distinguished by their large size and varied diet. Many large species evolved; some were specialized carnivores (meat eaters), and others were herbivores (plant eaters). Some tooth differentiation is apparent, indicating a more efficient mode of food preparation and probably a more varied diet. Some pelycosaurs had large dorsal sails—webs of membrane stretched across the body's protruding spines—

that could have been a crude precursor of the internal temperature-control systems later found in mammals. Perhaps when the animal was cold it turned its body to position the so-called sails to absorb more sunlight.

Pelycosaurs thrived for about 50 million years before becoming extinct. One pelycosaur suborder, the sphenacodonts, included members of the genus *Dimetrodon,* which may have given rise to the second subclass of mammal-like reptiles, Therapsida (Figure 3-2). Therapsids gave rise to more than 300 genera, which contained species ranging in size from rats to the rhinoceros. Some members were carnivores and others were herbivores.

A skull originally found in 1897 in Texas and dating to about 200 mya sheds light on the evolution of the therapsids. The skull, belonging to a creature called *Tetraceratops insignis,* was found in a drawer at the American Museum of Natural History. When the skull was first found, the animal was thought to be a pelycosaur. However, analysis by Laurin and Reisz (1990) suggested that the skull belonged to an animal that is intermediate between the pelycosaurs and the later therapsids, the mammal-like reptiles. The animals' dentition and certain traits of the jaw and face suggest that it is more advanced than the pelycosaurs but less advanced than previously described therapsids.

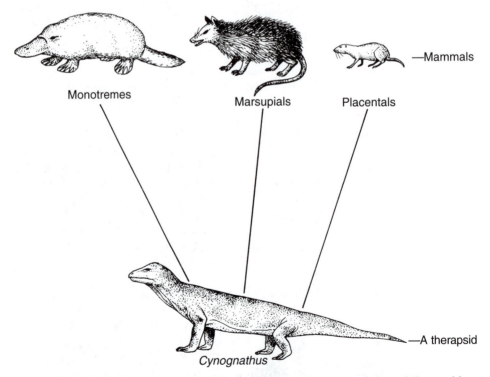

FIGURE 3-2 Divergence of the mammals. *Cynognathus* is representative of therapsids, from which the first mammals evolved. (*From* INTRODUCTION TO EVOLUTION by F. Racle, © 1979. Reprinted by permission of Prentice-Hall, Inc., Upper Saddle River, NJ.)

An important mammalian feature is the ability to generate heat and maintain a constant body temperature. Although some therapsids may have been warm-blooded, it is not known how precisely they were able to control their body temperature.

Like reptiles, therapsids may have laid eggs. Egg protection among mammal-like reptiles could have led to incubation and parental feeding, which may have paved the way for longer egg retention within the mother and then, as in mammals, to live births.

The line of advancing mammal-like features passed through the theriodonts, a diverse group of apparently efficient carnivores, to the cynodonts, from which the first true mammals evolved about 200 mya. Two major trends in cynodont evolution were an overall size reduction—they ranged in size from a rat to a wolf—and an increasing elaboration of mammalian features. The cynodonts were small and apparently were insect eaters like their mammalian descendants. The cynodonts may have been nocturnal like their ancestors.

Mammals began to move into and exploit new, relatively unoccupied habitats, resulting in rapid diversification, expansion, and proliferation. This process of rapid diversification and proliferation, known as **adaptive radiation**, is one of the first stages in the evolution of new groups.

One of the best preserved early mammals was recently found in China (Hu et al., 1997). This new fossil taxon, called *Zhangheotherium quinquecuspidens*, is a nearly complete postcranial skeleton and a partial skull with dentition. The fossil provides new insight into the relationship of the major mammalian lineages and the evolution of the mammal skeleton. The new taxon is part of a mammalian radiation occurring before the divergence of living marsupials and placentals. An early Cretaceous placement is suggested for the material based on faunal correlations and radiometric dates. Once fully analyzed, this new fossil will provide better understanding of the earliest stages of mammal evolution.

Mammalian Traits

A number of traits characterizing modern mammals are also typical of their earlier ancestors (Box 3-1), including the following: (1) Mammals are warm-blooded animals, a condition called *homeothermy*. Internal control of a constant body temperature allowed mammals to inhabit and exploit a wider range of environments than those available to reptiles. (2) Mammals have different kinds of teeth specialized for different functions; this is called *heterodontism.* Mammals generally have four types of teeth. The canines are jabbing teeth; the incisors are cutting and slicing teeth; and the premolars and molars are for grinding. (3) Mammals express play behavior as an important means of environmental exploration and learning. Play is an extremely important primate behavior through which youngsters practice survival skills, develop physical coordination, and learn social behaviors and communication skills, among others. (4) Mammals are more intelligent than their reptilian predecessors. (5) The mammalian mode of reproduction is significant in understanding mammalian evolutionary success (Box 3-2). The

---

BOX 3-1   Some Major Mammalian Evolutionary Traits

- Mothers nurse their newborn and provide protection.
- Fewer young are born each parturition than in amphibians and reptiles.
- Most mammals give birth to live young; the exception is the monotremes.
- There is a clear trend toward prolonged immaturity, which is correlated with the role intelligence and learning play in development.
- Mammals maintain internal control of body temperature—homeothermy.
- Many mammals lead social lives and are found in social groups.
- Mammals evidence dietary differentiation and heterodontism.
- Play behavior is important for normal social and physical development and is most important among primates.

---

reproductive mode of one group, the placentals, allows an extensive period of prenatal development. Mammals have fewer births per parturition, and those infants that are born are protected. (6) The developmental period among mammalian young is extended by nursing. Nursing young need not begin to feed or defend themselves immediately after birth; therefore they may be less prone to predation. The infant's longer period of attachment to its mother increases the potential period for learning behaviors necessary for survival.

These traits are not clear-cut indications of mammal status. For example, there is evidence suggesting that some dinosaurs were warm-blooded (de Ricqles,

---

BOX 3-2   Reproductive Specializations

Amphibians: Reproduction is external and water is an essential medium for reproduction. More young are born than survive; no parental care.

Reptiles: Amniotic egg negates the need to return to water to reproduce. Internal fertilization. Many more young born than survive; parental care is not common.

Mammals: Three different reproductive strategies occur:
- Monotremes: lay eggs like birds and reptiles.
- Marsupials: viviparous; young born very immature and mature in mother's pouch; internal fertilization.
- Placentals: during reproduction a specialized structure, the placenta, forms in females; internal fertilization; early stages of development in mother's womb.

Among mammals the number of young born each time is usually fewer than characteristic of amphibians and reptiles. Mammalian females nurse their young and protect them for various lengths of time.

1974; Desmond, 1975; Thomas and Olson, 1980). Of the mammalian traits previously noted, fossil evidence is useful primarily in regard to heterodontism.

Mammalian Subclasses

Reproductive specialties differentiate the three subclasses of mammals (see Box 3-2). One subclass, the Monotremata (monotremes), includes the duckbilled platypus and the spiny anteater. In common with birds and reptiles, monotremes lay eggs as their mode of reproduction.

A second subclass, the Marsupialia (marsupials), is more widespread than the monotremes and includes the opossum, kangaroo, and koala. Marsupials are **viviparous**; that is, they give birth to live young rather than lay eggs. Marsupials lack a placenta; their young are born at a very immature stage and migrate to the mother's pouch, where they attach themselves to her nipples. They remain within the pouch until they are adequately developed, and then they emerge.

The third subclass, the placental mammals, is the Eutheria. Placental mammals develop by a special process in which the egg is expelled from the mother's ovary, is fertilized, and then implants itself within the walls of the mother's womb. The early stage of the organism's development is termed the *embryo*, which produces a tissue, the **placenta** (absent in monotremes and marsupials), on the wall of the womb. The placenta permits an interchange of molecules between the mother and developing offspring. Whereas the bird's or reptile's egg must contain enough yolk to nourish the embryo until it has hatched, as well as storing waste products, placental mammals use the mother's physiological mechanisms for these functions and for supplying oxygen to the tissues of the embryo. In this way the offspring are protected until they are more fully developed than the offspring of egg-laying animals.

A tiny tooth, plus four teeth embedded in a 2-centimeter-long jaw, all from the same animal that lived in southern Australia 115 mya, may be evidence for rewriting the history of mammalian evolution (Rich et al., 1997; Wuethrich, 1997). The species, *Aukstribosphenos nyktos*, which belongs to a newly created genus, may be the oldest mammal fossil from Australia (Rich et al., 1997).

If some early diagnoses of the fossil are correct, and there is considerable debate on the relationship of this fossil to mammalian evolution, it is not an ancestor to Australia's marsupials or egg-laying monotremes, but to placental mammals. If this depiction is correct, it places placental mammals in Australia 110 million years earlier than previously thought, and this finding has great implications for mammalian evolution on a worldwide scale. Even if the jaw does not belong to a shrew-sized early placental, it could still rearrange the mammalian evolutionary tree by altering the timing of the branching of the major mammalian forms (Wuethrich, 1997).

Prior to this discovery it was thought that placental mammals originated in Asia and then migrated to North America. It was thought that placental mammals stayed in the northern hemisphere until about 65 mya and did not enter Australia until about 5 mya via island-hopping rodents from Southeast Asia. If the new fossil is a placental, it destroys this scenario. If placental mammals were in Australia 100 million years earlier than thought, it raises many questions as to the place(s) of origin of placentals. It opens the possibility that placentals could have arisen in any number of locales other than Southeast Asia. A placental in Australia by 115 mya pushes back the time of origin for higher mammals.

There are researchers who question the placental ties of *Aukstribosphenos*, noting that the jaw evidence is equivocal and may not be that of an ancient placental. It may, in fact, be an entirely new kind of animal. Perhaps *A. nyktos* is an advanced member of early mammalian group ancestral to both placentals and marsupials. Still others suggest that the evidence is too fragmentary to make any firm conclusions at this time (Wuethrich, 1997).

THE INSECTIVORA

The Insectivora (insect-eating forms) is the mammalian group most likely to have given rise to the placental mammals, including the order Primates (Table 3-3) about 55 or 60 mya. Living representatives of the Insectivora, including moles, hedgehogs, and shrews, are found throughout tropical and temperate regions of both the Old and New Worlds. The evolutionary history of the Insectivora goes back at least 130 mya.

The anatomical traits characteristic of insectivores make it likely that they were ancestral to several mammalian orders besides the order Primates. For example, insectivores may have been ancestral to rodents and bats.

TABLE 3-3   Primate Classification (Not All Categories Are Listed in This Table)

Order Primates	Some Living Examples
Suborder: Prosimii	
Superfamily: Lemuroidea	Lemurs, indris, sifakas (all found on island of Madagascar)
Lorisoidea	Loris, bush baby
Tarsiioidea	Tarsier (Southeast Asia)
Suborder: Anthropoidea	
Superfamily: Ceboidea	New World monkeys: e.g., howler monkey, spider monkey, woolly monkey
Superfamily: Cercopithecoidea	Old World monkeys: e.g. macaques, baboons, langurs
Superfamily: Hominoidea	
Family: Hylobatidae	Gibbons, siamangs (Asia only)
Family: Pongidae	
Genus: *Pan*	Chimpanzee (Africa only)
Genus: *Gorilla*	Gorilla (Africa only)
Genus: *Pongo*	Orangutan (Asia only)
Family: Hominidae	
Genus: *Homo*[a]	Humans

[a]The human genus of *Homo* has existed for about 2.4 million years. It was preceded by the genus *Australopithecus*. This topic is discussed in Chapters 8 and 9.

Insectivores have a curious mix of anatomical traits. Like primates they have five digits on their extremities. Unlike primates, however, the digits are tipped with claws, not nails. The Southeast Asian tree shrew is one animal having a mix of anatomical traits—some are like those of insectivores and some are like those of primates—making it difficult to classify tree shrews with either one or the other group. Unlike most insectivores, which are terrestrial or burrow into the ground, tree shrews are arboreal. Like primates, and unlike insectivores, tree shrews have large eyes and possess somewhat mobile hands and feet that can be used to grasp. They supplement their insectivorous diet with other foods. In common with insectivores, tree shrews have digits tipped with claws, no stereoscopic vision, multiple births, and a dental complement different from that of primates, as well as other traits.

Most researchers place tree shrews among the insectivores, but this was not always true. Because of anatomical and behavioral traits shared with primates, tree shrews are often the models referred to when trying to reconstruct the earliest stages of primate evolution. Unfortunately, there is virtually no fossil record to document the evolutionary transition from insectivores to primates. We must rely on inferences from later fossils and living representatives of both the insectivores and primates. Using insectivores as our model for what early primates looked like and how they may have behaved, it is suggested that the ancestors of the primates and the earliest primates themselves were small, nocturnal insectivores and relied more heavily upon the sense of smell than do modern primates. Primates diverged from the insectivores by adapting to a mode of life that included an omnivorous diet and life in the trees. This new diet and habitat led to fundamental anatomical and behavior changes as noted in the following pages.

THE PRIMATES

A number of anatomical traits that characterize Primates (Clark, 1970; Box 3-3) may be related to behavioral complexity. The free and precise movement of the hands and the forelimbs leads to our own tool manipulation abilities. A shift from an olfactory to a visual reliance leads to a different perception of the world. The cerebral cortex increases in size and complexity. There is a lengthening of the prenatal and postnatal life, which demands prolonged infant care by the care giver and allows time for the offspring to learn how to exploit environmental resources. Jolly (1985:230) stated, "If there is an essence to being a primate, it is the progressive evolution of intelligence as a way of life." Table 3-4 provides a chronological outline of primate evolution.

Primate Traits

Primates typically exhibit a number of the following traits:

- Nails instead of claws on their digits; the digits have dermal pads.
- Prehensile (grasping) hands and feet.
- Five fingers and five toes—a condition called **pentadactyly**.

- Tendency toward complete bony enclosure of the eye orbits.
- Forward placement of the eye orbits.
- Opposability of the toe and thumb to the remaining digits.
- Enlarged cerebral brain hemispheres, which are related to the primate's sense organs.
- One pair of thoracically placed mammary glands.
- Well-developed **clavicles** (the so-called collarbones).
- Reduced olfactory sense and increased visual sense.

BOX 3-3   Some Primate Traits

A. Locomotor adaptations
1. Retention of ancestral mammal limb structure; pentadactyly in hands and feet; separate ulna and radius; mobility of the limbs.
2. Evolution of mobile and grasping (prehensile) hands and feet; nails replacing claws in most forms.
3. Retention of a tail in most monkeys. In some New World monkeys the tail is prehensile and functions as an extra hand for grasping.
4. Evolution of an erect sitting posture, which was important for structural erectness; rotation of the foramen magnum to a position beneath the skull.
5. Evolution of nervous system to provide precise and rapid musculature control.

B. Sensory adaptations
1. Enlargement of the eyes.
2. Evolution of color vision and increased sensitivity to low light levels.
3. Medial (forward) rotation of the eyes, which allows stereoscopic vision (overlapping fields of vision).
4. In many primates, enclosure of the eye in a bone cup, which results in greater protection.
5. Reduction of the snout and loss of the naked rhinarium in monkeys and apes, both of which indicate a decreasing reliance on the olfactory sense.
6. The increasing reliance on vision and decreasing reliance on olfaction supported by a reorganization of the brain's structures.
7. Internal ear structures enclosed.

C. Dental traits
1. Simple cusp patterns in the molar teeth. Old World monkeys have bilophodont lower molars (four cusps in two parallel rows), and apes and humans have the Y-5 lower molar cusp configuration (five cusps) or some variant of the Y-5.
2. All Old World monkeys, apes, and humans usually have 32 teeth—2 incisors, 1 canine, 2 premolars, and 3 molars in each quadrant of the jaw. Most New World monkeys have 36 teeth as a result of an extra premolar in each quadrant of the jaw.

D. General characteristics
1. Lengthened period of maturation, infant dependency, and gestation compared with most mammals; a decreased number of young per parturition, usually one infant born each parturition; relatively long life span.
2. Relatively large and complex brains, especially those regions controlling vision, manipulation of the hands and feet, muscle coordination and control, and memory and learning.
3. Year-round, bisexual social groups organized on the basis of age, sex, and matrilineal kinship.

Some data from B. Campbell, *Humankind Emerging*, 1982. Boston: Little, Brown.

TABLE 3-4   Basics of Primate Evolution

Know This ⤷

Epoch (mya)	Habitat	Event
Paleocene (66–53)	Subtropical (cool/dry)	Possible primate remains at end of Paleocene
Eocene (53–37)	Tropical (warm/wet)	Prosimian-like adapids and omomyids in North America and Europe; anthropoids in Africa and Asia by later early Eocene
Oligocene (37–25)	Temperate (cool/dry)	New World monkeys; monkeys and hominoids in Africa and Eurasia
Miocene (25–5.2)	Temperate (warmer)	Hominoids in Africa and Eurasia; divergence of ape and human lineages
Pliocene (5.2–1.8)	Temperate (cool/dry)	Hominids in Africa ca 5 mya, first *Homo* around 2.4 mya
Pleistocene (1.8–0.01)	Temperate	Speciation of *Homo* and worldwide dispersal

• A reproductive strategy that usually includes one infant each birth and extensive parental care.

Not all primates have all these traits, and other mammals have some of these traits. For example, some marsupials have nailed digits and prehensile hands and feet, and a number of mammalian orders have clavicles, partially enclosed eye orbits, and pectoral mammary glands.

Primates are a good example of a diversified group. Most common primate traits stem from either (1) a retention of ancient or generalized vertebrate and mammalian traits or (2) the development of an **arboreal** (tree-living) adaptation. Primates are broadly spread throughout the Old and New World tropics. The order Primates is subdivided into four groups: **prosimians** (the most primitive and earliest members), **ceboids** (New World monkeys), **cercopithecoids** (Old World monkeys), and **hominoids** (apes and humans). We also often talk about **hominids**, a term most often used to characterize the earliest stages of human evolution, and **pongids**, a term referring to chimpanzees, gorillas, orangutans, and their ancestors.

The Human-Ape Relationship

In 1863, T. H. Huxley published a group of essays entitled *Evidence as to Man's Place in Nature*, in which he argued for a close relationship between humans and anthropoid apes (especially the chimpanzee and gorilla). Although an anthropoid ape derivation of humans was vaguely perceived by certain eighteenth-century philosophers, Huxley seems to have been the first to express it in modern, scientific form. Darwin supported Huxley's contentions in his 1871 book *The Descent of Man*. Sir A. Keith produced a plausible explanation of how **brachiating** (arm-swinging beneath the branches) apes could have evolved into bipedal humans. Keith's explanation is now mainly of historical value because it has been substantially revised based on current fossil evidence.

One way of clarifying the relationship between humans and chimpanzees is analysis of DNA (deoxyribonucleic acid), the genetic basis of all life. DNA strands can be compared by using the technique of DNA hybridization, in which the links between the double strands of the DNA helix are broken by heating. As DNA cools, the strands realign and pair again. The extent of relatedness of DNA strands is shown by the degree to which the strands reassociate. Single DNA strands from different species can be placed together to determine if they will link up again. For humans and chimpanzees, the single strands bond again—this bonding is called DNA hybridization. The next step compares human double-stranded DNA to the hybridized human–chimpanzee double-stranded DNA. Similarities and differences are measured in terms of thermal stability, that is, the difference between the dissociation temperatures (the temperature at which the strands separate) of hybridized chimpanzee–human DNA and reannealed (rejoined) human DNA. By comparing the temperatures at which human DNA and hybridized chimpanzee–human DNA chains dissociate, the percentage of identity in the nucleotide base pair sequences that form DNA is determined. DNA hybridization is useful for testing relationships of animals not too distantly related. Single DNA strands will not hybridize if organisms are too distantly related.

Washburn and Moore (1980) studied the similarity of human DNA to that of other primates. The numbers measure the thermal stability in degrees Celsius; the lower the number, the closer the relationship: chimpanzee, 2.4; gorilla 2.5; orangutan, 4.5; Old World monkey, 9; New World monkey, 15 (Figure 3-3).

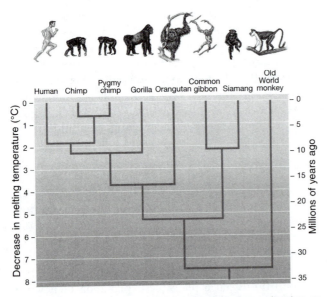

FIGURE 3-3 Evolutionary relationships among primates as indicated by DNA melting temperatures. (*From* LIFE ON EARTH by Audesirk/Audesirk, © 1997. Reprinted by permission of Prentice-Hall, Inc., Upper Saddle River, NJ.)

Protein sequences show a close human–chimpanzee relationship. Protein sequences support the view that humans and chimpanzees are so close that they can hardly be differentiated by this method. For example, a comparison of the percentage of difference in the chains of amino acids in proteins analyzed to date reveals that humans differ from chimpanzees by 0.3 percent; from gorillas by 0.6 percent; from orangutans by 2.8 percent; and from macaque monkeys by 3.9 percent (Goodman, 1975). The lower the percentage differences, the closer is the relationship.

Immunology is also informative; indirect measures of amino acid differences between homologous proteins from two species can be obtained relatively easily. The protein molecule to be compared is used as an antigen, a substance capable of stimulating the production of antibodies by the host organism. Homologous protein molecules from another species are reacted with these antibodies. Goodman's (1975) extensive immunological surveys supported a close human–chimpanzee relationship. The following numbers are immunological distance units measuring reactions of other primates to humans in immunological tests. The smaller the number, the greater is the reaction and the closer is the relationship: chimpanzee, 9; gorilla, 8; orangutan, 20; gibbon, 24; macaque, 34; *Cebus* (New World monkey), 71; prosimians, 100.

The human–chimpanzee relationship is closest in terms of DNA hybridization and protein chains in amino acids. The gorilla is closely behind in terms of its relationship to humans in all but the immunological distance units, where they are more similar to humans than are chimpanzees.

One result of the close molecular relationship of humans and apes has been a suggested revision of the taxonomic scheme. Most scientists place the apes and humans into two separate families, Hominidae for humans and Pongidae for apes. Yunish and Prakash's (1982) detailed comparative analysis of high-resolution chromosomes led to their suggestion for placing humans, chimpanzees, and gorillas into the Hominidae and recognizing two subfamilies, the Ponginae (orangutans) and the Homininae (humans, chimpanzees, and gorillas). It is too early to say if this suggested revision will take hold, but it has generated a good deal of discussion.

More recent information from molecular genetics and DNA studies indicates that humans and chimpanzees are closer genetically to each other than either is to the gorilla. This viewpoint is bolstered by the divergence times of the different forms (Table 3-5). For example, gorillas may have diverged from the common ancestor about 8 to 10 mya, while humans and chimpanzees may still have been united in the same evolutionary line until about 7.7 to 6.8 mya. However, using information from comparative anatomy (for example, comparing structures, muscles, and functions), the chimpanzee and gorilla appear to be each other's closest relative. The issue is obviously still not settled and is currently one of the most heatedly debated in primate evolution.

Based on multivariate analyses of the teeth, Mahaney and Sciulli (1983) concluded that extant humans and African apes might be subsumed into a single

TABLE 3-5 Comparison of Divergence Times among Primates Based on the Fossil and Immunological Records (in millions of years)

Species	Immunological Distance Time Estimates	Fossil Record Time Estimates
Human and chimpanzee	4 ± 1.5[a]	7–5
Human and gibbon	12 ± 3[a]	19–15
Human and rhesus monkey	22–20[b]	40–26
Human and New World monkey (capuchin)	38–35[b]	60–50

[a]Data from P. Andrews and J. Cronin, "The relationship of *Sivapithecus* and *Ramapithecus* and the evolution of the orangutan," *Nature*, 1982, 297:541.

[b]Data from V. Sarich and A. Wilson, "An immunological time scale for hominid evolution," *Science*, 1967, 158:1200.

family, the Hominidae, with subfamily distinction. This conclusion is in line with the suggestion of Yunish and Prakash.

Two major questions concerning the human–ape split from a common ancestor are, Do chimpanzees and gorillas share a slightly closer relationship to humans than do the other apes? and, Are humans more allied to one of the great apes to the exclusion of the others? Although Schwartz (1984, 1987) argued for a close human–orangutan relationship, most data stress that the closest human and ape relationship is between humans and chimpanzees.

Marks (1991) adamantly stated that the DNA hybridization data, and perhaps the molecular data generally, do not indicate that humans and chimpanzees are more closely related than either is to the gorilla. Marks argued that the evidence is inaccurate and that chimpanzees–gorillas–humans share an equally close genetic relationship.

Muscular and skeletal features also suggest a close human–African ape relationship. These commonalities result from a shared ancestral locomotor pattern, for example, brachiation. (A cautionary note must be added: The ancestors of modern humans and apes probably had a generalized locomotor pattern in which arm-swinging was complementary to quadrupedalism, walking on all fours. Ancestral hominoids were not specialized for one locomotor behavior.) Many of these shared features are ancestral traits, that is, traits inherited from their shared common ancestor. For example, the human trunk is similar to that of an ape in breadth and shortness of the lumbar (lower back) region. The similarity in the upper body of humans and apes extends to the length of the clavicle and many details of the bones, joints, and muscles. We share with apes major structural features of the trunk and motion, making possible such actions as stretching to the side and hanging comfortably by the arms. Humans and apes also share a number of similarities in the "soft" (non-bony) parts, most strikingly in the upper limbs.

THE HUMAN PRIMATE

What makes humans (members of the family Hominidae) unique among the primates (Table 3-6)? Why are we included in a different taxonomic group than other members of the order Primates? From an evolutionarily perspective, the most significant of our uniquely modern human traits are these: (1) a completely erect posture and habitual bipedal gait; (2) abstract and symbolical communication known as language; (3) capacity for abstract and symbolic thought; (4) cultural way of life, providing as it does immense opportunities for learning; (5) comparatively large brains; and (6) consistent tool use and manufacture and reliance on tools for survival.

We cannot deny that other animals, particularly other primates, learn by experience and observation. Some animals, including other primates, transmit learned behavior from one generation to another; this transgenerational passing of learned behavior is the basis for cultural behavior. Furthermore, some animals, such as chimpanzees, make and use tools—an activity once thought to be our preserve. Examples of chimpanzee tool use include modification of leaves to absorb water, modification of twigs by chimpanzees at Gombe in Tanzania to insert into termite mounds, and using branches to crack nuts, as is done by chimpanzees in the Tai Forest in the Ivory Coast. These and other examples of chimpanzee tool use are discussed in Chapter 4. Some animals also display behavioral patterns we

---

TABLE 3-6   Definitive Traits of the Family Hominidae

Skeletal and muscular adaptations allowing erect straight-knee bipedalism (discussed in Chapter 7).

A well-developed pollex, or thumb, and the loss of opposibility of the hallux, or big toe.

Increased cranial height associated with increased cranial capacities.

Cranial traits including forward placement of the occipital condyles (related to the position of the skull upon the vertebral column), reduced nuchal area on the occipital for neck muscle attachment, strongly developed pyramidal mastoid process.

Reduced projection of the face that is ultimately related to dental changes and reduced sizes of the maxilla and mandible, themselves associated with dental changes. (At least some of these changes are related to diet.)

Dental changes including spatulate-shaped canines and the lack of sexual dimorphism in canine size and shape, lack of canine diastema, bicuspid premolars, evenly rounded dental arcade. In later stages of human evolution there is a marked size reduction of the molar teeth.

Modified from W. LeGros Clark, *The Fossil Evidence for Human Evolution*, 1964, Chicago: University of Chicago Press.

readily understand. Yet there are dramatic differences between humans and other primates. We can sit and speculate about this proposition—that is one of our unique traits.

Although curiosity is a major primate trait, we are perhaps the nosiest of the nosy. We climb a hill simply to see what lies beyond. Dostoevski once wrote, "Man needs the unfathomable and the infinite just as much as he does the small planet which he inhabits." As far as we know, we alone among the primates have the capacity for self-reflection. The English author G. W. Corner wrote, "After all, if he is an ape he is the only ape that is debating what kind of ape he is." Seemingly, we alone of all the primates have the ability to communicate about the past and plan for the future—our language allows us this unique trait. Probably we alone of all the animals have moral and philosophical ideas. The English writer William Hazlitt notes, "Man is the only animal that laughs and weeps, for he is the only animal that is struck with the difference between what things are and what they ought to be."

SUMMARY

In 1863, T. H. Huxley suggested that humans were closely related to gorillas and chimpanzees. The most sensitive measure of that close evolutionary relationship is an analysis of genetic similarity. Genetic data strongly suggest that humans have the closest evolutionary relationship to the African chimpanzee. Humans and chimpanzees may have diverged from a common ancestor as recently as 6–8 million years ago.

Despite the fact that humans have a close evolutionary relationship to nonhuman primates, especially the chimpanzee, a number of features distinguish humans within the order Primates. Humans constantly locomote bipedally, have an abstract means of communication called language, and have a dependency on technology that is part of an elaborate survival mechanism called culture. Culture provides humans with an almost endless means of elaborating on their genetic capabilities.

SUGGESTED READINGS

Bruce, E., and F. Ayala. 1978. Humans and apes are genetically very similar. *Nature* 276:264–265.

Clark, W. Le Gros. 1970. *The Antecedents of Man.* Chicago: Quadrangle Books.

Gibbons, A. 1990. Our chimp cousins get that much closer. *Science* 250:176.

Lewin, R. 1984. DNA reveals surprises in human family tree. *Science* 226:1179–1182.

Lewin, R. 1987. My close cousin the chimpanzee. *Science* 238:273–275.

4

Reconstructing Ancient Human Behavior and Social Organizations: Use of the Comparative Approach

Overview
The Outlook
Foraging Societies
Nonhuman Primates
Social Carnivores
Summary
Suggested Readings

Because fossil and archaeological records provide limited data concerning behavior and social organization, researchers turn their attention to other sources of information to help reconstruct our past. Modern hunter-gatherers (or foragers), for example, serve as analogues for reconstructing how our ancestors adapted to their environment and how they may have made and used tools. Nonhuman primates, our closest phylogenetic relatives, are studied to generate information about ecological and behavioral adaptations. Useful information can also be obtained from watching how social carnivores hunt and dismember their prey. Using nonhuman primate models stresses phylogenetic relationships, whereas reliance on social carnivore models stresses ecological relationships.

If any model proves useful in helping reconstruct human behavioral patterns and social organizations, it will have to be a unique model. We must look not only for similarities between ourselves and other primates, but we must also explore our differences. Models allow new inferences to be drawn and new insights to be reached; they provide new meaning to data. Without the models discussed in this chapter, little could be said about the behavior, diet, social organization, and mating systems of long-extinct human ancestors.

OVERVIEW

This chapter discusses possible models for helping us understand and reconstruct early human behavior and social organizations. Models can be used in many ways, and various models have been proposed for the purpose of helping to understand human evolution. In this book, for example, various arguments (scenarios)* have been mentioned to try to help explain the appearance of a morphological or behavioral trait.

Many mistaken attempts have been made to rely on one model to explain unique traits in human evolution. Various definitions have been offered in an attempt to explain what it means to be called hominid or human. One of the earliest explanations is the "man the hunter" hypothesis. In this scenario, first proposed by Charles Darwin, hunting is promoted as the key behavioral feature redirecting human evolution. Despite the many deficiencies in the hunting scenario, it is clear that hunting and meat eating played important roles at some point in human evolution and that hunting has affected our evolutionary history (Tooby & DeVore, 1987).

According to Jolly's (1970) seed-eating hypothesis, the basic early hominid dietary adaptation was feeding on seeds and other small objects. This diet purportedly led to a number of unique dental traits shared by both hominids and such monkeys as the gelada. A diet of seeds and small objects supposedly led to the initial divergence of the human and ape lines from a common ancestor.

A third scenario was proposed by C. O. Lovejoy (1981). He argued that a key innovation enhancing the survival of our early human ancestors was monogamous pair bonding (leading to the early appearance of a nuclear family—a female, a male, and their offspring) and male provisioning. Both these patterns were related to bipedalism. This scenario stressed the male's provisioning of a female and her youngster as an enhancement of their survival and the development of bipedal behavior by males. It failed, however, to explain why females also become bipeds. An attempt to rectify this failure was provided by N. Tanner (1981), in the "gathering by females" scenario. Tanner's hypothesis has often been substituted for the male-provisioning-by-hunting hypothesis. However, because both the "gathering by females" and the "hunting by males" hypotheses stress the contributions of only one of the two sexes, each fails as an explanation. "Any account of hominid evolution that concentrates only on males, or only on females, or suggests that any specific age–sex class is responsible for hominid evolution is defective" (Tooby & DeVore, 1987:192). An explanation cannot merely assert, as do both of the preceding, that one subsistence pattern is superior to or more reliable than the other. It must show why such is true.

Rather than propose that one model or group of models is best for reconstructing human behavior and social organizations, we present information from different models to show what kinds of information can be gathered using a

---

* A *scenario* is a formal proposition about previously existing organisms, how they responded to their environment, and what specific evolutionary changes they underwent over time.

comparative approach. This approach is more eclectic. We look, for example, at the *possible* clues that can be provided from research on modern human foraging populations, nonhuman primates, and social carnivores. Each of these sources provides information that can give us useful clues in an attempt to reconstruct behavior and social organizations from bones and artifacts.

In using modern human populations and nonhuman primate models, we stress phylogeny (evolutionary relatedness) rather than ecology. When using social carnivore models, we stress ecological relationships (hunting and meat eating) instead of phylogeny. Nonhuman primate models stress similar behaviors that have appeared in evolutionarily related species. Social carnivore models stress similar behaviors that have appeared in evolutionarily unrelated species. In the latter, behavioral similarities are due to shared ecological pressures.

Any model useful in helping to reconstruct early human behavioral patterns and social organizations will have to be a unique model. Humans are unique animals—no one model is appropriate for reconstructing our past (Kinzey, 1987b, and Potts, 1987, both made this point). We need to not only look for similarities between ourselves and nonhuman primates, for example, but also explore our differences. Those differences making us unique may be more important in helping understand our evolutionary past than citing long lists of shared similarities with other phylogenetically or ecologically related species (Potts, 1987).

Despite the potential problems of using models, of misusing models, or of using inappropriate models, models allow new inferences to be drawn and new insights to be reached. Models give new meaning to data. Without models little could be said about the behavior, diet, social organization, and mating system of long-extinct human ancestors. According to Tooby and DeVore (1987:184), "Models are essential for the reconstruction of hominid behavioral evolution.... [They] offer the eventual prospect of alleviating the shortage of information about hominid evolution." The question is not whether we should use models. The question is, What models are useful and how can models best be used?

THE OUTLOOK

The comparative approach may help to determine the similarities and differences between certain phenomena in humans and other animal species, and it may help us begin to understand how we are like or unlike other primates. However, the comparative approach will not, by itself, establish the causes of similarities and differences. Delineation of these causes depends on one's theoretical and disciplinary approach. The comparative method does not consider all possible examples; thus a comparison is open to a voluntarily or involuntarily biased selection. Nonhuman primates, for example, are so varied that it is not difficult to find one or several examples of almost any point one espouses. Comparative discussions of human and nonhuman social behavior seem particularly vulnerable to culturally loaded generalizations with the assumption that they are true of all people. Despite these constraints, a comparative approach yields useful information and is a main reason why we can deduce a fair amount of information about the social organizations and behaviors of long-extinct humans from their cultural and skeletal remains.

Various lines of evidence can be employed to reconstruct a species' evolutionary history. The fossil and archaeological records preserve traces of past behavior and the bones of a species. All such evidence is important in understanding and reconstructing what a species looked like and how it lived. This record, however, is always incomplete because it is based on relative degrees of preservation and, more important, because many aspects of behavior do not fossilize. Vital questions about our behavior and social organization can, at best, be solved only partially by the fossil and archaeological records (Table 4-1).

TABLE 4-1   Major Human Behavioral, Anatomical, and Physiological Changes since the Human–Ape Divergence[a]

Trait	Visible in Fossil/ Archaeological Record	Inferred
Anatomical/physiological traits		
Postcranial modification for bipedalism	X	
Modification of hands for effective tool use and manufacture	X	
Reorganization and enlargement of brain	X	
Reduction of face and jaws; remodeling of cranium, face, and jaws	X	
Reduction of body hair and changes in glands of the skin		X
Modified estrous (ovulation) cycle		X
Modification of vocal tract for speech	X	
Changes relating to birth processes (i.e., lengthening of gestation, delayed maturation) (seen in fossil record)	X	
Behavioral/social changes		
Development and consistent use of tools	X	
Inclusion of meat protein in diet; hunting behavior	X	
Temporarily defined home base	X	
Food sharing and sexual division of labor	?	X
Controls on emotional displays		X
Larger social groups	X	
Permanent dwelling structures	X	
In much later periods, evidence of art, symbolism, and spiritualism	X	
Extension of social-bonding mechanisms	?	X

[a]These categories should not be considered absolute differentiators of human and nonhuman primates. For example, there are data on tool use and manufacture among some modern apes; consumption of animal protein, hunting, and scavenging among some monkeys and apes; and psychological attachment to a home area. More likely, the *combination* of these and other factors, rather than the presence of any one of them, resulted in the differentiation of human and nonhuman primates. More items will be added as fossil and archaeological records increase.

The modern world is full of potential comparisons yielding answers to some of the questions raised by the fossil record. The problem is to find the source(s) likely to yield the most appropriate answers. In terms of understanding human evolution, there are three major sources whose behavior can yield useful comparisons. The first source is contemporary human groups living in habitats somewhat resembling those occupied by earlier humans and following a food-getting pattern of hunting and gathering, or foraging. The few surviving groups of foragers may help us understand the quality of social and emotional life of times past because all humans lived in small social groups of hunters and gatherers prior to the appearance of agriculture about 12,000 years ago.

No modern foraging population can provide a perfect model for reconstructing early human social organization or behavior. However, such populations offer guidance in matters of interpretation. For example, early humans and most modern foragers (because of restrictions imposed by food and water sources) exist in relatively low density populations maintained by widely spaced births, perhaps infanticide, and occasional episodes of locally intensified death rates during droughts, food shortages, and so on.

Evidence from Australia helps clarify the social nature of ancient hunter-gatherers (O'Neill, 1994). Although foragers are usually described as small groups of individuals migrating about the landscape, evidence from Australia and some other places suggests that some foragers lived in relatively large and sedentary groups resulting from good environmental conditions. By at least 10,000 years ago, populations in several regions of the world had developed complex, non-agricultural societies.

Extant nonhuman primates are a second source of information for reconstructing our past because of our shared genetic relationship and because some, such as the savanna baboons and bonobos, or pygmy chimpanzees, live in a habitat similar to that which we assume was once inhabited by our ancestors. The nonhuman primates' mode of adaptation to habitat pressures, their food-getting and predator avoidance behaviors, and aspects of their social structure are all important clues to how humans adapted in similar circumstances. Tool use and manufacture, an important feature in human evolution, was once identified as a uniquely human trait. Chimpanzees, however, make and use tools in many circumstances. Because the chimpanzee is our closest nonhuman primate relative, it is relevant to understanding human evolution to know how and in what situations the chimpanzee uses tools. Furthermore, we should learn why the chimpanzee makes tools and many other nonhuman primates do not. This information can help reconstruct the adaptive situation leading to our ancestor's commitment to tool use and manufacture.

Social carnivores have provided clues to certain of our behavioral patterns. In contrast to nonhuman primates, who are basically vegetarians with an occasional addition of meat to the diet, wild dogs, lions, and hyenas provide clues to the earliest hunting methods, the adaptiveness of food sharing, and the use of communicative signals during hunting. However, the comparison of human hunting as a social pattern with the hunting of social carnivores misses the special nature of the human hunting adaptation. As Washburn and Moore (1974) noted, human females do not go out to hunt and regurgitate food to their young when they return. Human young do not stay in dens; they are carried by their mothers. Male wolves do not kill with tools, butcher, and share with females who have been gathering food. The human hunting pattern that appeared relatively recently in human evolution is new and unique. The archaeological record suggests that meat eating (but not necessarily hunting) and tool use were important at an early stage in human evolution. When considering the possible size of the home range, hunting techniques, and kinds and sizes of animals available to a hunter, social carnivores do provide useful insights.

The point is not that we are, or ever were, nothing more than social carnivores or that modern nonhuman primates are an adequate model for our evolutionary past. Modern social carnivores and nonhuman primates have evolved, as we have; therefore they can serve only as partial models. We can learn just as much when these models provide answers clarifying our uniqueness as when they provide answers highlighting our commonality. If we find a behavioral trait differentiating us from these models, we may be dealing with a uniquely human behavior. The more we know about the evolutionary history and ecological adaptations of our phylogenetically related primate relatives and the ecologically related social carnivores, the more we learn about processes that shaped our evolutionary past.

Nonhuman primates, social carnivores, and extant human hunting-gathering populations present an array of natural experiments in their various adaptations to multiple habitat demands. Their way of coping helps us better understand our ancestral coping skills.

FORAGING SOCIETIES

Because events in the prehistoric past cannot be directly observed, the anthropologist can reconstruct them only from material evidence recovered in modern times. Such reconstruction is based on analogy, whereby the identity of unknown forms is inferred from those already known. One problem with this approach is that living societies whose technology is similar to that inferred from the archaeological record may be incorrectly viewed as exact analogues for the reconstruction of the entire prehistoric culture.

Ethnoarchaeology utilizes living populations for reconstructing our past. Although ethnoarchaeological research provides many clues for the study of extinct populations, there is considerable debate concerning the nature and limits of ethnographic analogy for analyzing prehistoric human behavior. Modern cultural systems are unlikely to reflect the total range of prehistoric systems. Freeman (1968) argued that direct analogies between modern foragers and earlier humans in terms of their cultural systems and social organization can be misleading because we may be dealing with the material effects of cultural behavior in adaptive systems vastly different from those of today. Gifford (1980), who was concerned with the formation of prehistoric sites, stated, "The key to elucidation of the past by studies of the present lies in assuming a comprehensive approach to the study of process and effect. By closely defining site formation processes, one can frame and test hypotheses concerning areas of knowledge which at present remain hazy."

One individual to study foragers as a guide to the past was Richard Gould (1968a, 1968b, 1969), who worked in the Gibson Desert of western Australia with a two-family group of thirteen aborigines (three women, two men, and eight children). These people were once among the few people in the world still making and using stone tools regularly. Gould's objective was to collect information that might bear on the interpretation of prehistoric sites and the reconstruction of prehistoric social behavior. He and his wife observed the details of toolmaking, hunting, camping, composition of **living floors** (areas of intensive activity), and the aborigines' extremely complex system of social behaviors.

During the peak of the Australian summer, a day begins before sunup. Obtaining the daily food starts around 6:00 or 7:00 A.M., before the day becomes unbearably hot. The group divides into two parties to search for food, and everyone leaves camp. Women gather plant foods; men do the hunting, a less dependable way of obtaining food in the desert. Hunting generally occurs from ambush, and where possible, hunters take advantage of a water hole. On most occasions all that the men have to show for their hunting efforts is a lizard or two. Women are more apt to provide the daily food, since roughly 60 to 70 percent of the aborigine's diet is plant food.

The Australian aborigines' remarkable adaptation to their rather harsh desert environment includes a technology similar to that of a toolmaker of 30,000 years ago. A common tool is the "adz flake," which is thick with a fairly steep edge. It closely resembles scrapers common to many prehistoric sites. Aborigines use their teeth as tools or for making some kinds of tools. (They nibble flakes from stone with the premolar teeth.) Upper Paleolithic toolmakers may have used their dental structure similarly.

Aborigine tooth use is a useful example of how a study of modern foragers can help us understand some morphological traits encountered in the fossil record. Because dental remains comprise a large proportion of the fossil evidence and because a number of inferences are based on dental wear patterns, it would be of use to note how modern populations use their teeth. If teeth are used as tools, what types of tooth wear patterns result? What types of wear patterns result from different diets? Can gritty diets affect the crown surfaces, as is claimed for some human fossil samples? A study of dental use can also be of help in understanding cranial morphology. For example, how does the use of the teeth as tools affect the chewing musculature and surface features of the skull or **mandible** (lower jaw)? These questions can be partly answered from the ethnographic record.

Gould spent much time studying contemporary aboriginal living sites, which represent the daily activities of the people. Such observation provided a wider perspective for interpreting prehistoric living sites. Gould's approach to aboriginal life yielded important data and suggested new possibilities and new analogies.

A concentrated long-term effort was begun in 1967 to gather information on the San people living in the Kalahari Desert of Botswana in southern Africa. Approximately one-third of all existing foragers (some 9,000 persons), once inhabited this 350,000-square-mile expanse. Researchers concentrated on the inhabitants of one small area, which has a radius of fewer than 20 miles and includes 11 permanent water holes and wells, between 400 and 500 plant and animal species, and about 450 people.

The project investigated many aspects of San life. Archaeologists excavated San living floors, asking for explanations of what they uncovered in the hope of generating alternative interpretations of prehistoric sites. San garbage dumps were analyzed to see the kinds and amounts of accumulations left, in the hope of gaining a clearer understanding of the many seemingly prehistoric "garbage dumps"—for example, how many people it took to accumulate the debris and what items were most likely to survive.

Much time was spent watching what San eat and their manner of obtaining food. The basic San tools were a pair of unworked stones for cracking nuts and a digging stick. The most important item, the *kaross*, is a combination garment and receptacle draped over a woman's shoulder. Such foods as nuts, berries, and roots, as well as any small children, are stuffed into the pocket formed by the drape. Because of its utilitarian value, early populations may have developed some type of carrying device. Plant foods provide the bulk of the diet; obtaining meat is a riskier affair and has less predictable results.

Studies of San social behavior and organization were undertaken. A study was made of the choice of living sites to get a clearer idea of living-floor patterns found at long-deserted sites. Lee (1978) studied factors that force people to move from camp to camp. The San typically occupy a camp for weeks or months before they literally eat their way out of it. Such very basic data may help explain some of the migrations of prehistoric populations.

In addition to providing information on tool use and manufacture, dietary patterns, and the formation of living sites, foragers may provide a picture of the dynamics of the band existence of prehistoric people. One result of these studies was the "magic numbers" hypothesis proposed by Joseph Birdsell (1972). Birdsell noted that forager band sizes range from twenty to fifty persons, and he selected twenty-five as a representative size. This is often called a *microband*. Studies of the Kalahari San and of the Birhar of northern India supported the suggestion that twenty-five is an average group size. Prehistoric populations also probably averaged close to twenty-five members per band. Although there is nothing absolute about this number, it may have something to do with the most efficient working group of adults. The number is consistent with the size range of primate groups generally. A second "magic number," 500, is considered an average for a *dialect tribe* (a macroband or tribe) of foragers, that is, a group all speaking the same dialect. This is a purely human phenomenon.

The number 500 apparently reflects certain features of the human communication system. The unity of foraging societies depends on face-to-face contact, on intimacy among the band members, which creates the impression of belonging to an extended community. The intimacy involves not only the same language but also a store of shared knowledge. The number 500 may also have something to do with an effective size for a breeding population (Washburn & Moore, 1974).

There appears to be a basic limit to the number of persons who are capable of knowing one another well enough to maintain a group identity at the forager level. Murdock (noted in Pfeiffer, 1985) demonstrated the relevance of the number 500 in technological societies. For example, an architect's rule-of-thumb states that enrollment in an elementary school should not exceed 500 pupils if the principal expects to know them all by name.

The underlying mechanisms accounting for the "magic numbers" phenomenon are yet to be resolved; however, the memory capacity of the human brain is surely relevant. Other factors, an effective gene pool, the establishment of feelings of intimacy, and perhaps the effective functioning of informal social control mechanisms, may also be involved. The "magic numbers" hint at the existence of social regularities that we do not yet understand, and the numbers set reasonable limits for group sizes in the prehistoric past.

Studies of modern societies have forced scientists to reassess a number of ideas concerning the social organizations and behaviors of our ancestors. It was once argued that hunting was the pursuit that bonded males together and that it was the basis for an apparent male dominance in society. A strong male bias permeated theory building in human evolution. Hunting, primarily a male activity, was romanticized; supposedly it was an activity requiring considerable intelligence and a complex tool assemblage. Gathering, primarily a female activity, was supposedly a far simpler task requiring a simple tool assemblage and little specialized knowledge. Through a lack of information, and with evident cultural biases, females were relegated to a secondary role as food providers. Their role in human evolution was dismissed through the error of omission or conscious disregard.

This bias has begun to disappear. Not only is plant gathering a major economic strategy, with females often providing the majority of the food supplies, but it is also a complex activity requiring no less specialized knowledge than any other food-gathering activity. Plant gathering requires a knowledge of where to find the plants, in what seasons they are edible, how to obtain the plants, how to prepare them, and so on. In a bisexual species, such as humans, both sexes are important for survival and evolutionary success. The sexual inequality that characterized recent theories of human evolution reflected cultural biases, not biological realities.

NONHUMAN PRIMATES

Behavioral observation of the kind normally conducted by anthropologists and zoologists in the field is called *ethology*. The observer, the ethologist, searches for the functions of the observed behavior patterns, trying to understand what may have shaped their evolution. Ethological studies begin with a description of the behavioral repertoire, the *ethogram*, of the species. The ethogram should be a complete description of an animal's behavioral patterns as well as a discussion of the form and function of such behaviors.

Ethologists are also concerned with comparing the behavior of different populations of the same species. This intraspecific comparison provides an indication of the species' adaptability to different habitats; such adaptability is important as one ascends the phylogenetic ladder.

In an earlier chapter we noted the importance of social living among mammals. Primates are among the most social of the mammals. Primates are found in both the Old and the New World. Most primates reside in social groups that are organized according to established rules of age, sex, and relative dominance. For the most part, primate groups are permanent, year-long, bisexual organizations as opposed to the seasonal, sometimes unisexual groupings of many other social animals. Social behavior is keenly important for understanding primate adaptations and evolution. Because of the highly social nature of nonhuman primates, we must view natural groups, as well as individuals, as the adaptive units of the species.

Primate young are born relatively immature; they need the protection and care afforded not only by their mother but also by their social group. The pattern of prolonged immaturity, coupled with a relatively large brain size, means that life in a primate social group provides many opportunities for learning. Social living places a premium on learning. Most of the primate behavioral repertoire is learned, resulting in substantial individual behavioral plasticity that allows flexibility in response to environmental challenges and gives the primate an evolutionary advantage, especially in relatively unstable environments. Primates can, for example, respond to changing environmental conditions rather instantaneously by modifying their behavior. This behavioral flexibility has relevance for understanding human evolution. If we are to understand the habitat shift that occurred among our ancestors, we must be cognizant of the behavioral background of the monkeys and apes. This successful habitat shift obviously involved behavioral plasticity, that is, the ability to adapt to new surroundings, and a constant curiosity leading to the acquisition of new traits to meet new environmental challenges, such as new foods and new predators (Poirier, 1969). Our ancestors were not carbon copies of extant primates, but the rich variability of extant primate behavior makes it possible to reconstruct the most probable pattern of related forms in the past (Jay, 1968).

Two Primate Models: The Savanna-Dwelling Baboon and the Chimpanzee

Various nonhuman primates have served as models for reconstructing early stages of human evolution. One of the first was the savanna-dwelling baboon. It was argued that when early humans (or their immediate ancestors) moved out of tropical forests, they had to deal with problems similar to those of other terrestrial primates, such as baboons. These problems included predator avoidance and coping with scattered food resources. Early baboon studies stressed male dominance and female submissiveness, tightly organized social groups, and high levels of aggression. These features found their way into many evolutionary scenarios and were used to support such concepts as the so-called naturalness of domination by males over females among humans and the supposed innateness of human aggressive behavior.

Over time and after much more study, several fallacies appeared in the argument that extant savanna-dwelling baboons and extinct (as well as extant) humans share a number of close behavioral similarities. For example, forest-dwelling baboons do not exhibit the aggressiveness seen in savanna-dwelling baboons, nor do they display closed social groups and obvious male dominance. These differences show the baboon's range of behavioral plasticity and clearly indicate that the behavior patterns witnessed on the savanna are not genetically inherited. (This finding should caution any reader who unhesitatingly accepts claims for the innateness of human social behaviors.) Taking just one pattern, supposed male domination, we now know that female primates in many (most?) species play a far larger role in maintaining social order and social traditions than was previously credited. Female primates are not mere spectators in a male game for sexual dominance. They have a large say in who their mates will be, for example. (In the Tai forest, female chimps sneak away from males in their group to mate with males in another group. DNA studies indicate half of all female matings occur this way.)

Sherwood Washburn (1978), who, along with Irven DeVore, pioneered studies on savanna baboons, stated:

> Because of my early research on the social organization of baboons, my work is often cited to support theories about the animal origins of human behavior. Obviously, we studied animal behavior to find both possible similarities and possible differences. As time has passed it is the differences that seem more important, especially when considering social behavior. (p. 70)

Despite this caveat, baboons can provide useful data about some adaptations to savanna life. What is obviously needed is a host of studies on various savanna-dwelling forms, including nonprimates, to document the range of possible adaptations. For example, studies of savanna-venturing chimpanzees, who are more closely related phylogenetically to humans than are baboons, have added a needed dimension to our understanding of primate adaptations to savanna life.

We can give another example of the dangers involved in making naive comparisons between human and nonhuman primates. Nonhuman primates are often looked to as models for reconstructing the mating patterns of early humans. What has been generally lost in such comparisons is the fact that there is *no one* primate pattern of sexual behavior. It was once accepted that apes were similar in their reproductive behaviors and that humans were remarkably different from apes. This assumption is not true. Ape reproductive behavior varies so much from one form to another that reconstruction of an ancestral human reproductive pattern is unlikely.

Female orangutans, for example, have no external signs of ovulation (such as is common in the genital swelling among some monkeys and apes), and animals may mate on any day of the month. Orangutans employ a wide variety of copulatory positions, including face-to-face copulation, a common human pattern. Orangutans are usually solitary and the least social of the great apes (the chimpanzees, gorillas, and orangutans), despite their reproductive similarity to humans. These observations show that continuous sexual receptivity does not always lead to the formation of long-term social groups.

From the viewpoint of reconstructing human evolution, studies of the chimpanzee have generated many suggestions concerning our ancestral behavior and social organization. Of special interest are the facts of chimpanzee intelligence, communication, sociability and adaptability, duration of the mother–infant tie and sibling relationships, bipedalism, extent of object manipulation and tool use, heavy reliance on plant foods and some predation, and the important roles that social tradition and the environmental context have on social organization and behavior (Tanner, 1981).

As more data become available on chimpanzees, there is more emphasis on the diversity in almost every aspect of chimpanzee life and social organization. There are variations in hunting behavior, fighting, tool use and manufacture, and social interactions (Gibbons, 1992).

At least thirty-two populations of chimpanzees use and make tools. Chimpanzees in the far west of Africa use tools most extensively. These tools range from twigs (used for getting termites, ants, and honey from a bee's nest), to picks (for getting marrow from bones), to crude stone hammers and anvils for cracking nuts. In contrast, east African chimpanzees, except those at Gombe and Mahale, Tanzania, use tools less frequently. It has been suggested that at one east African study site, Kibale, Uganda, food supplies may be so rich that the use of tools to extract food is not needed.

Boesch-Achermann and Boesch's (1994) studies of rain forest–dwelling chimpanzees challenge the notion that tool use and toolmaking developed on the savanna. Their studies of rain forest–dwelling chimpanzees augment our understanding of variability in such activities by chimpanzees in different environments. Rain forest chimpanzees of the Tai National Forest, Ivory Coast, make and use more kinds of tools than chimpanzees dwelling in more open areas. Tai chimpanzees perform more modifications of their tools and transport them over longer distances. Tai chimpanzees combine various kinds of tools in one operation—for example, to access the contents of a favored nut. These tool operations are more complex than those among the chimpanzees in Gombe.

The Tai chimpanzees are quite purposeful in their use of stone tools to open the nuts they favor, those from the *Panda oleosa* tree. Because stones are rare in the Tai forest, chimpanzees regularly carry tools and nuts between cracking sites. Boesch-Achermann and Boesch (1994) found that stone hammers were purposely chosen; their weight and the distance they had to be carried seemingly were carefully considered. "Such selection requires mental operations, measurement and conservation of distance, comparison of several distances, permutations of objects in a given map, and permutation of the point of reference" (ibid., p. 13). Toolmaking is a complex task.

The limited distribution of nut-cracking behaviors suggests cultural differences between chimpanzee populations. Chimpanzees west of the Sassandra River crack nuts; those to the east do not. Nut cracking is a learned behavior, not unlike the skilled use and making of tools by the Gombe chimpanzees. Like Gombe, female chimpanzees in the Tai Forest are the skilled users and makers of tools. Females transport stone hammers between panda trees. Males are easily distracted from tool-using activities. Females generally are more attentive to nut-cracking activities. As at Gombe, female chimpanzees at Tai were found to be the predominant "ant dippers" and "termite fishers."

Hunting behavior and meat eating also show remarkable variability. Chimpanzees of the Tai Forest cooperate in hunting colobus monkeys. And, among these same chimpanzees, the ranking male of the group shares the meat with the female who killed the monkey before other males have a chance to share the meat.

These behaviors are further discussed in the next pages. What is becoming increasingly clear is that chimpanzees, like humans, show a range of *cultural diversity* in their behavioral patterns. This presence of cultural diversity, unthinkable to researchers only a generation or so ago, increasingly narrows the social and behavioral gap between humans and chimpanzees.

One of the best-known chimpanzee researchers is Jane Goodall, whose studies, begun in 1960 in the Gombe Stream Reserve, Tanzania, have added significantly to our knowledge about chimpanzees and have provided insights for reconstructing the earliest stages of human evolution (Goodall, 1986). Prior to Goodall's observations, a common anthropological definition of humans was "man the toolmaker." Humans made tools; that ability separated us from the rest of the primates. Goodall, however, has documented a number of instances of chimpanzee tool use and manufacture. Instances of tool use have also been reported by Japanese investigators, who noted that chimpanzees use tools to probe for and "capture" ants and termites (Nishida & Uehara, 1980). Goodall (1964) saw chimpanzees break off grass stems or thin branches, which they poke into termite holes to get at the termites. If the probe does not fit the hole, the chimpanzee shapes it until it does. Leaves are stripped away to make the tool suitable for "termite fishing." After termites become attached to the probe, the chimpanzee runs the probe across its front teeth and eats the termites. Thus, not only is a tool used, it is also made.

Chimpanzees have been observed chewing a wad of leaves to make them more absorbent and then using the wad as a sponge to sop up rainwater that cannot be reached with the lips. This modification of a handful of leaves is another example of tool use. Chimpanzees used leaves to wipe the remnants of brain from inside a baboon's skull and to dab at a bleeding wound on the rump. They used leaves as toilet paper in the case of diarrhea, and some chimpanzees have used leaves to wipe themselves clean of mud and sticky foods. They have used stout sticks as levers to enlarge the opening of an underground bees' nest and to pry open banana boxes stored at the observation camp, much to the chagrin of Goodall's staff.

Boesch and Boesch (1983, 1984) and Boesch and Boesch-Achermann (1991) described some fascinating instances of tool use by the chimpanzees in Tai

National Park. These chimpanzees break tree nuts with rocks. Among the toughest nuts to crack are those from the *Panda oleosa* tree. These nuts require an estimated 3,500 pounds of pressure to be broken open. The chimpanzees at Tai use stone hammers ranging in weight from 10 ounces to granite blocks of 4 to 45 pounds. Stones are rarely found in the forest, and the chimpanzees have the ability to remember the positions of many of the stones scattered about.

To extract the kernels from within the panda nut, a chimpanzee must handle the stone hammer with skill: "Time and time again, we have been impressed to see a chimpanzee raise a twenty-pound stone above its head, strike a nut with ten or more powerful blows, and then, using the same hammer, switch to delicate little taps from a height of only four inches. To finish the job, the chimps often break off a small piece of twig and use it to extract the last tiny fragments of kernel from the shell" (Boesch and Boesch-Achermann, 1991:53).

There is a sex difference in tool use—females use stone hammers more often than males to crack the panda nuts. Females share up to 60 percent of the nuts they open with their infants. The infant becomes able to fend for itself at about six years of age. Mothers also share other tool-acquired foods such as honey, ants, and bone marrow. Such sharing occurs less often among the females at Gombe.

Three traits differentiate chimpanzee tool use and manufacture from that of humans: (1) We use tools to make other tools—either chimpanzees do not, or they have not been seen to do so. (2) We use tools much more frequently and in more circumstances than do chimpanzees. (3) We depend on tools for survival; the chimpanzee does not. It has been argued that we make tools for the future, whereas other toolmaking animals drop the tool immediately after use. Chimpanzees, however, will carry "termiting" sticks for rather long distances and sometimes from mound to mound, looking for a meal. But they never carry tools for the distances that even early humans did (Toth, 1987). Humans make tools for later contingencies and save them for long periods. The chimpanzee evidently does not but may not need to do so as long as natural materials are so prevalent. Perhaps when we began to use scarcer materials, or materials more difficult to obtain, we began to save them for future use.

McGrew (1978) noted that chimpanzee tool use is basically done by females. Males can make and use tools, but tool use and manufacture is a learned and practiced behavioral tradition usually passed from mother to daughter. Sons are less apt to learn these techniques because they spend less time with their mothers and therefore have less time to observe how tools are made and used. Perhaps the close and usually lifelong association between mothers and daughters in most primates also means that early in human evolution females were more likely than males to make and use tools. Chimpanzee tool use and manufacture are also a function of intelligence and manual dexterity. Although baboons relish the ants and termites eaten by the chimpanzees, and although they have ample opportunity to observe chimpanzees as they "termite fish" or "ant dip," as these acquisition activities are called, baboons seem unable to learn the techniques and apparently lack the necessary manual dexterity.

Orangutans have joined the chimpanzees as documented tool users in the natural environment. C. Van Schaik (Zimmer, 1995), working in the Suaq Balimbing swamp in Sumatra, has seen orangutans using tools to extract food and for other purposes. Like chimpanzees, the Suaq orangs will fashion a stick and insert it into a hole in a termite nest to extract the termites. They also use sticks to scare ants from tree colonies. Most commonly, however, they use sticks to poke into a beehive to extract the honey. Sticks are used to clean prickly hairs from a fruit before the fruit is devoured. Tool use among the orangs at Suaq seems to be quite routine. However, other orangutan populations have not been seen using tools. Perhaps this population is under pressure to develop and use tools because the trees at Suaq are so heavily infested by insects and because the orangs at Suaq depend so heavily on insect food. Van Schaik notes that at other Sumatran swamps with traits similar to those in Suaq, orangs are not seen using tools. Perhaps tool use at Suaq is a cultural pattern, possibly developed originally by a particularly intelligent or dexterous ape.

Until recently it was assumed that humans were the only predatory, meat-eating, food-sharing primates. In fact, a number of nonhuman primates prey on birds, small reptiles, and small mammals. Baboons have been seen to hunt small game like hares and young gazelles. They have also been observed to share food. Chimpanzees hunt and eat meat, and more frequently than originally assumed: "The Gombe Stream chimpanzees are efficient hunters; a group of about 40 individuals may catch over 20 different prey animals during one year" (van Lawick-Goodall, 1971:281–282). Chimpanzee predatory behavior is of marked interest to anthropologists, who are used to considering humans the sole predatory primate.

During a twelve-month study of chimpanzee hunting at Gombe, Teleki (1973a, b) witnessed thirty episodes of predation, twelve of them successful. The prey most often taken was another primate. There is no evidence that chimpanzees take or even pursue animals weighing more than twenty pounds. Japanese investigators (Takahata et al., 1984) witnessed fifty-four instances of predatory behavior among chimpanzees in the Mahale Mountains, Tanzania. Most prey were small animals, and there was a concentration on juvenile members of solitary-living ungulates and small group–living primates. McGrew (1983) showed that chimpanzees prey mostly on mammals; amphibians and reptiles are ignored.

Chimpanzees in some study locations share the rewards of their predatory behavior (Teleki, 1973a). Teleki once observed fifteen chimpanzees spend nine hours devouring and sharing a small animal. Meat is the only food that is shared among group members. Although Teleki documented the sharing of meat, other investigators (Toshisada et al., 1979) have not seen this behavior in their studies. Sharing of prey may be an example of a group-specific behavior and another indication of the plasticity of primate behavior.

Gombe chimpanzees prey heavily on colobus monkeys, killing more than 100 red colobus per year, nearly one-fifth of the monkeys sharing the chimpanzee's range (Stanford, 1995). Most of the monkey prey are immatures under two years of age. Chimpanzees seem to most favor baby colobus, which comprise 75 percent of the kill. The colobus stand their ground against the chimpanzees.

If the colobus broke ranks and fled, the chimpanzees would rather easily catch a lone monkey.

The more males there are in a chimpanzee group, the more likely it is that hunting will occur. Gombe chimpanzees are most apt to hunt colobus when one or more estrous females are in their group. Males sometimes hunt to obtain meat that they offer to sexually receptive females. However, males also hunt when no estrous females are present.

An intense debate in paleoanthropological studies revolves around the issue of what part of the early human diet was vegetable and what part was animal protein. In the latter instance, the debate centers on whether humans hunted or scavenged their meat. Partially because hunting is seen as a more "noble" pursuit and scavenging as a "demeaning" one (thus, in many cultures scavenging carnivores such as hyenas are considered to be lowly animals), early humans were considered to have obtained much of their meat through hunting.

Chimpanzees can help put this debate into perspective. Hasegawa and others (1983) suggested that some reported instances of chimpanzee hunting may in fact have been examples of scavenging. In one chimpanzee population in Tanzania, chimpanzees ate meat that they were neither seen nor heard to kill. It was even suggested that chimpanzees may scavenge meat taken by carnivores. Evidence of such scavenging supports the contention that early humans also obtained some part of their meat through scavenging (Chapter 8).

Another common argument is that human males are the hunters and females are the gatherers. This conception often relegates human females to a secondary position in terms of food acquisition, ignoring the fact that among modern foraging populations females provide the bulk of the food—gathered vegetable food.

Chimpanzees again show that our conceptions of early human evolution may need reworking. For example, although male chimpanzees do most of the hunting at Gombe, females do hunt. Females, however, do not hunt as vigorously when males are present—and this may account for the scant reports of hunting by female chimpanzees. When males are absent, females may hunt on their own. Female chimpanzees at Gombe have scavenged meat killed by baboons. Although baboon males may be larger than female chimpanzees, the latter are not deterred by the former's presence. Japanese investigators (Takahata et al., 1984) showed that predation by female chimpanzees inhabiting the Mahale Mountains is more frequent than predation by female chimpanzees at Gombe. Sex differences were recognized in prey selection and hunting methods among the Mahale Mountain chimpanzees. Female chimpanzees in Mahale hunt alone and prey especially on bushpigs and blue duikers. Although a small group of male chimpanzees sometimes chases prey, definite evidence of collective hunting has not been obtained at Mahale. On the other hand, male chimpanzees at Gombe hunt in small groups, and Goodall (1986) noted that brothers cooperate in hunting behavior.

McGrew (1978) also noted sex differences in the mode of food acquisition among chimpanzees. Although the males at Gombe consume more meat from birds and mammals, females consume more insects. This difference may be related to the female's more frequent ant dipping and termite fishing. McGrew categorized the prey acquisition by male chimpanzees as hunting because it is a cooperative act and involves moving relatively great distances. He characterizes the female chimpanzee's behavior as gathering because it basically consists of an individual accumulating many small units of food that is concentrated at a few known permanent sources. McGrew's use of the words *hunting* and *gathering* suggested a continuity between chimpanzee and early human food-getting activities. The possible sex differentiation of chimpanzee food-getting behavior may suggest a reevaluation of the human fossil record.

Chimpanzee hunting behavior raises a number of other important issues for interpreting human evolution. Considering that chimpanzees at Gombe share their food, could predation, cooperative hunting, and socially structured food sharing be prehuman traits? If so, this would cast doubt on the hypothesis that the complex of erect posture, free hands, and tool use was a prerequisite to the emergence of hunting behavior. The hypothesis that the open savanna is the habitat where hunting most likely developed must also be questioned. It is in the woodland-savanna and the forested areas where today one finds the highest diversity of mammals and where chimpanzees have been seen hunting. One cherished belief must surely be abandoned—socially organized hunting among primates is not solely a human trait, nor is primate predatory behavior solely a male activity. Not only female chimpanzees but also female baboons have been observed in predatory behavior.

Chimpanzee social groupings are also of interest when trying to reconstruct early human social groups. (The plural form *groupings* is used rather than the singular form *group* because it is clear that any primate species manifests a number of variations in terms of its social groupings.) The adaptability and flexible nature of chimpanzee social groupings may have a bearing on understanding how early humans coped with environmental and predatory stress. Chimpanzees in the Budongo Forest, Uganda, for example, markedly change their behavior when approaching open terrain. They are relaxed and their social group is loose in the forest, but they become tense and vigilant in open spaces. Chimpanzees on the savanna move in structured groups more like savanna-dwelling baboons (Nishida, 1968). Did early humans change their social behavior and the nature of their social groups as they moved into the savanna grasslands to begin a long involvement in this habitat?

Chimpanzee communities, which may consist of fifty or more members, occupy a territory from which other male chimpanzees are excluded (Ghiglieri, 1985). Community members constantly search for fruit-bearing trees and other food sources. When fruit is scarce, they may leave and forage on their own. When fruit is abundant, however, chimpanzees tend to congregate in large parties to feed, mate, and socialize. This fusion-fission type of social organization is relatively rare among nonhuman primates. The changeable pattern in social groupings may maximize the efficiency of the search for fruit, which accounts for approximately 78 percent of the diet.

Much of the fruit in the chimpanzee's diet comes from rare species that tend to grow in clumps rather than being uniformly distributed throughout the range. The chimpanzee's way of life is based on finding a rare and quickly vanishing food supply before its competitors (such as the red colobus monkey). Ghiglieri (1985) suggested that the chimpanzee's excellent sense of spatial relationships and acute memory may be related to its feeding pattern.

The fission-fusion pattern of the social group is an accommodation to the food supply. Fissioning reduces competition for food in times of scarcity. Those chimpanzees were favored in the course of evolution who could split from larger parties and forage alone on scarce resources without losing their ties to the community. As the size of the foraging group increases, so must the number of fruit trees visited. The size of the foraging party is proportional to the crown volume of the tree. Large trees, with more fruit, are visited by more chimpanzees for a longer period of time. Chimpanzees are attracted to larger trees for repeat visits, and they forage in such trees more intensively.

Different chimpanzee groups have differing diets. For example, chimpanzees in West Africa use stone hammers and anvils to crack the hard-shelled panda nut. No other chimpanzee populations perform this behavior. The chimpanzees of Mahale and Gombe use sticks to "fish" for termites, but Ugandan chimpanzees ignore termite mounds. Chimpanzees of the Tai Forest favor adult red colobus monkeys as prey; those at Gombe prefer immature animals, especially infants. The chimpanzees at Gombe once ate baboons; no other chimpanzee groups have been seen doing so.

The chimpanzees of the Tai Forest tend to hunt in groups, while those at Gombe often hunt alone. This difference is probably due to variations in the habitat. The Tai Forest has tall trees; at Gombe more open woodlands with lower canopies predominate. The tall trees of the Tai Forest make it difficult and rather energetically costly to prey on colobus that live among the branches. For the effort to be worth expending, Tai chimpanzees prey on adult colobus. To catch the large and agile colobus, the Tai chimpanzees must hunt in groups. Because the low canopy at Gombe makes it difficult for colobus to escape, Gombe chimpanzees can be productive as solitary hunters.

The fact that female chimpanzees, rather than males, migrate from the natal group is rare among primates. Unlike most nonhuman primate males, the chimpanzee male resides within his natal group. A male ultimately becomes part of the male community that patrols the group's borders and fathers the next generation. Whereas male chimpanzees in a community are closely related, females may not be closely related to other females in the group. This is an anomaly among nonhuman primates.

Probably because of their close filial ties, male chimpanzees of a group are generally noncompetitive, a behavior pattern that extends to reproductive behavior. Male chimpanzees, unlike orangutans, spend little time vying with one another for mating opportunities. Female chimpanzees usually mate with several male group members during each estrus cycle. The male pattern of reproductive tolerance is striking, given that a male has only a limited opportunity to pass on his genes. A female is normally sexually receptive for only a few weeks every five years. Male tolerance toward reproductive competitors is tied to the fact that the group's males are related. Descent from the same small group of male patriarchs implies that any two males will share a genetic ancestry. Hence, if one male successfully mates, some of the genes of the other male are also passed on to the next generation. This pattern is termed *inclusive fitness.*

Using DNA extracted from shed hair in nests, Woodruff and Morin (1995) determined that the males at Gombe are significantly more closely related to each other than the females are. On average, these males are related at the level of half brothers. This close genetic relationship may help explain cooperative male hunting behavior and the lack of male-male aggression during mating. The lack of male-male aggression has typically been explained by kin selection; the new DNA data seem to confirm the veracity of this explanation.

Ghiglieri suggested that it is not altruism that spurs the male's behavior, but self-interest. When a male sires offspring, other group males share his success by way of increases in their inclusive fitness. The size of the shared increase varies with the number of shared genes between the males, and it is significant that chimpanzee group males are commonly quite closely related. According to Ghiglieri, genetic relatedness and inclusive fitness are key factors in the evolution of a community maintained by cooperating males. Cooperation by genetically related males in the defense of the home range is one foundation of the chimpanzee community.

The mature female chimpanzee must leave her natal group to avoid mating with related males. Once an infant is born, she must stay well within the territory of her mate; otherwise alien males patrolling the boundary of her group's home range may kill her infant. Goodall (1979) documented the death and destruction caused by marauding males. Reproductively successful females with infants confine their range within the limits of a single community of males.

Female chimpanzees also have community interests. Within her adopted community, a female tends to socialize only with a subset of other females, some of whom may be relatives from the natal group. Female chimpanzees tend to travel with one another. In some instances, they may collectively repel strange females trying to enter their group. This behavior implies a close female community. Ghiglieri suggested that if such observations are given weight, they could imply a separate female community superimposed on the male community.

High-ranking female chimpanzees tend to live longer, have more and healthier offspring, and produce rapidly maturing daughters. Daughters of high-ranking females mature at about age nine, four years earlier than daughters of lower-ranking mothers. As a result, daughters of high-ranking mothers can reproduce earlier and get a jump on establishing protective relationships with dominating males. Dominant females tend to control areas of food abundance, perhaps the key factor in explaining their reproductive advantage. During the first seven years of life, infant mortality is higher among offspring of low-ranking females, partly because of the slayings of some of the young by higher-ranking members of the clan (Pusey et al., 1997).

Perhaps in response to all-too-frequent intercommunity conflicts among themselves, humans have tended to look at nature in a benign way. Chimpanzees, for example, were first seen as peaceful animals, a model of the eighteenth century's elusive "noble savage." This idea has been replaced by new information. At Gombe, Goodall documented intercommunity clashes between chimpanzee groups, one of which extended its range at the expense of its neighbors. Three healthy males from one group disappeared, and Goodall suspected that they were victims of an intercommunity clash. In other clashes one small group was annihilated. Goodall (1979) suggested that overcrowding resulting from human destruction of the habitat may be a cause for such behavior.

There are some interesting behavioral and social differences between the chimpanzee and the bonobo (*Pan paniscus*). The bonobo weighs approximately the same as the smallest chimpanzee. However, the bonobo has a more slender body, longer legs, and a smaller head and shoulders than does the chimpanzee. Bonobos apparently diverged from chimpanzees about 1.5 mya, according to DNA data.

The chimpanzee ranges across the tropical rain forests from west to east Africa, but the bonobo seems only to be found in the Congo (Kano, 1982, 1990; Kuroda, 1979). Bonobos inhabit the humid rain forest of the Congo river basin in a much more homogeneous environment than that supporting the chimpanzee. Bonobos are primarily frugivorous.

Unlike the chimpanzees' situation at Gombe, *P. paniscus* was observed to eat meat on only three occasions (Ingmanson & Ihobe, 1992). All three instances occurred in one group and involved the consumption of a flying squirrel. Other potential prey were not taken. In two of the three instances, the carcass was possessed by adult females. Consumption occurred slowly and drew the attention of many group members, some exhibiting begging behavior. Once, adult females shared the prey among themselves, but not with the adult males. The meat and the bones of the prey were consumed. Predation appears to be opportunistic, and no cooperative hunting occurred.

Both chimpanzees and bonobos share similar social organization features; for example, they both reside in large communities composed of smaller subunits. However, there are a number of important differences. In one long-term study of bonobos by the Japanese primatologist Kano (1982, 1990), animals were provisioned by providing easy access to sugarcane. The provisioned group consisted of about sixty males and females, half of whom were adults. Bonobos reside in larger social groups than do chimpanzees.

The bonobo group often divides into smaller subunits, temporary associations whose size and membership change freely, depending on the amount and distribution of food and social interactions among subunit members. These small units are usually foraging units of about ten animals and are usually nonaggressive toward similar surrounding units. Foraging units become excited and vocalize in response to larger groups. Such larger groups are noisy in contrast to the quiet of the foraging units. There is extensive home range overlap among neighboring bonobo groups. However, unlike the tension and aggression, as well as the killing, that Goodall reported when chimpanzee social groups meet, similar aggression between overlapping bonobo groups has not been verified. Bonobos do not show the all-male patrols found among chimpanzees.

Bonobos have higher male–female and female–female affinities than do chimpanzees. The core of the bonobo group is bisexual, and there is little difference in the ranging patterns of males and females (Kuroda, 1979). Strong group cohesion is maintained by genitogenital rubbing in females, a lengthened period of female sexual receptivity, high tolerance of group members, and widespread food sharing (Susman, 1987).

At sexual maturity, around age seven or eight, female bonobos begin to show genital swelling and sexual receptivity. However, there are several years of adolescent sterility. Females bear their first infant around age twelve to fourteen. Female bonobos are seldom found alone with their offspring or in all-female social groups.

All females born and raised in the group that Kano (1990) studied left the group permanently shortly after the stage of adolescent sterility. New females continually joined the group, and some remained to become stable members. Males, on the other hand, were never seen to leave the natal group. The sexes are quite tolerant of each other. The core of bonobo society consists of strongly bonded females and the males associated with them (Badrian and Badrian, 1984). This is quite the opposite of the male kinship groups found among chimpanzees. Bonobo males were never seen to kill others of their kind, such as the cases of infanticide and killings that Goodall reported for chimpanzees. (However, such behavior was not reported for almost the first twenty years of Goodall's study.)

Bonobos engage in some interesting forms of sexual behavior. Kano (1990) discussed homosexual genital rump rubbing—unique to bonobos and used to quell excitement—and homosexual mounting behavior. Homosexual behavior in bonobo society serves as greeting, appeasement, and reassurance. Heterosexual copulation serves these functions and also seems to enhance female–male relationships without being merely a reproductive act. Sterile female bonobos copulate as frequently as do their fertile peers. Young females migrate from group to group over a period of three or four years. These females exhibit continual genital swellings and are among the most sexually active females. When a young female enters a new group, she actively solicits mating from resident males, as well as engaging in vigorous genital rubbing with resident females.

Unlike chimpanzee females, bonobos resume cycling rather soon after giving birth. Even nursing mothers frequently engage in copulation. These nonreproductive copulations seem to diminish hostility and maintain intimacy between the sexes.

Although males may dominate females (Kuroda, 1979), females are generally unafraid of males (Kano, 1990). Males are tolerant of females and rarely threaten or attack them over food. Dominance behavior is generally subdued among female bonobos. It is not difficult to find a receptive female; thus aggression over access to females is minimal. The ample supplies of food promote group use of the environment, rather than exclusivity to food resources.

Unlike chimpanzee males who may become estranged from their mothers, bonobo males often stay with their mothers long after they become adults. Grown sons occasionally beg food from their mothers. Adult males are tolerant of youngsters, who seek them out for play and grooming behavior. Males will carry infants for short periods. The males' tolerance of youngsters may be related to their prolonged family attachment, during which they become intimate with their siblings.

Field studies show that the bonobo presents a unique social strategy among primates: essentially a female-bonded society without female relatedness, male relatedness without male bonding, and a relative inability of males to dominate females. Bonobo parties are generally more stable—for example, changing less often than chimpanzee parties at Tai and Gombe.

Bonobo parties at the study site of Wamba are more stable than those at Lomako. Parties at both sites are mostly mixed, containing both adult males and females and low frequencies of groups of mothers. All-female parties with or without offspring can be highly stable. Lone animals are a rare occurrence and are usually males.

The most striking aspect of female–female affiliation is genitogenital rubbing. Usually two but sometimes more females clasp each other ventroventrally and rapidly rub together the fronts of their genitalia. The behavior is intimately associated with feeding, eases tension during group excitement, and is involved in heterosexual matings and begging for food. It is most commonly seen in situations of low feeding competition and has been interpreted as reflecting cooperative alliances among females for food-patch defense.

Bonobos do not appear to hunt mammalian prey, but they opportunistically take squirrels, duikers, and some monkeys. Unlike chimpanzee females, bonobo females can retain ownership of meat in the face of pressure from adult males. Bonobo mothers share plant foods with their infants, but adults also share. Adult females frequently share food with each other and with males. The occurrence of food sharing may be related to the availability of large fruits in the habitat.

The high degree of affiliation expressed by bonobos is not based on relatedness. Females transfer between communities; thus adult females within a community are unlikely to be related. Males appear to remain in their natal groups. At Wamba, adult male dominance rankings are strongly influenced by the presence of their mothers in the community. The importance of mothers to the dominance ranking of their sons is unclear.

Bonobo communities are composed of unrelated females who are highly affiliative with each other and related males who are not highly affiliative with each other. There is a male dominance hierarchy, with a single dominant male and with adults outranking adolescents. Female feeding priority with male social dominance implies some form of male deference during feeding by bonobos, which may influence female mate choice.

The absence of male bonding is probably related to the inability of males to cooperate in defending access to more than one female. Given the distribution of females in the community range, it does not benefit the males to cooperatively defend the community range, unlike the case with the chimpanzee. There is no bonobo equivalent of the male patrols seen among the chimpanzees at Gombe, for example.

If, as suggested by some, the earliest known human ancestor (see Chapter 8) was more forest adapted and arboreal than its descendants, then the bonobo may provide important clues for understanding its anatomy and behavior. Bonobos provide an important source of data for modeling early hominid behavior.

Despite problems, modern nonhuman primates can provide clues, as well as interpretive parameters, useful for reconstructing human evolution. It must be stressed, however, that modern nonhuman primates are not exact replicas of our way of life millions of years ago. They are the end product, as we are, of millions of years of evolution. Although the analysis of modern primate behavior has made it possible to reconstruct some of the early stages of human development, later phases may require a different approach, especially because of the importance of culture in later stages of human evolution.

SOCIAL CARNIVORES

Social carnivores such as hyenas can sometimes yield important clues for reconstructing human evolution (Schaller & Lowther, 1969; Thompson, 1975). Because social (e.g., group-living) carnivores like wild hunting dogs and hyenas, for example, coordinate hunts without resorting to symbolic language, and because they do not use tools to hunt, we can get clues as to how early human ancestors might have hunted without access to language or tools. Although the search for clues about our past among nonhuman primates is reasonable on genetic grounds, it is less reasonable on ecological grounds. Social systems are strongly influenced by habitat conditions. Although monkeys and apes are essentially vegetarians living in groups confined to small areas, we assume our ancestors were widely roaming foragers for perhaps 2 million years. This way of life is in strong contrast to that of modern nonhuman primates. Something can be learned about the genesis of our social system by studying phylogenetically unrelated but ecologically similar forms. Social carnivores are an obvious choice. Some selective pressures influencing the social existence of social carnivores might also have had an effect on human societies.

We are interested in the eating habits of social carnivores, plus such gnawing rodents as the porcupine, especially in the remains of their meals: Which bones are eaten, which bones are left, and the state of the leftovers are all important clues. Such studies allow a more scientific means of determining which archaeological bone deposits are the result of human or nonhuman activity.

SUMMARY

Various ways in which we can collect comparative data for reconstructing human evolution and behavior were highlighted (Box 4-1). Of all nonhuman primates, the chimpanzee and the bonobo offer the most fascinating insights into our past way of life, especially instances of their hunting behavior, use and manufacture of

---

BOX 4-1   Summary of Some Basic Kinds of Information Obtained Using the Comparative Approach

Modern Foraging Peoples

- Site formation
- Food sources
- Methods of tool manufacture and tool use
- Movement patterns—what social or environmental factors influence movement
- Use of teeth as tools and the resulting dental damage
- Size of the social groups—what mechanisms affect group sizes
- Sex roles—what part each sex plays in providing dietary requirements, for example
- Health—mortality and morbidity patterns

Nonhuman Primates

- The range of social organizations and behaviors
- Ecological adaptations—help reconstruct behavior and social organizations
- Food sources—help assess what part of the diet was plant and what part animal protein
- Sex roles and mating patterns
- The importance of social life and learning of social behaviors—helps us understand the importance of tool use and manufacture, the evolution of bipedalism, and the role of hunting
- Tool use and making

Social Carnivores

- How to hunt effectively without tools and language
- What the remnants of a social carnivore's meal look like and what part of animals they eat—help to interpret archaeological bone deposits

---

tools, and social organization. From the social carnivores, with whom we shared a similar habitat of social hunting, we can gather information concerning our social organization and way of hunting. From populations of modern foragers insights can be gained about a way of life that was a basic part of our evolutionary past.

SUGGESTED READINGS

Boesch, C., and H. Boesch-Achermann. 1991. Dim forest, bright chimps. *Natural History*, September: 50–56.

Gibbons, A. 1992. Chimps: More diverse than a barrel of monkeys. *Science* 255:287–288.

Gould, R. 1968. Living archaeology: The Ngatatjara of western Australia. *Southwestern Journal of Anthropology* 24:210.

Potts, R. 1987. Reconstructions of early hominid socioecology: A critique of primate models. In *The Evolution of Human Behavior: Primate Models.* W. Kinzey, ed. Albany: SUNY Press.

Pusey, A., J. Williams, and J. Goodall. 1997. The influence of dominance rank on the reproductive success of female chimpanzees. *Science* 277:828–831.

Schaller, G., and G. Lowther. 1969. The relevance of carnivore behavior to the study of early hominids. *Southwestern Journal of Anthropology* 25:307.

Stanford, C., and J. Allen. 1991. On strategic storytelling: Current models of human behavioral evolution. *Current Anthropology* 32:58–61.

Thompson, P. 1975. A cross-species analysis of carnivore, primate, and hominid behavior. *Journal of Human Evolution* 4:113.

Tooby, J., and I. DeVore. 1987. The reconstruction of hominid behavioral evolution through strategic modeling. In *The Evolution of Human Behavior: Primate Models.* W. Kinzey, ed. Albany: SUNY Press.

Washburn, S. 1978. What we can't learn about people from apes. *Human Nature* 1:70–75.

Washburn, S., and I. DeVore. 1961. The social life of baboons. *Scientific American* 204:62–71.

White, F. 1996. *Pan paniscus* 1973 to 1996: Twenty-three years of field research. *Evolutionary Anthropology* 5:11–17.

Woodruff, D., and P. Morin. 1995. Geneticists out on a limb. *Natural History,* January: 54.

Wrangham, R. 1997. Subtle, secret female chimpanzees. *Science* 277:774–775.

5

Early Primate Evolution

Overview
Dietary Patterns
Misidentification of Paleocene Fossils
Eocene Primates
Alternative Approaches
Origins of New World Monkeys
Summary
Suggested Readings

Early primates, the prosimians, probably evolved from an insect-eating stock during the Eocene geological epoch. Major aspects of primate evolution probably occurred within the arboreal niche, which represented a refuge zone from rodent competition. Early stages in primate evolution witnessed changes in the skull, face, and limb structure, changes related to diet and locomotor behavior. During the Eocene there was widespread extinction of many prosimian species.

Identifying where the earliest primates first appeared is difficult, with contending fossils in Africa, Asia, and North America. In Africa and Asia by the end of the Eocene we witness the evolution of new primates, the monkeys and the apes.

Two hypotheses have been offered to explain the appearance of major primate traits. The first, the arboreal hypothesis, was offered in the early 1900s by G. E. Smith and F. W. Jones, who argued that major primate anatomical traits were adaptations to life in the trees. M. Cartmill offered an elaboration of the arboreal hypothesis called the visual predation hypothesis, which concentrates on explaining the functions and evolution of the grasping hands and feet and the primate's visual system.

OVERVIEW

As the number and types of reptiles gradually decreased, mammals began to compete for the vacated habitat. The earliest primates appeared about 55 mya. Some early primates adapted to the ground and became extinct after about 10 million years. Others ascended the trees, where they fared better. The trees probably offered a refuge zone where competition was less intense but living more complicated. Early primates were forced to adapt to a strange new world, a new dimension of life among the dense foliage, branches, and canopies of the forest.

Rodents first appeared in the late **Paleocene** (60 mya), after which time no primate group evolved clear rodentlike adaptations. The main period of rodent radiation occurred during the middle and later **Eocene** and coincided with the decline and extinction of primitive primates in North America and Europe. Because the rodents and early primates probably utilized common resources, they were potential competitors.

The drastic reduction in the number of primate genera in the late Eocene and their complete disappearance from Europe and North America between 40 and 25 mya probably resulted from many causes. Through competition with rodents the primate adaptive zone became seriously constricted. The progressive cooling of the climate and the reduction of tropical forests may have driven primates from what are today the more temperate areas.

Sussman and Raven (1978) suggest that competition between some bats and early primates (the prosimians) led to the extinction of many of the latter during the Eocene. The Eocene may have been a time when bats and primates were refining their abilities to exploit fruit and flowers of the angiosperms, as well as the insects feeding upon the fruit and flowers. Primates and marsupials survived chiefly in regions where competition with flower-visiting and fruit-eating bats was limited. Primates endured in Madagascar and South Africa, and for marsupials survival occurred in Australia.

As noted in an earlier chapter, it has been argued that primates evolved from *insectivores* (insect eaters) and that there was a primate–insectivore transition. This notion is related to the fact that insectivores are rather generalized mammals, which, in turn, makes them suitable primate ancestors. There is, however, little fossil evidence to convincingly document this transition.

It is difficult to demonstrate the "primateness" of early fossils. No one trait or group of traits necessarily provides suitable criteria for analyzing extant taxa (Schwartz et al., 1978). Many mammals, such as marsupials, carnivores, and even some marine mammals, share some traits with primates. To circumvent this problem, some researchers have proposed a series of "evolutionary trends" that seemingly characterize the order Primates (see Box 3-3; Clark, 1969; Napier & Napier, 1970). These trends emphasize such traits as a reduction of the snout, reduction of a reliance on olfaction, and elaboration of the visual sense and the cerebral cortex. However, Martin (1968:391) noted that these trends are "largely an artificial feature developed in the minds of the 'highest' primates, which picture a line of progressive evolution ultimately leading to themselves." Others (Cartmill, 1972,

1974; Kay & Cartmill, 1977) maintained that such trends express an adaptive shift that should be considered crucial.

According to Schwartz et al. (1978) the order Primates is first distinguished by a set of shared molar traits. Apart from such dental traits, the primate ancestor appears to have retained primitive insectivore characteristics in virtually every other feature.

DIETARY PATTERNS

The majority of early primate evolution occurred within an arboreal niche; primate evolutionary trends are probably reflections of an adaptation to tree living. Major adjustments required for arboreal living stem from an exploration of the habitat, which both required and led to changes in the limbs and diet. Most foods readily available within the arboreal niche are vegetal; thus most primates are vegetarians. It may be more correct, however, to describe the feeding patterns of modern primates as that of opportunistic omnivores; that is, they feed on insects and other available foodstuffs. There are also examples of predation and carnivory among modern primates.

Teeth, the longest lasting of the skeletal parts, form a large portion of early primate remains. The major distinguishing features of early primate dentitions reflect an important shift in their dietary adaptation. The dietary change was not an absolute and total shift; rather, it involved a relative increase in the importance of fruit, leaves, and other herbaceous materials. Szalay (1969) postulated that the shift may have occurred as a series of overlapping shifts. First, a large sparsely inhabited or uninhabited **frugivorous–herbivorous** (a fruit, bud, and leaf) niche must have existed. Changes necessary to exploit these new food sources were largely behavioral, involving a slow shift in food preferences. Once a sustained interest in small fruits, berries, and leaves became established at the expense of a more **insectivorous** diet, selection favored populations that most efficiently utilized these foods. Dependency on these new foods led to modifications in the dental and digestive systems.

The early insectivore diet included soft-bodied invertebrates, which were quickly sliced and swallowed. This dietary pattern favored tall, sharp teeth with well-defined **cusps** (elevations of the tooth crown or the grinding surface). This configuration was poorly suited for chewing rough, tough-shelled seeds or fibrous fruits found within the arboreal niche. Rather early in primate evolution there was selection for shorter and more bulbous cusps and for grinding mastication. Chief among the subsequent modifications was a reduced snout, which was probably related to size reduction and/or crowding of the incisors, canines, and premolars and to increasing reliance on the hands for picking up objects. The **zygomatic arches** became laterally broad and strong. This change was presumably related to the increasing bulk of stronger **masseter muscles**, which attach to the zygomatic arches. The masseter muscles are the chief muscles for a grinding mode of mastication. Major craniofacial changes among Eocene primates included the development of **stereoscopic vision** and an increasing reliance on the visual senses.

It seems that there were dietary differences among Eocene primates. For example, one species of the genus *Cantius* seems to have specialized on soft fruit, while another had a more eclectic diet. One species of *Notharctus* may have been a leaf-eater (Broadfield, 1992).

MISIDENTIFICATION OF PALEOCENE FOSSILS

Cartmill (1972) first suggested that no Paleocene form can be called a primate, and he referred such fossils to the order Insectivora. Beard (1990a) placed these fossils among the so-called flying lemurs. Even if Paleocene forms are not primates, they at least suggest the direction that primate evolution was taking.

As suspected by a number of researchers, some families of so-called archaic primates may turn out not to be primates after all (Beard, 1990b; Kay et al., 1990; Martin, 1990). At issue are the Paleocene and Eocene families of Plesiadapidae, Paromomyidae, Picrodontidae, and Saxonellidae, all of which are usually referred to the infraorder Plesiadapiformes of the order Primates. Members of this infraorder resemble later primates in certain features of their molar teeth and ear region, but they lack many other traits considered diagnostic of primate status.

Until new discoveries of two partial skeletons of *Phenacolemur* and a virtually complete skull of *Ignacius* from very early Eocene deposits in Wyoming (Beard, 1990a; Kay et al., 1990), only the genus *Plesiadapis* was known from reasonably well-preserved skulls and skeletons. The new discoveries belong to the family Paromomyidae. Beard and Kay et al. concluded that these fossils belonged not with the order Primates, as some have argued based on analysis of less complete remains, but instead to the Dermoptera, a peculiar order of Southeast Asian gliding mammals often referred to as *flying lemurs*. Postcranial remains indicated that the middle phalanges of the fingers and toes of the newly found remains were markedly longer than the other phalanges. This is atypical among primates. Only the dermopterans among modern mammals provide a comparable condition. The gliding mechanism extends onto the digits of the hands and feet, which explains the elongated middle phalanges.

These new discoveries raised many taxonomic problems that are yet to be solved. For example, is there an evolutionary relationship between the Dermoptera and Primates? Other options are also being discussed.

EOCENE PRIMATES

The earliest primates appear suddenly at the beginning of the Eocene approximately 55 million years ago. These early forms represent two groups (clades) that apparently emigrated to Europe and North America essentially simultaneously. Currently the fossil record provides no conclusive evidence as to the origins of the order Primates. According to Rose (1995), suggestions of either an African or an Asian origin are speculative.

Among the earliest primates, the lemur-like forms are called Adapidae and are assigned to their own infraorder, Adapiformes. The tarsier- or galago-like Omomyidae are assigned to the Tarsiiformes or Omomyiformes. The most primitive of the adapiformes is *Donrussellia*, which is also the oldest known primate from Europe. It first appears in Spain and Portugal. The omomyids were small primates; all the early ones weighed less than 1 kilogram, and many weighed less than 100 grams. These forms are considered primates not only on dental similarities, but also because they share with recent primates details of the cranial and postcranial anatomies.

The Eocene was a time of maximal adaptive radiation for the early primates; as many as forty-three genera and three families are recognized from this time period. An important adaptation to the arboreal habitat was exploitation of its three dimensionality. Many adaptations, such as those related to arboreal locomotion and activity, including feeding, are evident in Eocene fossils from a time span of 54 to 36 mya. Major adjustments appear in the hands, feet, skull, and face. Included within the general structural adaptations of the limbs are grasping hands and feet equipped with nails. Primate hands and feet are characterized by a retention of five digits, pentadactyly, and by a grasping thumb and big toe. (Grasping hands and feet are not only adaptations to climbing but also allow the mother to carry the young primate, who clings tightly to her stomach. The grasping hand and foot reduce infant mortality in a species in which the mother is highly mobile.) The configuration of the foot bones of a 52-million-year-old primate, *Cantius*, provides the oldest evidence of a grasping big toe.

Another important trait of the primate upper limb structure, presumably also an adaptation to arboreal life, is the retention of two separate forelimb bones, the **ulna** (on the outer side) and the **radius** (the shorter of the forearm bones found on the thumb side). The retention of two separate bones, which are, for example, fused in ungulates, allows for greater mobility and rotation of the forearm, which would be useful in the jumping and grasping necessitated by an arboreal lifestyle.

Major changes in the primate skull also occurred during the Eocene. Chief among these changes is a reduction of the nasal area (Figure 5-1) and the forward rotation of the eye orbits from a location on the side of the head (as they are placed, for example, in dogs) (Figure 5-2). These alterations portend shifts of emphasis in the sensory modalities. The reduction of the nasal area rather early in primate evolution suggests a reduced reliance on the **olfactory** sense. This reduction is emphasized by the loss of the naked rhinarium (the moistened, hairless, tactile-sensitive skin surrounding the nostrils of many mammals) in most modern primates. Arboreal life emphasizes the visual over the olfactory sense, and few modern primates seem to rely heavily on olfactory communication. The shift in sensory reliance signifies a reduction of the olfactory and an enlargement of the visual brain centers.

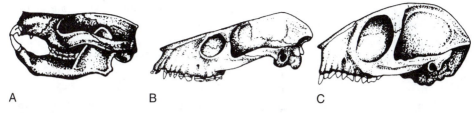

A   B   C

FIGURE 5-1 Comparison of three skulls: *A*, The Paleocene form *Plesiadapis* is no longer considered to be a primate; *B, Adapis; C, Necrolemur.* (*From* PHYSICAL ANTHROPOLOGY, 3/E by Kelso/Trevathan, © 1984. Reprinted by permission of Prentice-Hall, Inc., Upper Saddle River, NJ.)

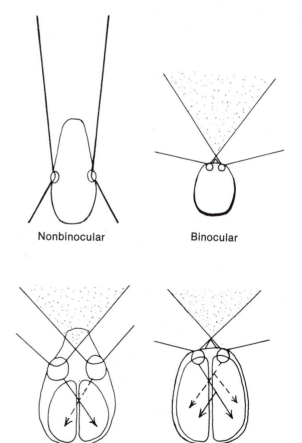

Nonbinocular   Binocular

FIGURE 5-2 Comparison of nonbinocular and binocular vision (*above*) and binocular, nonstereoscopic and binocular stereoscopic vision (*below*). Primates possess binocular, stereoscopic vision. (*From* PHYSICAL ANTHROPOLOGY, 3/E by Kelso/Trevathan, © 1984. Reprinted by permission of Prentice-Hall, Inc., Upper Saddle River, NJ.)

Binocular,
nonstereoscopic   Binocular,
stereoscopic

Fossil evidence of the shifting of the eye orbits from a lateral to a frontal position and enclosure of the eye itself within a protective bony casing points up the increasing importance of the visual sense. The forward rotation of the eye orbits resulted in stereoscopic vision, the convergence of two visual fields on one object. This may have been an adaptation to the locomotor pattern of jumping from one tree limb to another. Sometime during primate evolution the structure of the eye itself was reorganized; most modern primates are **diurnal** (active during the daytime) creatures with color vision.

Stereoscopic vision would be highly adaptive in the arboreal niche. Such activity as leaping from branch to branch in search of food requires the tree dweller to make distance judgments continually. To the degree that both visual fields overlap, image fusion and improvements of depth judgment are needed. Stereoscopic vision is highly adaptive because misjudged leaps can result in fatal falls. The early fossil record shows that the order Primates began diverging into perhaps a dozen or more forms before full forward eye rotation. All higher primates have a complete bone ring around the opening of the eye socket. Additionally, monkeys, apes, and humans have a bony wall between the eye and temporalis muscle. The eye socket thus becomes a closed, bony cup (called a **postorbital bar**). The primate postorbital bar may function as a protective device or strut for transmitting chewing stress. Cartmill (1972) suggested that it originally served to prevent deformation of the eye orbit caused by contractions of the chewing (masseter) muscles.

There is fossil evidence for the existence of these trends. One Eocene primate family, the Adapidae—which includes the genera *Notharctus* (Figure 5-3), found in North America, and *Adapis*, the first fossil primate genus described, found in France—exhibits some of these trends. The generalized structure of these forms is characterized by a grasping big toe and thumb. Although the snout is still quite long (resulting in a projecting or *prognathic* face), the orbits have rotated forward, indicating stereoscopic vision. Other Eocene forms show a general shortening of the snout and a shifting forward of the **foramen magnum** (the hole at the bottom of the skull through which the spinal cord passes), indicating that these creatures were erect while sitting. Coupled with forelimb shortening, the shifting forward of the foramen magnum suggests a locomotor pattern of hopping and climbing. The early pattern of primate locomotion seems to be moving away from true quadrupedalism during this period.

Alexander (1992) described rather complete *Notharctus* remains from Wyoming. Especially important are skull materials whose morphology changed our understanding of this early primate. Other remains include a complete jaw and an associated partial skeleton. *Notharctus* seems to have been a forest dweller with long and powerful hind legs that were used for leaping from tree to tree. *Notharctus* had a long hand with elongated fingers that were used to cling to trunks and tree branches. It also seems to have had a long tail.

Notharctus was a relatively advanced primate living in the first half of the Eocene, about 50 mya. Its grasping hands and feet, tipped with nails and not

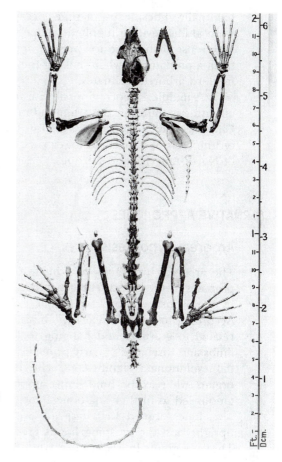

FIGURE 5-3 Skeletal reconstruction of *Notharctus osborni.* (Image # 37373, courtesy Department of Library Services, American Museum of Natural History.)

claws, were similar to those of later primates. *Notharctus* had eyes that seem to have accommodated stereoscopic vision, and it had a reduced muzzle.

A partial skeleton of *Cantius trigonodus* from the early Eocene Willwood Formation of Bighorn Basin, Wyoming, exhibits long hind limbs and short forelimbs (Rose & Walker, 1985). *Cantius* apparently used its hindlimbs extensively for locomotor purposes. Specializations in the hind limb indicate capabilities for leaping and for powerful grasping by the **opposable** big toe (the hallux). *Cantius* was an active arboreal quadruped with a propensity for leaping. Modern examples of this form of locomotion are found among primates known as lemurs, which today are found on the island of Madagascar.

It has been suggested that a major trend in early primate evolution was a reorganization of the structure and function of the middle ear (Beecher, 1969; Szalay, 1972a). This restructuring may have allowed better balance while leaping and may have enhanced the ability to make constant adjustments in body position. The ability to determine body position is important to an animal that habitually glides, leaps, or relies occasionally, but crucially, on exacting balance. Even animals with a highly developed visual sense would benefit from an accessory sense of balance for precise detection of movement when in rapid flight from a predator or when making the spectacular leaps so characteristic of many modern arboreal primates.

A middle Paleocene fossil with likely primate affinities and dating to about 60 mya was found in the Wanghudun Formation in Anhui Province, east central China (Szalay & Li, 1986). This fossil, called *Decoredon anhuiensis,* was identified on the basis of upper and lower jaws. It may be ancestral to the Eocene primates of North America and Europe.

ALTERNATIVE APPROACHES

Arboreal Hypothesis

The arboreal hypothesis of primate origins links the major adaptations of early primates to the tree-dwelling habitat. This hypothesis was originally propounded by the British anatomists G. Elliott Smith (1912) and F. Wood Jones (1916). According to the arboreal hypothesis, the primate's grasping hands and feet are related to grasping and hanging to thin branches. Jones argued that the hind limbs and forelimbs of early primates had different functions that were of potential evolutionary significance. The hands were the grasping and exploratory organs, whereas the hind limbs supported and propelled the body. These adaptations led to further anatomical and behavioral changes.

Jones argued that early in primate evolution the body posture became upright, and the grasping hands gradually replaced the jaws in obtaining food. The jaws gradually reduced in size, the face became smaller, and the eye orbits shifted to a more forward position. These changes were accompanied by alterations in the nervous system; the olfactory sense became reduced in importance, and the visual sense became elaborated. These changes led to a restructuring of the brain and further anatomical changes in the facial and jaw region. Cartmill (1975b:15) summed up this process as follows:

> The result of all these trends is a lemurlike primate. To make a monkey out of a lemur, all that is needed is to carry these trends a bit further, resulting in a larger brain, a shorter face, defter hands, more closely set eyes and so on. All these things are prerequisite for the evolution of humans. . . . The theory is persuasive, neat and fairly comprehensive. It does provide an explanation for most of the peculiarities of primates. I am going to argue, however, that it is not adequate.

Visual Predation Theory

Cartmill (1972, 1974, 1975b) offered an elaboration of the arboreal hypothesis, which is called the *visual predation theory.* He argued that the arboreal hypothesis of primate evolution, which states that the early primates lost their sense of smell, developed stereoscopic vision, had grasping hands and feet, and replaced claws with nails because of the demands of an arboreal existence, is erroneous and incomplete.

Cartmill's theory concentrates on explaining the functions and evolution of the grasping hands and feet and the distinctive primate visual system. Grasping hands and feet are found only among arboreal mammals or their secondarily terrestrial relatives (for example, gorillas). Most arboreal mammals, however, have hands and feet more like those found among squirrels than among monkeys. Only some climbing mice, arboreal marsupials (such as the opossum), and most nonhuman primates have a divergent and opposable big toe.

Cartmill argued that the opposable big toe and grasping hind foot function to anchor an animal as it steps on a rotten or unstable branch. Grasping hind feet help protect an animal against sudden falls, and they are also well adapted for locomotion on slender branches. The primates' hands and feet might have originated as part of an adaptation to cautious movement among relatively slender branches. Extensive food supplies consisting of leaves, flowers, fruits, and nuts are found at the terminal ends of these branches. Such growth attracts insects and other invertebrates. If they were able to get safely out on these branches, primates would encounter a rich food source.

Feeding at the terminal ends of branches does not itself require grasping hands and feet. However, if an animal feeding at the terminal ends of branches is a predator of invertebrates, it must be able to move quietly within striking distance of the prey and then either leap at it or grab it with a swift movement of the hand and arm. Grasping feet allow an animal to move quietly and cautiously among relatively thin branches and, by anchoring the animal, allow it to lift both its hands to grab at the prey. The primates' close-set eyes might also be an adaptation to predation.

Among the nonprimates, cats probably have the most primatelike visual system. They have stereoscopic vision and parallel optic axes (both eyes point in the same direction). Cats are similar to primates in the visual pathways in their nervous system. Cats catch their prey by stalking and suddenly pouncing; they rely on stereoscopic vision to estimate the length of the pounce. Cartmill used cat hunting behavior, with its coincident anatomical modifications such as stereoscopic vision and close-set eyes, as a model for understanding primate predation and the evolution of their visual system. According to Cartmill (1975b:19), "The grasping hind feet and close-set eyes characteristic of primates originated as part of an adaptation to visually directed predation on insects among slender branches in the undergrowth and lower canopy of tropical forests."

The visual predation theory can also explain the reduction of the primate olfactory sense. Reduction in olfaction may be a result of a convergence of the eye orbits. As the orbits move toward the middle of the face, they constrict the olfactory nerves that pass between them from the brain to the nose. Olfaction appears to be most reduced among those primates where the eye sockets are close together.

The replacement of claws by nails might also be an adaptation to moving on slender branches and feeding on fruits, seeds, insects (which are caught by hand), and nectar: "Clawless digits, grasping feet and close-set eyes: these and other features common to most living primates all suggest that the last common ancestor of the living primates was a small visual predator" (Cartmill, 1975b:21).

In Cartmill's scheme primate ancestors shared similarities with ancient hedgehogs, which underwent an adaptive shift toward eating more fruit and other plant materials. These insectivores gave rise to a form such as *Purgatorius*, a Paleocene genus that might be ancestral to Eocene primates, that climbed trees to get fruit. Early primates might have first eaten a somewhat mixed diet and led a double existence, climbing trees for fruit and searching the forest floor for insects. Occasionally, such a creature might grab an insect in the fruits of the tree. This unspecialized lifeway might have provided the basis for the evolutionary radiations witnessed in the Paleocene and Eocene.

Cartmill's visual predation theory of primate origins has several important implications. Because the feeding pattern represents the source of the basic primate pattern of adaptation, evidence for such feeding patterns must be present in all members of the order Primates. Cartmill used the following traits for his definition of a primate:

1. Internal ear structures enclosed by a hollow, rounded, bony prominence called the auditory bulla.
2. Presence of a complete postorbital bar.
3. Divergent thumb and first toe with flattened nails.

Cartmill's argument that these traits indicate a shift to visual predation and an insectivorous diet has been challenged. According to Cartmill the enclosure of the eye with a complete bony orbit is associated with the convergence of the eyes and stereoscopic vision. However, many nonprimate forms with stereoscopic vision have a complete postorbital bar. Additionally, many forms without a postorbital bar are neither insectivores nor predators.

Both the arboreal hypothesis and the visual predation theory agree that primates evolved in the trees. The ideas differ, however, in that Cartmill stressed what primates did within the trees, that is, visually preying on insects. Jones's arboreal hypothesis did not place heavy stress on feeding adaptations as crucial to understanding early primate evolution.

ORIGINS OF NEW WORLD MONKEYS

Primate evolution was drastically affected by such geological changes as continental drift (Figure 5-4). The shifting continents affected the movements and lifeways of many living forms. The relationship of the African and Euroasiatic plates as well as that of Africa and South Africa are important in understanding early phases of primate evolution.

It was traditionally thought that New and Old World monkeys shared similarities because of parallel evolution, that is, because both arose from the same North American stock and independently evolved in similar directions. Biochemical

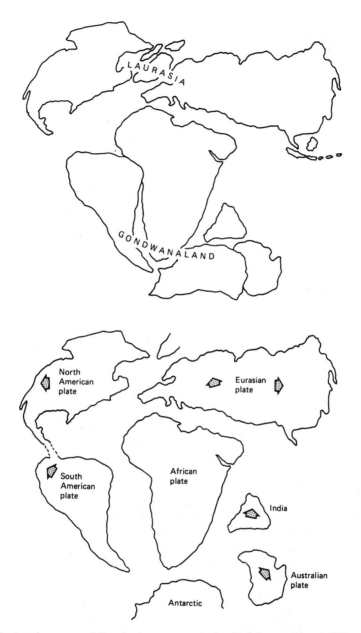

FIGURE 5-4   Land masses of the Cretaceous period, which began about 135 mya and lasted until about 65 mya. At the beginning of the Cretaceous, the continental plates were united in two major land masses, Laurasia and Gondwanaland (top). During the Cretaceous, these land masses separated, and the individual plates on which they rested began migrating to their present positions (bottom). Arrows indicate direction of movement. (*From* INTRODUCTION TO EVOLUTION by F. Racle, © 1979. Reprinted by permission of Prentice-Hall, Inc., Upper Saddle River, NJ.)

evidence from New and Old World monkeys shows, however, that both shared a very long period of common ancestry.

Primates first appeared in South America in the late Oligocene about 30–25 mya. Primates reached South America accidentally and probably through the process of some animals being stranded on rafts of natural vegetation swept out to sea. North and South America and South America and Africa were separated by water distances of a few hundred miles. However, there were probably intervening islands between North and South America and between the latter and Africa that served as way stations. The most plausible crossing was Africa to South America, a contention bolstered by the fact that African rodents reached South America in the Oligocene. Fossil evidence also shows a striking dental similarity between some Oligocene African primates and those in South America (Chapter 6). The biochemical record seems to show that South American and African monkeys are descended from a common ancestor.

Among the more interesting and latest of the South American monkey fossils is a skull found by John Flynn and André Wyss in the Chilean Andes. This well-preserved skull, dating to about 20 mya, has features suggesting an African heritage. The new fossil is named *Chilecebus carrascoensis*. The skull apparently belonged to a smallish animal weighing about 2 pounds.

The maxilla has nearly all its smallish teeth in place. The shape of the molars and the shape of the ear region look like the molars and ear region of older monkey fossils from Africa. These similarities indicate an African, not a North American, origin of the South American monkeys.

Assuming a seafloor spread of approximately 2 centimeters a year, Africa and South America must have been about 1,900 miles apart in the south and about 300 miles apart in the north by the end of the Eocene epoch. Tarling (1980) assumed that falling sea levels in the early Oligocene exposed a number of stepping-stone islands. Perhaps deep oceanic water never exceeded about 120 miles in width.

Although South American monkeys probably trace their origins to Africa, there was a land bridge or island chain connecting North and South America in the early Oligocene. However, ocean currents flowing in a northerly direction probably hindered any drifting southward of vegetation rafts. On the other hand, there is evidence of a north–south migration of some dinosaurs, herbivorous mammals, and other vertebrates.

Branisella, which dates to about 27 mya, is the oldest South American primate. The *Branisella* fossil comes from Bolivia and consists of parts of the upper jaw preserving some teeth and part of a lower jaw. Two other genera, *Tremacebus* and *Dolichocebus*, date to the late Oligocene or early Miocene in Argentina. *Tremacebus* is known from a fairly complete skull and lower jaw fragment, and *Dolichocebus* consists of a distorted skull and several isolated teeth. Meldrum (1990) suggested that there are at least four fossil species in Argentina—two of which may be related to living New World monkeys. Fossilized monkey remains found in Colombia and dating to 15–12 mya seem to be directly ancestral to the modern South American night monkey. The long independent evolutionary history of the night monkey has no comparable situation among Old World monkeys. The oldest traceable evolutionary lineage in Old World monkeys belongs to the genus *Macaca* (the macaques). That evolutionary line is tentatively traceable to the late Miocene, only about 8 mya.

In 1990 fossils of a previously unknown extinct monkey species were found in Cuba. The bones indicated that the animal weighed about 10 pounds and that it may be a distant relative of the living howler monkeys found in South and Central America. Cuba apparently once supported a rather diverse monkey population, as did a number of Caribbean islands. Today they are all gone, victimized by some unexplained occurrence.

SUMMARY

The earliest primates seem to have appeared during the Eocene geological epoch. Paleocene fossils once thought to be primates are now generally identified as dermopterans. The earliest primates are identified by molar traits and changes in the limb, skull, and facial skeletons. By 40 mya, the center of primate evolution shifted to Asia and Africa. The evolutionary history of South American monkeys can be traced to fossils found in what is today Egypt. By the late Eocene we witness the beginnings of the ape evolutionary line.

Two hypotheses have been offered to explain the appearance of major primate traits. The first was offered in the early 1900s by G. E. Smith and F. W. Jones, who argued that major primate anatomical traits were adaptations to an arboreal lifestyle. Their suggestion is termed the arboreal hypothesis. M. Cartmill offered an elaboration of the arboreal hypothesis that is called the visual predation hypothesis. Cartmill's hypothesis concentrates on explaining the functions and evolution of the grasping hands and feet and the distinctive primate visual system.

SUGGESTED READINGS

Beard, C. 1990. Flying lemurs, primates and fossils. *American Journal of Physical Anthropology* 81:192.

Cartmill, M. 1974. Rethinking primate origins. *Science* 184:436–443.

Cartmill, M. 1975. Primate evolution: Analyses of trends. *Science* 189:129–133.

Martin, R. 1991. New fossils and primate origins. *Nature* 349:19–20.

Rose, M., and A. Walker. 1985. The skeleton of early Eocene *Cantius*, oldest lemuriform primate. *American Journal of Physical Anthropology* 66:73–89.

Szalay, F. 1968. The beginnings of primates. *Evolution* 22:19–36.

Szalay, F. 1973. A review of some recent advances in paleoprimatology. *Yearbook of Physical Anthropology* 17:39–64.

Szalay, F., and E. Delson. 1978. *Evolutionary History of the Primates.* New York: Academic Press.

6

The Transition to Apes

Eocene Fossils
Oligocene Fayum Deposits, Egypt
Miocene Hominoids
Gigantopithecus
Summary
Suggested Readings

In recent years a great diversity of hominoid remains has been recovered from African, Asian, and European sites (Table 6-1). The earliest hominoids, ancestors of extant apes and humans, appeared about 50 mya in Eocene geological deposits. One Miocene group, the dryopithecines, was once touted as the last common stock (the stem group) of apes and humans. New fossil remains and evidence suggesting a late divergence of apes and humans has led to a serious reconsideration of a dryopithecine ancestry. The human–ape divergence from a common ancestor is now set in the late Miocene and early Pliocene. The issue of what fossil or group of fossils constitutes the stem group is hotly contended. Major environmental shifts during the Miocene are key to understanding hominoid evolution and the appearance of the ancestors of modern apes and humans.

TABLE 6-1 Some Fossils Relevant to Anthropoid Origins

Genus and Species	Fossil Material
Algeria	
Algeripithecus minutus	Isolated upper and lower teeth
Tabelia hammadae	Isolated upper and lower teeth
cf. *Tabelia* sp	Isolated teeth
Burma	
Amphipithecus and *Pondaugnia*	Mandibular fragments and teeth
China	
Eosimias sinensis	Two lower jaws showing mandibular P4–M2
Fayum, Egypt	
See Table 6-2.	
Oman	
Omomyidae?	Two isolated molars
Oligopithecus savagei	One lower molar
Thailand	
Siamopithecus eocaenus	Dental remains
Wailekia orientale	Mandibular fragment

Some data from E. Simons and T. Rasmussen, A whole new world of ancestors: Eocene Anthropoideans from Africa, *Evolutionary Anthropology*, 1994, 4:128–139.

EOCENE FOSSILS

Relatively recently discovered primitive anthropoids or anthropoid-like forms from North Africa and Asia suggest the possibility that the ape line represents one of the initial branches from the primate stem. The oldest of these forms are *Algeripithecus* and *Tabelia* from the early or middle Eocene of Algeria, and *Eosimias*, from the middle Oligocene of China. The fossils consist of isolated teeth and jaw fragments. The teeth of the Algerian forms are very small, while *Eosimias* displays several features presumed to be primitive for primates (Rose, 1996).

The *Eosimias* material is the complete lower dentition having a combination of primitive and derived traits not exhibited in other living or extinct primates. Numerous derived aspects of the jaw and dental morphology of *Eosimias* support its anthropoid affinities.

A new species, *E. centennicus*, is established from materials dated to the late middle Eocene and collected in 1995 from the Yuanqu Basin in southern Shanxi Province, China. The specimen includes the first ever complete lower dentition of the Eosimiid primates. The incisors are smaller relative to the cheek teeth than is true in other basal anthropoids. There are striking similarities in the morphology of the lower premolars between *Eosimias* and the Burmese *Amphipithecus* described below in the following paragraphs (Beard et al., 1994; Gibbons, 1994). By the middle Eocene the anthropoids ranged from western Algeria to eastern China, implying that the anthropoid clade is more ancient than most thought (Beard et al., 1996). Because early anthropoids appear in both Africa and Asia, the fossil record currently cannot specify the continent of first origin.

Southern Asia is a focal point of hominoid origins, a suggestion based on finds dated to about 40 mya and placed within the genera of *Amphipithecus* and *Pondaungia,* both of which come from the Pondaung Hills, upper Burma. Since their original discovery in the mid-1930s, anthropologists have debated the evolutionary affinities of both forms.

The remains of *Amphipithecus* and *Pondaungia* consist of mandibular fragments and teeth. *Amphipithecus's* mandible was deep and heavy relative to the molar teeth (Figure 6-1). The left and right halves of the jaw were fused, unlike those of nearly all extinct and living prosimians. Jaw fusion was probably a response to chewing tougher foods. *Amphipithecus's* dental formula is reconstructed as possibly 2 incisors, 1 canine, 3 premolars, and 3 molars. It had one extra premolar compared to modern apes. The cusps on the chewing surfaces of the teeth were relatively flat, a trait found in fruit-eating primates. Both *Amphipithecus* and *Pondaungia* exhibit a combination of lower and higher primate traits, with the latter predominating (Ciochon, 1984/1985). *Amphipithecus* was approximately the size of the smallest of the modern apes, the gibbon, and weighed about 15 pounds. An artist's reconstruction of *Amphipithecus* appears in Figure 6-2.

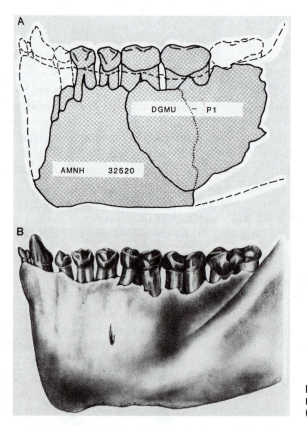

FIGURE 6-1   The reconstructed mandible of *Amphipithecus.* (Courtesy R. L. Ciochon.)

FIGURE 6-2 Artist's reconstruction of *Amphipithecus* based on actual fossil evidence and the order of development of anatomical features observed in primate evolution. (Courtesy R. L. Ciochon.)

The late Eocene locality of Krabi in southern Thailand yields primate remains. *Siamopithecus eocaenus* is about the size of the Oligocene-dated *Aegyptopithecus* from the Fayum in Egypt; that is, its estimated body weight is 6.5–7 kilograms (Chaimanee et al., 1997). Its anthropoid status is supported by numerous features, but it differs in some ways from known anthropoids. It is not clear if its ancestor was an Asian or African form, and it may represent a branch arising from an African–Southeast Asian anthropoid radiation. *Siamopithecus*'s ancestor may have originated in Africa and migrated into South Asia during or after the early Eocene and before the middle Eocene.

A fragment of a primate mandible also found at Krabi is attributed to *Wailekia orientale*, which is closely aligned to *Oligopithecus savagei* from Egypt (pages 99–100). If *Wailekia* is a preoligopithecine or an intermediate taxon in the anthropoid evolutionary line, then an African origin for Anthropoidea is not as clearly indicated as Fayum and northwestern African fossils once seemed to suggest.

In 1992, Godenot and Mahkoubi described three tiny fossilized teeth from the Algerian Sahara that may be 50–46 million years old. These are older than the Fayum sample described below. The teeth belong to a new genus and species, *Algeripithecus minutus*, weighing 5 to 11 ounces. There is a relationship between this material and the Fayum genus *Aegyptopithecus*, described on pages 101–103.

OLIGOCENE FAYUM DEPOSITS, EGYPT

Deposits in the Fayum area south of Cairo, Egypt, have been excavated since the 1960s (Simons, 1962b, 1965a, 1967a, 1968a, 1984). Fayum deposits yielded hominoid fossils, as well as fossils of monkeys. Modern monkeys and apes are generally distinguished by anatomical traits related to locomotor or dental adaptations or both. Modern monkeys have tails and are generally quadrupedal; modern apes lack tails, and some locomote by brachiating, that is, by arm-swinging beneath branches through the trees, and by **knuckle-walking** and **fist-walking** on the ground. The hands are placed on the ground, and the weight is borne by the knuckles in knuckle-walking and by the fists in fist-walking. The brain sizes of apes are generally larger than those of monkeys. In many respects Fayum hominoids resembled monkeys. They had relatively small brains and were arboreal quadrupeds, and some species possessed tails. Their dental structure, however, was already unique to hominoids. The four-cusp to five-cusp pattern of the lower molars was particularly diagnostic. These were monkeylike forms possessing an ape's teeth.

Elwyn Simons (1965b) and his colleagues identified between 19 and 21 primate species from the Egyptian Fayum site that could belong to six or more families (Table 6-2). The oldest dates are from Locality 41, the late Eocene about 37–36 mya. Fossil plants and birds suggest a wet, warm, tropical, forested, and swampy environment. Limb bones from the locale probably belong to *Catopithecus browni* (Simons, 1993), a form about the size of a South American squirrel monkey, 600–900 grams. Although its face was small like a squirrel monkey, its brain was not as big, so the head was smaller overall. Eye orbit size indicates a diurnal primate.

Simons (1995) cites the shovel-shaped front incisors, flattened face, forward-looking eye orbits, and fused frontal suture as significant higher primate traits of *Catopithecus*. He argues that *Catopithecus*'s teeth are very similar to those of

TABLE 6-2 Fayum Primates

Genus and Species	Approximate Age (mya)
Aegyptopithecus zeuxis	33.1 to 33.4
Propliopithecus chirobates	
Apidium phiomense	
Parapithecus grangeri	
Qatrania fleaglie	
Afrotarsius chatrathi	
Propliopithecus haeckli	33.8 to 34.0
Propliopithecus ankeli	
Apidium moustafai	
Oligopithecus savagei	34 to 35.1
Qatrania wingi	
Catopithecus browni	35.6 to 35.9
Proteopithecus sylviae	
Serapia eocaena	
Arsinoea kallimos	
Plesiopithecus teras	

Some data from E. Simons and T. Rasmussen, A whole new world of ancestors: Eocene Anthropoideans from Africa, *Evolutionary Anthropology*, 1994, 4:128–139.

adapids; this similarity suggests evolution from that primate branch. *Catopithecus* was an arboreal form feeding on seeds and occasionally insects.

Catopithecus is one of three genera that Rasmussen and Simons (1992) refer to as the oligopithecines. The largest genus, *Oligopithecus savagei*, weighing 700–1000 grams, is described on page 100. The smallest and least well known genus, *Proteopithecus sylviae*, weighed 500 grams. The oligopithecines were probably frugivores and insectivores.

The geographical range of *Oligopithecus* is extended with a lower molar found in Oman. The Fayum remains date to 34 mya, while the Oman molar dates to about 35.8 mya. These late Eocene ages make the oligopithecines contemporaneous with such Asian materials as *Amphipithecus* and *Pondaungia*, as well as Eocene-dated North American and European primates.

Three other species of higher primates come from Locality 41 (Simons, 1993). *Serapia eocaena* is a small creature resembling the later dating *Parapithecus*. The still smaller *Arsinoea kallimos* was about the size of the smallest modern monkey, the South American pygmy marmoset. The smallest of the three is the 36-million-year-old *Plesiopithecus teras*. Its molar vaguely resembles those of the other Fayum higher primates, but the greatly enlarged lower canine or incisor is unlike the front tooth of any Fayum primate. It was arboreal and likely nocturnal.

Simons (1993) argues that the diversity of primates seen at Locality 41 suggests 5–10 million years of evolution since they diverged from a common ancestor. Thus, African higher primates may be as old as 46 million years.

The Fayum habitat at 37 to 30 mya was quite different from today's desert. Studies of fossilized seed pods, pollens, and wood indicate that in the Oligocene the site was part of a tropical gallery forest. There were probably areas of open savanna or coastal plains nearby.

The recovery of quantities of fish and land vertebrates helped in reconstructing the habitat. Most fossils occur in stream-channel deposits and consist largely of disassociated skeletal parts waterborne to their final interment. Fish bones abound in the finer sands and gravels. The rarity of shark and ray fish dental remains suggests that the beds were deposited in fresh water, but near the coast. Most mammal skull parts are damaged, and the bones of one individual are rarely found together. Perhaps the material was moved about by water and catfish, turtles, crocodiles, and other predators.

Skeletal remains of large amphibians resembling sea cows were recovered. Reptiles are represented by land tortoises similar to those existing today in the Malay archipelago and the Galapagos Islands. Turtles and crocodiles were also apparently abundant. There is no evidence of grazing animals or other fauna characteristic of modern Africa. The total Fayum assemblage indicates a warm, well-watered lowland, with vegetation-clogged rivers.

The lower geological levels at the Fayum feature an abundant and diverse fauna of medium and large herbivores, and very few primates. The upper geological levels feature a diverse group of arboreal primates and a reduced diversity of large herbivores. Open vegetation and dry conditions typify the lower levels, and more densely forested and more humid conditions appear in upper levels. This apparent change in ecology could explain the explosive radiation of arboreal pri-mates seen in the upper section of the Fayum sediments (Gagnon, 1992).

The Oligocene Fayum primates may have inhabited the forest canopy, as do many modern primates. The suggestion that the environment had tropical, lush, stream-watered growth is supported by the rarity of small mammalian fauna other than primates and rodents. Undergrowth near the Oligocene streams was proba-bly too dense or wet to maintain an abundance of small mammals. Primates and rodents, the most common fauna at the site, might have reached this relatively inaccessible riverbank area through the forest canopy.

A large portion of the Fayum primate assemblage consists of animals whose young age is indicated by incomplete tooth eruption on many of the jaw frag-ments. The frontal bones of the skull show that these so-called dawn apes had a comparatively narrow snout situated between relatively forward positioned eyes, some forebrain expansion, and a relative reduction of the olfactory lobes. These animals depended on the visual sense. Four relatively complete frontal bones indi-cate that they were fused into one bone along the midline, as is the case in one of the Fayum hominoids, *Aegyptopithecus*. Fusion of the frontal bones is character-istic of the more highly evolved primates.

Limb bones of the Fayum apes indicate that they were quadrupeds. Some Fayum fossil apes had tails, unlike their modern descendants (Ankel, 1972).

Oligocene Fayum deposits yielded two anthropoid families, the Propliopitheci-dae and the Parapithecidae, and a prosimian family, the Tarsiidae. The Proplio-pithecidae includes the genera *Aegyptopithecus zeuxis*, *Propliopithecus haeckli*, *P. markgrafi*, *P. ankeli*, and *P. chirobates*. The Parapithecidae includes *Parapithecus fraasi*, *P. grangeri*, *Apidium moustafai*, *A. phiomense*, and *Qatrania wingi*. The tarsiid species is *Afrotarsius chatrathi*. The affinities of *Oligopithecus savagei* were previously discussed.

Oligopithecus savagei, first found at the Fayum in 1964, is dated to approxi-mately 35 mya. The *Oligopithecus* material consists of the left half of the mandible, from which both incisors and the last molars are missing. Simons (1962b) reconstructs the **dental formula** as 2-1-2-3 (2 incisors, 1 canine, 2 pre-molars, and 3 molars) in each quadrant of the jaw, like that of all modern Old World monkeys, apes, and humans. *Oligopithecus* is related to recently recovered Eocene fossils from the Fayum.

Apidium is represented by an ancestral and a descendant species. Simons (1960, 1972) suggested that these genera may be ancestral to Old World monkeys. The genus *Apidium* forms the largest group of Fayum primate fossils; more than fifty mandibular fragments have been recovered. *Apidium* has an extra premolar when compared with modern Old World primates. Its dental formula, 2-1-3-3, a total of thirty-six teeth, is the same as that of most New World monkeys. Those holding to the possibility of continental drift as one explanation of the similarity between Old and New World monkeys point to this shared feature as proof of an African origin for New World monkeys.

The dental formula of the 30-plus-million-year-old *Propliopithecus* is 2-1-2-3 like that of a modern chimpanzee (Figure 6-3). Its canines are fairly short and light, and the premolars lack the sectorial (one-cusped) condition characteristic

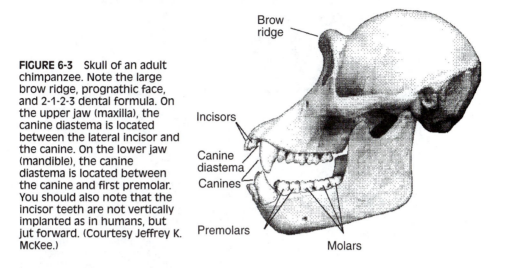

FIGURE 6-3 Skull of an adult chimpanzee. Note the large brow ridge, prognathic face, and 2-1-2-3 dental formula. On the upper jaw (maxilla), the canine diastema is located between the lateral incisor and the canine. On the lower jaw (mandible), the canine diastema is located between the canine and first premolar. You should also note that the incisor teeth are not vertically implanted as in humans, but jut forward. (Courtesy Jeffrey K. McKee.)

of modern apes. In primates with large canines the canine overlaps the premolar tooth in the opposing jaw. The overlapping maxillary canines are accommodated by a gap (the **canine diastema**) between the premolar and adjacent teeth (Figure 6-3) and by the presence of one instead of two cusps (the **bicuspid** condition) on the premolar, against which the overlapping canine shears. *Propliopithecus*'s incisors appear to have been vertically implanted rather than jutting forward as in monkeys and apes.

Propliopithecus ankeli was described by Simons et al. (1987). This species dates to the early Oligocene period and is one of the oldest of the Fayum primates. It differs from other species of *Propliopithecus* in being larger and having relatively larger or more robust canines and broader premolars. This form emphasizes the remarkable diversity of primates from the Oligocene levels at the Fayum.

Propliopithecus was probably a generalized small-faced arboreal stock and probably a representative of a large stock, some of whose members may have given rise to *Aegyptopithecus* and later to modern apes. Leaping is its possible mode of locomotion.

Aegyptopithecus (Figure 6-4) is dated at approximately 34–33 mya. More than twelve skull fragments, over fifty teeth, and several limb bones have been recovered. The skull material provides one of the best-preserved indications of early hominoid skulls. Simons (1987) reported considerable individual variability in the four most recently discovered male cranial bones. Some *Aegyptopithecus* males had large sagittal crests. The large sagittal crests, to which chewing muscles attach, develop in response to the heavy chewing musculature associated with large teeth. There are indications that *Aegyptopithecus* was increasing in size. *A. zeuxis* weighed 9 to 10 pounds, having evolved from smaller-bodied forms. Numerous dental and facial similarities between it and the 20- to 16-million-year-old East African **Miocene** fossil hominoid *Proconsul* suggest that *Aegyptopithecus* was in that ancestry (Simons, 1987).

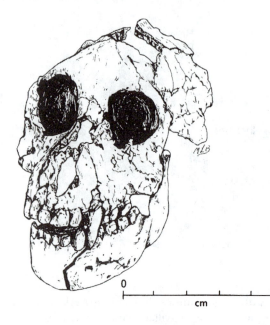

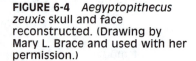

FIGURE 6-4 *Aegyptopithecus zeuxis* skull and face reconstructed. (Drawing by Mary L. Brace and used with her permission.)

An *Aegyptopithecus* endocranial cast suggests that it had a rather small brain for an evolving ape (Radinsky, 1973, 1977). The brain had a relatively large visual cortex, a relatively small olfactory region, and a smaller frontal lobe than that of modern apes. *Aegyptopithecus* had an increased emphasis on vision and a decreased reliance on smell, in a manner similar to that of modern apes (Kay & Simons, 1980).

Aegyptopithecus is also known from four incomplete mandibles and about fifty teeth. Several dental traits suggest that it could have evolved from the earlier *Propliopithecus. Aegyptopithecus* had large canines for an animal its size. The jaw is apelike and deepest under the canines.

Simons (1984) described *Aegyptopithecus* remains that seem to represent both sexes. The jaws and canines assigned to males are larger than those assigned to females. In extant primate species in which such size differences exist, the animals live in social groups containing adults of both sexes. Like modern-day primates, *Aegyptopithecus* may have resided in relatively large social groups.

The limb skeleton of *Aegyptopithecus* is documented by more than a dozen arm bones and several leg and foot bones. A nearly complete right ulna compares favorably with the ulna of arboreal primates. The length of the ulna compares well with ulnar length of the arboreal New World howler monkey *Alouatta* or the Old World *Presbytis cristatus,* an arboreal Asian leaf-eating monkey.

Aegyptopithecus was probably an arboreal quadruped that moved with its elbows slightly bent. It must have been capable of walking rather long distances and of galloping while moving terrestrially (Schon Ybarra, 1984). It was well adapted to climbing and possibly to leaping. Two incomplete humeri belonging to *A. zeuxis* suggest a robust, slowly moving arboreal quadruped (Fleagle &

Simons, 1982). It probably favored twigs and small branches for support while in the trees and shrubs.

Three partial femora of *A. zeuxis* suggest that this was an arboreal quadruped rather than a leaping or suspensory primate (Ankel-Simonds, Fleagle, & Chatrath, 1998). The femur seems relatively robust and short for its body mass. In its femoral anatomy, *Aegyptopithecus* is intermediate between the more primitive oligopithecines from the late Eocene Fayum and the early Miocene proconsul fossils of East Africa.

Morphologically and chronologically, *Aegyptopithecus* could be ancestral to a Miocene group of hominoids, the dryopithecines. It seems to occupy an early position in the hominoid lineage. Although features of the skull and dentition suggest a relationship to late Old World primates, the postcranial skeleton differs from Old World primates in many significant details.

Body weights of the Fayum primates range from about 1 pound or less to about 10 pounds for *A. zeuxis*. A similar range is found among extant New World monkeys. Body size is a part of a species' adaptation to exploiting various food sources (Kay, 1973). The choice of leaves or insects as a protein source for fruit-eating (frugivorous) primates is an important element in selection for body size. Fayum primates tend to be larger than is common for modern arboreal insectivores, and this may rule out insectivory as a feeding strategy. The body size of *Aegyptopithecus* falls within the size range of such arboreal apes as the gibbon and far below the range of terrestrial apes such as chimpanzees and gorillas. This further indicates an arboreal habitat (Kay & Simons, 1980).

Kay and Simons summarized the data on Fayum primates as follows:

1. They were primarily frugivorous, although one form, *Parapithecus*, may have been somewhat more folivorous (leaf eating) than other Fayum primates.
2. A predominately arboreal habitat is indicated for all forms, with the possible exception of *Parapithecus*.
3. The relatively small eye orbits of *Apidium* suggest that it was diurnal, as is true of most extant primates. Nocturnal animals have large eye orbits. *Apidium* and *Aegyptopithecus* had a poorly developed tactile sensory apparatus in the snout, as is true of modern primates.
4. Probably the closest living ecological analogues of the Fayum primates are found among living New World monkeys, who are similar to Fayum primates in body size, are diurnal, and have a predominantly frugivorous diet.

Although they share a dental pattern of two premolars with modern Old World primates, both *Aegyptopithecus* and *Propliopithecus* retain more primitive, New World monkeylike traits in many respects of the skull and postcranial skeleton. It has been argued that the Fayum forms precede the monkey–ape divergence (Fleagle et al., 1986); however, Simons (1987) argued that at least *Aegyptopithecus* is on the ape evolutionary line. The virtually simultaneous appearance of monkeys and apes in the Fayum deposits and the similarities—small size, teeth designed for fruit eating, and quadrupedal posture—strongly indicate that they evolved either from a common ancestor or from a separate ancestor, but not one from the other (Whitten & Nickels, 1983).

MIOCENE HOMINOIDS

During the Miocene geological epoch (25–6 mya), hominoids were represented by a number of genera, some of which are placed in a fossil group known as the *dryopithecines,* a name that means "oak ape." In Greek mythology a dryad is a wood nymph, often said to have inhabited oak forests—a possible habitat for European dyropithecines. A likely ancestor is the Oligocene genus *Aegyptopithecus.*

Early apes dominate the African Miocene primate record, whereas monkey fossils are rare. However, by the middle Miocene, 16–10 mya, the proportions change and monkeys predominate. This situation exists today. By the late Miocene, 10–5 mya, primitive apes are almost nonexistent in the African fossil record, although they survive in some abundance in southern Asia and China until about 7 mya.

Compared with Oligocene primates, Miocene apes are morphologically more like modern apes. All Miocene hominoids have at least a few distinctly ape-like traits. There is a considerable morphological gap between the early apes of the Fayum and the monkeys and apes of the early East African Miocene. Miocene forms more clearly document the divergence of the monkeys and apes.

During the Miocene epoch, great mountain ranges arose and continents continued to drift apart. Although Africa and Eurasia were still one continent, volcanoes were actively changing the African continent. A series of geological disturbances in Africa formed the Great Rift Valley. There seems to have been a mixture of wet and dry and warm and cool weather. The vegetation, a patchwork of forest and grasslands not much different from modern African savannas, provided a rich environment of plant and animal foods.

Hominoids of the early Miocene, 20 to 18 mya, lived in quite different habitats than did hominoids in the middle Miocene of 15 to 12 mya (Andrews, 1981). The habitat of the former seems to have been more heavily forested, whereas that of the latter appears to have been dominated by temperate to tropical woodlands. Fossil soils and grasses from the site of Fort Ternan, Kenya, may indicate a mosaic of grassy woodland and wooded grasslands from about 14 mya. Others argue that the habitat is forest and woodland. Perhaps grassland habitats were available in east Africa long before the evolutionary divergence of apes and hominids some 10–6 mya (Retallack et al., 1990).

Andrews suggested that the ecological shift is accompanied by dental and skeletal changes in the hominoids, for example, the development of thickened molar tooth enamel, and by skull and postcranial modifications. These features probably reflected a changing dietary pattern and a new means of environmental exploitation. Although early Miocene hominoids retained mainly primitive traits, middle Miocene hominoids shared many derived traits with extant great apes (chimpanzees, gorillas, and orangutans) and humans. They may have been able to exploit habitats beyond the range of modern apes.

The ancestors of extant great apes and humans may have passed through a very different adaptive phase than the one characterizing their present way of life. The members of one Miocene genus, *Sivapithecus*, were probably the size of modern orangutans, and animals of this size living in temperate or tropical woodlands must have been at least partially terrestrial because of discontinuities in the woodland canopy. Because woodland habitats have greater seasonal variation than forests, fruits comprised only a minor dietary item. The ecological evidence suggests that hominoids of the middle Miocene were omnivorous and partially terrestrial (Andrews, 1981).

Andrews (1993) suggests that the various hominoid genera fall within three large groups. The Afropithecini are restricted to the East African Turkana sites of Buluk and Kalodirr, yielding *Afropithecus*, which date older than 17 mya. The Arabian site of Ab Dabtiyah, yielding *Heliopithecus*, also dates to 17 mya. The East African sites of Maboko Island and Nachola, yielding *Kenyapithecus africanus*, date to about 15 mya.

The second group is the Kenyapithecini. The sparse African fossil record includes the middle Miocene site of Fort Ternan, yielding *K. wickeri*, dated to about 14 mya. Similarly aged sites are rare in Eurasia, but hominoids similar to *Kenyapithecus* come from Pasalar and Candir, Turkey, and from two eastern European sites. These sites date to about 15–14 mya.

The third group includes European fossils commonly assigned to *Dryopithecus*. The Dryopithecini date from 12 to 8 mya from sites in Austria, France, Germany, Hungary, and Spain; similar fossils have been found in Georgia and China.

The Afropithecini seem to be associated with tropical forests with perhaps some aridity. The Kenyapithecini appear to have thicker enamel than the Afropithecini, although their postcranial anatomies are quite similar. Their habitat appears to have differed little from that of the afropithecines. The Dryopithecini retain the primitively thin enamel of early hominoids. The upper extremities are similar to modern great apes. The dryopithecine environment appears to have been forested.

Andrews suggests that the early hominoids were primarily arboreal frugivores. Two trends appear in hominoid evolution. The first led to increased molar enamel thickness combined with little change in the postcranial anatomy. The second trend produced postcranial anatomical changes, leading to functional complexes similar to modern great apes. These changes were likely associated with habitat shifts, perhaps from tropical forest habitats in Africa to the subtropical and warm temperate forests of Europe. The latter would have been more seasonal and open. Dietary changes, not seen in dental, facial, or cranial anatomies, may also have occurred.

Distribution

Around 18 to 15 mya a land corridor existed between Africa and Eurasia via Arabia, permitting migration of African mammals into Eurasia (Table 6-3). During this time hominoids made a major appearance in Eurasia. The climate was

TABLE 6-3 Miocene Hominoids Discussed in Text

Genus	Locale	Approximate Date (mya)
Africa Primarily		
Proconsul	Kenya, Uganda	20?, 18.5–17.5
Afropithecus	Kenya	17
Turkanopithecus	Kenya	18–16
Nyanzapithecus	Kenya	16–15
Rangwapithecus	Kenya	16–15
Kenyapithecus africanus	Kenya	15
Kenyapithecus wickerii	Kenya, Turkey	15–14
Dendropithecus	Kenya	Lower Miocene
Otavipithecus	Namibia	13
Micropithecus	Uganda	Miocene
Morotopithecus	Uganda	20.6
Heliopithecus	Arabia	17
Asia Primarily		
Sivapithecus	Asia primarily	17–14
Ankarapithecus	Turkey	10
Dionysopithecus	China	Early Miocene
Ramapithecus?	China	Mid-Miocene
Lufengpithecus	China	Mid-Miocene
Gigantopithecus	India	9–5
Gigantopithecus	China, Vietnam	500,000 years
Europe Primarily		
Dryopithecus	Europe primarily	16–10
Oreopithecus	Italy, East Africa	12–10
Ouranopithecus	Greece	11–10

more seasonal, and more open-country woodland habitats appeared. About 15 to 8 mya the Tethys Sea shrank and formed the Mediterranean, Black, and Caspian sea basins, and open-country habitats expanded. As environments became increasingly seasonal, the hominoid range shrank further. By 8 to 7 mya, Eurasian and African hominoids were vastly diminished in numbers and range.

There were several episodes of lower sea levels during the Miocene that increased the likelihood of migration from Africa into Asia. The potential land corridor linking Africa, Saudi Arabia, and Iran/Iraq allowed primates to reach southwestern Asia during lowered sea levels in the early or middle Miocene. Subsequent dispersal into China came from southwestern Asia through India and Pakistan.

Considerable Miocene hominoid remains come from Africa, especially from sites in Kenya and Uganda (Figure 6-5). These animals range in size from that of a small gibbon (10 pounds) to that of a large male chimpanzee (110 pounds). Most African Miocene species are well known dentally; however, little skull material is preserved. Postcranial materials are becoming more abundant. Although some specimens may date to 20 mya, most probably date to between 18.5 and 17.5 mya.

A significant African Miocene hominoid assemblage was found at the Kaswanga primate site on Rusinga Island, Kenya. This site yielded nine whole or

FIGURE 6-5 Distribution of Miocene hominoids, by country in which fossils were found (shaded). See Table 6-3 for a list of sites and specimens. (Courtesy Jeffrey K. McKee.)

partial *Proconsul* skeletons that were washed into a small gully. The bones sample apes ranging from very small youngsters to adults of both sexes. Practically every part of the *Proconsul* skeleton is known from one or more of the individuals (Walker & Teaford, 1989).

Leakey and Leakey (1986a, 1986b, 1987) and Leakey et al. (1988a, 1988b) report the recovery of specimens from sediments along the western side of Lake Turkana, Kenya, at a small rich early Miocene locality called Kalodirr. The estimated age of these remains is 18 to 16 mya. The relatively complete material offers new insights of the morphological diversity in the Miocene Hominoidea.

One new genus, *Afropithecus turkanensis*, contains forty-six specimens. Its mosaic of features, typical of a variety of Miocene hominoids (Leakey et al., 1988a, 1988b), suggests a greater complexity in the early Miocene ape fossil record than was previously apparent. It shares a number of traits with the Oligocene genus *Aegyptopithecus*, which may indicate a phylogenetic link. The type specimen of *Afropithecus* consists of the snout, facial skeleton, and some cranial fragments. The relatively large size of the canine teeth suggests that the new specimen is a male.

The second new specimen from Kalodirr, *Turkanopithecus kalakolensis*, may be slightly older than *Afropithecus*. The skull of the type specimen is slightly smaller than a previously described female *Proconsul africanus*. It is reasonably complete and includes the facial skeleton, partial skull cap, and examples of all the permanent maxillary teeth except the incisors. The associated lower jaw includes much of the left side and some teeth. A complete right femur and other bone fragments are probably associated with the skull and lower jaw. The relationship of *Turkanopithecus* to other known hominoids is not clear. There are important skull differences when compared with the other similarly sized African Miocene hominoid skull of *P. africanus*.

Material from a site on Maboko Island, Kenya, is assigned to a new genus, *Nyanzapithecus*, with two species, *N. pickfordi* and *N. vancouveringi*, and dates to about 16 to 15 mya (Harrison, 1986). *Nyanzapithecus* shares a distinctive suite of traits, especially in the upper molars and premolars, with *Oreopithecus*, a late Miocene (8.5–6.5 mya) hominoid from Tuscany, Italy. In both genera the molars increase in size from the first to the third molar. *Oreopithecus*, dating from approximately 12 to 10 mya, has been called a monkey, an ape, and even an early human. East African members of the genus seem to confirm its hominoid status. *Oreopithecus* may show the evolution of bipedalism in a hominoid line distinct from that leading to the hominids.

Nyanzapithecus is a medium-sized primate with a highly distinctive dental morphology, a relatively short face with a low and broad nasal opening, and a relatively large jaw containing small and robust incisors. *Nyanzapithecus*, *Oreopithecus*, and a closely related 17-mya genus from Songhor, Kenya, called *Rangwapithecus*, are placed in the family Oreopithecidae (Harrison, 1986), which seems to have diverged from the basal hominoid stock in Africa by at least the early Miocene. *Rangwapithecus vancouveringi* is small species found in lower Miocene deposits at three sites in Kenya. The two species of *R. gordoni* and *R. vancouveringi* are closely related.

Another small-bodied African hominoid is *Dendropithecus macinnesi*, known from several lower Miocene sites in Kenya. The fossilized remains contain the maxilla and mandible with all the teeth, as well as some postcranial bones. Dentally, *Dendropithecus* is the size of the Asian siamang—a 15–20-pound arboreal-dwelling primate.

Leakey and Leakey (1987) gave the name of *Simiolus enjiessi* to a new genus and species of small-bodied ape found in Kenya. It differs from other small-bodied Miocene African apes, such as *Micropithecus*, in dental features.

In 1991 hominoid remains were recovered from a mine dump in the Otavi region of northern Namibia in southern Africa. The mandible with four cheek teeth, a broken premolar, the canine root socket, and the incisor sockets, dates to about 13 mya (Conroy et al., 1993). The fossil, called *Otavipithecus namibiensis* in honor of its location, is the first hominoid remain found south of equatorial east Africa. According to Conroy et al. (1992) the Otavi mandible differs from other middle Miocene hominoids of both Africa and Eurasia. The most appropriate comparisons are with the east African and Eurasian hominoids *Kenyapithecus*, *Sivapithecus*, and *Dryopithecus*.

Andrews (1992) hesitates to accept *Otavipithecus* as a new hominoid genus. Perhaps it is linked with the previously described east African *Afropithecus*. However, Andrews accepted a species distinction for the Namibia find.

Otavipithecus weighed between 14 and 20 kilograms, the same weight estimated for *Proconsul africanus*. The diet was probably leaves, berries, seeds, buds, and flowers—foods not needing much anterior tooth preparation. Estimation of age at death is about 10 years. The habitat was more humid than it is today. Perhaps like some other Miocene hominoids, the Otavi specimen dwelled in a forest environment.

By the mid-Miocene, hominoids apparently inhabited almost the full length of Africa, including what is today the Arabian peninsula. Soon after, they apparently dispersed from Africa, the first occurrence thereafter being in Turkey. About 3 million years later they are known from southern France and western Pakistan, and they extended their range into China later in the Miocene (Andrews, 1992).

Dating of the Indian-subcontinent hominoids is based on faunal associations. The Nagri faunal zone in North India is generally accepted as of later Miocene or early **Pliocene** age. Because the Nagri overlies the Chinji, the latter is considered to be older, perhaps of middle Miocene dating.

Eighteen localities in the Siwalik Hills of Pakistan yielded forty-three hominoid individuals (Pilbeam et al., 1977b). The Lower and Middle Siwalik fauna can be separated into two groups: one group dating to around 12 mya, and another dating about 17 to 10 mya (Pilbeam et al., 1977a). The mammalian community at these sites suggests a woodland or bush habitat with open patches of grassland rather than extensive forests. In Nagri times the habitat was more or less open rather than extensively forested. The evidence suggests a shift from a mainly subtropical forest habitat to more open, less low-lying habitats from Chinji to Nagri times and, thus, a nonevergreen forest context for at least some of the major primate localities.

At least four hominoid species are recognized from the Siwaliks: *Sivapithecus punjabicus*, *S. sivalensis*, *S. indicus*, and *Gigantopithecus bilaspurensis* (Pilbeam et al., 1977b). *Sivapithecus* specimens range in age from 13 to 8 mya, and *Gigantopithecus* is dated to about 9 to 5 mya.

The Miocene hominoid assemblage from the Dam formation in Saudi Arabia, dated to 15 to 14 mya (Andrews and Tobien, 1977), suggests linkage with East African Miocene hominoids. Free migration occurred between Arabia and North and East Africa at this time. Saudi Arabia yielded hominoid materials dated to the early Miocene about 17 mya.

Because Saudi Arabia must have been close to migration routes between Africa and Eurasia, it is interesting that Saudi specimens are not linked with contemporaneous *Sivapithecus* species in Turkey. The Turkish deposits are similar in age to the Saudi deposit, but Turkish species share traits with later Miocene *Sivapithecus* from India and Pakistan. These findings indicate that the Saudi Arabian specimens represent a primitive hominoid branch not directly related to later ape evolution.

The face and skull of a 60-pound female fruit-eating ape that inhabited the woodlands of central Turkey belongs to *Ankarapithecus meteai*. This fossil dates to approximately 10 mya, close to the hominid-pongid divergence date, and similar to the age estimated for *Ouranopithecus* (which Cameron, 1997, calls *Graecopithecus*) in Greece and *Dryopithecus* from the Indian subcontinent. Fossil hominoids from this time period are very rare and crucial for sorting out hominoid evolution. The material, the most complete fossil ape face found dating between 18 and 3 mya, joins a jawbone and lower face from the same species found in the 1950s in the same area. The face and skull suggest that *Ankarapithecus* is not matched with any extant or fossil hominoids. The configuration of traits may support its placement as a stem member of the great ape and human clade (Alpagut et al., 1996; Cameron, 1997).

Numerous jaws and teeth come from a site near Salonika, Greece, that is dated to about 11 or 10 mya. A site near Athens yielded similar materials. This gorilla-sized hominoid, named *Ouranopithecus macedoniensis*, has an African-ape subnasal morphology. It shares its molar size with modern gorillas. The small size of the canines relative to the molars and premolars and thick molar enamel are shared traits with all late Miocene hominoids. It might be argued that *Ouranopithecus* is a viable Africa ape–human ancestor.

The habitat of *Ouranopithecus* was a large grassy plain, home to ungulate herds. Trees and bushes provided food for giraffes and mastodonts and likely provided refuge and sleeping sites for the hominoids. The climate was probably fairly hot, with two well-marked seasons. Fossils recovered from the Ravin de la Pluie contain male and female specimens, as well as those of young and old, indicating life in a social group (deBonis and Koufos, 1995).

Ouranopithecus was comparable in size to female gorillas. Size disparity among the specimens indicates sexual dimorphism. *Ouranopithecus* had powerful jaws and probably powerful chewing muscles. Dental dimensions suggest a weight of 160 pounds for males, if tooth and body size were closely correlated (deBonis and Koufos, 1995).

While the canines of male *Ouranopithecus* were larger than those of females, they were relatively smaller than those of hominoids excepting *Australopithecus* and *Homo*. *Ouranopithecus* has a short, rounded mandibular second premolar more like that of *Australopithecus* than apes. The wear pattern is similar to that of *A. afarensis*.

A partial skull with a reasonably complete face was recovered at the Xirochori locality (deBonis et al., 1990). The orbital area is more similar to that of a male gorilla or an early hominid. In other ways this material is more like African than Asian hominoids. DeBonis and Koufos (1995) state that *Ouranopithecus* presents a suite of primitive traits but shares several derived traits with the later *Australopithecus* and *Homo*. They consider *Ouranopithecus* to be a sister group of *Australopithecus* and *Homo*. Cameron (1997), who prefers the genus designation *Graecopithecus*, refers the form to the Homininae. Begun (1994) disagrees and suggests that *Ouranopithecus* became extinct.

Several Miocene hominoids from northeastern Hungary date to about 12 mya and come from a subtropical climate with traces of wet forest to grassland and higher mountain elements (Kretzoi, 1975). Some materials are grouped with either *Dryopithecus* or *Sivapithecus*. European hominoids were primitive forest or woodland dwellers and were probably quadrupedal and arboreal. Larger species may have come to the ground to feed on relatively soft foods.

Morphology

The morphological reconstruction of Miocene apes is largely based on material gathered from around Lake Victoria in East Africa. This material probably represents bones washed into the deposits from which they were dug, perhaps after they were consumed by large carnivores and vultures, or perhaps crocodiles preyed on the animals when they came to the water to drink. The primate population at this time was evidently large and diverse, and known specimens most likely represent only a small portion of that population.

The presence of so many animal remains in shallow-water lake deposits suggests that the animals were vulnerable when they came to the water to drink and that they were attacked and killed there. The relative absence of limb bones may be because of their high marrow content. The majority of the limb bones were probably broken and eaten by carnivores. This hypothesis would also account for the almost complete absence of skulls, whose brain content was liable to be eaten by larger carnivores.

Cranium, Face, Brain.   Well-preserved Miocene East African cranial material belongs to *Proconsul africanus*. The skull is lightly built and rather small, suggesting a creature more the size of an Old World monkey than a modern ape. (However, its age and sex are unclear.) Walker and Pickford (Walker, 1983) suggested a body weight close to 24 pounds. Conroy (1987) estimated that it weighed 26 pounds and was a female; others suggest a weight closer to 33 pounds. *Proconsul's* skull differs from that of modern apes. It lacks the heavy bony structures characteristic of the sagittal (top of skull) and **nuchal** (back of skull) regions. When present, these crests are sites for the attachment of heavy chewing and neck muscles, respectively. There is no heavy bone ridge (**supraorbital torus**) above the eye orbits as found in modern apes and larger Old World monkeys (Figure 6-6).

The East African *Proconsul* had a limited degree of brain development. The general shape of the brain is similar to that of Old World monkeys. However, Walker and Teaford (1989) reported a cranial capacity about 167 cubic centimeters and concluded that *P. africanus* was more encephalized than modern monkeys of comparable body size. The presence of a frontal air sinus, or air space, within the frontal bone of the skull is significant. Such sinuses are found in humans and African apes, but not in Asian apes or among the monkeys. The presence of a frontal air sinus in *Proconsul* suggests that these animals had some affinities with modern apes (Walker & Teaford, 1989).

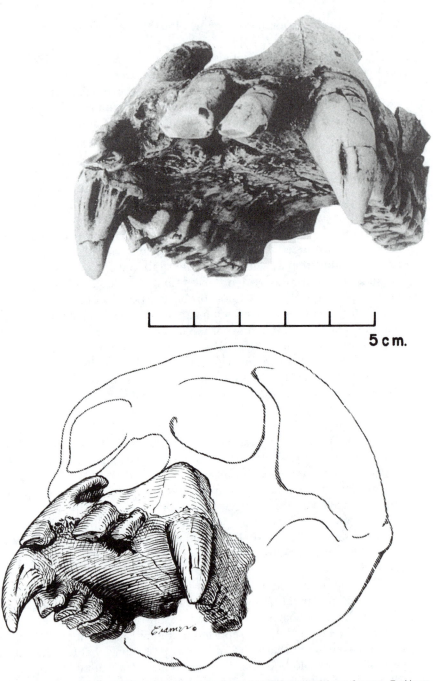

5 cm.

FIGURE 6-6 *Top,* Palate of *Proconsul major,* one of the larger African forms. *Bottom,* The face and skull reconstructed about the palate. (Photo of casts courtesy Wenner-Gren Foundation for Anthropological Research, Inc., and with permission of the owners of the original specimens.)

Micropithecus clarki, found in Miocene deposits in Uganda, is the smallest hominoid, living or extinct, yet known (Fleagle & Simons, 1978). Its facial skeleton, similar to that of the smallest of the living apes, the gibbon, had a relatively broad snout, broad nasal region and large eye orbits and was shallow. Although the molars and premolars were rather small, the incisors and canines were relatively large. Dentally, *Micropithecus* is most similar to small Miocene hominoids from Kenya.

In 1978 an early hominoid was discovered in the Xiacowan Formation, northern Jiangsu Province, eastern China. It dated to the early Miocene about 19–17 mya. The specimen, a partial upper jaw with three teeth, is called *Dionysopithecus* (Li, 1978). This specimen is almost identical to the small primate upper jaw belonging to *Micropithecus.* This is the first indication of a link between the East African early Miocene localities and similarly aged localities in eastern China. Based on the apparent lack of Oligocene higher primate fossils in Asia, the Jiangsu material argues for a dispersal out of Africa into Asia about 20 mya.

S. Moya Solá and M. Kohler (1993) recovered cranial fragments of *D. laietanus* in northern Spain in 1991. They claim that the fragments demonstrate that *Dryopithecus* is a member of the group including great apes and humans and is most closely affiliated with the Asian orangutans. Begun (1992), on the other hand, argues that *Dryopithecus* is a close relative of African apes.

Postcranial Bones. A sample of Miocene apes from Africa dramatically increased the postcranial bone sample of these forms (Walker and Teaford, 1989). The hands and feet exhibited both apelike and monkeylike features and showed that *Proconsul* was a slow-moving quadruped. The limb proportions also indicate both apelike and monkeylike features. There are no modern animal models of *Proconsul's* anatomy, and each of *Proconsul's* anatomical complexes is unique. The ankle bones are slender and monkeylike while the big toe is robust and apelike. Similar unique combinations are found in the pelvis.

Originally it was concluded that *Proconsul* was an active, leaping quadruped that moved like today's Asian langurs and perhaps also had a limited ability to swing by its arms. The new fossils described by Walker and Teaford (1989) reveal that *Proconsul* was a relatively slow-moving, arboreal species that had no obvious specializations for leaping, arm-swinging, or terrestrial living. *Proconsul* was not well adapted for running and rapid, frequent leaping. It may have spent most of its time climbing and bridging in the upper canopy and between trees. There seems to have been an emphasis on slow climbing with some evidence of fore and hind limb specialization beyond what occurs in modern monkeys, and a tendency toward more upright posture. However, there is also some evidence that *Proconsul* had a tail. If a tail was present, it does not help solve the taxonomic status of *Proconsul*; that is, was it a hominoid or a primitive member of Old World monkey stock?

Begun (1992) argued that based on postcranial remains, fossils traditionally assigned to the European *Dryopithecus* group actually fall into three groups with different evolutionary relationships to other Miocene hominoids and different locomotor behaviors. Miocene hominoids probably exhibited a variety of locomotor behaviors, some, perhaps, not exhibited (or seldom exhibited) by modern apes.

Dryopithecine material in Spain may be especially relevant to discussions of dryopithecine locomotion. There is a partial skeleton from a 9.5-million-year-old animal that may have been a male weighing about 75 pounds. The skeletal material shows a creature with a semierect posture much like today's great apes. Although this posture was previously suggested based on finds in Hungary, the Spanish fossils are the strongest evidence yet of a semierect posture. Fist-walking or knuckle-walking like that of modern great apes may be a good representative of the locomotor behavior of this animal.

The oldest evidence for brachiation may come from Uganda in the form of a partial shoulder bone and parts of two femurs. The glenoid fossa on the shoulder suggests that the animal's shoulder joints were mobile. Dated to 20.6 mya, the shoulder bone of a 90–110-pound animal called *Morotopithecus bishopi* belonged to an animal that could swing as well as arm-hang from the branches. It probably moved quadrupedally on the ground. The mobility of the shoulder joint allowed this animal to distribute its body weight over the branches, allowing it to feed in many areas of the branches.

Arm and ankle bones from *Kenyapithecus* are claimed to resemble those of modern apes, but the claim may be premature. The shape of the ankle bone suggests that the animal could rotate its foot sideways, a feature of modern chimpanzees that allows them to cling to trees with their feet and also to walk flat-footed on the ground.

Dentition.   Much has been written about dryopithecine dentition, not only because their teeth comprise a large part of the fossil sample but also because of the characteristic Y-5 mandibular molar crown pattern. The Y-5 pattern persists with variations among modern and fossil apes and humans. This pattern has been a persistent hominoid trait for at least 30 million years.

In the Y-5 pattern the mandibular molar surface has five cusps (elevations) separated by grooves in the form of a Y. Although this pattern of cusps and grooves is commonly found in the lower molar teeth of human fossil remains, in modern humans there is frequently a reduction or absence of the fifth cusp and the formation of a plus fissure pattern (that is, a + 5 or + 4), especially on the second and third molars. Although some consider the Y-5 pattern to be an important diagnostic trait, Morris (1970) raised doubts about the value of using this trait to draw evolutionary relationships.

Dryopithecine dentition shows certain differences from that of modern apes. The incisors are relatively smaller, the tooth rows tend to converge anteriorly, and on the upper molars the internal **cingulum** (extra enamel at the side of the tongue base) is strongly developed and rather elaborately crinkled. The canines and premolars are apelike; when the upper and lower teeth are in contact (in occlusion), the canine teeth overlap each other and are strongly projecting. The first lower premolar is sectorial (the medial surface is sheared away to accommodate the upper overlapping canine) as in all modern primates with large, overlapping upper canines.

Evolutionary Relationships

For many years it was suspected that the origins of the Pongidae (apes) and the Hominidae (humans) were probably to be found among the diverse array of Miocene hominoids. For some time it was suggested that one member of the Miocene hominoid stock was probably ancestral to the first hominids. This view has been replaced, based largely on the questioning of the hominid status of a form called *Ramapithecus* and on evidence suggesting that the human–ape divergence from a common ancestor occurred later than originally thought.

Ramapithecus was first found in 1934 by G. E. Lewis (1934a), who described fragmentary dental and jaw remains and remarked on traits that appeared to be superficially associated with the human ancestral line. That line of reasoning was later supported by Louis Leakey (1968, 1969, 1970) on the basis of dental remains found in Kenya. *Ramapithecus* was once considered to be the first hominid, a form that diverged from the common ape–human line about 14 to 12 mya.

The question of whether this fossil group belongs on the hominid line is at least partially dependent on where one chooses to recognize the split of that line from the common human–ape stock. This boundary is likely to be arbitrary, and of the criteria used to differentiate humans from apes—postcranial features, dentition, and cranial and facial features—until recently only dental traits belonging to this group were available. A number of anatomical traits at first led to the conclusion that this form had a short, flat, and deep face and a number of dental traits superficially resembling those of the first hominids, the australopithecines (Chapter 8).

Many (Frayer, 1974; Greenfield, 1979; Robinson, 1972) have stressed the nonhominid traits of *Ramapithecus* and called for placing it in the genus *Sivapithecus* (from India and China), with which it shares many similarities. The demise of the *Ramapithecus*-as-hominid viewpoint began with the wide acceptance of the argument that the human–ape split occurred only about 8 to 6 mya (Chapter 4), long after the first appearance of *Ramapithecus* at about 14 to 12 mya.

More important in understanding the *Ramapithecus*-as-hominid viewpoint was the notion that the human and ape evolutionary lines diverged from one another perhaps as early as 20 mya. The argument that the Miocene hominoids could be divided into ape and human ancestors led to the assumption that simple markers, such as tooth enamel thickness—considered a response to dietary pressures where rough, hard-to-chew foods required thick enamel crowns in order to slow the process of erosion—could be used to place species into either the human or ape group. Although much was made about the relationship between enamel thickness and diet, and more specifically the appropriateness of using enamel thickness to assess phylogenetic relationships, Martin (1985) showed the error in this line of thinking.

Ramapithecus's fate as a nonhominid and its inclusion within the genus *Sivapithecus* was all but sealed with the recovery of a multitude of new materials. Hominoid fossils from the Lufeng basin of Yunnan Province, People's Republic of China, constitute one of the most extensive collections of hominoid materials ever assembled (Figure 6-7). There are nearly 1,000 specimens (dating to about 8 mya) representing tens if not hundreds of individuals of both sexes.

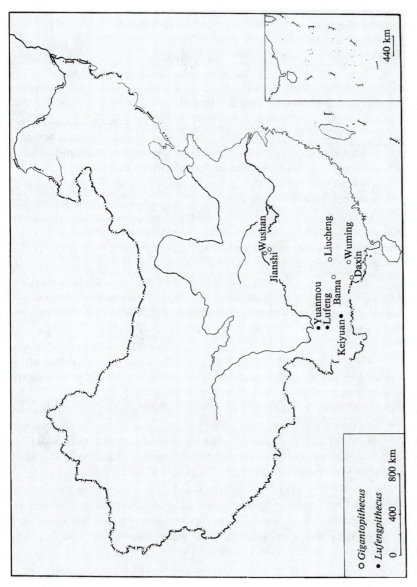

FIGURE 6-7 Hominoid locations in China. (Courtesy X. Wu and F. E. Poirier.)

The taxonomic situation concerning the Lufeng fossils is still not resolved (see Etler, 1984; Wu and Poirier, 1995). Many scientists place all the Lufeng hominoids into the taxon *Sivapithecus yunanensis* and put these forms within the orangutan lineage. The similarity with orangutans is particularly vivid in the sloped and slightly concave facial profile of *Sivapithecus* and the forward jutting of its canine teeth (Figure 6-8).

Conroy (1990) accepted that the differences within the sample are due to sexual dimorphism and noted that the Chinese crania bear no resemblance to other *Sivapithecus* crania. Therefore, he proposed a new genus, *Lufengpithecus*, to accommodate the Chinese material.

Postcranial remains belonging to *Sivapithecus* include arm and leg bones and a few finger and foot bones (Pilbeam et al., 1980). The forearm and foot were mobile; the big toe (the hallux) was opposable and capable of powerful gripping, as in modern orangutans (Badgley, 1984). These forms were apparently fully capable of moving through large and perhaps small branch zones of an arboreal habitat. The once-held view that they were evolving a bipedal mode of locomotion is not substantiated. Unless the fossil record unexpectedly forces us to reconsider the importance of bipedalism as the human hallmark, forms, such as *Sivapithecus*, not showing consistent bipedalism, cannot be considered to be within the Hominidae.

The view that sivapithecids might be ancestral to the Hominidae was further undermined when Pilbeam and his coworkers recovered the remains of an adult male *Sivapithecus* skull in Pakistan dating to about 8 mya. The skull, which includes about two-thirds of the facial bones, looks distinctively non-

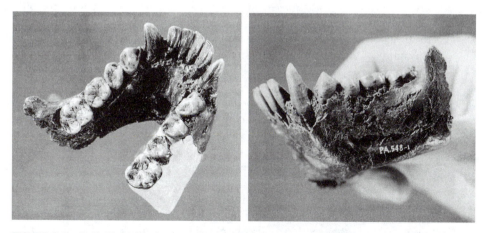

FIGURE 6-8 *Left*, Note the large canines and the canine diastema (situated between the canine and the first premolar) of this *Sivapithecus* mandible. *Right*, A side view of the same mandible. (Courtesy Zhou Guoxing, Beijing Natural History Museum.)

human. It has close-set eyes, a protruding jaw, and flaring cheekbones. It looks very much like the skull of the orangutan (Pilbeam, 1982, 1983, 1984; Preuss, 1982).

The downfall of the argument that members of the Hominidae might be found among some middle Miocene hominoids began with the wide acceptance of a late divergence date of humans and apes and has been substantiated with fossil evidence found in China, Pakistan, and Africa. The hominoid group known as the sivapithecids may have already split off from the common ape stock and may be ancestral to the orangutans rather than to the gorilla, chimpanzee, and humans. Dental similarities between the sivapithecids and the australopithecines are not indicative of an ancestral–descendant relationship but are the result of parallelisms (Wolpoff, 1982).

GIGANTOPITHECUS

The remains belonging to a form called *Gigantopithecus* have been called everything from an ape to a giant human. *Gigantopithecus* has been designated as the ancestor of the elusive yeti or abominable snowman and linked to China's elusive "Hairy Wildman" (Greenwell & Poirier, 1989; Poirier et al., 1983). Early mention of *Gigantopithecus* was made by G. R. von Koenigswald in 1935 on the basis of teeth found in a Chinese drugstore in Hong Kong. The Chinese have collected fossilized teeth and bones, referred to as "dragon bones," for use in herbal medicines. Since the recovery of the original material, other *Gigantopithecus* remains have been found in India as well as in China (Wu & Poirier, 1995). *Gigantopithecus* is known from a number of lower jaw remains and well over a thousand isolated teeth. No other skeletal parts are available. *Gigantopithecus* may have weighed between 400 and 600 pounds and stood at least 6 feet tall. It seems to have ranged in time from 9 to 5 mya in India to as recently as 250,000–500,000 years ago in China. In China and Vietnam, *Gigantopithecus* remains are found in the same deposits as those yielding bones belonging to the ancestors of the giant panda and the human fossils of *Homo erectus*.

In 1955, forty-seven *Gigantopithecus blacki* teeth were found among a shipment of "dragon bones" in China. Tracing those teeth back to their source resulted in the recovery of more teeth and a rather complete large mandible. By 1958 three mandibles and more than 1,300 teeth had been recovered. *Gigantopithecus* remains have come from sites in Hubei Province, Guangxi Province and Sichuan Province—from warehouses for Chinese medicinal products as well as from cave deposits (Wang, 1980). Not all the Chinese remains come from the same time period, and the fossils in Hubei appear to be of a later date than elsewhere in China. The Hubei teeth are also larger. These materials are described in Wu and Poirier (1995).

The Indian version of *Gigantopithecus* belongs to the species *G. bilaspurensis* (actually the species name *giganteus* has precedence and is gaining favor)—the species designation referring to a 1968 find from the village of Bilaspur in India. The Indian materials are dated between 9 and 5 mya.

Ciochon (1984/1985, 1991) reported on *Gigantopithecus* remains found in northern Vietnam. This find represents the southernmost distribution of *Gigantopithecus* and possibly its latest temporal occurrence. It is found in conjunction with *Homo erectus* at two sites in Vietnam. Some have suggested that *H. erectus* preyed on *Gigantopithecus*, a speculation not supported by any evidence. In China, *Gigantopithecus* is known to coexist with a very large orangutan form and occasionally with *H. erectus*.

Gigantopithecus's mandibles and teeth are very large (Figure 6-9). The teeth are largely composed of enamel, possibly an adaptation to heavy chewing stress. However, Daegling and Grine (1987) argued that *G. blacki*'s mandible is comparatively slender compared to the size of its molars. They also reject the popular notion that the *Gigantopithecus* diet was adapted to hard-object chewing.

The jaws of *Gigantopithecus* are deep and very thick. The molars are low crowned and flat and exhibit heavy enamel suitable for tough grinding. The premolars are broad and flat and configured similarly to the molars. The canine teeth are neither pointed nor sharp, and the incisors are small, peglike, and closely aligned (Ciochon, 1991). The features of the teeth and jaws suggested that the animal was adapted to chewing tough, fibrous food by cutting, crushing, and grinding it. *Gigantopithecus* teeth also have a high incidence of cavities, similar to that found in giant pandas, whose diet, which includes a large amount of bamboo, may be similar to that of *Gigantopithecus*, as Ciochon and others suggested.

In addition to bamboo, *Gigantopithecus* consumed other vegetable foods, a fact proven by the analysis of the phytoliths adhering to its teeth. Phytoliths, tiny pieces of silica or plant stones, can provide dietary information. Silica dissolved in water enters plants through their roots and solidifies in the plant's cells. Phytoliths can bond to tooth enamel, and because phytoliths differ in every species where they exist, they become clues to the diet. An examination of the microscopic scratches and gritty plant remains embedded in *Gigantopithecus* teeth suggests that they ingested seeds and fruit as well as bamboo.

Gigantopithecus probably evolved in India and spread north and east; the Indian form predates the Chinese variety by millions of years. *Gigantopithecus* seems to be a relatively long-lived side branch of hominoid evolution. However, Eckhardt (1972, 1975) and Gelvin (1980) suggested some close parallels between *Gigantopithecus* and early hominids. If Jolly (1970) is correct, the similarities in jaws and teeth are a reflection of independently acquired adaptations to a similar habitat and diet. Whatever the final resolution of its evolutionary affiliation, *Gigantopithecus* may represent a trend toward nonarboreal apes.

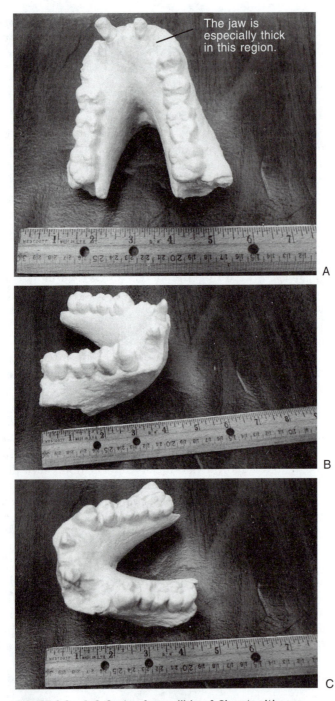

The jaw is especially thick in this region.

A

B

C

FIGURE 6-9   *A–C,* Casts of mandible of *Gigantopithecus blacki* from China. The missing teeth include the two medial incisors, two canines, and the two third molars.

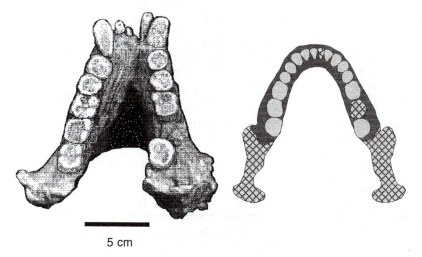

5 cm

D

FIGURE 6-9 *(continued)* The thickness of the mandible is evident; *D*, A comparison of the *Gigantopithecus* mandible (*left*) with that of a modern human mandible (*right*). Note the differences in size and shape. The hatched areas on the human mandible represent parts lost from the fossil specimen. (Photos *A–C* courtesy Frank E. Poirier; cast provided by X. Wu. *D*, Courtesy Jeffrey K. McKee.)

SUMMARY

The most complete early evidence of fossil hominoids comes from Oligocene Fayum deposits in Egypt. These forms were apelike in their teeth and monkeylike in the rest of their morphology and locomotor behavior. They were small, quadrupedal, arboreal primates.

Some Fayum form, perhaps *Aegyptopithecus*, was probably ancestral to the Miocene dryopithecines. Early and middle Miocene hominoids such as *Proconsul* and *Dryopithecus* were, in many respects, quite different from later hominoids. They were predominantly frugivorous or omnivorous, mainly arboreal, and living mostly in forested habitats. Until quite recently, it was assumed that extant apes and humans were rather closely related to the Miocene hominoids. Now, however, the ancestor–descendant relationship is considered more complex and unclear. *Sivapithecus*, once considered a hominid ancestor known as *Ramapithecus*, is now thought to be ancestral to orangutans.

Gigantopithecus's evolutionary position vis-à-vis other hominoids is unclear. Attempts to relate it to human evolution have not been widely accepted.

SUGGESTED READINGS

Andrews, P. 1993. Evolution and environment in the Hominidae. *Nature* 360:641–646.

Ankel-Simons, E., J. Fleagle, and P. Chatrath. 1998. Femoral anatomy of *Aegyptopithecus zeuxis*, an Early Oligocene anthropoid. *American Journal of Physical Anthropology*. 106:413–424.

Begun, D. 1994. Observations on the cranial anatomy of *Ouranopithecus*: Taxonomic and phylogenetic implications. *American Journal of Physical Anthropology.* Supplement 18:54.

Conroy, G. 1990. *Primate Evolution.* New York: W. W. Norton.

Culotta, E. 1995. New finds rekindle debate over anthropoid origins. *Science* 268:1851.

deBonis, L., and G. Koufos. 1995. Our ancestor's ancestor: *Ouranopithecus* is a Greek link in human ancestry. *Evolutionary Anthropology* 3:75–83.

Frayer, D. 1974. A reappraisal of *Ramapithecus. Yearbook of Physical Anthropology* 18:19–30.

Gibbons, A. 1994. Primate origins: New skull fuels debate. *Science* 266:541.

Gibbons, A., and E. Culotta. 1997. Miocene primates go ape. *Science* 276:355–356.

Greenfield, L. 1980. A late divergence hypothesis. *American Journal of Physical Anthropology* 52:351–366.

Martin, L., and P. Andrews. 1993. Renaissance of Europe's ape. *Nature* 365:494.

Pilbeam, D. 1979. Recent finds and interpretations of Miocene hominoids. *Annual Review of Anthropology* 8:333–352.

Pilbeam, D. 1984. Bone of contention. *Natural History,* June: 2–5.

Rose, K. 1996. The earliest primates. *Evolutionary Anthropology* 5:159–172.

Simons, E. 1984. Dawn ape of the Fayum. *Natural History,* May: 18–20.

Simons, E. 1993. Egypt's simian spring. *Natural History* 102:58–59.

Simons, E., and D. Pilbeam. 1965. Preliminary revision of the Dryopithecinae (Pongidae, Anthropoidea). *Folia Primatologica* 3:81–152.

Wu, R. 1984. The crania of *Ramapithecus* and *Sivapithecus* from Lufeng, China. In *The Early Evolution of Man.* P. Andrews and J. L. Franzen, eds. Frankfurt: Senckenberg Museum.

Wu, X., and F. Poirier. 1995. *Human Evolution in China.* New York: Oxford University Press.

7

Trends in Human Evolution

The major trends in human evolution include a restructuring of the pelvis and lower limbs permitting upright bipedalism, exploitation of the terrestrial environment, increasing brain size, tool use and manufacture, and the addition of meat protein to the diet. Bipedal locomotion is the major trait differentiating early humans from the common ape–human ancestor. The first evidence of hominid bipedality in the fossil record appears about 4.2 mya.

The effective exploitation of the habitat by humans involved such behavioral adjustments as life in a social group, a sexual division of labor, and the development of a capacity for symbolic language. The increase in brain size was neither rapid nor consistent and was likely associated with increasingly complex social organizations and means of environmental manipulation.

Stone tools first appear in the archaeological record about 2.5 mya, approximately 2.5–3 million years later than the first identified human fossil remains. Primate visual acuity, manual dexterity, and inquisitiveness were preadaptations to human tool use and manufacture. Humans are the only primate to rely on tool technology for survival. Most nonhuman primate diets include heavy amounts of vegetable materials, unlike many human diets, which include large amounts of meat. It is not entirely clear when meat protein began to play a large role in the human diet, nor is it clear how much meat was obtained by hunting or scavenging.

TREND 1: THE EVOLUTION OF BIPEDALISM

Trunk erectness developed early among primates: All major primate groups include species that sit or sleep in an upright position. On occasion, many primates assume an upright posture. (Although birds, some lizards, and some dinosaurs assumed a bipedal posture, it is quite different from that exhibited by humans.)

Primate bipedalism usually takes the following forms: (1) Consistent bipedalism characterized by standing erect with straightened knees is practiced by humans. (2) Bipedal running occurs in many nonhuman primates. However, to compensate for the restrictions of the pelvis and hind limb musculature, they use a bent-knee gait. (3) Bipedal walking is less common among monkeys than among the great apes, whose gait, however, is a bent-knee gait. Only humans can stand bipedally erect for long periods of time. The distinguishing feature of human locomotion is that we are bipedal all the time as our normal mode of locomotion.

Because we are the only primate to have intensively taken up bipedalism, we are interested in how and why we did so. The anatomical changes necessary for bipedalism have been detailed in many places, and there is general agreement with Washburn's (1971) scheme presented here (Table 7-1). There were major changes in the human lower limbs to accompany the shift to habitual bipedalism not only in general skeletal proportions but also in the form of the muscles and in general limb functioning. Structural changes in the lower limbs include an elongated femur (upper leg bone) and restructuring of the foot. Major changes in the lower limb skeleton include elongation of the bones (our lower limbs are longer than our upper limbs, opposite of the great ape configuration), reorientation of bones, and different positioning of the muscles on the bones (Figure 7-1).

The human foot has shifted from the nonhuman primate pattern of a grasping organ to a weight-bearing platform. Major anatomical changes in the foot

TABLE 7-1   Important Skeletal Modifications Needed for Human Bipedalism

Skull
Foramen magnum moves forward with flexion of the cranial base. Position is common in primates generally and is related to upright sitting.

Pelvis
Major change is the shortening and broadening of the ilium.

Vertebral Column
Rotation of sacral vertebrae and sigmoid-shaped spine.

Lower Limbs and Feet
Feet change from grasping to weight-bearing platform.

Change in muscle size and structure, especially gluteal and hamstring muscles.

Elongation of lower limbs, most noticeable in genus *Homo*.

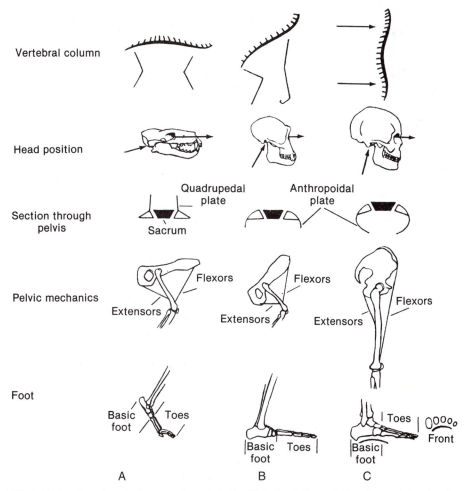

Vertebral column

Head position

Section through pelvis

Quadrupedal plate

Anthropoidal plate

Sacrum

Pelvic mechanics

Flexors

Flexors

Flexors

Extensors

Extensors

Extensors

Foot

Basic foot   Toes

Basic foot   Toes

Toes

Basic foot

Front

A   B   C

FIGURE 7-1 Structural changes associated with bipedalism. *A*, Quadrupedal animal; *B*, Chimpanzee; *C*, Modern human. (*From* HUMAN EVOLUTION by J. Birdsell, © 1981. New York: Harper and Row. Reprinted by permission of Addison-Wesley Educational Publishers Inc., Glenview, IL.

region occurred early in human evolution. The structure of the human foot indicates that it evolved from the kind of foot typical of apes and atypical of quadrupedal monkeys. The essential points are that weight is borne on the first toe and that in walking and standing, the foot toes out rather than points in. Monkeys bear almost no weight on the first toe, and the axis of the weight-bearing stress is through the middle toes rather than between the first and second toes as in humans.

A number of important features distinguish the human from the ape pelvis. The pelvis is actually comprised of three distinct bones: the **ilium**, **ischium**, and **pubis** (Figure 7-2). The structural basis of bipedalism is anatomically complex

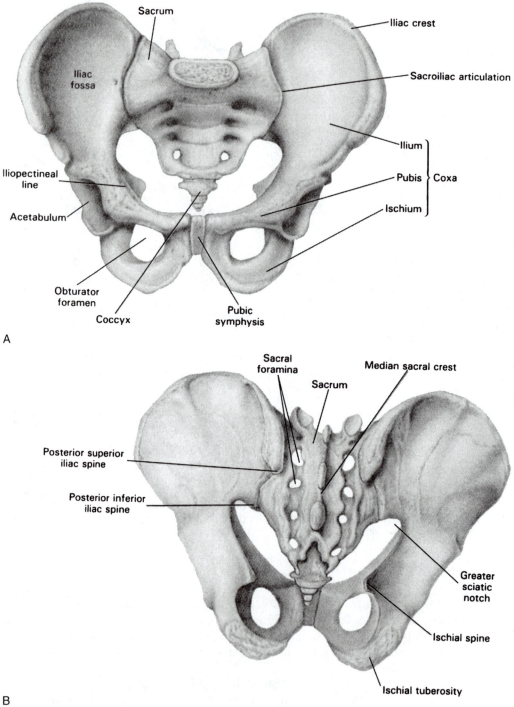

A

B

FIGURE 7-2 The pelvic girdle. *A*, Anterior view; *B*, Posterior view;

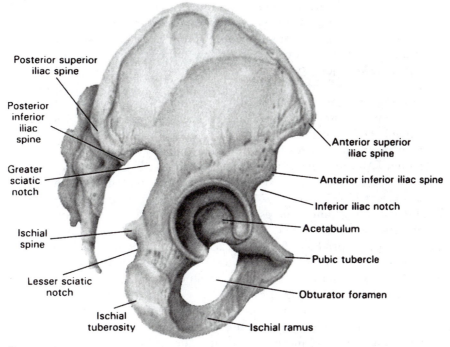

Posterior superior
iliac spine

Posterior
inferior
iliac
spine

Greater
sciatic
notch

Ischial
spine

Lesser sciatic
notch

Ischial
tuberosity

Anterior superior
iliac spine

Anterior inferior iliac spine

Inferior iliac notch

Acetabulum

Pubic tubercle

Obturator foramen

Ischial ramus

C

FIGURE 7-2 *(continued)* *C,* Lateral view. *(From* FUNDAMENTALS OF ANATOMY AND PHYSIOLOGY by F. Martini, © 1989. Reprinted by permission of Prentice-Hall, Inc., Upper Saddle River, NJ.)

and involves a reorganization of the pelvis. The ilium appears to have evolved to human form prior to the ischium (Zihlman, 1967). The essential problem for bipedal humans was the transfer of the landing and balancing functions from the forelimbs to the hind limbs. In quadrupedal monkeys or knuckle-walking chimpanzees, the principal locomotor force derives from muscles posterior to the femur. If the main drive is from the right leg, the animal lands on the left forelimb. When the human foot strikes the ground, it must first perform the landing–balancing functions of the ancestral forelimb, then give the push resulting in the step.

The major pelvic changes involved a shortening and broadening of the ilium. The ilium tilted backward, allowing the trunk to be held vertically, followed by rotation of the sacral vertebrae (vertebrae at the end of the spinal column) and compensated for by a curving of the spine (referred to as a *sigmoid* or *S-shaped* curve). The change in curvature developed with the onset of walking. This change allows an opening in the birth canal and the maintenance of an erect posture.

Muscular changes essential for the maintenance of balance and stabilization of the trunk accompanied skeletal reorganization. Although most human and ape thigh muscles do not differ with regard to the type of action produced, they do differ in the effect of the muscle's action. Of special importance are the gluteus maximus, the largest muscle in the human buttocks, and the hamstring muscles (the semitendinous, semimembranous, and biceps femoris), which are important thigh extensors in humans and apes. Upon contraction, extensor muscles tend to straighten a bone around a joint. These muscles are also powerful flexors of the leg at the knee joint (when they contract, they allow bending at the knee, decreasing the angle between the thigh and calf) and are important rotators of the thigh. The muscles that move the leg forward are the flexors because they bend the leg at the hip; those that move the leg backward are the extensors because they extend the leg at the hip joint. In humans these muscles are more developed than in other primates because humans alone depend on them for their locomotion. Also in humans the leg is proportionately heavier and larger.

The ape's ischium is relatively longer, and the femur relatively shorter, than in upright bipeds (Figure 7-3). This relationship influences the functioning of the hamstrings and gluteus maximus. With a long moment arm (stable element)—the ischium—and a shorter lever arm (movable element)—the femur—the muscles produce power of action. In upright bipeds with the reverse proportions (short ischium and long femur), the hamstrings produce a speed rather than power action. Gluteus maximus in humans is more a speed-of-action muscle than it is among apes.

Power is apparently more valuable in animals that spend time climbing; speed and range of movement are of greater importance to a biped less dependent on tree life and more dependent on its abilities to cover long distances in the shortest possible time. The upright biped sacrificed power of action for endurance.

Ideas on the origin of human bipedalism, the first change that differentiated apes and humans, require the reconstruction of many unknowns. Darwin (1871) suggested that when primates came to the ground they could have

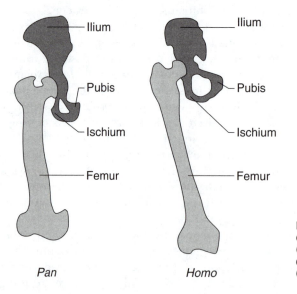

FIGURE 7-3 Pelvis and femur of chimpanzee (*Pan, left*) and human (*Homo, right*) show shape differences discussed in the text. (Courtesy Jeffrey K. McKee.)

become bipedal or quadrupedal. He suggested that the reason that humans alone among the terrestrial primates became bipeds is tied to how they use their hands.

> But the hands and arms could hardly have become perfect enough to have manu-
> factured weapons, or to have hurled stones and spears with a true aim, as long as
> they were habitually used for locomotion and for supporting the whole weight of the
> body, or, . . . so long as they were especially fitted for climbing trees. Such rough
> treatment would also have blunted the sense of touch, on which their delicate use
> largely depends. . . . it would have been an advantage to man to become a biped; but
> for many actions it is indispensable that the arms and whole upper part of the body
> should be free; and he must for this end stand firmly on his feet. (p. 141)

Many ideas have been given for the origin of bipedalism, but we will concentrate on the more recent suggestions (Table 7-2).

Shipman (1984) suggested that human bipedalism was an adaptation to the pattern of scavenging meat. Although bipedal running is neither fast nor efficient when compared to the quadrupedal gaits, bipedal walking is more energetically efficient than quadrupedal walking. Bipedalism increased the energetic efficiency of human travel, and this increased efficiency was an important factor in the origin of bipedalism (Rodman & McHenry, 1980). Bipedalism is an efficient means of covering large areas slowly, and Shipman argued that it is an appropriate adaptation for a scavenger who must cover large areas. Bipedalism elevates the head, thereby improving the ability to locate distant items. Combining bipedalism with agile climbing ability (of which there may be evidence in such early hominids as *Australopithecus afarensis*) further improves the opportunities to exploit the environment. Bipedalism frees the hands and makes them available for carrying items.

According to Shipman (1984:26–27), "Bipedalism is compatible with a scavenging strategy. I am tempted to argue that bipedalism evolved because it provided a substantial advantage to scavenging hominids. But I doubt hominids could scavenge effectively without tools and bipedalism predates the oldest known tools by more than a million years."

Leonard and Robertson (1995) have shown that at normal walking speeds, the energetic efficiency of human bipedalism relative to generalized quadrupedalism

TABLE 7-2 Some Explanations for Bipedalism

Explanation	Source
Energetically more efficient	Rodman and McHenry, 1980
Reduces incidence of solar radiation	Wheeler, 1984
Facilitates tool use and making	Darwin, 1871
Male provisioning and monogamy	Lovejoy, 1981
Infant dependency on mother	Tanner, 1981
Posture for small tree feeding	Hunt, 1994
Energetically efficient for meat scavenging	Shipman, 1984
Long-distance migration and scavenging	Sinclair et al., 1986

is greater than previously thought. The relative efficiency of bipedalism varies with speed of gait and gender. The energetic effects are most evident at slower speeds, consistent with the argument that bipedalism among hominids is an adaptation to long-distance walking. Energetic efficiency is likely part of a suite of adaptive traits that allowed hominids to expand into an open African habitat.

Sinclair and others (1986) suggested that bipedalism developed along with long-distance migration, and they agree with Shipman that scavenging was important to the evolution of bipedalism. They argued that early hominids scavenged migrating ungulate (hooved mammal) populations, the only population that existed in large enough numbers to provide sufficient food for scavengers. Because many migratory animals die from starvation, carcasses are available to scavengers, who would not necessarily have to contend with predators for a kill. A migratory scavenger has access to an abundant and constant food supply.

There was an unfilled niche in Africa for a mammalian scavenger that could follow migratory ungulates. However, if the scavenger was a bipedal human, it had to carry its young. Access to a rich and constant food supply encouraged bipedalism among humans. Those who developed the ability to walk long distances might have rapidly increased their numbers and displaced the less numerous sedentary quadrupeds dependent on plant gathering.

Sinclair and others' (1986) protohominid was a quadrupedal plant gatherer and occasional scavenger, much like the baboon. Two changes were needed for such a form to follow migrating ungulates. First, the young had to be carried. Among humans this purpose was accomplished by using the hands and arms, which were freed from locomotion to carry the youngster, and by assuming an upright posture. A prolonged upright stance for efficient carrying required adaptations of the pelvis. Second, they must be able to travel long distances efficiently. The primate foot with an opposable big toe changed to the modern human foot as a propulsive lever. This change must occur coincident with the hip changes.

The migration hypothesis suggests that habitual tool use developed from a need to quicken the butchering of carcasses and avoid competition with other, stronger mammal predators. The opportunity for hominid migration was enormous because savanna Africa was dominated by migration ecosystems.

Lovejoy (1981, 1984) suggested that perhaps bipedalism was necessary to a new and effective reproductive strategy—pair bonding in a kind of rudimentary family unit. The link between reproductive strategy and bipedalism lies in primate sexual behavior, according to Lovejoy. Some female monkeys and apes have a well-defined and rather short estrous period, the time of ovulation. Males attracted to estrous females seek the best chance of mating by competing (not necessarily through physical altercations) for them. The degree and kind of such competition varies among species. Except among human males and a few other primates, if males provide infant care they usually do so with minimal skill and interest. The offspring's care is almost exclusively left to the mother, who must care for both herself and her infant. The mother usually cannot care for more than one infant at one time and normally does not become sexually receptive again until the infant can forage on its own.

Birthrates of monkeys, whose offspring mature rapidly, are not much reduced because of a mother's preoccupation with her infant. For apes and early humans, however, the problem is and was more critical. An ape mother may spend five years raising one infant; this long period of care lowers the birthrate because primate mothers rarely give birth to another infant while still nursing previous offspring. Because of the long birth intervals among apes, when compared to monkeys, Lovejoy argued that apes would be at an evolutionary disadvantage if they were in direct competition with monkeys.

According to Lovejoy, the solution to this dilemma is to space infants more closely, as monkeys do, while still providing each infant with quality care. That solution necessitates adopting a better strategy of offspring care, for example, providing the mother with a food supply so that she does not have to forage for her own and her infant's needs. If this occurs, the mother can care for two or more infants simultaneously. Because she moves less, her offspring may have a greater chance of survival.

One possible auxiliary food source is the male. If an adult male is to be incorporated into a food-sharing role, his attention must turn to the female and infants—or to one female and one infant. A monogamous male could indirectly help his infant survive by bringing food to its mother, giving her more time to be a parent and to protect the infant. To provide greater quantities of food, the male must be able to carry it; thus he would find bipedalism adaptive.

According to Lovejoy's scenario, the female benefited from male provisioning. For example, her ability to care for her offspring was increased. She could spend less time searching for food and more time directly caring for and protecting her young. The provisioning bipedal male was able to obtain food farther away from the area occupied by the female and infant; thus he increased their food supply without depleting local food resources. The female was thereby able to collect more foods locally, reducing possible dangers both she and her young might encounter from roaming over a larger area.

Because the bipedal male increased the female's food supply through his provisioning behavior, she had more energy available for parenting. According to Lovejoy (1984:26), "Therein lies the ultimate advantage of provisioning." Females who benefited from provisioning were better able to manage overlapping offspring. Selection would have rapidly favored females that chose mates whose interest in them continued after fertilization. Any behavior of a potential mate that improved a female's reproductive rate would be favored.

Lovejoy found anatomical evidence among early human ancestors favoring his position of a monogamous situation. Among extant polygynous primates, where male conflict determines reproductive success, the male's canine teeth are enlarged. Females of the same species, however, have relatively small canines. In *A. afarensis* (Chapter 8), an early example of the human lineage, males also show relatively small canines. Lovejoy suggested that this is evidence for the presence of a monogamous unit.

Lovejoy's hypothesis concentrated on the acquisition of bipedalism by males as a means of supplying food for a female encumbered by a slowly maturing infant, but Tanner (1981) suggested a hypothesis that centers on the acquisition of bipedalism by females. Tanner noted that bipedalism accommodated the increased infant dependency on its mother. "With effective baby and child care, the young can be born more physically immature—which was certainly fortunate, for this was becoming necessary due to changes in the pelvis for bipedalism. Because infants and young must in any case be cared for already, increasing immaturity at birth would not be selected against" (pp. 157–158).

The ability to walk great distances while carrying items was essential to early humans. Mobility over long distances and effective carrying for both females and males were made feasible by the development of bipedalism. There was much to be carried by the gathering females—their infants, digging implements, and the gathered foods. It was suggested in Chapter 4 that because of these demands on the female some sort of carrying device was a likely first tool.

Tanner argued that with the development of bipedalism, learning to walk required more time to develop motor coordination prior to independence. Prolonged infant dependency on the mother became necessary. "This meant that the mother—or older sibling, mother's sibling, or mother's friend—had to carry a child that could no longer cling as effectively because the changed anatomy of bipedalism required loss of the foot's ability to grasp the mother. Even young who were already able to walk would have to be carried frequently and often, because they would tire" (pp. 156–157). Tanner's hypothesis suggested a restructuring of social life in response to the rigors imposed by bipedalism.

McHenry (1982) questioned Lovejoy's scenario. For example, (1) evidence indicates that early humans were polygynous and not monogamous, as Lovejoy suggested, and the provisioning of immobile females and their offspring by males is unlikely. (2) Among monogamous primates, sexual dimorphism is nearly absent, but in early humans it is pronounced, as one might expect in a polygynous species. (3) All monogamous nonhuman primates are territorial, the adult male and female with their young living in an exclusive territorial social unit. Early hominids apparently lived in larger groups. (4) In no known monogamous nonhuman primate do we have a pattern whereby a male provides food for the female and her offspring. (5) Parental care of infants is not limited to monogamous primates, and a decrease in birth spacing may not be a sufficient cause for the origin of monogamy and parental care.

Wheeler (1994) suggests that the body of bipedal animals is raised off the ground away from heat radiating from the surface and that additional cooling might occur through contact with air movements several feet above ground. However, Chaplin et al. (1994) argue that the increased time in open habitats that thermoregulation supposedly afforded to early hominids because of bipedalism was relatively short and of little or no adaptive significance. They suggest that thermoregulatory considerations, including those implicated with brain growth, cannot be cited as a primary cause in the evolution of bipedalism.

Hunt (1994) proposes an explanation for bipedality that incorporates feeding ecology and for which there is some proof in the fossil record. Hunt's explanation is titled the small-tree postural feeding hypothesis. Hunt suggests that bipedalism evolved during climatic changes in the Miocene. Using extant chimpanzees as his models, Hunt notes that bipedalism was observed most commonly when chimpanzees fed erect on the small fruits of small, open-forest trees while standing bipedally erect. Animals fed bipedally by reaching to pick fruit while standing on the ground, or from within the tree, standing bipedally and being stabilized by grabbing an overhead branch. According to Hunt, the food-gathering function of chimpanzee bipedalism suggests that hominid bipedalism may have evolved in conjunction with arm-hanging as a feeding adaptation that allowed fruit harvesting in open-forest or woodland trees.

Hunt's suggestion has support in the anatomy of *A. afarensis*, in which anatomical features of the hand, shoulder, and torso have been related to climbing (Chapter 8). While there are differences of opinion, Hunt suggests that *A. afarensis*'s pelvis and hind limb indicate a less than optimal bipedal adaptation compared to modern humans. If such locomotor insufficiency existed, according to Hunt, it supports the hypothesis that bipedalism evolved more as a terrestrial feeding posture than as a locomotor posture.

Several problems in locating the origins of bipedalism can be tied to the fact that investigators tend to look for one cause. As in most cases of evolutionary change, a number of interrelated pressures probably result in the onset of a new adaptation.

TREND 2: EFFECTIVE EXPLOITATION OF THE TERRESTRIAL HABITAT

Behavioral adjustments were needed to cope with the terrestrial habitat. Major adjustments were probably reflected in the social group. Based on comparative evidence from extant foragers, nonhuman primates, and the archaeological record, early humans may have lived in groups with an average of twenty-five members per group, and there was a sexual division of labor and sexual role differentiation.

Tanner's (1981) picture of early hominid communities assumed a plant-gathering economy in which mothers were the regular gatherers. Tanner suggested that the early hominid social group probably contained a mother and one to several young. This genealogical unit could have comprised three generations, an old mother, adult daughter(s), and her infant or juvenile offspring. This unit is typical of many nonhuman primates. Because generations were short and these creatures relatively short-lived, units of more than three generations would be rare. This mother-centered (matrifocal) genealogical unit was the most stable group; individuals within the unit would probably travel and gather together. Several units, especially those composed of sisters, may have met frequently and camped together with some regularity around well-known water sources.

Among most nonhuman primates each animal is a separate subsistence unit. Once infants are weaned, they must depend on their own skills in food acquisition for survival. Among humans, however, weaned young still depend on adults for food. Because of this long-term dependence, much of the day for both male and female humans is spent in activities that provide food for the young: "Because of the long-term dependence of children, a division of labor evolved in which the adventurous, wandering male became the hunter and the female developed the less mobile role of gatherer and mother" (Lancaster, 1975:78–79).

Females have the major responsibility for the early care, feeding, and rearing of the young. Therefore, any sexual division of labor, by increasing reproductive fitness (that is, the infant's survival), is beneficial. The human infant is born relatively immature and unable to fend for itself. The human mother lacks the body hair common to nonhuman primates that the infant can grasp, allowing the mother the usual range of movement. The human mother must carry the infant. Given the long period of immaturity among human infants, once foraging developed as a way of life, a sexual division of labor must have occurred.

The division of labor allowed a flexible system of joint dependence on plant and animal foods, which were provided by both sexes. The sexual division of labor was an efficient coping strategy quite different from that characterizing nonhuman primates. The human hunting-gathering pattern provided great flexibility in coping, for it allowed adjustments to daily, seasonal, and cyclical variations in food supply and geographical and habitat variations.

There is no archaeological evidence supporting the contention that early humans exhibited a sexual division of labor (although there is evidence of anatomical sexual dimorphism). The adaptive advantages provided by this system, however, suggest the likelihood that such a division existed. A sexual division of labor may help explain why early humans could successfully compete and establish themselves in their new habitat.

A concomitant of the human sexual division of labor was increasing parental care, which can be explained by referring to what evolutionary biologists call *K* and *r selection*. The *r* stands for the intrinsic rate of population increase and is a measure of how prolific a population can be. The *K* symbolizes the saturated carrying capacity of the environment. K and r selection may have a bearing on understanding the evolution of the human family. Stable, predictable environments with a great deal of complicated structure tend to select for larger adult size, long lifespans, and periodic reproduction with reduced numbers of young. If food supplies are scarce, specialized, and otherwise difficult to extract, selection favors prolonged immaturity to provide more time for learning. Predation pressures also call for increased parental protection. All these factors combine to favor increased parental care for survival, which probably enhanced the sexual division of labor.

It is likely that early hominids were under K selection; they exhibited adult sexual dimorphism, prolonged immaturity, heavy parental investment, and a reduced number of young at birth. All these factors are essentially primate traits, and all are elements of K selection. K selection factors are self-reinforcing. Longer life, as part of a function of year-round resources, selects for longer developmental periods and larger body sizes, both useful for effectively exploiting the environment. Prolonged nurturing brings pressure for reduced numbers of young and greater birth spacing to allow parental care to aid in learning the complicated environment, in this case also to learn tool use and manufacture. Because offspring live to an age when they compete with their parents for food, there is increasing pressure to reduce birthrates.

The acquisition of tool use among humans, with its concomitant muscular and neural requirements, helped initiate other adaptations for effective environmental manipulation and exploration. Tool use and terrestriality probably placed a premium on the development of an effective signaling system. Language can be seen as a means of environmental exploitation. Language may be a partial response to continuing pressures to communicate effectively about increasing complexities of life—for example, how to make tools, where to find food, and passing social traditions from a mother to her infants.

Although much has been written about the evolution of human language, we do not know when language first evolved. Furthermore, few of the anatomical modifications necessary for human speech fossilize because many of the speech structures are either muscle or cartilage.

Many have tried to link an increasing brain size with the onset of language, which was supposedly tied to coordinating hunting behavior, and Poirier has tried to link the onset of language to food sharing. Calvin (1983) argued that it was the sequential skills and coordination developed in throwing that subsequently made language possible. Calvin suggested that learning to throw with one hand produced the very first lateralization of the brain, the first concentration of a brain function in one hemisphere. Language skills eventually became lateralized, and both throwing and language are most commonly concentrated in the brain's left hemisphere.

Calvin further suggested that the lateralization of throwing behavior was the spurt for rapid brain enlargement. He saw a link between the muscle sequencing and visual perception that allowed one to hit a rapidly moving distant target by throwing a rock with one hand and an increasingly sophisticated tool complex. "The same rapid-movement sequencer in the left brain could have gone from throwing to talking to chipping rocks into scrapers and knives, incidentally providing the sparks that made possible fire on demand."

The communication system and brain structure of some nonhuman primates indicate that vocalizations often carry information about the sender's sex, group membership, and social relationship. Such vocalizations can also refer to external objects or events. Some species show hemispheric asymmetries in auditory perception as well as in vocalization. As a result, Stekelis (1985:157) has commented that "these data suggest that the vocal-auditory machinery of the earliest hominids was far more ready to take on 'primordial' speech function than has been previously supposed." If true, then selection may have occurred rather early in hominid evolution for an increase in these capacities in conjunction with tool use and manufacture, food-getting activities, problem solving, and other activities.

Laitman (1984) attempted to explain the anatomical modifications involved in the evolution of human language by noting the shift in the position of the larynx (voice box) in the neck. The position of the larynx determines how an animal breathes, swallows, and vocalizes. In almost all mammals, at all stages of development, the larynx is situated high in the neck, lying roughly opposite the first to third cervical (neck) vertebrae. In this position, the larynx allows a direct passage of air between the nose and lungs. While an animal is breathing, liquids can still be swallowed. A nonhuman primate, for example, can simultaneously breathe and swallow liquids. However, the larynx's position severely limits the range of sound production.

In contrast, the position of the larynx shifts downward around the second year of life in modern humans. From birth to approximately two years of age, the human larynx is high in the neck, much like any other mammal. The human newborn can breathe, swallow, and make sounds much like monkeys and apes. Around two years of age, however, the larynx begins to descend, altering forever the way the child breathes, swallows, and vocalizes. Once descent occurs, the larynx is in a position unlike that of any other mammal. In human adults, the position of the larynx can appear from the fourth to almost the seventh cervical vertebrae.

Although human adults cannot breathe and drink simultaneously, the descent of the larynx has produced a greatly enlarged pharyngeal chamber (the pharynx is the internal passage from the nose to the throat) above the vocal folds. Sounds produced in the larynx of human adults can be modified to a greater degree than is possible for newborns and any other nonhuman mammal. The expanded pharynx seems to be the key to our articulate speech.

Laitman reconstructed the laryngeal positions among early hominids. He suggested that the early hominids, the australopithecines, had a condition approaching that of monkeys or apes. Consequently, they probably had a very restricted vocal repertoire compared to modern humans. The high position of their larynges would have made it impossible for them to produce some of the universal vowel sounds found in human speech, and it is unlikely that they could speak the way we do today. Laitman suggested that the modern laryngeal condition allowing articulate speech appeared first among archaic *H. sapiens* some 300,000 to 400,000 years ago.

Until recently, there was no good fossil evidence that could be used to solve the dilemma of which early humans had speech. However, the discovery of a well-preserved hyoid bone from Kebara Cave, Israel, dating to about 62,000 years ago suggests to some researchers that Neandertals may have had the capacity for speech (see Chapter 12). The hyoid is a small, U-shaped bone that lies between the chin and larynx. It anchors the muscles that move the tongue and the larynx. The fossilized hyoid is almost identical to that of the modern human hyoid in its size and shape. At least for some researchers, the discovery of this fossil bone negates any arguments against the Neandertals having speech (Arensburg et al., 1989; Arensburg et al., 1990).

Arensburg et al. (1990) conclude that the Kebara hyoid is quite similar to that of modern humans. The relation of the hyoid to the mandible and cervical vertebrae probably did not differ from that of modern humans. These findings suggest that Middle Paleolithic peoples did not differ much from modern humans in terms of the anatomy of the vocal tract. However, Lieberman (1992) disputes Arensburg et al.'s contentions. The same linear measurements that Arensburg et al. used on the Kebara hyoid apparently would identify a pig's hyoid as that of a modern human (Laitman et al., 1990).

However, Laitman et al. (1990) stated that although the fossilized hyoid may hold valuable clues for interpreting vocal tract evolution, the absence of both other fossil hyoids for comparison and an understanding of what metric analysis of an individual bone actually signifies severely limits the value of the Kebara hyoid.

Kay et al. (1998) suggested that Neandertals may have had the nerve complex needed to control the subtle and varied movement of the tongue needed for speech. Kay et al. said that the hypoglossal canal, the bony canal that carries a nerve connection between the brain and the tongue, is about the same size in Neandertals and early humans as it is in modern humans. The nerve that goes through the hypoglossal canal controls most voluntary muscles in the tongue. Without such control, the tongue is unable to perform the motions necessary for speech. The presence of the canal and its size allows one to reasonably suggest that the Neandertals may have been capable of speech; however, it does not prove that they had speech.

TREND 3: INCREASING BRAIN SIZE AND COMPLEXITY

There has been a trend toward increased brain size and complexity during human evolution; however, the trend was neither consistent nor steady (Table 7-3). The size increase was slight during the approximately 3 million years of the evolutionary history of the *Australopithecus* and early *Homo* lineages but rather rapid during the middle Pleistocene in *H. erectus* and later *H. sapiens*. Increased brain size and complexity were probably related to tool use and manufacture, increasing environmental challenges, and more complex social groups, among other factors.

Increased brain size and complexity may be related to the infant's slower maturation rate, which required extended parental investment. Extending the

TABLE 7-3 Cranial Capacity Comparisons among Some Primates

Form	Cranial Capacity Range (cc)	Average Cranial Capacity (cc)
Great Apes		
Chimpanzee	282–500	383
Gorilla	340–752	505
Hominidae		
Australopithecus afarensis	380–500	413
A. africanus	435–530	441
A. robustus	—	530
A. boisei	506–530	513
Homo habilis	590–752	640
H. erectus	750–1250	937
H. s. sapiens	1,000–2,000	1,330

Note. Especially for the fossil forms these figures are based on limited and incomplete materials. In the case of *A. robustus*, for example, the cranial capacity given is from one specimen only. Cranial capacities are related to an animal's size and are thus also influenced by one's sex.

Cranial capacities are given in cubic centimeters (cc).

period of maternal care allowed more time for infant socialization and placed a premium on learning abilities (Poirier & Hussey, 1982). Learning may have been enhanced by increasing brain sizes and complexity. Size increases could have led to earlier births requiring longer learning periods.

Culture has as a major component learned behavior that is transmitted across generations. One prerequisite for culture is adequate memory storage facilitating relatively complex learning. A threefold increase in brain size occurred from early hominids to modern humans. This increase likely enhanced the capacity for information storage and the ability to learn. Although early hominids had relatively small brains, even the smaller-brained forms had relatively larger cranial capacities than contemporaneous apes. The functional significance of the larger cranial capacities of later humans is that they probably reflect increased abilities for technology and long-term memory.

Anthropologists have long speculated on the amount of feedback between increased brain size and complexity and tool use and manufacture. Although some aspects of this interaction have been questioned (for example, Holloway, 1967), there is little doubt about its importance. Tool use and manufacture are best understood as related to hemispheric specialization, especially brain lateralization (specialization of the right and left hemispheres for different functions). We cannot say which appeared first, hemispheric specialization or manual skills. However, increasing verbal ability, skilled tool use and fabrication, and later hemispheric specialization probably evolved together (Tunnell, 1973).

Martin (in Lewin, 1982) suggested that the upper limit of brain development is determined while the infant is still in the womb. After birth, the brain follows a set trajectory, which in nonhuman primates typically involves doubling of the brain's weight; in humans the brain weight quadruples. Differences in gestation times apparently have consequences for potential brain growth.

Dietary patterns and the nature of the resources exploited for food seem to affect brain size. Among bats, for example, fruit eaters have larger brains in relation to their body size than do insectivores. The reason typically offered is that as fruit is more widely dispersed and difficult to find than insects, fruit eaters need to be smarter to gather their food.

Milton (1981) hypothesized that the element of predictability associated with the spatial and temporal distribution patterns of plant foods in tropical forests stimulated primate intelligence. What appears to set most primates apart from other relatively long-lived and large-brained animals is their ability to store and retrieve a great amount of independently acquired information about their environment (Eisenberg, 1973). Milton (1981) noted, "The extreme diversity of plant foods in tropical forests and the manner in which they are distributed in space and time have been a major selective force in the development of advanced cerebral complexity in certain higher primates" (p. 535).

Given the dynamic nature of tropical forests, it seems maladaptive for a tropical forest dweller to genetically code a large amount of dietary information. What appears to be required is a great deal of behavioral flexibility, allowing a response to continually changing forest conditions. Increasing mental complexity, which places a strong emphasis on learning and retention, might have been selected for.

Milton noted that among later members of the human line, for example, the genus *Homo*, a behavioral shift favoring an increased ability to exploit mobile big game, so that it could become a dependable addition to the diet, may have required some major changes in certain areas of the brain. Additionally, mobile prey typically evolve at the same or a faster rate than their predators: "Lacking powerful jaws and claws characteristic of hunting carnivores and already *predisposed* to solve their dietary problems primarily through behavioral rather than morphological or physiological adaptations, these hunting hominids may have depended heavily on mental acuity to outwit and capture prey" (1981:544).

The reliance upon intelligence as a primate way of life has been stressed by researchers. Jolly (1985:230) noted, for example, "if there is an essence to being a primate, it is the progressive evolution of intelligence as a way of life." She may have been the first to link sociality to the evolving primate brain. As has been noted, primates are social animals whose daily existence depends on their ability to socialize with their peers. Primates are socially sophisticated animals who recognize and differentiate between their kin, their friends, and their mates. This social acumen "may be the fundamental selective force behind the evolution of primate intelligence" (Small, 1990:38). However, Small also noted that "any proposal that the need for these social machinations must have favored large and complex primate brains is equivocal, because no one has yet demonstrated a direct relation between social acumen and individual reproductive success" (p. 42). This caveat not withstanding, it must be remembered that increasing encephalization characterizes the order Primates.

Holloway (1982, 1983) questioned the commonly held assumption that the brain was one of the last structures to change in human evolution. He suggested that the brain was reorganized early in human evolution and that only the enlargement of the brain occurred late. The development of bipedalism was probably integrated with neuropsychological restructuring. Tobias (1982) noted that cerebral enlargement was not striking for the first 100,000 generations of human existence, but cerebral changes other than enlargement occurred.

Given Holloway's position, analyses examining brain size alone are likely to provide misleading and possibly erroneous conclusions regarding the dynamics of human evolution. Natural selection has operated on the evolution of the human brain, and the selection pressure has been in the realm of social behavior. Holloway suggested that selection pressure on brain organization and size continued throughout most of human evolution, or at least until the Neandertals appeared (Chapter 12). The brain was not the terminal organ to evolve in the overall mosaic of human evolution, according to Holloway, unless one talks only about absolute size and ignores relative brain size, cerebral cortical organization, and cerebral asymmetry.

Absolute and relative increases in brain size were probably interspersed with evolutionary episodes of brain reorganization and other changes. Holloway's understanding of brain evolution changes our understanding of its mode and importance in human evolution.

Falk, like Holloway, spent years studying primate endocranial casts (or endo-casts); however, her views differ from those of Holloway. Falk (1984) noted that endocasts belonging to members of an early hominid lineage, the South African australopithecines, resemble ape brains in both size and external form. This resemblance does not mean, however, that the australopithecine and the ape had the same thought processes or mental capacities. In contrast to apes, australo-pithecines were bipedal and may have had tools and other cultural attributes. Some evolutionary changes occurred in the early human brain that were not evi-dent in the gross organization of the brain's outermost portion.

Australopithecine brains were still very apelike; the first humanlike endocast belonged to a more advanced species, *Homo habilis,* from northern Kenya, which dates to approximately 2 mya. This endocast exhibits a humanlike frontal lobe, including what appears to be Broca's area, an area on the cerebral cortex named after Paul Broca. Broca's area is crucial for human speech (Figure 7-4), and Broca's area appears in the australopithecines. On the parietal lobe of *H. habilis* is also an expansion of Wernicke's area, an association area of the brain neces-sary for comprehension of spoken language. Tobias (1987, 1994) suggested that the developed presence of Broca's and Wernicke's areas of the brain implies that *H. habilis* was the first hominid to have the neural capacity for language. There is, however, no agreement on the issue of whether or not *H. habilis* had language.

Carl Wernicke was a German neurologist who studied brain damage associ-ated with the loss of comprehension in aphasia. The site he studied, now called

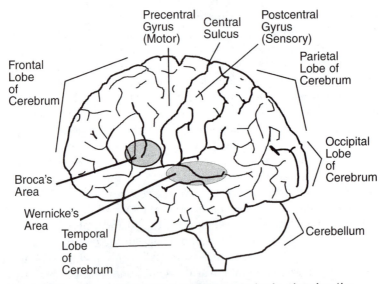

FIGURE 7-4 Schematic drawing of the human brain, showing the major lobes of the cerebrum as well as the gyri responsible for motor and sensory functions. Broca's and Wernicke's areas of the cerebral cortex are responsible for speech and association, respectively. (Courtesy Jeffrey K. McKee.)

Wernicke's area, is located on the dominant hemisphere in the temporal lobe. A bundle of nerve fibers sends signals from Wernicke's to Broca's area, allowing the vocal repetition of heard and memorized sounds. Broca's area is located toward the front of the dominant hemisphere. Broca's area sends the code for the succession of speech sounds to the motor cortex of the brain, which controls the muscles of the face, jaw, tongue, pharynx, and larynx, thus helping to set the speech apparatus in motion.

Falk suggested that until early humans acquired language, "early ancestors may not have been very human" (1984:39). Falk did not accept Holloway's view that the brains of the South African australopithecines were reorganized along human lines some 2.5 to 3 mya. She suggested that their brains were still apelike, judging from their external appearance, and that this apelike condition persisted for a long time. Given the scanty nature of australopithecine cranial materials, no resolution to this argument is in sight.

With the continuing increases in brain size and complexity and with continuing and perhaps heightened awareness of the surroundings that such increases allowed, all distinctive features of a protocultural stage were being elevated to a new level of sociopsychological integration. This new level would eventually affect every aspect of the earlier modes of protocultural adaptation and lead, according to Hallowell (1961), to "more inclusive, complex, and diversified sociocultural systems" (p. 250).

Not too long ago, the leading theory of hominid brain evolution was tied to a combination of bipedalism, forelimbs freed from locomotion and used for other purposes (such as tool use and manufacture), hunting and meat consumption, and brain enlargement. Washburn (1960) best exemplified this viewpoint. This theory has lost favor, largely because of the discovery of 3.5–3.7-million-year-old footprints indicating the presence of hominid bipedalism long before brain size began its dramatic increase. These prints are discussed in Chapter 8.

Many other theories attempt to explain hominid brain reorganization and enlargement. Some include parts of Washburn's earlier explanation. One of the more interesting recent theories is called the "radiator" theory (Falk, 1990). (Falk's interesting article was followed by responses from other researchers who supported, clarified, or rejected the "radiator" theory.) Human brains have relatively large cooling needs, and the evolving brain had to make crucial adjustments for heat dissipation. Because humans have more stamina for exercise than do many other mammals, they must be able to dissipate metabolic heat for longer durations. Furthermore, early humans occupied high-light and high-heat regions in the African savannas. Fialkowski (1986) suggested that increased brain size during hominid evolution provided structural redundancy that prevented cognitive impairment during heat stress. Fialkowski argued that increased brain size was a by-product of heat dissipation. Falk (1990) added that the increased brain size and danger of heat stress led to important changes in blood flow to and from the brain.

Wheeler (1984) drew a connection between upright body posture and heat stress. He argued that an upright hominid presented to the sun only about 40 percent of the body area that it would present if it were a quadruped. Thus, the bipedal hominid would reduce its heat load, and bipedalism would have been a factor allowing early hominids to occupy a noonday scavenging niche that was out of harm's way and avoided competition from other scavengers who rested during the heat of the day (Blumenschine, 1987).

Combining elements from these different ideas, there seems to be a connection between a scavenging daytime savanna niche, bipedalism, increasing brain and body size, heat dissipation, and change in blood flow patterns to and from the brain.

TREND 4: EXTENSIVE MANIPULATION OF NATURAL OBJECTS AND THE DEVELOPMENT OF MOTOR SKILLS TO FACILITATE TOOLMAKING

Extensive manipulatory behavior was facilitated by hands freed of locomotor functions, stereoscopic vision, increasing brain size, and more effective hand–eye coordination. The selective pressure for extensive environmental manipulation probably grew out of increasing tool use, which was, in turn, related to increasing problems of survival. Manipulation of the environment was an outgrowth of primate inquisitiveness. Table 7-4 presents a chronology of the development of stone tools, and Figure 7-5 gives some examples.

The primate grasping hand permits detachment of objects from the environment. Knowledge about our environment stemmed from, among other things, just naturally picking up objects and examining them. This appears to be a natural outgrowth of primate curiosity, which is often expressed in play behavior. Nonhuman primate tool use and manufacture were discussed in Chapter 4.

TABLE 7-4   Approximate Time and Characteristics of Stone Tool Industries

5.0–2.5 mya
No known stone technology. Suspected use and discard of sticks and stones with little or no modification.

2.5–2.0 mya
Oldowan tools in Africa. All-purpose tools. Associated with *Homo habilis* fossils.

1.8 mya–200,000 ya
Developed Oldowan traditions in Africa, with Acheulian tools first recorded at 1.4 mya. Perhaps use of bamboo tools in Asia. Large bifacially flaked tools associated with *H. erectus* (or *H. ergaster*) in Africa.

150,000–40,000 ya
Often referred to as the Middle Stone Age. Several regional tool traditions, such as the Mousterian, associated with many Neandertal sites.

35,000–Present
Often referred to as the Late Stone Age. Specialized and composite tools. Many regional traditions are named. Associated with modern *H. sapiens*.

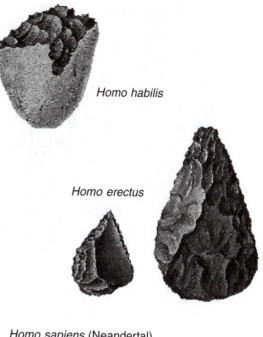

Homo habilis

Homo erectus

Homo sapiens (Neandertal)

FIGURE 7-5 Tool types. *Top*, Oldowan tool associated with *Homo habilis*; *Middle*, Acheulian tools associated with *H. erectus*; *Bottom*, Mousterian tools associated with the Neandertals. (*From* LIFE ON EARTH by Audesirk/Audesirk, © 1997. Reprinted by permission of Prentice-Hall, Inc., Upper Saddle River, NJ.)

Grooming (Figure 7-6), a primate behavioral pattern, uses the hands to pick through another animal's hair and requires sophisticated hand–eye coordination. Most nonhuman primates who engage in grooming can oppose the thumb to the forefinger. Such opposability is required in holding and handling objects. These seemingly inauspicious beginnings involving play and grooming behavior were preparation for picking up and examining objects. In time, such actions might have led to tool use and manufacture. Although other arboreal animals have some of the same adaptations to the arboreal niche as nonhuman primates, rarely do any approach the primate's fine manipulative abilities and hand–eye coordination.

Let us return to the proposition that the ability to detach objects from the environment using the hands is a major advance that was most important for the development of primate perceptual skills. We owe recognition of different kinds of

A   B

FIGURE 7-6   *A*, Grooming behavior by Indian rhesus monkeys, *Macaca mulatta* (photo courtesy Frank E. Poirier); *B*, Grooming behavior by Kenyan savanna baboons, *Papio* (photo courtesy Sevanne Epperson).

objects to our visual acuity and tactile examination. Given the upright sitting position of nonhuman primates, vision became "a supervision, a guide and control of fine manipulations" (Sphuler, 1957:41). The relation between the evolution of keen vision—which was possibly an adaptation to locomoting through the trees and grasping at swift insects (Cartmill, 1975)—and fine manipulation is two-dimensional. Vision itself became more refined, and intellectual absorption and mental utilization were more complete and lasting as the skilled movements became more complex and efficient (Polyak, 1957).

Primates extract objects from the environment with their hands; they smell and taste them, visually and tactilely examine them, and then perhaps replace them: "In this way the higher primates have come to see the environment not as a continuum of events in a world of pattern but as an encounter with objects that proved to make up these events and this pattern" (Campbell, 1966:129).

Susman (1994) may have provided anatomical proof for early hominid toolmaking abilities. By noting that the human first metacarpal (thumb) bone has a broad head in relation to its length, Susman may have provided a way to determine which early ancestors had hands that functioned like our own (Aiello, 1994). Human thumbs are much stronger than the thumbs of other primates, so the thumb, like some of the wrist bones, can resist increased pressures. Compared to the thumbs of other primates, the human thumb has three additional muscles that add strength and refined motor control. The broad head in relation to the length of the metacarpal bone in the human hand has no peers among the other primates. When such a configuration is matched in the hominid fossil record,

Susman concludes that the bone must have come from a hand capable of generating the force needed for human tool use and making.

Susman investigated the metacarpals of *Australopithecus afarensis, A. robustus, Homo habilis,* and *H. erectus.* He concluded that only *A. afarensis* was anatomically unable to make and use tools. However, *A. robustus* had a thumb that could make and use tools. The problem here is that the metacarpal Susman attributes to *A. robustus* is attributed by others to *H. erectus,* widely acknowledged to be a consistent tool user and maker.

It is widely recognized that some of the nonhuman primates make and use tools of both stone and vegetation. These primates, however, do not have the stout human thumb. The stout metacarpal allows humans a type of manual dexterity thought necessary for stone use and manufacture (Aiello, 1994).

TREND 5: THE INCREASED ACQUISITION OF MEAT PROTEIN

Although most nonhuman primates are vegetarians, we have already noted that some kill and eat other vertebrates (Chapter 4). The time when meat first assumed importance in the human diet is not known. (This topic is discussed in Chapter 8.) Consistent meat eating required behavioral adjustments and changes in dentition and jaw musculature. Once meat became basic to the diet, means would have developed whereby it could be most efficiently obtained and butchered. Methods for carrying meat, rules for sharing (perhaps one of the first sets of societal rules), and even a linguistic system naming those who were to receive shares would have appeared.

Sometimes analyses of tooth surfaces can tell us the role of certain foods in an animal's diet. Using an electron microscope one can examine the minute scratches left on tooth enamel and dentine as the animal chews and crushes food. Tooth surfaces of an early hominid *Australopithecus* (= *Paranthropus*) *robustus* (discussed in Chapter 8), for example, suggest that it was basically vegetarian. More precisely, the tooth wear patterns resemble those of chimpanzees. Because the chimpanzee ingests a large number of dietary items, the statement that the teeth of *A. robustus* resemble those of a chimpanzee under an electron microscope does not conclusively define its diet. It does, however, exclude grass eating, bone crushing, and root eating, all of which would have left distinctive scratches and pits on the tooth enamel.

A shift in enamel wear patterns on the teeth of a later human species, *Homo erectus,* suggests that a large amount of grit was incorporated into the diet. Perhaps this grit came from the discovery that roots and tubers were a good food source. The grit may also have been adhering to meat that was lying on the ground, but the teeth show no signs of bone crushing.

Too much emphasis may have been placed on hunting as an important factor in human evolution. With most interest focused on the hunting half of the hunter-gatherer food-getting complex, gathering has been underemphasized. Many researchers have ignored the probable evolutionary importance of gathering vegetable foods or have dismissed its results as "casually collected foods." Coon (1971) referred to the primacy of hunting and contended that it had more impact on social structure than did gathering. However, Lee (1968), among others, criticized this view. Food sources other than those offered by meat were important, and it is very unlikely that any human group ever relied primarily on meat.

When scenarios of human evolution refer to ingestion of meat protein, they usually refer to meat that has been hunted. The idea that scavenging might have represented a complete ecological adaptation has only recently come to the forefront. Several researchers, such as R. Potts (1984) and P. Shipman (1984), who worked with animal bones found at the 1.8-million-year-old Bed I site at Olduvai Gorge (also spelled Oldupai Gorge), Tanzania, have indicated that scavenging was probably quite an important component of early human life.

Based on an analysis of more than 2,500 antelope bones from Bed I, Olduvai Gorge, Shipman (1984) suggested that "instead of hunting for prey and leaving the remains behind for carnivores to scavenge, perhaps hominids were scavenging from carnivores" (p. 24). Scavenging has different costs and benefits than hunting. For example, the scavenger can be relatively sure that the prey is dead, for predators have already performed the task of chasing and killing the prey. However, "while scavenging may be cheap, it's risky" (p. 24). Both predators and scavengers face the danger of possibly fighting over a carcass. The major energetic costs to scavengers come from the fact that they must survey much larger areas than predators to find food. Predators tend to be specialized for speed, scavengers for endurance. Scavengers also need an efficient means of locating carcasses. Shipman suggested that bipedalism was an adaptation to this need for endurance and for locating carcasses.

There are few full-time mammalian scavengers. The bulk of the scavenger's diet comes either from other food sources or from hunting small game. Such game as rats or hares are consumed on the spot, eliminating the problem of having to defend a carcass against larger carnivores. Because small carnivores such as jackals and striped hyenas often cannot defend a carcass, much of their diet consists of fruit and insects.

There is dental evidence that early humans ate both meat and fruits. Shipman noted, "The evidence of cut marks, tooth wear, and bipedalism, together with our knowledge of scavenger adaptations, . . . is consistent with the hypothesis that two million years ago hominids were scavengers rather than accomplished hunters" (1984:27). Hunting as a way of life may not have appeared until 1.5 mya with *H. erectus.*

Blumenschine (1987) provided an interesting discussion of the potential niche of an early hominid scavenging strategy, although he, like others, is not convinced that early hominids did in fact scavenge. Hominid scavenging success would have been influenced by the size of the carcass scavenged in relation to the animals scavenging from the carcass and the degree of competition for the carcass.

If early hominids did scavenge meat, they could have secured carcasses during the dry season from within or on the margins of riparian woodlands, that is, woodlands on the banks of rivers or streams. Most carcasses that would have been encountered there would be from medium-sized adults that were killed, partially eaten, and abandoned by felids during the dry season.

Cavallo (1990) suggested that early hominids may have scavenged from leopard kills cached in trees. If, as has been suggested, some early hominids were more arboreal than their ancestors, scavenging carcasses from trees would not have presented a problem: "By scavenging from the leopard's temporarily abandoned larder, early hominids could have obtained the fleshy and marrow-rich bones of small-to-medium-sized prey animals in relative safety" (Cavallo, 1990:56). Cavallo also suggested that the sharp, broken limb bones from partially eaten prey could have been used by hominids to peel back the hide to expose the flesh of a carcass. This activity might have provided early hominids with the initial impetus to manufacture and utilize tools to prepare and extract meat from a carcass.

The "man the hunter" hypothesis argues that the development of hunting had a profound effect on human evolution. This hypothesis suggests that males are both the cooperative and competitive sex, cooperating with one another in pursuit of big game and competing (this competition is often mistakenly viewed as aggressive physical confrontation) for access to female mates (Cheney, 1982). Male bonding (Tiger & Fox, 1971) is viewed as having an old evolutionary history, and females are portrayed as infant-producers, whose reproductive functions demand neither cooperation nor competition with members of their sex.

This long-standing interpretation of human evolution has been vigorously challenged by those arguing that food gathering, traditionally a female task, was easily as important as hunting in the evolution of human behavior. Food gathering exerted strong selective pressures on intelligence and technological skills, but proponents of this view are divided about the importance of competition and cooperation in the evolution of human behavior. Female reproductive success is assumed to be less dependent than that of males on competition for mates, and it is often argued that there has been little selection for competition or aggression in females. This stress on noncompetitive females ignores the important element of competition among them for access to the "most desirable" male mates (Poirier, 1997).

SUMMARY

There were five major trends in human evolution. A number of skeletal and muscular modifications are associated with bipedalism. Although bipedalism surely characterized early human evolution—the first evidence coming from footprints dated to 3.75 mya and bones dated to 4.2 mya—there are differing opinions concerning why it developed. One factor affecting an effective exploitation of the terrestrial niche was the sexual division of labor; both females and males contributed to the daily larder. Although meat protein became increasingly important in the human diet, the role of gathered plants cannot be overlooked, nor can the role that females played in gathering such foods. The male's role and the concept of "man the hunter" have been overemphasized in past theoretical constructs of human evolution. Another feature characterizing human evolution was an increase

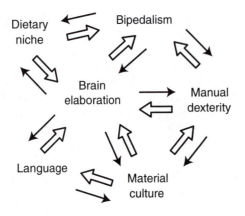

FIGURE 7-7   Positive feedback loops in the evolution of the unique hominid form. Solid arrows represent functional or behavioral correlates; open arrows represent positive directional natural selection. (Courtesy Jeffrey K. McKee.)

in brain size and complexity. In neither case was the trend consistent or rapid. Brain lateralization and increasing complexity seem to have preceded dramatic enlargement of the brain, which occurred only during later stages of human evolution. This pattern is an example of mosaic evolution.

Figure 7-7 is a depiction of how the trends discussed in this chapter interact with each other. There is a clear feedback between these variables.

SUGGESTED READINGS

Arensburg, B., L. Schepartz, A. Tillier, B. Vandermeersch, and Y. Rak. 1990. A reappraisal of the anatomical basis for speech in Middle Paleolithic hominids. *American Journal of Physical Anthropology* 83:137–146.

Blumenschine, R. 1987. Characteristics of an early hominid scavenging niche. *Current Anthropology* 28:383–408.

Cartmill, M. 1990. Human uniqueness and theoretical content in paleoanthropology. *International Journal of Primatology* 11:173–192.

Chaplin, G., N. Jablonski, and N. Cable. 1994. Physiology, thermoregulation and bipedalism. *Journal of Human Evolution* 27:497–510.

Falk, D. 1990. Brain evolution in *Homo*: The "radiator" theory. *Behavioral and Brain Sciences* 13:333–381.

Fialkowski, K. 1986. A mechanism for the origin of the human brain: A hypothesis. *Current Anthropology* 27:288–290.

Laitman, J. 1984. The anatomy of human speech. *Natural History* 93:21–27.

Laitman, J., J. Reidenberg, P. Gannon, and B. Johansson. 1990. The Kebara hyoid: What it tells us about the evolution of the hominid vocal tract. *American Journal of Physical Anthropology* 81:254.

Lancaster, J. 1971. On the evolution of tool-using behavior. In *Background for Man*, ed. P. Dolhinow and V. Sarich. Boston: Little, Brown.

Lovejoy, C. O. 1981. The origin of man. *Science* 211:341–350.

Shipman, P. 1984. Scavenger hunt. *Natural History* 93:20–27.

Washburn, S. 1960. Tools and human evolution. *Scientific American* 203:62–75.

Washburn, S., and C. Lancaster. 1968. The evolution of hunting. In *Man the Hunter*, ed. R. Lee and I. DeVore. Chicago: Aldine-Atherton.

Wheeler, P. 1984. The evolution of bipedality and loss of functional body hair in hominids. *Journal of Human Evolution* 13:91–98.

8

The Earliest Hominids

The earliest known hominids come from East Africa, dating possibly as early as 5.5 mya. By about 4.2 mya, the genus Australopithecus *was established on the continent, characterized by an upright stance and bipedal locomotion with a brain only slightly larger than that of a modern chimpanzee. Early* Australopithecus *fossils range from East Africa to Chad (Central Africa) to South Africa, comprising a number of closely related species. There is no evidence that they possessed stone tool technology, but they appear to have been quite adaptable to a range of environments.*

HISTORICAL PERSPECTIVE

Well over 2 million years ago, a young child met a premature demise while walking near a small stream, tottering on two legs. His body fell into the water, or was dropped there by a predator, and floated to the back of a nearby cave. Eventually the body sank into the soft sediments below, beginning the process of fossilization. Over many millennia the boy's skull became encased in rock as the sediments hardened. The skull resurfaced in 1924 when it was blasted out with dynamite during quarry operations near the village of Taung, South Africa (Figures 8-1 and 8-2).

Through a set of fortuitous circumstances, the skull was taken to Raymond Dart, then an anatomy professor at the University of the Witwatersrand, South Africa. In 1925, Dart announced the discovery of early hominid remains and attributed them to a newly created genus, *Australopithecus*. A short description of his findings appeared on February 7, 1925, in the British journal *Nature*. Dart's preliminary description was based on the skull and an associated endocast (Figure 8-3) of a three- or four-year-old child, probably a male, who had become entombed in the ancient cave deposit and recovered at the site of Taung.

It had taken Dart seventy-three days to clear away enough of the adhering limestone matrix to reveal the face and part of the skull, using his wife's knitting needles. It took a full four years to extract the bone completely from the rock encasement. Dart later remarked that when he was first able to see the face in late December, "What emerged was a baby's face, an infant with a full set of milk (or deciduous) teeth and its first permanent molars just in the process of erupt-

FIGURE 8-1 Quarry activity at the Buxton Limeworks, Taung, in 1927. The pinnacle on the right is close to the spot from which the Taung hominid skull was blasted out by dynamite in 1924. The photo was taken by the late Italian anthropologist Lidio Cipriani. (Courtesy Jacopo Moggi-Cecchi.)

FIGURE 8-2 Remnant pinnacles of quarried tufa and breccia at the Buxton Limeworks, Taung. The Taung hominid skull came from a spot near the pinnacle in the foreground. (Courtesy Jeffrey K. McKee.)

ing. I doubt if there was any parent prouder of his offspring than I was of my 'Taung baby' on that Christmas of 1924" (Dart and Craig, 1959:9).

Dart was convinced that the skeletal remains belonged to a "manlike ape" that stood erect and walked bipedally. This belief was based on the relatively forward position of the foramen magnum at the base of the skull, suggesting that the spinal cord entered from below as in humans, rather than from behind the skull as in apes. He named the fossil *Australopithecus africanus*, the southern ape of Africa. He stated, "The specimen is important because it exhibits an extinct race of apes intermediate between living anthropoids and man" (Dart, 1925:195).

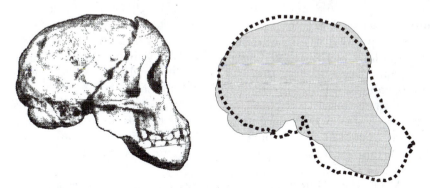

FIGURE 8-3 *Left*, The Taung hominid skull, type specimen of *Australopithecus africanus*; *Right*, The silhouette of the Taung skull is compared with the outline of juvenile chimpanzee skull of approximately the same developmental age (dashed line). (Courtesy Jeffrey K. McKee.)

Although Dart was convinced of both the importance of his find and its place in human evolution, most other scientists rejected his contentions (Lewin, 1985). At the time of Dart's writing, there were many competing theories of human evolution, all based on very fragmentary remains and not unduly restrained by the facts. The Taung fossil was rejected as a human ancestor because it did not fit into the theories then being championed by recognized scholars. Besides belonging to a juvenile—and it is improper to propose a new taxon based on immature specimens—the fossil, in light of the then championed theories, was found in the wrong place, was dated too late in time, and possessed the wrong morphological characteristics.

In 1925, Asia, not Africa, was considered the place of human origins because of earlier *Homo erectus* finds. When material was recovered from Zhoukoudian, China (Chapter 10), it was cited as proof of the correctness of the Asia-as-homeland viewpoint. The material from Zhoukoudian (the so-called Peking Man) was readily accepted into the human fold.

The Taung child was initially given a late Pleistocene dating, which was considered by most to be too late in geological history for an early human ancestor. Said Arthur Keith, one of Dart's chief critics: "A genealogist would make an identical mistake were he to claim a modern Sussex peasant as the ancestor of William the Conqueror" (Keith, 1925:492). Most authorities accepted a human–ape branching during the much earlier Oligocene geological epoch. This idea was based in part on a mistaken notion of the geological time scale. At the turn of the twentieth century, the age of Earth was considered to be only about 65 million years, and the total period of mammalian evolution was relegated to the last 3 million years of geological time. Humans were considered to have appeared early in mammalian evolution. Even when geological time was revised backward, some scientists continued to suggest that the Taung child appeared too late to be a human ancestor.

Another factor that led to Taung's rejection was the notion that the brain preceded the rest of the body in evolving toward a human form; Taung's small cranial capacity did not fit this conception. Furthermore, Taung had a more human face and dentition than were expected. But the strongest argument against a position in human evolution came in the form of the Piltdown material. Piltdown was a site in England that had yielded a humanlike skull with an apelike face—material that had been cleverly doctored and planted in the site (Chapter 2). Until this material was finally shown to be a hoax in the early 1950s, many fossils were measured against Piltdown's incongruous nature (that is, a human skull, large cranial capacity, and an ape's jaw). The faked Piltdown material fit preconceived notions of human evolution; Taung did not. (Arthur Keith, Dart's most vigorous critic, has been implicated as a perpetrator of the fraud.)

While Dart's interpretations concerning early human evolution in Africa were being rejected, Robert Broom entered the fray, and he soon became convinced that Dart was correct. From the cave site of Sterkfontein, South Africa,

Broom recovered a remarkable series of *Australopithecus* fossils, including adult crania and limb bones. These verified Dart's contention that Taung represented an upright, bipedal animal, and was a valid contender as a possible human ancestor. Despite Broom's additional proof of Dart's interpretations, others remained unconvinced that the South Africa fossils represented an early member of the human lineage. As has been too often true, Broom overindulged himself by naming his fossils, establishing a number of taxa without genetic reality. These errors further tainted his testimony on Dart's behalf.

Dart had another supporter in the famed neuroanatomist Grafton Elliot Smith, an old friend and mentor. Elliott Smith (1925) noted that the scientific community should not be surprised by Dart's discovery . . . not if they "know their Charles Darwin." He was referring to something Darwin had written in *The Descent of Man* in 1871:

> In each great region of the world the living mammals are closely related to the extinct species of the same region. It is therefore probable that Africa was formerly inhabited by extinct apes closely allied to the gorilla and chimpanzee; and as these two species are now man's nearest allies, it is somewhat more probable that our early progenitors lived on the African continent than elsewhere. (p. 199)

Dart's discovery proved Darwin's prescient insight that human origins probably began in Africa. Today there are hundreds of early hominid fossils vindicating Dart's analysis of Taung. A number of species of *Australopithecus*, collectively known as the australopithecines, have been found in South Africa, East Africa, and Chad. (Reports of *Australopithecus* remains in China are dubious.) Clearly human origins began with small-brained, bipedal animals living during the Pliocene in Africa.

GEOGRAPHICAL AND TEMPORAL RANGE OF THE EARLY AUSTRALOPITHECINES

Darwin's logic and Dart's fossils provided sufficient reason to search for fossil evidence of early human ancestors in Africa, but gave no indication as to what time period may yield the earliest forms—those that first diverged from the other hominoids and started on the path to bipedalism. *Australopithecus africanus* fossils date to the late Pliocene, between 3.2 and 2.5 mya, and although they have many primitive and apelike traits, they are not the earliest hominids. How do we then determine when the hominid lineage first arose?

One type of evidence for the timing of hominid origins comes from the **molecular clock**. The genetic techniques discussed in Chapter 3 which show the degree of relatedness among living primates can be used to predict how long ago various species shared a common ancestor. The accumulation of mutations in DNA (and the molecules coded by DNA) represent the "ticking" of the molecular clock—the accumulation of more mutations represents a greater length of time. If one assumes that such mutations are selectively neutral (i.e., not subject to natural selection), then they may accumulate at a stochastically regular rate. Data from varied molecules and DNA suggest that hominids diverged from ancestral apes sometime between 7 and 4 mya, probably about 5 mya.

The earliest known fossils that might be attributable to an early hominid come from Lothagam and Tabarin, Rift Valley sites in Kenya (Figure 8-4). The best estimated dates for these sites are about 5.5 mya and 5.0 mya, respectively (Ward & Hill, 1987), close to the hypothesized time range of the hominid–ape divergence.

A mandibular fragment from Lothagam contains a first molar tooth, with a cusp pattern and a bulbous expansion on the buccal (cheek) side that are suggestive of hominid affinities. The mandible from Tabarin has a first and second molar, also with a buccal flare. The teeth of both specimens are most notable for their **serrate root** patterns: in this pattern, the mesial (front) roots are longer than the distal (back) roots, and the roots are angled in a distal direction (Hill, 1985; Hill & Ward, 1988; Ward & Hill, 1987). The serrate pattern is characteristic of later hominids and suggests an adaptation for strong bite forces. Although the Lothagam and Tabarin mandibular fragments resemble *Australopithecus afaren-*

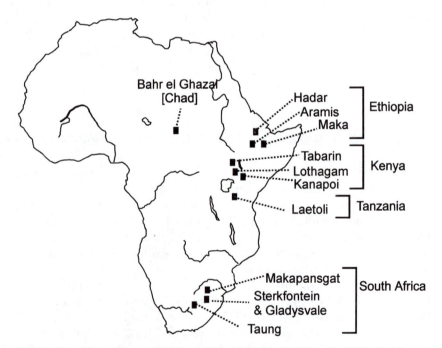

FIGURE 8-4 Map of the early hominid fossil sites of Africa. See Table 8-1 for further details. (Courtesy Jeffrey K. McKee.)

sis (discussed later), many diagnostic features are not preserved. It is not possible on the basis of current evidence to establish whether or not the animals represented at these sites were bipedal.

Another possible hominid was recently discovered at the Ethiopian site of Aramis, dating to 4.4 mya. Originally described as *Australopithecus ramidus*, the enigmatic fossils were later given a new genus name, *Ardipithecus* (White et al., 1994, 1995). With a mixture of primitive and advanced traits, there is a suggestion of a forward-positioned foramen magnum from a fragment of the cranial base, which like that of the Taung child suggests a bipedal animal.

Confirmed bipedalism appears by as early as 4.2 mya with fossils from Kenya known as *Australopithecus anamensis*; these fossils include a tibia that clearly shows that these forms walked on two legs. Although australopithecines did not have the full set of locomotor traits of modern humans, bipedal locomotion was established very early after the divergence from other hominoids.

Australopithecus afarensis, another East African hominid found in Ethiopia and Tanzania, is best known for the remarkable "Lucy" skeleton. This species may date to as early as 3.9 mya, and appears in the fossil record until 2.9 mya. A possible representative of *A. afarensis* was recently found in Chad, with an age of sometime between 3.5 and 3.0 mya (Brunet et al., 1995). The significance of the Chad discoveries is that the site is 2500 kilometers west of the East African rift valley, where most of the earliest hominids were found, thus greatly extending the known geographic range of the genus *Australopithecus*.

The South African *Australopithecus africanus* sites generally fall later in time, between about 3.2 and 2.5 mya. However, the dating is tentative because it is based primarily on faunal analysis; the cave sites are not conducive to radiometric dating techniques. Taung, at what is now the southeastern margin of the Kalahari desert, is the southernmost early hominid site and the farthest from the equator.

South Africa

Most South African fossil hominids come from deposits in large caves that formed in the extensive dolomites that span the northeastern parts of the country. Dolomite is a Precambrian limestone in which massive caverns were formed when the lime was dissolved by underground water; with the uplift of the African continent and subsequent erosion, the caverns became exposed to the surface and provided shelter for a wide variety of animal inhabitants over millions of years. Many such animals became interred in the cave, leaving their bones for the process of fossilization. In the early 1900s, the limestone stalactites and stalagmites that had formed inside the caves attracted miners who were in search of lime for gold processing, construction, and agriculture. In the process of mining, the solidified cave infill that contained fossil bones—a rock conglomerate known as **breccia**—was discarded. Many fossil finds have been made in the miner's "dumps" of breccia, and only later were fossil remains excavated in situ once scientists had access to the sites.

Makapansgat (Figure 8-4) is the northernmost of these dolomitic caves and probably contains the oldest deposits (McKee et al., 1995). About 30 fossil hominids were recovered, primarily from sorting miners' dumps, and attributed to Members 3 and 4 of the Makapansgat Limeworks, probably spanning a time period between 3.2 and 2.9 mya. The *Australopithecus africanus* fossils were accompanied by more than 200,000 fossils of other mammals. It is important to note that the caves were not habitation or occupation areas for *Australopithecus,* but merely a site of deposition—probably due to the hominids having become meals for the carnivorous felids and hyaenids that occupied the caves.

Sterkfontein is Africa's richest single site for early hominid remains, having yielded over 500 fossils of *Australopithecus* and early *Homo* (Clarke, 1994) (Figure 8-5). Most of the *Australopithecus africanus* remains come from Member 4, dating to about 2.5 mya. Hominid foot bones from Sterkfontein Member 2 are presumably older than those of Member 4, based on superposition of deposits, but the age of the deposit is unclear (Clarke & Tobias, 1995; McKee, 1996). The nearby site of Gladysvale recently yielded an australopithecine tooth (Berger et al., 1993); an age of the deposit has yet to be established.

Taung is unusual not only in its far southern location, the greatest latitude from the equator of any *Australopithecus* site, but also in the type of caves in which animal bones were deposited. At Taung the caves are formed in accretions of **tufa**, another type of limestone (Figure 8-6). Tufa is formed from the lime-rich water that comes from springs in the dolomitic bedrock; successive layers of tufa are deposited over many years, leaving a large apronlike accretion. Within the

FIGURE 8-5   The Sterkfontein fossil site, showing excavations of breccia below the dolomitic roof. The Swartkrans fossil site (Chapter 9) is on the hill in the background. (Courtesy Jeffrey K. McKee.)

FIGURE 8-6 Tufa is a limestone accretion formed by water and algae. The small cave opening in tufa accretion pictured here leads to a small chamber similar to that in which the Taung child was interred. (Courtesy Jeffrey K. McKee.)

tufa accretions, small caves can form—much smaller than those that form in dolomite. The spring water that forms the tufa also attracted many animals—including a juvenile *Australopithecus africanus.*

East Africa

The Rift Valley system in East Africa has yielded a great deal of information on early human evolution. The extensive rift opened as a result of geological tension associated with the tectonic uplift of the African continent, particularly during the Miocene and Pliocene (Partridge et al., 1995). Along the resulting valleys, Pliocene fossil sites are strewn from the Afar depression of Ethiopia, down through ancient lake beds of Kenya and Tanzania, and as far south as Lake Malawi.

In contrast to the South African cave sites, the East African sites mostly formed out in the open as bones became deposited in the sediments at the edges of lakes and rivers. Deposits of volcanic ash, resulting from exceptionally high volcanism in the geologically turbulent Pliocene of East Africa, rest above and below the fossil bones and provide an ideal context for radiometric dating (potassium-argon, argon-argon, and fission track methods). In one case, at Laetoli in Tanzania, the volcanic ash also left a suitable surface for the imprinting and preservation of *Australopithecus* footprints.

Arguably the oldest of the East African Rift Valley sites that may contain hominid material is Lothagam, between the Kerio and Lomunyenkupurat rivers in northern Kenya. The Lothagam sequence of sediments is extensive and has posed problems for accurate dating. The most recent assessment, based on the fossil fauna, puts the age of the hominid deposit in excess of 5.6 mya (Hill et al., 1992).

The Tabarin site, in the Tugen Hills near Lake Baringo, Kenya, yielded a possible hominid mandible from an outcrop of the Chemeron Formation. Isotopic dates of the volcanic sediments underlying the Tabarin mandible date to around 5 mya, while the associated fauna confirm that a date no later than 4.15 mya is most likely (Ward & Hill, 1987). Particularly useful in the faunal dating was a suid (pig), *Nyanzachoerus jaegeri*; suids evolved rapidly throughout the East African sequence and thus are quite valuable in establishing faunal chronologies.

The site of Aramis is in sedimentary deposits of the Middle Awash, in the Afar depression of Ethiopia. The fragmentary fossils of 17 *Ardipithecus ramidus* fossils were recovered in sediments overlying volcanic **tuff** (consolidated volcanic ash) that was dated by $^{40}Ar/^{39}Ar$ (similar to K/Ar, Chapter 1). The 4.4 mya age of the tuff is thus a maximum age for the fossils (WoldeGabriel et al., 1994). The associated fossil mammals are consistent with an early age determination.

In Kenya, the *Australopithecus anamensis* site of Kanapoi has water-deposited sediments that include datable volcanic components; nine hominid specimens come from this site. These have been dated by the $^{40}Ar/^{39}Ar$ method to approximately 4.2 mya (Leakey et al., 1995). The site of Allia Bay, containing 12 further fossils of this early hominid, dates to 3.9 mya. The fossil record shows that the hominid lineage, as recognized by bipedal animals, was clearly established before 4 mya.

Most of the sites yielding *Australopithecus afarensis* come from the Afar depression of Ethiopia. Some of the most significant hominid remains were recovered from the Hadar site, which encompasses an area of roughly 65 square kilometers. The sediments generally represent lake, lake margin, and associated river and stream deposits related to an extensive lake that periodically filled the entire sedimentary basin. Well over 200 hominid fossils have been recovered from the early Hadar sequence, largely from surface finds of fossils that had eroded from the ancient sediments. These fossils come from a sequence of deposits dating from 3.4 to 2.9 mya, thus overlapping in time with the earliest of the South African *Australopithecus africanus* fossils.

Australopithecus afarensis has also been found in older deposits at Laetoli, Tanzania. The Upper Laetoli beds, accumulated from windblown tuffs, are radiometrically dated to between approximately 3.8 and 3.5 mya (Leakey et al., 1976). Laetoli not only yielded a spectacular array of hominid fossils, including a mandible that serves as the type specimen of *A. afarensis*, but also preserved a most unusual type of fossil: hominid footprints. The coincidence of freshly laid volcanic ash with a light rainfall provided conditions for the imprinting, hardening, and preservation of footprints dated from 3.6 mya. The best preserved trail has 34 hominid prints covering a distance of 23.5 meters, representing a stroll taken by three bipedal individuals of varying sizes.

Other sites which have yielded *Australopithecus afarensis* fossils are listed in Table 8-1, along with the site of Bahr el Ghazal (Arabic for "River of the

TABLE 8-1   Key Early Hominid Sites of the African Pliocene

Location	Species	Maximum Age (million years)
East Africa		
Ethiopia		
Aramis	*Ardipithecus ramidus*	4.4
Maka	*Australopithecus afarensis*	3.4
Hadar Sidiha Koma	*Australopithecus afarensis*	3.4
Hadar Denen Dora	*Australopithecus afarensis*	3.2
Kada Hadar	*Australopithecus afarensis*	3.2
Kenya		
Lothagam	*Australopithecus* sp. (?)	5.5
Tabarin	*Australopithecus* sp. (?)	5.0
Kanapoi	*Australopithecus anamensis*	4.2
Tanzania		
Laetoli	*Australopithecus afarensis*	3.8
Central Africa		
Chad		
Bahr el Ghazal	*Australopithecus afarensis* (?)	3.5
South Africa		
Makapansgat Member 3	*Australopithecus africanus*	3.2 (?)
Makapansgat Member 4	*Australopithecus africanus*	3.0 (?)
Sterkfontein Member 2	*Australopithecus* sp. (?)	3.5 (?)
Sterkfontein Member 4	*Australopithecus africanus*	2.6 (?)
Gladysvale	*Australopithecus africanus* (?)	?
Taung	*Australopithecus africanus*	2.8

Gazelles"), Chad. *A. afarensis* had a large geographic range and was an established species on the African landscape for perhaps as much as 1 million years.

THE FOSSIL EVIDENCE

Let us now turn to the skeletal evidence of early hominid morphology. Very important facts often overlooked when discussing the morphology of skeletal remains are their scattered nature and the unequal preservation potential of bones (Chapter 1). Interpretations are often skewed by the amount of the material; for example, some sites yield disproportionate numbers of remains. An analysis of almost any anatomical entity over the entire African sample is likely to be heavily biased by characteristics and samples from certain sites. One well-preserved skeleton, such as Lucy from Hadar, makes a major difference to the composition of any of the anatomical samples. Likewise, the type specimen of a species is the "norm" by which we judge other fossils and assign them to the same species; yet until a large sample has accumulated, we do not know if the "type" reflects an average individual.

The history of discovery also plays a role in shaping our interpretations. The early hominids discussed in this chapter are often referred to as "gracile" australopithecines. This term stems from an early attempt to distinguish them from a closely related group of hominid bipeds, the "robust" australopithecines, who are characterized by a massive expansion of the face and teeth accompanied by robust facial architecture (discussed in the next chapter). Before it was known that the robust forms were the later descendants of the so-called graciles, it was even considered possible that the robust were the males and the graciles the females of the same species (Brace 1972). These early distinctions in the literature left us with the misleading term "gracile"—for the faces of the early hominids are anything but gracile when compared to modern humans.

Numerous as the samples may appear to be, some parts are poorly represented, and the remains of a small number of well-preserved specimens dominate. The preburial survival potential of bones is related to the great variability in their size, shape, and density. Relatively light bones, such as vertebrae, or bones with a high surface-to-volume ratio, such as ribs, are more easily transported and weathered than are limb bones and teeth. Teeth are more likely to survive stream transport than the larger and more fragile skull. However, in conditions with extremes of temperature and soil moisture, as is typical of East African savannas, teeth may crack and disintegrate long before the skull.

Carnivore and scavenger activity cause initial alteration of the number of different bones available for fossilization. Most early hominid fossil remains were probably scavenged before burial; in the case of South African caves, scavenging is often the reason that bones were initially brought into caves. Lighter elements would be less susceptible to burial and more likely to be destroyed by abrasion and weathering than denser bony elements, and may be more easily washed away.

As an example of the survival potential of bones, Behrensmeyer (1977) cited the Lake Turkana sample. As of 1973, this sample contained 120 individuals, representing a time span of 1.5 million years. Assuming an average life span of 25 years (Mann, 1975) and a stable average population of 50 individuals, the sample of 120 may come from an actual total of 3 million individuals. Only 0.00004 of the original number of individuals are represented in this fossil sample, one of the best-known hominid fossil collections.

We must be cognizant of the taphonomic processes leading to the fossilization of bone. They tend to skew our interpretations in favor of jaws and teeth, as well as other parts naturally favored for preservation. Other parts of the anatomy, however, may be just as important in an accurate assessment of the function and phylogeny of early hominid beings.

Characteristics of the Fossil Species

Ardipithecus ramidus is an enigmatic genus and species, currently known only from seventeen fossils found at the 4.4-mya site of Aramis, Ethiopia. The individuals represented were the victims of carnivore activity, scarred by tooth marks of their predators. The term "ramid" translates from the Afar language as "root" and is meant to imply that the species lies at the root of our hominid family tree. When the fossils were first published by Tim White and his team (White et al., 1994), they were referred to the genus *Australopithecus* and touted as the earliest hominids. With second thoughts, White et al. (1995) named a new genus, *Ardipithecus*, for the fossils may indeed represent a species at the root of the chimpanzee family tree.

The fossils from Aramis, comprising craniodental as well as postcranial specimens, carry a number of plesiomorphic (ancestral) features of the early hominoids (White et al., 1994). The tooth enamel is thinner at the crown, and the premolars have a number of primitive traits. The molars have not yet undergone the expansion that characterizes the later australopithecines. The humerus has a mixture of ancestral and derived features, even though the ulna looks more like that of the later hominids.

So why might the fossils be considered early hominids? There are a few subtle clues. The canines are less projecting than those of Miocene hominoids—and this characteristic may be the beginning of a trend that continues throughout the early phases of hominid evolution. The molar root patterns are serrate, as in later hominids that have strong bite forces. The feature most suggestive of hominid affinities is the apparent position of the foramen magnum; recall that Dart's initial claim for the Taung skull as a biped was also based upon the relatively forward position of this key feature. A piece of the cranial base from Aramis has characteristics that imply a forward position for the foramen magnum, indicating upright posture and bipedal locomotion. Further fossils recently recovered at Aramis may resolve the issue of the bipedalism of *A. ramidus*.

Australopithecus anamensis is the earliest fossil species that was undeniably a bipedal hominid. Discovered and named by Meave Leakey and her colleagues, the name "anam" ("lake" in the Turkana language) refers to its discovery near the present Lake Turkana in the sediments of a more ancient lake (Leakey et al., 1995). This early australopithecine shares a number of traits with later *Australopithecus afarensis*, but the presence of some more primitive traits suggests that it may be designated as a separate species. In particular, the mandibular tooth rows are parallel, yielding a U shape like that of modern apes. Other dental traits, such as the shape of the canine and pattern of tooth roots, are also shared with other hominoids. And, as with apes, there appears to be a high degree of sexual dimorphism in the sample.

Despite these hominoid plesiomorphies, *A. anamensis* was definitely a bipedal animal. The flattening at the top of the tibia (where it articulates with the femur at the knee joint) is characteristic of all bipeds. The fossil teeth also show the beginnings of a significant hominid trend—the thickening of the enamel. Unlike *Ardipithecus ramidus*, the thick enamel of *Australopithecus anamensis* would have allowed for the crushing of harder objects in the diet (such as nuts and seeds).

A much larger sample of fossils gives us a good understanding of *Australopithecus afarensis*. This species designation was initially based on materials found at Hadar, Ethiopia, and Laetoli, Tanzania (Johanson & White, 1979, 1980; Johanson et al., 1978). In essence *A. afarensis* was an animal like *A. africanus*, a small-brained bipedal animal with a face characterized by a mixture of apelike and humanlike characteristics.

The naming of the species initially elicited considerable controversy (as was the case with *A. africanus*, and is expected to be the case with *A. ramidus*, *A. anamensis*, and *A. bahrelgazali*—a putative species to be discussed later). The morphological overlap of *A. afarensis* with *A. africanus* suggested to some researchers that the East African finds were geographic variants of the South African australopithecines (Tobias, 1980; Zhilman, 1985). Some regard the East African fossils as representing two species, whereas others see the variability as being the product of sexual dimorphism. The naming of the species was also criticized, as the type specimen was from Laetoli, not from the Afar (as in *A. afarensis);* but Dart was also criticized for naming *Australopithecus africanus* with a mixture of Latin and Greek terms. Although such disputes may add zest to the popular perception of anthropology, they add little to our understanding of human evolution. Whether or not *A. afarensis* (or *A. anamensis*) represents a truly distinct biological species is a question that cannot be resolved with the current fossil sample; and the rules of species nomenclature are only of esoteric interest to those who hold to the pre-Darwinian system of Linnaean taxonomy (see Chapter 2). Indisputably, the fossils referred to *A. afarensis* represent a distinct and interesting stage of human evolutionary origins in East Africa.

What distinguishes the fossils known as *A. afarensis*? Most importantly they were clearly bipedal animals, or at least had the morphology allowing habitual bipedalism. The first knee joint found by Johanson and his team, as well as the "Lucy" skeleton, are of a short but stout biped. Mary Leakey's discovery of fossil footprints at Laetoli only served to confirm what was clear from the postcranial morphology of the fossil bones. As Dart had recognized, bipedality was the first step on our peculiar evolutionary path.

A. afarensis, unlike earlier hominoids, had enlarged molars and premolars. These dental traits were accompanied by a fairly prognathic face—one large enough to house the teeth. The canine teeth were still a bit projecting, but nowhere near the size of the large, threatening canines utilized for defense by most other primate species. There was a small canine diastema in the upper jaw, a slight gap between the lateral incisor and adjacent canine. This trait would disappear in most subsequent hominids. In this dental complex, the first lower premolar (or P_3) was not fully bicuspid as in modern humans, but sectorial—sort of a transitional tooth between the cutting canine and the grinding molars. The molars were beginning their expansion of breadth.

The australopithecine mandible from Bahr el Ghazal, Chad, is similar to *A. afarensis* in its canines and bicuspid premolars. Detailed differences exist in the mandibular symphysis and the apelike three-rooted system of the premolars (*A. afarensis* has one or two roots). The fossils may represent a distinct species, *A. bahrelghazali* (Brunet et al., 1996), or a regional variant of *A. afarensis*.

The arms of *A. afarensis* were proportionally longer than those of modern humans, suggesting an ability to climb. Climbing of trees or sharp cliffs may have been important to the survival of these early hominids, as with modern baboons. Yet sheer cunning may have been a feature setting this ancestral hominid apart; its cranial capacity ranged from 380 cubic centimeters to possibly as much as 500 cc.

In relation to its body size, this is a slight but potentially important advance over other hominoids.

A. afarensis put our ancestors on the path to humanity; in southern Africa, *A. africanus* perpetuated some trends and initiated others. Some scientists suspect that *A. africanus* took a step to the side of our hominid lineage, toward the robust forms that eventually went extinct (e.g., Johanson & White, 1979; Rak, 1985). Others place *A. africanus* squarely on the line leading to the genus *Homo* (e.g., McKee, 1989; Tobias, 1980). Either way, *A. africanus* represents the next phase, showing a larger cranial capacity and a more humanlike dentition than the earlier forms from East Africa. It should be noted, however, that fossils attributed to *A. africanus* are quite variable, particularly the sample from Sterkfontein Member 4. It has been suggested that the deposit may contain more than one *Australopithecus* species (Clarke, 1988).

The cranial capacity of *A. africanus* ranges from 425 to over 500 cc (Conroy et al., 1998), not counting a projected adult cranial capacity for the Taung child of 540 cc (Tobias, 1971). The average of 451 cc is above the *A. afarensis* average of 413 (Tobias, 1994). The cranial capacity, presumably reflecting the size of the hominid brain, was beginning to expand disproportionally to the enlargement of the rest of the body. The recently discovered partial cranium STW-505 (Tobias, 1992), a partial cranium from Sterkfontein Member 4, has the greatest adult cranial capacity of *A. africanus*, estimated between 500 and 530 cc (Conroy et al., 1998).

Like *A. afarensis*, *A. africanus* was bipedal with upper limb adaptations for climbing (Berger, 1994). But the teeth and jaws were a bit more modern: the canines were reduced, there was no canine diastema, the premolars were fully bicuspid (and more like the grinding molars), and the dental arcade had a more parabolic (archlike) shape. The face was still fairly prognathic and was strongly built.

EVOLUTIONARY TRENDS

Body Size and Limb Proportions

Body weight estimates are possible when sufficient samples of a species have been collected. *A. afarensis* was in the range of 29–45 kilograms (64–99 pounds), and *A. africanus* had a similar range of 30–41 kg (66–90 pounds) (McHenry, 1992). McHenry's (1991a) height estimates for these hominids showed considerable sexual dimorphism, particularly in *A. afarensis*. *A. afarensis* females would have stood approximately 105 centimeters tall (3 feet 5 inches), as compared to 151 cm for males (4 feet 11 inches). *A. africanus* females were about 115 cm in height (3 feet 11 inches), and males on the order of 138 cm (4 feet 6 inches). One gets a picture of some fairly short but sturdily built early hominids.

The apparent limb proportions of *A. afarensis* and *A. africanus* are perplexing. New postcranial fossils of *A. africanus* from Sterkfontein Member 4 reveal that it had somewhat primitive limb proportions, with relatively large forelimb and small hind limb joints (McHenry & Berger, 1998). These proportions are in contrast to the joints of *A. afarensis* and *A. anamensis*, which had more humanlike proportions of forelimbs and hind limbs. On the basis of craniodental evidence, in which the earlier East African species have more primitive traits, the later-appearing *A. africanus* of South Africa with its more derived craniodental traits was not expected to have such primitive morphology in the limbs.

Jaws and Teeth

Australopithecine dental traits have been studied in more detail than any other skeletal remains belonging to this group. Although their dental traits comprise a pattern of considerable complexity, the dental pattern conforms to that of the Hominidae. The human characteristics of the permanent (adult) dentition hold true as well for the deciduous (immature) dentition. The upper incisors in all adult specimens are consistently smaller than those of apes. Although the canines are larger than commonly found among modern humans, they too are reduced in size relative to the apes. The canine teeth in the Hadar and Laetoli sample are particularly large. However, some canines are spatulate (not pointed) and show some sexual dimorphism; in the earliest stages of wear the canines are worn flat from the tip to the level of adjacent teeth. The first lower premolars are usually bicuspid and usually do not show any alteration that would allow for an overlapping canine tooth; this pattern would allow for more rotary chewing motions.

The premolar and molar teeth are large, the third lower molar commonly exceeds the length of the second, and the **lingual** (on the tongue side) cusps of the first lower premolar teeth are relatively large. These are evidently primitive human traits, as they also appear later in *Homo erectus*.

Early hominids had relatively vertically implanted incisors, relatively large premolars, and molars with thick enamel. *A. anamensis* and *A. afarensis* exhibit the most generalized dentitions, thus providing a link between Miocene hominoids and the Plio-Pleistocene hominids. Dental variability increased over time, eventually leading to the divergence of the hominids into a *Homo* lineage and a "robust" australopithecine lineage (Chapter 9).

There has been considerable rethinking concerning the timing and the meaning of australopithecine dental development patterns. There are currently four main alternatives (Conroy & Vannier, 1991):

1. Australopithecine dental development is similar to that of modern humans, and this similarity implies prolonged maturation. This idea is most consistent with the work of Mann (1968, 1975).
2. Australopithecine dental development patterns are most similar to those of the apes. This comparison suggests more rapid maturation rates, thereby implying a shortened period of learning and intellectual development. This idea was first proposed by Bromage and Dean (1986).
3. "Gracile" and the later "robust" australopithecines have differing rates of dental development, but both forms matured rapidly and early. This idea was first suggested by Dean (1985).

4. Because modern human and ape dental development patterns are so variable, perhaps neither is a good model for australopithecine patterns (Conroy & Vannier, 1991; Kuykendall, 1996). Smith (1991) argued that the unique rate and pattern of human life history did not exist among the australopithecines and that growth and aging evolved substantially in the Hominidae over the last 2 million years.

This disagreement over tooth growth patterns reflects the way we look at the early hominids. By comparison with apes, modern humans have an extended period of infancy that is important for greater intellectual development and social nurturing. If our earliest ancestors also had prolonged infancies, then they were experiencing a different social life from that of the apes. The signs of prolonged immaturity are looked for in tooth eruption patterns.

If the suggestion by Bromage and Dean (1986) and by Smith (1986) that the teeth of early hominids were more apelike than humanlike in their maturation pattern is correct, it has implications for reconstructing early hominid behavior patterns and society (see Grine, 1987, for a different view). A reduced period of immaturity might also mean a reduced period for learning, which would have an impact on potential cultural development. The implication is that the period of infancy in early hominids is not much prolonged, if at all, over that of apes. In fact, contrary to what is now the majority view, Bromage and Dean and Smith hold that there is no evidence for prolonged immaturity even among the earliest members of the genus *Homo*, despite considerable advances in brain size over the australopithecines.

Skull, Brain Size and Structure, and Face

Throughout this book we discuss changes in skull and facial shape and size. It is necessary, therefore, to consider some factors affecting them. In terrestrial vertebrates, a group including humans, overall skull shape depends on the form of the chewing apparatus (teeth, jaws, and associated muscles), the sense organs, brain size and shape, and the position of the skull on the spinal column. Skull shape reflects the function and size of different parts of the skull. Skull and facial size and shape are formed as an evolutionary compromise among a number of separate functional complexes, such as those related to vision, bipedalism (Chapter 7), mastication, and brain development.

The head and face are highly integrated structures, and changes in one area result in changes in others. The amount of development of any of the muscles attaching to the skull or the face (especially the chewing muscles) will produce tensions and stresses in the bony architecture that affect its form. Bone is a very plastic substance, and its size and shape change in response to the stresses imposed on it by the muscles attached to its surface. Thus some changes we see in the fossil record have to do with natural selection for particular bony structures, and other changes are the developmental result of how those bones were used during life.

Largely because of the shape and dimensions of the skull (e.g., Figure 8-3), many scientists were first inclined to the position that *Australopithecus* was an ape allied to the gorilla or chimpanzee rather than an early member of the human family, Hominidae. The small brain cases, combined with massive and projecting jaws, gave a superficially apelike appearance. This view was overcome as more skulls were uncovered and their morphological patterns critically examined.

Considerable argument raged over the subject of the australopithecines' cranial capacity; many held that the estimated brain size was too small for them to be included within the Hominidae. The early assumption was that there was some arbitrary point in brain expansion (some suggested a cranial capacity of 750 to 800 cc) that formed a dividing line between human and ape. There was considerable variation in early hominid cranial capacities. Overall, the range of variation is from perhaps less than 400 cc for *A. afarensis* (although some had cranial capacities of 500 cc) to over 500 cc for *A. africanus*. Body size and stratigraphic age of the specimens help explain much of the variation.

Cranial capacity measurements give a general idea of brain volume, without regard for body size. Estimates are usually based on reconstructions from the preserved portions of skulls, or from the volumes of endocranial casts such as that of the Taung child. Using a computer imaging technique with 3-D computed tomography (CT scan), Conroy et al. (1990) were able to "see" inside a matrix-filled *Australopithecus* cranium from Makapansgat and electronically "reconstruct" the missing portions of the endocranial cavity in order to determine endocranial volume.

McHenry (1994) utilizes the data of cranial and postcranial measurements to determine an **encephalization quotient** (EQ). The EQ is calculated as estimated brain weight in relation to the expected brain weight for a typical mammal of a particular body size. In other words, most mammals should have an EQ value of 1. The higher the EQ, the greater the brain size for body size. Those with a greater relative brain size are said to be more encephalized.

A. afarensis has an EQ of 2.2, as compared to a chimpanzee EQ of 2.0 (McHenry, 1994). Thus *A. afarensis* began the hominid trend of increased encephalization. *A. africanus* was determined by McHenry to have an EQ of 2.5, thus showing a further increase. As a point of comparison, modern humans have an EQ of about 5.8.

The functional significance of larger human cranial capacities may reflect increasing capabilities for technology and complex social behavior. Long-term memory may also have been facilitated by the increasing cranial capacities (Peters, 1979).

Taken by themselves, the several endocasts available do not permit firm statements regarding the convolution pattern of the brain. Surface irregularities seen in the casts provide little information regarding morphological details commonly regarded as of particular interest in contrasting human and ape brains.

There appear to be a number of important ways in which the australopithecine brain differs from that of the apes. These differences correspond to some of the unique developments of the human brain. Holloway (1974, 1975) argued that the australopithecine brain differed from ours more in size than in organization (this subject was discussed in more detail in Chapter 7). On the other hand, Falk et al. (1989) suggested that the australopithecine brain was extremely simple and apelike. Tobias (1994) noted the important morphological characters distinguishing australopithecine cranial endocast features from those of apes. Among these were the following: The brainstem is positioned further anteriorly; the parietal lobe of the cerebrum is more developed; there is a degree of asymmetry; and there is a slight protrusion in the area of Broca's area (the speech center—see Chapter 7 and Figure 7-4). Most would agree that the aus-tralopithecine brain represents the first steps of the important increases in brain size and complexity that characterize human evolution.

The cranial specimens from the Hadar sample of *A. afarensis* are character-ized by pronounced sexual dimorphism. One of the obtrusive features of the exceptionally well-preserved *A. africanus* skull (STS 5) from Sterkfontein, South Africa (Figure 8-7), is the height of the cranial vault above the eye orbits. A com-parison of the australopithecine skulls with those of gorillas, chimpanzees, and orangutans shows that the relative height of the former exceeds the range of vari-ation in ape skulls and comes within the range of human skulls. Among the large adult anthropoid apes, the **occipital torus** forms a crest that reaches high up on the skull, considerably extending the nuchal area for the attachment of powerful neck muscles, which hold the head erect on the spinal column (Zuckerman, 1954a). Among the australopithecines, the nuchal area is very restricted and faces downward instead of backward (Zuckerman, 1954b). The conditions of skull height and level of the occipital torus are related to the poise of the head on the vertebral column. The australopithecine skull was positioned as one would expect in a bipedal creature.

In all sufficiently preserved australopithecine skulls, there is a well-marked pyramidal **mastoid** process, similar in many respects to that of modern humans. Although some adult male gorillas have such a process, when it appears it is of a different shape. Unlike the case in gorillas, the mastoid process is a consistent

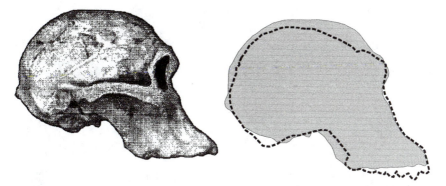

FIGURE 8-7 *Left,* A skull of *Australopithecus africanus*, STS 5 or "Mrs. Ples" from Sterkfontein Member 4. *Right,* The silhouette of STS 5 is compared with the shape of a reconstructed *Australopithecus afarensis* (dashed line). (Courtesy Jeffrey K. McKee.)

element of human skull anatomy. It is not possible to ascertain the exact functional significance of the australopithecine mastoid process. However, it is probably related to the relative degree of development and pull of the muscles attached to it, particularly those that are used for turning the head side to side.

Pelvis and Limb Bones

No part of the postcranial anatomy shows a more marked contrast between modern apes and humans than does the pelvis (Figure 8-8). The primary factor determining the evolutionary separation of the human from the ape family, the Hominidae from the Pongidae, was the modification of their respective locomotor skeletons for different modes of life. The pelvis of *Homo sapiens* and that of its ancestors is modified to accept an upright bipedal posture. If the australopithecines are representatives of a human and not an ape stock, as has been argued, their limb and pelvic structures are relevant to the determinations of their taxonomic status.

Several australopithecine pelvic remains have been recovered. Pelvic materials from Sterkfontein, South Africa, and that belonging to Lucy from Hadar, Ethiopia, were virtually complete. Two immature pelvic specimens were also recovered at Makapansgat Limeworks, South Africa. All the pelvic remains exhibit a typically human configuration, although there are deviations from modern human pelvises. Broom et al. (1950) noted the humanlike ilium along with the

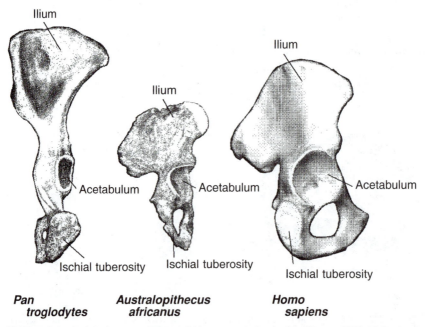

FIGURE 8-8 Pelvic bones of *Pan* (chimpanzee), *Australopithecus* (STS 14 from Sterkfontein), and modern human. Note the differences in size, shape, and orientation, particularly in the ilium and ischium. (Courtesy Jeffrey K. McKee.)

more chimplike pubis and ischium of the *A. africanus* pelvis from Sterkfontein. Likewise, pelvic remains belonging to Lucy show enough evolution for bipedalism; but the second step, further pelvic evolution for the birth of large-brained infants, had not yet occurred (Lovejoy 1973, 1975, 1988).

The australopithecine pelvis (Figure 8-8) strongly contrasts with the ape pelvis and approaches most closely the human pelvis. For example, the broadening of the ilium (the large, flat bone that forms the upper part of the pelvis) in humans extends the anteroposterior attachment of the gluteal (buttocks) muscles, which are used to balance the pelvis and trunk on the lower limbs. The bending down of the posterior extremity of the iliac crest brings the largest of the gluteal muscles in humans, the gluteus maximus, into a posterior position in relation to the hip joint, permitting it to function as a thigh extensor (for example, permitting the leg to move backward when standing up from a sitting position), an essential action in walking erect. The positioning of the articular surface of the acetabulum (the cup on the pelvis into which the head of the femur fits and revolves) allows great stability in the transmission of weight from the trunk to the hip joint. Other functional implications tied to the organization of the australopithecines' pelvis are related to the assumption of an erect posture and bipedalism.

Changes in pelvic shape, especially in the ilium, that have accompanied the evolution of human bipedalism have had different results in males and females. Changes in the ilium of females were tempered by the need to provide a fairly large birth canal, whose size is functionally related to the size of the infant's head. Lovejoy (1973, 1975, 1988) noted that the birth canal in modern females has enlarged to accommodate the birth of larger-brain infants. Given the small head size (because of the small cranial capacity) of early hominid infants, Lovejoy argued that there would have been less conflicting selection for bipedalism on the one hand and a large birth canal on the other. The pelvic structure of early hominid females may have been better adapted to bipedalism than that of the modern female. On the other hand, Berg (1994) argues that australopithecines had less ability to maintain hip and knee extension during walking, and probably would have moved the pelvis and lower limbs differently. Australopithecines, according to this view, may have walked with a waddling gait. If so, this mode of walking required greater energy expenditure than the walking of modern humans.

The size of the birth canal in males is controlled mainly by locomotion and is unrelated to having to give birth. Lovejoy reasoned that the male pelvis has changed less than the female pelvis during human evolution and that the modern male pelvis more closely resembles the pelvis of early hominids than does the female pelvis (Lovejoy et al., 1973). Sexual differences in the pelvis cause the difference in locomotion and posture seen among modern males and females. At Sterkfontein, which yielded many remains of *A. africanus*, a number of specimens of the lower (distal) end of the femur were recovered. Its morphology indicates that the knee joint could be locked in an erect posture. Some femoral traits, however, are difficult to assess, other than to say that they indicate some differences in the mechanism of the knee joint when compared with *Homo sapiens* (Heiple & Lovejoy, 1971; Lovejoy & Heiple, 1970).

The two bones of the lower leg, the tibia and fibula, indicated that the bony adaptation for bipedalism was well advanced in the ankle (Day & Wood, 1968). Evidence from one of the anklebones, the talus, however, indicates a general construction in some ways intermediate between that of *Homo sapiens* and apes. The human condition of the talus would have permitted enough stability at the ankle joint for bearing weight in the erect position. However, the articular surface on the head of the talus suggests considerable mobility of the front portion of the foot, as seen in apes.

The thirty-seven foot bones and fragments from the Hadar formation comprise the largest and most complete collection of Plio-Pleistocene foot bones. They present a distinctly human morphological composite. The toes of *A. afarensis* may have been longer and more curved than those in modern humans. Stern and Susman (1983) suggested that this configuration is tied to adaptations to arboreal activity. Tuttle (1985) suggested that the feet typified by the Hadar remains could not have belonged to the species making the Laetoli footprints. On the other hand, a close look at the hallux (big toe) convinced Latimer and Lovejoy (1990) that *A. afarensis* was a fully efficient terrestrial biped. They noted that *A. afarensis* did not have an opposable hallux and that the toe functioned as it does in modern humans. In fact, *Homo* and *Australopithecus* are the only two primate genera lacking an opposable hallux. The absence of such "is direct and virtually absolute confirmation that climbing behavior was negligible in *A. afarensis*" (Latimer & Lovejoy, 1990:133). They argued that only a virtually complete terrestrial habitat can account for the absence of an opposable big toe.

More recent results from an analysis of metatarsal heads are inconclusive regarding the functional anatomy of *A. afarensis* feet (Duncan et al., 1994). Overall, the results are consistent with other evidence indicating that *A. afarensis* was a capable climber. This viewpoint differs from that of Latimer and Lovejoy, who argued that *A. afarensis* demonstrated a humanlike articular set. Duncan et al.'s results are consistent with a model of australopithecine locomotion that includes both terrestrial and arboreal postural behavior.

The debate over the degree of australopithecine arboreality took a new turn with the discovery of a set of foot bones from Sterkfontein Member 2, dubbed "Little Foot" by Clarke and Tobias (1995). Little Foot has a distinctly humanlike calcaneus at the heel, but the bones become increasingly apelike toward the toe. The hallux, or big toe, was clearly divergent. Either *Australopithecus* retained some primitive features during the evolution of bipedalism, or these features were used for climbing as well as walking.

Spoor et al. (1994) took an unusual approach to assessing australopithecine bipedalism. They used CT scans to view the inner ear of fossil skulls. The vestibular system of the inner ear is important in sensing and maintaining balance. They found that the inner ear morphology of *A. africanus* resembled that of great apes; only with *Homo erectus* (Chapter 10) did the modern morphology appear.

The thumb of *A. afarensis* is relatively short compared to *H. sapiens* but relatively long compared to the thumb of modern apes (Bush, 1980). The hand possessed an opposable thumb (it could touch the remaining digits), allowing the finer manipulative movements required for holding and grasping small objects. Early australopithecines did not have the hand morphology to make tools, but may have been able to throw stones and utilize their hands in novel ways (Marzke, 1997).

Forelimb proportions of *A. afarensis* and *A. africanus* are similar to those of modern humans, but the hind limbs are relatively much shorter. The relative and absolute elongation of the hind limbs represents a major evolutionary change in later human evolution. Lucy's bodily proportions are compatible with bipedalism, but some argue that functional equivalence with the bipedalism of modern humans seems improbable (Jungers, 1982). Lucy's relatively short hind limbs imply differences in her bipedal gait from the modern condition. The relative elongation of the hind limb in later humans permitted an increase in the velocity of gait at only a slight increase in energy cost because increased speed could be achieved by increased stride length rather than by increases in step frequency. Selection to reduce the energy costs of bipedalism would favor elongation of the hind limb, especially in a foraging form having to cover long distances diurnally in the heat of the day.

Early hominids were clearly bipedal. Whether they were as efficient or consistent in their bipedal locomotor behavior as modern humans is being debated (Abitol, 1987). The major changes that occurred in early hominid postcranial anatomies occurred in the lower limbs. Some traits in the upper limbs, the thumb, the shoulder girdle, and the length of the forelimbs may indicate a more arboreal mode of life than is common to modern humans. It should also be realized that even consistent bipeds like modern humans can and do spend time in the trees on occasion. It has also been suggested that the shoulder girdles of *A. afarensis* and *A. africanus* show evidence of suspensory/climbing adaptations.

Australopithecine morphology has thus led to disagreement over the extent of bipedalism among early hominids. Some of the confusion may be based on use of the terms "apelike" and "humanlike"; no single bone is completely either, and it should be remembered that modern apes have also diverged from the form of the common ancestor. Australopithecine forelimbs retain more ancestral or plesiomorphic traits than the hindlimbs. Perhaps some species were more arboreal than *Homo*. Furthermore, the adoption of bipedalism may have led to a relatively rapid reorganization of the hind limbs but to slower changes in the forelimbs, resulting in the retention of primitive features. In other words, the evolution of the early hominid postcranial structures may have evolved in a mosaic manner.

Sexual Dimorphism

It was noted earlier that whereas some scholars attributed variability in the Hadar sample to sexual dimorphism, others thought perhaps more than one species was represented. This is an important consideration, as *Homo sapiens* has a very small degree of sexual dimorphism as compared to the greater dimorphism exhibited by the great apes and many other primates. Sexual dimorphism carries social and behavioral implications for many species. Without a large sample of fossils, it is often difficult to distinguish male/female differences from species differences.

Johanson and White (1979) indicated that *A. afarensis* exhibited a good deal of sexual dimorphism (see also McHenry, 1991a, 1991b). Stern and Susman (1983) noted sexually dimorphic differences in the postcranial bones of *A. afarensis*, especially differences in the lower limbs and pelvis. Leonard and Hegmon (1987) found sexually dimorphic differences in the *A. afarensis* lower first premolar. Such sexually dimorphic differences might signal sexual differences in habitat exploitation, with females being more arboreal.

If females were more arboreal, there may have been selection for smaller body sizes and limb proportions suited to a partially arboreal existence. Among the supposed advantages accruing to the arboreal females would be access to a higher quality of food and greater protection of a female's dependent young against predators. (One of us, FEP, noted in a study of South Indian monkeys, Nilgiri langurs, that mothers with young infants usually left the youngsters in the trees when females went to the ground to collect food.) Selective pressures on the more terrestrial males would favor larger body sizes and increased molarization of the teeth as an adaptation to more low-quality terrestrial food in the diet.

A model of sexual differentiation in habitat exploitation does not negate the argument for bipedalism among female members of *A. afarensis*; they were certainly at least facultative bipeds. Rather, it suggests that there was not a complete overlap in habitat use by both sexes. The orangutan of Borneo may be a good analogy of sexual differentiation of habitat use. Male orangutans tend to exploit the ground and lower levels of the canopy more fully than do the females. Although the orangutan may be a useful analogy, the large degree of body size dimorphism among orangutans is not seen in *A. afarensis*.

Three field seasons at Hadar since 1990 have yielded fifty-three new hominid specimens, including the first relatively complete adult skull (A.L. 444–2) (Kimbel et al., 1994). These may bear on the question of sexual dimorphism. The skull has a heavy brow, jutting jaw, and small braincase—and has been attributed to a male. Kimbel and his colleagues are of the opinion that the new skull and other material provide proof that *A. afarensis* was a single but highly dimorphic species.

Could Lucy have been a male? It has long been argued that Lucy's pelvic structure looked more like that of modern males than modern females. The explanation is often given that because of the pelvic structure, Lucy and her kind were able to give birth only to small-brained infants. However, for some the thought has lingered that if the pelvis resembled that of a male, perhaps Lucy was not a female (as the name implies) but was instead a male. Hausler and Schmid (1995) argue that Lucy was a male because its pelvis was too narrow to accommodate an australopithecine birth. Wood and Quinney (1996) countered, and still relegate Lucy to a female status.

Recent research on the configuration of the zygomatic arch (the cheekbone) suggests that some other early fossil hominids were missexed. "Mrs. Ples" (STS 5) of Sterkfontein may be a male skull. Utilizing the shape of the zygomatic, Loth et al. (1995) assessed a number of fossil crania. They contend that in male primates the zygomatic typically rises sharply near the ear and juts back into the skull, creating a trapezoidal shape. In females the arch curves gently into the skull, making a more triangular shape. On a similar basis, the flexure of the mandibular ramus on the Taung child seems to indicate that he was a boy. If these diagnostic tools prove consistent, there will be a new means of sexing fossil hominids independently of size (which is somewhat inconsistent) and of pelvic materials (which are rarely recovered).

EARLY HOMINID PALEOECOLOGY

The early discovery of the Taung hominid at the margin of the Kalahari desert not only focused the search for human origins in Africa, but also spawned an ecological perception of the cause of hominid origins. Dart noted that the treeless plain of Taung was far from the central African forests that provide a habitat for the closely related apes of today. He postulated what has since become known as the savanna hypothesis. Wrote Dart (1926:317):

> It is obvious, *prima facie*, that the Australopithecoid group which forced this barrier into the remote Southland had evolved an intelligence (to find and subsist upon new types of food and to avoid the dangerous enemies of the open plain) as well as a bodily structure (for sudden and swift bipedal movement, to elude capture) far in advance of that of the slothful, semi-arboreal, quadrupedal anthropoids.

Later finds, particularly those at Olduvai Gorge, seemed to confirm that the environmental impetus for bipedality was an adaptation to the growing savannas of Africa as the former forest home of the anthropoids shrank to mere remnants.

It is true that Africa was a changing continent during the Pliocene. Global temperatures were dropping, beginning at about 3.2 mya. The tectonic uplift of the African continent further contributed to the cooling and drying trends (Partridge et al., 1995). Forests gradually shrank, and the savanna grasslands and open woodlands expanded (Cerling, 1992). Hominids, like other animals, had to adapt.

Bipedalism, however, is far from the "swift" form of locomotion envisioned by Dart. It would have been quite dangerous on the savanna with a host of carnivores and scavengers—many more than characterize the African landscape today. It has been suggested that standing up gave *Australopithecus* the ability to see over the tall grass of the savanna (Robinson, 1972)—but such a stance would have made the early bipeds more visible to predators.

It has been suggested that the erect posture of *Australopithecus* was important for maintaining a cooler body temperature (Wheeler 1991, 1993). When the sun strikes an animal's body at an angle, it generates less heat than when it bears down directly onto the surface, such as onto the back of a quadruped. Furthermore, the body is raised above the ground for greater dissipation of heat. But such thermoregulatory advantages are not seen as the primary selective value of bipedalism, and further changes in body proportions that favor heat dissipation only come with the evolution of the genus *Homo*.

Recent paleoecological reassessments of early hominid fossil sites are now providing us with a different picture of the *Australopithecus* habitat. It appears that forests, particularly along lakes and streams, may have been the preferred environments for *Australopithecus*. Not surprisingly (Poirier, 1993), this view has led to a serious questioning of the "savanna hypothesis."

Dart had been correct about the paleoenvironment of Taung, but for the wrong reason. He had assumed that Africa's ecological characteristics had not changed much since the time of the australopithecines. We now know that the continent went through numerous climatic and ecological cycles; even Taung had at one time in the past 100,000 years been quite wet and lush (Klein et al., 1991). But recent work at Taung demonstrates that it was probably a savanna environment when *A. africanus* lived there in the Pliocene (Denys, 1992; McKee, 1998).

The site of Laetoli may have also been quite an open habitat for *A. afarensis*, but paleoecological reconstructions vary (Reed, 1997). Taung and possibly Laetoli appear to be the exceptions among early hominid fossil sites. Most sites have yielded fossil fauna that imply a much more lush environment—leaf-grazing bovids, leaf-eating monkeys, and a high biodiversity of primates and other mammals.

At Hadar, Maka, and Bahr el Ghazal, *A. afarensis* must have lived in closed woodland or forested environments (White et al., 1993; Brunet et al., 1995; Reed, 1997). *A. africanus* lived in a subtropical forest at Makapansgat and a woodland at Sterkfontein (McKee, 1991; Rayner et al., 1993; Reed, 1997). *A. anamensis* was found in former riparian forest (i.e., a forest along a river or lake margin) (Leakey et al., 1995). Should *Ardipithecus ramidus* prove to be bipedal, then the wooded environment of Aramis, some 4.4 mya, is consistent with an early hominid adaptation to life among the trees—not in the open savanna.

One other point contributes to the case against the savanna hypothesis. We now have fossils of confirmed bipeds back to as early as 4.2 mya. Although savannas existed at the time, forests still covered much of Africa. The early hominids were not forced out of the trees, as some have suggested. The greatest expansion of savanna environments postdated the origin of bipedalism, and was a slow process. Kingston et al. (1994:958) note that "while the course of human evolution was surely affected by environmental change . . . interpretations of the origin of hominids in East Africa . . . should be considered within the context of a heterogenous mosaic of environments rather than an abrupt replacement of rain forests by grassland and woodland biomes."

If it was not an adaptation for life on the savanna, what selective value did bipedalism hold for early hominids? Hunt (1994) noted the slowness and inefficiency of australopithecine bipedalism, and proposed that bipedalism was favored for feeding behavior—not for locomotion alone. Bipedalism allows for terrestrial feeding on the small fruits on trees, picked by hand from parts of trees that are above the range regularly utilized by other animals. In other words, early hominids adapted to an open niche by standing up.

The presence of hominids at the Pliocene savanna sites of Taung and Laetoli supports the notion that bipedality arose as part of a niche expansion. Bipedalism, for whatever reason, was suited for life on the savanna as well. All we can really conclude is that the australopithecines were not adapted to a specific environment, but were *adaptable*. Such adaptability was a key feature of hominid evolution, eventually allowing the descendants of *Australopithecus* to spread throughout Africa and beyond.

LIFEWAYS

Several inferences about early hominid lifeways can be made with the evidence currently available. We are, of course, on safest grounds when talking about fossilized relics of behavior, for example, tools. But we can also make statements about dietary patterns and social organization.

Did Early Hominids Have Tools?

There is no evidence from the fossil record that the earliest hominids made or used stone tools. The first stone tools documented in the archaeological record appear about 2.4 mya, perhaps 2 or 3 million years after the first appearance of hominids. One might suspect that the australopithecines used some kind of tools. Even chimpanzees use rudimentary tools (Chapter 4); the most common tool of modern foragers is the digging stick—a tool that would not usually be preserved. Darwin (1871) was the first to suggest that freeing of the hands for tool use may have been a selective advantage of our upright stance. To what degree *Australopithecus* made or used tools must remain an open question.

Dart's Osteodontokeratic Culture

Raymond Dart made a painstaking analysis of several thousand bone fragments from Makapansgat, South Africa, and concluded they were used and left in the cave by *Australopithecus* (Dart 1955, 1956, 1957, 1971). Certain animal bones predominated in the deposits, whereas other body parts were not represented at all—suggesting to Dart that particular animal bones were intentionally brought into the cave for specific purposes. For example, mandibles were most common, leading Dart to suggest that the teeth were utilized as scrapers, saws, or "slashing" tools. Broken bones, many with jagged edges and sharp points, could have been daggers or knives. The bone cores of bovid horns were also commonly preserved—the horns were seen by Dart as pounding, digging, or jabbing tools, or even weapons wielded in the hands of *Australopithecus*. Virtually every bone in the Makapansgat deposit was postulated to have had a function, from scapular blades to cranial bowls.

Dart thus envisioned *Australopithecus* as a successful hunter, making tools from the remains of its prey. He named the tool technology the **osteodontokeratic culture**, literally the bone-tooth-horn culture. With his characteristic flare for vivid description, Dart (1953:209) wrote:

On this thesis man's predecessors differed from living apes in being confirmed
killers: carnivorous creatures, that seized living quarries by violence, battered them
to death, tore apart their broken bodies, dismembered them limb from limb, slak-
ing their ravenous thirst with the hot blood of victims and greedily devouring livid
writhing flesh.

Even some of the *Australopithecus* bones, particularly a broken juvenile mandible,
were seen to be the product of a "killer ape" that sometimes turned its predatory
habits on its own kind.

Brain (1967a, 1967b, 1968, 1981) offered an alternative explanation, based
on taphonomic observations of carnivore behavior. Brain raised serious questions
about Dart's osteodontokeratic culture because Dart maintained that early
humans selectively collected particular skeletal parts for tools, as evidenced by the
cave deposits. Brain argued that the South African cave sites were not actual
human occupations but that the bone accumulations reflect passive collections by
natural agents. Hyenas and porcupines have been suggested as the possible bone
collectors in the caves, as they are today. Brain's (1968, 1970) studies of hyena
scavenging of carnivore kills note that only minor portions of bone remained
after intensive scavenging; the most common remains are the same as those in
the Makapansgat cave deposits.

Leopards also seem to have played some role in the South African bone accumulations. Brain (1981) concluded that australopithecine cave deposits are mostly
the remnants of animal deposits. Leopards carry their prey into trees to avoid scavenging and to consume their food at leisure. Trees in the high veld of South Africa
today are frequently found near cave openings, suggesting that some leopard
remains may have fallen into the cave site. Leopards also occasionally use the caves
themselves to store their prey. In fact, Brain (1974) has shown that the two punc-
ture marks on the occipital bone of a partial *Australopithecus robustus* skull at
Swartkrans (Chapter 9, Figure 9-2) match the lower canines of a fossil leopard.

Brain (1981) concluded that early hominids were not the hunters but the
hunted. It is now known that from the earliest possible hominids from Aramis to
later remains at Taung, our earliest ancestors were at the mercy of a host of carnivorous animals. The osteodontokeratic culture has thus been dismissed. This is
not to say that *Australopithecus* never used bone tools—indeed, there are still unexplained remains at Makapansgat such as small bones thrust inside larger bones as
if used as reamers for marrow—but there is no evidence that early hominids were
regular toolmakers or that they were ever efficient predators.

Diet

Craniodental morphology and tooth wear among australopithecines suggest that
they were primarily vegetarians. Ryan (1981), who completed a microscopic study
of the teeth of *A. afarensis*, suggested that *A. afarensis* was probably a vegetarian
that used its teeth to strip tough outer portions off plant stems to eat the softer
interiors. Ryan and Johanson (1989) suggested that the wear on the incisor teeth

of *A. afarensis* is most similar to that seen in *Gorilla* and that the incisors were used to strip leaves and to chew hard foods such as roots, seeds, and rhizomes. The canine/premolar tooth complex was used to puncture-crush food and for shearing/slicing as in modern apes or such monkeys as baboons. Grine (1981) used scanning electron microscopy to look at the microwear on *A. africanus* deciduous dentition. He found on the tooth surfaces the characteristic polish and fine scratches associated with shearing vegetation. The enlarged molars and thickened enamel were probably adaptations to a vegetarian diet; evidence for scavenging and hunting of meat only comes later in the hominid fossil record.

SUMMARY

Since 1924, hundreds of early hominid fossils have been discovered and excavated from Pliocene deposits in Africa. These establish Africa as the continent of human origins, as predicted by Darwin. The key feature implicating these early species as human ancestors is their bipedal locomotion. The earliest hominid fossils come from East Africa. Fossils from 4.4 mya, known as *Ardipithecus ramidus*, may represent the earliest known fossils of a biped, and 5.5–5.0-mya fossils from Lothagam and Tabarin may have hominid affinities. The australopithecines were all confirmed bipeds. *Australopithecus anamensis*, from 4.2 to 3.9 mya, is the earliest of the named species, found in Kenya. It retains a number of hominoid craniodental features. *A. afarensis* was its likely descendant, also known from East Africa as well as Chad. It shows a number of advances in morphology, including a slight increase in cranial capacity and EQ over other hominoids. *A. africanus* appears later in the fossil record of South Africa, found at sites tentatively dated between 3.2 and 2.5 mya.

The australopithecines were primarily vegetarians, living in both forest and savanna environments. They neither manufactured nor possessed any known stone tools. Their morphology suggests that whereas they walked bipedally, they were quite capable of climbing and exploiting trees for food and shelter.

SUGGESTED READINGS

Behrensmeyer, A. K., N. E. Todd, R. Potts, and G. E. McBrinn. 1997. Late Pliocene faunal turnover in the Turkana Basin, Kenya and Ethiopia. *Science* 278:1589–1594.

Brain, C. K. 1981. *The Hunters or the Hunted? An Introduction to African Cave Taphonomy.* Chicago: University of Chicago Press.

Brunet, M., A. Beauvilain, Y. Coppens, E. Heintz, A. H. E. Moutaye, and D. Pilbeam. 1995. The first australopithecine 2,500 kilometers west of the Rift Valley (Chad). *Nature* 378:273–274.

Hill, A., and S. Ward. 1988. Origin of the Hominidae. *Yearbook of Physical Anthropology* 31:49–84.

Hunt, K. D. 1994. The evolution of human bipedality: Ecology and functional morphology. *Journal of Human Evolution* 26:183–202.

Johanson, D., and B. Edgar. 1996. *From Lucy to Language.* New York: Simon & Schuster.

Kimbel, W. H., D. C. Johanson, and Y. Rak. 1994. The first skull and other new discoveries of *Australopithecus afarensis* at Hadar, Ethiopia. *Nature* 368:449–451.

Leakey, M. G., C. S. Feibel, I. McDougall, and A. Walker. 1995. New four-million-year-old hominid species from Kanapoi and Allia Bay, Kenya. *Nature* 376:585–571.

McHenry, H. M. 1994. Tempo and mode in human evolution. *Proceedings of the National Academy of Sciences* 91:6780–6786.

Reed, K. E. 1997. Early hominid evolution and ecological change through the African Plio-Pleistocene. *Journal of Human Evolution* 32:289–322.

White, T. D., G. Suwa, and B. Asfaw. 1994. *Australopithecus ramidus*, a new species of early hominid from Aramis, Ethiopia. *Nature* 371:306–312.

9

The Hominid Divergence

At least two hominid lineages diverged from the early australopithecines of Africa: the "robust" australopithecines and the earliest members of our own genus, Homo. *The robust lineage specialized in the evolution of the masticatory system, acquiring a robust facial architecture and large molars and premolars, presumably for grinding vegetation. Species of this lineage comprise* Australopithecus robustus *of South Africa, and* A. boisei *(and possibly* A. aethiopicus) *of East Africa. The evolutionary beginnings of the genus* Homo *initiated the trends of cranial expansion and facial reduction.* Homo habilis *and possibly* H. rudolfensis *are the earliest representatives of this lineage, first appearing at about 2.4 mya in East Africa.* H. habilis *has also been found in South Africa, thus being the first hominid species recognized over such a wide geographic expanse. At 2.5 mya the first stone tools of the archaeological record are found in East Africa. The tools were simple cores and flakes known as the Oldowan industry, and are generally thought to have been made by* Homo. *Early* Homo *may have used the tools in scavenging meat and processing plant foods. The hominid divergence took place during a time of significant changes in the climate and environmental composition of faunal and floral communities.*

HISTORICAL PERSPECTIVE

Robert Broom, who had confirmed Dart's analysis of the Taung child with discoveries of adult australopithecines at Sterkfontein, South Africa, happened upon a different type of early hominid at a nearby cave site. The first hominid fossils from Kromdraai, just a short walk from Sterkfontein, were found by a young schoolboy in 1938. Broom (1938) noted the particularly robust nature of the maxilla and mandible—strong, thick bones to support large molar teeth. Broom named a new genus and species, *Paranthropus robustus* to accommodate this material. In the following years, further fossils came from Swartkrans (across the valley from Sterkfontein), confirming the remarkable facial architecture of these early hominids. The Kromdraai and Swartkrans fossils were similar in many respects to *Australopithecus africanus*, in being relatively small-brained bipeds, and thus are often referred to the same genus. *Australopithecus (= Paranthropus) robustus* was a lineage of facially robust australopithecines that eventually became extinct.

In 1949, Broom and John Robinson discovered a somewhat different type of hominid at Swartkrans. It was much more similar to modern humans in many respects. Although the fossils were originally given a new genus name, *Telanthropus*, we now recognize them as early members of the genus *Homo*. The significance of Swartkrans was that it was the first fossil site to reveal the apparent coexistence of two types of hominids.

East Africa eventually revealed a similar dichotomy of hominids. Through the dedicated efforts of the Leakeys, Olduvai Gorge, Tanzania, has unfolded some of its vast secrets to the scientific world. (For an insightful look at the Leakeys and their work, see Cole, 1975.) The well-stratified gorge, part of the Rift Valley system, stretches about 25 miles across the Serengeti Plain. It originated from river action cutting through sedimentary layers, some of which contain chronometrically datable volcanic lavas from a nearby crater.

The Leakeys began work at Olduvai in the early 1930s, a full generation after the gorge was discovered. During early excavations, tool and bone concentrations were uncovered, but there were no significant human fossil remains. The first important early human discovery from Olduvai came in July 1959, when Mary Leakey noticed a part of a skull and two very large premolar teeth. It took nineteen days to free the teeth and parts of the fossilized palate from their interment. Olduvai has since yielded a number of significant fossils and cultural remains of early humans.

The 1959 cranium from Olduvai was not merely a robust-faced hominid, but hyperrobust with inflated molar teeth. Originally given the name *Zinjanthropus boisei*, its general similarities to the South African robust australopithecines eventually led to a generic referral of *Australopithecus* or *Paranthropus*. (In this text we opt to include the robust forms in the genus *Australopithecus*, since the generic distinction of the robust australopithecines remains a point of discussion.) This hyperrobust australopithecine (of extremely large facial and dental proportions) was found in deposits that harbored primitive stone tools. The Leakeys doubted that the small-brained, robust-faced *A. boisei* species could have made stone tools, despite the temporal association of stone tools with robust hominid fossils. Their predilections were justified to much of the scientific world with the discovery of yet another hominid species in the same deposits: *Homo habilis* (L. Leakey et al., 1964).

Homo habilis, with a more gracile face and larger cranial capacity, was deemed to be the likely toolmaker. Its scientific name means "handy man." Its acceptance as a species, as is often the case, took time. Some saw the fossils as representing a late *Australopithecus*; others saw it as early *Homo erectus*. Further discoveries from the Rift Valley and South African caves confirmed the existence of this "transitional" species; indeed, there may be more than one species represented.

The fossil evidence clearly shows the existence of two main types of hominids from the late Pliocene (2.5 to 1.75 mya), early *Homo* and a robust australopithecine. Variability within those types has led to a continuing debate as to the number of species represented by the fossils. We term this increase in variability the *hominid divergence*. The appearance of these hominid types was accompanied by significant climatic changes on the African continent and the first appearance of primitive stone tools, about 2.5 mya, making the origin of our genus *Homo* an intriguing and perplexing time period to study.

GEOGRAPHICAL AND TEMPORAL RANGE OF LATE PLIOCENE HOMINIDS

The robust australopithecines first appear in the East African fossil record at about 2.5 mya (Figure 9-1). The earliest forms, from west of Lake Turkana, Kenya, as well as from the Omo basin, Ethiopia, are sometimes referred to *Australopithecus aethiopicus*. These include the remarkable cranial remains known as the "Black Skull" (WT 17000). The latest fossil of this possible species comes from East Turkana, at about 1.8 mya.

The remaining hyperrobust fossils, *A. boisei*, come primarily from the Turkana region, starting at about 2.3 mya, as well as from Olduvai Gorge, Bed I (approximately 1.8 mya) in Tanzania. The latest occurrences are at Chesowanja, Kenya, a poorly dated site on the order of 1.4 mya, and Konso, Ethiopia. The *A. boisei* skull from Konso, securely dated to just over 1.4 mya, is the most northerly occurrence of the species.

Either the two species, *A. boisei* and *A. aethiopicus*, coexisted for half a million years, or there was one variable species, *A. boisei*, which lived in East Africa for more than a full million years.

The South African fossils of *A. robustus* first appear later in time at Kromdraai, relatively dated on the basis of the cave fauna to about 2 mya. *A. robustus* is known from geological Members 1, 2, and 3 at Swartkrans, covering a period roughly dating between 1.8 and 1.4 mya. Recent discoveries of robust australopithecine remains, at the nearby South African cave sites of Drimolen and Gondolin (Kuykendall, personal communication), have yet to be dated but do not extend the limited geographic range known so far. Drimolen has a large hominid sample, including some remarkable infant fossils.

Homo habilis, even in its strictest sense, is the earliest hominid species known from both South Africa and East Africa. The earliest possible member of the

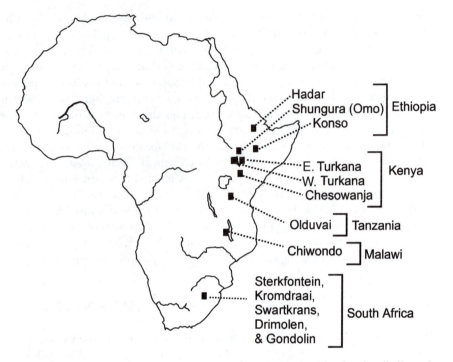

FIGURE 9-1   Map of the early *Homo* and robust australopithecine fossil sites of Africa. See Table 9-1 for further details. (Courtesy Jeffrey K. McKee.)

species comes from late deposits at Hadar in the Afar depression of Ethiopia, dating to 2.4 mya (Kimbel et al., 1996). In the Chiwondo beds of Malawi, part of the "hominid corridor" between East and South Africa, comes an early *Homo* fossil mandible that may represent a distinct species: *Homo rudolfensis* (Schrenck et al., 1993). On the basis of faunal dating, the Malawi fossil may be as old as 2.4 mya. Additional sites and dates are listed in Table 9-1, with Olduvai Gorge Bed II yielding the most recent *H. habilis* fossils at 1.65 mya.

In South Africa, *H. habilis* has been identified from Sterkfontein Member 5. This cave deposit (formerly known as the Sterkfontein Extension site) is geologically complex and may represent a mix of time periods. A tentative estimate places it around 2.2 mya. Swartkrans Member 1 also yielded a fossil considered by some to be *H. habilis* (as discussed in the next section), dating to about 1.8 mya.

The dating problems and taxonomic considerations render some confusion in the picture of the emergence of our genus, *Homo*. What is clear is that early *Homo* ranges from 2.4 to 1.65 mya, overlapping in time and space with the robust australopithecines of East Africa (2.5–1.4 mya) and South Africa (2.0–1.4 mya).

The fossil sites during this time period are often characterized by primitive stone tools, known as the **Oldowan** industry. Oldowan artifacts first appear at Gona, Ethiopia, at about 2.5 mya (Semaw et al., 1997). Although it is interesting that stone tools appear before the earliest known fossils of the genus *Homo*, this

TABLE 9-1 Key Early Hominid Sites of the African Late Pliocene and Early Pleistocene

Location	Species	Maximum Age (million years)
East Africa		
Ethiopia		
Hadar Makaamitalu	*Homo* cf. *habilis*	2.4
Konso	*Australopithecus boisei*	1.4
Shungura C	*Australopithecus aethiopicus*	2.6
Shungura E,G	*Australopithecus boisei*	2.4
Kenya		
West Turkana Upper Lomeki	*Australopithecus aethiopicus*	2.6
East Turkana Upper Burgi	*Australopithecus aethiopicus* *Homo rudolfensis* *Homo erectus*	1.9
East Turkana KBS Tuff	*Australopithecus boisei* *Homo erectus*	1.9
East Turkana Okote	*Australopithecus boisei*	1.6
Chesowanja	*Australopithecus boisei*	1.4
Tanzania		
Olduvai Gorge Bed I	*Australopithecus boisei* *Homo habilis*	1.8
Olduvai Gorge Bed II	*Homo habilis* *Homo erectus*	1.7
Malawi		
Chiwondo Beds	*Homo* cf. *rudolfensis*	2.4
South Africa		
Sterkfontein Member 5	*Homo habilis*	2.2 (?)
Kromdraai B	*Australopithecus robustus*	2.0 (?)
Swartkrans Member 1	*Australopithecus robustus* *Homo habilis* (?)	1.8 (?)
Swartkrans Member 2	*Australopithecus robustus* *Homo erectus*	1.6 (?)
Swartkrans Member 3	*Australopithecus robustus*	1.4 (?)

fact may be a product of the incompleteness of the fossil record. This stone tool technology persisted throughout Africa for over a million years before any significant advances appeared, and persisted in some regions of Africa until 600,000 years ago (Clark et al., 1984).

THE FOSSIL EVIDENCE

The definitive species characteristics of early *Homo* and the robust australopithecines are largely dependent on craniodental features. It is important to note that all of these early hominids were clearly bipedal. Furthermore, although there were postcranial differences among these lineages, the term "robust" applies specifically to the facial architecture and not to the body as a whole.

The Robust Australopithecines

Australopithecus (= *Paranthropus*) *robustus* was the first robust australopithecine species to be recognized. This South African species was defined by Broom (1938) in terms of its robust facial bones and robust mandible. This robusticity of the bones associated with mastication was able to withstand heavy chewing forces. A final buttress to absorb the masticatory forces formed above the eye orbits—the supraorbital torus (Figure 9-2).

A powerful temporalis muscle, one of the muscles that close the jaw, spread across the parietal region of the skull to the center, resulting in the development of a sagittal crest. The flaring zygomatic arches allowed the large temporalis muscle to pass to the mandibular ramus, and were strongly built to support the masseter, the other main muscle closing the jaw.

Along with the strong masticatory muscles, the focus of the *A. robustus* dentition was on the grinding teeth—the premolars and molars. These teeth were expanded buccolingually (side to side toward the cheek and tongue) to provide large, flat chewing surfaces, and they had thickened enamel. The anterior teeth, the incisors and canines, were reduced in size; the selective advantage of this reduction would have been for the space left in the dental arcade for the massive posterior grinding teeth.

A. robustus had an average cranial capacity of about 530 cc. As their body sizes were not significantly expanded over that of *A. africanus*, their encephalization quotient (EQ) was 2.9 (an increase from the *A. africanus* EQ of 2.5) (McHenry, 1994). Nevertheless, this cranial expansion did not characterize all robust species, and in no case did it match the relative cranial expansion of early *Homo* (with an EQ of 3.1).

Australopithecus boisei, of East Africa, accentuated the features of *A. robustus*. Their faces were "hyperrobust" (Figure 9-2). Not only did they have a strong sagit-

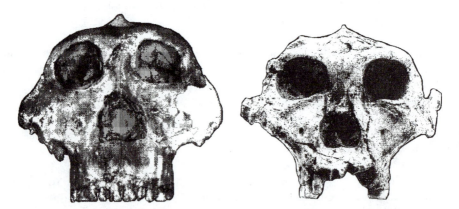

FIGURE 9-2 Frontal views of *Australopithecus boisei* (OH 5 from Olduvai Gorge, Tanzania, *left*) and *Australopithecus robustus* (SK 48 from Swartkrans, South Africa, *right*). (Courtesy Jeffrey K. McKee.)

tal crest for the attachment of the temporalis muscles, but they also had a pronounced nuchal crest on the posterior (occipital) aspect of the skull. The nuchal crest provided attachment for the neck muscles that hold up the head; their faces had become so large and heavy that it probably took strong neck muscles to counterbalance the weight.

The entire face was oriented toward powerful mastication. The supraorbital torus of the fossil skulls overshadows the front of the braincase, leaving no forehead. The zygomatic arches are widely flared and robust; coupled with considerable postorbital constriction of the cranium, there was a substantial area for a large temporalis muscle. A strong maxilla and a thick, deep mandibular body support "molarized" premolars and massive grinding molars.

There was little focus on brain evolution during the long existence of *A. boisei.* The cranial capacities of these animals averaged about 410 cc, leaving them with an EQ of only 2.6 (McHenry, 1994).

It has been argued (e.g., Kimbel et al., 1988; Wood, 1988) that there is more than one species of hyperrobust australopithecine in East Africa. Some fossils are referred to *A. aethiopicus,* as best represented by the "Black Skull" (Walker et al., 1986), a manganese-stained cranium from west of Lake Turkana. The Black Skull (WT 17000) is one of the earliest representatives of the robust species, and retains many characteristics reminiscent of *A. afarensis,* most notably the significant prognathism and features of the cranial base. However, the recent discovery of an *A. boisei* skull at Konso, from deposits dating to over a million years later than the black skull, revealed an individual with a combination of *A. boisei* and *A. aethiopicus* (as well as *A. robustus!*) features (Suwa et al., 1997). The combination of traits in one skull suggests that the taxonomic splitting of the East African sample may not be warranted.

Early *Homo*

Homo habilis, in its broadest sense, initiated two important trends that characterized the evolution of our genus: increased cranial size and complexity, and facial reduction. Its facial construction contrasts markedly with the robust australopithecines, becoming more gracile—even more so than the so-called gracile australopithecines. *H. habilis* maintained large incisors but had reduced canines and premolars. The molars were variable in size, but particularly the third molar was reduced. The masticatory system weakened from the muscularity of the australopithecines, and in association with this trend the supraorbital torus became less prominent. The face became more **orthognathic** (a flat, vertical face), but maintained more alveolar prognathism than modern humans (i.e., the portion of the mandible and maxilla housing the teeth protruded) (Figures 9-3, 9-4).

The frontal expansion of the brain was marked by the beginning of a forehead. The cranial capacity averaged 610 cc, but given the diminutive body size, *H. habilis sensu lato* (in the inclusive sense of the species name) had an EQ of 3.1 (McHenry, 1994). Not only was there a significant increase in relative brain size, but the endocranial remains also reveal an increased complexity of the brain.

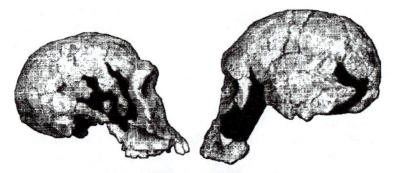

FIGURE 9-3 Fossil crania of early *Homo*, KNM-ER 1813 (*left*), and KNM-ER 1470 (*right*), both from Koobi Fora, Kenya. These may be considered to be variants of the same species, *Homo habilis*, but some researchers refer KNM-ER 1470 to *Homo rudolfensis*. (Courtesy Jeffrey K. McKee.)

According to Tobias (1987, 1991), *H. habilis* had developed enlargements of both Broca's area (the speech center) and Wernicke's area (the association area), suggesting the neural capacity for language (see Chapter 7). Furthermore, there was greater asymmetry of the brain, implying a greater degree of lateralization in brain function (as in modern humans).

The postcranial anatomy of *H. habilis* maintained some primitive features: although the hands were adapted for gripping, the phalanges were still curved. The limb proportions were remarkably apelike, despite the clear orthograde stance and bipedal locomotion (Johanson et al., 1987). However, the hallux (big toe) of the foot was adducted (i.e., not divergent as in some early australopithecines and nonhuman primates).

Some *"Homo habilis"* individuals were larger, with comparatively more robust facial features. A number of scholars refer these fossils (from east of Lake Turkana, 1.9–1.8 mya, and Chiwondo beds in Malawi, approximately 2.4 mya) to

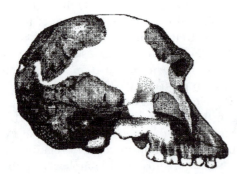

FIGURE 9-4 Reconstruction of a *Homo habilis* cranium, STW 53 from Sterkfontein Member 5, South Africa. (Courtesy Jeffrey K. McKee.)

a separate taxon, *Homo rudolfensis* (Wood, 1992). *H. rudolfensis* fossils are characterized by the plesiomorphic traits of a large palate, a more robust mandible, and larger premolars and molars. They also exhibit some apomorphies, including a more orthognathic face, no supraorbital torus, and a more *Homo*-like femur. Their cranial capacity averaged 751, but the EQ was only 3.0 (compared to *H. habilis sensu stricto* of 3.5) (McHenry, 1994).

If *H. rudolfensis* proves to have been a separate species, then two similar forms would have coexisted in East Africa, perhaps for as much as half a million years. We shall return to this theme later in the paleoecology section.

EVOLUTIONARY TRENDS

Body Size

Body size estimates for early *Homo* and the robust australopithecines, listed in Table 9-2, show a degree of sexual dimorphism, particularly in *Homo habilis*. Size variation seen in both East and South African "robust" remains may indicate a degree of sexual dimorphism much beyond that typical of modern human populations. However, the variation is less than seen in modern gorillas and orangutans, the two largest living apes.

Because of the heavy mandibles and large teeth, it was often assumed that the robust australopithecines also had large body sizes. Until 1988 the sample of postcranial remains associated with this group was too limited to make conclusive decisions concerning overall body size and weight, other than to use projections based upon tooth and jaw size (as is often the basis for calculating the body sizes of early fossil primates). McHenry's (1991b) study of a partial skeleton attributed to the East African robust group, together with his work on a trebled sample of South African robust forms, has immensely clarified the situation.

McHenry's work shows that a large portion (35 percent) of the postcrania attributed to robust australopithecines from Swartkrans (Member 1) are from extraordinarily small-bodied individuals, perhaps weighing about 28 kg (62 pounds). A smaller percentage, 22 percent of the postcrania, are attributed to an individual

TABLE 9-2   Stature of Early Hominids

	Age (mya)	Female (cm)	Male (cm)	Average
Australopithecus afarensis	4.0–2.9	105	151	128
Australopithecus africanus	3.0–2.4	115	138	127
Australopithecus boisei	2.0–1.3	124	137	131
Australopithecus robustus	1.8–1.6	110	132	121
Homo habilis	2.0–1.8	125	157	141
African *Homo erectus*	1.7–0.7	160	180	170

From H. McHenry, Early hominid stature, *American Journal of Physical Anthropology*, 1991, 85:149–158.

weighing about 43 kg (95 pounds), and about 43 percent of the bones come from an individual less than or equal to about 54 kg (119 pounds). Postcrania from other Swartkrans members are similar in size to the 45-kg standard.

The partial skeleton of an East African robust form (KNM-ER 1500) has hind limb joints that would correspond to a modern human weighing as little as 34 kg (75 pounds). The largest estimated East African robust form weighed about 54 kg (119 pounds). McHenry's studies showed that robust australopithecines "ranged from quite small to only moderate in body size relative to modern humans. These were petite-bodied vegetarian cousins of our ancestors" (1991b: 445).

Postcranial Morphology

An almost complete foot skeleton (OH 8, Figure 9-5) was found in Bed I, Olduvai Gorge. The foot is small and shows a remarkable anatomical resemblance to the foot of *Homo*; there is no evidence of a divergence between the first and second toes, typical of the grasping foot of the ape. The Olduvai foot does show, however, differences from the foot skeleton of modern *Homo*. For example, the thick-

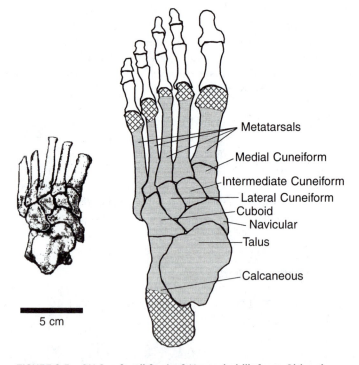

5 cm

FIGURE 9-5   OH 8, a fossil foot of *Homo habilis* from Olduvai Gorge, Tanzania (*left*). Compare the size and shape to a modern human foot on the right. (Shaded area are bones represented by the fossil specimen, with hatched areas showing the parts broken off of OH 8.) (Courtesy Jeffrey K. McKee.)

ening of the small metatarsal bone (Figure 9-5) of the middle toe led Day and Napier (1966) to conclude that the transmission of weight and propulsive effort through the forefoot was not as fully evolved as in modern *Homo*. Oxnard and Lisowski (1980) argued that the foot bones of OH 8 display features that resemble those found in the feet of arboreal creatures. They suggested that the OH 8 foot may have belonged to an animal capable of some type of bipedal walking, but it is also likely that the form placed its feet on the ground more in the manner of the chimpanzee and gorilla. They visualized a creature capable of both arboreal and terrestrial activities, and rejected the position that the foot is from a creature with strictly human bipedal locomotion. More recent analyses by Kidd et al. (1996), using a multivariate analysis of the OH 8 hind foot, indicate a mixture of traits supporting the notion of a combined arboreal and terrestrial form of locomotion. The apelike limb proportions of an *H. habilis* partial skeleton, OH 62, tend to confirm this position.

In 1986, fossil *H. habilis* bones were recovered at Olduvai Gorge, not far from the site (FLK NN) of the Leakeys' original *H. habilis* find (Johanson et al., 1987). These fossils, collectively known as OH 62, consist of teeth and bone fragments from the right arm, skull, and both legs, and date to 1.8 mya (Johanson et al., 1987; Wood, 1987). This is the first time that skull and limb bones possibly attributable to *H. habilis* were recovered from the same site—presumably representing a single female individual.

OH 62 provided an unexpected look at materials called *H. habilis*. Until the OH 62 find, *H. habilis* was considered to be taller and more modern looking in its postcranial skeleton, that is, more like its possible successor *H. erectus*. OH 62 came from an individual who was only 3.6 feet tall, approximately the same height as estimated for Lucy (*A. afarensis*). The long arms of OH 62 were particularly unexpected. The upper arms are 95 percent as long as the legs; they probably dangled to the knees. A comparable figure for the much older Lucy material, who also had long arms compared to her legs, is 85 percent. Among modern humans, the arms comprise 70 to 75 percent of the leg length.

The similarities in body size and arm length between OH 62 and *A. afarensis*, which predated OH 62 by more than 1 million years, suggest that little change occurred in the postcranial bones over a long period of time. The long arms of OH 62 also suggest that it spent time in the trees, despite its basically bipedal pattern, possibly for feeding, predator avoidance, and sleeping. Perhaps *Homo erectus* was the first fully terrestrial hominid.

Hartwig-Scherer and Martin (1991) argued that the postcranial skeleton of OH 62 shows closer affinities to African-ape limb proportions than does the postcranial morphology of Lucy. These authors find it difficult to accept an evolutionary sequence in which *H. habilis*, with its less humanlike postcranial skeleton, is intermediate between *A. afarensis*, with its more humanlike postcranial skeleton and bipedalism, and fully bipedal *H. erectus*. They concluded that OH 62 may be a different East African evolutionary line coexisting with the robust australopithecines and early *Homo*. Such a view adds some credence to an argument for a separate *Homo* species, *H. rudolfensis*, which has a more modern femur.

If OH 62 belongs in *H. habilis* as Johanson and his colleagues suggested, then its shared traits with *Australopithecus* present some interesting problems. The time span of East African *H. habilis* materials is 2.4 to 1.65 mya. Some of the earliest *H. erectus* (or *H. ergaster*) fossils in East Africa date to 1.8 mya, penecontemporaneous with OH 62. (This material is discussed more fully in the next chapter.) If OH 62 represents *H. habilis,* and if *H. habilis* was ancestral to *H. erectus* as many suggest, then the morphological change was completed in an exceptionally short period of time.

The hand bones of *H. habilis* and *A. robustus* provide further grist to the complexities of late Pliocene hominid evolution. Susman and Stern (1979) argued that the hand of OH 7 *(H. habilis)* from Olduvai had the functional capacity to allow suspensory locomotor behaviors. They suggested that "early hominids may have retained a capacity for climbing even past the point at which the foot became adapted for bipedalism" (p. 572). This suggestion is particularly interesting in light of Darwin's early insight: "But the hands and arms could hardly have become perfect enough to have manufactured weapons, or to have hurled stones and spears with a true aim, as long as they were habitually used for locomotion . . . or as long as they were especially well adapted . . . for climbing trees" (Darwin, 1871:141).

Napier (1959, 1962) concluded from a study of *H. habilis* OH 7 hand bones dating to 1.75 mya, from Bed I, Olduvai Gorge, that *H. habilis* was capable of a **power grip**, that is, the kind of grip used when wielding a hammer. It may have also been capable of some **precision grip**, the type of grip employed in holding small objects by opposing the thumb and second finger. Modern humans use this grip when writing. Napier demonstrated that the power grip alone is adequate for constructing not only stone tools called **pebble tools** but also even more advanced types of **handaxes**. The hand was anatomically suited for producing the tools found at early hominid sites, but it was not fully human.

Despite the fact that most have argued that the only early hominid maker and user of stone tools was *H. habilis,* there is the possibility that at least one member of the robust hominids, *A. robustus,* also made stone tools (Lewin, 1988; Shipman, 1986; Susman, 1988). The argument that *H. habilis* was the first stone-tool maker was based primarily on the fact that the earliest occurrence of stone tools in the archaeological record was close in time to the earliest appearance of the genus *Homo.* This is circumstantial evidence of a causal relationship. As noted earlier in this chapter, recent finds at Gona, Ethiopia, of stone tools at 2.5 mya predate the earliest known fossil *Homo,* but not *A. boisei,* leading some to question the temporal correlation of stone tools and *H. habilis* (Wood, 1997). On the other hand, there were thirty-four stone tools found in direct association with the earliest fossil of *Homo habilis* at Hadar (Kimbel et al., 1996). The morphological evidence is being debated as well.

Susman (1988) argued that finger bones attributed to *A. robustus* from Swartkrans, South Africa, indicated the ability to make stone tools. The fossil evidence consists of twenty-two hand bones dating to about 1.8 mya. Although both *A. robustus* and early *Homo* are found at the Swartkrans site, the context yielding the hand bones has mostly yielded *A. robustus* remains. Susman's argument for tool manufacture by *A. robustus* was based primarily on the width of its fingertips. Human fingertips are quite broad, in contrast to the narrow pattern found among apes and the earliest hominid species. The broad human fingertip, with a large pad of tissue richly supplied with blood vessels and sensory nerve endings, allows fine control in object manipulation. Susman argued that *A. robustus* had the broad fingertips characteristic of modern humans.

Marzke (1997) was more circumspect regarding primate hand functions in the precision grips that are essential to effective manipulation of stone tools. She proposed a suite of eight morphological features that distinguish human hands from those of nonhuman primates. *Australopithecus afarensis* (Chapter 8) had three of these features, but limitations of their hand morphology would not have permitted effective toolmaking. Early *Homo* hand fossils from Olduvai strongly suggested the capacity for tool manufacture. The single feature used in Susman's analysis of the Swartkrans fossils was seen by Marzke as insufficient evidence for inferring effective tool manufacture and use capabilities by *A. robustus*. Moreover, Trinkaus and Long (1990) suggested that the Swartkrans metacarpals are just as likely to be attributed to *Homo erectus* as to the robust australopithecines and that inferences concerning the manual dexterity and toolmaking behaviors of *A. robustus* are tentative.

LIFEWAYS

Tool Use and Manufacture

The advent of the manufacture and use of stone tools was clearly an important factor in the lifeways of early *Homo*, and perhaps the robust australopithecines. Early tools are difficult to recognize because they were stones, bones, or sticks picked up from the environment, used once or a few times, and discarded. Many of these earliest examples of tools are lost because materials such as wood or bone have decayed or are indistinguishable from surrounding rocks, bones, and fossilized wood. The earliest recognizable tools were made from stone.

There is evidence of a few wooden tools dated to 1.5 mya (Keeley & Toth, 1981). If further studies show that such tools are common at early sites, their manufacture as digging sticks and spears may eventually be inferred as part of the early human adaptive pattern.

The earliest known stone tools from Gona, Ethiopia, dating between 2.6 and 2.5 mya, are not associated with hominid fossil remains (Semaw et al., 1997). However, the earliest likely representative of *H. habilis*, from later Hadar deposits of 2.4 mya (Kimbel et al., 1997), are found in association with stone tools. Stone tools possibly as old as 2.4 mya have been recovered from the site of Senga 5A, located on the eastern bank of the Semliki River in eastern Congo (Harris et al., 1987). There are 435 stone artifacts of Oldowan character, 100 fragmentary fossilized faunal specimens, and 5 fragments of fossilized wood from Senga. There are no hominid skeletal remains.

There are variations in tool manufacturing techniques and in the raw materials used. Nevertheless, there are two basic tool categories: the core tool and the flake tool. To make a core tool, chips are knocked off a lump of stone until the lump (the core) is the desired size and shape. The **prepared core** of the stone that remains is the tool. A flake tool is a chip struck from a core. The size and shape of the flake may vary depending on the shape of the core from which it is taken. The flake may be used as is, or it may be further modified.

Most researchers have argued that for early toolmakers the core was the primary tool and that the associated flakes and fragments were largely waste material. Toth (1987) suggested, however, that too much emphasis has been put on cores at the expense of flakes. He proposed that the traditional relationship might be reversed: flakes may have been the primary tools, and the cores often the by-products of flake manufacture.

Toth also suggested that cores were likely transported from place to place and worked on a bit at a time. Early hominids may have carried partially flaked cores with them, perhaps in simple containers. The cores may have been chipped at resting places. Places of prolonged and frequent occupation would contain heavier concentrations of flaked material. Toth suggested that such a pattern appears at Koobi Fora, Kenya. The fact that early hominids seem to have transported tools or potential tools over long distances differentiates human and chimpanzee tool use (Chapter 4). The latter rarely transport objects farther than 100 meters.

The first recognized stone tools belong to the Oldowan tradition. The **chopper**, a tool typically found in Lower Pleistocene sites, is a smooth, rounded cobblestone or oblong block given a rough cutting edge by knocking flakes from both sides (bifacially flaked). Most of the earliest choppers found at Olduvai, where their earliest occurrence dates to 1.75 mya, are about the size of a tennis ball or slightly smaller. Some tools must have been held between the thumb, ring, and index finger and used to prepare pieces of plant or animal food. The Olduvai sites also contain possible bone tools.

Experimental data concerning the manufacture and use of the Olduvai bifaces were provided by Jones (1979). Quartzite bifaces are efficient tools because the tool edges remain sharp during use and can be easily resharpened by secondary flaking. Such bifaces are very useful in skinning and cutting meat. Although primary flake edges of basalt bifaces are easy to produce, they cannot be effectively resharpened.

The properties of the stones used to make the Oldowan bifaces at Olduvai vary, leading to differences in work capabilities and their apparent effectiveness as tools. The size, shape, and flaking properties of raw materials must be considered when assessing the tool manufacturer's technological sophistication. Some tools considered to be crude or primitive are, according to Jones's data, the products of sophisticated and efficient techniques of stone tool manufacture.

Four different types of artifact deposition at Lake Turkana, Kenya, were recognized by Isaac and Harris (1978):

A. Concentrations of artifacts with little or no associated bone.
B. Modest numbers of artifacts with bones from the carcass of a single large animal.
C. Artifact concentrations with conspicuous patches of broken bone from the carcasses of several animals of different species.
D. Artifacts dispersed with a very low density over ancient land surfaces or throughout sediment beds.

Isaac and Harris noted that the occurrences of type B denote cutting of carcasses by the toolmaker; thus these sites are called *butchery sites* and are treated as representatives of a camp or home base. Some type A sites may be camps where plant foods rather than meat constituted the principal food. Type A sites could, however, result from the decay of bone at type B and C sites.

Other Possible Cultural Remains

Other possible evidence of cultural remains has been recovered, but as with Dart's putative osteodontokeratic culture, the fossil record can be deceptive and appear to give evidence of culture where none exists. Volcanic dust, an excellent preservative, covers most "living floors" (places where objects remain in their original context) at Olduvai Gorge. Mary Leakey mapped the 2,400-square-foot living floor at the Olduvai Bed I site of FLK, which is dated to 1.8 mya. The map shows the exact location of more than 4,000 artifacts and fossils. Leakey (1967) suggested that what she described as a stone circle found at Bed I, dated to about 1.8 mya, may have formed the base of a rough windbreak or a simple shelter. The evidence suggesting an artificial structure includes the small heaps of piled-up stones that form part of the circle and the fact that occupation debris did not appear in comparable density within the circle and in surrounding areas.

Mary Leakey suggested that the Olduvai living floors in Beds I and II may represent a seasonally occupied home base. The accumulated remains suggest the possibility that the inhabitants may have achieved a new type of social stability and may have possessed a sense of belonging to a particular social group.

Leakey's interpretation of the Olduvai living floors implies that hominids of the terminal Pliocene had shifted to a lifestyle similar to that of modern hunter-gatherers. The home-base interpretation implies a long-term continuity between early and modern humans. The early existence of supposed campsites implies that basic components of hunter-gatherer subsistence and social behavior existed, representing a way of life with deep evolutionary roots in human history. The problem is that no other evidence of shelter appears in the archaeological record until about 300,000 ya at Terra Amata (Chapter 11), and other interpretations of the site may be more likely.

Potts (1984, 1988) questioned whether food sharing, meat consumption, and tool use, associated with home bases, existed as early as 2 mya, or even before. In discussing the purported stone circle found at Olduvai site DK, Level

3, the assumed earliest possible representation of a shelter and the basis for the home-base interpretation, Potts noted the possibility that such a configuration may have been produced by the radial distribution of tree roots. A tree would have grown into a stony area, spreading the stones into a circle. He also suggested that the stone flakes and bone fragments found within the stone circle could have been deposited by a water flow.

Using taphonomic analysis, Potts concluded that the Olduvai bone assemblages have no features typical of modern animal death sites. The Olduvai faunal assemblages were probably not favored ambush sites. The preponderance of limb bones indicates that some bone-collecting animal was responsible for carrying these remains away from the death sites to other specific locales. The problem is, however, who was that bone collector?

There are several reasons to assume that carnivores restricted hominid activity at the Olduvai sites. Some bones there exhibit tooth marks and breakage patterns attributable to carnivores. Furthermore, the presence of both cut marks (made by a stone implement) and tooth marks (made by a nonhuman carnivore) indicates that humans and carnivores were interested in parts of the same carcasses, and sometimes even in parts of the same bone. Who came first is in question—sometimes the carnivore tooth marks are overlain on a bone by stone tool marks, suggesting hominid scavenging, and sometimes the opposite appears to be the case (Potts & Shipman, 1981).

There is no evidence at Olduvai that whole or nearly whole carcasses were transported to the sites. Primarily limb bones, even those of small ungulates, appear at the sites of bone concentration. This occurrence is consistent with opportunistic foraging by scavenging and hunting, without food sharing at a home base, as is true with a hunter-gatherer type of food sharing. Bone accumulations at Olduvai show no evidence of the complete processing of meat or bone. Such incomplete processing and the evident attraction of carnivores to meat-bearing parts suggest that early hominids abandoned considerable portions of meat and marrow at each site.

Potts concluded that it is impossible to assume that food sharing, avoidance of carnivore competition, or other behaviors associated with hunter-gatherer home bases occurred at the early Olduvai sites: "The available evidence suggests that hominids would have minimized the time spent at these sites, rather than have used them as the primary focus of social activity" (1984:344–345).

Using a computer simulation, Potts suggested that an alternative interpretation of the putative home-base accumulations would be a simultaneous use of multiple caches of stone tools, rather than a single home base. Stone caches, Potts argued, were an energetically efficient way to use both stone and food sources at the same time: "Thus, the accumulation of stone artifacts and animal bones at the same locations does not necessarily mean that hominids used these sites as home bases" (1984:345). According to this interpretation, stone raw materials and manufactured tools were carried and left at various places in the foraging area. As a result, multiple stone caches were created, useful for processing carcasses and possibly other foods.

The time and energy spent in handling and transporting portions of meat could be minimized by taking the bones to the nearest cache, where stone tools and bones remained from a previous visit. The time spent at a cache was minimized by quickly processing the new materials. By immediately abandoning the site, hominids could probably often avoid direct confrontation with carnivores attracted to the remains. In contrast, modern foragers occupy their campsites or home bases for as long as several months before moving.

Potts's hypothesis suggested an outline for the development of early hominid home bases. In the early stages, widely separated food and tools (or raw materials) were carried to the same well-defined areas to be used together. Humans thus produced sites, and also foraged and used resources, in ways generally seen among higher primates, with limited social activity at a site. Once humans began to forage and collect animal meat, no matter how often, a premium was placed on avoiding the threat of well-adapted carnivorous predators and scavengers. The use of these sites, the stone caches, primarily as processing areas implies that social activity was not focused there as it is in modern forager campsites. As areas to which resources were carried, however, these early sites were the precursors of home bases.

Food Sources

Early hominids were probably foragers, scavengers, and hunters, perhaps in that order of importance. It is difficult to assess the nature and acquisition of early hominid food sources. Most observers think that early hominids were to some degree carnivorous; however, vegetable foods not only were incorporated into the diet but were probably the staples. Although a great range of vegetable materials were potentially available as food sources, many could not be exploited until a way was found to store and ferment or cook them to remove toxic ingredients.

Sixty to 80 percent of the food of most modern foragers consists of vegetable matter, and the food of early humans was likewise predominantly vegetable (that is, consisting of herbaceous plants). J. D. Clark (1976) suggested that numerous stones found in the early sites could have been used for "preparing the otherwise unpalatable parts of plants by breaking down of fibrous portions" (p. 23). The all-purpose tools could easily process both plant and animal foods and serve multiple functions. There may be a relationship between butchering and such tools as flake knives, small scrapers, and chopping tools. However, large cutting tools appear to be only incidentally associated with meat eating and other hunting pursuits. Because cutting tools are often found at waterside sites, they were probably general-purpose tools that could be related to vegetable collecting and preparation.

In the dry season, plant harvesting from various woodland-bushland tree legumes and from a variety of liana species in thickets and groves could have regionally supported relatively large numbers of hominids (Peters, 1979). During the dry season, scavenging and hunting would be likely where game was concentrated near water holes in rivers and at springs. (Modern baboons tend to hunt more often in seasons of low food resources.)

A number of studies have described archaeological evidence for meat eating by Plio-Pleistocene hominids from Koobi Fora, Lake Turkana, and Olduvai Gorge (Bunn, 1981; Keely & Toth, 1981; Potts & Shipman 1981). The evidence for meat consumption consists of scattered stone artifacts and fragmentary animal bones. Taphonomic analysis of bone assemblages from both sites reveals direct evidence of butchering and marrow-processing activities.

Microscopic examination of one bone assemblage from Olduvai and Koobi Fora showed three major categories of bone modification: (1) human-induced damage features, including butchery (cut) marks and hammer-related fracture patterns; (2) carnivore and rodent-induced damage, including gnaw marks and tooth-related fracture patterns; and (3) weathering and postdepositional alterations. A series of very fine linear grooves on the bone surfaces provides the clearest evidence of human involvement with the bones: "The grooves are cut marks made by hominids using knife-like stone flakes to remove skin from carcasses, separate articulated bones and detach meat adhering to bones" (Bunn, 1981:574).

The presence of what appear to be cut and percussion marks on significant numbers of bones from Olduvai and Koobi Fora may document early hominid involvement in cutting animal carcasses and breaking open bones, presumably to obtain the meat and marrow, nearly 2 mya. Besides indicating the use of stone tools, this direct evidence of early diets allows us to dismiss models of human evolution that do not incorporate some meat eating. The mode of acquisition of the meat, whether it was hunted or scavenged or both, still remains uncertain.

In a sample of seventy-five bones with eighty-five surface markings from twelve excavated levels in Beds I and II, Olduvai Gorge, 24 percent had cut marks probably produced by slicing, chopping, or scraping (Potts & Shipman, 1981). Several bones in the assemblage showed both slicing marks and tooth scratches. Humans and carnivores used the same parts of the carcasses in some cases.

One problem in trying to interpret the incidence of meat eating in early human diets by relying on the evidence of cut marks on bone is that natural forces can leave marks on bone that are similar to those produced by human activity (Behrensmeyer et al., 1986; Hill, 1986; Morell, 1986). The type of soil in which assumed human altered bone lies is important because trampling by hooved animals of bone lying on sandy ground might produce marks similar to those produced by a stone tool cutting meat and tendon from bone. Sand lodged in an animal's hoof cuts across bone, leaving deeply grooved scratch marks. Trampling alone will not produce a scratch, "but a hoof with sand on it leaves a mark that . . . is indistinguishable from those made with a stone tool" (Behrensmeyer, quoted in Morell, 1986:71). Although it is unlikely that multiple trample scratches could be mistaken for slicing or scraping marks, isolated trample marks might be misidentified as cut marks. Because of the low incidence of identified cut marks in bone assemblages attributed to human action, the misidentification of even a few trample marks could affect interpretations of early hominid behavior by overestimating the amount of meat either eaten or butchered.

There is a further problem in trying to decipher the nature of bone and tool assemblages. Nearly all the associations appear at ancient lakeside or streamside sites where bones and tools may intermix by chance. For any site, the a priori possibilities include (1) human hunting, possibly followed by scavenging; (2) natural death assemblages due to diseases, predation, and so on, followed by human scavenging; (3) human accumulation of bone at a central place, perhaps followed by carnivore scavenging; (4) animal accumulation of bone at a den, followed by human scavenging; (5) the coincidental association of tools and bones at watering holes; and (6) association possibly due to water movement of the tools and bones (Klein, 1989). Various researchers have used different techniques, including taphonomy, to try to separate these phenomena.

Potts argued that bones found at several Olduvai sites dated between 1.85 and 1.7 mya accumulated over a period of at least five to ten years. Although inhabitants returned to these sites over a number of years, there is no clear notion of how often meat was eaten at these places, whether food sharing or other social activities occurred, and what proportion of the bones was the result of hunting as opposed to scavenging.

Potts's interpretation contrasts with that of Binford (1985, 1987), who argued that the Olduvai remains largely represent animal death sites rather than bone collections transported by hominids. Hominids may have scavenged from carcasses abandoned by carnivores and consumed more bone marrow than meat.

The ease with which meat was obtained may have varied seasonally. The four major methods of obtaining meat may have included scavenging among migratory animals, driving other predators from their kills, capturing sick animals or the newborns of large mammals, and hunting. The hunts of early hominids must have had a relatively high rate of failure, and as is consistent with the Olduvai remains, much of the prey must have been weak, young, or old.

Meat consumption may have been important for the evolution of the brain of early *Homo.* Aiello and Wheeler (1995) point out that five major organ systems use up to 60–70 percent of the body's energy at rest, although they account for only about 7 percent of the total body mass. These expensive organs are the gut, heart, liver, kidney, and brain. Unless an animal eats a lot more high-calorie foods, or one of these organs gets smaller, there is no energy budget left to feed a larger brain. The gut seems to be the organ system that got smaller, which could be because of a higher quality diet or partial digestion of food outside the body (through the use of tools). Lucy's barrel-shaped rib cage suggests that *A. afarensis* had an enormous gut and body proportions more like that of a gorilla than a modern human. The oldest relatively complete skeleton of early *Homo* (WT 15000), had a larger brain and a more delicate waist, as indicated by the more humanlike flattened rib cage.

Hunting and Scavenging

Hunting in the open savanna implies a rather cohesive social organization; coordination and cohesion of group activities depend on the establishment of some subtle communication system. This is not to imply, however, that these hunters were capable of articulate speech. Social carnivores cooperate during hunting without articulate speech. Even without an elaborate communicatory network and with their small brains, social carnivores use a variety of cooperative hunting techniques. A carnivorous hominid could have used such techniques as relay races to wear down the prey, driving it to members lying in ambush (techniques known to be used by modern baboons), and encircling and attacking it from many directions. Lacking technologically advanced implements and much speed of locomotion, early hominids must have hunted from ambush or by such means as driving the prey into rivers, over cliffs, or into deep mud. They probably used methods less dependent on speed and physical prowess than on group cooperative behavior.

Based on the remarkably complete and intact elephant skeleton found in Bed I, Olduvai, Tanner (1981) suggested that butchering was not well developed by 1.8 mya. Meat eating was probably still largely confined to predation on small animals without the use of tools, and only rarely were attempts made to butcher large animals such as elephants: "The fact that the Olduvai Bed I elephant carcass is largely intact, despite the association of stone tools, seems to indicate that butchery skills had not yet advanced to the point where large pieces could be removed and carried away" (p. 240).

Although scenarios of human evolution frequently refer to probable occasional indulgence in scavenging, the idea that scavenging might have represented a complete ecological adaptation has only recently come to the fore. Several studies indicate that scavenging may have been an important component of early hominid food-getting practices for obtaining meat (Shipman, 1986).

The scavenging hypothesis argues that the early inhabitants at Olduvai were poor hunters, infrequently capable of killing and butchering their prey. Shipman (1986) argued that they relied instead on scavenging to obtain meat, skin, and other products of the carcass. Scavenging supplemented plant-food foraging and was not the major dietary pattern. Shipman estimated that about 33 percent of the diet was provided by scavenging.

Bunn and Kroll (1986) argued that butchery by the Olduvai hominids was common and that they had access to meaty carcasses of many small and large animals prior to any substantial meat or marrow loss through feeding by predators and scavengers. They suggested that the Olduvai hominids were butchering carcasses by an efficient and systematic technique that involved skinning, dismemberment, and defleshing operations. Unlike Shipman (1986), they also argued that scavenging from natural deaths was unlikely to be a principal means of meat and marrow acquisition. Nevertheless, Bunn and Kroll suggested that active confrontational scavenging at large predator kill sites might have enabled ancient hominids to achieve at least temporary control of carcasses during the time when high-yield meaty limbs were available. They argued that the data support a subsistence strategy combining hunting of at least small animals and transporting of carcasses to favored locales.

PALEOECOLOGY

The global decline in temperatures that began during the time of the early australopithecines, starting about 3.3 mya, continued until about 2.5 mya. At that time the temperatures began to fluctuate above and below present day levels in 41,000-year cycles (Figure 9-6). The African continent experienced continued, gradual aridification and forest reduction, with a particular increase in savanna grasslands at about 1.7 mya (Cerling, 1992).

Amid these environmental changes, the hominid divergence took place. Other fauna were evolving and diversifying as well—the bovids in particular adapted to the savanna environments, as evidenced by new species appearing around 2.5 mya (Vrba, 1985a, 1995a). Other animals were going extinct, resulting in a novel environment and mammalian community to which the hominids

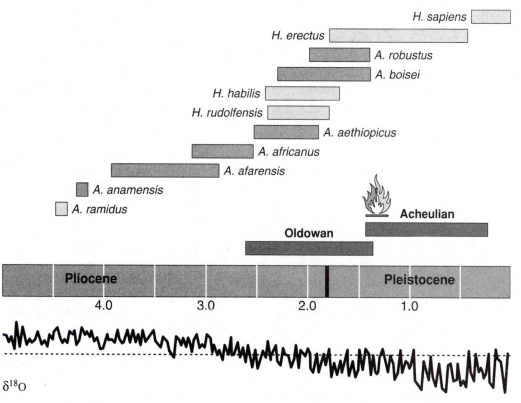

FIGURE 9-6 Time intervals represented by fossil hominid species and putative species, as well as early tool technologies and the first appearance of fire, in relation to climatic change. The curve at the bottom is an inverted oxygen isotope curve (data from Shackleton, 1995), reflecting fluctuations in global temperature (solid line) relative to today's temperature regime (dashed line). (Courtesy Jeffrey K. McKee.)

had to adapt. Yet neither the forest nor the savanna was a particularly inviting environment, because there was a great diversity of carnivores. The predators known from Africa today, such as lions, cheetahs, leopards, and hyenas, had established their presence, and they were accompanied by other large predators. *Dinofelis* cats, with moderately enlarged upper canines, and the saber-toothed cat *Megantereon* were predators, along with a variety of hyaenids that scavenged and may have hunted as well. Despite the potential disadvantages in this faunal array, early hominids survived. They must have had biological or cultural advantages enhancing survival.

Assessments of the hominid niche depend upon paleoecological reconstructions of the sites in which we find their fossil remains, along with observations of their morphological adaptations. The specialized masticatory apparatus led many to suspect that the robust australopithecines would have preferred the more heavily vegetated areas in which they could find sufficient food resources for their vegetarian diet. Early members of the genus *Homo*, presumed to have used tools and perhaps have had a more omnivorous diet, were expected to have occupied more varied environments and survived on the savanna. The paleoecological record has changed this view.

Key hominid fossil sites are listed in Table 9-3 with the reconstructed environments. The robust australopithecines are found in a wide variety of environments, with no evident habitat "preference." Likewise, early *Homo* seems to have covered the full range of available habitats. The question arises, If the two hominid lineages were sharing habitats, how did they coexist for more than a million years without one outcompeting the other?

"Gause's principle" is an ecological principle stating that two species cannot coexist in space over much time and occupy the same niche when resources are in limited supply, because one will tend to competitively exclude the other. This principle was initially used to question the existence of two hominid lineages, but the fossil record has established at least two coexisting species with little doubt. One must be careful in applying this principle, for two similar species may occupy the same habitat and apparently exploit the same resources (Ayala, 1970). Incidences of sustained sympatry (species overlap) may be mediated through mechanisms dependent on related frequencies of the species that promote the net of fitness of one species over the other without, however, driving one or both to extinction (Ayala, 1972). The terms *fundamental niche* and *realized niche* describe the limits of niche utilization for a species along the continuum from noncompetitive situations (where species can operate at full potential) to competitive situations, respectively. Coexistence is possible (Winterhalder, 1980), especially if the fitness of neither species is reduced below some crucial dimension (Ayala, 1972; Morse, 1974).

As discussed in the next subsection, the robust australopithecines and early *Homo* may have shared habitats but divided the dietary niche to allow coexistence. But according to some researchers, there were more than two coeval hominid species. In the most liberal scheme, there would have been four hominids in East Africa, coexisting for up to half a million years: *H. habilis, H. rudolfensis, A. boisei,* and *A. aethiopicus.* Toward the end of the period, a fifth species (*H. erectus* or

TABLE 9-3 Hominid Fossil Sites

Site	Location	Age Range (mya)	Species	Reconstructed Environment
Aramis	Ethiopia	4.4–4.3	*Ardipithecus ramidus*	Forest
Kanapoi	Kenya	4.2–4.0	*Australopithecus anamensis*	Riparian woodland/grassland
Laetoli (upper levels)	Tanzania	3.8–3.6	*Australopithecus afarensis*	Open woodland
Hadar Sidiha Koma	Ethiopia	3.4–3.3	*Australopithecus afarensis*	Woodland
Hadar Denen Dora	Ethiopia	3.2–3.1	*Australopithecus afarensis*	Woodland
Bahr el Ghazal	Chad	3.5–3.0	*Australopithecus afarensis*	Wooded lakeside
Makapansgat Member 3	South Africa	3.2–3.0	*Australopithecus africanus*	Forest, woodland
Makapansgat Member 4	South Africa	3.0–2.8	*Australopithecus africanus*	Woodland
Taung Dart Deposits	South Africa	2.8–2.6	*Australopithecus africanus*	Dry grassland, shrub
Shungura formation–C	Kenya	2.7–2.6	*Australopithecus aethiopicus*	Riparian woodland, shrubland
West Turkana–Upper Lomekwi	Kenya	2.6–2.5	*Australopithecus aethiopicus*	Open woodland/ riparian woodland
Sterkfontein Member 4	South Africa	2.6–2.5	*Australopithecus africanus*	Woodland
Hadar Makaamitalu Basin	Ethiopia	2.4–2.3	*Homo* cf. *habilis*	Open woodland
Chiwondo Beds	Malawi	2.4–2.3	*Homo* cf. *rudolfensis*	Mosaic vegetation, lake shore
Shungura Formation–E	Ethiopia	2.4–2.3	*Australopithecus boisei*	Riparian woodland
Shungura Formation–G	Ethiopia	2.3–2.2	*Australopithecus boisei*	Open woodland/grassland
Sterkfontein Member 5	South Africa	2.2–2.0	*Homo habilis*	Open grassland
Kromdraai B	South Africa	2.0–1.9	*Australopithecus robustus*	Open savanna grassland
East Turkana– Upper Burgi		2.0–1.9	*Australopithecus aethiopicus, Homo rudolfensis* (?), *Homo erectus*	Savanna woodland
East Turkana/KBS tuff	Kenya	1.9–1.8	*Australopithecus boisei, Homo erectus*	Open grassland
Olduvai Gorge Bed I	Tanzania	1.8–1.7	*Australopithecus boisei, Homo habilis*	Savanna grassland/woodland
Swartkrans Member 1	South Africa	1.8 (?)–1.7	*Australopithecus robustus, Homo erectus* (?)	Savanna woodland/ riparian woodland
Olduvai Gorge Bed II	Tanzania	1.7–1.5	*Homo habilis, Homo erectus*	Riparian forest/ grassy woodland
East Turkana–Okote	Kenya	1.6–1.5	*Australopithecus boisei*	Wetlands/grasslands
West Turkana–Natoo	Kenya	1.6–1.4	*Homo erectus*	Woodland savanna, swamp
Swartkrans Member 2	South Africa	1.6 (?)–1.5	*Australopithecus robustus, Homo erectus*	Savanna woodland
Swartkrans Member 3	South Africa	1.5 (?)–1.4	*Australopithecus robustus*	Open grassland

H. ergaster) appeared. Aside from questioning this scheme on the basis of hominid morphology alone, Gause's principle casts doubt on the coexistence of so many species. The two species within each genus would have had to diverge into distinct niches, despite the remarkable similarity in adaptive morphology. Alternatively, the East African environmental resources would have to have been sufficient to support a number of similar species. Under a scheme with fewer species, intraspecific competition in variable species rather than interspecific competition would explain the ultimate direction of each lineage.

The Dietary Hypothesis

The dietary hypothesis was originally expounded by John T. Robinson to explain morphological differences between the "gracile" and "robust" australopithecines, *A. africanus* and *A. robustus*. Robinson (1962, 1963, 1965) argued that the architecture of the robust form's skull and face is closely associated with biomechanical specializations related to diet. He saw *A. robustus* as a specialized vegetarian, and *A. africanus* as a more omnivorous hominid. Since the time of his original arguments, the hominid fossil record has expanded considerably, and the issues of concern have changed. It is worth considering the dietary hypothesis in terms of the divergence of the robust australopithecines and early *Homo*.

One of the main pillars of Robinson's argument was the size disparity between the anterior and posterior teeth in the robust form. He argued that the teeth of the robust form were specialized for crushing and chewing food, and he supported his contention by noting the presence of tooth damage in the form of enamel flakes detached from the chewing surfaces. According to Robinson, this flaking was caused by application of considerable pressure in a small area, resulting from biting hard on grit particles adhering to the roots and tubers that were supposedly a large part of the diet of the robust form. Such detached flakes, however, are characteristic of many australopithecines and may not be diagnostic of dietary differences. Nevertheless, microwear studies have shown that both the permanent and deciduous molar teeth of robust australopithecines were used more for crushing and grinding than were the teeth of *A. africanus* (Grine & Kay, 1988). It has also been suggested that the thick enamel of robust australopithecine molar teeth may have been important for reducing hard dietary items during the dry season when most plant foods were comparatively tough.

Grine and Kay (1989) analyzed the diet of the robust australopithecines on the basis of microwear patterns of the molars. The dental wear evidenced in the fossil teeth is strongly suggestive of a diet of hard food items that included seeds. Whereas dental wear patterns confirm a vegetative diet, the robust australopithecines may also have supplemented their diets with meat, as evidenced by analysis of trace elements in the teeth.

Sillen (1992) tested the ratio of strontium to calcium in fossil bones of *A. robustus* from Swartkrans Member 1. Animals that eat more plants, which are rich in strontium, have a higher ratio of strontium to calcium in their bones than those that eat meat. There are some problems when applying this analytical technique to fossils because exposure to water and acids in the soil can change the strontium and calcium levels over time through *diagenesis* (low-pressure changes to the composition of a bone during fossilization). Sillen took the problems of diagenesis into account by testing a wide variety of animals of known or suspected dietary habits. He found relatively low ratios of strontium to calcium in bones from nine specimens of *A. robustus*, indicating that they may have eaten meat along with plant matter. Studies of carbon isotope ratios (Lee-Thorp et al., 1994) tend to confirm the conclusion that *A. robustus* had a more omnivorous diet than previously suspected, possibly including animal matter. Yet one must be cautious in envisioning *A. robustus* as a hunter or scavenger; whether the meat component came from large mammals or from insects, invertebrates, and small vertebrates must also be considered.

Environmental Change and Hominid Evolution

As with the savanna hypothesis discussed in the previous chapter, it is often asked whether or not environmental change served as the catalyst for particular events and trends in hominid evolution. There is undoubtedly a temporal coincidence between climatic and biotic changes on the African continent, and the divergence of the hominids into two or more lineages, all around 2.5 mya. Might climatic change have *caused* the hominid divergence?

Elisabeth Vrba (1985b, 1995b), building upon the observations of Brain (1981) and Brain and Meester (1964), proposed a causal connection between climatic change and mammalian evolution. Vrba (1985a, 1995a) noted that a disproportionate number of bovid species first appear in the fossil record around 2.5 mya. New hominid species appeared approximately at the same time. She proposed that these speciation events were ultimately caused by the dramatic cooling and aridification of Africa; without the impetus of environmental events of change, most species and ecosystems would remain in equilibrium most of the time and resist change.

Vrba formulated her ideas into the **turnover-pulse hypothesis**. "Turnover" refers to changes in the species composition of a community due to immigration, emigration, speciation, and extinction. In Vrba's model, turnover of most species tends to occur simultaneously during short periods of time—that is, a "pulse" of turnover. Climatic change allegedly causes the pulses. At other times, with little climatic change, there is very little turnover. The origin of hominid, bovid, and other mammalian species at about 2.5 mya was proposed by Vrba (1988, 1995b) as a significant pulse.

The proposed mechanism for the speciation component of turnover has to do with the fragmentation of species into small, isolated subpopulations. With the decline of forests across Africa, many subpopulations became isolated in the small patches of remaining forest. This isolation allowed for the rapid evolution of disparate trends through genetic drift, and eventually to complete divergent speciation of subpopulations from one another.

Vrba derived support for the turnover-pulse hypothesis from the fossil record of African bovids. However, further tests of the fossil record have failed to confirm the existence of pulses. The main problem is that the fossil record is notoriously incomplete. We do not know when past speciation events occurred; we can only observe when species first appear in the fossil record—possibly a few hundred thousand years later. For example, it was noted earlier that the first appearance of stone tools predated fossil deposits yielding early *Homo*; but the stone tools at Gona were probably not the first stone tools made, and we may yet find earlier fossils of *Homo habilis*, and so cannot dismiss *Homo* as the toolmaker.

Behrensmeyer et al. (1997) did an in-depth study of the Turkana Basin, Kenya, one of the more complete fossil records known. Although they saw signals of significant environmental changes and mammalian adaptations between 3.0 and 1.8 mya, they detected no pulses. The Turkana evidence suggests that the fauna was steadily nudged toward grassland-adapted species by global cooling and drying in Africa. It is unclear why Vrba's fossil record of African bovids appears punctuated and the Turkana record is not, but the reason may have to do with the limits of the fossil record. Using a series of computer simulations, McKee (1995, 1996, 1997) showed that the apparent patterns of evolution and turnover seen in the fossil record were an artifact of the record's incompleteness; in both East Africa and South Africa, a model of continuous (nonpulsed) turnover could result in the observed fossil data once the disparities in the fossil record were taken into account. The sudden appearance in the fossil record of a number of bovid species may thus be more an artifact of the fossil record than a sudden evolutionary event at 2.5 mya.

Kimbel (1995) and White (1988, 1995) focus on the hominid fossil record. They note that we have a very small sample of fossils and that first-appearance dates are unlikely to reflect the true time of speciation events. Whereas the turnover-pulse hypothesis has not been disproved, there are at present insufficient fossil data to test the hypothesis adequately.

One must also take into account the variability of environments exploited by early *Homo* and even the robust australopithecines. Kingston et al. (1994:958) note, "While the course of human evolution was surely affected by environmental change . . . interpretations of the origin of hominids in East Africa . . . should be considered within the context of a heterogenous mosaic of environments rather than an abrupt replacement of rain forests by grassland and woodland biomes." Foley (1994) notes that the primary result of climate may be on levels of diversity and extinction patterns; there is no correlation in Foley's data between climatic change and species origins, but there does appear to be a correlation between environmental change and species extinctions (see Figure 9-6).

Potts (1996a, 1996b) has proposed a different ecological model, which he calls *variability selection*, to explain hominid evolution. He has proposed that climatic changes favor animals that can readily adapt to new environments. There is a trend toward "survival of the generalist": those lineages capable of living in varied environments and adapting to change, such as hominid species, are perpetuated, whereas more specialized species go extinct when they fail to adapt to new conditions. Perhaps this model may explain the ultimate success of the *Homo* lineage, whereas the presumably more specialized robust australopithecines eventually went extinct in the Pleistocene.

SUMMARY

The Late Pliocene of Africa ushered in two main hominid lineages, the robust australopithecines and early *Homo*, along with gradual changes in the climate, vegetative cover, and mammalian communities. At least one of the hominid species mastered adaptations to environmental change with the aid of simple stone tools, known as Oldowan tools. The evolution of the robust australopithecines focused on craniofacial adaptations to a diet requiring heavy grinding, but they may not have been exclusively vegetarian. The increases in brain size and complexity that characterized early *Homo* suggest that natural selection favored greater behavioral adaptability in that lineage, initiating a trend that continued throughout human evolution. Yet early *Homo* retained some primitive features in the postcranial anatomy. Early *Homo* evolved into *Homo erectus* before the end of the Pliocene, and the robust australopithecines went extinct in the Pleistocene.

SUGGESTED READINGS

Kimbel, W. H., D. C. Johanson, and Y. Rak. 1997. Systematic assessment of a maxilla of *Homo* from Hadar, Ethiopia. *American Journal of Physical Anthropology* 103:235–262.

Marzke, M. W. 1997. Precision grips, hand morphology, and tools. *American Journal of Physical Anthropology* 102:91–110.

McKee, J. K., J. F. Thackeray, and L. R. Berger. 1995. Faunal assemblage seriation of southern African Pliocene and Pleistocene fossil deposits. *American Journal of Physical Anthropology* 96:235–250.

Potts, R. 1996. *Humanity's Descent—The Consequences of Ecological Instability.* New York: William Morrow.

Schrenk, F., T. G. Bromage, C. G. Betzler, U. Ring, and Y. M. Juwayeyi. 1993. Oldest *Homo* and Pliocene biogeography of the Malawi Rift. *Nature* 365:833–836.

Suwa, G., B. Asfaw, Y. Beyene, T. D. White, S. Katoh, S. Nagaoka, H. Nakaya, K. Uzawa, P. Renne, and G. WoldeGabriel, G. 1997. The first skull of *Australopithecus boisei*. *Nature* 389:489–492.

Tobias, P. V. 1987. The brain of *Homo habilis*: A new level of organization in cerebral evolution. *Journal of Human Evolution* 16:741–761.

Tobias, P. V. 1991. *Olduvai Gorge*, vol. 4: *The Skulls, Endocasts and Teeth of* Homo habilis. Cambridge: Cambridge University Press.

Vrba, E. S. 1995. On the connections between paleoclimate and evolution. In *Paleoclimate and Evolution*, ed. E. Vrba et al. New Haven, CT: Yale University Press.

Wood, B. 1992. Origin and evolution of the genus *Homo*. *Nature* 355:783–790.

10

Homo erectus

Overview
General Morphology
Review of Sites
Acheulian Tradition
Homo erectus and the Use of Fire
Summary
Suggested Readings

Homo erectus *fossils were first recovered in Java in 1891, but skeletal and cultural remains have since been recovered in Africa, Asia, and Europe (Figure 10-1). The oldest* H. erectus *fossils are from East Africa and possibly Java and date to about 1.8 mya. Some argue that the African fossils are more modern than their Asian counterparts and that they warrant a separate species named* H. ergaster. *Supposedly the more modern* H. ergaster *and not* H. erectus *is ancestral to* H. sapiens.

Homo erectus *is distinguished from earlier members of the genus* Homo *by a number of features including larger cranial capacities, which range from 750 to 1,250 cubic centimeters. The flattened skull vault is distinctive, and behind large brow ridges is a marked postorbital constriction. There is a sagittal ridge and thick skull bones, and the face and jaws are prognathic.*

Beginning with H. erectus, *the story of human evolution is increasingly associated with cultural elaborations and geographic spread into new environments. In Africa its tool tradition is called the Acheulian.* H. erectus's *apparent migration out of Africa was aided by its cultural adaptations. It seems to have hunted big game, and one of* H. erectus's *most important cultural innovations was the use of fire.*

FIGURE 10-1   Distribution of *Homo erectus* by country in which fossils or artifacts have been found (*black*). The European sites (*gray*) have transitional forms that some may refer to archaic *Homo sapiens* or *Homo heidelbergensis*. See Table 10-3 for a list of the sites and specimens. (Courtesy Jeffrey K. McKee.)

OVERVIEW

The first fossils eventually called *Homo erectus* were found in 1891 in Java, Indonesia, by Eugene Dubois, a Dutch physician. Dubois joined the medical division of the Dutch Colonial Service and traveled to Indonesia hopeful of recovering the remains of the link between apes and humans—the so-called missing link. Several years before Dubois's journey, the German biologist Ernst Haeckel postulated a theoretical human ancestral line based on fragmentary information. The only well-known fossil remains were comparatively recent bones discovered years earlier in the Neander Valley of Germany. Haeckel suggested that the human evolutionary line began among some extinct Miocene apes and reached *Homo sapiens* by way of an imagined speechless group of "ape-men" that he called *Pithecanthropi*.

Soon after his arrival in Indonesia, Dubois reported the discovery of a skull, femur, and several bone fragments at Trinil, a locale on the Solo River. Dubois eventually applied the name Haeckel suggested, "Pithecanthropus," to the bones that he recovered. Dubois first called his find "Anthropopithecus erectus" (upright manlike ape), the genus name indicating that he thought the form was closely related to chimpanzees. He changed the name to "Pithecanthropus" (upright apelike man) when he realized he had underestimated the brain size, which was larger than that of a modern ape. The name *Pithecanthropus* indicates that Dubois thought the fossil to be a link between humans and apes. Because the *Pithecanthropus* femur resembled that of modern *Homo*, Dubois concluded that his "ape-man" walked erect in the same manner as *Homo sapiens*. He christened his form *Pithecanthropus erectus*. The original generic name was subsequently dropped, and the form renamed *Homo erectus* (subspecies designation *erectus* to distinguish it from other *H. erectus* finds). For years many scientists doubted Dubois's contention that he had recovered an ancestral human. Most were hesitant to accept the association of an archaic skull with a relatively modern looking femur. (Refer to the discussion of mosaic evolution in Chapter 2.) By the time most scientists became convinced of Dubois's claims, he had rejected his original interpretation and died unconvinced of the immense value of his discovery.

Dubois's role with *Pithecanthropus* has been badly misunderstood and misrepresented. Readers interested in this story should consult Theunissen's (1989) excellent biography or Gould's (1990) shorter explanation of Dubois's role in the understanding and acceptance of *P. erectus* as our ancestor.

Quite some time has passed since *H. erectus* was first described by Dubois, but the story is still not done. The record is incomplete, and recently there have been unprecedented finds with fascinating dates from heretofore unsuspected regions in the world. There are continuing problems with the chronology in Asia because in China, one of the most important centers for *H. erectus,* datable strata are rare. The nature of evolution in *H. erectus* and the question of the number of species are intriguing. The origins of *H. erectus* are unclear. It must have descended from an earlier *Homo*, probably *H. habilis*. But *H. habilis* is still poorly known, and the species may incorrectly include fossils that belong elsewhere. If *H. erectus* is the true ancestor to *H. sapiens*, where did the transition occur and when? There seem to be a number of intermediate fossils, sharing traits with both the *H. erectus* and *H. sapiens* species. This group may include *H. heidelbergensis* and *H. antecessor.*

The number of species in *Homo* prior to *H. sapiens* is debated but continues to increase. Added rather recently were *H. rudolfensis* and *H. ergaster.* The most recent addition is the Spanish material from Atapuerca that is being called *H. antecessor* by some researchers. Even the number of genera is proliferating with *Homo* in Africa, *Pithecanthropus* and *Meganthropus* being revived in Indonesia, and some Chinese colleagues continue to use *Sinanthropus*. Others use different generic names for the North African forms. We really must ask if the names are taxonomically relevant.

Why *Homo* appeared is debatable, but many pin its appearance on disputable climatic changes. Some find evidence for cooling and drying and a shrinking of forests, constituting an environmental thrust. Not everyone agrees that this change happened, over what areas it may have happened, and what its effect was. There is general agreement that *H. erectus* (or *H. ergaster*) was adapted to the more arid, open grasslands and less stable environments that spread across tropical Africa. Its long and linear body build in Africa signals its adaptation to tropical and subtropical regions. By at least 1 mya it was adapted to the arid highlands of Ethiopia and the cold regions of China and Siberia. Because of the range of habitats, modern human diversity may have had its start with *H. erectus*.

 H. erectus is differentiated from the earlier *H. habilis* or *H. rudolfensis* by continuing changes in the face and skull and increases in cranial capacity (Table 10-1). The tool assemblage, the Acheulian handaxe culture, is primarily African based. In Asia it may have relied heavily on bamboo. *H. erectus* seems to have been the first hominid to inhabit caves and to exploit fire. Intelligence seems to have reacted to climatic stress, although fire was being exploited in less extreme climates in Africa as well. Fire was exploited for warmth, light, cooking, and perhaps art and magic. Perhaps manipulation of fire—where to find it and how to keep it alive, led to the first social stratification among hominids. Fire exploitation may be a root of magic, ritual, and religion.

 Some researchers recognize more than the species *H. erectus*—for example, *H. ergaster* in Africa and *H. heidelbergensis* and *H. antecessor* in Europe. Some retain the Chinese fossils in the originally suggested genus, *Sinanthropus,* and others retain the original Indonesian genus *Pithecanthropus.* We refer to all of the materials as *H. erectus.*

TABLE 10-1   Cranial Traits of *Homo erectus*

Long and low skull whose greatest breadth is situated low down on the skull. Skulls generally referred to as platycephalic.

Midline of skull often exhibits a sagittal ridge or elevation.

A relatively flat frontal bone characterized by prominent brow ridges continuous across the brow (supraorbital torus). Postorbital constriction is prominent.

Relatively small mastoid process.

Cranial bones almost twice as thick as those in modern humans.

Mean value of adult cranial capacity about 833 cc.

Very broad nasal bones.

Dental and Jaw Traits
Relatively robust mandibles, absence of a chin, broad ascending ramus (indicating large masseter muscles).

Molars that generally have large pulp cavities (taurodontism); upper central incisors that are typically shovel-shaped; enamel of molars in Asian forms generally wrinkled.

GENERAL MORPHOLOGY

The genus and species designation *H. erectus* is based on skeletal remains of samples from Africa, Asia, and Europe. Although there is a moderate degree of individual and geographical variation, these remains comprise a group whose morphological characters are sufficiently consistent and distinctive to justify their inclusion in the genus *Homo*. That being the case, what morphological features distinguish them from *H. sapiens* and *H. habilis*?

H. erectus has a cranial capacity varying between 750 and 1,250 cc. The lower values are found among earlier representatives and the higher values among later representatives of the species. The mean cranial capacity of twelve Asian skulls in 929 cc. Considering the *H. erectus* sample as a whole, an increase in cranial capacity over the preceding australopithecines may be partly the result of increased body size (Wolpoff, 1980).

Leigh (1991) has shown a significant cranial capacity increase through time in both *H. erectus* and early *H. sapiens* (where there is a relatively marked increase in a short period of time). Among *H. erectus,* the increase is especially apparent in some Chinese and Indonesian specimens, although other *H. erectus* samples do not show the increase.

It has been argued that with increased body size *H. erectus* also had an increased cranial capacity. However, Alan Walker (1993) estimates that WT 15000 (material from Lake Turkana, Kenya) had a cranial capacity of 909 cc, equivalent to that of earlier members of *Homo*. Perhaps the relative brain size often thought to characterize *Homo* is only found in *Homo* after the Middle Pleistocene.

There is marked flattening, **platycephaly,** of the *H. erectus* skull vault. A sagittal ridge runs across the skull's midline, and the skull bones are quite thick. The greatest width of the skull is low on the skull vault; in modern humans it is higher on the skull vault because of decreasing bone thickness, reduced mass of the chewing muscles, and increased cranial capacities. Posterior to the large brow ridges above the eye orbits, the skull is marked by **postorbital constriction.** The nasal bones are broad and flat, and the face more prognathic than in modern *Homo* (Figures 10-2 and 10-3).

The heavily constructed *H. erectus* mandible lacks a chin. The teeth are larger than those found in *H. sapiens*. The canines are sometimes slightly projecting, with a small diastema in the upper dentition; however, the first lower premolar is bicuspid with subequal cusps. The molars have well-differentiated cusps complicated by wrinkling of the enamel surfaces. This wrinkled enamel pattern found in many extant Asian populations has been used by some scientists to show a direct evolutionary link between modern Asian populations and Asian *H. erectus*. The second upper molar may be larger than the first, and the length of the third lower molar may exceed the second. Premolar and molar tooth size reduction is one of the most dramatic changes that occurred between the australopithecines and *H. erectus,* and an equally great reduction occurred over the *H. erectus* time span. The mandible also reduced in size.

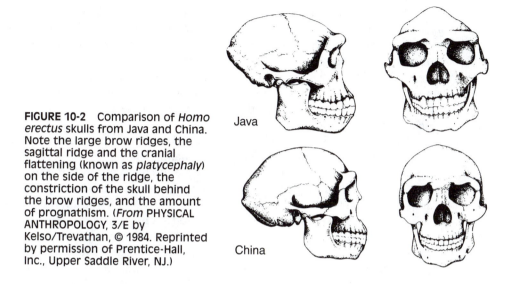

FIGURE 10-2 Comparison of *Homo erectus* skulls from Java and China. Note the large brow ridges, the sagittal ridge and the cranial flattening (known as *platycephaly*) on the side of the ridge, the constriction of the skull behind the brow ridges, and the amount of prognathism. (*From* PHYSICAL ANTHROPOLOGY, 3/E by Kelso/Trevathan, © 1984. Reprinted by permission of Prentice-Hall, Inc., Upper Saddle River, NJ.)

Java

China

H. erectus is perhaps the first hominid to have displayed a projecting nose (Waters, 1990). Although there are no fossils of noses because they are comprised of soft cartilage, the nose's profile can be determined from the shape of the bones around the nasal opening. With a projecting nose, *H. erectus* may have found it easier to conserve water in a hot and dry climate. This may have been one factor that allowed *H. erectus* to move across the hot African savannas to colonize other regions of the world.

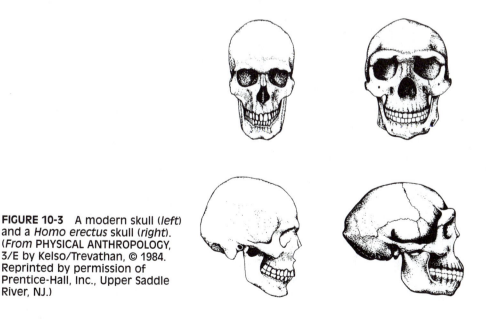

FIGURE 10-3 A modern skull (*left*) and a *Homo erectus* skull (*right*). (*From* PHYSICAL ANTHROPOLOGY, 3/E by Kelso/Trevathan, © 1984. Reprinted by permission of Prentice-Hall, Inc., Upper Saddle River, NJ.)

One important function of the modern human nose is to moisten inhaled air. Inhaled air must be 90 percent saturated and be at the body's core temperature when it reaches the lungs, or oxygen will not pass from the air to the blood and the lung tissue will be destroyed. A projecting nose wets the air. Because the inner walls of the nose are colder than exhaled air, moisture from this air condenses on the walls. The dry, inhaled air then picks up the condensed moisture left on the walls of the nose by the exhaled air. The larger the nose, the more efficiently this process works.

The nose serves as a radiator to warm inhaled air. The larger nasal cavities associated with the European Neandertals dating about 55,000 years ago (see Chapter 12) are said to be an adaptation to life in cold regions. If the nose moistens dry inhaled air and warms cold inhaled air, hominids inhabiting dry or cold conditions are well served by a large projecting nose. In its evolutionary history, *H. erectus* is the first hominid to have witnessed such climatic diversity.

H. erectus's limb bones are essentially modern. However, Day (1971) and Day and Molleson (1973), on the basis of material from Olduvai Gorge, suggested that there are some differences distinguishing the postcranial anatomies of *H. erectus* and *H. sapiens*. As will be noted later, a similar conclusion is drawn from preliminary study of *H. erectus* material (WT 15000) from Lake Turkana. Whatever the differences between the postcranial anatomies of *H. erectus* and *H. sapiens,* both species were bipedal.

The *H. erectus* morphology can be summarized as follows:

1. The cranial capacity is about the size of a modern one-year-old child.
2. The rib cage is like that of modern humans.
3. The hips are more narrow than those of other hominids, giving it greater speed. Its longer legs allowed it to cover more distance. The robust bones of the leg indicate a demanding life.
4. *H. erectus* was generally a tropic dweller. The finding that *H. erectus* was physiologically adapted to warm and humid climates means that a humanlike physiology with a dependence on sweating as a major cooling mechanism was established by 1.5 mya. African *H. erectus* are at least 158 centimeters tall and weigh no less than 51 kilograms. WT 15000 is estimated to be 185 cm tall and weighed 68 kg, a well-nourished and healthy creature. African *H. erectus,* with a mean stature of 170 cm, would be in the tallest 17 percent of modern populations, even if we make comparisons only with males.
5. The lowest thoracic vertebra, T7, had a small opening through which the spinal cord passed. Nerves in the T7 area allow fine control of the rib cage muscles used in exhaling. Walker (1993) suggests that WT 15000's spinal cord could not carry enough nerve tissue for him to control his breathing as well as modern humans. Linking words into long sentences would have been impossible.

The overall similarity between early *H. erectus* and modern humans is clear. The limb proportions are like those of modern humans who inhabit extremely dry, hot places. The facial skeleton is quite modern, although the face is certainly more prognathic. The upper limb skeleton is quite like modern humans. The major exceptions to modern morphology are in the size and shape of the braincase, size of the thoracic neural canal, narrowness of the pelvis, long femoral necks, and other limb traits.

Although a number of traits distinguish *H. erectus* from *H. sapiens* (Table 10-2), there is a general consensus that the former or some closely allied species stands in an ancestral relationship to the latter, based on the following observations (W. L. G. Clark, 1967): (1) The morphological traits of *H. erectus* conform very well with the theoretical postulates for an intermediate stage in the evolution of later species of *Homo;* (2) the existence of *H. erectus* in the early part of the Pleistocene, antedating well-authenticated fossil remains of *H. sapiens,* provides it with an antiquity conforming well with its supposed evolutionary position; and (3) some *H. erectus* materials appear to illustrate a graded series of morphological changes leading from *H. erectus* to *H. sapiens*. In fact, there is disagreement about whether some of the fossils belong with the species *H. erectus* or *H. habilis*.

Questions have been raised concerning the exact role *H. erectus* played in subsequent evolution and the validity of maintaining the African and east Asian samples in the same species. Some African fossils such as KNM-ER 3733 and 3883 are particularly different from the classic east Asian *H. erectus*. For example, the African skulls have thinner skull bones. The African fossils generally have larger brains than Asian forms. These larger brains are housed in flat and long but elevated braincases that are expanded higher up in the parietal region. Because they are older than east Asian specimens, these specimens could represent an African population that was ancestral to Asian *H. erectus*. However, when the African skulls differ from the east Asian *H. erectus,* they tend to be more like *H. sapiens* (Andrews, 1984b). This observation raises the possibility that the African specimens are directly ancestral to *H. sapiens* and that the east Asian *H. erectus* repre-

---

TABLE 10-2 Some Critical Morphological Features of *Homo erectus*

Cranial capacity: range of 750–1,250 cc. The lowest values are for the earliest forms.

Skull: platycephaly, sagittal ridge, thick skull bones; greatest width of skull is low down on the skull.

Facial skeleton: supraorbital torus and postorbital constriction, heavy mandible lacking a chin, prognathism, projecting nose.

Dentition: large teeth, wrinkled dental enamel quite apparent in Chinese fossils.

Body size: increased body size (weight and stature), mean stature of 170 cm for African fossils.

Limb skeleton: modern upper limbs, narrow hips, long and robust leg bones.

This table assumes that all the fossils are *H. erectus,* whereas some of the traits listed for the African species are referred to as *H. ergaster* by other researchers.

sents a specialized evolutionary side branch that became extinct. Louis Leakey was perhaps the first researcher to call attention to morphological differences between African and Asian early *Homo*. Although Leakey's contention for different taxonomic status for the African and Asian forms originally did not gain wide support, there is currently considerable favor for placing the African materials into the species *H. ergaster,* different from the Asian *H. erectus.*

REVIEW OF SITES

Africa

North Africa. North African *H. erectus* material was recovered in Morocco, Algeria, and Tunisia (see Table 10-3) for all sites discussed). The time span of the North African sample is estimated to be from the late Middle Pleistocene back to the older but uncertain age of the Ternifine (Algeria) remains. The relative ages of this material, from the oldest at Ternifine to the most recent at Salé, is as follows: Ternifine, Sidi Abderrahman, Rabat, and Salé (the latter three are from Morocco). The Ternifine remains may date to 730,000 to 600,000 years ago. Sidi Abderrahman may be 500,000 years old. Middle Pleistocene material from Algerian and Moroccan coastal sites is mostly mandibular remains. The exception is the Salé partial cranial vault and lower face, which dates to about 160,000 years ago.

These materials are variously referred to as late *H. erectus* or early *H. sapiens* because they combine traits from both species. Primitive *H. sapiens* traits are especially noticeable in the most recent remains from Salé and Rabat.

Lake Turkana. The oldest *Homo erectus* remains come from Lake Turkana, Kenya. A pelvic fragment, KNM-ER 3228 (Gleadow, 1980; McDougall et al., 1980), and two incomplete femurs (upper leg bones) labeled KNM-ER 1472 and 1481 date to about 1.8 mya. These femurs show a strong resemblance to later *H. erectus* from Olduvai.

Homo erectus remains (cataloged as WT 15000) from Lake Turkana found in 1984 are from a site known as Nariokotome III. The remains of a young male are dated to approximately 1.6 mya (Brown & Feibel, 1985; McDougall et al., 1985). Its chronological age is based on tooth wear and tooth eruption patterns. WT 15000 has a dental age of 11, but the skeletal age corresponded to a modern 13–13.5-year-old, and his stature corresponded to a modern 15-year-old. The remains were found in what was once a marshy habitat. The skeletal remains are the most complete known for *H. erectus*. Missing are the left arm and hand, the right arm from below the elbow, and most of both feet. Postmortem damage occurred, and some parts of the bones are crushed. There are no signs of carnivore or scavenger damage (Brown et al., 1985).

One of the most interesting features of WT 15000 is his estimated adult height. He had already grown to 5 feet 4 inches tall, the height previously postulated for adult *H. erectus*. When fully grown he might have reached a height of

TABLE 10-3   *Homo erectus* Sites Discussed in Text

	Site	Evidence	Date (years ago)
Africa			
Ethiopia	Plain of Gadeb	Tools, fire	1.4 million
	Konso	Tools, human remains	1.5–1.4 million
	Bodo	Human remains, tools	600,000
Kenya	Lake Turkana	Human remains, footprints	1.8–1.5 million
	Olorgesailie	Tools, living site	900,000–400,000
Namibia		Tools–*H. erectus?*	Middle Pleistocene
North Africa	Algeria, Morocco, Tunisia	Tools and human remains–*H. erectus?*	Middle Pleistocene
South Africa	Swartkrans	Human remains	Middle Pleistocene
Tanzania	Olduvai Gorge, Bed II	Human remains, tools	1.2 million
	Olduvai Gorge, Bed IV	Human remains, tools	700,000–400,000
	Ndutu	Human remains–*H. sapiens?*	600,000–400,000
Asia			
China	Longgupo Cave (Wushan Hominid Site)	Human remains–*H. erectus?*	1.9 million?
	Yuanmou	Human remains	1.7 million?
	Xiaochangliang	Tools	1 million–700,000
	Lantian	Human remains	800,000–590,000
	Zhoukoudian	Human remains, tools, fire	600,000–414,000
	Hexian?	Human remains	200,000–150,000
	Yunxian	Human remains	Middle Pleistocene
Java	Djetis, Trinil Beds	Human remains, tools	1.8–1.6 million? 53,000–27,000?
Malaysia, Burma,		Tools?	Middle Pleistocene
Thailand	Kao Pah Nam	Tools, hearth	700,000
Vietnam	Tham Khuyan, Tham Hai, Nui Do, Quan Yen	Human remains, tools	400,000?
Middle East			
Saudi Arabia	Shuwayhitiyeh, Najran, Saffaqah, Wadi Tathlith	Tools	900,000–600,000
Europe			
England	Boxgrove	Human remains, tools	515,000–485,000
France	Montmaurin	Human remains	300,000?
Georgia	Dmanisi	Human remains	1.6 million–900,000?
Germany	Mauer	Human remains, tools?	300,000–250,000
Hungary	Vértesszöllös	Human remains	400,000–185,000?
Italy	Ceprano	Human remains	900,000–800,000
	Fontana Ranuccio	Human remains, tools	700,000 and 450,000
Spain	Orce	Human remains?, tools	1.6 million
	Gran Dolina	Human remains, tools	780,000
	Torralba, Ambrona	Tools, animal remains	500,000
	Aridos 1, 2	Tools	Middle Pleistocene
Siberia	Diring Yuriakh	Tools	500,000?, 300,000?

6 feet, much taller than previously envisioned for any of our early ancestors. In fact, WT 15000 was taller than most modern people. WT 15000 weighed about 48 kg at the time of death and might have weighed about 68 kg fully grown. The height and weight estimates reinforce the view of early African *H. erectus* as tall, relatively thin individuals, physically similar to some modern human populations living under the same general climatic conditions. *Australopithecus* was apparently shorter and relatively heavier, and this difference may reflect a shift in both the ecology and behavior of *H. erectus*.

Body size is a fundamental species adaptation that affects the development of the species' evolutionary strategies. More recent studies on body size in African and Asian *H. erectus* suggest that they were larger than originally thought (Gauld, 1996). The average estimated height of six African *H. erectus* skeletons dated between 1.7 and 0.7 mya is 170 cm, tall even by modern standards (Ruff, 1993). *H. erectus* from Zhoukoudian are shorter than their African brethren.

H. erectus was likely dwelling in relatively open, at least semiarid places, for this is where their physique is most adaptive. Australopithecines could have inhabited either closed and wet or open and dry habitats. Given their smaller size and small stride length, the australopithecines likely lived in relatively closed, wet environments—perhaps something like a riverine forest.

WT 15000's skull, assembled from about seventy pieces, is small, and his cranial capacity may be 909 cc (Lewin, 1984). The overall shape of the upper region of the thigh differs from that in extant or extinct humans. The vertebrae show some interesting differences from those of modern humans. The Turkana youngster has a narrow and flared pelvis and a combination of a large femoral head and long femoral neck. These features of the upper leg are not found in other human femurs, and the functional significance in terms of the locomotor pattern of WT 15000 is unknown.

Birth canal diameters of early *H. erectus* were significantly smaller than those in *H. sapiens,* and the passage of a modern-sized full-term fetus would have been impossible. *H. erectus* infants must have exhibited considerable postpartum development and long-term dependence upon their primary caretaker, probably the mother.

Excavations at Lake Turkana in 1978 revealed several deep, four-toed impressions of hippopotamus feet and a shallow depression resembling a human footprint (Behrensmeyer & Laporte, 1981). Further excavations revealed two more complete humanlike footprints in line with the first. Excavations in 1979 revealed another two complete human tracks along with tracks of many other vertebrates. The footprints were apparently formed when the mud surface in the area was submerged under quiet water. Tracks of a small wading bird indicate that the water was shallow. The human prints date to about 1.5 mya and were made by an individual 5 to 5.6 feet tall and weighing about 120 pounds.

An almost complete *Homo erectus* skull, KNM-ER 3733 (Figure 10-4), from Lake Turkana is dated to 1.5 mya (R. Leakey, 1970a, 1970b; Walker & Leakey, 1978). The skull looks almost identical to *H. erectus* skulls found in China that date to only 360,000 years ago.

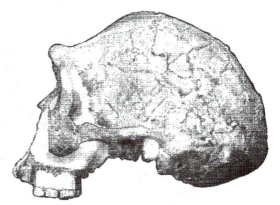

FIGURE 10-4 KNM-ER 3733, a *Homo erectus* cranium from Koobi Fora, Kenya. Some researchers refer this skull to *Homo ergaster.* (Courtesy Jeffrey K. McKee.)

Slightly older than KNM-ER 3733 is a very similar skull belonging to KNM-ER 3833. Its brow ridges, nuchal region, mastoids,* and cranial base are somewhat thicker than similar areas in KNM-ER 3733. Wolpoff (1980) suggested the possibility that KNM-ER 3733 is a female and KNM-ER 3833 is a male.

The KNM-ER 1805 skull from Lake Turkana dates to approximately 1.5 mya. The face is broken away from the skull, the brow ridge is missing, and there is an associated mandible. Although the specimen shows closer similarity to the preceding australopithecines than to KNM-ER 3733, Wolpoff suggested that it belongs with *H. erectus* and that it may represent a transitional stage.

Olduvai Gorge. In Bed II at Olduvai Gorge, in deposits near the margin of an ancient lake, L. Leakey (1961) recovered a human skullcap, which was labeled OH 9. Some 100 yards away lay numerous handaxes and abundant remains of large mammals, the long bones of which were apparently split for marrow. The material is dated to 1.2 mya. The skullcap resembles Far East *Homo erectus.* It is thick; the frontal region is flattened; and there are a prominent nuchal crest, small mastoids, and large, flaring brow ridges. There is no face.

OH 9 shows similarities to the smaller but more complex KNM-ER 3733 material. The two finds resemble each other in enough ways that Rightmire (1979) suggested the possibility of the Turkana population being ancestral to that at Olduvai.

Other artifactual and skeletal remains associated with *H. erectus* come from Bed IV at Olduvai (Day, 1971; M. Leakey, 1971) and date between 700,000 and 400,000 years ago. A left femoral shaft and hipbone associated with an Acheulian

---

*The mastoid process is a bony protuberance found on each side of the skull behind the ear. It carries the insertion of the sternomastoid (or sternocleidomastoid) muscles, which function to allow humans to rotate the head sideways. With the enlarging of the mastoids the muscles obtain leverage to pull the head forward and make it possible for the sternomastoid muscles to raise the head after it has tipped back.

industry (the stone tool industry of *H. erectus*) in Bed IV represented the first well-defined artifactual assemblage of *H. erectus* at Olduvai. A sample of the occupational debris from Bed IV yielded 494 artifacts, 347 unmodified cobbles, and 257 largely fragmentary faunal skeletal remains. Handaxes from Bed IV resemble those of the Early Acheulian series in Middle Bed II. Handaxes, the characteristic tool of the Acheulian tradition, are pear-shaped implements with sharp edges all around.

Femoral and pelvic remains attributed to *H. erectus* and referred to as OH 28 were found in situ during the 1970 Olduvai excavations. The femur has most of the shaft but lacks the head and greater trochanter (a bony eminence on the upper part of the femur to which muscles that extend and flex the leg are attached). Femoral and pelvic fragments from the left side of the body are probably from the same individual. There is every indication of habitual bipedalism.

Ethiopia. *H. erectus* inhabited Ethiopia, as indicated at the sites of Omo, Konso, and the Plain of Gadeb. At the Konso site *H. erectus* and a robust australopithecine species have been shown to overlap. The *H. erectus* tool tradition, the Acheulian, has been recovered from the Plain of Gadeb on the southeast plateau in Ethiopia (Clark, 1987). Clark and Kurashina (1979) suggested that humans appeared on the Ethiopian high plateau (the altitude was 2,300–2,400 meters) perhaps about 1 mya. **Artifacts** (cultural remains) from this locale include tools of an advanced Oldowan assemblage, the *Developed Oldowan Industry,* and the Acheulian tradition. Although many elements of the artifact assemblage are provisionally classified as Developed Oldowan, some tools show a refinement more usual in the Acheulian tradition. If the Developed Oldowan assignation does hold, this is the first appearance of such assemblages outside Olduvai Gorge. The Gadeb sites show an alternating sequence of Acheulian and Developed Oldowan dating between 1.5 and 0.7 mya. These must have been contemporaneous traditions. The sites are generally found close to or in stream channels. Although remains of grazing animals are found at some sites, judging from the preponderance of the remains, the preferred food animal seems to have been the hippopotamus.

The Bodo material found in 1976 and hominid materials found in 1981 and 1990 have been dated to approximately 0.6 mya (J. D. Clark et al., 1994). The Ethiopian sites yielding this material also seem to show a transition from the Oldowan chopper and flake assemblages, present in lower stratigraphic units, to Acheulian bifaces, consistently prevalent and widespread in directly overlying deposits (or a relationship between these artifacts). These older dates from the Middle Awash region of Ethiopia and from Olorgesailie in Kenya combine with the older occurrences of Acheulian bifaces at other Ethiopian sites to emphasize the long duration of the Acheulian. Together with the older *H. erectus* from Java, the Ethiopian finds emphasize that the Old World origins and migration, as well as the culture, of *H. erectus* were complex (J. D. Clark et al., 1994).

Clark and Kurashina suggested that there was probably contact between groups inhabiting this region of the Ethiopian highlands and those to the south in the Rift Valley. They also suggested the possibility that these early humans were experimenting with fire.

Tanzania.   The Ndutu skull discovered in Tanzania in 1973 (J. D. Clark, 1976) is a fairly well-preserved specimen dated about 600,000 to 400,000 years ago. Ndutu was roughly contemporaneous with material from Bed IV, Olduvai, and Zhoukoudian, China, which it resembles. The Ndutu skull vault is thick, with prominent brow ridges, which are damaged, but with a rather vertical forehead. The back of the skull (the occipital region) is also thick. On the other hand, the skull shows less robusticity of the muscle markings on the occipital. There is no sagittal ridge across the midline. Ndutu appears to be morphologically intermediate between *H. erectus* and *H. sapiens*. Rightmire (1983) stressed Ndutu's affinities to archaic *H. sapiens* (discussed in Chapter 11).

South Africa.   At Swartkrans, South Africa, Broom and Robinson (1949, 1950) found three fragments of a lower and upper jaw. The best of the three pieces is a mandibular fragment (SK 15). There is also an almost complete skull (SK 847). When the material was first discovered, some argued that it was contemporaneous with members of the robust australopithecine lineage. W. L. G. Clark (1967) suggested that it belonged to a female *A. robustus*. The argument continues, but most suggest that Swartkrans provides evidence for the contemporaneity of *H. erectus* and *A. robustus*.

Olorgesailie Occupation Remains.   Olorgesailie, located in the Rift Valley about an hour's drive from Nairobi, Kenya, is an extensive living site that may contain the relics of a *H. erectus* group. Because there are no human skeletal remains, any designation concerning the human species inhabiting the area must be made on cultural remains and on associated dating. Neither yardstick is satisfactory.

Geological and paleobotanical evidence from Pleistocene sediments indicates that for prolonged periods there was a stable freshwater lake in the area. Former climatic conditions were wetter than today. The site dates between 700,000 and 400,000 to 900,000 years ago (Bye et al., 1987; Isaac, 1977).

The occupation areas have stone and bone accumulations that may have coincided with natural boundaries, such as the bank of a sandy brook or the limit of shade provided by a larger tree. The inhabitants might have built shelters of hedges that disappeared over time. Smaller occupation areas may have been used by four or five adults in a group; larger areas may have accommodated more than twenty adults.

Based on the accumulation of a ton or more of stone artifacts and **manuports** (materials carried into the site, but which do not necessarily show use), it seems the site was continuously occupied for two or three months. Archaeological assemblages at Olorgesailie are later than the lower Acheulian assemblages from Olduvai Bed II. Within one oval-shaped area, measuring 19 by 13 meters, excavators found 2,200 pounds of stone artifacts, rubble, and unmodified cobbles (Figure 10-5).

The abundance of bone of an extinct nonhuman primate (*Theropithecus*) seemed at first to attest to continued, extremely successful hunting of a single troop (Figure 10-6). One analysis of the primate remains stressed that butchering

FIGURE 10-5 Stone tools of the Acheulian tradition from the site of Olorgesailie, Kenya.

D

E

F

FIGURE 10-5 (continued) (Photos courtesy Lori J. Fitton
[*E, F*], Alyson Poirier [*B, C*], and Frank E. Poirier [*A, D*].)

FIGURE 10-6 The skull of an extinct baboon, *Theropithecus,* from Olorgesailie, Kenya. (Photo courtesy Lori J. Fitton.)

occurred but dismissed the contention that the animals were somehow killed as a troop by humans (Shipman et al., 1981). Binford and Todd (1982) suggested that the primates were initially preyed on or at least scavenged by a relatively small predator-scavenger. Later, the bones were subjected to considerable attritional breakage by nonbiological agents or simply by trampling. Humans may have had little to do with this bone accumulation.

If the other faunal remains are the result of human activity, their abundance suggests that the Olorgesailie inhabitants were hunters and scavengers. Large mammalian remains predominate; rodent, bird, and reptilian bones are relatively scarce. However, the lighter bones of smaller rodents, birds, and reptiles are less likely to fossilize than the heavier and larger bones of larger mammals. Most bone is splintered; either the inhabitants pulverized the bone or scavengers moved in after they left camp.

Potts (Gibbons, 1990) found two areas where hominids at Olorgesailie left major concentrations of fossil bones and tools. At one site a nearly complete elephant skeleton intermingled with stone tools was recovered. Potts thought he had uncovered a butchery site.

Potts also suggested that the Olorgesailie hominids had home bases. Bones scarred solely by stone tool marks have been recovered from Olorgesailie. These are unlike bones found at Bed I, Olduvai, that show both stone tool marks and carnivore tooth marks, indicating, according to Potts, that the Olduvai hominids shared carcasses with large predators and scavengers and were unable to keep them from their bases.

The spread of *H. erectus* out of Africa probably involved moving through the Dardanelles, which were often dry during glaciations, facilitating movement from southwest Asia to Europe. The importance of the east Mediterranean route through southwest Asia is indicated at the site of 'Ubeidiya in the Jordon Valley, Israel (Bar-Yosef, 1980), which contains evidence that people emigrated from Africa 1 mya or earlier (Tchernov, 1987).

The strong volcanic activity in the Rift Valley region about 1.6 mya was perhaps one factor leading (forcing) *H. erectus* from Africa and into other parts of the world.

Large numbers of Pre-Acheulian stone tools were found in 1977 from sixteen sites near Ash Shuwahitiyah in northern Arabia. These tools are typologically similar to those from Lower Pleistocene sites in East Africa—especially Oldowan, Karari, and Developed Oldowan materials.

Another site, Najran, located on the eastern side of the Asir Mountains and the Rub' al Khali desert also has tools. Artifacts at both sites are similar in type and percentage, raw material, and technology. The high percentage of choppers at Najran resembles Oldowan sites. However, the Najran sample is too small for positive attribution.

The site near Saffaqah has the largest collection of artifacts from a single Saudi Arabian site. It was found in 1979 and is located southeast of al-Dawadmi. The site is located in a valley and contains large areas of handaxes, cleavers, picks, spheroids, and other materials. It also has choppers and core axes. There are seven Middle Pleistocene artifact clusters—those referred to butchering and meat slicing, to bone splitting, to hide scraping, to plant gathering and processing, to stone tool making, to wood making, and to bone working.

Saffaqah contained almost 8,000 stone tools. The site was abandoned when the large lake in the area disappeared. It had good plant and animal communities to exploit, and there was considerable stone for toolmaking. The period of human occupation stretched from the Middle Pleistocene through the Mousterian and into the Neolithic.

The Saudi sites were occupied by migrations out of Africa. The land route is the longest route and was down the Nile river from the Ethiopian highlands and east across the Sinai into Western Asia. A shorter route was through the Rift Valley and across the Afar depression to the narrow strait of Bab al Mandeb separating Asia and Africa. The strait is about 28 kilometers wide with a small island situated off the Yemen coast. If the migrants could use rafts to reach the island, they could penetrate southwestern Asia from that point.

These materials are described in Whalen and Pease (1990), Whalen and Schatte (1997), Whalen et al. (1982), Whalen et al. (1984), Whalen et al. (1986), and Whalen et al. (1989).

Stone tools perhaps dating to 1 mya were recovered in Qatar (Abdul Nayeem, 1998).

If the new *H. erectus* dates in Indonesia are correct (pages 224–225), *H. erectus* left Africa much earlier than assumed. Such an early migration is possible. Indonesia was once connected to the rest of Asia by lower sea levels that provided a land route from Africa. Java is 10,000 to 15,000 miles from Kenya, depending on the route traveled. At one mile of migration per year, *H. erectus* could have moved from Kenya to Java in 15,000 years.

Asia

Java. Human fossil remains have been recovered from Java, which among other islands of western and northern Indonesia received invasions of Pleistocene animals from both India and China. The Djetis faunal beds, the earliest Javanese human-bearing beds, contain fossil species thought to have come from the tropical region of south China. The overlying Trinil faunal beds, containing fauna largely of south Chinese origin, yielded a host of human fossil remains, including Dubois's original "Pithecanthropus erectus." The dating of the Trinil faunal beds is approximately 750,000 to 500,000 years ago.

The Trinil faunal beds contain fossils of widely varying age. Doubt exists about the relationship of the Trinil fossil skullcap of *H. erectus* and the femur attributed to the same individual. The site yielding the femur is about 15 meters away from the skullcap. The femur's antiquity can only be inferred from association and from its supposedly archaic features. Such indirect evidence, however, has not stilled criticism about the claimed association of the femur and skullcap. Modern chemical analyses can neither confirm nor deny the femur's antiquity—an enterprise not aided by Dubois, who boiled the specimen in glue in the mistaken notion that doing so would aid its preservation.

Dubois apparently mixed materials from two different levels, and the skullcap and femur were not associated. It is ironic that the femur indicating the modernity of *H. erectus*'s bipedalism probably derives from *H. sapiens*. Later *H. erectus* finds do, however, support claims for bipedalism.

The Trinil faunal beds may contain examples of the earliest Javan tools, the Patjitanian (or Pacitanian) tools. These are advanced over earlier Anyathian tools found in Malaysia, which are not associated with human remains. Both industries are considered to be in the Acheulian tradition. Jacob and others (1978) announced the discovery of two stone tools from the Sambungmachan deposits that may range from 900,000 to 700,000 years old.

Tantalizing evidence suggests a far older appearance of *H. erectus* in Asia than previously thought. There are claims for old appearances of *H. erectus* in China at Gongwangling, for example (Wu & Poirier, 1995). Recent redating of two important cranial samples from Java, the Modjokerto and the Sangiran materials, further suggests a long time span. The Modjokerto skull material (Modjokerto 1 or Perning 1) found in 1936 belongs to an approximately 5-year-old individual. It was thought to date to about 1 mya based on the age of the sediment layer with which it is associated.

Two fragments (S27 and S31), the Sangiran materials named *Meganthropus*, were found in the 1970s. This material consists of a crushed face and partial cranium from two individuals. Their robusticity led some to originally suggest that they were closely related to the African robust australopithecines. They were thought to date to 900,000 to 700,000 years ago.

Using argon-argon dating, Swisher et al. (1994) suggested that the Modjokerto material dates to 1.81 mya and the Sangiran to 1.6 mya. The argon-argon dating technique is similar to the potassium-argon technique, but it can be used on a single crystal that yields more accurate isotope ratios than do the larger samples, and, since the argon-argon technique compares two argon isotopes, not potassium, the rarity of potassium in Java is not a problem.

These dates are approximately the same as the earliest appearance of *H. erectus* (or *H. ergaster*) in Africa and suggest that either (1) *H. erectus* left Africa far earlier than imagined (if *H. erectus* evolved first in Africa and then migrated to Asia, the new Asian dates demand a much older *H. erectus* yet to be found in Africa) or (2) perhaps *H. erectus* evolved independently in Asia and in Africa. If this is true, then Asia must also contain *H. habilis,* currently the suspected ancestor of *H. erectus,* or even possibly *Australopithecus* as some suggest is the case in China.

The new dates may answer why no Acheulian tools are found in Asia. Acheulian tools are widely found with African *H. erectus* and should, therefore, be expected to appear in Asia. They do not. Redating of the Javan hominids suggests that if the Asian forms are related to African *H. erectus,* the latter may have left Africa before the invention of the Acheulian tool. If so, this explains its absence in Asia.

Redating the Java materials calls into question the exact evolutionary relationship of the Asian and African fossils normally called *H. erectus.* Noting morphological variation between the Asian and African remains, some suggest that the African forms should be placed in a species called *H. ergaster.* If this viewpoint holds, the Asian forms are put onto a side branch of human evolution. The possibility of an evolutionary line linking Chinese *H. erectus* and *H. sapiens* populations (Wu & Poirier, 1995) refutes this possibility.

One of the most unexpected discoveries is the suggestion that *H. erectus* lived on Java between 53,000 and 27,000 years ago (Gibbons, 1996; Swisher et al., 1996). These dates indicate that *H. erectus* may have survived on Java at least 250,000 years longer than on the Asian mainland and perhaps 1 million years longer than in Africa. If the dating holds, this is the first time that *H. erectus* and *H. sapiens* have been shown to coexist. If this coexistence occurred, *H. erectus* likely became trapped on Java after having spread there over land from the rest of Asia. *H. sapiens* probably arrived after 40,000 years ago by boat. *H. sapiens*'s arrival in Java perhaps led to the demise of *H. erectus.*

The new dates come from water buffalo teeth, not the hominid remains. The animal teeth have high levels of uranium that can compromise ESR dating. Furthermore, the bovid teeth may not be the same age as the human skulls, because flooding or erosion may have washed older skulls from their original resting places.

These findings challenge the multiregional evolutionary model (discussed in Chapter 13), which proposes that *H. erectus* in Asia was among the ancestors of modern humans. Swisher et al.'s (1996) work questions whether the Solo skulls from Java are the ancestors of modern Australian aborigines as predicted by the multiregional model. If the new dates are correct, *H. erectus* persisted in Southeast Asia into the latest Pleistocene overlapping *H. sapiens.*

Morwood et al. (1998) suggest that *Homo erectus* in Indonesia actually used boat travel—perhaps bamboo rafts. This is a startling claim given most current thought on the abilities of *H. erectus,* and, if the claim is true, it will necessitate a serious rethinking of *H. erectus's* cognitive and technical skills. Prior to this announcement the earliest widely accepted evidence of major water crossings was the colonization of Australia by anatomically modern *H. sapiens* perhaps 60,000–40,000 years ago.

According to Morwood et al., *H. erectus* reached the island of Flores sometime between 900,000 and 800,000 years ago via a water crossing of at least 19 kilometers from mainland South Asia. It will take considerably more evidence, more widely accepted dates, and time and argument before boat travel is an accepted means of travel for *H. erectus.*

China. A review of the Chinese hominids appears in Wu and Poirier (1995). *H. erectus* in China is found in the cold climates of the north at Zhoukoudian and in the warm and wet climes of southern China. This species had a wide geographical range and had cultural adaptations (e.g., fire, clothing, housing) allowing it to adapt to environmental diversity.

The skeletal remains of Chinese *H. erectus* are mostly teeth and skull fragments. Limb bones are quite rare. Taphonomic analyses are needed at many sites, but some are certainly carnivore accumulations.

There are at least fifteen *H. erectus* sites in China (Figure 10-7). The time span is mostly the Middle Pleistocene, but some Lower Pleistocene sites are possible. Nine sites yield archaeological materials, six sites yield skull and facial materials, twelve sites yield dental and jaw remains, and two sites yield postcranials.

The earliest representatives of human fossil remains from China belong to *H. erectus* and perhaps date to 1.7 mya. Although this date has been confirmed by three different laboratories, a date of 700,000 to 500,000 years ago also appears in the literature. This material from the Yuanmou basin in Yunnan Province consists of teeth and limb fragments (Figure 10-8). The incisors are large and may belong to a young male. The environment at Yuanmou was a grass-forest and the average temperature was about 10 degrees Celsius, lower than the present-day average. According to G. Zhou (1987, unpub. ms.), the material should be referred to as *H. erectus yuanmouensis.*

Until rather recently most Chinese representatives of *H. erectus* came from Zhoukoudian (once spelled Choukoutien), which lies about 25 miles southwest of Beijing (Peking). The remains are often referred to as "Peking Man." Zhoukoudian is a limestone cliff that was long the haunt of "dragon-bone" (fossilized bone) collectors whose finds ended up in Chinese pharmacies. In the early 1900s, the German paleontologist K. A. Haberer found a human tooth in a Beijing drugstore and traced it back to Zhoukoudian. For twenty-four years various scientists worked in or watched the site, which had once been a large cave. In 1921 they were led to Locality 1, where they immediately found bits of quartz recognized as a tool. More quartz tools were found in subsequent excavations. The presence of tools at Zhoukoudian indicated human occupation.

In 1923 and 1926 human teeth were sifted from the Zhoukoudian debris. In 1927 the Swedish paleontologist B. Böhlin produced one more tooth. This was subsequently shown to Davidson Black (1931), who allocated the tooth to a new hominid genus and species that he named "Sinanthropus pekinensis." Zhoukoudian was excavated continuously from 1927 to 1937, and the remains were described by Franz Weidenreich (1936, 1938, 1941, 1943). Work resumed in the 1950s, and a new mandible was recovered and described in 1959 (Chang, 1962; Jia & Huang, 1990).

Human remains from Locality 1 included at least 14 skullcaps without faces, 12 mandibles, 150 teeth, and several postcranial remains. Much of the material was fragmentary; however, enough remained to allow a rather complete reconstruction. Early in World War II, at the beginning of the Japanese occupation of China, all the skulls were lost, and no one seems to know what happened to them (Shapiro, 1971, 1974). All that remained was a fine set of casts, a lone tooth, and a very complete set of monographs by Weidenreich based on the original materials.

Deposits at Zhoukoudian were laid down over an extensive time period (Huang, 1960). The *H. erectus* remains seem to date back to approximately 360,000 years ago according to the K/Ar dating method. However, estimates range from 600,000 to 414,000 years ago. This postdates Djetis faunal beds and is perhaps contemporaneous with the later Trinil faunal beds from Java.

A number of animal bones were associated with the hominid material. It was a time when *Crocuta crocuta,* the living spotted hyena, was crowding its older cousin out of its habitats in Africa, Europe, and China. Deer bones were the most numerous faunal remains, but there were numerous elephant, rhinoceros, and giant beaver bones. High and low in the fill were layers of ash and burnt bone.

Scattered about were a few human trunk and limb bones and skull fragments (Figure 10-9). A good many pieces of the face and jaw were present, but these were not affixed to the braincase. Some suggested that the Zhoukoudian inhabitants were cannibals. If so, cannibalism was probably ritualistic; that is, human protein was not an important part of the diet.

Numerous pollen grains were collected at Zhoukoudian; 28 percent of the arboreal species were of beech and 11 percent of grasses. Seeds of the hackberry, a relative of the wild cherry, were common. Pollen analysis indicates that Zhoukoudian lay near the border zone that separated the northern coniferous belt, or boreal forest, from the temperate steppe. The hills about Zhoukoudian were covered in pine and spruce, the slopes bearing trees that grow today in the far north of Maine (Coon, 1962).

Floral and faunal remains suggest a northern temperate zone. Mammalian remains associated with a tropical or polar climate are rare. Evidence from different cave layers suggests climatic shifts during the long history of Zhoukoudian. There is, however, disagreement among Chinese researchers concerning the climate during *H. erectus* times at Zhoukoudian (Li & Ji, 1981; Wu & Poirier, 1995).

Mountainous areas north and west of Zhoukoudian had mixed forests of pine, cedar, elm, hackberry, and Chinese redbud. Bison, saber-toothed tigers, tigers, leopards, cheetahs, horses, woolly rhinoceroses, striped hyenas, sika deer,

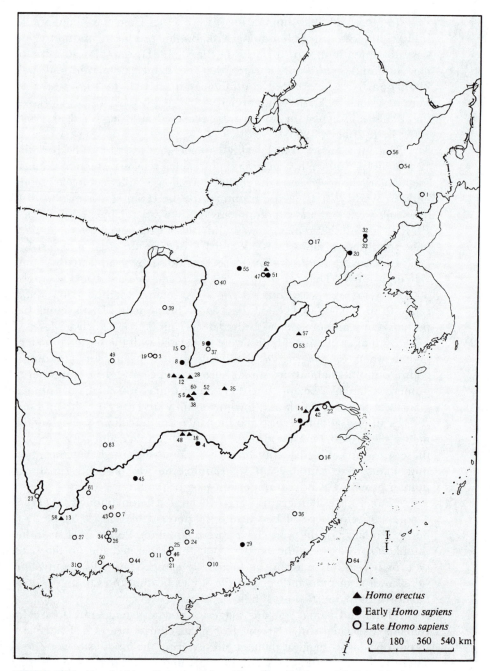

FIGURE 10-7 Hominid locations in China. (Courtesy X. Wu and F. E. Poirier.)

FIGURE 10-7 (continued)

1. Antu	17. Jianpin	33. Miaohoushan Dongdong	49. Xichou
2. Baojiyan	18. Jianshi	34. Nalai	50. Xichuan
3. Changwu	19. Jinchuan	35. Nanzhao	51. Zhoukoudian (Locality 4)
4. Changyang	20. Jinniushan	36. Qingliu	52. Xintai
5. Chaoxian	21. Laibin	37. Quwo	53. Xuetian
6. Chenjiawo	22. Lianhua	38. Quyuan River Mouth	54. Xujiayao
7. Chuandong	23. Lijiang	39. Salawusu	55. Yanjiangang
8. Dali	24. Lipu	40. Shiyu	56. Yiyuan
9. Dingcun	25. Liujiang	41. Shuicheng	57. Yuanmou
10. Dongzhongyan	26. Longlin	42. Tangshan	58. Yuanyang
11. Du'an	27. Longtanshan	43. Taohua	59. Yunxi
12. Gongwangling	28. Luonan	44. Tiandong	60. Yunxian
13. Guojiabao	29. Maba	45. Tongzi	61. Zhaotong
14. Hexian	30. Maomaodong	46. Tubo	62. Zhoukoudian (Locality 1)
15. Huanglong	31. Mengzi	47. Zhoukoudian (Upper Cave)	63. Ziyang
16. Jiande	32. Miaohoushan	48. Wushan (Damiao)	64. Zuozhen

and elephants inhabited this region. A big river and possibly a lake located to the east contained various water species; along the shorelines grew reeds and plants. Buffalo, deer, otters, beavers and other animals inhabited the area (Jia, 1975).

Some of these species may have formed the diet for *H. erectus*. *H. erectus* at Zhoukoudian hunted big game; however, the daily meal consisted as much of small animals such as hedgehogs, frogs, and hare. Ash layers in the cave abounded with the bones of these animals and others such as hamsters, mice, black rats, and harvest mice. There are fragments of ostrich eggs.

The inhabitants of Zhoukoudian may have exploited vegetable foods; however, these fossilize poorly. Charred hackberry seeds are the only evidence to date of possible plant food.

FIGURE 10-8 Upper median incisors of *Homo erectus* from Yuanmou, China. (Courtesy Institute of Vertebrate Paleontology and Paleoanthropology [IVPP], Beijing, China.)

FIGURE 10-9 Skull bones and reconstructed face and skull of *Homo erectus* from Zhoukoudian, China. *A,* First *H. erectus* skull found in Zhoukoudian in 1929 at Locality E; *B,* Anterior (mostly the frontal) and posterior (mostly the occipital) parts of skull H found in 1966; *C,* Right-side view of the reconstructed skull H; *D,* Left-side view of skull H; *E,* Superior view of skull H; *F,* Bust of *H. erectus* from Zhoukoudian; *G,* Reconstructed face and skull. (Courtesy Institute of Vertebrate Paleontology and Paleo-anthropology [IVPP].)

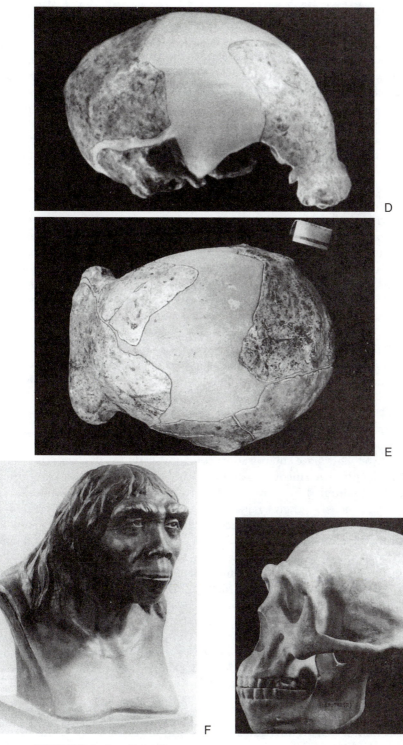

D

E

F

G

FIGURE 10-9 (continued)

Numerous quartz stone tools were uncovered from Locality 1. The characteristic tool was a pebble trimmed to make an edged chopping tool. Zhoukoudian yielded flake scrapers and points made with a crude beak. Many tools are large, massive, and crudely worked; few display an even, uniform retouch. Possibly some of the tools were used to work animal skins that could have been worn or used as enclosure walls to keep out the cold.

The tool manufacturers often selected oval-shaped pebbles to make single-edged or doubled-edged axes. These were found in most layers in the cave deposit. Most tools were made from sandstone and varied in shape from round disks to irregular triangles and long slabs. These tools were easily blunted, and there is bountiful evidence of blunt and resharpened artifacts in the cave.

Binford and Ho (1985) and Binford and Stone (1986) questioned many of the notions associated with the finds at Zhoukoudian. Binford and Ho rejected arguments that *H. erectus* at Zhoukoudian was a cannibal, an argument posited at least in part because the skulls lack faces, supposedly removed to gain access to the brain. They argued that hominid remains at the site are instead the work of other scavenging carnivores. Once inside the cave, these remains were dispersed throughout the cave by secondary scavenging, probably by wolves and hyenas.

Although many have stated that *H. erectus* used fire and perhaps cooked food, Binford and Ho and Binford and Stone suggested that the traces of fire at Zhoukoudian do not reflect purposeful burning and do not indicate the use of hearths.

Binford and Ho and Binford and Stone questioned whether bone deposits indicate that *H. erectus* at Zhoukoudian was a big-game hunter. They stated that the deposits, including the human bones, were the remains of carnivore activity. They also doubt that the hackberry seeds represent the remains of *H. erectus*'s dietary practices. They have shown rather conclusively that earlier reports of bone tools at Zhoukoudian are incorrect, and that the so-called bone tools are instead bones that were modified by carnivore chewing and not human handiwork.

Jia (1989) reacted strongly against many of the propositions stated by Binford and Ho and Binford and Stone. Jia suggested that the broken bone at Zhoukoudian may be attributed to an attempt to extract marrow. He also stated quite adamantly that the human inhabitants at Zhoukoudian not only used but also controlled fire. Given the cold climates at the time when the cave was inhabited, fire use could have been an important means for keeping warm.

Another important Chinese *H. erectus* site is at Chenjiawo in Lantian District, Shaanxi Province (Woo, 1964). In 1963, Chinese paleontologists recovered a mandible from the site; in 1964 at Gongwangling Hill, about 20 kilometers away, they recovered facial bones, a tooth, and a fairly complete skullcap (Figure 10-10)—all from the same individual. Both sites predate Zhoukoudian. The cranial material may date to 800,000 to 750,000 years ago. The mandible may be dated to 590,000 to 500,000 years ago. The Lantian jaw is robust, and in many respects the skullcap is similar to material from the Javan Djetis faunal beds. The skullcap is low and excessively thick; the massive brow ridges are arched near the middle. The cranial capacity is estimated to

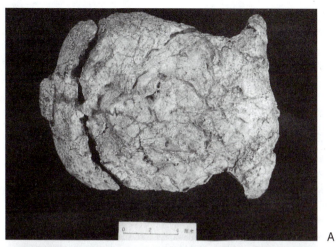

A

B

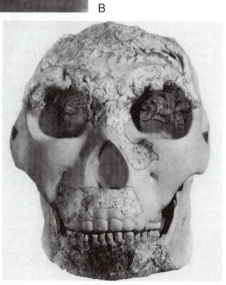

C

FIGURE 10-10 *Homo erectus* from Gongwangling, Lantian, China. *A,* Skullcap; *B,* Lateral view of reconstructed skull and face; *C,* Anterior view of reconstructed skull and face. (Courtesy Institute of Vertebrate Paleontology and Paleoanthropology [IVPP].)

be approximately 780 cc, close to the estimate for the skull from the Djetis faunal beds.

The mandible is well preserved except for small parts of the vertical ramus. All the teeth are present except the right first premolar, which was lost before death. There is no mandibular third molar on either side. This was a congenital condition. Indications in the bone and teeth suggest that Lantian suffered from periodontal disease and manifested a condition known as periodontoclasia.

According to Woo (1964), the Lantian material is allied with Zhoukoudian. However, Woo maintains that differences exist, and he first classified the Lantian material as "Sinanthropus lantianensis." Most paleontologists prefer the designation *H. erectus lantianensis.*

A heavily fossilized *Homo erectus* skull (Figure 10-11) belonging to a young male was unearthed in southern China in 1980 from Longtang cave in Hexian County, Anhui Province (Wanpo et al., 1981). Excavations in 1980 and 1981 exposed parts of the frontal and parietal bones from the skull, the left side of a fairly robust mandible (which may belong to a female), and nine teeth. As many as four individuals may be represented by the fossil sample. The skull has similarities and differences from the skulls found at Zhoukoudian. The fission track date is 190,000 to 150,000 years old and the amino acid racemization date is about 200,000 years old.

Mammalian fauna associated with the human remains consist largely of animals that probably inhabited forests and woodlands. There are indications that the climate at this time in the middle-late Middle Pleistocene was cool.

Fossil and archaeological material from Longgupo Cave (called the Wushan Hominid Site in Wu and Poirier, 1995), situated near the eastern border of Sichuan

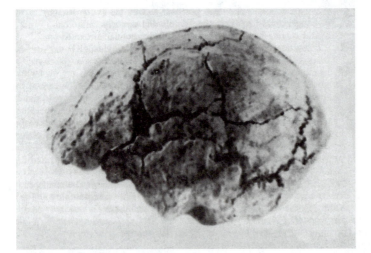

FIGURE 10-11 *Homo erectus* skullcap from Hexian, China. (Courtesy Institute of Vertebrate Paleontology and Paleoanthropology [IVPP].)

Province, lends support for the notion that hominids were established in Asia by 1.9 mya. (This is also suggested by the most recent dates for some *H. erectus* sites in Java.) The Longgupo materials may support an early hominid lineage in Asia, and the morphology of the left side of mandibular piece from an adult suggests to Wangpo et al. (1995) that the materials may not be those of *H. erectus* but instead are from *H. ergaster*. The root structure of an isolated upper incisor from the site suggests likewise.

The dating of Longgupo is a crucial matter for understanding hominid evolution in Asia. Paleomagnetic and ESR dating and faunal associations are consistent with an old date (Wu & Poirier, 1995).

The bifed root (a trait of *H. ergaster*) of the mandibular premolar and the primitive features of the mandible lead some to exclude the materials from *H. erectus* (Ciochon, 1996; Wangpo et al., 1995). The in situ molar has five cusps like *H. habilis* and *H. ergaster* and is unlike the six cusps found in Asian *H. erectus*. If this is a species more primitive than *H. erectus*, it implies that the first hominid out of Africa was not *H. erectus* and that *H. erectus* may have evolved in Asia and spread back into Europe and Africa (Wood & Turner, 1995).

Two items from the site that may be early stone tools were made of a type of rock not found elsewhere at the site (Wangpo et al., 1995).

Having said this, it must also be said that some doubt that the dental remains are even those of a hominid. Also recovered from the site were *Gigantopithecus* remains (Wu & Poirier, 1995). Perhaps the Longgupo specimen was not hominid but was related to the Chinese hominoid *Lufengpithecus* (Chapter 6). Longgupo may have no special affinity to early African hominids.

At the 700,000-to-1-million-year-old site of Xiaochangliang many artifacts and fossil animal bones, some with cut marks, were found. Taken together, these are the earmarks of a workshop or possible campsite. The ratio of waste flakes to artifacts that were used as tools is consistent with the ratios expected at sites where tools were actually made. An open-air campsite is a rare find in China. Until the Xiaochangliang finds, the only clearly occupied early sites in Asia were caves, notably Zhoukoudian, located 65 miles southeast.

The artifacts seem to be homegrown and show no indication of having been introduced from outside populations, such as a migration from Africa. Artifacts from Xiaochangliang show that relatively sophisticated technologies arose in localized parts of the Far East as early as, or earlier than, in Europe.

In 1989 a human skull was found in Yunxian County, Hubei Province, central China. Another skull was found in 1990. Both skulls are without mandibles, are big and robust, and have distinct postorbital constriction. There is no median sagittal ridge, the parietal bone is short and flat, and there is no angular torus.

These skulls have features usually seen in *H. erectus*, such as very distinct postorbital constriction and the low position of the maximum breadth of the braincase. However, there are other features concordant with archaic Chinese *H. sapiens*. The advanced features favor a *H. sapiens* attribution, but final taxonomic ascription must await further analysis.

Based on the associated fauna, the site dates to the middle part of the Middle Pleistocene. It has been suggested that the site may be at least 1 million years old. Some stone artifacts were surface collected and some appeared in situ.

Placing the Javan and Chinese *H. erectus* fossils in the same species affirms their close evolutionary relationship. The major features differentiating the Zhoukoudian and Javan specimens are in the skull and teeth; the cranial capacity of the Zhoukoudian fossils is larger, and the teeth are significantly smaller compared to earlier fossils. The Zhoukoudian skulls vary greatly in length, and cranial capacities range from 915 cc to 1,225 cc. Asian *H. erectus* samples do not differ in their postcranial anatomies and approximate *H. sapiens* in this respect.

Asian *H. erectus* specimens have equally thick skull bones, and all have large brow ridges, but there are major differences in cranial capacities. The mean cranial capacity of the Javanese material is estimated at 975 cc, or lower; the Lantian material at 780 cc; and the material from Locality 1, Zhoukoudian at 1,075 cc. The increased brain volume differentiating the Javanese and Chinese Locality 1 samples is matched by other modernizations of their skull morphology.

When compared with older Javanese material, the dental arch of the Zhoukoudian sample is shorter and more rounded in front, and there is no sign of a diastema in the upper tooth row. The Zhoukoudian mandible is also shorter and more compact. In the Zhoukoudian sample the first upper molar is the largest (it is the second largest in the Javan sample), but the lower third molar is shorter than the second (Howells, 1966).

Fossil evidence for the presence of Middle Pleistocene humans has been reported from Vietnam. There are human remains from the sites of Tham Khuyen and Tham Hai and tools from the sites of Nui Do and Quan Yen. The Vietnam fossils have a preliminary date of about 400,000 years ago (Ciochon, 1984/1985).

Thailand. A rock shelter dating to approximately 700,000 years old has been found in northern Thailand. The Kao Pah Nam rock shelter, located in a heavily eroded limestone landscape, yielded animal bones, stone tools, and the remnants of a hearth. Faunal remains include forest-dwelling animals such as the hippopotamus, and giant ox, deer, bamboo rat, and porcupine—all or some of which may have been included in the diet.

Europe

The first recovered human skeletal material dating from Middle Pleistocene Europe is the Heidelberg or Mauer mandible. It was recovered in 1907 from a sandpit in the village of Mauer, Germany, located 6 miles southeast of Heidelberg. It lay 78 feet below the surface in soils containing bones of the spotted hyena, *Crocuta crocuta*, and is dated to between 300,000 and 250,000 years ago, although the date is insecure.

The mandible is well preserved; most of the teeth are moderately worn, except for four left molars and premolars, broken at the time of discovery and only partially restored. It is chinless and massive—one of the largest human mandibles yet recovered. Compared with other human mandibles, Mauer's most striking feature is the great width of the ascending ramus. This vertical strut of bone underlies the back of the cheek and carries at its posterior corner the condyle that articulates the jaw with the skull. The functional implications of the mandibular breadth are related to the fact that the temporalis muscle (the largest of the muscles that close the jaw) attaches to the coronoid process of the mandible and fans out on the side of the skull. The masseter muscle attaches to the outer surface of the lower portion of the ramus. Although the width of the ascending ramus is undoubtedly related to mandibular length, it also suggests powerful chewing muscles and wide-flaring, strong cheek bones. Despite the large size of the mandible, the teeth are not proportionately large.

Beyond guessing that it had a wide, not strongly projecting face, we cannot reconstruct the Heidelberg (Mauer) skull. Despite its large size, the jaw and teeth place the specimen in the genus *Homo*. Some scientists refer Mauer to a *H. erectus* subspecies, for example, *H. e. heidelbergensis*. Others include it with early *H. sapiens*. Increasingly, however, Mauer is referred to as *Homo heidelbergensis* and is touted as ancestral to Neandertals. Some newly recovered English (Boxgrove—page 241) and Spanish (Atapuerca—page 239) fossils and other materials are also being referred to as *Homo heidelbergensis*.

Middle Pleistocene human remains have been recovered from the site of Vértesszöllös, situated west of Budapest, Hungary. Vértesszöllös appears to have been a campsite with a small saucerlike depression, no bigger than an average room. The area was apparently formed by rising waters of a hot spring, which may have made it an attractive gathering place during cooler weather. In and around the site were a number of pebble tools—the first undisputed early tools found in Europe (Kretzoi & Vértes, 1965). The only human skeletal remains were an occipital bone and quite a large amount of burned bone, indicating the use of fire. The site was first dated at approximately 400,000 years ago, but this date may be too old, and there exist estimates of 350,000 years to as recently as approximately 185,000 years ago.

The occipital is rather thick and has a well-marked angle and ridge for the attachment of the neck muscles. Despite its thickness, some argue that the skull bone is from a population advanced over African and contemporaneous Asian *H. erectus*. The reconstructed angle formed by the roof and floor of the skull appears to have been wider than that in *H. erectus,* indicating that the cranial capacity was considerably larger. Thoma (1966) estimated that the cranial capacity was about 1,400 cc, close to the average of modern *H. sapiens* and well above the previously described *H. erectus* sample.

Because of the morphological differentiation from the Middle Pleistocene Asian sample, and because of its estimated large brain size, Thoma (1967, 1969) suggested that the Vértesszöllös occipital might be designated *H. sapiens paleohungaricus*. Thoma's suggestion would place a population of more progressive *H. sapiens* contemporaneous with the *H. erectus* population. It has been suggested that an evolutionary line ran from Mauer through Vértesszöllös to later *H. sapiens* populations. According to Wolpoff (1977), the potential importance of Vértesszöllös lies in the information it provides concerning evolutionary changes at the end of the *H. erectus* lineage or the very beginning of *H. sapiens.*

The occipital bone probably belonged to a large individual. It exceeds *H. erectus* occipitals in total height; however, it shows general affinities to *H. erectus*. Although its cranial capacity has been used to assess its phylogenetic position, direct determination of taxonomic status is impossible from the Vértesszöllös occipital alone.

The site of Přezletice, Czech Republic, is probably older than either Mauer or Vértesszöllös. Přezletice is located near Prague and was first recognized in 1938. The site is rich in early Pleistocene mammalian fauna. Stone tools were recovered, but no undoubted human remains appeared. Most of the bone assemblage was broken, and it has been claimed that one end of a long bone fragment from a deer had been worked to form a keel-like point. Simply on the basis of its time placement, Přezletice might possibly represent an early *H. erectus* site in Europe; but without human skeletal remains, one cannot be sure.

A significant *Homo erectus* find was made recently in the country of Georgia, at a site called Dmanisi. The find is a large and heavy mandible, with all its teeth in place. The mandible was found in conjunction with stone tools, the skulls of two saber-toothed tigers, and the ribs of an elephant.

The dating of this material is 1.6 mya or 900,000 years ago, based on paleomagnetism. Gabunia and Vekua (1995) date the site to between 1.8 and 1.6 mya. This is an important find because of the paucity of early *H. erectus* remains outside of Africa. Although there are *H. erectus* materials of 1 mya in Asia, most European remains are in the range of 500,000 years ago. The materials from Georgia will help focus the issue of when *H. erectus* migrated from Africa (Gibbons, 1992). The Dmanisi mandible seems more similar to African than Asian *H. erectus.*

A Middle Pleistocene site, Fontana Ranuccio in Italy, yielded limestone tools dating to 700,000 years ago and a bone industry dating to 450,000 years ago. The two human teeth (one an incisor) date to the latter level. This is the earliest well-dated association of Acheulian stone tools with human remains to be found in Italy (Serge & Ascenzi, 1984). It is not clear if the material belongs to a member of *H. erectus,* although the 700,000-year-old date for the choppers is in the *H. erectus* time span.

Another site in Italy, Castel di Guido, is estimated to date about 300,000 years ago. The site yielded animal remains, Acheulian stone and bone tools, and small tools. Fragments of human remains, including a temporal bone, were recovered. The temporal bone shows traits of *H. erectus* and has a number of features associated with *H. sapiens* (Mallegni & Radmilli, 1988).

In 1994 a 900,000-to-800,000-year-old *Homo* skullcap called Ceprano Man was recovered in Italy. Unlike classic *H. erectus,* this find has no crest dissecting the midline of the skull, and the brain is significantly larger than classic *H. erectus.* Italian researchers find more resemblance between this material and that from Algeria than with the Mauer find.

The Montmaurin mandible from France may date to about 300,000 years ago. It resembles the Mauer mandible in its robustness but is about the same size as the early *H. sapiens* mandible from Steinheim, Germany (Chapter 11). Montmaurin differs from Mauer in having less broad rami. The mandible has no chin, and in other features resembles *H. erectus* (Wolpoff, 1980).

Some of the newest *H. erectus* materials are from Europe, and fossils from Spain are among the most exciting. Gran Dolina, one cave site from Atapuerca, yielded hundreds of hominid remains and tools paleomagnetically dated to at least 780,000 years ago. (Gran Dolina is only a few hundred yards removed from Sima de los Huesos, described in the next chapter.) There are four to six individuals (perhaps victims of cannibalism), including a child and an adolescent. Some facial traits suggest the remains are more aligned with African fossils that some call *H. ergaster.* Others call the materials *H. heidelbergensis.*

Some Spanish researchers refer to the young boy's remains as *H. antecessor,* a species they consider ancestral to modern humans and Neandertals. The name *H. antecessor* comes from the Latin word meaning explorer or one who goes first. Unfortunately, this new species is based on a juvenile specimen. If it is accepted, it will bump *H. erectus* and *H. heidelbergensis* off the main line of descent to modern humans, placing them among the proliferating side branches of the human family tree.

The young boy from Atapuerca had a face with modern features, sunken cheekbones, and a projecting nose and midface. There is a prominent brow ridge and multiple roots for the premolars. The multiple roots of the premolars are not found in any other European fossil, all having a single root. Only African *H. erectus* (= *ergaster*) has multiple roots. It is an unusual mosaic that de Castro et al. (1997) think cannot be accommodated within *H. heidelbergensis.*

De Castro and his colleagues suggest that *H. antecessor* is a close kin of *H. ergaster* in Africa and is ancestral to *H. heidelbergensis,* which many agree led to the Neandertals. De Castro et al. suggest that *H. ergaster* gave rise to *H. antecessor,* probably in Africa, although it is still only seen at Atapuerca. They think *H. antecessor* dispersed to Europe about 1 mya, leaving remains at Atapuerca about 780,000 years ago. It further evolved into *H. heidelbergensis* and to the Neandertals, but not to modern humans. The southern branch of *H. antecessor,* probably still in Africa, gave rise to modern humans through another, yet unidentified species. This form may be revealed in the Kabwe and Bodo specimens (Chapter 11).

Bone fragments and stone tools come from three sites at Orce in Spain. The sites are situated around an ancient lake basin. Disputed hominid bones date to 1.6 mya, making Orce possibly among the oldest European sites with hominid remains.

Dates at Orce are based on paleomagnetism and micro- and macromammalian fauna. Fuentenueva 3 contains more than 100 flint artifacts from three distinct layers and nonhuman bones. Barranco Leon contains more than sixty artifacts similar to the Developed Oldowan of Africa. A cranial fragment of highly contentious affinity and two small pieces of humerus were found. The Venta Micena site yielded more than 15,000 bones comprising more than thirty species. The nearby Cueva Victoria site yielded four fragmentary hominid fossils.

While some claim the bones from Venta Micena are human, others claim they are from horses. The cranial fragment is the most contentious item, while the small pieces of humerus are more readily accepted as hominid. Immunological tests of proteins confirm both human and horse presence. Recent studies by Borja et al. (1997) that seem to confirm human albumin from the skull fragment have not stilled the controversy. While the bone remains are vigorously debated, the archaeological remains dated to 1.4 mya are generally accepted.

Although the migration route to Europe is usually thought to be a land route running north from the Middle East and then west across land bordering the Mediterranean or regions further inland, humans could have traveled across the Strait of Gibraltar from northern Africa or across the Bosporous from Turkey. Declines in sea level between 2.4 and 1.6 mya reduced the distance across the Bosporous to about 3 miles, with a small island approximately halfway. African fauna associated with tools and butchery support the notion that humans entered Europe prior to 1 mya.

European Middle Pleistocene human populations were possibly pursuing a big-game hunting way of life as is suggested at the sites of Torralba and Ambrona, located in the rolling countryside of north-central Spain (Howell, 1965; Pfeiffer, 1972) and at the sites of Aridos 1 and 2 also located in Spain. The Ambrona Valley was part of a major migration route for herds of deer, horses, and elephants. Concentrated in a relatively small area at Torralba are the remains of approximately thirty elephants, twenty-five horses, twenty-five deer, ten wild oxen, and six rhinoceroses. Detailed stratigraphic and pollen analysis at Torralba and Ambrona yields a data of 500,000 years ago.

Binford (1981, 1985, 1987a, 1987b) raised serious doubts concerning the interpretations of the Torralba and Ambrona sites (see also Klein, 1987, and Villa, 1990, for a review of Binford's argument). It is generally conceded that the Torralba data were overinterpreted. It no longer seems feasible to view Torralba as an elephant-hunting site.

Aridos, a Middle Pleistocene locale containing elephant bones and stone tools, is located 18 kilometers southeast of Madrid and provides evidence for organized exploitation of elephant remains by hominids. The evidence appears quite different from the marginal scavenging and minimal involvement by hominids with the Torralba elephant remains (Villa, 1990).

Aridos 1 and 2 are 200 meters apart and are dated to the Middle Pleistocene based on microfauna and tool associations. Both are individual death sites containing elephant remains (Villa, 1990). There is no evidence of projectile points, spears, or natural traps to indicate hunting behavior. However, both sites clearly indicate meat acquisition through early access to the carcass. There is extensive evidence of knapping and tool resharpening. The Aridos finds conform to patterns documented at butchery sites. There is no convincing evidence to support a hypothesis of elephant drives at Aridos, and the newer analysis at Torralba no longer supports the possibility of elephant drives there.

Potentially exciting and quite unexpected finds were recovered from the Siberian site of Diring Yuriakh by Y. Mochanov and S. Fodoseeva (Morell, 1994). Diring

Yuriakh, located above the flood plain of the Lena River, is at 62 degrees north latitude and had annual temperature fluctuations of −70 degrees F to +70 degrees F. Occupation of Diring may represent an opportunistic movement of people into the area during a warm climatic interval. Even then the climate would have required clothing, fire, and shelter to keep warm. It is not clear how long Diring was occupied or whether occupation in the Lena Basin was uninterrupted for a long period of time. Other sites in the region date from 10,000 to 30,000 years old.

Russian researchers thought the purported tools at Diring to be similar to East African Oldowan materials. The purported archaeological record has large rocks that look as if they were used as anvils. Flake debitage surrounding these "anvils" is supplemented by a few unifacially flaked choppers or scrappers. Some purported tools had only a few flakes struck from the core; others appear to be extensively worked. Richard Potts suggests that Diring was a quarrying site. While Waters et al. (1997) report the finding of 4,000 artifacts, other archaeologists remain skeptical and suggest the materials are geofacts.

Dating at the site is disputed (Gibbons, 1997b) with Russian researchers giving dates of 1.6 mya and M. Waters giving a date of about 500,000 years ago. A TL date of 260,000 is also suggested. All these dates are unexpectedly early for an area previously assumed uninhabited by early hominids. We are not considering the 1.6 mya date as possible. Waters' date is within the *H. erectus* time span, previously thought to have migrated no further north than Zhoukoudian, 2,500 kilometers south of Diring.

The 14-inch-long tibial fragment from Boxgrove, England, is dated to 515,000–485,000 years ago. Based on the length and thickness of this lower leg fragment, it is estimated to come from a very muscular person about 6 feet tall and weighing more than 168 pounds. Since Boxgrove predates the Neandertals, some suggest it may be the common ancestor of modern humans and Neandertals.

Two human lower incisors found in the fine silt layer below the tibia may belong to another individual living after the owner of the tibia. The teeth look like teeth in the Heidelberg mandible, and some refer Boxgrove to *H. heidelbergensis*. Root damage suggests periodontal disease.

The human remains are associated with handaxes and remains of elephants, rhinoceroses, hyenas, deer, bears, and wolves. Cut marks on rhinoceros and horse bones show that the carcasses were skinned, disarticulated, and defleshed, prior to the smashing of the bones for the marrow. There is no evidence of secondary scavenging by other animals.

Although other European sites date to about the same time as Boxgrove, none shares its detailed archaeology. More than 125 flint handaxes are scattered about the dismembered animal remains.

ACHEULIAN TRADITION

The Acheulian tool tradition associated mostly with African *H. erectus* sites first appeared about 1.5 mya. It seems to be an advance over the preceding Oldowan tool tradition associated with *H. habilis*. Acheulian tools were made from a wider range of raw materials, which may indicate a greater awareness by the toolmakers of their environment. In contrast to the all-purpose Oldowan tools, different Acheulian tools were apparently tailored for different purposes. They appear to be more standardized and specialized than Oldowan tools.

The basic Acheulian tool kit includes a versatile range of cutting, scraping, piercing, chopping, and pounding tools used to prepare animal and plant materials. Bones were broken and trimmed to use as tools, and wood was worked into spears.

The precision evident in the manufacture of Acheulian handaxes apparently resulted from a new flaking method, the **soft-hammer technique,** in which a stone flake is detached from the core with a wood, bone, or antler hammer (Figure 10-12). The use of these softer materials as a hammer allowed more control of the final product in terms of flake length, width, and thickness. The core surface was flaked all over, resulting in a bifacial flat and pear-shaped tool with more regular, longer, and thinner edges. With this technique a new type of core tool—the cleaver, shaped like a "U" with a straight transverse cutting edge—was developed.

The evolution of Acheulian industries in *H. erectus* populations involved two factors: a marked improvement in manufacturing skills and an ability to translate the idea of the tool into a better-made product. Wolpoff (1980) argued that the second factor led to an increasing number of different tool types, the appearance of fire, and eventually fire-hardened spears.

Three waterlogged spears dated between 400,000 and 380,000 years ago were recovered in Germany (Thieme, 1997). The spears are shaped with the thickest end toward the front and with a long tapering end, like modern javelins. They were apparently meant for throwing. Grooves on the spear suggest that flint tools may have been joined to make them a composite tool. The spears were found with 10,000 animal bones, mostly bones of horses, many of which were butchered. Flint artifacts and a possible hearth were also uncovered.

The Acheulian tradition is the most widespread and, aside from the Oldowan, the longest-lasting archaeological tradition. The tradition first appears at Olduvai above volcanic tuffs separating the upper and lower members of Bed II and dates to about 1.5 mya. A possibly related industry from the Karari Plateau, Lake Turkana, dates between 1.5 and 1.3 mya. At Lake Natron, to the north of Lake Turkana, two other Acheulian occupation floors date to about 1.3 mya. Evidence exists of an East African Acheulian tradition lasting until about 190,000 years ago. Elsewhere, evidence of an evolved Acheulian tradition continues until 125,000 to 115,000 years ago, although by that time it acquired a more specialized and regional character (J. D. Clark, 1976) and is associated with *H. sapiens* populations.

The Acheulian tradition represents a mode of life that appears to have persisted for a relatively long time and that allowed adaptation to a variety of tropical, temperate, and even cold environments. There is evidence that the makers of Acheulian tools, although it is not known if they were *H. erectus*, inhabited arid and climatically harsh regions. For example, by 250,000 years ago human populations managed to adapt to harsh semiarid uplands in Tadzhikistan (Davis et al., 1980).

Pope (1989) suggested that the distribution of bamboo forests in Asia coincided with the distribution of the chopper-chopping tools. He thinks that bam-

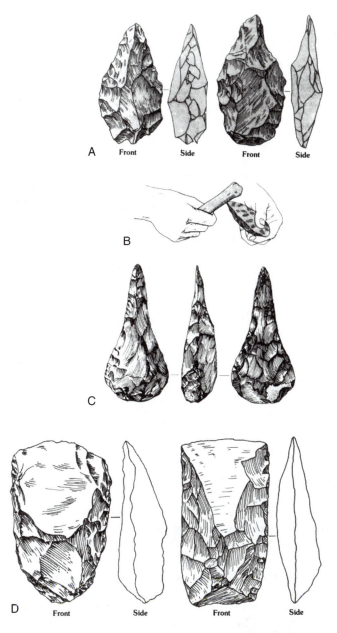

FIGURE 10-12   Handaxe production. *A,* Early handaxes from
Bed II, Olduvai Gorge; *B,* Use of an animal bone to make a
handaxe; *C,* Acheulian handaxe from Swanscombe, England,
one-third actual size; *D,* Acheulian cleavers, one-half actual
size. (After *Olduvai Gorge, Excavations in Beds I and II* by
M. Leakey, © 1971. Oxford: Cambridge University Press.)

boo must have been an extremely important resource, not because appropriate rock was scarce but because bamboo tools would have been efficient, durable, and highly portable.

HOMO ERECTUS **AND THE USE OF FIRE**

The control of fire has probably been among the most momentous and far-reaching of human discoveries. Controlled and purposeful use of fire involved conquering the fear that exists toward fire among mammals generally. With purposeful use of fire, humans began to shape the world according to their design. By bringing fire into its living space, *H. erectus* carved zones of light and warmth out of darkness that provided relative protection from predators. Fire, by changing living habits, may have indirectly altered the brain's structure and enhanced the ability to learn and communicate.

The earliest evidence of fire with possible human connections comes from sites at Lakes Baringo and Turkana in Kenya. Burnt clay at these sites dates between 1.5 and 1.4 mya. Although some researchers (Gowlett et al., 1981) suggest an association between this evidence and human occupation, most are unconvinced of such a purposeful association. It is not difficult to find traces of fire early in Africa. The problem is distinguishing between controlled fire used by humans and naturally occurring fires.

The Ethiopian sites of Gadeb and Melka Konture would have extreme daily temperature fluctuations, with freezing or near freezing temperatures at night. It is significant that some of the earliest evidence of hominid control of fire occurs at Gadeb at 1.4 mya.

If fire at Lakes Baringo and Turkana is not associated with humans, then the earliest possible evidence of fire use associated with humans may be the discoveries from the South African cave site of Swartkrans. The evidence from Swartkrans Member 3 dated between 1.4 and 1 mya, has been reported by Brain and Sillen (1988). The Swartkrans site contains skeletal remains of both *A. robustus* and *H. erectus,* and it is not certain who was using the fire. Evidence of fire use from other parts of the world is only found in association with *H. erectus.*

The evidence for controlled use of fire at Swartkrans is in the form of burned bone, which is found in several distinct layers of limestone within the cave. The 270 charred bone fragments were heated to a range of temperatures that occur in campfires. If controlled use of fire in South Africa is verified, this is among the oldest incidence of humans using fire in Africa.

Fire was probably originally obtained from such ready-made sources as volcanic eruptions, brush fires, or gas and oil seepages. Hunters may have camped near fire, which was a natural resource as were game, water, and shelter. From the beginning fire may have been used to keep predators away. Perhaps humans became regular cave dwellers only after they learned to use fire to drive predators away from the cave.

Sillen and Brain (1990) suggested that one possible use of fire at Swartkrans was to keep away predators. There is evidence from Swartkrans that leopards were human predators, and modern leopards at least are wary of fire. Sillen and Brain dismissed the use of fire for cooking food at Swartkrans because the burned bone does not indicate temperatures found in cooking of food. Conceivably, the bones were used as the fodder for the fire—they may have been burned for warmth.

Perhaps each social group took smouldering embers with them when they moved. Each group may have had its own fire-bearer, responsible for carrying and keeping the embers alive. Control of this potent material may have conferred an aura of respect and invincibility on its keeper. Could such an individual have become an important leader? Could the use and control of fire confer status on those who possess the knowledge of where to find and how to use fire? Perhaps this control and knowledge were prized possessions guardedly passed from generation to generation.

Fire may have been used in hunting to stampede prey. Fire may also have been used to produce more effective spears. Fire hardens the core and makes the outer part crumbly and easier to sharpen. The earliest possible fire-hardened spear, however, dates to only approximately 80,000 years ago and was found in Germany.

The presence of fire-hardened wooden spears is important because they indicate an ability for rather complex problem solving. A set of primary stone tools was needed to chop, cut, carve, and scrape a secondary tool made of wood. That wood was chosen from among the best available varieties. The secondary product, the wooden spear, was then fire-hardened, representing still another technology and a tertiary process that altered the nature of the wood (Marschak, 1989).

Psychological changes may have accompanied the use of fire; for example, cooking may have produced behavioral restraint, that is, control of a tendency to do things on the spur of the moment. Cooking of food suggests that less food is eaten on the spot and more is carried back to the camp. If the assumption that food sharing requires elaborate social rules is correct, it follows that the more there is to share, and the more individuals there are to share with, the more rules are needed. A continuing elaboration of the communication system would be in order.

Introducing fire into the living spaces creates an artificial day independent of the sun's movements; evening hours could be illuminated and one's attention turned to other pursuits. Extra time could be used to make tools, and to think about food-getting and migration routes. Fire may be a potent stimulant that served early ceremonial functions.

We can raise a number of unanswerable questions at this time. For example, what did early cave dwellers think of shadows dancing on dark cave walls as they sat around their fires? Did willowy shapes on the walls lead to thoughts that may have had magical or ritual overtones? Were any of the shadows construed as friends or foes, as animals of the hunt? Did the place that fire holds in many of the world's religions have such beginnings as these?

SUMMARY

If *H. erectus* originated in Africa, the early dates such as 1.8 mya at Sangarin, Indonesia, suggest that the species left Africa soon after it appeared. Others suggest that another species, *H. ergaster*, left Africa before *H. erectus*. If true, then *H. erectus* may have evolved elsewhere and migrated to both Java and Africa.

One migration route from Africa could have involved the Middle East and North Africa. Sites in Saudi Arabia may date to 900,000 years ago. The best known site on the way out of Africa is 'Ubeidiya in Israel, which contains more than 10,000 tools, including dozens of handaxes. Fauna from the site dates to 1.4 mya.

The early establishment and long continuity of *H. erectus* traits in Asia suggested to some that it was marginalized in and perhaps even endemic to Asia. If so, the African materials might better be called *H. ergaster*. If *H. sapiens* later replaced *H. erectus* in Asia, we should expect to find evidence of late *H. erectus* and *H. sapiens* overlapping, as seems true in Java.

H. erectus cultural associations such as the Acheulian tool tradition from Africa are elaborations of earlier Lower Pleistocene activities. Some morphological features distinguishing *H. erectus* from earlier forms—for example, changes in brain size, facial morphology, and perhaps dental structure—may be correlated with cultural activities. If culture is the basis of the human adaptation, natural selection furthered a more efficient cultural adaptation. One cultural adaptation seemingly new to *H. erectus* was the use of fire. (See Box 10-1 for a list of critical features.)

BOX 10-1   Some Critical Features Associated with *Homo erectus*

- Time Span: 1.8 million to 150,000 years ago. The earliest forms come from East Africa.

- Distribution: Africa, Asia, and Europe.

- Associated Tool
  Culture: Most often the Acheulian tool industry. Soft-hammer technique used for first time. Bone and wooden tools found.

- Lifeways: Use of fire. Inhabited caves and built shelters. Evidence of big-game hunting. Entered new habitats.

- Morphology:
  Cranial capacity: 750 cc in the earlier and perhaps smaller-bodied forms to 1,250 cc in the latest and perhaps larger-bodied forms

  Face and skull: Flattened skull vault
                      Greatest width of skull low on skull
                      Thick skull bones
                      Sagittal ridge is common
                      Large brow ridges and marked postorbital constriction
                      Protruding nose
                      Prognathism, heavy mandible lacking a chin, large teeth

  Limbs: Essentially modern limb structure and pelvis; there are some differences, but the functional significance of these is unknown
                      Bipeds

SUGGESTED READINGS

Bräuer, G., and M. Schultz. 1996. The morphological affinities of the Plio-Pleistocene mandible from Dmanisi, Georgia. *Journal of Human Evolution* 30:445–481.

Cachel, S., and J. Harris. 1995. Ranging patterns, land-use and subsistence in *Homo erectus,* from the perspective of evolutionary ecology. In *Evolution and Ecology of* Homo erectus, pp. 51–68, ed. J. Bower and S. Sartono. Leiden: DSWO Press.

Carbonell, E., et al. 1995. Lower Pleistocene hominids and artifacts from Atapuerca-TD6 (Spain). *Science* 269:826–830.

Ciochon, R. 1996. The earliest Asians yet. *Natural History* 104:50–55.

Clark, J. D. 1987. Transitions: *Homo erectus* and the Acheulian: The Ethiopian sites of Gadeb and the Middle Awash. *Journal of Human Evolution* 16:809–826.

de Castro, J. B., J. Arsuga, E. Carbonell, A. Rosasa, I. Martinez, and M. Mosquera. 1997. A hominid from the Lower Pleistocene of Atapuerca, Spain: Possible ancestor to Neandertals and modern humans. *Science* 276:1392–1395.

Gabunia, L., and A. Vekua. 1995. A Plio-Pleistocene hominid from Dmanisi, East Georgia, Caucasus. *Nature* 373:509–512.

Gibbons, A. 1992. Jawing with our Georgian ancestors. *Science* 255:401.

Gibbons, A. 1994. Rewriting—and redating—prehistory. *Science* 263:1087–1088.

Gibbons, A. 1996. *Homo erectus* in Java: A 250,000-year anachronism. *Science* 274:1841–1842.

Gibbons, A. 1997a. Doubts over spectacular dates. *Science* 278:220–222.

Gibbons, A. 1997b. A new face for human ancestors. *Science* 276:1331–1333.

Gutin, J. 1995. Remains in Spain now reign as oldest Europeans. *Science* 269:754–755.

Holden, C. 1994. Old human bones found in Spain. *Science* 265:755.

Holden, C. 1997. Tooling around: Dates show early Siberian settlement. *Science* 275:1268.

Howells, W. 1973. *Evolution of the Genus* Homo. Reading, MA: Addison-Wesley.

Jia, L. P. 1975. *The Cave Home of Peking Man.* Peking: Foreign Languages Press.

Jia, L. P., and W. Huang. 1990. *The Story of Peking Man.* New York: Oxford University Press.

Leakey, L. 1966. *Homo habilis, Homo erectus,* and the australopithecines. *Nature* 209:1279–1281.

Morell, V. 1994. Did early humans reach Siberia 500,000 years ago? *Science* 261:611–612.

Pfeiffer, J. 1971. When *Homo erectus* tamed fire, he tamed himself. In *Human Variation,* ed. H. Bleibtreu and J. Downs. Beverly Hills, CA: Glencoe Press.

Pope, G. 1993. Ancient Asia's cutting edge. *Natural History,* May: 55–58.

Stringer, C. 1984. The definition of *Homo erectus* and the existence of the species in Africa and Europe. In *The Early Evolution of Man,* ed. P. Andrews and J. Franzen. Frankfurt: Senckenberg Museum.

Swisher, C., W. Rink, S. Anton, H. Schwarcz, G. Curtin, A. Suprijo, and Widiasmoro. 1996. Latest *Homo erectus* of Java: Potential contemporaneity with *Homo sapiens* in Southeast Asia. *Science* 274:1870–1874.

Walker, A. 1993. The origin of the genus *Homo.* In *The Origin and Evolution of Humans and Humanness,* pp. 29–47, ed. T. Rasmussen. Boston: Jones and Bartless.

Walker, A., and R. Leakey. 1993. *The Nariokotome* Homo erectus *Skeleton.* Cambridge, MA: Harvard University Press.

Wangpo, W., R. Ciochon, G. Yumin, R. Larick, F. Qiren, H. Schwarcz, C. Yonge, J. de Vos, and W. Rink. 1995. Early *Homo* and associated artefacts from Asia. *Nature* 378:275–278.

Waters, M., S. Forman, and J. Pierson. 1997. Diring Yuriakh: A Lower Paleolithic site in Central Siberia. *Science* 275:1281–1284.

Weidenreich, F. 1936. The mandibles of "Sinanthropus pekinensis." *Paleontologia Sinica,* New Series D 1.

Weidenreich, F. 1943. The skull of "Sinanthropus pekinensis." *Paleontologia Sinica,* New Series D 10:1–485.

Wood, B., and A. Turner. 1995. Out of Africa and into Asia. *Nature* 378:239–240.

Wu, X., and F. E. Poirier. 1995. *Human Evolution in China: A Metric Description of the Fossils and a Review of the Sites.* New York: Oxford University Press.

11

Early *Homo sapiens*

The evolutionary relationships of many of the forms discussed in this chapter are unclear because the specimens show some morphological traits belonging to Homo erectus *and some to* H. sapiens *and the dating of many specimens is uncertain. These specimens are referred to as early* H. sapiens *rather than late* H. erectus *because of changes in skull size and shape and to a lesser degree facial changes. The faces and skulls of a number of early* H. sapiens *specimens are less robust than in the preceding* H. erectus *sample. The general time span of these forms is perhaps 100,000 to 250,000 or 300,000 years ago. Evidence of the lifeways of some of these fossils has been recorded from the sites of Arago and Terra Amata in France.*

OVERVIEW

There is a lack of agreement as to which anatomical traits precisely define early *Homo sapiens*. A series of African and Eurasian fossils are different from *Homo erectus* and yet are not clearly modern *Homo sapiens* (Table 11-1). Some of these remains have large cranial capacities approaching and even exceeding those of modern *H. sapiens*. Nevertheless, some are robustly built and have large faces, jaws, and teeth.

    The dating and taxonomy problems associated with a number of these fossils cannot be overstressed. Some forms listed as early *H. sapiens* here are listed with *H. erectus* by others. Besides the dating problems, this uncertainty is attributable to the fragmentary state of the materials and the equivocal nature of some of the anatomical traits exhibited. Although a number of the early *H. sapiens* forms have been so designated on scanty evidence and debatable grounds, there are important differences between these fossils and *H. erectus*. The major problem in trying to decide on either a *H. sapiens* or *H. erectus* designation is related to the fact that we are somewhat arbitrarily subdividing an evolutionary continuum. There is a continuity between the earliest members of *H. sapiens* and the latest *H. erectus* fossils in areas with large samples. There will probably always be specimens that cannot

TABLE 11-1   Early *Homo sapiens* Sites Discussed in Text

Country	Site	Evidence	Date
Africa			
South Africa	Saldanha	Human remains, tools	100,000 years(?)
	Florisbad	Human remains	200,000–100,000
Zambia	Kabwe (Broken Hill)	Human remains, tools	130,000(?), 800,000–600,000 very unlikely
Ethiopia	Bodo	Human remains	200,000+
Eritrea	Afar	Human remains	1 mya?
Asia			
Indonesia	Solo	Human remains, tools	250,000(?) or much later, perhaps Upper Pleistocene
China	Jinniushan	Human remains	270,000–100,000(?)
India	Narmada River	Human remains, tools	??
Europe			
England	Swanscombe	Human remains, tools	225,000–200,000
Wales	Pontnewydd cave	Human remains, tools	200,000
Germany	Bilzingsleben	Human remains, tools, dwellings(?)	225,000
	Steinheim	Human remains	Riss Glaciation
Greece	Petralona	Human remains	Hotly debated
France	Terra Amata	Tools, dwellings	300,000
	Arago (Tautavel)	Human remains, tools	200,000+(?)
	Biache	Human remains	Riss Glaciation
Spain	Sima de los Huesos	Human remains	300,000–200,000
Italy	Altamura	Human remains	400,000

be satisfactorily placed within any one group. There is also an element of personal choice in the classification of some forms as *H. erectus* or early *H. sapiens.*

The main differences between the early *H. sapiens* and late *H. erectus* sample are found in skull size and morphology and to a lesser degree in facial anatomy. Dental differences from *H. erectus* include size reduction in the posterior teeth and an expansion in the size of the anterior teeth (Wolpoff, 1980). Some early *H. sapiens* specimens, however, have immense posterior teeth that surpass the average size in the *H. erectus* sample. The major postcranial change between *H. erectus* and early *H. sapiens* is a reduction in muscular robusticity.

Major skull changes are associated with a generally increasing cranial capacity. The cranial capacity of early *H. sapiens* averages 1,166 cubic centimeters, representing an 11 percent increase over that of *H. erectus.* Some early *H. sapiens* cranial capacities, however, fall below the capacities of later *H. erectus* specimens. There is a marked decrease on the back of the skull (the occipital region) for neck muscle attachment when comparing late *H. erectus* and early *H. sapiens* specimens (Wolpoff, 1980). Most changes in the skull appear to result from increasing cranial capacities and the reduction of the area of muscle attachment. Brain size increases appear to reflect actual evolutionary changes in the brain rather than merely being associated with body size increases.

SUB-SAHARAN AFRICA

The uncertain dating of sub-Saharan African remains confuses taxonomic attribution. The sub-Saharan African forms discussed here, Kabwe (or Broken Hill) from Zambia and Saldanha from South Africa, are variously referred to as late *H. erectus* or early *H. sapiens,* the designation used here. The Kabwe or Broken Hill specimen was found in 1921. Klein's (1973) faunal studies and amino acid racemization determinations suggested a date of about 130,000 years ago. Murrill (1983) suggested a far older date, perhaps on the order of 800,000 to 600,000 years ago. If Murrill is correct, attribution to the *H. erectus* taxon is quite in order because it is highly unlikely that *H. sapiens* dated back to 600,000 years or more. Rightmire (1979) and Bilsborough (1979) agreed that Kabwe has many *H. erectus* traits.

The Kabwe skull (Figure 11-1) has a complete face that shows a combination of robust and gracile traits. The skull has a very large brow ridge, low forehead, and a well-developed occipital region—characteristics of *H. erectus.* On the other hand, the skull has several traits seen in early *H. sapiens:* an expanded cranial capacity (about 1,300 cc), thinner skull bones, and a gracility of the structures supporting the facial musculature (Wolpoff, 1980).

The Saldanha skull is quite similar to that of Kabwe, although its face and base are not preserved. It was found in 1953 near Saldanha Bay, 90 miles north of Cape Town. Handaxe and flake tool implements were also recovered. Although the date has not been firmly established, it may be about 100,000 years old. Both Rightmire (1979) and Bilsborough (1979) placed this skull with *H. erectus;* Wolpoff (1980) placed it with *H. sapiens.*

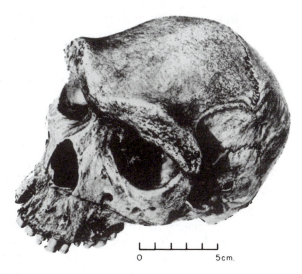

FIGURE 11-1 Broken Hill (Kabwe) cranium and face. (Photo of cast courtesy Wenner-Gren Foundation for Anthropological Research, Inc., and owner of original specimen.)

0   5cm.

There is a fragmentary cranium consisting of the sides and part of the face of an adult from Florisbad, South Africa. Various dates have been assigned to this specimen, ranging from 200,000 to 100,000 years ago. Recent ESR dating of the hominid tooth associated with the skull yielded a date of 259,000 ± 35,000 years (Grün et al., 1996).

Human material from the Bodo region, Ethiopia, approximately 53 percent of a skull and face, was found with stone tools. Preliminary indications reveal a date between 500,000 and 200,000 years ago. In addition to the human remains and stone tools, there are many remains of elephants, hippopotamuses, horses, rhinoceroses, giraffes, pigs, rodents, reptiles, and fish. The Bodo individual apparently camped near the edge of a lake.

The Bodo material is morphologically intermediate between *H. erectus* and some early *H. sapiens* samples in such traits as the thickness and total breadth of the brow ridges and face. In other features, such as the form of the nasal bones and frontal region of the skull, Bodo is more like archaic *H. sapiens*. Bodo most resembles fossils from Broken Hill (Kabwe), Zambia, and Petralona, Greece, which many now designate as early *H. sapiens*.

Electron microscope studies of the Bodo skull revealed a series of cut marks on the forehead and cheek bones. Bodo had been intentionally defleshed after its death. The marks on the bone were left by the cutting edge of a stone tool (White, 1986).

Yet to be fully analyzed, a million-year-old skull (found with two lower teeth and two pelvic fragments) from the Afar Depression, Eritrea, East Africa, may eventually have an important bearing on understanding early human evolution (Abbate et al., 1998). This is the only skull from Africa that dates from between 1.4 mya and 600,000 years ago. The site was biochronologically and paleomagnetically dated. Very preliminary analysis of the well-preserved skull suggests that it may combine features of both *Homo erectus* (= *H. ergaster* in Africa) and early

Homo sapiens, but it cannot yet be assigned to either species. The skull has brow ridges like those of *H. erectus*. However, the skull is widest at a higher point on the skull than is true of *H. erectus* skulls. This width higher on the skull may signal a larger brain, a trait of the later-appearing *H. sapiens*. The skull may have important bearing on the hotly debated issue of when and where *Homo sapiens* arose.

ASIA

The Solo remains are possible early *H. sapiens* fossils from the Ngandong Beds along the Solo River in Indonesia. Thirteen skulls and skull fragments lacking faces were recovered between 1931 and 1941. There are two incomplete lower leg bones (tibias). The skulls are morphologically similar to Kabwe and have marked cranial flattening (platycephaly), powerful brow ridges, and thick cranial walls. Cranial capacities range between 1,150 and 1,300 cc. The Solo crania are generally larger than those often associated with *H. erectus,* and Wolpoff (1980) suggested an average 10 percent increase in cranial capacity over *H. erectus.*

Dating the Solo remains has been a persistent problem. The remains were once relegated to the Upper Pleistocene, but other estimates suggest the possibility of a date of 250,000 years ago. This would be the time span of the latest *H. erectus* and earliest *H. sapiens* samples. Although there are broad similarities between the Solo remains and Chinese *H. erectus* material from Zhoukoudian, the Solo sample exhibits the gracility of certain skull features that characterize later *H. sapiens* samples. The material may be transitional between *H. erectus* and *H. sapiens.*

Most early *H. sapiens* remains from China are teeth (Wu & Poirier, 1995). The major exception is the Jinniushan assemblage. Many traits in the Chinese late *H. erectus* and early *H. sapiens* samples are transitional between the two species. Most dates from early *H. sapiens* sites in China are based on the uranium series and vary rather widely in age. The oldest early *H. sapiens* site may be more than 280,000 years old, and the youngest may be about 83,000 years old. The range is mostly between 200,000 and 100,000 years ago. Most sites have associated tool assemblages.

Remains discovered in 1984 from Jinniushan (Gold Ox Hill), Liaoning Province, northeastern China, include an almost complete skeleton from a twenty-five- to thirty-year-old male. The materials were first referred to *H. erectus* but are now referred to early *H. sapiens*. There are bones of the hands, feet, spine, ribs, and ulna. The well-preserved skull (Figure 11-2) has a relatively low cranial vault and prominent brow ridges, as well as other traits associated with post–*H. erectus* and pre–*H. sapiens* specimens. There are a few stone tools, burned animal bones, burned clay, and carbon, which is evidence of fire. A uranium series of dates suggests an age of 270,000 to 150,000 years ago. However, other dating methods yielded dates of 184,000 to 100,000 years ago. This is a cave deposit, and it must still be established that the human remains are of the same date as the surrounding materials.

The Narmada skullcap was found along the Narmada River in Madhya Pradesh state, India (de Lumley & Sonakia, 1985). The estimated cranial capacity of 1,200 cc exceeds that typical of *H. erectus*. Kennedy et al. (1991) concluded that

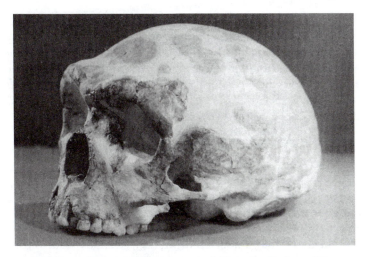

FIGURE 11-2 Early *Homo sapiens* skull from Jinniushan, China. (Courtesy Institute of Paleontology and Paleoanthropology [IVPP].)

although the Narmada skullcap shares some features with Asian *H. erectus,* it shares a broader set of traits with early *H. sapiens.* Narmada shares traits with such finds as Petralona, Bilzingsleben, Kabwe, Dali, and Ngandong (Solo)—all or some of which are referred to early *H. sapiens.* Kennedy et al. suggested that Narmada is an adult female. They accorded the specimen the nomen *H. sapiens narmadensis.*

EUROPE

European remains of possible early *H. sapiens* are the most numerous of this otherwise scant set of fossils. They date to about 300,000 or 250,000 years ago to less than 100,000 years ago. Although there are a number of such European sites, the fossil specimens are limited, and there remains a problem with their derivation and proper dating. Petralona in Greece and Bilzingsleben, Germany, for example, have been referred to *H. erectus* by some researchers. In some cases, it may be difficult to decide whether fossils should be classified as *H. erectus* or early *H. sapiens.*

The 700 human remains from Sima de los Huesos (Pit of the Bones), a small chamber within a cave located in the Sierra de Atapuerca, northern Spain, are from at least thirty-two people and date to about 300,000 years ago with a minimum age of 200,000 years (Arsuga et al., 1993; Stringer, 1993). This is the world's largest repository of Middle Pleistocene hominids. More than three-quarters of the human postcranials from this period, plus the late Lower and early Upper Pleistocene, come from this one site. For several bones the site has the only known representatives. It is not yet possible to conclude how the human fossil assemblage accumulated.

The unusually large skeletal sample provides a unique chance to examine variability in Middle Pleistocene populations and to help decide who are the Neandertal's ancestor. Postcranial bones, for example, show that the morphological complex of the Neandertal shoulder and arm was present in the Middle Pleistocene hominid assemblage before the Neandertals appeared. Thus, it seems fruitless to try to relate this morphology specifically to Neandertal specializations or way of life.

Three hominid crania were recovered in 1992. One (number 4) is complete, the second (5) is virtually complete, and the third (6) is a more fragmentary cranium of an immature individual. There is a large size difference between the two adult crania. The cranial capacity of number 4, 1,390 cc, is one of the largest in the Middle Pleistocene hominid assemblage. The cranial sample best fits with an archaic *H. sapiens* group and appears to document an early stage in Neandertal evolution. There are further similarities between some facial and cranial remains from Atapuerca and those from Petralona and Steinheim. Stringer (1993) suggests that materials from Vértesszöllös and Bilzingsleben might be linked with the Petralona-Atapuerca grouping. Perhaps all the materials fall into an early (archaic) *H. sapiens* group.

Important fossil remains were found in October 1993 in a cave in southeastern Italy near the town of Altamura (Dorozynski, 1993). This may be the most complete skeletal remains ever recovered from this time period, about 400,000 years ago, in Europe. The traits of its face suggest that this is a form evolutionarily placed between the Neandertals and *H. erectus*. Although the pronounced brow ridges are common to Neandertals, the morphology of the ridges, the skull vault, and the maximum facial width are not fully Neandertal.

Swanscombe is a gravel pit located near London along the Thames River. The area appears to have been a favorite hunting site for prehistoric populations, because several hundred thousand stone tools were recovered. The first human material came to light in 1935, when workers recovered an occipital bone (Figure 11-3) protruding from a gravel bank. This was the first lucky happening associated with Swanscombe (Ovey, 1964).

A second fossil was found the following March near the site of the original find. A left parietal (the parietals are the two bones on the top of skull) was uncovered, and it belonged with the 1935 occipital bone. The third skull fragment, the right parietal, was recovered in 1955, 75 feet from the original find. It also belonged to the same individual.

Deposits yielding the Swanscombe remains appear to be about 225,000 years old. The associated fauna includes elephant and rhinoceros. Fluorine analysis of the faunal remains yielded a figure of 2 percent, common for Middle Pleistocene bone deposits (Oakley, 1952). Stone implements associated with the skeletal remains have been assigned to the early Middle Acheulian handaxe tradition, usually associated with *H. erectus*.

Swanscombe was inhabited during a temperate climatic period. The presence of elephants and rhinoceroses indicates that the English climate was warmer than it is today. African fauna migrated across the Dardanelles land bridge and browsed in the warm Thames Valley along with wild boar, deer, and other wood-

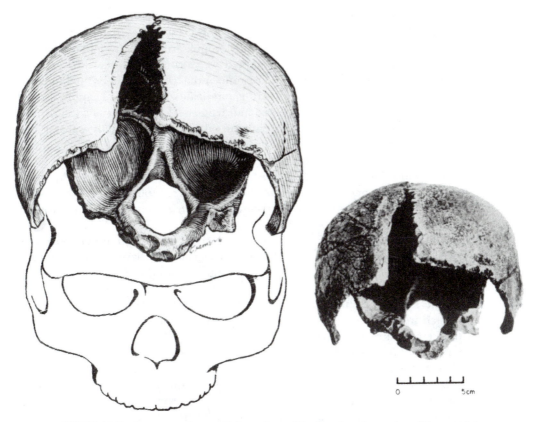

FIGURE 11-3   Swanscombe partial cranium. (Photo of cast courtesy Wenner-Gren Foundation for Anthropological Research, Inc., and owner of original specimen.)

land types. The approach of colder times is indicated by a decrease in the tropical African faunal assemblage and an increase of open-grassland species, which indicate a forest recession. These changes preceded the Riss glaciation.

The three Swanscombe skull bones (occipital and two parietals) are well preserved. Because the sutures were still open, the individual is estimated to have been twenty to twenty-five years old, based on suture closure in modern populations. The cranial capacity, between 1,275 and 1,325 cc, according to Coon (1962), or closer to 1,250 cc by other estimates, is within the range of capacities of modern populations. A major feature differentiating Swanscombe and modern *H. sapiens* is the thickness of its skull bones.

The larger brain and general suggestion of rounded and expanded skull contours typical of the Swanscombe skull approach modern conditions. On the other hand, the relatively low braincase height and certain other traits suggest a form morphologically intermediate between *H. erectus* and modern *H. sapiens*. Swanscombe is usually referred to as an archaic member of *H. sapiens*, that is, *H. sapiens swanscombensis*.

Four skull fragments and a molar tooth were recovered from Bilzingsleben, Germany (Vlček, 1978). The skull morphology resembles that of the African *H. erectus* from Olduvai Gorge. The brow ridges are well developed, the skull bones are thick, and the occipital is marked by a strong horizontal strut of bone. The bones are associated with a flake stone industry and numerous butchered animal bones. Thorium-uranium dating indicates an age of approximately 228,000 years for the human remains and artifacts (Harmon et al., 1980). Associated fossils indicate a forest environment with a climate slightly warmer than present and without winter frost (Harmon et al., 1980).

Some researchers suggest that the Bilzingsleben remains belong to an archaic Middle Pleistocene *H. sapiens;* others classify the material as *H. erectus.* The Bilzingsleben material is similar to that of Vértesszöllös (which is probably *H. erectus*) but also bears some resemblance to *H. sapiens* material from Petralona, Steinheim, and Swanscombe.

Over 60,000 flint implements, as well as rock, bone, and antler tools, were recovered. Evidence of two possible dwelling structures have been recognized. The presence of fish bones indicates freshwater fishing, an activity previously unknown at this early date.

The Petralona skull was recovered from a Greek cave in 1959. The skull is encrusted with limestone and is in an excellent state of preservation. The dating of the Petralona cave material is disputed. Kurtén (1983) suggested a date on the order of 800,000 years ago. Based on studies of associated faunal remains and on skull morphology, Murrill (1983) suggested a date of 800,000 to 600,000 years ago. If these early dates are verified, they suggest attribution to a late *H. erectus,* not early *H. sapiens.* Dating problems at Petralona stem from the fact that the fauna have been variously attributed to different time periods. Hennig and others (1981) questioned whether the fauna are associated with the human skull. They suggested that the human remains date to less than 200,000 years ago—that is, within the *Homo sapiens* time range.

The Petralona skull is large; however, cranial capacity estimates are disputed. Although estimates of 1,440 cc and 1,384 cc have been proposed, Howells (1973) accepted an estimate of 1,220 cc as more accurate. Murrill (1981), who spent years working on the Petralona skull, estimated 1,155 cc. Howells (1973) suggested that the skull is a specimen in the *H. erectus* lineage and differs from the Olduvai and Far Eastern *H. erectus* samples. The Petralona skull exhibits many features found on the Hungarian Vértesszöllös and Zambian Kabwe specimens.

Stone tools dating to approximately 200,000 years ago were found in Greece (Hoffman, 1991). Among them was the first handaxe of this age to be found in Greece. It is not clear which human species, *H. erectus* or early *H. sapiens,* made the stone axe. Archaeological and human fossil remains from Greece are important because Greece was probably on the migration route of early humans out of Africa into Europe.

Arago cave in France yielded cultural and bone material dated to at least 190,000 to 180,000 years ago, with some estimates as old as 300,000 to 200,000 years ago. The human remains include many isolated teeth, phalanges (the small bones of the fingers and toes), parietal fragments, a mandible with six teeth (Arago 2), a half mandible with five teeth (Arago 13), the anterior portion of an adult skull recovered in 1971, and some fragmentary postcranial remains recovered in 1978. At least twenty-three individuals, including at least eight youngsters, may be represented.

The most complete specimen (Arago 21) consists of the front portion of a skull with a complete face and a crushed frontal bone. Arago 21 has massive brow ridges, a flat forehead, and a narrow elongated braincase. The skull has traits reminiscent of Far Eastern *H. erectus* specimens. Because of the absence of maxillary tooth wear, the skull is thought to belong to a young adult approximately twenty years of age.

Two mandibles, probably belonging to a male and female, were found in 1969 and 1970 at approximately the same level. Neither apparently belongs with the Arago 21 skull. The mandibles seem to have been prognathic, and there are indications of a considerable amount of chewing stress. The Arago 2 mandible may belong to a female, and it shows one of the earliest traces of a possible chin. The mandibles are considerably thicker than the older Mauer mandible. The teeth of Arago 13 are very large, and the posterior dentition surpasses the size for *H. erectus.*

Among the most complete skulls dated to the Riss Glaciation, the Biache skull from France shows many similarities to the material from Swanscombe. In addition to the parietals and occipital, Biache includes the back of the temporals (the bone found on the side of the skull) and a palate with all the molar teeth. Unlike Swanscombe, the Biache skull is flattened in the area where the occipital meets the parietals. The skull vault is small and fairly low, the area for nuchal (neck) muscle attachment is weakly developed, the occiput is rounded, and the mastoids are small. The Biache specimen may be a female.

The Steinheim (Figure 11-4) skull and face were found in 1935 approximately 25 feet deep in a gravel pit located north of Stuttgart, Germany. The material may not date as old as once suggested. There is considerable resemblance between the Steinheim and Swanscombe remains. The Steinheim skull is damaged behind the left eye and has a sizable hole in the base of the skull, suggesting possible cannibalism. The skull materials were associated with many nonhuman bones, but no tools were found.

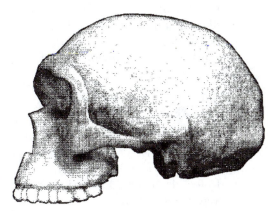

FIGURE 11-4 Reconstruction of an archaic *Homo sapiens* skull based on a fossil from Steinheim, Germany. (Courtesy Jeffrey K. McKee.)

As a result of being covered by wet earth before fossilization, the skull is warped and crushed. The left side, forward of the auditory (ear) opening, has caved in, and much of the left side of the face is detached. The shape of the occipital bone is similar to that of Swanscombe, but the estimated cranial capacity is smaller, at between 1,150 and 1,175 cc, similar to preceding *H. erectus* finds. The skull differs from *H. erectus* in several ways. As in modern skulls, the occipital is smoothly rounded, and the markings of the neck muscle attachments are slight and set low. This configuration indicates gracile neck muscles.

Steinheim has heavy brow ridges and a low forehead, but not quite as archaic a condition as found among *H. erectus*. Although low, the forehead is fairly steep, and the brow ridges are obvious. Although large and heavy, the brow ridges are slightly separated over the nose. Steinheim's face is less prognathic than that of the Chinese *H. erectus* but more prognathic than modern populations. The nose seems to have been rather broad.

The front teeth are missing, but the posterior teeth appear to be modern and not suggestive of having been placed in a large mandible. The teeth are moderately taurodont; there is a tendency toward an enlarged pulp cavity and perhaps fusion of the molar roots. Except for taurodontism, nothing notable distinguishes these teeth from those of modern Europeans.

Steinheim seems to have been a member of a population intermediate between *H. erectus* and modern *H. sapiens,* and a number of traits distinguish it from succeeding European Neandertals. The Steinheim brow ridges seem to adumbrate those of the western European Neandertals; however, the characteristic does not diverge to such an extent as to warrant a species distinction from *H. sapiens.* The cranial capacity falls within the lower end of the range of modern populations (Clark, 1967). Judging from the Steinheim skull, evolutionary processes leading to the emergence of modern humans were working more swiftly on the back of the skull than on the face.

Steinheim exhibits a combination of "advanced" and "archaic" traits. The skull is small and low, cranial capacity is low, and the brow ridges are large. Along with these features typical of *H. erectus* are features of a more modern aspect. The face is relatively small and has minimal prognathism. The skull also appears to be tucked under at the brow ridges. Maximal skull breadth is higher on the occipital than in earlier *H. erectus,* indicating that although the skull is small, it morphologically approaches *H. sapiens.* The teeth are small, the third molar is reduced, and the occipital is rounded without a sharp angle. All these are modern features. Steinheim may be an early member of the Neandertal lineage.

LIFEWAYS

Two French sites provide the best data concerning the lifeways of early *Homo sapiens* populations. Arago cave is located north of the Rousillon plain, at the southern tip of the Corbieres Mountain, near the village of Tautavel in the Pyrenees. Arago is 15 feet deep and 33 feet wide at its maximum. As early as 1838, nonhuman bones were recovered there. One cave level was formed during a dry, cold period when the cave was intermittently occupied. When it was abandoned, sand blew in, covering the human relics and providing a clean floor for subsequent inhabitants.

The de Lumleys (1973) hypothesized that the cave was inhabited by groups who regularly returned to an established camp. The inhabitants lived in a dimly lit area some distance from the cave's entrance, in a sandpit between a dune accumulating in the entry and another dune being formed at the cave's rear. Habitation areas are littered with bone fragments and flint or quartz tools; in some areas the abundance and disposition of the remains suggest a toolmaking area. In other places piles of bones more than 50 cm deep represent bone debris. The de Lumleys stated that stone slabs were brought into the cave and were perhaps used to avoid sinking into the sand. More than 100,000 artifacts were uncovered. Arago yielded many pebble tools, including choppers and chopping tools. Handaxes, an important component of *H. erectus* living sites, were rare.

One of the best examples of a later Middle Pleistocene site is located at Terra Amata on the French Riviera near Nice (de Lumley, 1969). The site, dating to less than 300,000 years ago, was first uncovered in 1959 during construction of a shipyard. A few years later during the building of apartments, bulldozers uncovered an extensive sandy deposit containing many Paleolithic tools.

The only clue to the physical appearance of Terra Amata's inhabitants is an imprint of a right foot, 9.5 inches long, which is preserved in the sand. The individual making the print is estimated to have been 5 feet 1 inch tall. The site is included in an early *H. sapiens* sample, according to Wolpoff (1980), although earlier reports placed it within the *H. erectus* sample.

The landscape during the time of occupation was quite different from today. The backdrop of the Alps was much the same, but the seas reached further inland. Although temperate, the climate was brisker and more humid. Pollen grains indicate that fir and Norway pine grew farther down on the Alpine slopes than is true today.

Superimposed living floors were uncovered in three separate locales: four on a beach section that formed a sandbar, six on the beach, and eleven on a dune island. On the slopes of an ancient sand dune, de Lumley uncovered what may be remains of a number of oval huts that ranged from 26 to 49 feet long and 13 to 20 feet wide and may have housed ten to twenty people. The huts may have been constructed of sturdy branches, bent to interlock at the top, with an entrance at one end and a hole in the top to allow smoke to escape. Presumably the branches were supported by posts and rocks of varying sizes placed against the posts.

A basic feature of each hut was a hearth at its center. The presumed hearths were usually shallow pits scooped from the sand, a foot or two in diameter. A low wall, made of piled pebbles, stood at the northwest quadrant of each hearth and may have served as a windscreen. Areas closest to the hearths were cleared of debris, indicating that people may have slept there. The hearths were apparently designed for rather small fires; however, judging from the larger accumulations of charcoal and ash, those located in the huts closest to the sea may have accommodated larger fires.

More recent work, however, sheds doubt on the existence of huts. Terra Amata was more disturbed than originally thought. The low-density scatter of stone and bone with localized patches of burning may not indicate a series of beach huts, as so often is suggested.

Faunal remains include birds, turtles, and eight mammalian species. There is abundant evidence that the inhabitants were big-game hunters; in order of the abundance of their remains, they hunted stag, elephant, wild boar, ibex, and Merck's rhinoceros. Most faunal remains were those of younger animals. There are also indications that the inhabitants ate oysters, mussels, and limpets—the shells of which are present. The presence of fish bones indicates that the inhabitants also fished.

Pollen evidence suggests that the inhabitants were seasonal migrants who arrived in late spring and early summer. Presumably, they chose the sheltered cove as a camping site because of the presence of a nearby fresh water supply. On their arrival they erected huts and built hearths and windscreens. They probably hunted for a day or two, gathered seafood, and left. A short stay is indicated by the fact that the living floors show no signs of compaction characteristic of longer occupation and the fact that the huts probably collapsed soon after they were erected. (Many tools on the living floors were bleached. Freshly chipped stone tools left lying in the sun quickly bleach on the exposed side; therefore, for the implements to be exposed to the full force of the Mediterranean sun, the huts must have fallen soon after they were abandoned.)

Little of the previous year's occupation floors survived. However, evidence suggests that the visitors erected their new huts on or near the old locations. This may have been facilitated by the hearth windscreens, which protruded above the sand, being used as markers. Eleven living floors are so precisely superimposed that they seem to represent eleven consecutive years of occupation. All this suggests that the inhabitants had a stable and fairly complex social organization; perhaps these were family groups that returned to the same site every year. However, any discussion of huts and implications drawn from their presumed existence awaits verification.

There are large numbers of stone tools. Some tools were probably locally made; the hut floors show evidence of toolmaking activity. The toolmaker's place in the hut is indicated by a patch of living floor surrounded by a litter of tool manufacturing debris. Ground impressions may have been left at places where they sat, sometimes perhaps on skins. At another French site, the cave of Lazaret, dated at approximately 130,000 years ago, there is a suggestion that inhabitants slept on seaweed beds (Butzer, 1970).

Some domestic furnishings have been recovered. Flattened limestone blocks may have provided convenient surfaces for sitting or for breaking animal bone. A semispherical imprint in the sand was filled with a whitish substance, which may have been an impression left by a wooden bowl. If so, it would be the earliest trace of a container. Near the imprint were lumps of the natural pigment red ocher. Several ends of these lumps were worn smooth and pointed like a pencil; these "pencils" may have been used to color the body in preparation for some sort of ceremony. Velo (1984) suggested that ocher could also have been used to treat wounds and stem bleeding.

The red ocher found at Terra Amata is not the only evidence from this time indicating possible decoration. The earliest direct evidence of such decoration—perhaps it was art—is found in Riss layers at Pech de l'Aze, France, along with an Acheulian tool complex. An engraving from Pech de l'Aze consists of a series of connected double arcs running from left to right. The marks were made by different tools, and perhaps at different times. Other simple marks were added, including a series of angles and double marks that resulted in a complex set of engravings. Although not completely understood, the marks may signify a complex cultural context (Marschak, 1972).

SUMMARY

Different taxonomic assignments have been suggested to accommodate the fossil sample discussed in this chapter (Box 11-1). This lack of agreement is due to the facts that these samples show a combination of *H. erectus* and *H. sapiens* traits and that the dating of many specimens is disputed. Until we better understand the

---

BOX 11-1 Some Critical Features Associated with Early *Homo sapiens*

- Time Span: Many of the remains have a disputed dating. The time span usually given is from 300,000 to 100,000 years ago. However, at least one researcher suggested that one form, Petralona, may date to 800,000 years ago. If so, it must then be included with *Homo erectus*.

- Distribution: Africa, Asia, Europe.

- Lifeways: Lived in caves and built dwellings. Possible use of aquatic food and big-game hunting. Possible decoration of body.

- Morphology: Exhibit traits that characterize both *Homo erectus* and *Homo sapiens*. Much disagreement concerning the taxonomic status of many of these fossils.
  - Cranial capacity: The largest is about 1,325 cc. Average cranial capacities are 1,166, an 11% increase over that of *Homo erectus*. Some early *H. sapiens* cranial capacities are smaller than those of *H. erectus*.
  - Face and skull: Some show reduced brow ridges; others have large brow ridges.
  - Some have thinning of skull bones.
  - Some have a low forehead and a flat skull vault like *H. erectus*.
  - Marked decrease of robust musculature on the back of the skull in many of the fossils.
  - Prognathism and lack of a chin in all the fossils except Arago 2.
  - Evidence of decreasing bulk of chewing muscles.
  - Many have immense molar and premolar teeth, while others have a reduction in size of these same teeth.
  - Postcranial skeleton: Bipedal, less robusticity in lower limbs than seen in *H. erectus*.

selective factors working on various morphological complexes, we will be unable positively to attribute these specimens to one or the other species.

Most researchers agree, however, that *H. sapiens* evolved from an *H. erectus* lineage. Louis Leakey (1966) argued that no *H. erectus* was ancestral to *H. sapiens*. Accepting this position, the only ancestor to *H. sapiens* would be *H. habilis* or its African descendant, *Homo ergaster; H. erectus* would be an extinct side branch of human evolution. This position has not yet gained widespread support. A third position is that some, if not all, *H. erectus* populations gave rise to *H. sapiens*. This position, essentially accepted here, allows for different rates of evolutionary change in different populations and for some competitive replacement of one population by another as a way of speeding the establishment of *H. sapiens*.

SUGGESTED READINGS

Arsuga, J.-I., I. Martinez, A. Garcia, J.-M. Carretero, and E. Carbonell. 1993. Three new human skulls from the Sima de los Huesos Middle Pleistocene site in Sierra de Atapuerca, Spain. *Nature* 362:534–537.

Arsuga, J.-I., J. M. Bermudez de Castro, and E. Carbonell (eds.). 1997. The Sima de los Huesos hominid site. *Journal of Human Evolution* 33:105–421.

de Lumley, H. 1969. A Paleolithic camp at Nice. *Scientific American* 220:42–50.

Dorozynski, A. 1993. Possible Neandertal ancestor found. *Science* 262:991.

Hennig, G., W. Herr, E. Weber, and X. Xirotiris. 1981. ESR-dating of the fossil hominid cranium from Petralona cave, Greece. *Nature* 292:533–536.

Stringer, C. 1993. Secrets of the Pit of the Bones. *Nature* 362:501–502.

White, T. 1986. Cut marks on the Bodo cranium: A case of prehistoric defleshing. *American Journal of Physical Anthropology* 69:503–509.

12

Neandertals and Their Immediate Predecessors

European Eemian (or Riss-Würm) Interglacial Sample
The Neandertals: The Background
The Neandertals: The Fossil Sample
Cultural Remains and Lifeways
Evolutionary Relationships
Summary
Suggested Readings

European Neandertal* remains were among the first human fossils to be discovered. When they appeared in the 1800s they were dismissed as aberrant examples of modern humans. Neandertal remains have been and continue to be the source of considerable taxonomic debate. The Neandertals are currently referred to as either Homo sapiens neanderthalensis, *making them direct ancestors to ourselves, or to a different species,* Homo neanderthalensis, *which places them on a side branch of the evolutionary line to modern* Homo sapiens. *Finds in the Middle East provide some of the strongest evidence for excluding the Neandertals from our evolutionary lineage. Finds in France suggest that the Neandertals in Europe existed after the appearance of modern H. sapiens in Europe. Evidence in Africa and the Middle East suggests to some researchers that modern* Homo *is not derived from a Neandertal population. There is an array of Neandertal cultural remains. The tool assemblage commonly associated with the European Neandertals is called the Mousterian. For the first time in human history, there is evidence of extensive burials accompanied by rituals. Neandertal cranial capacities exceed the range of those for modern humans, although the Neandertal sample is much smaller and more homogeneous than that of modern humans. Neandertals have robust facial skeletons that indicate large chewing muscles, and they have a distinctive cranial morphology. These and other anatomical traits are more marked in specimens from the colder regions of western Europe. Some remains from eastern Europe and the Middle East, regions outside the influence of the European glaciation, exhibit less skeletal robustness.*

*The name is also spelled Neanderthal.

EUROPEAN EEMIAN (OR RISS-WÜRM) INTERGLACIAL SAMPLE

Europe provides a human fossil sample from the Eemian (Riss-Würm) Interglacial period dating approximately 100,000 years ago. This sample is regionally diverse and is foreshadowed by the slightly earlier sample discussed in Chapter 11. There are uncertainties concerning the dating of some of these fossils, which derive primarily from France, Germany, Croatia, and Italy, although there is also some fragmentary material from elsewhere (Table 12-1). Some of these forms played a major role in earlier taxonomic controversies involving the exact role of the subsequent Neandertals in our evolutionary history. This topic will be discussed in a later section in this chapter.

Fontéchevade, France

In 1947, G. Henri-Martin broke through a limey crust cave floor at Fontéchevade to find fossil deposits containing tools associated with an interglacial warmweather fauna. Embedded in the same deposits were parts of two skulls: a patch about the size of a silver dollar from the brow of one skull and most of the top of another, which exhibited signs of having been charred. Fluorine analysis established the contemporaneity of the human and nonhuman skeletal material. Beneath this layer was an older tool assemblage, but without associated skeletal remains.

TABLE 12-1   Neandertals, Their Immediate Predecessors, and Contemporaneous Fossils

Geographical Area	Site
400,000 to 200,000 Years Ago	
Italy	Altamura
Spain	Sima de los Huesos
Eemian (Riss-Würm) Interglacial Sample	
Croatia	Krapina
France	Fontéchevade
Germany	Ehringsdorf
Würm Glacial Sample	
China	Dali, Mapa
Croatia	Vindija
Czech Republic	Ochoz, Sipka, Gànovce, Külna, Šala
France	Hortus, La Ferrassie, Le Moustier, La Chapelle-aux-Saints, St. Césaire, Arcy-sur-Cure
Germany	Neander Valley
Hungary	Subalyuk
Italy	Monte Circeo
Iraq	Shanidar
Israel	Tabūn, Skhūl, Kebara, Qafzeh, Amud
Syria	Dederiyeh
Spain	Zafarraya

The cranial capacity of the fragmentary Fontéchevade materials has been estimated at about 1,350 cc. The most complete skull, number 2, is a left parietal bone, an upper half of the right parietal, and the upper portion of the frontal. It was argued that enough of the frontal bone exists to indicate that the skull lacked massive brow ridges, a trait of the subsequent western European Neandertal sample (Vallois, 1949a). The evidence for the nonexistence of the large brow ridges is inconclusive; after all, the brow ridge area is missing on the larger skull. Some scientists claim the smaller fragment is from an immature individual in whom the large ridges characteristic of European Neandertals might not yet have developed. Those holding the non–brow-ridge point of view counter that the skull is from a mature individual because the frontal sinus is well developed. The major furor caused by this discovery stemmed from early assertions that the Fontéchevade materials were not demonstrably different from modern *H. sapiens* and were more advanced, more "sapienslike," than subsequent western European Neandertals.

Fontéchevade is distinguishable from modern *H. sapiens;* it most closely approaches Swanscombe in skull thickness and in breadth across the back of the skull. Either Fontéchevade is ancestral to later European populations, or it is a member of a separate and more advanced evolutionary line with little genetic link to European Neandertals.

Ehringsdorf, Germany

The Ehringsdorf skull was found in 1925 at a depth of 54 feet near Weimar, Germany, associated with warm-temperature forest fauna and flora. Common among the faunal assemblage were bones of immature *Elephas, Dicerorhinus, Bos,* and *Equus.* Hunters may have been using pitfalls to catch their prey because young and inexperienced animals are more prone to fall victim to such trapping methods than are adults.

Implements associated with the human remains belong to the **Mousterian** tool tradition (see pages 284–285) but were not a simple and homogeneous industry. Based on the heterogeneity of the cultural and skeletal sample, some suggested that Ehringsdorf is the product of a mixture of several related populations; however, this possibility is unlikely. The major human remains include four parietals and a broken and faceless braincase, which may have belonged to a twenty- to thirty-year-old adult female. The bones separated during deposition, and because their edges were scraped along the ground, they do not articulate perfectly.

The cranial capacity is large, 1,450 cc according to some estimates, or somewhat smaller if this reconstruction was faulty. The heavy brow ridges are like those of Steinheim but thicker and approach the size and shape of those of subsequent Neandertals. The braincase is low and archaic looking with a well-developed **occipital bun** (a bony protuberance on the occipital at the rear of the skull), and the greatest width is low on the occipitals. Ehringsdorf closely approximates the earlier Steinheim and Swanscombe materials.

Krapina, Croatia

The Krapina material comes from the floor of a rock shelter in northern Croatia, which was excavated between 1895 and 1906. K. Gorjanovic-Kramberger (1906) and associates recovered 800 skull fragments, postcranial skeletal material, and teeth. Krapina is the largest human bone sample ever recovered from a single site. One reason for the fragmentary nature of the material is that the skeletons were broken after death. It is generally agreed that the human-bearing deposit at Krapina belongs to the Eemian Interglacial period. More than a thousand stone implements have been recovered.

The Krapina human skeletal material includes postcranial bones from almost every body part and more than 282 teeth. Estimates as to the number of individuals represented range from twenty-eight to eighty. All adult skulls show a strong development of the brow ridges; in other features such as a sloping forehead, powerful jaws, and small mastoid processes, some approximate later Neandertal skulls. There is considerable variation in skull form; the frontal region of some skulls closely resembles that of more modern *H. sapiens* (Figure 12-1).

The Krapina material is morphologically like that of subsequent Neandertals. The skulls exhibit no feature that would categorically exclude them from being classed with the skulls of other European Neandertals. The skulls do, however, exhibit notable variation in the expression of certain features. Some variation is due to temporal differences in the sample; however, much of the variation is attributable to sexual dimorphism. In several features of the postcranial skeleton, the Krapina sample is typically Neandertal in appearance. The Croatian sequence (including remains from Velika Pećina, which are discussed in Chapter 13) suggests that the Neandertals evolved directly into modern *H. sapiens,* at least in eastern Europe. This suggestion is contrary to the view that the Neandertals may have been replaced by a more modern population from outside Europe.

The bone breakage on the Krapina bones was thought to indicate cannibalism, but Russell (1987a) refuted this contention. The bone breakage at Krapina is more likely due to sedimentary pressure and/or roof falls. Russell (1987b) presented evidence that the Krapina hominids developed mortuary practices. She argued that the cut marks on the bone are consistent with a pattern of defleshing in preparation for secondary burial. Trinkaus (1985b), noting the high incidence of relatively fragile bones like the scapula in the Krapina sample, suggested that the remains were the result of burial. According to Trinkaus (1985b:213) the Krapina remains "represent one of the oldest, as well as the largest samples of human burials yet known."

A number of other interesting finds have been reported from Croatia. Vindija cave yielded a large but fragmentary series of human remains. The majority of the material belongs with the Neandertals (Malez et al., 1980). Human remains from Vindija number about eighty-eight specimens. The earliest layer roughly dates to between 40,000 and 32,000 years ago, later than Krapina. The Vindija material will be discussed more fully later in this chapter.

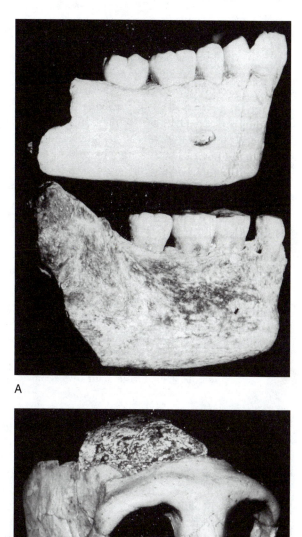

A

B

FIGURE 12-1 *A,* Two mandibles from Krapina, Croatia; *B,* Partial skull and face from Krapina. (Courtesy Croatian Natural History Museum, photos by Dr. F. H. Smith.)

In many respects the interglacial sample discussed in this section adumbrates subsequent European Neandertal populations, and in other respects it seems somewhat more modern. A number of schemes have been proposed to accommodate its physical variability. The alternatives, discussed later in the chapter, can be summarized as follows: (1) These forms are ancestral to European Neandertal populations; (2) these forms are the basis of a separate, more advanced evolutionary line with little or no genetic connection with European Neandertals; and (3) some members of the sample might be ancestral to European Neandertals, while others, like Swanscombe and Fontéchevade, are the basis of a separate evolutionary line, the Presapiens, leading to modern *H. sapiens*. Each scheme is based on the importance one attaches to the range of variation within these limited samples.

THE NEANDERTALS: THE BACKGROUND

Howell (1965:123) noted that

> of all the different kinds of prehistoric peoples, certainly the one who projects the clearest image is Neandertal man. For most of us he is Stone Age man, the squat, shaggy, beetle-browed fellow that inevitably comes to mind when we think of our ancient relatives. We see him standing in the mouth of a cave—stone ax in hand, a few rough furs over his shoulder, some mammoth bones piled in the background— staring out over a snow-choked landscape as he ponders the ever-present problems of the ice age and the giant cave bear.

This image persists because there is some truth to it. In some ways the Neandertals were morphologically different from us. Sometimes they lived in caves, wore skins, and inhabited cold climates. The first fossil skull positively identified as belonging to an ancient population was that of a Neandertal, and having nothing else to compare it with except the skulls of modern populations, many were struck by the differences between the two.

Broadly defined, Neandertals and their culture (usually designated as the Mousterian) have been traced from sites in the Near East, Africa, Europe, and possibly Asia. There are more than 275 individual Neandertals from more than 70 sites. Understanding the problem of the Neandertals is complicated by the fact that we have so many skeletal representatives and we know so much about their culture from undisturbed cave deposits. This statement may seem contradictory; if we know so much about the Neandertals, why is there so much trouble interpreting the data? The answer may be that we know "too much"; we may be too accustomed to dealing with limited population samples. One factor involved in this array of morphological and cultural traits is that of adaptive radiation, the process whereby organisms diversify to meet particular habitat demands. Neandertals lived in a variety of habitats in divergent parts of the globe to which they had to adapt biologically and culturally.

With minor variations most anthropologists accept the following criteria as a definition of the Neandertal stage of human evolution: The geographical range was primarily Europe and the Middle East; the culture was the Mousterian, itself a complex of derivatives from earlier toolmaking traditions. The term *Neandertal* usually refers to a form possessing a modern-sized brain coupled with an archaic-looking skull and robust postcranial skeleton. Neandertals were large headed and had big brains, big noses, strong brow development, low foreheads, and little chin development. These traits are even true of youngsters. Some Neandertal traits first appear about 230,000 years ago, with a full suite of Neandertal traits visible by 130,000 years ago (Box 12-1). The last known Neandertal comes from France and dates to about 33,000 years ago.

Neandertals in Portugal may have survived after 30,000 years ago. Their tools did not mimic Upper Paleolithic industries, as happened in Spain and France.

Neither the people nor their culture sprang from a vacuum. Earlier populations have already been described. The Mousterian culture is a derivative of what are commonly called the Acheulian, Clactonian-Tayacian, and Levalloisian flake techniques. That the Neandertals had ancestors is not in question; what many argue is whether they (at least the western European sample) have descendants—and who they are.

Discovery of Neandertal Remains

To appreciate some of the problems of interpretation, a word is needed on the scientific climate of the times of the earliest Neandertal discoveries. The discovery of

---

BOX 12-1   Some Critical Features Associated with Neandertals

- Time span: Approximately 130,000–33,000 years ago.

- Distribution: Primarily Europe and Middle East.

- Lifeways: Mousterian tool tradition, prepared core technique, big-game hunters, burial of dead, possible personal ornamentation.

- Morphology: Varies with location. Western European Neandertals are the most distinctive.
  - Cranial capacity: 1,524–1,640 cc for males and 1,270–1,425 cc for females.
  - Face and skull: In many European forms the skull is low and has a flat crown; in some Middle Eastern forms the skull has a high crown.
  - Occipital bun common in European forms.
  - Large brow ridges common in many fossils.
  - Maxillary prognathism common to Western European fossils.
  - Receding or absent chin.
  - Large and robust jaws.
  - Broader anterior teeth than in modern populations.
  - Distinct bony labyrinth of middle ear.
  - Postcranial skeleton: Short and powerfully built, some differences in pelvic morphology, differently shaped foramen magnum.

the first Neandertal remains only slightly preceded the publication of Darwin's evolutionary theory; thus they drew more attention than might have otherwise been true. People were searching for the "missing link," and the Neandertal was characterized as big, burly, and hairy, with a sloping head and slouching back, a club-wielding creature dragging his mate to his den by her hair.

The first reported Neandertal find came from Germany in 1856. Workers originally mistook the material for nonhuman bones and immediately disposed of it. At the last moment the owner of the excavation site saved the bones and gave them to a local teacher who, in turn, passed them on to H. Schaaffhausen, an anatomist in Bonn. He termed the material *ancient*, a pronouncement pleasing to the budding group of evolutionists; antievolutionists, however, thought that the material represented a pathological individual. In 1863, Thomas Huxley discussed this find in *Man's Place in Nature*. Further Neandertal finds came to light in 1866 from La Naulette, Belgium, when a jaw associated with a Mousterian cultural assemblage and bones of rhinoceros, mammoth, and bear were uncovered—all of which provided clues to the age of the specimen. In 1886 additional skeletal remains came from Spy in Belgium; now talk of pathological individuals was minimal.

The years preceding World War I witnessed the recovery of much European Neandertal material, most coming from the Dordogne region of southwestern France. Other finds were recovered in Spain, Italy, southeastern Europe, Russia, Iraq, and Turkey. The French paleontologist M. Boule described them in detail but erroneously pointed to what he considered to be their highly uniform, specialized archaic nature.

Until the early 1930s, there was no particular Neandertal "problem" beyond the diligent search for more fossils. Many scientists assumed that European Neandertals were slowly driven to extinction by later and more advanced populations. Human remains from cave sites in Israel showed general characteristics not quite like those of the European Neandertals, but they were also distinguishable from modern *H. sapiens*. These discoveries raised doubts.

THE NEANDERTALS: THE FOSSIL SAMPLE

Western Europe

Western European Neandertal remains are found in sheltered and well-watered valleys of southern France and similar parts of the Spanish and Italian peninsulas, regions outside the main zone of frozen ground and tundra vegetation. There was also at least sporadic penetration, perhaps seasonally for hunting and collecting, into adjacent areas. The numerous remains from this area result from high population concentrations, good preservation conditions, and heavy archaeological exploration.

Since the discovery of a skull and portions of the limb skeleton in 1856, most scientists have recognized the Neandertals as being morphologically fairly distinct. European Neandertals were a morphologically heterogeneous population. More than with any other fossil group, the interpretation of the European Neandertals has been plagued by the "type" concept and the downplaying of intrapopulation and interpopulation variability. Wolpoff (1980) suggested that sexual dimorphism is one major factor contributing to systematic variation among the Neandertals.

The following traits are representative of western European Neandertals (Table 12-2): Cranial capacities range from 1,525 to 1,640 cc in six male skulls and from 1,300 to 1,425 cc in three female skulls. The skulls are more capacious than those of modern *H. sapiens,* although the sample from which Neandertal cranial capacity estimates are based is much smaller. The larger brain may be related to the Neandertal's heavier body. Arguments by Trinkaus (1984, 1986) that the large Neandertal brain sizes are related to a twelve-month gestation period are rejected by Frayer (1985), Greene and Sibley (1986), and Rak and Arensburg (1987). The significance of the size and shape differences between Neandertal and modern brains is uncertain.

The Neandertal cranium has a low flat crown and achieves its interior space by being longer and more bulging in the back and sides. A fairly consistent trait is the presence of an occipital bun (Figure 12-2), a bulging of the occipital bone at the rear of the skull. The occipital bun, or chignon, has long been considered a Neandertal trait; however, neither its function nor its distribution among other humans was carefully surveyed until Trinkaus and LeMay (1982) rectified that problem. The occipital bun appears to have attained its peak occurrence among western European Neandertals of the early Würm Glaciation. Even among these forms, however, there is variation in the relative size (expression) of this trait. Some forms such as La Chapelle-aux-Saints 1 and La Quina 5, both from France, have large, projecting occipital buns, whereas La Ferrassie 1 from France and Spy 2 from Belgium have relatively small ones.

TABLE 12-2   Traits of the Neandertal Face, Skull, Dentition, and Skeleton

Face: Overall facial skeleton is massive; midfacial prognathism, large nasal apertures, well-developed but discontinuous brow ridges.

Skull: The cranial vault is long, low, and wide. The occipital bones have occipital ridges, and many have occipital buns. Perhaps differently shaped foramen magnum and middle ear bones.

Dentition and jaws: No canine diastema in maxillary region; molars have large pulp cavity (taurodontism); large incisors, no chin.

Postcranial Skeleton
Spinal column: Heavily built; the cervical vertebrae have long projecting spinous processes.

Upper limb skeleton: Broad scapula, robust humerus with massive head.

Pelvis: More dorsally rotated ilia than in modern humans.

Lower limb skeleton: Massive femurs, short and strong tibiae, large and thick kneecaps.

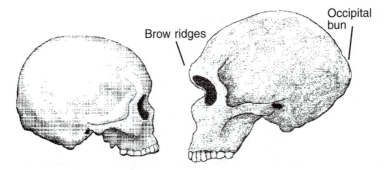

FIGURE 12-2 Crania of modern *Homo (left)* and a western European Neandertal *(right)*. Note the distinctive brow ridges and occipital bun of the Neandertal. (Courtesy Jeffrey K. McKee.)

The presence of an occipital bun does not automatically indicate inclusion in the western European Neandertal group. It also appeared among earlier European, archaic African, and European early Upper Paleolithic *H. sapiens*. It is possible that some Near Eastern Neandertals exhibited the trait. Some evidence of an occipital bun also appeared in recent human populations.

Various interpretations have been forthcoming concerning the origin or function of the occipital bun. Trinkaus and LeMay suggested that the occipital bun is related to the extent of posterior brain growth, and its timing is relative to the formation of the bones of the cranial vault. The occipital bun may be due to a posterior displacement of the occipital bone as a result of later posteriorly directed brain growth. It may be dependent on the timing of brain growth relative to the developmental sequence of the cranial vault bones. Trinkaus and LeMay suggested that the occipital bun results from a significant increase in brain size relatively late in the normal development of the childhood brain, especially in relation to the growth patterns of the individual's cranial vault bones. The occipital bun is, therefore, not distinctive of the Neandertals, or any human group; rather, it is a product of human neurocranial development. Only the high incidence and large size of the occipital buns among Upper Pleistocene humans are unique.

Trinkaus and LeMay argued that Upper Pleistocene humans had a slightly delayed pattern of brain growth relative to the timetable of twentieth-century humans. An additional contributory factor in the incidence of the occipital bun may be the relatively large brain sizes of many Upper Pleistocene humans, especially as exhibited among males.

Graves (1991) suggested the possibility that the Neandertals may have had a different developmental program than modern humans. (There is scant evidence to support Graves, but the point is worth exploring.) He suggested that more precocial infants, that is, more rapidly developing infants, were advantageous to cold-adapted humans and that less physically dependent young should be expected if Neandertal females were engaged in confrontational hunting. More rapidly developing young were also able to contribute to subsistence activities. However, there is a negative side to precocial young—a shorter period of postnatal development might have meant less behavioral flexibility.

Graves also suggested that Neandertal females reproduced at a slower rate than their modern replacements, which might have led rapidly to the extinction of the Neandertals, with preferential selection against genes producing developmental patterns associated with Neandertal reproduction.

Four major traits distinguish the Neandertal face: The chin is receding or is absent; there are large cheek bones; the prominent brow ridges curve over the eye orbits and connect across the bridge of the nose; and there is a rather large nasal cavity and maxillary prognathism. European Neandertal jaws and teeth are distinctive. The jaws are usually large, and all indicate strong muscle attachments. Some jaw features are related to facial size; however, some features are related to the size and use of the masticatory muscles. Certain traits of the Neandertals' teeth support the contention of specialized use (Smith, 1976). The most important features distinguishing Neandertal dentitions from those of extant humans are in size rather than in structure. Major distinctions occur in the incisors and canines (Brace, 1962a, 1964, 1968a, 1968b; Wolpoff, 1971a). Neandertal anterior dentitions are larger than those in modern *H. sapiens,* especially in breadth.

Neandertals seem to have used their anterior teeth in gripping, holding, exerting torsion, and other manipulations (Brose & Wolpoff, 1971; Coon, 1962). The anterior teeth have robust roots and supporting structures.

The Neandertal postcranial skeleton suggests that they were short, powerfully built individuals when compared to modern populations. Neandertals were over 5 feet tall. Their extremities were short, and their long bones were robust and slightly curved. The hands and fingers were short and stubby. Their feet were similar to ours; in fact, a Neandertal footprint cast appears in the wet clay of an Italian cave. For many years it was argued that European Neandertals were incapable of erect bipedalism because the foramen magnum was supposedly slanted rearward, as it is in quadrupedal animals, rather than being directly beneath the skull, as in bipeds. This mistaken notion arose because of a faulty reconstruction of the cranial base of the La Chappelle-aux-Saints specimen.

Holliday (1997) describes European Neandertal postcranial anatomy as "hyperpolar." That is, their limb and body proportions are extremely cold adapted; they surpass modern-day Eskimos in this regard. He explains the cold adaptation as resulting from intense selection pressure that was due to the cold of glacial Europe and/or less effective cultural buffering.

Besides being an adaptation to climatic stress, the short and stocky body builds of the western European Neandertals may also have been a response to nutritional stress. Many Neandertal teeth exhibit hypoplasia—that is, they are not fully developed—often an indication of dietary stress. Studies of modern human populations show that one possible response to dietary stress is short stature. However, in modern populations these short statures are often accompanied by lean body builds—a trait not exhibited by western European Neandertals.

Climatic conditions in which European Neandertals lived were less than hospitable. Ice descended on the British Isles and to the northern edge of Europe from Scandinavia and came down out of the Alps as well; central Europe was an arctic province. South of the ice the ground was frozen, and the Mediterranean climate of preceding interglacial times gave way to tundra, cold steppe, and plains (Howells, 1967). Some traits of European Neandertal morphology were probably adaptations to a cold environment (Coon, 1962; Steegmann, 1972). Neandertal nasal prognathism is best explained as a cold adaptation (Wolpoff, 1968). Nasal prognathism generated a massive face, combined with a relatively long and low skull, and an expanded nuchal area for neck muscle attachment. The postcranial skeleton, with short, stubby limbs and phalanges, was similarly adapted to cold. There is a rough gradient of what are considered to be Neandertal traits; their most extreme expressions are prevalent in the colder regions of Europe and decrease as one moves eastward and southward in the Middle East. Western European Neandertals are the most readily identifiable, as climatic selection was maximized in Western Europe.

Nasal morphology and associated features are the most distinctive traits of the Neandertal face. The size and shape of the nose are related to the function of warming and moistening inspired air. Perhaps Neandertal noses dissipated body heat during frequent periods of heightened activity. Nasal breadth is also affected by the width between the canine teeth because the canine roots run along the sides of the nose. Among Neandertals, the breadth across the canines was large because of the large incisors. This feature may account for the large nasal breadths in early *H. sapiens* samples. As Wolpoff (1980) pointed out, before the emergence of cold-adapted Neandertals, there was a background of broad nasal openings in early *H. sapiens*.

Laitman (in Fischman, 1992) suggested that western European Neandertals had an elevated larynx that affected their speech. Laitman suggested that they may not have been able to articulate some vowel sounds, such as *a, i,* and *u,* as clearly as modern humans. The elevated larynx also left the Neandertal's large nose free, helping to warm incoming air. The heated and moistened air protects the throat and lungs. Neandertals may have taken in more air through their noses and less through their mouths to deal with the cold air temperatures they faced in western Europe. With warming climates, the same conditions that favored warming of cold air would have favored sinus infections. Laitman asks, Could recurrent respiratory infections have been a problem?

The Neandertal face is extraordinarily robust. Rak (1986) suggested that the face is constructed to counteract the considerable forces that Neandertals developed between their upper and lower teeth. Individuals exhibit very heavy wear on the front teeth, indicating heavy chewing stress. Perhaps this stress came as a result of chewing hides or other materials. Rak thought that the Neandertal's face is morphologically more similar to preceding than to subsequent humans. He has doubts about the Neandertal's place in the evolutionary lineage of modern *H. sapiens sapiens.*

Hublin et al. (1996) suggest that Neandertals have a distinct bony labyrinth of the middle ear. Based on their analysis of the Arcy-sur-Cure juvenile temporal from France, this Neandertal specimen seems to have had smaller anterior and posterior semicircular canals than modern humans. The smaller canals are striking if it is considered that body mass, which is positively correlated with canal size, was probably higher in Neandertals than modern humans. Unlike great apes and other hominids, the Neandertals show an inferiorly positioned but relatively small posterior semicircular canal.

Central and Eastern Europe

Although less numerous than western European remains, eastern and central European Neandertal samples are very important. It has been argued that the apparently sudden appearance of late Paleolithic populations in western Europe presupposes their origin elsewhere in the east and that the settlement of western Europe during the Würm Glaciation was made by immigrants from the east. A number of finds from eastern and central Europe fill some of the geographical and chronological gaps in the Neandertal fossil record and, in so doing, have blurred the boundary between western European Neandertals and fully modern humans (Brose & Wolpoff, 1971; Jelinek, 1969). These forms seem to be transitional between the Neandertals and modern *H. sapiens sapiens,* as some have argued.

Vindija cave, Croatia, yielded about eighty-eight fragmentary specimens. The earliest stratigraphic level dates from 40,000 to 32,000 years ago. The Vindija remains can be divided into three groups. The first group of *H. s. sapiens* contains thirty-three specimens, whose only remarkable feature is a somewhat unusually thick cranial vault. The second group contains four specimens, which are anatomically close to the Neandertals, but they could also be accommodated within an early Upper Paleolithic *H. s. sapiens* sample. The third group of forty specimens is placed among the Neandertals. In some respects, however, they are intermediate between the central European *H. s. sapiens* condition and older central European Neandertals. Adult specimens preserving the brow region exhibit a characteristic Neandertal brow ridge.

The Vindija Neandertals represent a group intermediate between most central European Neandertals and early *H. s. sapiens.* The "existence of such a group of comparatively late-dated Neandertals, along with the Neandertal-reminiscent morphology exhibited by certain early Upper Paleolithic specimens . . . strengthens the hypothesis of a direct ancestral position for at least central European *H. sapiens neanderthalensis* in the lineage of *H. sapiens sapiens* in Europe" (Malez et al., 1980:367). The Vindija Neandertals support the hypothesis of an in situ transition to *H. s. sapiens* in south-central Europe.

The Ochoz jaw is a well-preserved but incomplete mandible from the Czech Republic that was originally recovered in 1905. Investigations conducted from 1953 through 1955 date the jaw and associated Mousterian remains to a Neandertal time period. The mandible has some traits found in western European Neandertals. The Sipka jaw is from a Czech Republic cave site discovered in 1880; it dates to the Würm I glacial period. The jaw, which belongs to a child about ten years old, can be regarded as late Neandertal with certain features reminiscent of modern *H. sapiens* (Jelinek, 1969). The Šala frontal bone from the Czech Republic has the typical Neandertal brow ridge, although the bony shelf is less heavy. For this find, as for those from Ochoz and Sipka, certain morphological traits indicate an evolutionary tendency toward modern *H. s. sapiens*. An endocranial cast and remnants of a braincase were recovered from the Slovakian site of Gánovce. A final Czech find is the right part of a maxilla from Kůlna cave, recovered in July 1965. This jaw, like other central and eastern European remains, is characterized by a mixture of archaic and advanced traits (Jelinek, 1969).

In 1952 an adult female mandible was recovered in a Mousterian tool layer in Subalyuk cave, Hungary. The mandible shows the beginning of a chin, while at the same time it has some archaic traits. The teeth exhibit the same mix of traits. A child's skeleton, found with the mandible, was badly smashed during excavation. Only the child's skull has been studied.

Until now we have remarked on the fact that the lower jaws of all human fossil remains lacked a chin. As you are fully aware, a chin is a common feature of the lower jaw of most humans today. What accounted for this change? Why does the chin only appear rather late in human evolution? What is its function?

A great deal of stress passes through the lower jaw while food is being ground by the teeth. In earlier humans and in large monkeys and apes, this stress is dealt with by large, thick mandibles. In species with a powerful side-to-side grinding action of the molar teeth, there is a thickening of the body of the mandible. This thickening is most evident in the midline of the mandible (that is, the chin area). In larger monkeys and apes the midline is strengthened by the development of internal buttressing (known as a *simian shelf*) and by external buttressing (known as the *mandibular torus*) halfway up the body of the mandible.

Both kinds of buttressing were lost during human evolution. In modern humans the internal buttress was replaced by the chin. Although the stresses in the mandibles of modern humans are not great, the molar teeth still grind the food, and this action produces some stress. Therefore, some strengthening of the mandible is still required—and is provided by the chin. The eversion of the mandible, the forward jutting of the midline of the mandible, has produced the chin. The forward projecting may also be an accommodation to the location of the head on the spinal column.

The eastern and central European fossils are important for the following reasons (Jelinek, 1969): (1) To varying degrees and frequencies, they display many traits found in fully developed *H. s. sapiens*. (2) Chronologically these forms extend to the time period in which the oldest finds of European *H. s. sapiens* occur. (3) Even some forms designated as *H. s. sapiens* exhibit cultural and morphological traits linking them to previous samples.

Smith (1982) argued that the central European sample shows all the traits of the Neandertals. The only systematic difference between western and early central European Neandertals is in body size. Central European Neandertals appear to be shorter, but this impression may be the result of an overabundance of subadult material in the Krapina sample.

Late Neandertals from central Europe have basically the same morphological pattern as the earlier sample. The late sample, however, exhibits traits that more closely approach *H. s. sapiens* to a consistently greater degree than the earlier group. The late group, for instance, shows a reduction in robusticity in certain facial traits. The early *H. s. sapiens* sample from central Europe exhibits several traits indicating a close connection with preceding central European Neandertals. The morphological continuum in Upper Pleistocene central European human remains indicates some degree of local genetic continuity between Neandertals and *H. s. sapiens*. The transition may have been a local process.

Western Europe does not provide as convincing an indication of morphological continuity as does central Europe (Smith, 1982). It is tempting, therefore, to hypothesize that extraneous factors affected the transition from the Neandertals to early *H. s. sapiens* and to suggest that the immediate source of this influence was central Europe. Perhaps gene flow from outside western Europe was responsible for the anatomical change from a Neandertal to a *H. s. sapiens* morphology in western Europe. This is an old puzzle that has not been resolved to everyone's satisfaction. As noted earlier, Rak thought that the anatomy of the western European Neandertal face precludes Neandertals as direct ancestors to modern *H. sapiens*. A case has also been made that the change through time in the Neandertal Mousterian tool assemblage indicates such a basic difference in the intellectual capabilities of Neandertals and modern humans that the former should not be considered a member of our species. According to some researchers, they should be classified *Homo neanderthalensis*.

The Middle East

Some Middle Eastern finds appear to be morphologically transitional between Neandertals and *H. s. sapiens*. Some, such as Qafzeh 6 and Skhūl 5, anatomically closely approach *H. s. sapiens*, whereas others dating from an earlier time, such as Tabūn and Shanidar 1, closely approach western European Neandertals, except for the adaptation to extremes of cold. Some scientists argue that there is good archaeological and skeletal evidence for considering all Middle Eastern specimens members of a late non–cold-adapted Neandertal group, imperceptibly grading into fully modern *H. s. sapiens* (Brose & Wolpoff, 1971).

The Middle East has long been a crossroads of humanity; many consider the Middle Eastern corridor, stretching along the coastline of Israel, Lebanon, and Syria and bordered on the west by the Mediterranean and on the east by the Lebanon mountains, as an evolutionary focal point. Abundant game has allowed rather heavy local human population centers to develop. Pollen analysis indicates that approximately 45,000 to 40,000 years ago the climate shifted toward somewhat drier conditions, leading to local concentrations of grazing lands, grazing animals, and their hunters. The richest fossil sites from this time period are most abundant in the valleys along the western slopes of the coastal ranges. Mount Carmel, Israel, lies in such a valley, as do some of the other sites mentioned.

The most complete Middle Eastern record comes from Israel and Iraq. Two major sites at Mount Carmel, Israel, are the cave of et-Tabūn (Cave of the Oven) and the cave of es-Skhūl (Cave of the Young Goats). A third cave, el-Wad, yielded fragmentary remains. Mount Carmel lies approximately 12 miles from Haifa.

Human fossils from et-Tabūn cave were associated with a mammalian fauna suggestive of a fairly warm climate and, at a higher level, with fauna of a somewhat damper climate. Skulls from both caves show pronounced brow ridge development, but they display a remarkable variability in the degree of development of other features typically associated with western European Neandertals. In the rounded and vertical forehead and height of the cranial vault, some (especially some material from es-Skhūl) rather closely approximate anatomically modern *H. sapiens.* This resemblance is enhanced by the rounded occipital contour; the strongly developed mastoid process; smaller sphenoidal angle of the skull base; development of a distinct chin in some cases; moderate size of the facial skeleton; and the slender, straight-shafted limbs (Clark, 1967).

The et-Tabūn cave remains, a large male mandible and a female skeleton, date to about 53,000 years ago, although some material may date to 80,000 to 70,000 years ago. The et-Tabūn female (Tabūn 1) has a low skull, arched brows, and heavy, continuous brow ridges like her western European contemporaries; however, she lacks an occipital bun. She appears to have been rather delicately built and approximately 5 feet tall. Her cranial capacity was estimated at about 1,270 cc. The mandible lacks a chin. The male mandible, et-Tabūn 2, is large, deep, and rather squarish in front. Morphologically the et-Tabūn material falls between the central and western Neandertals and has some resemblance to the Shanidar materials from Iraq, especially Shanidar 1. The et-Tabūn remains fit into a rather loosely defined group, including members from Shanidar in Iraq and Amud cave in Israel.

Es-Skhūl contained ten buried skeletons, perhaps dating to between 35,000 and 55,000 years ago, in varying states of preservation. However, a more recent date is between 100,000 and 81,000 years ago (Stringer et al., 1989). Although the et-Tabūn group manifests some Western European Neandertal traits, those from es-Skhūl show a general similarity to later *H. sapiens.* The es-Skhūl braincases are similar to those of modern humans in shape and size; they are high, flat sided, and round—not projecting in a bun at the rear. The forepart of the skull is reminiscent of earlier Neandertals. The brows are large but not heavy or bulbous as among earlier Neandertals. The mandible has a chin (Howells, 1967), and the teeth are large.

There are differences in the es-Skhūl skulls: The forehead of one is rather heavy and sloping; in another it is higher and more rounded. In one of the skulls the nose and mouth are somewhat prognathic. One group of es-Skhūl skulls, numbers 2, 4 (which is well preserved), 7, and 9, are intermediate between Neandertals and modern *H. sapiens.* Skulls 5 (the best known and best preserved) and 6 are more like *H. s. sapiens.* Skull 5 (Figure 12-3) belonged to a male aged about thirty-five years and had a cranial capacity of 1,518 cc (Coon, 1962).

The fossils at Mount Carmel seem to represent an evolutionary trend away from the Neandertal line, as represented at Tabūn, and toward the *H. s. sapiens* line as represented at Skhūl. It has been suggested that a population such as that represented by Tabūn was replaced by a population such as that represented by the latest Skhūl specimens.

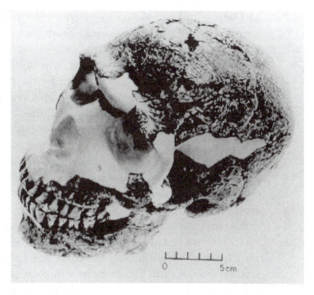

FIGURE 12-3 The skull of es-Skhūl 5. (Photo courtesy Wenner-Gren Foundation for Anthropological Research, Inc., and owners of original specimen.)

Although there are earlier suggestions based on the archaeological and human remains found in the Mount Carmel caves that the Neandertals evolved into modern *H. sapiens*, the more recently excavated Kebara and Qafzeh caves in the same region cast doubt on this possibility (Stringer, 1987; Valladas et al., 1987a, 1987b). Finds from Qafzeh suggest that *H. s. sapiens* lived in the Middle Eastern region for more than twice as long as generally accepted based on such sites as Skhūl cave. The Qafzeh cave remains are dated to 92,000 years ago by TL dating of burnt flint or ESR on tooth enamel to 115,000 years ago plus or minus 15,000 years (Schwarz et al., 1988). The oldest dated Neandertal remains, those from Kebara cave, date to 62,000 to 52,000 years ago. The older date for the Qafzeh remains suggests that *H. s. sapiens* preceded the Neandertals in the region.

Prior to the discoveries at Qafzeh cave, Neandertals were usually viewed as members of our own species. They are distinguished from modern humans by a subspecies designation; that is, they are called *H. s. neanderthalensis*. However, if the modern subspecies of *H. s. sapiens* preceded its supposed ancestors, the Neandertals, then the latter could not be ancestral to the former, as many have suggested. The dates from Qafzeh cave indicate that the model of the Neandertals evolving into modern *H. sapiens* lacks credence. The Qafzeh dates approach those dates for the oldest possible *H. s. sapiens* sites, which are found in eastern and southern Africa and which date to between 130,000 and 90,000 years ago. These sites are discussed in the next chapter.

If the dates from Qafzeh and Kebara are correct, then Neandertals and modern *H. sapiens* coexisted and maintained a separate gene pool in the Middle Eastern region for about 60,000 years before the Neandertals were replaced by modern *H. sapiens* in Europe about 35,000 years ago. If there was genetic separation for that length of time, as is suggested by the dates of the human remains at Qafzeh and Kebara caves, then the Neandertals should be classified as a separate species *(H. neanderthalensis)* from us rather than as a separate subspecies, *H. s. neanderthalensis.*

Pelvic morphology may shed light on the taxonomy of specimens from Qafzeh and Kebara caves (Rak, 1990). The pelvis of Qafzeh 9 is dated by thermoluminescence to approximately 95,000 years ago. The Kebara pelvis is dated to about 60,000 years ago. Substantial morphological differences between the two pelvises provide another set of anatomical arguments for two separate and parallel evolutionary lines. The Qafzeh specimen comes from a population ancestral to modern *H. sapiens,* whereas Rak argued that the Kebara specimen and other Neandertal specimens contemporaneous with it have little bearing on the evolution of modern humans.

New ESR dates suggest that the Skhūl and Qafzeh specimens are of approximately equal age. If this finding is accurate, then it also offers proof that modern pelvic anatomy is found in hominids living contemporaneously with the Neandertals.

The partial skeleton of a ten-month-old infant, Amud 7 from Amud cave, Israel, dates to about 60,000 years ago. Although the skull is damaged, many cranial bones and a relatively complete mandible are present. The vertebral column and ribs are fairly well preserved, but other postcranial bones are incomplete. A red deer upper jaw leaning against the pelvis of the buried infant may be a sign of ritualized burial. The mandible lacks a chin, as is so for other Neandertal youngsters. In contrast, juvenile early *H. s. sapiens* young have a chin. The size and shape of the foramen magnum are typical of Neandertals.

Shanidar cave is in the western Zagros mountains of northern Iraq. Periodically, because of local earthquakes or the formation of ice on the cave ceiling, slabs of limestone plummet from the cave roof, killing many of the cave's inhabitants. In 1953, R. Solecki recovered an infant's skeleton; in 1957, three adult skeletons; and in 1960, three more skeletons. The Shanidar cave remains have been described by Solecki (1960, 1971), Stewart (1958a, 1958b, 1958c, 1961, 1962, 1963), and Trinkaus (1983).

The Shanidar remains lay in Mousterian culture-bearing deposits. Shanidar 1 has been C^{14} dated at 46,000 years ago plus or minus 1,500 years (Solecki, 1960). Shanidar 3 is perhaps a few hundred years older. Shanidar 2 and the infant are close to 60,000 years old. Several features of Shanidar 3's pelvis suggest an age of forty to forty-five years.

The Shanidar material is morphologically closer to a Tabūn than the more modern es-Skhūl sample. The female from Tabūn and a male specimen from Amud share a degree of kinship with the Shanidar sample. Although all immediately strike one as being Neandertals, each had a somewhat rounder head than found among Western European Neandertals. The Shanidar sample suggests a population allied to, but slightly distinct from, that of Europe.

Shanidar 3 appears to have been recovering from a projectile point found embedded in his ribcage when he was killed by a rockfall (Solecki, 1989). He was subsequently buried against the cave wall. Shanidar 1, who died at about thirty to thirty-five years of age, is one of the largest fossil skulls ever found. Its cranial capacity is estimated at over 1,700 cc, about 400 cc above the average for modern

H. sapiens. Shanidar 1 was probably born with his right arm, shoulder blade, and collar bone not fully developed. He was severely wounded by the blows of some sharp instrument around and above the right eye. He had a healed bone lesion from a blow on the right parietal. Despite these infirmities, which surely must have affected his ability to contribute to the social group, he survived and was subsequently crushed by a slab of falling limestone, apparently while standing erect.

Four adults from Shanidar, Shanidar 1, 3, 4, and 5, exhibit evidence of pre-death trauma. A critical factor in understanding these traumas is the chronological age of the skeletons. All four died at a relatively advanced age; the average age of the four adults was about forty years. The high prevalence of trauma may reflect the number of elderly individuals in the sample (Trinkaus, 1978; Trinkaus & Zimmerman, 1982).

The risk of injury seems to have been high in the Neandertal sample. Neandertal skeletons of advanced age show evidence of bone trauma—which suggests that Neandertal life was harsh and dangerous. Nevertheless, the fact that they survived despite these injuries indicates that the Neandertals had a level of social development in which disabled individuals were well cared for by members of the group. Shanidar 1 and 3 lived many years with severely debilitating injuries, which might have prevented them from normal participation in the group's subsistence. Such individuals, therefore, may have contributed in a more indirect way (but see Tappen's caveat on page 290); thus it is not surprising that many were intentionally buried.

The cranial vaults of Shanidar 1 and 5 suggest deliberate cranial deformation (Trinkaus, 1982a). The most noticeable features of the cranial vaults are their frontal flattening and parietal curvature, features associated with cranial deformation among recent humans. The inferred presence of deliberate skull deformation among the Shanidar Neandertals suggests a heretofore poorly documented personal aesthetic sense. The appearance of this practice at the same time in human evolution as intentional burial and prolonged survival of the infirm suggests a behavioral pattern allied with that of modern humans.

Contemporaneous Fossils

Sometimes the term *Neandertal* or *Neandertaloid* is extended to include some African and east Asian fossils. However, the best-known African and east Asian forms are almost certainly older than the Neandertals. Furthermore, the large brow ridges, low frontals, and other features that the so-called African and east Asian remains share with their European counterparts characterize virtually all nonmodern *Homo* skulls. At the same time, African and east Asian skulls generally lack a cluster of traits that tend to characterize European Neandertals (Santa Luca, 1978; Stringer et al., 1984). Referring to these forms as Neandertals or Neandertaloids confuses their taxonomic significance.

The Maba skullcap was recovered in a limestone cave in Guangdong Province, China in 1958. The skullcap consists of the frontal, parietal, and nasal bones and the lower border of the right eye socket (Figure 12-4). Although the

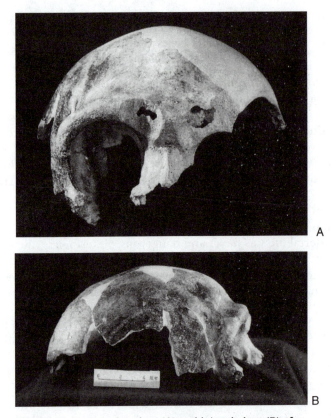

A

B

FIGURE 12-4 Anterior view *(A)* and lateral view *(B)* of early *Homo sapiens* skull from Maba, China. (Courtesy Institute of Vertebrate Paleontology and Paleoanthropology [IVPP].)

fragmentary nature of the material complicates taxonomic allocation, in a number of details Maba approaches the Neandertals. However, there are differences from the Neandertals in the facial skeleton.

The Dali skull (Figure 12-5), from Shaanxi Province, appears to be a complete version of the Maba skullcap. The face is short, and the occipital lacks the flattening common in European Neandertals. Both Maba and Dali seem to represent the same evolutionary grade as archaic *H. sapiens* populations in Europe.

The Dali skull was found in 1978. It may date between 71,000 and 41,000 years ago or be as old as 200,000 years based on uranium dates on ox teeth from the site. The right portion of the braincase and the left zygomatic are missing. The skull presents a mosaic of archaic and more advanced traits. It is the most complete cranium found from the Middle Pleistocene period. The vault is very low, with bone thickness at least equal to the Zhoukoudian sample and with an

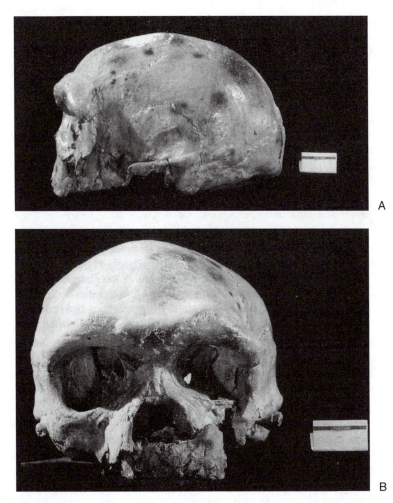

FIGURE 12-5   Lateral view *(A)* and anterior view *(B)* of early *Homo sapiens* skull from Dali, China. (Courtesy Institute of Vertebrate Paleontology and Paleoanthropology [IVPP].)

estimated cranial capacity of 1,120 cc. The brow ridges are heavy and slightly arched, and the occipital is rounded and without a bun. Braüer (1984) rejected an attribution of Maba and Dali to the Neandertal lineage. The skulls might fit somewhere on a *Homo erectus*–early *Homo sapiens* continuum.

Human fossils recovered in Changyang County, Hubei Province, China in 1956 are associated with vertebrate fossils of various kinds of animals. The human remains include part of the left maxilla. The material is dated to about 195,000 years ago—before the Neandertal samples discussed previously. The Changyang fossil is similar to Maba and other materials, such as Dingcun (Shanxi Province), Tongzi (Guizhou province), and Dali (Wang, 1980), all from China.

CULTURAL REMAINS AND LIFEWAYS

The Neandertal cultural assemblage is the Mousterian, a name derived from the southwestern French village of Le Moustier, where the type site (the site to which others are compared and from which the assemblage was first recognized) is located. The tool categories, the scrapers, points, and knives, tell us something about the lifeways and concerns of their fabricators.

Not all Neandertal remains are associated with a Mousterian cultural assemblage. A late-appearing Neandertal is a skeleton excavated at St. Césaire in southwestern France, dating to 35,000–34,000 years ago. Tools associated with this skeleton belonged to the Upper Paleolithic Châtelperronian assemblage usually found with *H. sapiens sapiens* populations.

Neandertal remains from Arcy-sur-Cure, France, date to about 34,000 years ago—contemporaneous with European *H. s. sapiens.* The stone and bone tools and the pierced or grooved animal teeth and ivory rings apparently used for jewelry resembled materials found with *H. s. sapiens.* What are they doing with this Neandertal find? A similar admixture of Neandertal bones and *H. s. sapiens* cultural remains occurs in Israel, but at a much earlier date. Hublin et al. (1996) suggest that Neandertals were actively trading with their anatomically more modern contemporaries. However, there is no evidence of genetic admixture. Despite having the same cultural assemblage as contemporaneous populations, Neandertals seem to have died out while their contemporaries survived.

New stone-working techniques appear in Europe and Africa about 100,000 years ago. Like the preceding Acheulian, the European Mousterian tradition gradually replaced earlier stone-working techniques. By 40,000 to 30,000 years ago, the Mousterian itself was being supplanted. Perhaps the most important change in material culture was an increase in the number of tool traditions. Five Mousterian traditions are identified in Europe. In the Near East, the Mousterian is associated with both Neandertals and *H. s. sapiens,* but in Europe it is found only with Neandertals.

The site of Zafarraya in Spain is roughly contemporaneous with Saint-Césaire and Arcy-sur-Cure in France. Zafarraya provides clear evidence of the late persistence of the Mousterian Industry between 35,000 and 30,000 years ago (Hublin et al., 1998).

The apparent specialization of Mousterian tool types indicates specialized economic pursuits and a wide range of environmental manipulation. The Mousterian is typified by prepared core techniques for tool production. In this technique a stone is shaped before the final blade-producing blow is struck. The resultant *Levallois blades* are relatively long and have a sharp cutting edge. Toward the end of the Middle Paleolithic (a period of tool production, including Mousterian tools) and characterizing the Upper Paleolithic (a period of tool manufacturing usually associated with finely made tools produced by early *H. s. sapiens* populations), tool preparation involved striking off thin, fine flakes of predetermined size and shape with great precision. In this **Levallois technique,** a core is prepared by removing a large number of flakes to produce the desired shape. The core from which the flake is removed is not the primary tool.

The Levallois technique is not invariably associated with the Mousterian assemblage. It goes back much further in time and is associated with the Acheulian **percussion flaking,** a method in which a stone is used to chip flakes from another stone. The Mousterian appears to be a Middle Paleolithic industry derived without major discontinuities from the preceding Acheulian.

The Mousterian, *sensu stricto,* is a set of stone tool assemblages suggesting versatility and sophistication in applying the overall technology mastered in the Acheulian. Handaxes appear to be replaced by a new range of tools made from prepared cores. At their best, these tools were meticulously prepared and trimmed, suggesting a special purpose rather than the multipurpose tools of preceding times. Butzer (1971) suggested that most Mousterian tools are characterized by careful manufacture because an increasing number of good artisans produced new artifactual types to accommodate a wider range of activities. Although similar tools are found in northern Africa and the Near East, the true European Mousterian includes a greater proportion and diversity of highly refined tools.

Much of the cultural evidence used to reconstruct the European Neandertal's way of life comes from near the French village of Les Eyzies, located more than 300 miles southwest of Paris. Here, rivers have cut into a great limestone plateau, creating gorges and wide open valleys bounded by steep cliffs hundreds of feet in height. There are many caves in the cliffs; some are small, but others extend deep into the rocks. The cliffs and overhangs provide such good shelter that even today houses are built by using the rock as a natural back wall.

The cultural record from this area of France reveals much about how European Neandertals adapted to their physical surroundings. The area around Les Eyzies offered advantages in the struggle with the environment. The cliffs provided shelter and an unlimited source of raw materials for fabricating tools; mountain runoff assured a plentiful water supply. An abundance of game, particularly reindeer, seems to have provided a large measure of the Neandertals' nourishment. Some 200 prehistoric sites are found within a 20-mile radius of Les Eyzies, and most archaeologists are certain that many more sites remain to be discovered. Most sites are located in caves, rock shelters, and open-air locations within a mile or two of well-traveled routes.

The Neandertals were big-game hunters; animal meat may have provided a large part of their caloric intake. Archaeological evidence from an open-air site such as Lebenstedt, Germany, supports the assumption that during the summer some Neandertals followed gregarious herds of grazing animals northward into open tundras.

There is also some evidence suggesting that the Neandertals were scavengers, raiding the kills of other predators and carrying off the legs of the fallen prey. Bone accumulations at a number of Neandertal campsites consist largely of bones from small mammals and only the lower limbs of larger animals.

According to Bordes (1953), the fine Mousterian flakes may have been worked as tools for long-term use by seasonal or permanent cave occupants, whereas rougher flakes may have been manufactured for brief use by groups wandering the tundra during the summer. Some Neandertals may have been seasonal migrants, tracking the herds onto the forest tundra in winter and returning with them onto the broad expanse of herbaceous tundra in summer.

Some members of the Neandertal population may have been sedentary. On the basis of reindeer antler and dentition from sites in southwestern France, Bouchud (1954) has shown that most of these sites must have been occupied year-round. Furthermore, it has been suggested that the complex nature of the Mousterian assemblage, as expressed in southern France, precludes anything but well-established territoriality and semipermanent settlements (Bordes, 1953, 1961).

Perhaps migration was confined to populations inhabiting the fringes, whereas Neandertal groups in less severe conditions, and where good shelter was available, basically remained sedentary. Seasonal movement was perhaps a localized adaptation of some populations to certain environmental stresses.

Faunal remains indicate that Neandertals were successful hunters. Woolly mammoths and rhinoceroses were successfully hunted; fish and fowl remains at the Lebenstedt site, for example, are evidence of the hunters' success. The killing and eviction of bears must have been a cooperative effort. The Drachenhöhle (Dragon's cave) site at Mixnitz, Austria, is one site where, judging by the bone accumulation, it appears that hibernating bears, including females with cubs, were attacked and killed on numerous occasions. There is a narrow passage by the foot of a waterfall where Neandertals may have waylaid and perhaps stoned the bears to death (Cornwall, 1968). Although there are reports of a supposed cave bear worship cult among Western European Neandertals, most data supporting such a conclusion can be dismissed (Kurtén, 1976).

Certain implements were probably used for hide preparation and butchery. Points—broad, triangular, retouched flakes—may have been hafted to wooden spears to improve the penetrating power of the plain wooden implement. Based on their anatomical study of the scapula (shoulder blade) and its joint surface, Churchill and Trinkaus (1990) concluded that Neandertals made frequent use of throwing behavior. Familiarity with fat-dressed skins could have led the Neandertals to use rawhide lashings and thongs. They may have discovered the running noose of rawhide that could be used as a snare and perhaps thrown as a lasso.

Neandertals may have employed trapping devices. The use of pitfalls is likely; and a rawhide noose tied to a bent sapling as a spring to tighten it, and with some kind of tripline, could have been used to catch both small and large game. During extreme cold periods, when large game might be scarce, Neandertals could have turned to smaller game that are most easily taken by trapping. Although no evidence of such traps exists, the large quantities of small game at Mousterian sites make a guess at trapping justified (Cornwall, 1968).

Evidence of a hunting way of life comes from Shanidar cave, Iraq (Solecki, 1971), whose inhabitants were hunters, gatherers, and foragers. Animals hunted include goat, sheep, wild cattle, pig, and land tortoise, and there are scattered remains of bear, deer, fox, marten, and gerbil. The most common mammalian remains are of the more docile, gregarious herbivorous mammals that may have been the mainstay of the Neandertal diet. These were probably caught by running grazing herds either off cliffs or into a blind canyon and slaughtering them there. Several such canyons are within easy reach of Shanidar cave. Small traps may have been used to capture solitary animals.

Two examples of Neandertal living sites document the life of their inhabitants. One, Salzgitter-Lebenstedt, located in northern Germany and excavated in 1952, is an open-air summer campsite dated to about 55,000 years ago. Reindeer accounted for the largest percentage (72 percent) of the remains (19 percent were of juveniles); woolly mammoth comprised 14 percent of the assemblage; bison, 5.4 percent; horse, 4.6 percent; and woolly rhinoceros, 2 percent. There were also single specimens from several carnivore, fish, and mollusk species.

The Mousterian cultural inventory from here is mostly flake tools, mainly scrapers and points, with careful retouching on both surfaces. The stone tools are functionally related to butchering—no surprise if this was a seasonal hunting site. Evidence exists of worked reindeer antlers (used as clubs?), bone points of mammoth ribs (used as digging sticks?), and barbed bone points (used as spearheads?), which may represent part of the weapons of hunting. A band of forty to fifty individuals may have temporarily occupied the site during the summer months.

The French site of Combe Grenal is located in a little valley about 14 miles from Les Eyzies. The site was originally dug by Bordes (1972) over an eleven-year period. When work terminated, Combe Grenal was a 40-foot hole in the ground, which yielded sixty-four separate layers of geological and archaeological deposits.

The richest and most important layers at Combe Grenal yielded an almost continuous record of Neandertal occupation from about 90,000 to 40,000 years ago. Combe Grenal seems to have been a center for Neandertal activity. Groups of thirty-five to forty individuals may have lived and died there over many generations.

An interesting discovery at Combe Grenal is a posthole, perhaps one of several at the mouth of the cave, where stakes were driven into the ground to support skins or woven branches to provide shelter from wind, rain, and snow, or they may have supported a meat-drying rack.

Combe Grenal has an especially rich accumulation of tools. Bordes (1961) discovered that the tools showed a number of unique and characteristic patterns. Different occupation layers contained different tool kits, which may hint at basic differences in living habits. Bordes collected and classified 19,000 tools from Combe Grenal. The posthole occupation layer alone contained 766 tools and a great many tool types. Of the 766 tools, 600 items belong to a single broad class of flints with one or more notches struck off the side. Most pieces are sawtooth (denticulate) tools, but there are also single-notched tools that could be used to help scrape bark from narrow branches for making stakes and spear shafts.

Although a second type of tool kit, found in fourteen other layers, includes a variety of different types, one tool class predominates. Nearly two of every three pieces is a scraper, a high proportion of which are the so-called Quina scrapers, named after the La Quina shelter about 70 miles northwest of Combe Grenal. These implements might have been used as heavy-duty tools for cleaning hides to make clothing.

Bordes identified four basic types of tool kits, which he suggested might belong to different tribes or traditions. The Binfords (1966), however, argued that different tool types at Combe Grenal reflect different everyday activities, not tool traditions of different bands. The Binfords suggested that the tools were used by the same people but for different purposes. Their analysis yielded about fourteen different tool kits.

Twenty-five of forty tool-bearing layers contain one or more of the three tool kits associated with maintenance activities. These layers may have been camps, home bases for all the group's members, or places away from the home site reserved for intensive activities associated with hunting or food processing, such as areas where tools are manufactured and repaired. Other layers may represent temporary occupation for more specialized activities. Some layers contain charcoal traces, generally characteristic of intensive settlement.

The Binfords speculated that because women are more likely to stay close to the base camp, they might tend to make their tools from local, readily available materials. Tools manufactured from local flint were predominately denticulate, or notched. These items are most commonly associated with food processing, activities that might be predominantly the women's task. Tools thought to belong to the male's hunting kits, for example, spear points and certain kinds of scrapers, were made from remote sources. The variety of materials used to make hunting tools may indicate that men were away from the base camp and had ready access to more kinds of materials.

Based on Bordes's and the Binfords' analyses, there are suggestions of a connection between hunting and the Levallois technique. Hunting tools often require large and relatively standardized flakes with a fine cutting edge, such as that produced by this technique. The Binfords also found a relationship between climate and cultural activities as indicated by the tool kits. There are six clusters of faunal remains. The greatest number occurs with tool kits characterizing base-camp layers, suggesting that inhabitants chose to settle there to exploit the game. The least variety of game was found at more temporary and specialized stations.

Neandertals present some of the earliest evidence of mortuary practices. Neandertal burials and other indications of ritualistic behavior provide insights into their culture. The Neandertals appear to have treated death as something of a special social phenomenon: "He buried his dead, which suggests an awareness of the transitoriness of life, concern over the future, and also a willingness to care for the aged" (Howell, 1965:190). Neandertal burials have been uncovered in western and eastern Europe, Iraq, and central Asia. Four French sites, Le Moustier (dating between 56,000 and 40,000 years ago), La Ferrassie, La Chapelle-aux-Saints (dating between 75,000 and 60,000 years ago), and possibly Combe Grenal, yielded Neandertal burials. At Le Moustier a young male (aged fifteen to twenty) is said to be buried in a cave lowered into a trench and placed on his right side, with his knees slightly drawn and his head resting on his forearm, reminiscent of a sleeping position. Several stone implements and a number of animal bones were buried with the body. Faunal remains contained charred remnants of wild cattle, which may be relics of a roasted meat offering to the deceased. However, the bones at Le Moustier were buried and reburied several times to provide visiting dignitaries with the thrill of discovery. Their original condition on first excavation is not known. In the cave of La Ferrassie, two adults and six children were buried in the floor, all with their bodies oriented in an east–west direction.

There is other evidence of Neandertal burials. A site at Teshik-Tash, Uzbekistan, held the remains of a young boy, supposedly surrounded by a half dozen goat frontlets with their horn cores rammed into the soil. However, goat horns are found throughout the deposit, and no plot of their overall distribution has been published to demonstrate the special nature of the horn circle.

One of the most interesting of the many possible Neandertal burials is at Shanidar cave, Iraq (Solecki, 1971). One Shanidar skeleton, number 4, may have been buried with flowers (not all agree, however, for example, Brace, 1971). Leroi-Gourhan (1975) identified eight flower species representing mainly small, brightly colored wild flowers. It has been suggested that the blossom period for the flowers was sometime between early May and early June. Leroi-Gourhan concluded that someone ranged the mountainside in the mournful task of collecting floral offerings. However, others argue that the bones and flowers are not contemporaneous. Although the grave fill at Shanidar contains clumps of flower pollen, the fill was heavily disturbed by rodent burrows, and the pollen may be intrusive and not associated with any burial site (Chase & Dibble, 1987).

A Neandertal infant burial was revealed at Dederiyeh cave, Syria (Akazawa et al., 1995). The infant was found in situ in a deposit of Mousterian tools. It lay on its back with the arms extended and legs flexed, features indicative of an intentional burial. A limestone slab, of a type rare at Dederiyeh, was found at the head of the body, and a small piece of triangular flint appeared just at the level of the infant's heart. The age estimate of the youngster is two years, but the maximum breadth of the skull equaled that of a modern six-year-old Japanese child. Akazawa et al. (1995) suggest that perhaps the infant had a relatively large brain for its age.

Originally it was claimed that the Monte Circeo male cranium, dating between 57,000 and 51,000 years ago (Schwarcz et al., 1991), from the site of Grotta Guattari, Italy, showed signs that indicated Neandertal ritual behavior. There were claims of modification of the human remains prior to burial and claims that humans were responsible for the accumulated animal bones at the site. Ritualistic cannibalism was suspected because the foramen magnum was broken and widened to get at the brain. Analyses by Stiner (1991) and White and Toth (1991) indicated instead that the remains at Grotta Guattari are the result of hyena accumulation, specifically that the bones represent a spotted hyena maternity den. When White and Toth examined the foramen magnum area, they found that the hole was broken outward, not inward as would be the case if someone hit the skull from outside to widen the hole. Toth observed that similar inside-out fractures of the foramen magnum were the result of hyenas apparently inserting their teeth into the foramen and pulling outward. Grooves on the inside of the skull also are apparently caused by hyena teeth. There is no evidence to support the earlier claim of human cannibalism at Monte Circeo.

A further caution about Neandertal burial sites is necessary. Neandertal burials in caves and rock shelters may indicate only that carnivores were not using these sites at the time.

The findings of possible ritualistic behavior mark a new stage in human evolution. Presumably death and life now held new values. Burial implies a new kind of concern for the deceased. Further evidence for this concern is suggested by the recovery of individuals who survived serious injuries and who must have been cared for by their contemporaries. Shanidar 3 was apparently recovering from a spear or knife wound in the ribs when he was killed by a rock fall. Shanidar 1 was missing his lower right arm and had healed wounds above his eyes and on the right parietal. Survival of these injuries suggests that persons who received such care were possibly kept alive, nursed back to health, and supported because of some concern for either the individual or for that individual's knowledge. In any case, it suggests a more complex, extensive social organization.

Much is made of what appears to be altruistic behavior among Neandertals. Tappen (1985), however, chides those who overemphasize this apparent altruism. His close study of the dentition of the "old man" from La Chapelle-aux-Saints, France, casts doubt on overly ambitious attempts to document altruism. (According to Trinkaus, 1985a, the "old man" was between forty and forty-five years of age when he died.) It was argued that because the "old man" had lost many of his teeth someone might have chewed his food before giving it to him. Tappen shows, however, that the tooth loss occurred after death and therefore could not have affected his survival. La Chapelle could chew with moderate effectiveness up to the time of death. Because the case for altruism is weak here, it may also be weak in other instances. For example, "evidence of advanced social organization and cultural capacities is strikingly tenuous" (Tappen, 1985:50). Tappen states that without documented proof of social concern, the case that the Neandertals are directly related to modern humans is weakened.

Neandertal burials have yielded considerable interesting data. Some Neandertal burials are tightly flexed and sometimes bound, either to save space in burial or to possibly restrain the wandering "spirit" of the dead, a practice seen in historical times. Some burials seem to have been aligned in an east to west direction, perhaps in recognition of the rising and setting of the sun; this practice is also historically documented. Stones seem to have been placed on some Middle Eastern Neandertal burials. The practice of placing stones on graves persists in the Near East. Some of the practices seemingly associated with Neandertal burials thus have been retained into historical times (Marshack, 1989).

Not all Neandertal sites indicate burials. The Neandertal cave site of l'Hortus, France, provides no evidence of burial. Human remains of more than twenty people are indiscriminately mixed with bones of animals they presumably hunted.

EVOLUTIONARY RELATIONSHIPS

The relationship of Neandertals to subsequent *H. s. sapiens* is unclear. The two major viewpoints are these: (1) The Neandertals are directly ancestral to modern *H. s. sapiens;* or (2) the Neandertals were basically a western European population that became extinct, so they are not implicated in the evolution of our subspecies. The latter argument contends that both the Neandertals and early representatives of modern *H. sapiens* coexisted in Europe and the Middle East—therefore, the Neandertals were probably not ancestral to modern *H. sapiens.* Proponents of this viewpoint argue that the origin of *H. s. sapiens* occurred in Africa sometime between 120,000 and 90,000 years ago. (This theory is discussed in the next chapter.) These populations gradually spread from Africa to other parts of the world.

In contrast to the argument that modern *H. s. sapiens* evolved only in Africa and spread from there to other parts of the world is the argument that *H. s. sapiens* evolved from a Neandertal stock in many parts of the Old World. This view of the evolution of modern *H. s. sapiens* includes a direct ancestral–descendant relationship between the Neandertals and ourselves. Nevertheless, as Wolpoff (1980) noted, "the argument that this early Upper Pleistocene sample represents a more or less worldwide evolutionary grade, broadly ancestral to more modern populations, is not meant to prejudge the question of whether a specific ancestral–descendent relation can be demonstrated in each area of the world. This must be decided on local evidence" (p. 253).

One of the problems inherent with arguments concerning the evolutionary placement and taxonomy of the Neandertals is the fact that the term *Neandertal* was originally applied to and meant to describe specific fossil materials from western Europe. The term is now used to describe a wide array of fossils, many of which barely resemble the original material. There is considerable morphological variability in fossils now referred to as Neandertals.

The morphological variability in European forms designated as Neandertals has been explained in many ways. It has been suggested, for example, that some of the more gracile specimens from eastern and central Europe and the Middle East, which are sometimes referred to as "Progressive Neandertals," are intermediate between the earliest *H. sapiens* and the earliest *H. s. sapiens* populations, if not already *H. s. sapiens.* On the other hand, their more robust looking contemporaries, those fossils from western Europe that are sometimes referred to as "Classic Neandertals," are considered outside our direct evolutionary lineage. The European Neandertals were replaced by modern *H. sapiens* populations about 35,000 years ago. How did this replacement occur? Did it involve indigenous European gene pools, or was gene flow from outside Europe necessary?

Some European remains postdating the Neandertals continue to show such morphological traits as large brow ridges and large teeth, which are typical of the Neandertals. The continuance of such traits may be due to genetic admixture with the Neandertals, or the traits may be retentions from more primitive ancestors elsewhere. A skull fragment from Hanofersand, Germany, dated to 36,000 years ago, has been interpreted as a Neandertal–modern *Homo sapiens* hybrid. However, it may also be a very robust early *H. s. sapiens* and not a hybrid.

Although European Neandertals, especially those in western Europe, retained a number of archaic traits, there are African and Middle Eastern fossils that seem to be members of our subspecies, *H. s. sapiens.* If dates for fossil sites in the Kebara and Qafzeh caves in Israel are correct, they clearly indicate that

H. s. sapiens populations moved out of sub-Saharan Africa and into the Middle East and then much more recently entered Europe (Stringer & Andrews, 1988).

Europe may have been a backwater in the evolution of modern *H. sapiens.* Stringer and Andrews (1988) suggested that the Neandertals genetically contributed little or nothing to modern populations. Because modern *H. sapiens* in Africa predate the Neandertals, the notion that the Neandertals evolved into modern humans is thrown into question. Stringer and Andrews argued that there is no evidence in any part of the world for a morphological transition from the Neandertals to modern *H. sapiens.* If they are correct, then the Neandertals should be classified as a separate species from ourselves, *H. neanderthalensis,* rather than as a separate subspecies *H. s. neanderthalensis.* The position that excludes the Neandertals from our direct evolutionary lineage harks back to earlier arguments by adherents of the Presapiens school (for example, Keith, 1925; Vallois, 1949a, 1952, 1954), who also excluded the Neandertals from our direct evolutionary lineage.

Some fossil material supports a species designation *H. neanderthalensis* for the Neandertals. The Kebara Neandertals may have lived about 40,000 years after making contact with *H. s. sapiens* in the Middle East, for example, at the sites of Qafzeh and Skhūl. Although the Kebara Neandertals overlapped with *H. s. sapiens,* they show no sign of hybridization. In fact, Kebara is one of the most robust Neandertal skeletons. Furthermore, early modern fossils from Israel and Lebanon dated 40,000 to 30,000 years ago show no features suggesting hybridization with Neandertals.

The late Neandertal material from St. Césaire, France suggests coexistence, perhaps without hybridization, between western European Neandertals and modern humans. Neandertal skeletal material from St. Césaire is dated to approximately 36,000 plus or minus 3,000 years (Mercier et al., 1991). The thermoluminescence date is on burnt flint associated with the human remains. This is one of the last known Neandertals and supports the idea that the last Neandertals coexisted with the earliest *H. s. sapiens* for several thousand years in western Europe. This inferred coexistence raises many questions (Stringer & Grün, 1991). For example, (1) how long was the coexistence, and how rapidly did western European Neandertals disappear, and (2) was there hybridization, and, if so, how can it be detected in the fossil remains? To answer these and other questions, a better chronological framework is needed in Europe for the time period of 30,000 to 50,000 years ago.

The Neandertal remains at St. Césaire are associated with tools previously thought to belong only with succeeding *H. s. sapiens* populations. The same situation pertains with the similarly aged Arcy-sur-Cure materials from France. Neandertals in western Europe did make Upper Paleolithic Aurignacian and Châtelperronian tools previously associated only with later, Upper Paleolithic humans. It is still unsettled whether the Châtelperronian industry represented at St. Césaire represents the last Neandertal innovations in a long Mousterian tradition or whether they were created through contact with the newly arrived modern humans (Mercier et al., 1991).

The St. Césaire skull does not indicate an evolutionary shift in the direction of modern *H. s. sapiens,* casting further doubt on the argument that Neandertals evolved into *H. s. sapiens.* However, those arguing for a Neandertal heritage of modern humans retort that the St. Césaire skull only negates any strong possibility that Neandertals evolved into modern humans in western Europe. This still leaves eastern Europe as a possible area for local evolutionary change from Neandertals to modern humans.

Stringer (1990) suggested that modern humans and Neandertals may be distinct evolutionary lines that diverged from a common ancestor more than 200,000 years ago. As noted in Chapter 10, this ancestor may be *Homo heidelbergensis* from sites in Spain, Germany, and England. The Neandertals would have evolved in Europe and *H. s. sapiens* in Africa.

It is still unclear why, if *H. s. sapiens* evolved in Africa, they took so long to reach Europe and replace the European Neandertals. Perhaps there was a climatic impediment to movement into Europe. Perhaps early *H. s. sapiens* populations did enter Europe, and we still have not found their remains.

Krings et al. (1997) announced extraction of a DNA sample from the Neandertal humerus found in the Neander Valley of Germany in 1856. After 141 years, the bone has shed light on the Neandertal genome.

There are many difficulties obtaining DNA from ancient specimens. DNA begins to degrade from the moment of death. The damaged state of ancient DNA makes the amplification method—the PCR—prone to error. Furthermore, it is hard to distinguish ancient DNA from modern DNA that may have contaminated it. Despite problems of extraction, preservation, and amplification, a small amount of DNA was extracted. Comparing 378 base pairs of the Neandertal's mtDNA to that of modern humans, researchers found an average of 27 differences between modern and Neandertal DNA—much more than the typical variation of 8 found among modern humans. The results lend support to the notion that Neandertals were a side branch of human evolution, not our immediate ancestors.

Taking the analysis one step further, trying to put time estimates on the divergence of Neandertals from modern humans, it is suggested that Neandertal DNA began to diverge some 690,000–550,000 years ago, compared to 150,000–120,000 years ago for the ancestral sequence of all modern humans. The new data also suggest no mixing in mitochondrial genes between Neandertals and modern humans.

This one bit of evidence will not still arguments about the Neandertal's evolutionary history. The lack of a trait or gene sequence in moderns that is found in ancients does not mean that one is not ancestral to the other. The trait might have vanished over time. Furthermore, the sample does not preclude the fact that Neandertals and modern ancestors may have interbred in the distant past. Commingling could have occurred long before modern humans lost many genetic variants, as seen, for example, among Neandertals.

SUMMARY

The role the European Neandertals played in the evolution of modern *H. sapiens* has been debated almost since the first fossils were recovered. Among the options is the contention that the Neandertals are directly ancestral to modern populations. Others contend that the European Neandertals became extinct without contributing to the modern gene pool. A variation of this contention is that Neandertal populations in western Europe may have become extinct, but contemporaneous populations in eastern and central European and elsewhere are part of our direct evolutionary heritage.

Whatever is the case for human evolution in Europe, modern *H. s. sapiens* remains apparently appear in Africa before appearing in Europe. Modern *H. s. sapiens* may have appeared in Africa as early as 120,000 to 90,000 years ago. The best evidence for the appearance of modern humans in Europe dates to only 35,000 years ago. Possibly Europe was populated by modern *H. sapiens* migrating out of Africa.

The exact role that the Neandertals played in our evolutionary history is still unclear. The problem will only be resolved with the recovery of new fossil materials and the analysis and reanalysis of more fossil evidence. It is not clear when these things will happen.

SUGGESTED READINGS

Brace, C. 1968. Ridiculed, rejected, but still our ancestor, Neanderthal. *Natural History* 77:38–42.

Graves, P. 1991. New models and metaphors for the Neanderthal debate. *Current Anthropology* 32:513–542.

Howell, F. 1951. The place of Neanderthal man in human evolution. *American Journal of Physical Anthropology* 9:379.

Howell, F. 1957. Pleistocene glacial ecology and the evolution of "classical" Neanderthal man. *Quarterly Review of Biology* 32:330.

Kahn, P., and A. Gibbons. 1997. DNA from an extinct human. *Science* 277:176–178.

Kolata, G. 1974. The demise of the Neanderthals: Was language a factor? *Science* 186:618–619.

Krings, M., A. Stone, R. Schmitz, H. Krainitzki, M. Stoneking, and S. Pääbo. 1997. Neandertal DNA sequences and the origin of modern humans. *Cell* 90:19–30.

Lewin, R. 1996. *The Origin of Modern Humans.* New York: W. H. Freeman.

Rak, Y. 1986. The Neanderthal: A new look at an old face. *Journal of Human Evolution* 15:151–164.

Rak, Y. 1990. On the differences between two pelvises of Mousterian context from the Qafzeh and Kebara Caves, Israel. *American Journal of Physical Anthropology* 81:323–333.

Smith, F. 1982. Upper Pleistocene hominid evolution in south central Europe: A review of the evidence and analysis of trends. *Current Anthropology* 23:667–686.

Solecki, R. 1989. On the evidence for Neanderthal burial. *Current Anthropology* 30:324.

Stringer, C. 1987. The dates of Eden. *Nature* 331:565–566.

Stringer, C. 1990. The emergence of modern humans. *Scientific American,* December: 98–104.

Stringer, C., and C. Gamble. 1996. *In Search of the Neanderthals: Solving the Puzzle of Human Origins.* New York: Thames and Hudson.

Trinkaus, E. 1983. *The Shanidar Neanderthals.* New York: Academic Press.

Trinkaus, E. 1986. The Neandertals and modern human origins. *Annual Review of Anthropology* 15:193–218.

13

The Appearance of *Homo sapiens sapiens*

Homo sapiens sapiens, *the subspecies to which we belong, colonized the Americas and some of the Pacific Islands, in addition to spreading throughout Africa, Asia, and Europe. The cultural tradition of early* H. s. sapiens *is called the Upper Paleolithic, during which time there is a noticeable acceleration of cultural and technological innovation and an explosion of artistic expression.*

The earliest evidence of H. s. sapiens *remains comes from Africa and dates to about 120,000 years ago. By at least 40,000 or 30,000 years ago populations had colonized Australia. There is considerable debate as to when human populations entered the Americas; the earliest date under serious consideration is about 40,000 years ago. However, many accept the earliest possible date to be only about 15,000 to 10,000 years ago. These populations crossed the Bering land bridge, then joining Siberia to Alaska, and migrated south.*

OVERVIEW: MODELS AND DNA

Homo sapiens sapiens, the subspecies to which we belong, inhabited large parts of the world by 40,000 years ago (Table 13-1). At this time a noticeable acceleration of cultural and technological innovation and the flowering of aesthetic expression occurred. The cultural tradition of early *H. s. sapiens,* the *Upper Paleolithic,* contains a number of different tool traditions. The oldest *H. s. sapiens* samples appear in Africa perhaps by 120,000 years ago, and it is likely that the subspecies first evolved in Africa.

TABLE 13-1   Some *Homo sapiens sapiens* Sites Discussed in Text

Geographic Region	Site	Date (years ago)
Africa	Omo, Ethiopia	130,000
	Eyasi, Tanzania	130,000
	Laetoli, Tanzania	120,000 ± 30,000
	Klasies River Mouth, South Africa	115,000–90,000
	Border Cave, South Africa	115,000–90,000
	Equus Cave, Taung, South Africa	100,000–40,000
	Katanda, Congo	90,000–80,000 (?)
Asia	China; Java	34,000–10,000
Europe	Croatia	33,000
	France; Italy	about 30,000
	Czech Republic	30,000
	Makarovo-4, Varvarina Gora, Siberia	40,000–34,000
New Guinea and Australia	Huron Peninsula	40,000
	Kosipe	35,000–25,000
	Lake Mungo	35,000 (?), 28,000 (?)
	Devil's Lair	35,000
	Jinmium	200,000 (?); archaeology, 75,000
Tasmania	Fraser Cave	20,000–15,000
	Bluff Rockshelter and ORSA	32,000
	Warreen Cave	35,000
New World		
Early Paleo-Indian	Santa Rosa Island, California	30,000+
	Lewisville, Texas	30,000+ (?)
	La Jolla, California	30,000+ (?)
	Orogrande Cave, New Mexico	38,000 (?)
	Brazil, Chile	32,000
Middle Paleo-Indian	Fort Rock Cave, Oregon	28,000–11,500 (many dates disputed)
	Old Crow Basin, Bluefish Caves, Yukon Meadowcroft Rock Shelter, Pennsylvania, Puebla, Tlapacoya, Mexico	25,000+ (?)
Late Paleo-Indian	Quite common in North and South America; associated with Folsom, Clovis, and Plano point traditions	less than 11,500

H. s. sapiens populations inhabited most of the world, having moved into North America by perhaps 40,000 years ago, although this date is hotly disputed; Central America over 30,000 years ago; and Australia perhaps 40,000 years ago. The migration of human groups out of the Old into the New World was facilitated by cultural adaptations allowing them to meet the requirements of new environments. Until about 12,000 years ago, members of our subspecies continued to live as small-band hunters and foragers.

Wolpoff (1980) argued that the evolutionary development of *H. s. sapiens* can be best understood in terms of worldwide changes in selection acting on already differentiated local populations of archaic *H. sapiens*. The earliest *H. s. sapiens* populations did not look especially modern. They were probably as different from living populations as they were from the preceding archaic *H. sapiens* samples. They are designated *H. s. sapiens* because they show a higher incidence of *H. s. sapiens* traits and a lower incidence of archaic *H. sapiens* traits.

Wood (1994) mentions two problems complicating the investigation of modern humans. Because of a lack of consensus about a definition of "modern human," it is hard to find them in the fossil record. For example, if anatomical modernity exhibits different forms because of climatic stress, then climate needs to be considered when making comparisons in fossil populations. If the Neandertal anatomy was studied in terms of the extent to which it resembled modern humans adapted to a similar climatic regime, Wood suggests, then perhaps Western European Neandertals would not look so distinctive.

Wood suggests that the second problem is that the "problem" of the origin of modern humans is rarely qualified. What constitutes a modern human morphology? Is it one trait or a combination of traits? How does one weight the complicating factor of mosaic evolution, for example?

H. s. sapiens fossils are distinguished from previous fossils by a size reduction in the anterior teeth, facial and brow ridge reduction, and increased cranial height. In all early *H. s. sapiens* samples these attributes are less marked than in today's populations. Morphological change among *H. s. sapiens* seems to have occurred at different times in different parts of the world. For example, the brow ridge in the East African sample was already largely reduced, whereas in the contemporaneous European sample, especially in individuals designated as males, the brow ridges were large and well developed (Wolpoff, 1980; Box 13-1).

Smith et al. (1990) succinctly reviewed various models of the origins of modern humans. As previously noted, until the early 1980s modern human origins were explained in the context of the so-called Neandertal, Presapiens, and Preneandertal schools of thought. These models belonged to a distinctly Eurocentric viewpoint that began to lose ground in the 1970s as evidence of modern humans became more prevalent in Africa and Asia. At present, the focus centers upon Africa.

As Smith et al. noted, three different models, built upon earlier models, have come to the fore: the Afro-European Sapiens Model (AES), the Recent African Evolution Model (RAE), and the Multiregional Evolution Model (MRE) (Table 13-2). The first model, proposed by G. Braüer (1984a, 1984b, 1984c) sug-

---

BOX 13-1   Distinguishing *H. s. sapiens* **from the Neandertals**

The following traits can distinguish these two from one another:

1. In *H. s. sapiens* the forehead is more vertical; the brow ridges are absent or reduced and are never continuous.
2. *H. s. sapiens* has a higher skull vault, shows little or no evidence of an occipital bun, and has thinner skull bones.
3. *H. s. sapiens* shows relatively little prognathism. A distinct chin is present.
4. *H. s. sapiens* exhibits reduced bone thickness throughout the body that is probably related to reduced muscle mass.
5. *H. s. sapiens* shows a size reduction in the anterior teeth.

---

gests an early, indigenous African transition to modern *H. sapiens.* This early African *H. s. sapiens* moved into Europe and possibly into Asia (Figure 13-1).

Brauer argued that modern humans evolved from an early archaic African *H. sapiens* stock (such as witnessed at Bodo, Kabwe, and Ndutu—see Chapter 11). These forms shared many traits with *H. erectus,* and from this group emerged a late archaic *H. sapiens* stage, transitional to modern Africans. Brauer argued that anatomically modern humans were present in southern Africa by 100,000 years ago and are represented by fossils from Border Cave and the Klasies River Mouth Site in South Africa and Omo 1 from Ethiopia. These fossils are discussed later in this chapter.

TABLE 13-2   Two Hypotheses for the Evolution of *Homo sapiens* **and Their Underlying Predictions**

Out of Africa (RAE Model)

1. Anatomically modern humans appear first in Africa and significantly earlier there than elsewhere.

2. Fossils transitional between archaic and anatomically early modern *H. sapiens* should only appear in Africa.

3. There should be little or no hybridization between archaic and anatomically early modern *H. sapiens.*

4. There will be little or no anatomical link between preceding and anatomically modern *H. sapiens* in regional areas. They will anatomically distinct.

Multiregional Evolution (MRE Model)

1. Anatomically modern *H. sapiens* will appear broadly contemporaneously throughout the Old World.

2. Anatomically transitional populations will appear regionally throughout the Old World.

3. There will be anatomical continuity between ancient and modern populations regionally throughout the Old World. This continuity leads some multiregional adherents to suggest that without a clear break between *H. erectus* and *H. sapiens,* the lineage should just be referred to as *H. sapiens.*

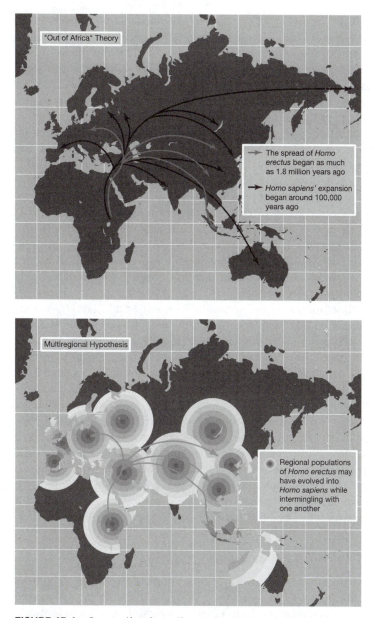

FIGURE 13-1   Competing hypotheses for the evolution of *Homo sapiens* from *Homo erectus*. *Top,* Out of Africa (RAE) model proponents hypothesize that *H. sapiens* evolved in Africa, then migrated throughout the rest of the Old World. *Bottom,* Multiregional (MRE) model proponents state that populations of *H. sapiens* evolved in many areas simultaneously from regional *H. erectus* populations. (*From* LIFE ON EARTH, Audesirk/Audesirk, © 1997. Reprinted by permission of Prentice-Hall, Inc., Upper Saddle River, NJ.)

Braüer suggested that when early *H. s. sapiens* slowly moved out of Africa, an emigration partly due to environmental dessication, they absorbed some archaic human populations into their gene pool. The disappearance of archaic humans in Europe was the result of replacement and hybridization. Braüer's model recognizes some local continuity between archaic and modern humans in Eurasia. However, he argued that the dominant feature in the appearance of modern humans in Eurasia was the influx of a modern gene pool from Africa.

The RAE model also posits an African origin for modern humans and suggests that the transition to modern humans occurred only in Africa. Proponents of the RAE model, like Stringer and Andrews (1988), concurred with Braüer and drew heavily upon his research. Unlike Braüer, Stringer and Andrews argued that once modern humans emerged in Africa and began to radiate into Eurasia, there was no significant admixture between them and the archaic Eurasians. Stringer and Andrews denied admixture and argued that the African migrants were a different species than the archaic Eurasians. Stringer and Andrews' model is characterized as a total replacement model. More recently, Andrews modified his position to allow that some hybridization could have occurred between the Neandertals and modern humans.

The MRE model is associated with Wolpoff et al. (1984), among others. According to this model, there is considerable morphological and genetic continuity across the archaic/modern human boundary in Eurasia and in Africa. Unlike the AES and RAE models, the MRE model does not require hybridization from outside Eurasia, that is, from Africa, for the transition to anatomically modern *H. sapiens*. In the MRE model, the timing and mode of evolution from an archaic to a modern human form would vary from region to region (Thorne & Wolpoff, 1992). The MRE model has roots in the earlier position of Weidenreich (1943) and later in the work of Coon (1962). Proponents of the MRE model trace regional morphological variability in archaic *H. sapiens* to the initial radiation of *H. erectus*. The MRE model posits that genetic exchange across population boundaries would have maintained the total world's human population as one species. According to Wolpoff (1990), the modern human form need not have occurred earliest in Africa; thus there is no need for a migration out of Africa to explain the appearance of modern *H. sapiens*.

Mitochondrial DNA

One of the newest attempts to unravel the origins of *H. s. sapiens* comes from the study of mitochondrial DNA (mtDNA). Unlike nuclear DNA, which one inherits from both parents, mitochondrial DNA is inherited from one's mother. Mitochondrial DNA is found outside the cell nucleus, from a part of the cell called the *mitochondrion,* which produces most of the energy needed to maintain cell life. Because mtDNA is inherited only from the mother, it is useful for tracing genealogy. Mitochondrial DNA can be altered only by mutations, which appear more frequently in mtDNA than in nDNA.

Three biochemists, R. Cann, M. Stoneking, and A. C. Wilson, analyzed the mtDNA of 147 women from five different world geographic regions—Africa, Asia,

Europe, Australia, and New Guinea—and discovered that the differences among the whole set were very small (Cann et al., 1987; Lewin, 1987; Wainscoat, 1987). This indicated that all the women from diverse regions of the world shared a relatively recently inherited form of mtDNA. The different populations separated out; one set was formed by women of African origin only and another set by individuals of all the groups. In terms of mtDNA all humans are more closely related than almost any other mammalian species.

There was more diversity in the mtDNA found in women with an African ancestry, suggesting that it had accumulated more mutations because it was the oldest population with the mtDNA. In other words, this was the oldest branch of the human family. Cann et al. suggested that the mtDNA tree began in Africa and from there spread to the rest of the world. An African origin of all modern mtDNA agrees with some interpretations of the fossil record, which suggest that all modern human populations ultimately trace their roots to Africa, perhaps to such fossil representatives as are found in Tanzania, Ethiopia, and South Africa and dating between 120,000 and 90,000 years ago.

According to the proposal by Cann and others (1987), all human females can trace their mtDNA ancestry to a woman who resided in Africa approximately 200,000 years ago (the range is 290,000 to 140,000 years ago). This mtDNA "Eve," as she has been dubbed, may have "mothered" the entire population of modern women. Her genetic structure, through the reproductive success of her female line, overrode that of females in all other populations. As her female relatives fanned out from Africa sometime about 100,000 years ago, they replaced local populations and eventually genetically settled the whole world. There are many ramifications of this proposal; one of the most important is that all of the world's populations are closely related to one another—no matter the phenotypic (outward) appearance.

One potential problem with Cann's study concerns the African sample, eighteen of twenty-five females were African-Americans. Perhaps diversity in "African" mtDNA was created by admixture with other population groups and not by mutation. Cann et al. (1987) argued that mtDNA changes are selectively neutral and accumulate at a constant rate. Based on estimates of when humans reached Australia, New Guinea, and the New World, they calculated that the mtDNA of human populations diverges at a rate of 2–4 percent per million years. Using these figures, Cann et al. estimated that the common ancestor of all surviving mtDNA types existed between 290,000 and 140,000 years ago and that the ancestral stock of Eurasians diverged from an African type between 180,000 and 90,000 years ago. On the other hand, a mutation rate slower than 2–4 percent would date the last common African ancestor to 850,000 years ago.

Some paleoanthropologists question the time scale for the origin of modern *H. s. sapiens* as postulated by the mtDNA data (Eckhardt, 1991). Fossil evidence suggests a more recent origin of 130,000 or 120,000 to 90,000 years ago rather than the 200,000-year-old figure of the mtDNA data. Others question the possibility that one female and her female relatives could genetically swamp the genotypes of the world's females. Still others question the rapidity of the genetic swamping that the data of Cann and her colleagues suggested. And others suggest that the similarity in mtDNA might be due, not to a common ancestor, but to the effects of random genetic drift.

The mtDNA data generally provide older dates than the archaeological or fossil records for the human entry into the New World, the populating of Upper Pleistocene Europe, and most especially the *H. s. sapiens* migration out of Africa. These older dates are based on a mtDNA clock predicated on the fact that mtDNA mutates at a regular and slow rate. However, several new studies suggest that mtDNA mutates more often, as much as twenty times faster than previously thought—at least for short-term rates. However, other studies did not find this higher mutation rate (see Gibbons, 1998, for a review).

Many evolutionists assume that the mtDNA clock is constant, producing mutations every 6,000 to 12,000 years or so. However, if the clock ticks more rapidly, if mutations occur more frequently than has been assumed, dates of when *H. s. sapiens* left Africa and when *H. s. sapiens* first entered Europe or the New World may be much more recent than the touted older dates. (If the mtDNA clock ticks more rapidly, the more recent dates are often more in line with the archaeological evidence.)

Perhaps there is a short-term rapid rate and a much slower long-term rate of mtDNA evolution (Gibbons, 1998). Short-term rates may not affect long-term rates, and the younger dates for migrations out of Africa and of migration into Europe and the New World would not be affected. If mtDNA mutates slowly (if fewer mutations occur) the "mitochondrial Eve"—the mother of us all—could have inhabited Africa 100,000 to 200,000 years ago. If, however, mtDNA mutates rapidly (if more mutations occur) she may have lived as recently as 6,000 years ago. Mitochondrial DNA studies based on slow mutation rates estimate that the New World was populated 34,000 years ago; however, some of the oldest non-controversial archaeological evidence dates sites to no more than 12,000 years ago—more in line with rapidly (frequently) mutating mtDNA.

Vigilant et al. (1991) provided what seemed to be further support for the "African Eve" hypothesis. They sequenced mtDNA for 189 people of diverse geographic origin, including 121 native Africans. Their study supported the notion that mtDNAs found in modern populations stem from a single ancestral mtDNA that was present in an African population about 200,000 years ago, give or take 50,000 years. From the African homeland, *H. s. sapiens* migrated to other parts of the world. This study failed to find human mtDNAs that diverged from one another more than about 280,000 years ago, leading the authors to infer that migrating human populations from Africa probably replaced resident Eurasian populations that descended from earlier migrations of *H. erectus* out of Africa.

However, Vigilant et al.'s study has been questioned by one of its coauthors (Barinaga, 1992; Hedges et al., 1992; Templeton, 1992). This latest revision does not totally reject an "African Eve"; rather it casts doubt upon the hypothesis. Using complicated computer analyses, Hedges et al. (1992) and Templeton (1992) have shown that various evolutionary trees are possible, some showing non-African roots. Their studies suggested that Cann et al.'s and Vigilant et al.'s analyses of the mtDNA sequence are flawed.

Ayala (1995) disputes the African Eve idea, noting that the preponderance of evidence argues against a population bottleneck before the emergence of modern humans. He notes that the so-called Eve "is not the mother from whom all humans descend, but rather a mtDNA molecule (or the woman carrier of that molecule), from which all modern mtDNA molecules descend. The inference that all humans descend from only one or very few women is based on a confusion between gene genealogies and individual genealogies." Despite his position on the so-called Eve, Ayala views Africa as the home of modern humans.

Y Chromosome

Other genetic information from the Y chromosome may challenge the Out of Africa model. The Y chromosome is the male equivalent of the female mtDNA in that it is passed from father to son, and mutations on large sections of the chromosome are neutral with respect to natural selection. As the Y chromosome genes do not undergo recombination, variants of the genes may be used to trace a male lineage back to a theoretical "Adam." If the Out of Africa scenario were true, then the Y chromosome data should mimic that of mtDNA. However, gene genealogies of males and females may be distinct if they do not associate with events of population or species origins.

A useful section of the Y chromosome is known as the YAP (Y Alu polymorphic) element. Hammer (1995) initially found evidence in tacit support of the Out of Africa hypothesis, concluding that the common origin of the human YAP element occurred 188,000 years ago (with a 95 percent confidence interval from 51,000 to 411,000 years ago). No geographic location was determined for the origin of YAP.

Hammer et al. (1997) studied geographic variations of five YAP haplotypes and found that the story of human origins, with respect to this section of the Y chromosome, may have been quite complicated. Haplotype 1, which is the oldest haplotype and is distributed throughout populations globally, was postulated to have originated in Africa. Haplotype 5 also appears to have originated in Africa, but was distributed much more recently. YAP Haplotype 3, however, has greater diversity in Asia, suggesting that it originated there and then spread back to Africa. Altheide and Hammer (1997) studied another section of the Y chromosome, SRY, which also is suggestive of Asian origins. Different models may explain the data, but one possibility included an Asian origin for the YAP element itself. What emerges is a picture of multiple migrations out of and back to Africa, contradicting the single Out of Africa hypothesis.

Further genetic evidence of an Asian lineage comes from the beta-globin gene on chromosome 11, which is inherited from both parents. The oldest version of the gene, haplotype B2, gave rise to a set called C haplotypes. These are common in Asian populations and very rare among Africans, suggesting that the

C haplotypes arose in Asia. Other C haplotypes might suggest that some Asian markers are older than African versions.

Nuclear DNA

Tishkoff et al. (1996) conducted one of the largest studies to date of nuclear DNA, which, unlike mtDNA, is passed by both sexes. This study looked at genetic patterns in a single chromosome (chromosome 12) from 1,600 people in 42 worldwide populations. They found extensive variety in the DNA of sub-Saharan groups, but few differences in populations living elsewhere. The pattern of variation looks like a series of smaller populations repeatedly diverging from larger groups, and losing variety during the budding process. Of the 24 possible variations in the DNA sequence on this chromosome, 21 occurred in sub-Saharan Africa. Three variants were found in Middle Eastern and European populations, and only two occurred in Asian and American populations.

The amount of variation is a measure of how long the DNA sequence has existed in a population and is a rough measure of time. According to Tishkoff et al., the variation found in chromosome 12 suggests that all non-Africans derive from a single common ancestral population migrating out of northeastern Africa about 100,000 to 70,000 years ago. This ancestral population might have been as small as 1,000 individuals.

Data from the MHC (i.e., the major histocompatibility complex) molecules imply that at some stage in its evolutionary history the hominid line split into at least two populations (Klein et al., 1993). One of these lines led to *Homo sapiens*. Klein et al. suggest that the population that led to *H. sapiens* consisted of at least 500 but more likely at least 10,000 breeders. These carried most of the MHC alleles present in modern populations. While this larger population may have divided into smaller units, these units remained in genetic communication.

Fossils versus DNA

As so often happens with these arguments, there are many doubters, and the information is still in the formative stage. Much more information needs to be gathered. However, the genetic information supports some fossil data suggesting an important role for Asian human fossils in the final determination of the species of *H. s. sapiens* (e.g., Wu & Poirier, 1995).

Thorne and Wolpoff (1992) examined the fossil record of Asia and Europe for evidence of African skeletal features. They also looked for evidence of an anatomical discontinuity between the human fossils before and after the assumed replacement of local populations by the more advanced African *H. s. sapiens*. They noted that the hominid fossils from Australasia (Indonesia, New Guinea, and Australia) show an anatomical continuity uninterrupted by African migrants. Their study of Chinese fossils found no evidence that African features displaced those of ancient fossils from China. The same is true of the work of Wu and Poirier (1995).

Looking at the Neandertals, Thorne and Wolpoff saw no evidence of replacement by a more advanced *H. s. sapiens* stock. (They rejected placing the Neandertals in a separate species; see the previous chapter.) Thorne and Wolpoff argued for a genetic continuity of the Neandertals into modern populations.

Thorne and Wolpoff (1992:79) noted, "Contrary to the Eve theory predictions, the evidence points indisputably toward the continuity of various skeletal features between the earliest human populations and living peoples in different regions." They argued for a multiregional evolution of *H. s. sapiens* rather than a singular origin in Africa. They also rejected suggestions that the earliest *H. s. sapiens* fossils are found in Africa. They questioned the taxonomic assessment of materials from Klasies River Mouth and argued that fossil samples from Omo and Border Cave are too fragmentary to make concrete conclusions and have questionable datings.

Some recent fossil finds in China are used to challenge the Out of Africa hypothesis (Li & Etler, 1992). Two Chinese skulls dated to approximately 350,000 years ago come from Yunxian. The crania have aspects of both *Homo erectus* and *Homo sapiens,* not unlike other materials discussed in Chapter 11. The most notable *H. erectus* features are the sharp and angular features of the back of the skull (Li & Etler, 1992, place the material with *H. erectus*). *H. sapiens* features include a broad, flat face and high cheekbones. The faces and the teeth have some distinctly modern Chinese traits (Wu & Poirier, 1995).

The appearance of *H. sapiens* features suggests an indigenous evolution of *H. sapiens* in Asia. Furthermore, the appearance of modern Chinese traits found in skulls dating to 350,000 years ago is used to argue that these fossils represent a population that has continuously inhabited the area until the present day.

These Chinese fossils are used to support the argument that there was no replacement of ancient Asian populations by a modern people from elsewhere in the world. The so-called archaic *H. sapiens* found in Africa show different (some argue less modern) features in some aspects. On the other hand, the rear of the African skulls are more rounded, more modern, than that seen in Asia. As has often been the case in interpreting the hominid fossil record, how traits are weighted is the key to settling many arguments. Until this issue is settled, the Asian skulls suggest two scenarios: that modern humans may either have evolved in different world regions independently or that modern humans could be the result of interbreeding during large-scale movements of people around the world.

THE HUMAN FOSSIL SAMPLE

Africa

Evidence for early *H. s. sapiens* in southern Africa dating to about 100,000 years ago is primarily based on fossil remains from Klasies River Mouth Site (KRMS) and Border Cave. Smith et al. (1990) conclude that it is impossible to unequivocally date either site. The fewest dating problems are associated with KRMS, a complex of overhangs and caverns originally discovered in the late 1960s. Grün et al. (1990) suggested a minimum date of the human remains to be 90,000 years ago based on ESR dating. Others suggested that the upper jaw fragments date between 100,000 (or 120,000) and 80,000 years ago. A break in human occupation was followed by a period of regular human habitation, at a time when the sea was close enough to the cave for the inhabitants to carry numerous seashells into the cave. Heavy reliance on shellfish is unusual for a site dating to this early of a time period. This seashell layer dates after 80,000 years ago. The last early occupation of the site is associated with hearths and dates to a time between 80,000 and 60,000 years ago (Deacon & Geleijinse, 1988).

More serious dating problems are associated with Border Cave because the adult skull did not come from controlled excavations but was found in a dump outside the cave. Sediments wedged into cracks in the skull most closely match sediments that yield a date of 115,000 years ago.

The human materials from KRMS include 5 partial mandibles, a maxilla, about 12 small skull fragments, isolated teeth, and 4 postcranial bones. A skull found in 1934 by R. Dart is morphologically similar to the South African Cape Flats skulls discussed later. The former has a cranial capacity of 1,430 cubic centimeters, about 200 cc more than Cape Flats. Although some tout the modernity of the KRMS hominid specimens, Wolpoff and Caspari (1990) cast doubt about this position as well as claims for modernity of any contemporaneous specimens. Rightmire (1979) claimed a link between the Border Cave skull and modern black African populations.

Churchill et al. (1996) state that if the isolated ulna from KRMS is indicative of the general postcranial morphology of these hominids, then early hominids from KRMS may not be as modern as claimed based on the craniofacial material. However, the skeletal material from KRMS may reflect mosaic evolution—retention of archaic postcranial features, perhaps indicative of the retention of archaic habitual behavior, in hominids that were becoming craniofacially modern.

The Cape Flats skull comes from an open-air site near Cape Town, South Africa, and was discovered in 1929. The skull is long and narrow, with a cranial capacity of 1,230 cc. Coon (1962) suggested that the skull runs in the line from Kabwe (Broken Hill) and may be ancestral to some modern black African populations; however, his evidence is not convincing. The Boskop braincase, found in 1913, is estimated to have had a cranial capacity of between 1,800 and 1,900 cc. Along with the South African Fish Hoek remains, these forms are often considered to be ancestral to the modern South African San people.

Footprints dated to 117,000 years ago and preserved in a ledge of sandstone at the edge of Langebaan Lagoon, about 60 miles north of Cape Town, South Africa, are the oldest found of modern *Homo*. The prints were made by a person 5 feet 3 inches tall walking downhill through wet sand toward water. Once made, the prints were rapidly covered over and preserved.

Equus Cave, South Africa, is a tufa cave in the same limestone quarry that yielded the Taung child (*Australopithecus africanus,* Chapter 8). Excavations there have produced one of the world's largest samples of Pleistocene fauna, probably collected by brown hyenas, as well as Middle Stone Age artifacts. Equus Cave dates to between approximately 100,000 and 30,000 years ago (Klein et al., 1991). Among the Pleistocene fossils are eight isolated human teeth and a human mandibular body with two molars. The teeth are within the range of size and morphology of modern *H. sapiens,* excepting one canine and one lower molar that are slightly elongated (Grine & Klein, 1985).

Evidence for an early appearance of *H. s. sapiens* in sub-Saharan Africa also comes from the Omo River valley, Ethiopia. In 1967, R. Leakey recovered parts of three skeletons, including two broken skulls and some postcranial bones, plus skull fragments of a third individual. The two incomplete crania have been described by Day (1969, 1971). Omo 1 and 2 show some variation in skull morphology; however, Rightmire (1975) suggested they should be classified together. Omo 1, which lacks a face, is quite heavily built and has a long and low skull. There is a well-developed ridge of bone across the back of the skull. Omo 2 is more modern looking; it lacks frontal bone flattening and has a more rounded back of the skull.

Associated faunal remains may be of Middle Pleistocene derivation, and an age of 130,000 years ago has been obtained for the geological formation containing the Omo 1 and 2 skulls. However, the dating method used, thorium–uranium, is in some doubt.

Day and others (1980) reported the discovery of a skull from Laetoli, Tanzania, designated Laetoli hominid 18 (L.H. 18); its age is estimated at 120,000 plus or minus 30,000 years. The almost complete skull includes bones of the skull vault, much of the base, both temporals, part of the face, and part of the upper dentition. The age at death is estimated at between 20 and 30 years; wear on the third molar indicates that the upper end of the age range is most likely.

The skull, an early East African example of sub-Saharan *H. sapiens,* shows a number of points of resemblance to Omo 1 and 2, Broken Hill (Kabwe), Saldanha, and Bodo. Its anatomical features are a mix of modern and archaic traits. The Laetoli material may be near the root of the evolution of *H. sapiens* in East Africa. At Eyasi, located about 30 kilometers from Laetoli, three *H. s. sapiens* molars and some tools have been dated to about 130,000 years ago.

What may be 80,000-to-90,000-year-old (e.g., Middle Stone Age) bone tools from the site of Katanda in the Congo suggest that *H. s. sapiens* were making advanced tools in Africa (Brooks et al., 1995; Gibbons, 1995; Yellen et al., 1995). However, the dates from Katanda are ESR dates from hippopotamus teeth in the tool layer. These teeth could have been washed in from older deposits. There are also questions about a TL date from the site. However, both faunal and stratigraphic data are consistent with the ESR and TL dates. Coupled with abundant fish remains, the bone tool assemblage indicates a complex subsistence specialization. These tools appear 66,000 years before similar tools in Europe, indicating that African *H. s. sapiens* invented sophisticated tools long before their European counterparts. It is not clear whether Europeans developed a similar technology independent of earlier African discoveries or relied on African innovation.

Although there is evidence that anatomically modern humans evolved in Africa at least 100,000 years ago, it has been argued that modern behavior may have arisen only about 40,000 years ago and in Europe. The Katanda evidence challenges this notion.

It is argued that aspects of the site suggest the ability to plan for the future (Brooks et al., 1995; Gibbons, 1995; Yellen et al., 1995). For example, the inhabitants appeared to be camping at Katanda during the catfish spawning season. There is also evidence of use of ocher and of grinding stones made from non-local materials. Katanda is at present the only site in Africa dating to this time period with MSA tools. Until there are signs of such sophisticated activity from other African sites dating to the same time period, there will be doubts about Katanda's contribution.

Europe

The rather large Upper Pleistocene European human fossil sample contains many rather complete skeletons, at least partly because of burial. Early researchers (for example, Coon, 1962) were enamored of creating various racial groups from European Upper Paleolithic samples; however, there is no evidence to support this practice. The stature of these specimens varied; males attained a height comparable with modern males, but females seem to have been somewhat shorter. Limb proportions are as variable as those in modern populations. Generally, the bones indicate a robust build, but not as robust as among the Neandertals. Upper Paleolithic European samples had large heads, modern cranial capacities, wide faces, prominent chins, and high-bridged noses.

Southern France seems to have been a favorite living spot during the Upper Paleolithic, although remains found there also reflect considerable work in the area. The first European Upper Paleolithic remains appeared in the nineteenth century and were discarded as modern burials. Close to ninety individuals are known from European Upper Paleolithic sites. One of the first examples of fossil hominids was found in 1868 in the Cro-Magnon shelter located in limestone cliffs at the French village of Les Eyzies. Six skeletons were buried deep in the rock at the shelter: three males, two females, and one infant. One of the older male specimens is the type specimen (Figure 13-2). The sample had distinctly broad faces, high foreheads, protruding chins, and a cranial capacity estimated at 1,590 cc. Their height has been variously estimated at between 5 feet 4 inches and 6 feet.

Fossil remains were recovered from Combe Capelle in the same district as the Cro-Magnon shelter. The Combe Capelle material had a long face; a long, high, and narrow forehead; and a strong jaw. Perhaps the teeth were used as tools and the jaw as a vise. These people seem to have been of medium to small body size. Another French skeleton, Chancelade, belongs to the later Upper Paleolithic stage known as the Magdalenian (named after the La Magdeleine shelter, which is about 3 miles from Les Eyzies). Chancelade lived when cool weather prevailed in Europe. Chancelade was about 4 feet 11 inches tall and had wide zygomatic arches and a heavy jaw, possibly indicating heavy chewing stress. The long and

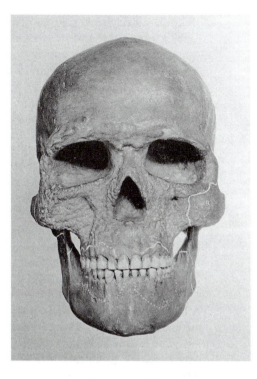

FIGURE 13-2 Restored skull of "Old Man" from Cro-Magnon shelter, France. (Image # 109229, courtesy Department of Library Services, American Museum of Natural History.)

narrow skull had a high keel in the middle; the nose was narrow. A pair of interesting skeletons, possibly a mother and her teenage son, were uncovered from the Grotte des Enfants, one of the Grimaldi caves on the Riviera located at the Italian-French border.

There are many central and eastern European representatives from the Upper Paleolithic (Jelinek, 1969). Předmostí, Brno, and Lautsch are three major finds in the Czech Republic. The Předmostí site is a common grave containing twenty individuals that may date to over 30,000 years ago. Only the male skull (number 3) and the female skull (number 4) are generally known; these show a mixture of archaic and progressive traits. There is evidence of brow ridges; however, the ridges are separate and not continuous. Other archaic traits include the low shape of the skull, marked muscular tuberosities, and a rather small chin. The Předmostí material was associated with more than 1,000 mammoth bones; the inhabitants were apparently effective big-game hunters.

The Brno skull of an adult male exhibits archaic and progressive features. In comparison with the Cro-Magnon material, it has a more accentuated brow ridge, a less rounded occipital region, some alveolar prognathism, and a low-placed maximum breadth of the skull. On the other hand, the forehead is high and bulging, the mastoid processes are large, and the chin is prominent. Other material from Moravia includes the Dolni Věstonice skull caps, to which have been added the grave of an adult female and the remnants of another grave

(Jelinek, 1961; Vlček, 1961b). The burial sites of three finds—a child's found in 1928, a woman's found in 1949, and a man's found in 1957—are similar to those found at Brno and Předmostí.

An adult male (between 45 and 50 years old) burial found in 1987 had the skeleton in a shallow grave, and the corpse facing a hearth. The body was buried in a flexed position on the right side. Several healed traumas marked the skull, and the dentition was heavily worn. Four perforated carnivore canines, two found in the pelvis area and two at the elbow, accompanied the skeleton. The head and pelvic areas were plastered with ocher (Svoboda, 1987).

Three young individuals, about 20 years old, were found at the same site (Klima, 1987). The three lay in a single pit; two were placed on their backs, and the third was on its stomach. The three seem to have been buried simultaneously. Two individuals might have been males and one a female. The woman's skeleton exhibited deformities, such as uneven length of the lower limbs, a deformed right femur, and scoliosis of the spine, which must have been incapacitating and painful. One male skeleton had a thick pole stuck into his hip.

Both of the male skulls were circled with pendants of pierced arctic fox and wolf teeth, as well as small droplike pendants of mammoth ivory. The bodies seem to have been covered by branches that were set afire. The fire was soon extinguished by soil thrown to cover the bodies.

The Dolni Věstonice site covers the span from 28,000 to 26,000 years ago. This material is morphologically intermediate, like that found in Brno and Předmostí. Similar morphological variability is seen in the Mladeč material from Central Moravia. Finds similar to those from the Czech Republic were unearthed in Russia and Rumania.

The Velika Pećina specimen from northwestern Croatia represents the earliest absolutely dated human fossil associated with the European Upper Paleolithic tool industry (F. Smith, 1976). The human discovery came from a cave that contained 138 different faunal species and subspecies. The most common species was the cave bear, which accounted for over 90 percent of the total faunal remains. The lower levels of the cave were characterized by a particular type of Mousterian industry called the *denticulate Mousterian*. This was its only occurrence in southeastern Europe.

The right half of a human frontal bone from Velika Pećina dates to 33,000 years ago and seems aligned with early Upper Paleolithic inhabitants of eastern Europe. This specimen is morphologically similar to later *H. s. sapiens* remains. Smith concluded that "it is very logical to view the transition from Neanderthals to Upper Paleolithic people in Eastern Europe as a continuum without significant migration of people from other areas" (1976:131).

Two Siberian sites for *H. s. sapiens* yielded the unexpectedly old dates of at least 40,000 years ago—nearly 10,000 years older than previously thought. The sites were dated using the accelerator radio carbon technique. Because bones from the Siberian sites were buried in permafrost conditions, they were very well preserved and assumed to be quite free of contamination. These dates rival those for modern humans in Europe and raise intriguing questions (Morell, 1995).

Makarovo-4, situated on a high bluff, yielded thousands of artifacts, two possible hearths, and a dense accumulation of animal bones. The artifacts resemble those in the Middle East dating about 45,000 years ago. Varvarina Gora, dated about 34,000 years ago, yielded similar materials, as well as bone and ivory tools.

If the dates are correct, the Siberians had a tool kit whose sophistication does not appear in Europe until after 40,000 years ago. There is a tentative connection between the Siberian artifacts and those from the western United States Clovis Industry (page 323). However, the region of Siberia where these new sites are located is about 4,000 kilometers from the Bering Straits, the land connection between Siberia and North America.

Asia

Upper Paleolithic human remains are quite prevalent in China except from the vast western regions of Xizang (Tibet), Qinghai, and Xinjiang. *H. s. sapiens* remains in China are mostly fragmentary; teeth, jaws, and cranial materials predominate (Wu & Poirier, 1995). The dating has mostly been done by C^{14} and TL, but some sites were dated on faunal correlations. Most of the thirty-seven *H. s. sapiens* sites in China are located in the north, northeast, or northwest. Many fossil assemblages are associated with artifacts. The dates range widely, but the oldest may be between 100,000 and 67,000 years old. Most sites date to 35,000–25,000 years ago, but some are as recent as 10,000 years ago. One of the most complete and earliest dated of the Chinese materials comes from Liujiang County, in southern China. The material consists of a skull and face (Figure 13-3) and portions of the axial and limb skeletons. The dates range from 67,000 YBP to 101,000–227,000 YBP.

The Upper Cave of Zhoukoudian yielded human fossils dated from 34,000 to 10,000 years ago. These materials disappeared during World War II along with the *H. erectus* materials from Zhoukoudian. The cultural assemblage appears to be of local origin. Skeletal parts of at least seven individuals were recovered; only three skulls are described (Weidenreich, 1938/1939, 1943). Skull fractures indicate that all seven individuals died unnatural deaths, perhaps killed in a mass murder. Skull number 101 is from an individual killed by an arrow or small-headed spear that pierced the skull. Skulls 102 and 103 belong to individuals who seem to have been killed by a stone dropped on the sides of their heads.

Many other Upper Paleolithic materials from China are described in Wu and Poirier (1995). Some argue that the Chinese material is ancestral to modern Chinese populations. Coon (1962) following Weidenreich (1945) suggested that the Upper Paleolithic Chinese material is related to the Chinese *H. erectus* materials, especially those from Zhoukoudian, and represents the end of that evolutionary line. Not everyone agrees.

Southern China from 100,000 to 70,000 years ago was possibly the area of dispersal for the earliest *H. s. sapiens* in Asia. This population had such recognizable Mongoloid traits as shovel-shaped incisor teeth. Beginning perhaps about 70,000 years ago, populations from southern China radiated south, moving through insular southeast Asia, crossing Wallacea, and reaching Australia.

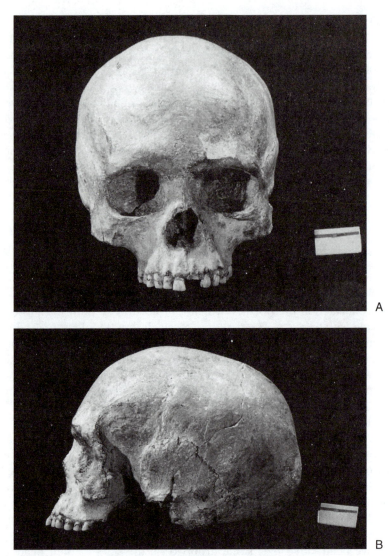

FIGURE 13-3 Anterior view (*A*) and lateral view (*B*) of the face and skull of *Homo sapiens sapiens* from Liujiang, China. (Courtesy Institute of Vertebrate Paleontology and Paleoanthropology [IVPP].)

The earliest well-documented artifacts in Japan date to about 50,000 years ago. A new tool technology appeared in Japan about 30,000 years ago when Japan was severed from the mainland; therefore, it is possible that this technology (if not indigenous) was introduced by a seafaring people. Further evidence of sea travel comes with a 32,000-year-old *H. s. sapiens* skeleton found on the southern island of Okinawa.

In 1890, prior to his discovery of *H. erectus,* E. Dubois was given two fossil skulls from Wadjak, central Java. These were cemented in limestone and unaccompanied by any cultural assemblage. The site has long been destroyed, and the exact dating of these materials is unknown. It was not until the 1920s that Dubois showed the skulls to the scientific world. Wadjak 1 (W-1) is a nearly complete skull, the base of which is mainly intact, and a piece of mandible. Wadjak 2 is comprised of five pieces, which Weidenreich reconstructed. The cranial capacity of W-1 is estimated at 1,475 cc; W-2 may be similar. Coon, following Weidenreich, suggested that Wadjak represents the ancestral line of modern Australian aborigines, a theory still being debated.

Kramer (1991) conducted an intensive analysis of the mandibular remains from Indonesia to determine whether they are representative of the ancestral population of the Australian Aborigines or represent a population completely replaced by an African migration of *H. sapiens* more than 100,000 years ago. Kramer was testing the efficacy of two competing models for the evolution of modern humans, the Out of Africa model and the Multiregional model.

Kramer's analysis suggested that the Indonesian fossil material is representative of the Australian Aboriginal ancestral population. This suggestion of a morphological continuity implies the presence of a genetic linkage in Australasia dating back at least 1 million years. Fossil material from Indonesia may support the Multiregional Model, in this case the regional evolution of Asian *Homo erectus* into modern *Homo sapiens*. Looking at the same fossils, Lahr and Foley (1994) conclude that the morphological evidence does not support a multiregional model.

Australia and the Pacific Region

The geographical position of New Guinea suggests that it may have been an early departure point for the Pleistocene settlement of Australia from the Indonesia–Indochina region. New Guinea's position as a point of origin for the colonization of Australia has been strengthened with the find of artifacts dating to about 40,000 years ago. These Australian finds of stone axes show a similarity to stone axes from the site of Kosipe in New Guinea, which dates to about 26,000 years ago.

The colonization of Australia poses a number of interesting problems, such as when and how humans first reached Australia; to what Asian forms they are related; and what the relationships are among Australia, Tasmania, and New Guinea, on the one hand, and with Indonesia and China, on the other. The first inhabitants of Australia arrived by boat and foot via two major island routes: (1) Java via Timor or (2) Borneo via the Celebes and the Moluccas. The widest distance to be crossed over water was approximately 50 miles, and this was probably navigated with small rafts or boats. Which route was used is still unknown; however, a broad anatomical relationship exists between modern Australian Aborigines and fossil materials from Ngandong and Wadjak, Java; Aitape and Kosipe, New Guinea; and Niah in Borneo.

Once in Australia, populations crossed the Bass Strait and moved into Tasmania. Prior to 10,000 years ago a broad, level causeway may have linked the two land masses. Based on this alone, apart from similarities in implements, it is probable that the original Australian inhabitants migrated to Tasmania. There are claims of stone tools and other artifacts from Australia that may date up to 200,000 years ago, although such claims are highly controversial. The claims are made for a site called Jinmium. Rock art, dotlike engravings, found there may date to 75,000 years ago. The site contains enormous sandstone boulders, some covered with thousands of small, pecked cup marks. A detached fragment having these pits lies in sediments TL dated to between 58,000 and 75,000 years ago. There are doubts about the TL date, and others suggest a date of 10,000 years ago. The thousands of marks were probably produced by a number of people or over a longer period of time (Bahn, 1996a). The Jinmium date and the rock art date both exceed all known dates in Australia.

Already hanging by a tenuous thread, the claim that art began in Upper Paleolithic Europe is shattered by the Australian dates if they prove to be correct. In fact, art attributed to *H. erectus,* comes from an Israeli site dating between 800,000 and 233,000 years ago. It resembles a female figurine with grooves around its neck and along its arms. Bones from the Bilzingsleben site in Germany bear a series of what seem to be decorative parallel incisions (Bahn, 1996a).

The evidence that Australian habitation may date back far beyond previous estimates of 40,000 or so years ago has startled many researchers. Attempts to confirm the archaeological dates (176,000–116,000 years ago) have been made. A TL date and core sediment samples suggest a date about 200,000 years ago. Vegetational changes attributed to human colonization of Australia suggest inhabitation at least 60,000 to 54,000 years ago or even as early as 140,000 years ago. The discovery of a stone tool assemblage dated to about 700,000 years ago on the Indonesian island of Flores shows that the technology existed that could have made seagoing craft.

Old dates for the habitation of Australia affect theories about the origins of modern humans. If the Jinmium inhabitants were *H. sapiens* or even a late *H. erectus* stock, then they are evidence supporting a multiregional theory of human evolution.

Two sites in Tasmania, Bluff rock shelter and ORS 7, date to about 32,000 years ago. These sites support the argument that Tasmania and Australia may have been intermittently connected during the past 50,000 years. Human migrants may have reached Tasmania about 36,000 years ago when a drop in sea level of 55 meters exposed a land bridge from Australia to Tasmania (Cosgrove, 1989).

Fraser cave in southwest Tasmania (Bailey, 1982; Kiernan et al., 1982) provides evidence of a specialized hunting economy focused on the large wallaby. The site was occupied between 20,000 and 15,000 years ago. Stone tools support the contention that the Tasmanian tool industries were derived from Australia.

The hunters at Fraser cave were the most southerly dwelling humans on Earth. By about 20,000 to 18,000 years ago, the inhabitants of Fraser cave were as close to the great Antarctic ice sheet, then 1,000 kilometers further south, as some European Upper Paleolithic hunters were to the northern ice sheets. They probably lived in tundralike conditions similar to those that existed in parts of northern

Europe. The European hunter's dependence on reindeer bears comparison with the emphasis on wallabies by the sub-Antarctic paleo-Tasmanians.

The 35,000-year-old Warreen Cave, the oldest site in Tasmania, contains stone tools and fauna. The site seems to have been abandoned about 12,000 years ago. Of similar age are the archaeological sites at Pamerpar Meethaner rock shelter. Prehistoric Tasmanian artists stenciled images of their hands on caves. Some of the stone used for tools shows that the cave dwellers traveled widely or engaged in trade with distant groups. As the climate became milder and the glacier melted, sea levels rose, and Tasmania became isolated about 10,000 years ago.

Human occupation of Australia is found at 35,750 years ago plus or minus 1,250 years at Lake Mungo (Barbetti & Allen, 1972; Bowler et al., 1972). Habgood (1986), however, gives a date of 28,000 years ago for Lake Mungo. Other dates from the same unit are older, 38,000 to 34,000 years ago, but less certainly associated with human activity. Slightly more recent human occupation, 30,000 to 24,000 years ago, seems better documented. The Lake Mungo remains include human cremations and hearths with burnt bone and stone artifacts. Before burial in a shallow grave, the human remains were burned, resulting in charred bones that are extensively smashed.

There is some doubt about the Lake Mungo date because it was derived from freshwater mussel shell, which often yields overly old results. If the Lake Mungo date is unacceptable, a date of 35,000 years ago for the Devil's Lair site in southwestern Australia would be the oldest date for human occupation in Australia.

There are many other finds from Australia. The Green Gully site, situated 9 miles from Melbourne, dates from 11,000 to 10,000 years ago. The material is fragmentary and is a mixture of male and female bones (Macintosh, 1967), the result of delayed burial after most of the flesh had rotted away. Delayed burial is practiced by modern Australian Aborigines. The Green Gully bones indicate that this practice has a long cultural tradition. The size of the Green Gully bones falls within the range of modern Australian Aborigines.

The Keilor skull, found in 1940, may date to 13,000 years ago. There is a strong similarity between this skull and Wadjak from Java. The heavily fossilized and badly crushed Talgai skull, found in 1884 in South Queensland, is undated. The skull, apparently of a male about fifteen years of age, is smaller than Keilor and has a cranial capacity of 1,300 cc. The skull falls within the middle range of modern Australian Aborigines. The Cohuna skull dating from 14,000 to 9,500 years ago, found in 1925, shows signs of having been twice mutilated; apparently after death it was dislodged to get at the brain (Macintosh, 1952; Mahoney et al., 1936). The Mossgiel skeletal material is comprised of skull parts and about three-quarters of the postcranial skeleton (Macintosh, 1967). The postcranial bones are very robust but within the upper ranges of modern Australian Aborigines. The date is not less than 6,000 years ago. Kow Swamp in southern Australia yielded skeletal remains that supposedly date from 14,000 to 9,500 years ago (Kennedy, 1984; Thorne & Macumber, 1972).

The Australian human fossil sample is heterogeneous, and although some features reflect the range of variation in modern Aborigines, other specimens have combinations of features that cannot be duplicated in today's Australian Aborigines. There are clear resemblances in the Australian fossil sample with the Solo skulls in Java, Indonesia.

New World Populations

Migration Routes.   The date of the entrance of human populations into the New World is very hotly disputed. Theories concerning the initial peopling of the New World are tied to late Pleistocene sea levels and glaciations because it is generally agreed that populations probably passed from the Old to the New World by way of an emergent Bering land platform, went through central Canada, and then moved south. Because the vast continental glaciers grew at the expense of sea waters, sea levels were lowest when glaciation was at its peak. During the glaciation the emergence of the Bering land platform made Alaska part of the Asian continent and tied it to North America, creating a migration route from Siberia to Alaska.

The maximum depth of the Bering Strait today is 180 feet; on a clear day one can see across the strait from the heights of Cape Prince of Wales, Alaska, to Cape Dezhnev, Siberia. A number of small islands form steppingstones between these points.

The Wisconsin Glacier covered much of North America about 40,000 years ago, lowering the sea level by as much as 460 feet. Oceans receded as the glacier grew, and a broad highway was revealed at the Bering Strait. A sea level fall of only 150 feet would have created a 200-mile-wide corridor connecting Alaska and Siberia. The slope of the sea floor is gentle, 3 or 4 inches to a mile, so a further drop of sea level would uncover much larger regions. A drop in sea level to 450 feet would have revealed a corridor 1,300 miles wide for the flow of biological traffic between the joined continents.

Haag (1962) argued that a bridge wider than present-day Alaska joined the Old and New Worlds during much of the Pleistocene. The land surface of this bridge was smooth and unbroken, and large animals may have moved freely across it during the 80,000 years of the Wisconsin glacial stage. The first humans probably crossed the bridge before the end of the Wisconsin Glaciation.

Others (for example, Bryan, 1969; Haynes, 1969) argued, in contrast, that the bridge first appeared 28,000 to 25,000 years ago. After a period it closed and reopened at between 14,000 and 12,000 years ago, and it may have opened and closed several times in conjunction with glacial fluctuations. Resolution of the dating of the opening and closing of the Bering land bridge is of major importance in settling the story of New World colonization.

If emigrants arrived in Alaska before 25,000 years ago, they could have moved south through a relatively narrow, inhospitable ice-free corridor in western Canada. By at least 22,000 to 19,000 years ago, the western ice sheet (Cordilleran) and the eastern ice sheet (Laurentide) drew apart, creating an ice-free north–south route. Southern movement would have been relatively free after 14,000 years ago, when the ice had melted.

The critical period for most human paleoecologists concerned with Beringia was from 30,000 to 14,000 years ago, the Duvanny Yar or Sartan Maximum. Sea levels reached their minimum some 18,000 years ago, creating a continuous land mass about 1,800 miles wide, north to south. The land mass was breached about 14,000 years ago; however, much of the platform was still exposed.

According to Aigner (1984), Beringia from 30,000 to 12,000 years ago was low-lying with a mosaic of vegetational communities, some of which supported such megafauna as mammoths, horses, and bison, and even camels and rhinoceroses (the last in Asia). Elsewhere, the poor quality of cover was a limiting factor on the distribution of the fauna. By 30,000 years ago Beringia was treeless. The steppe-tundra of 40,000 years ago was more productive for animal life than after 30,000 years ago, when increased cold and reduced precipitation provided fewer grazing areas. At 10,000 years ago the habitat was even more impoverished, and the megafauna was at or near extinction. The best time for human movement across Beringia was the earliest period; the glacial maximum period was less productive, and extreme cold may have precluded Arctic occupation. The terminal Pleistocene period was the least attractive in terms of game animals, but the climate had ameliorated; there is a clear record of human occupation of the high arctic at this time.

Recent evidence suggests that Beringea was not a very hospitable place. Plant and animal remains from cores in the Bering Strait suggest that migrants across Beringea, people and migrating ungulates, would have found little to sustain them except for tundra and small shrubs. This evidence runs counter to some speculations that the bridge was a grassy plain that lured grazing herds, including bison and mammoths, to the Americas. Twenty core samples from beneath the Bering and Chukchi seas found plant and insect fossils native to the tundra rather than a grasslands habitat.

At least some of the first humans entering North America may not have followed the inland route that most advocate. Instead, perhaps they hopped along the coast by boat. Evidence from Prince of Wales Island implies that not all the coast was icebound during the late Ice Age. Therefore, migrants might have found game-rich coastal havens. Skeletons of black and grizzly bears, the oldest dating to about 12,300 years ago, suggest that the area was not overburdened by ice and snow (Busch, 1994a). The possibility of the use of boat travel does not restrict migrations to the New World to times of glacial maxima and opens a wider window of opportunity for possible migration.

Perhaps populations in coastal Siberia were seafarers who could have crossed the Bering Straits by boat and sailed on down to South America. Using kayaks and umiaks, perhaps human populations reached from Siberia to the tip of South America. (Humans crossed 60 miles of ocean to reach Australia 40,000 years ago.) If these migrations occurred, it is likely that any coastal settlements were long innundated by the rising sea levels that have submerged coastal regions.

Whatever the true nature of the migration, many agree that it may have occurred as two or three major waves. Chard (1963), for example, suggested that an initial move from eastern Asia, along the Pacific shores about 40,000 years ago, brought an industrial tradition of choppers and bifaces. A second migration, perhaps following the Arctic coastal plain, brought with it a Middle Paleolithic tool tradition of flint working.

Based on her mtDNA studies, Cann suggested three migrations comprising at least eleven major genetic lineages. To accumulate that much genetic diversity requires multiple migrations or a smaller number of large migrations containing many unrelated females. Cann's data indicate a migration possibly beginning about 40,000 years ago (Morell, 1990).

Information on the Y chromosome is helping solve the ancestry of North and South American Native Americans. Phillip Underhill revealed that a mutation on the Y chromosome has been found only among North and South American Native Americans and among Eskimo groups. The change involved a switch from what is called the C allele to the T allele in a specific segment of the Y chromosome. This seems to have been a unique mutation event that may have occurred about 30,000 years ago and was passed along. The mutation, found in blood and hair samples of three far-flung Native American language groups, suggests that the genetic mutation may have occurred before the split and subsequent language differentiation among people in Asia before the migration across Beringea.

Bordes (1958) argued that the diversity of Paleo-Indian cultures suggests that several successive migrations occurred. The movement of immigrants south out of Alaska and Canada was largely controlled by the glacial fluxes. When avenues opened, people moved south. The emptiness of the American continent accelerated this spread, as did the abundance of game. Eight or nine thousand years has been estimated as the time needed for the journey from Alaska south to the tip of South America at Tierra del Fuego. The rather rapid southern expansion must have meant similar rapid loss of contact between various groups, leading to cultural changes and genetic drift.

Various other lines of evidence hint at when the human migration occurred. One approach is an analysis of the Gm allotypes, protein found in the serum portion of the blood (Suarez et al., 1985). Researchers sampled Gm allotypes of thousands of Native Americans from four cultural groups in North America. Their Gm types divided into two distinct groups, with the Aleuts and Eskimos of the far north in a third distinctive group. One group is thought to relate to the earliest Asian migrants to the New World. The geneticists suggested that there was one early migration, followed by two later ones.

Turner (1984, 1986) investigated tooth crowns and roots to try to pinpoint the origins of the earliest settlers to the Americas. He produced what he called "dentochronological" separation estimates of when the ancestors of Native Americans diverged from their Asian ancestor. He dates the appearance of the first Native Americans to about 14,000 to 13,000 years ago.

Turner found that the teeth from New World natives fall into three groups. Teeth of the Inuit and natives of the Aleutian Islands differ from those of North and South American Indians, which in turn differ from the teeth of natives of the northwest coast and the Alaskan interior. This investigation suggests three distinct waves of migration into the New World.

Greenberg (1986) used linguistic evidence to group Native American populations and to date their entrance to the New World. He estimated that the earliest populations arrived in the New World about 11,000 years ago, a date that agrees with Turner's estimates but is challenged by other linguists.

Like their colleagues in other research fields on the peopling of the New World, linguists disagree on dates of entry. The linguist Johanna Nichols provides a rather old date for New World entry using estimates based on the time required for some 142 New World language families to have evolved. Nichols suggests that the diversity of native languages in the Americas is so extensive that it would have taken at least 19,500 years and perhaps as long as 35,000 to 40,000 years for them to develop.

Evidence that humans may have entered the New World by about 40,000 years ago comes from the rock shelter site of Toca do Boqueiraõ da Pedra Furada in northeastern Brazil dating to perhaps 31,000 years ago. The Pedra Furada site is one of the most controversial of the claimed early sites. There are at least three sets of dates. There is evidence of 17,000-year-old red ocher cave paintings depicting birds, deer, armadillos, and stick-figure hunters and scenes of childbirth and sexual activity. Stone artifacts and hearths are said to date to 33,000 years ago. Some skeptics suggest that this date on charcoal came from a forest fire and not a controlled burn, such as hearth. Vance Haynes argued that the stone chips claimed to have been tools are not human products: "Big cobbles on that cliff can work loose and whizz down with enough force to produce chips that look man-made" (quoted in Wolkomir, 1991:143). In 1990 what appears to be an ash-filled hearth ringed with stones dated to 47,000 years ago.

Monte Verde, Chile, lies under a peat bog whose lack of oxygen has inhibited decay. The site was excavated from 1977 to 1985 by T. Dillehay, who discovered an unparalleled collection of plant remains and wooden artifacts (Dillehay, 1989). Wooden digging sticks, mortars, spear tips, and building foundations are said to date to 13,000 years ago. The artifacts have undergone twenty-five radiocarbon datings. Across the creek from this site Dillehay found three stone hearths and twenty-six pebbles that appear to have been deliberately chipped. These are dated to 33,000 years ago.

The remnants of a row of huts recovered from Monte Verde may have housed thirty to fifty people. Dillehay estimates that the site was occupied for about one year. Each hut was a wooden framework covered with animal skins. The hut remains come from the level dated to 12,500 years ago. There is also a footprint, possibly left by a youngster.

The inhabitants of Monte Verde left behind at least forty-two species of plant foods, including the wild potato. They may have cooked communally in two hearths. Possible food remains include mastodon, an extinct relative of the modern llama, rodents, fish, amphibians, and crayfish.

Dillehay found twenty specimens of medicinal plants; some appear to have been burned or chewed. At least half the medicinal plants were imported from outside the region and come from the highlands or the coastal region. Stone tools fashioned from ocean-beach pebbles come from a distance of at least 60 miles away. Either the settlers walked this distance, or they traded with distant populations.

Given the minimal date of 12,500 years ago for Monte Verde it is obvious that people were in the New World long before that. It must have taken thousands of years for them to migrate from the north to Chile. They probably arrived before the ice sheets blocked off Canada about 20,000 years ago. If Dillehay is correct that there are also remains at Monte Verde dated at 33,000 years ago, then they arrived even earlier.

Old Crow Basin and Bluefish Caves, in the Yukon, yielded mammoth bones that may have been worked by early human migrants. Both sites are located in the area known as Beringia. Possible artifacts from Old Crow Basin have been dated from 25,000 years B.P. to more than 40,000 years B.P. Bluefish Caves yielded stone tools and animal bones. A mammoth bone and a bone flake both date to about 24,000 years B.P. Bluefish Caves may have been a campsite.

The easiest way to view the New World situation is to divide it into three periods: the Early, Middle, and Late Paleo-Indian periods (Haynes, 1969). Many early sites are contested, and many researchers will not accept evidence of New World habitation prior to about 13,000 years ago (see, for example, Diamond, 1987). Most Early and Middle Paleo-Indian sites are plagued by context problems, questions about the authenticity of the artifacts, multiple dating problems (including poorly excavated samples and controversial dating techniques), and a lack of agreement about what constitutes reasonable evidence for an ancient New World human presence. Until these matters are satisfactorily settled, evidence for early New World sites such as those previously discussed and those noted in the following paragraphs will not gain wide acceptance.

Over the last decade, human remains from at least thirteen localities in the New World—most in southern California—have been assigned ages greatly exceeding a date of 11,000 years ago. Although data from several New World sites discussed here suggest human appearance at an earlier time, the number of such sites has been greatly reduced by the redating of Taylor and others (1985, see especially p. 137) and Taylor (1996). It is assured, however, that this redating will itself generate considerable controversy.

Not only are entry dates hotly contested, but the origins of the migrants is also controversial. Controversial skeletal remains found in several Western states and as far east as Minnesota may suggest that non-Asian populations migrated early on to the New World. Skeletons that some argue are phenotypically European, found in North America and dating to 9,000 years ago, are causing considerable debate. The most recently discovered of these is skeletal material from Kennewick, Washington (Lahr, 1997).

Both Asian and non-Asian genotypes may have migrated to the New World, perhaps doing so in separate waves. This possibility may help explain the phenotypic variation in Native American groups. Some are suggesting that some skeletal material may be linked with both Polynesians and with the long-puzzling Ainu of Japan.

Early Paleo-Indian Period.   The Early Paleo-Indian period began prior to 30,000 years ago. (Possible Early Paleo-Indian sites were discussed in the preceding subsection.) Most possible Early Paleo-Indian sites do not meet the minimal criteria for inclusion in the category of early sites. Although the geological age may be relatively well understood, either the association or nature of the possible artifacts is questionable.

An interesting possibility for an early New World site is Orogrande Cave, located in New Mexico's Chihuahua desert. The site, excavated by R. MacNeish (Appenzeller, 1992; Turnmire, 1990), awaits full scientific documentation and has the potential to help rewrite our thoughts about an early entrance into the New World. The oldest suggested date for the site is 38,000 years old. The site is a relatively small limestone cavern with a rich stratigraphic record of alternating layers of burned ash. MacNeish suggested that the burning resulted from cooking fires that got out of control.

Among the faunal evidence is a horse's toe bone with an embedded spear point and a clay fireplace, with what appears to be a human palmprint dating from 27,900 years ago, a date based on nearby charcoal. The rich faunal record dating from 30,000 to 40,000 years ago may shed light on late Pleistocene megafauna extinctions. There seems to be differential extinction of the megafauna represented at Orogrande, indicating that the animals did not die off in a relatively short period of time and perhaps death was not due to one single event, such as overhunting, as is often claimed to have happened to the New World Pleistocene megafauna.

The simple chipped pebbles and rock flakes excavated from the site look nothing like the finely worked points found at Clovis-era sites (page 323). However, MacNeish and his coworkers argued that the chipping was not produced by animal trampling or by debris falling from the cave ceiling. He also stated that only humans could have introduced the stone to the cave because nearly half of the stone represents rock types found nowhere in the cave. Further work will prove if MacNeish is correct; however, there are detractors for his position (Appenzeller, 1992).

Middle Paleo-Indian Period.   The Middle Paleo-Indian period dates from 28,000 to approximately 13,500 years ago. Human bones are often lacking from Middle Paleo-Indian sites; no site has yet produced any quantity of cultural material, and there is scanty evidence of a cultural stratigraphical sequence. The earliest possible sites of this period yield unifacial scrapers, blades, and flake points; the later sites yield more refined flakes.

A partial human cranium and seven other bones were accidentally uncovered in 1939 at a site along the Los Angeles River near Los Angeles. Less than two months after the original finds, workers discovered large animal bones in the same geological stratum. Teeth and bone fragments identified as belonging to an imperial mammoth were also found. It was impossible to date the material when first discovered because it could not be shown that it was undisturbed. However, several dating techniques have now been applied. There is some confusion about a radiocarbon date; Stewart (1973) cited a date of less than 23,600 years ago, but Bada and others (1974) gave a date of 26,000 years, using aspartic acid racemization. Others suggest a much more recent date of 10,000 to 5,000 years ago. The date is suspicious because amino acid racemization should not be used in warm climates (see Chapter 1).

A south-central Idaho site yielded stone artifacts and cut bone assigned dates of 15,000 to 14,500 years ago. A radiocarbon date of 13,200 years ago plus or minus 170 years was obtained at Fork Rock Cave, Oregon, from charcoal reportedly associated with a projectile point. A layer dated about 14,500 years ago at Wilson Butte Cave, southern Idaho, yielded a significant assemblage of tools. The Midland skull from western Texas has been dated to 18,500 years ago.

Meadowcroft Rock Shelter is located 47 miles west of Pittsburgh. The dates from the earliest habitation layers strongly support an arrival date to the New World of more than 20,000 years ago. If immigrants reached the upper Ohio River at Meadowcroft by at least 17,000 B.C., as the oldest dates suggest, allowing for the time for eastern migration, they crossed the Bering land bridge at least 2,000 to 3,000 years earlier. Although the older dates at Meadowcroft are not unanimously accepted, Adovasio and Carlisle (1984) counter claims that the dates are artificially inflated by contaminated dated material.

There are many skeptics on Meadowcroft. For example, pollen and botanical debris from the 16,200 YBP strata suggest an oak forest, similar to today's growth. However, it has been argued that Meadowcroft was only 70 miles south of the Pleistocene glacier, much too close for a temperate ecosystem. Adovasio and Carlisle (1988) countered that Pleistocene ecosystems were more complex than those today and cannot be judged by modern standards.

The early inhabitants at Meadowcroft left some of their tools and food remains; 150 artifacts were recovered. Meadowcroft was a temporary shelter for wandering bands who subsisted on local game and plants. The site may have been continuously used until European contact.

A number of Middle Paleo-Indian sites have been uncovered in Mexico. The Mexican sites near Puebla and Tlapacoya constitute some of the strongest possible evidence of a Middle Paleo-Indian occupation in the New World. At Tlapacoya, near Mexico City, a blade, associated with a date of 23,150 years ago plus or minus 950 years, was recovered from immediately beneath a fallen tree (Mirambell, 1967) and a hearth from a beach deposit yielded a date of 24,000 years ago plus or minus 4,000 years (Haynes, 1967). A site of questionable dating of 21,850 years ago plus or minus 850 years, based on shell, which commonly yields erroneous dates, was excavated near Puebla. A number of artifacts associated with bones of extinct game were also found. Hueyatlaco, about 75 miles southeast of Tlapacoya, yielded a sequence of artifacts associated with extinct animals (Irwin-Williams, 1967). One locality at the site yielded a scraper associated with shells radiocarbon dated to 21,850 years ago plus or minus 850 years.

Late Paleo-Indian Period.   Many New World archaeologists accept only evidence here referred to as the Late Paleo-Indian period as substantive proof of New World habitation. This period dates from 11,500 years ago, and sites are rather numerous. Human populations were well established in the New World, with their hunting sites and camps found from Tierra del Fuego in South America to Nova Scotia.

Situated atop a mesa in Alaska's remote Northern Slope, the Mesa site may be the oldest well-documented campsite in Alaska and perhaps in North America (Amato, 1993; Kunz and Reanier, 1994). Excavations at Mesa provide evidence for human habitation of Beringia, adjacent to the Bering Strait. The site, found in 1978, was not generally announced until 1993.

Carbon-14 dates on hearths associated with projectile points place humans at the site between 11,600 and 9,700 years ago. The presence of Paleo-Indians in Beringia at this date challenges the notion that Paleo-Indian cultures arose exclusively in midcontinental North American.

Not everyone accepts that Mesa held a population ancestral to groups in North America's interior. Meltzer (in Busch, 1994b) notes that only two charcoal samples from Mesa were dated at older than 11,000 years; all other dates centered on 10,000 years ago. If Mesa is 10,000 years old, its importance as one of the first North American sites is in doubt.

Mesa seems to have been a weapons-repair and game-spotting station. There are nine shallowly buried and unlined hearths associated with artifacts. The artifacts do not resemble those from other Alaskan sites such as the more southern Nenana complex dating to at least 11,000 years ago. This fact suggests that more than one cultural group migrated into the New World. The artifacts from Mesa strongly resemble those from the oldest undisputed Paleo-Indian sites in the lower United States and offer a link between Paleo-Indians in the high plains of the Southwest and their presumed northern predecessors (Amato, 1993).

The earliest part of the Late Paleo-Indian period is characterized by remains of technologically advanced and highly skilled hunters utilizing a distinctive fluted projectile point known as the **Clovis point** for killing mammoths and other big game. Most Clovis remains come from the American southwest dating between 12,000 to 11,000 YBP. Clovis points take their name from an early site located between Clovis and Portales, New Mexico. Work began there in 1932; the most important discoveries were made in 1936 and 1937, when artifacts were found in unmistakable association with mammoth remains (Cotter, 1937). Two points are grooved about halfway up the face. In addition to stone artifacts, two polished bone pieces were found in situ. These are tapering cylindrical bone shafts with a beveled point; one lay near the foreleg of one of the mammoths, the other by a tusk. Similar finds have been made near Goldstream, Alaska; near Lower Klamath Lake, northern California; at the Lind Coulee site in Washington; and in the Itchtucknee River bed in north-central Florida.

A discovery having far-reaching effects on American archaeology was made in 1926, 8 miles from the town of Folsom, New Mexico, on a small tributary of the Cimarron River (Cook, 1927; Figgins, 1927). While excavating a fossil bison, a team uncovered two pieces of chipped flint. A third piece was later found embedded in clay surrounding a rib of one of the animals. This discovery of manufactured objects in association with articulated bones of a long-extinct fauna, in apparently undisturbed deposits, suggested a far greater antiquity of human populations in North America than previously envisioned. At first, most scientists rejected the evidence: after three field seasons, nineteen flakes, and positive proof of a Pleistocene geological age, the date of the Folsom points was accepted. Most Folsom materials date between 10,000 to 8,000 YBP.

Points of the **Folsom tradition** are pressure flaked, about 2 inches long, thin, more or less leaf shaped, with concave bases, and they show removal of a longitudinal flake from each face. This manufacture produces their fluted shape, with grooves or channels extending from one-third to almost the entire length of the flake. Why these points were fluted is debatable. Folsom points and their derivatives have been found in many locales, often as surface finds uncovered by wind or water erosion.

The peoples of the Clovis tradition apparently specialized in hunting mammoth, whereas those of the Folsom tradition concentrated on a now extinct form of bison. Perhaps this change was linked to changing habitat conditions and the growing scarcity of mammoths. The transition from the Clovis to the Folsom point seems to coincide with the extinction of mammoths, horses, camels, and other members of the Pleistocene megafauna. A major question in New World prehistory is what role humans played in the extinction of many of the associated fauna of the time.

The **Plano tradition** dates to 12,000 to 8,000 years ago, and Plano points occur in sites from the Rockies to the Atlantic and from Mexico to Canada. Plano points are not fluted; instead they have parallel pressure-flaked scars. Some of the oldest Paleo-Indian housing remains date to Plano occupations. The houses seem to have been circular and from 6 to 8 feet in diameter. The most recently discovered structure dates to about 8,000 years ago. The oldest Paleo-Indian dwelling structures date to about 10,000 years ago and are located in the Stanislaus National Forest, California. Spear points found 30 miles away and dated to 12,000 years old add to the evidence of the nearby structures in Stanislaus. Manufacturers of the Plano points were big-game hunters specializing in fauna that exist yet today.

Not all Paleo-Indian groups were primarily hunters. Because of the ages of these sites, more perishable food items, floral forms and small faunal remains, may have been destroyed or decayed. The remains of large, more durable bones may give a skewed impression of the dietary pattern. Archaeological data from southern Arizona, for example, suggest that Paleo-Indians were both gatherers and hunters. Two types of early sites located in different environmental zones are found in Arizona: kill sites and sites containing ground stone tools used for woodworking and plant processing (Duncan, 1972). These sites may have been seasonal settlements within a single subsistence settlement system.

South American Sites. A number of Late Paleo-Indian sites were uncovered in South America. One of the most important is the 11,000- to 10,000-year-old Fells cave site in Tierra del Fuego, where an assemblage of stone and bone artifacts was associated with skeletal remains of extinct game animals. Because of the distances involved, there are differences in tool technology between the North and South American sites. An example of one of the South American tool traditions, the Andean Biface tradition, comes from El Jobo, Venezuela, dated at 16,000 to 12,000 years ago. Other examples come from a Peruvian site dated to about 13,000 years ago (Lanning & Patterson, 1967) and from northwestern Argentina (Cigliano, 1962). The Los Toldos cave, Argentina, yielded bone dated to 12,650 years ago. Piaui caves, Brazil, yielded chipped stone dated from 16,650 to 11,950 years ago. Guitarrero cave, Peru, yielded a human mandible and teeth. Although campfire remains from the site provided a date of about 12,000 years ago (Lynch & Kennedy, 1970), most information from the sites dates much later.

UPPER PALEOLITHIC LIFEWAYS

Dietary Patterns

Upper Paleolithic peoples were big-game hunters whose hunting techniques were comparable to those of preceding times. Their weapons included spears, javelins, harpoons, clubs, stone missiles, and boomerangs or throwing sticks. Snares and pitfalls almost certainly trapped big game, and herds of gregarious animals were chased off cliffs. Some French and Spanish cave drawings contain images that may be snares, traps, pitfalls, and enclosures.

Although fishing long preceded the Upper Paleolithic, the technique was refined during this time with the introduction of harpoons. Aquatic foods may have formed a sizable part of some local diets.

Some sites indicate that Upper Paleolithic inhabitants relied strongly on reindeer for food. The reindeer–human relationship seems to have been very close. Reindeer supplied raw materials for clothing and tents, sinew for thread, bones and antlers for tools and weapons, and teeth for ornaments, in addition to animal protein. There is abundant evidence at the German sites of Schleswig-Holstein of reindeer antlers being fashioned into harpoons. The frequency of bone sewing needles, bodkins (large-eyed blunt needles), and belt fasteners suggests that elaborate wearing apparel, presumably of tanned hides and furs, was common.

Group hunting economies may have been specialized for certain animals. Although the reindeer was certainly the most important food animal in France and Germany, the woolly mammoth was important to populations farther east. Horses were a locally important food source. If the game animals were seasonal migrants, their predatory hunters presumably followed the same pattern. If herds of gregarious animals were sedentary, semipermanent dwellings were possible.

Dwellings

Upper Paleolithic populations inhabited a variety of dwellings; rock shelters (for example, rock overhangs as distinguished from deep caves) were widely used. Trees were felled and propped against the rock face, perhaps trellised by branches and skins. Large caves were inhabited, and huts or tents built inside them were heated with wood or bone fires. There are remains of permanent dwellings where rock shelters are rare, as in central and eastern Europe. At Pushkari, Russia, long huts were sometimes sunk into the ground. One hut measures 13 × 39 feet. At the Kostenki I site located in the Don Valley, Russia, there are traces of two dwellings, each 49 × 120 feet, along with evidence of other dwellings of various sizes. The framework of these structures was probably wood and/or bone covered with skins and hides. There are also nine hearths situated on the long axis and numerous silos of varying shapes and heights. It is unlikely that this complex was accommodated under one roof. Human occupation layers at Kostenki-Borshevo date to 25,000 years ago; however, most occupation layers have a date of 15,000 to 12,000 years ago.

Group Organization

Although Upper Paleolithic groups still lived in bands, larger social organizations may have appeared. A tribal structure, an association of many bands cemented by mate exchange and economic bonds, may have been developing. Upper Paleolithic populations may have developed rituals for coming and remaining together. Mating and kinship rules may have created an intricate and cohesive relationship among large numbers of people.

Upper Paleolithic populations still had high mortality rates; the mortality pattern is similar to preceding Neandertal populations. Less than 50 percent of the seventy-six Eurasian skeletons were from individuals who had reached twenty years of age. Only 12 percent were past forty, and almost no female had reached the age of thirty.

Tool Inventory

Upper Paleolithic populations produced a culture that far exceeded in variety and elegance anything known to their predecessors. Fine stone tools and delicately worked bone implements were produced (Figure 13-4). Eurasian tool samples were characterized by an abundance and variety of long, parallel-sided implements called *blades*. Specific tools of the blade tool industry were devised for working bone and wood. **Burins** (chisel-shaped blades) were probably used for engraving and working wood, bone, or antler that may have been employed as handles or shafts. Scrapers may have been used to scrape wood or hollow out wood or bone. Laurel-leaf blades were carefully made into thin, sharp-edged knives or arrowheads.

European Upper Paleolithic tool industries have an emphasis on bone- and wood-working tools. Stone tools reflect only a small portion of the cultural changes that occurred during this period, although differing styles and the appearance and frequency of different tool types are used to define Upper Paleolithic cultural traditions. What was once considered to be a progressive series of industries, each evolving into or being replaced by another, may be a single technological stage representing basic adaptive strategies.

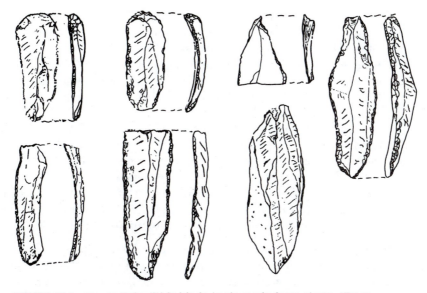

FIGURE 13-4   Upper Paleolithic blade tools made from stone. (*From* PHYSICAL ANTHROPOLOGY, 3/E by Kelso/Trevathan, © 1984. Reprinted by permission of Prentice-Hall, Inc., Upper Saddle River, NJ.)

The earliest Upper Paleolithic sites in eastern and central Europe may be older than their counterparts to the west. Although dates in excess of 35,000 years ago seem questionable, eastern European tool industries seem to have begun several thousand years before the earliest Upper Paleolithic in western Europe, and most early *H. s. sapiens* fossils from western Europe are later than those from eastern Europe.

The Aurignacian and the Perigordian are the two earliest European Upper Paleolithic tool traditions. Bone and stone tools characterize the former, whereas Perigordian assemblages have few bone implements.

New items such as polished pins or bone or antler awls are found in Upper Paleolithic tool kits. Points were probably hafted (affixed) to sticks. The later Magdalenian inventory (a cultural complex from western Europe dating from about 17,000 to 12,000 years ago) includes hooked rods used as spear throwers, barbed points and harpoons, fishhooks, needles, bone and ivory bodkins, belt fasteners, and tools of undetermined use. Many tools are highly decorated, depicting hunted animals, and they may have served as ceremonial items.

Major Features

The major cultural features of the Upper Paleolithic are as follows (Mellars, 1989; R. White, 1982):

1. A greater population density than in previous times.
2. A greater stylistic component to stone artifacts. Stylistic differences in tools may have played a role in information exchange (for example, in

noting territorial or social boundaries), in the context of rituals, in support of ethnicity, or in maintaining and strengthening mating networks and exchange relationships (Wobst, 1977).

3. A far greater emphasis on use of bone and antler and a proliferation of bone tools. The use of bone may reflect a shift toward the hunting of large numbers of herd animals, such as deer, in which both sexes have antlers for most of the year.

4. A broadening subsistence base to include greater amounts of fish and birds.

5. Indications of the use of personal ornaments. In addition to bone and antler, shell and stone were used for ornamental purposes.

6. Materials obtained from distant sources, presumably through structured exchange networks, at the beginning of the Upper Paleolithic humans.

7. Appearance of artistic expression in some parts of the world.

There seems to be a restructuring of social relationships across the Middle-Upper Paleolithic boundary in the course of which group affiliation and individual identity become important and are noted by regional differences in worked stone, antler and bone, the fabrication and wearing of ornaments, and the regular aggregation of a set of otherwise dispersed local groups. The desirability of antler as a communicative and technological medium is reflected in the hunting of large numbers of reindeer. Structured relationships between inhabitants of different geographical areas are evident in the presence of materials from distant sources.

AESTHETIC EXPRESSION OF UPPER PALEOLITHIC POPULATIONS

European Upper Paleolithic populations left numerous traces of their artistic work that tell much about their daily life, ritual practices, and concerns. Upper Paleolithic populations provided many provocative assortments of animal bones, skulls, and paintings.

The impression is that most prehistoric art is confined to cave recesses. One reason for this impression may be that cave art is among the most dramatic of the artistic representations and that, because it is in a protected environment, it is more likely to survive. However, prehistoric art is not confined solely to caves. Magnificent sculptured friezes are found in French rock shelters, such as Angles-sur-l'Anglin and Cap Blanc (Leroi-Gourhan, 1965). Large sculptured or engraved blocks were recovered from rock shelters and in sites at the foot of cliffs, such as Roc de Sers and Fourneau du Diable. Some deep and eroded, linear and zoomorphic (concerned with animal representations) engravings were found in cave mouths and shelters in Spain. Linear incisions in and around several caves at Mount Carmel, Israel, are attributed to the terminal Pleistocene, but they may be older. Some of the most recent prehistoric noncave art has been found in the Pyrenees; however, its dating is not yet verified (Bahn, 1985).

Although most attention concerning cave art focuses on Europe, there are also cave paintings in North Africa and south of the Sahara in Tanzania and South Africa. Art in the Hun mountain regions of Namibia, southern Africa, dates to 28,450 to 26,350 years ago, older than European cave art. Unlike European paintings, however, African paintings have unfortunately been disregarded. The longest continuous artistic tradition belongs to the Australian Aborigines and their ancestors. There is an artistic tradition among the Aborigines that dates back beyond 30,000 years in Australia and may date to 200,000 years ago.

When art first appeared is undecided. It was once claimed that a battered lava rock dating over 1 mya was a barely discernible piece of sculpture. There have been other claims of art from long ago such as what may be incised bone found at a *Homo erectus* site. One of the more recent, and unsubstantiated, possibilities is a small piece of volcanic rock dating to about 233,000 years ago and found in Israel. It has been claimed that the rock might be a heavily-worn female figurine.

Until much more collaborative evidence is found, no claims for early art can be substantiated. There are tantalizing clues awaiting further research and more finds for verification.

Cave Art

Upper Paleolithic art is divided into two categories: mobile art (Figure 13-5) applied to small objects normally found in archaeological deposits, and cave art restricted to the walls, roofs, and occasionally floors of caves and rock shelters. About 200 sites containing art have been discovered in western Europe, 90 percent are located in France and Spain in three major clusters: the foothills of the central Pyrenees; along the Bay of Biscay coast of northern Spain; and the heaviest concentration within a 20-mile radius of the village of Les Eyzies, southwestern France. Since the first viewing of Paleolithic cave art in 1879, at least 150 painted caves have been found in southwestern France. Reliefs were made by cutting away the rock to varying depths; there are examples of drawings on clay films on walls, ceilings, and floors and modeling of clay figures. Coloring includes various kinds of ocher, manganese, and charcoal.

There are many and varied explanations of why art developed (Diamond, 1993). The explanations include the following: (1) The depictions are copies of nature seen by the local people; (2) they are exemplars of magical rites to ensure hunting success; (3) they are learning devices for youngsters in a culture without a written language; and (4) they may represent local myths.

The oldest and most widely discussed explanation is the relationship between the art and magic. Much of Upper Paleolithic art, placed on walls deep in relatively inaccessible caves, is very difficult to see. Caves were probably entered by people using light from torches or fat-burning lamps. Much of the art is in areas badly situated for viewing—in narrow niches, behind rock bumps, and sometimes in areas that must have been dangerous for both artist and viewer to enter.

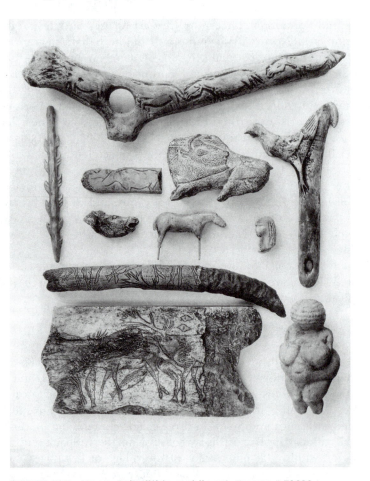

FIGURE 13-5   Upper Paleolithic mobile art. (Image # 39686, courtesy Department of Library Services, American Museum of Natural History.)

Some scientists see Upper Paleolithic art as being related to the food quest, as examples of magical rituals bound to the hunt. Much of the art is zoomorphic, that is, concerned with animal representations. Some pictures seem to depict masked figures with animal heads, antlers, and skins strapped over human forms (Figure 13-6).

Upper Paleolithic cave art represents an adjustment to daily life. Much of the artistic expression seems to reflect concern with food procurement. Many animal figures are painted with spears in them or marked with blows from clubs. The French cave of Font-de-Gaume has several drawings of traps or enclosures with animals suggestively caught in them. One drawing depicts a mammoth in a pit-like trap. Although naturalistic animal forms have always generated much discussion, there are more examples of Paleolithic art than carved or painted animals.

FIGURE 13-6 "Sorcerer," height 0.75 meter, Les Trois Frères, France. (Image # 329853, courtesy Department of Library Services, American Museum of Natural History.)

Among 1,200 engraved bones and antlers that came from 26 Magdalenian sites, including the famous site of Altamira, only 70 animal depictions were identifiable.

Many paintings are superimposed one atop another; some paintings in the magnificent cave at Lascaux, France, are four layers deep. If these paintings are actually attempts at sympathetic magic, that is, a way of ensuring a good hunt, were there also magicians? There are some fifty paintings of human figures clad in animal skins, sometimes wearing animal heads or horns. Many of these are in the midst of a dance.

Bahn (1996b) is dismissive of most attempts to explain the origins or functions of cave art. He writes:

> Attempts to resurrect old ideas of hunting magic . . . are based on a good deal of wishful thinking. They remove figures from their context. . . . The few figures that can be made to fit this hypothesis are so rare and unrepresentative of the whole that

it is self-evident that the vast majority of paleolithic art has nothing whatsoever to do with hunting or teaching in such simple terms. The same applies to the other currently fashionable theory of shamanism and "altered states of consciousness." (p. 213)

Pfeiffer (1983) argued that it is necessary to remember that humans at this time were illiterate; the only way to store knowledge was to memorize it. Without writing, everything had to be dramatized to help memorization, and our ancestors organized ways to attach emotion to information for memory's sake. Cave art helped to achieve this end, so Pfeiffer argued.

Pfeiffer suggested that cave art may have required elaborate and systematic planning. Three stages may have been involved: (1) leading the uninitiated through an eerie and difficult route, "a kind of obstacle course to soften them up for indoctrination" (Pfeiffer, 1983:39); (2) catching and holding their attention with shocking and frightening displays; and (3) using every technique to imprint information intact and indelibly in the memory. To prepare people for indoctrination, it helps to place them into a strange environment, a place without familiar landmarks, a place producing a feeling of loss. Caves meet these requirements.

To increase the sense of awe inspired by a cave and its paintings, early populations may have further assaulted the senses. Russian archaeologists recovered a set of red-painted mammoth bones, which may have been used as drums, and other possible percussion instruments. Bone and ivory instruments resembling bullroarers have been found in some caves. Bullroarers produce an unearthly sound that may have further stimulated the senses and increased the sense of awe.

Circumstantial evidence that cave art may have served as an educational tool comes from children's footprints found in some caves. Children may have been undergoing training in some of the caves adorned with artistic works.

Prehistoric art may be a reflection of increased social complexity. Art appeared when there was a burst of change in the economy, toolmaking traditions, and social behavior.

According to Leroi-Gourhan (1967), Paleolithic art is an expression of an entire organizational, perceptual world view, a cosmology, a system of thought. According to Leroi-Gourhan, this system is based on the division of the natural world into female and male components. Certain parts of caves as well as certain groups of animals and signs also have a masculine or feminine association. The way in which depictions are arranged on a panel, where they are placed in a cave and in relation to each other, supposedly all derive from this organizational structure.

Leroi-Gourhan's numerical counts of artistic subject matter showed that Paleolithic artists were selective in their choice and placement of art. These counts challenged long-held beliefs that most cave art is in the deep, dark, inaccessible regions of presumably sacred caves. Some specific forms or themes, such as depictions of females, tend to be in rock shelters or daylit locales. Among the portable (mobile) art, some themes or depictions are significantly correlated with certain artifact types or forms. Horses are frequently found on most kinds of artifacts except harpoons, whereas bison do not appear on spears.

It is not likely that all the activities seen in Upper Paleolithic art can be attributed to ritual and sympathetic control over hunting of desired but scarce resources. Surely there is some connection between the art and subsistence patterns, but these activities apparently do not alone cause or create art. Quite to the contrary of what is often assumed, Delaporte (see Lewin, 1986) suggested as a result of his examination of more recent representations of animals in pottery and sculpture that artists mostly paint or carve images of animals they *do not* eat. If this suggestion is true for early art, it contradicts the possibility that the art was a magical intervention to the hunt. Jared Diamond gives a rationale for why artists seem to have concentrated on some types of animals and not others. "Cro-Magnon artists may have preferred painting speedy horses and powerful bison to depicting the slimy little clams that filled their stomachs" (Diamond, 1993:28).

An extraordinary cave art site is in the mountains of southern France. The huge and undisturbed cavern, known as Grotte Chauvet, was found near Vallon-Pont-d'Arc in the Ardèche region (Clottes, 1995). Four chambers within the cave contained about 300 animal depictions, and more may yet be found. They date to about 20,000 years ago. This is the highest concentration of depictions in any French cave containing art.

The animals include woolly-haired rhinoceroses (the predominant depictions), bears, mammoths, oxen, and others. The rhinoceroses look very similar. All have distinctive ears, spherical feet, and a large black stripe dividing the body down the middle. Lions are second in number of representations. None have the mane associated with African lions; doubtless, these are cave lions. The lone panther is the only image of panthers in Paleolithic art, and the same is true for the lone engraved owl. The depictions may also include a rare image of a red, slouched hyena. Most depictions are rendered in yellow ocher, charcoal, and hematite.

Among the interesting features of the art is the exceptional prominence of carnivores; lions and bears are featured. The prominence of rhinoceroses is mysterious. Unlike other caves in France and elsewhere, Grotte Chauvet does not display such possible food animals as reindeer, whose bones are common in sites dating to this time.

In one small chamber a bear skull was placed on a large rock set against a backdrop of bear paintings. This intriguing assemblage raises the possibility that it is associated with ritual. On the cave floor are preserved human footprints, pieces of torches, and well-preserved artifacts.

Unlike other cave art, depictions in Grotte Chauvet seem to be grouped into compositions rather than consisting of unrelated animals on the same walls. No human likenesses are depicted; however, there are tracings of hands, possibly three vulvas, and a half-human and half-bison depiction.

New techniques are being employed in dating and deciphering cave art (Bahn, 1990). When human blood was found to have been mixed with red pigments used in paintings in some Australian rock shelters and caves dating from 20,000 to 11,000 years ago, a new dimension of research began. In some French cave art, pigments were consistently mixed with iron oxide (to produce red) and manganese dioxide (to produce black). Analyses of the organic components of pigments reveal that some paintings took a great deal of preparation and time to accomplish while others were simpler in their fashioning. New analyses are helping to detect fakes and later additions or alterations to cave paintings. Some cave paintings were rendered using only natural pigments, while others used concocted new pigments. Bahn (1990:426) noted, "Pigment analysis is providing a tool, applicable at least regionally, for dating Magdalenian paintings and is revealing that behind apparent stylistic homogeneity there is technological heterogeneity. Styles lasted longer than was thought, and are of limited use in dating."

Sculpture and Engravings

Upper Paleolithic inhabitants also engaged in sculpture and engraving (see Figure 13-5); there are incised animal outlines on cave walls, some produced in bas relief. At Cap Blanc, near the French village of Les Eyzies, a set of horses is carved in bas relief. The natural rock curves accentuate the sides of the horses' bodies.

Female statuettes of bone, stone, and ivory of varying design and merit are widely distributed in Europe. Their most obvious trait is an exaggeration of the torso, focusing on the stomach, breasts, and buttocks; the head and limbs are disproportionately small. A few Venuses have facial features rudimentarily depicted. These statuettes have been interpreted as tiny goddesses or fertility figurines. A major example is the so-called Venus of Willendorf, a 4-inch statuette with a wavy hairdo and accentuated breasts, stomach, and thighs. Some figurines also represent males, but most are sexless. The suggestion of a continent-wide fertility cult has been greatly exaggerated.

Some astonishing examples of sculpture dating to at least 15,000 years ago were found accidentally in the French cave of Le Tuc d'Audoubert. Access to the cave is by way of an underground river. Two molded clay bison, each almost a meter long, propped up in the middle of a low, round chamber were found in a larger chamber filled with stalactites. A third and smaller bison lay on the floor close to the main figures. A pit in the cave floor was the source of the clay for the figures. The sculpture was shaped with the artist's fingers as well as with a spatula, while a pointed object was used to insert the eyes, nostrils, and other features. The sculptors of the bison left their footprints in the wet clay of the side chamber.

Another cave in the Pyrenees, the Grotte de Montespan, also contains clay figures. Although these have deteriorated with age, one can still recognize a clay lion and clay bears, which lie against the walls of a cavern 1.2 miles from the cave's entrance. Once again there is a scattering of footprints, some belonging to children.

The site of El Juyo, dating to about 14,000 years ago, has been uncovered in Spain (Freeman et al., 1983). This site yielded an elaborate sanctuary—the clearest evidence yet of possible early human religious activity. The site includes almost 1,100 square feet of undisturbed strata. Faunal remains show that shellfish were gathered in large numbers. The hunting of such animals as red deer, roe deer, bison, horses, and ibex seems to have been very important. The most important animal in the diet seems to have been the red deer, probably because of its local abundance.

Level 4 at El Juyo reveals structures thought to have been used for ceremonial purposes. The most remarkable artifact is a free-standing, crudely made stone sculpture. The right half reveals the visage of a benign, smiling human male, and a simple curved nose, moustache, and beard. The left side reveals features of a large member of the cat family, perhaps a lion or leopard. The cat's features are seen in a deeply chiseled tear duct, a long and deliberately polished muzzle, a single projecting fang, and lines of black dots, which hint at the roots of whiskers.

The dualism expressed by the El Juyo sculpture, and the depiction of opposed animal and human natures utilizing a right and left polarity, are commonly found among living peoples but are rarely discernible in prehistory. Level 4 has been viewed as a "space that has been symbolically structured and set aside for the performance of patterned religious rituals dedicated to one or more culturally postulated supernatural beings. These rituals were not everyday activities essential to the economic survival of the group" (Freeman et al., 1983:52).

Although Neandertal burials and the later Upper Paleolithic paintings have been viewed as possibly religious in nature, the El Juyo sanctuary provides stronger evidence for religious practices. The stone face may be the most convincing depiction of a supernatural being yet discovered in Paleolithic art.

SUMMARY

Where fully modern *H. sapiens* first evolved is still being debated; however, Africa seems to be the origin of this new stage in human evolution (Box 13-2) about 100,000 years ago or perhaps earlier. In various places during the Upper Pleistocene, populations appeared who were basically migratory hunters, although

---

BOX 13-2   Some Critical Features Associated with *Homo sapiens sapiens*

- Time Span: Perhaps as early as 125,000 years ago in Africa, 92,000 years ago in the Levant, and 35,000–40,000 years ago elsewhere.

- Distribution: Worldwide. Populations entered the Australian region at least 35,000 years ago and perhaps the New World as early.

- Lifeways: Upper Paleolithic tool assemblage includes materials made from bone, antler, and wood. Fishing appears. Art and sculpture appear. Inhabited a variety of dwellings. Possibility of trade and magic or religion.

- Morphology: Included in same subspecies as modern humans but with anatomical differences from modern populations. There is reduction in facial robusticity and in the brow ridges, especially in the East African sample. Reduction in tooth size, increase in brain size, and the appearance of a chin.

- Postcranial skeleton: Robust body build, but less so than in Neandertals.

there is evidence of some sedentarism. During the Upper Paleolithic, art and sculpture came of age.

The exact dates of population movements into Australia and the New World are continually being revised backward in time.

SUGGESTED READINGS

Amato, I. 1993. American family tree gets new root. *Science* 260:22.

Ayala, F. 1995. The myth of Eve: Molecular biology and human origins. *Science* 270:1930–1936.

Bahn, P. 1996. New developments in Pleistocene art. *Evolutionary Anthropology* 4:204–215.

Barinaga, M. 1992. "African Eve" backers beat a retreat. *Science* 255:686–687.

Braüer, G. 1984. The Afro-european sapiens hypothesis and hominid evolution in Asia during the Middle and Upper Pleistocene. In *The Early Evolution of Man*, ed. P. Andrews and G. Franzen. Senckenberg: Courier Forschunginstitut Senckenberg.

Cann, R., M. Stoneking, and A. Wilson. 1987. Mitochondrial DNA and human evolution. *Nature* 325:31–37.

Diamond, J. 1993. Drowning dogs and the dawn of art. *Natural History* 3:23–29.

Fischman, J. 1996. Evidence mounts for our African origins—and alternatives. *Science* 271:1364.

Gibbons, A. 1993. Geneticists trace the DNA trail of the first Americans. *Science* 259:312–313.

Gibbons, A. 1997a. Ideas on human origins evolve at anthropology gathering. *Science* 276:535–536.

Gibbons, A. 1997b. Y chromosome shows Adam was an African. *Science* 278:804–805.

Gibbons, A. 1998. Calibrating the mitochondrial clock. *Science* 279:28–29.

Haag, W. 1962. The Bering Strait land bridge. *Scientific American* 206:112–123.

Kramer, A. 1991. Modern human origins in Australasia: Replacement or evolution? *American Journal of Physical Anthropology* 86:455–473.

Lahr, M., and R. Foley. 1994. Multiple dispersals and modern human origins. *Evolutionary Anthropology* 3:48–60.

Mellars, P. 1989. Major issues in the emergence of modern humans. *Current Anthropology* 30:349–385.

Meltzer, D. 1997. Monte Verde and the Pleistocene peopling of the Americas. *Science* 276:754–756.

Morell, V. 1995. Siberia: Surprising home for early modern humans. *Science* 268:1279.

Pfeiffer, J. 1983. Was Europe's fabulous cave art the start of the Information Age? *Smithsonian,* April: 36–45.

Smith, F., G. Falsetti, and S. Donnelly. 1990. Modern human origins. *Yearbook of Physical Anthropology* 32:35–68.

Stringer, C. 1990. Replacement, continuity, and the origin of *Homo sapiens.* In *Continuity or Replacement: Controversies in* Homo sapiens, ed. G. Braüer and F. Smith. Rotterdam: Balkema.

Stringer, C., and P. Andrews. 1988. Genetic and fossil evidence for the origin of modern humans. *Science* 239:1263–1268.

Templeton, A. 1992. Human origins and analysis of mitochondrial DNA sequences. *Science* 255:737.

Vigilant, L., M. Stoneking, H. Harpending, K. Hawkes, and A. Wilson. 1991. African populations and the evolution of human mitochondrial DNA. *Science* 253:1503–1507.

Wolpoff, M., X. Wu, and Z. Thorne. 1984. Modern *Homo sapiens* origins: A general theory of hominid evolution involving the fossil evidence from east Asia. In *The Origins of Modern Humans*, ed. F. Smith and F. Spencer. New York: Alan R. Liss.

Wu, X., and F. Poirier. 1995. *Human Evolution in China.* New York: Oxford University Press.

14

Conclusion?

RETROSPECTIVE

We have chronicled an evolutionary journey through time, from the earliest vertebrates through to ourselves and the living forms that share the planet with us. This
book has focused on the primate era of evolution. We have recounted the fossil discoveries and gleaned from them notions of the evolutionary process that led to our
own existence. Primate origins were traced to a time during the Eocene geological
epoch approximately 55 mya, shortly after the demise of the dinosaurs—if "shortly"
can be perceived on the scale of geological time. Only within the past 5 million
years or so, another "short" period of time, do we have clear evidence, as well as
some that is not so clear, of our human origins—distinct from the evolutionary
paths of all other animals.

The hominid evolutionary process, that of natural selection on genetic
variation, has *not* been distinct from other life forms. For much of the life span
of the hominid lineage, our nearest ancestors lived like other animals, subject
to the pressures of predation and the challenges of exploiting natural
resources. The earliest hominids were distinct primarily in their novel form of
locomotion, bipedalism. This eventually gave them a degree of independence
from the trees, which had been a necessity for many of the primates that preceded them, and opened up opportunities for the exploitation of new habitats.
Bipedal hominids survived the rigors of natural selection, setting an evolutionary course involving both the benefits and the consequences that came
with such a peculiar stance.

Charles Darwin anticipated two important correlates of human evolution:
that our earliest ancestors began in Africa, and that our upright posture freed
the hands for the use of tools. On the first count he was undoubtedly right; on the
second, we only have clear evidence of tool manufacture and use long after the
first bipedal hominids appear. Yet we do not know what the earliest bipedal
hominids did with their hands or what would have become of possible tools
not made of stone.

The earliest hominids, the australopithecines of East, South, and apparently West Africa, persisted and evolved through a period of cooling and drying
on the African continent. At some point around 2.5 mya, at about the same time
in the fossil record as a climatic shift and continental uplift, the hominid lineage
diverged. The divergence led to at least two different lineages, the robust australopithecines and the earliest progenitors of the genus *Homo*. Perhaps even
more hominid species arose, but varied interpretations of the fossil record and
general principles of ecology leave the question open.

What is clear is that humans did not evolve at once as a complete entity
(Table 14-1). Bipedality and orthograde (upright) posture were precursors of
later trends in the evolution of the brain and the face. Our evolution proceeded
in a mosaic fashion. Once bipedality and terrestrial locomotion had taken hold,
the evolution of the brain and face continued throughout the *Homo erectus*
phase, starting as early as 1.8 mya. Evolution within *H. erectus* was not static, but
continued for more than a million years until the precursors of our species, or

TABLE 14-1 Time of Appearance of Physical Traits of Human Species

	Homo habilis[a]	Homo erectus[b]	Archaic Homo sapiens	Neandertals	Early Modern Homo sapiens
Height (meters)	1–ca. 1.5	1.3–1.5	?	1.5–1.7	1.6–1.85
Physique	Relatively long arms and short legs	Robust skeleton	Robust skeleton	Robust; some adapted for cold	Modern skeleton
Brain size (cubic centimeters)	500–800	750–1,250	1,100–1,400	1,200–1,750	1,200–1,700
Skull/face	Relatively small face, some with larger and flatter faces	Flat, thick skull with large occipital and brow ridge; protruding face	Higher skull; face less protruding; projecting nose	Reduced brow ridge; thinner skull; large nose; midface projection	Small or no brow ridge; shorter, high skull
Jaws/teeth	Thinner jaw, but some with thicker jaws; narrow molars that are larger in some samples	Robust jaw in larger individuals; smaller teeth than H. habilis	Similar to H. erectus but teeth may be smaller	Similar to "archaic" H. sapiens; teeth smaller except for incisors; chin development in some	Shorter jaws than Neandertals; chin; teeth may be smaller
Distribution	Eastern (and southern?) Africa	Africa, Asia, Europe	Africa, Asia, Europe	Europe, western Asia	Africa, western Asia
Known dates (years ago)	2.3–1.6 million	ca. 1.8–0.3 million	400,000–100,000	150,000 (or slightly earlier)–30,000	130,000 (or slightly earlier)–60,000

[a]There may be considerable sexual dimorphism manifested in the range of features characterizing H. habilis. Perhaps more than one species is represented, e.g., H. rudolfensis.

[b]This includes African samples that some refer to the separate species of H. ergaster.

Some data from Reconstructing Human Origins, by G. Conroy, © 1997. New York: W. W. Norton & Co., Inc.

perhaps the earliest *members* of our species, appeared sometime within the past million years.

The time and place of the origin of our own species, *Homo sapiens,* is a subject of much debate. Evolution is a continuous process, and so the boundaries between species are obscure, especially when there is a good fossil record showing subtle changes. We see transition among the fossils through time, but it is difficult to discern which fossils represent species or subspecies. For example, Neandertals may have been variants of the lineage leading to our contemporary species, or an offshoot (like the robust australopithecines) that went terminally extinct. As we get closer in time to modern human origins, data aside from the fossils come into play, and so the genetics of late Pleistocene forms add to our understanding . . . as well as to our scientific debates about the details of human evolution.

From the standpoint of understanding human evolution, few points are more crucial than the mechanisms leading to the appearance of the first hominids and to members of our genus, *Homo.* Nevertheless, few issues have raised more controversy than determining these points in our evolutionary history. To use a phrase of Albert Einstein, "This huge world stands before us like a great external riddle."

QUESTIONS TO BE ANSWERED AND GAPS TO BE FILLED

There are many reasons for disagreements about when, how, and why humans diverged from the common ape–human stock and about when, how, and why the genus *Homo* appeared. Putting aside fossil remains for a moment, one useful means for understanding problems of interpretation is to refer to a thought experiment designed by the physicist John Archibald Wheeler. Imagine, as the paleoanthropologist must do, that an evolutionary world exists whose major components can be comprehended. The development and arrangement of forms in that evolutionary world relate to the kinds of questions the scientist raises about that world. If the scientist asks different kinds of questions, the order of that world may change. If the scientist performs different kinds of experiments, a different world of realities may emerge. Because the nature of the evolutionary world reveals itself in bits and pieces, and because it does not reveal itself until it emerges from the questions the scientist asks, no conceptual scheme is correct until the correct questions are raised. We must realize that disagreements will always appear when interpreting the fossil record.

The study of human evolution has engendered many controversies. Various individuals champion widely divergent theories. Some theories are plausible, whereas others can be forthrightly rejected. Such is the self-correcting nature of science, and particularly of a relatively young science such as paleoanthropology. We have made many strides forward in reconstructing the pattern and process of human evolution, but many key questions remain. Following are some major questions yet to be answered, perhaps in the near future:

1. Which form(s) is the last common ancestor of the human and great ape lineages?
2. What is the evolutionary sequence and context of the Pliocene and Lower Pleistocene hominid divergence? Was the genus *Homo* the only (major?) user and maker of stone tools at this time?
3. What role did the environmental changes in Africa play in shaping and propelling hominid evolution?
4. How many species of *Homo* preceded *H. sapiens?* What was the role of *H. erectus* in the evolution of *H. sapiens?*
5. Where do Neandertals fit in the human evolutionary lineage?
6. When and where did *H. s. sapiens* first appear?

There are also a number of still-to-be-filled gaps:

1. Late Miocene hominoid fossils are virtually unknown between 8 and 5 mya, a time when *Australopithecus* probably first appeared. Research in several areas throughout Africa, as well as Iran, Pakistan, Burma, and China, may provide the necessary information. One way of resolving the issue of the human–ape split would be to fill this gap.
2. By 2.4 mya at least two hominid lineages, *Homo* and the robust australopithecines, appear to have coexisted in Africa. There is a relative paucity of sites between 2.9 and 2.5 mya that may be able to document the divergence between the two lineages, and we need more data about the species that existed before and after this crucial phase of evolution. By focusing on African geological deposits dated 4 to 2 mya, we may expand our understanding of the human evolutionary process.
3. There are few sites between Africa and Asia that may help to explain when *Homo* first expanded its population to new continents, and what routes were followed.
4. The time period for the first appearance of *H. s. sapiens* presents the problem of trying to determine whether the evolutionary change from more archaic to modern-looking humans was gradual or abrupt, widespread or localized. The many determinants of this transition are still poorly understood.

The remains uncovered in the last few decades exceed those recovered in the preceding 100 years, and it is possible that remains recovered next year may exceed those of the past ten. As more trained workers are produced and as technological advances allow once inaccessible sites to become accessible, more material will appear. However, even with the recovery of more material all the answers may not be available. Sometimes what is needed is not more evidence but novel approaches and new interpretations of the available evidence. The dates for some sites may change, and evolutionary scenarios may be altered, but the basic fact will remain—we are related to the nonhuman primates. Their evolutionary development and ours are inextricably joined.

WHAT CONSTITUTES HUMAN STATUS?

Are we simply another of the primates, or are there major differences between human and nonhuman primates? The answer is complex. On one hand, we are just another primate in many respects. We share many aspects of our biology with other primates, particularly the great apes, as first elucidated by Thomas Huxley more than 130 years ago. Since then we have learned that other primates share much of our behavioral and social repertoire. On the other hand, we differ from other primates along a number of parameters. First among these are the results of the feedback between biology and culture; we are, after all, culture-bearing animals. The biocultural feedback is manifested in anatomical, social, or technological traits that are usually assumed to be basic to humans, such as the large and complex brain, symbolic communication, bipedal locomotion, consistent tool use and modification of tools with other tools, use of fire, and life within a large, bisexual, complex social group in which social roles are learned.

When did these characteristics considered so important in human evolution arise? For some traits, such as speech, there is little anatomical or artifactual material of much help. Fortunately, hints about brain size and bipedal locomotion are fossilized in the human skeletal record. Other factors such as tool use and fabrication, use of fire, hunting behavior, and larger, complex social groups (which imply complex social rules and communication systems) can also be identified in the fossil record.

By the Lower Pleistocene, there is evidence of a modest increase in brain size, bipedal locomotion, and tool use and fabrication, as well as circumstantial evidence of large and somewhat complex social groupings. However, we can do little but speculate about the possibility of language, report no conclusive evidence of the purposeful use of fire, and suggest that these creatures may have been hunting and scavenging meat—although vegetable foods are the dietary mainstay. By the time of *Homo erectus,* we note a larger brain size, hunting, and the likelihood of complex and large social groups. Perhaps language appears at this time, or advances from the rudiments of language possibly employed by earlier forms of *Homo.* In the later Middle Pleistocene, during the time of early *H. sapiens* and subsequently, there is a further increase of brain size, more complex and effective hunting practices, more efficient tools and tool use, continual use of fire, and large and complex social organizations.

In asking what is "human," a nonscientific term, we must answer with multiple defining features. Birds and kangaroos are bipeds of a sort, as were dinosaurs; whales and dolphins have relatively large brains; and some nonhuman primates exhibit a rudimentary culture. Some nonhuman primates and other animals use tools. Leslie White stated that the symbol is the universe of humanity, yet some have argued that chimpanzees and gorillas have at least the rudimentary ability to symbolize. Among insects, the honeybee can communicate such things as direction, distance, and quantity of food with a dance. Even such abstract emotions as love can possibly be identified among nonhumans. It should be clear that it is often difficult, if not impossible, to say which traits are purely human and which are not. Yet even the nonscientist can distinguish between human and nonhuman because we distinguish different forms on the basis of a combination of traits.

As with distinguishing what is "human," it is highly unlikely that one trait can be used to distinguish the first appearance of hominids or the genus *Homo*. Instead, several distinctive traits, when combined, will give an independent but mutual testimony to hominid and *Homo* status. Four traits are germane to all our basic concepts of defining ourselves: *bipedalism, a large and complex brain, language,* and *a cultural way of life.* Except for bipedalism, these traits did not characterize the first hominids. They were our ancestors, but perhaps they were not quite "human."

Bipedalism, a large brain, language, and culture all appear even in our stories and cartoons as indications of human character. When we attempt to humanize animals we have them walk on two feet, give them a mental ability similar to our own, have them speak, and bestow upon them our own cultural attributes and motives. Babies are urged to walk bipedally erect because only nonhumans move on all fours. Parents continually speak to their children, eliciting speech responses from them. Recent controversies over the use of life-support machines center on the common belief that when the brain stops functioning, the individual no longer exists. Contemporary arguments over the morality of abortion focus on that time when the fetus attains human status. Understanding the concept of "human" is not without consequence.

Whatever theoretical or philosophical approach we take, if we ignore the four basic attributes of "humanness"—bipedalism, a large and complex brain, language, and a cultural lifestyle—we ignore a construct that consciously and unconsciously permeates our daily activities and attitudes. These criteria, however, cannot be forced into a strict interpretative framework because they exhibit a wide range of variability. What is "human," as opposed to what is *Homo sapiens,* may fall outside the scientific realm and depend on personal views. Scientific inquiry serves to define and elucidate the most relevant parameters of what makes us "human."

PROSPECTS FOR CONTINUING EVOLUTION

In order to cast our eyes to our evolutionary future, we must observe the course set in the past. Two extreme views of human evolution, one a fairly straight line of evolutionary change, the other a "bushy" phylogeny with many branches, are depicted in Figure 14-1. The truth of our past evolutionary path probably lies somewhere between these two views. At present it is not possible to decide on an accurate phylogeny. New fossil finds will clarify some issues and undoubtedly lead to other perplexing surprises.

The discrepancies in interpretation of hominid evolution are not without consequence. The mode of species origins and differentiation, among hominids and other life forms as well, bears on questions of what will become of life on this planet. Will humans continue to evolve and adapt, or has the evolutionary process within our species come to a conclusion? Will the rapid rate of extinction

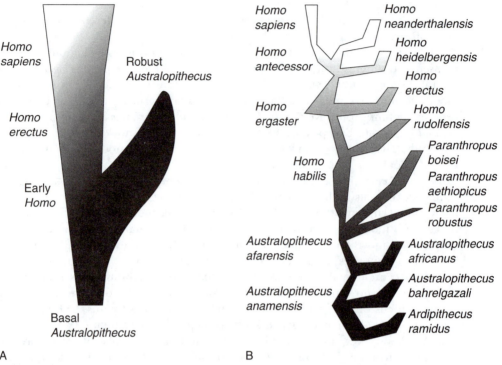

FIGURE 14-1 Two extreme views of hominid phylogeny. *A,* A gradualist perspective with little evolutionary branching; *B,* A punctuated view with numerous speciations. (Courtesy Jeffrey K. McKee.)

that characterizes the Holocene continue, and ultimately include *Homo sapiens,* or is life rapidly evolving to fill the void?

It sometimes appears that human evolution has ceased. There are visible changes in our populations, such as increases in height and longevity, but these are not evolutionary trends; they are **secular trends** that are a consequence of changes in our diets and lifestyles. In looking at the prospects for continued human evolution, the first question to answer is whether or not we have biologically reached an evolutionary optimum, a veritable pinnacle of success with the species *Homo sapiens,* leaving no room for improvement through natural selection. From the perspective of functional anatomy, the answer is an unqualified no. Krogman (1951) articulated such a view in his article "The Scars of Human Evolution," in which he looked at the maladaptations that were a consequence of our peculiar evolutionary path.

Bipedalism is the hallmark of hominid evolution, but the architectural shift to an orthograde posture left us with a somewhat poor "design." For example, the vertebral column of a quadrupedal mammal is a strong and sure biological construction. In changing its orientation for our hominid stance, evolution left us with an S-shaped vertebral column that is adequate but weak. The lower-back pains we often suffer, along with slipped disks, are a consequence.

Krogman listed numerous unfortunate biological consequences of our evolution, from varicose veins and hemorrhoids to impacted teeth. Perhaps the most serious malady comes from the mismatch of a bipedal pelvis with an enlarged head, making the birth process extremely difficult and sometimes not possible without surgical intervention.

With Krogman's perspective, we humans have the potential for further adaptations, subject to the rules of natural selection and the other forces of evolution. We also have new conditions to which we may need to adapt, many of which are of our own making: environmental toxins, increased solar radiation from ozone depletion, and decreased food and natural resources for a growing population. Our very culture requires either behavioral or evolutionary adaptations; in most animal species, limitations of food and other natural resources often lead to increased aggression (Poirier, 1974). Humans, however, have a degree of choice in their responses to environmental pressures.

The question of our future evolution is largely one of evolutionary mechanisms: whether a global, cultural species can evolve or becomes evolutionarily static, and by what means the evolution may proceed. On this question we can learn from varied interpretations of the fossil record. Those who construct a "bushy" phylogeny tend to hold to the theory of punctuated equilibrium. In this view, large populations of species remain static through time. New species would arise from small, isolated populations, perhaps having been cut off from the parent species by environmental change. The speciation would be relatively quick, largely a product of changes through genetic drift, and little morphological change would follow the speciation event. If this were the case, then there is little chance for further human evolution. Our population of about 6 billion people is seen as being too large and too mobile for isolates to break off as new species. Furthermore, the concept of genetic inertia implies that new genetic variants would be swamped by existing variation and have little chance of spreading throughout the population.

An alternative view sees human evolution as a continuous process, with little branching. This concept of evolution relies more on natural selection in large populations than on the speciation process among small populations. Large populations have considerable genetic variability, constantly replenished with new mutant alleles. The chance effects of genetic drift are less likely, so fewer adaptive variants are lost. As long as there is differential reproduction among those carrying the variants, natural selection would take its course. In this scenario, the current human population is poised for significant evolution—toward what kind of descendant we do not know.

It is interesting to speculate about the future of our species, but it is probably of more immediate concern to understand the evolutionary process as it applies to other species. Our evolutionary success and adaptability to environments across the globe has had a detrimental effect on many other species. For the past 10,000 years, and perhaps for much longer, human activity has contributed to the extinction of many species. This is due not only to hunting, but also to the displacement of other life forms as we moved into and took over their habitats—or replaced native species with the new life forms we created through domestication. The planet is now going through an extinction phase that is unparalleled since the last of the great extinctions some 65 million years ago that led to the demise of most dinosaurs (Chapter 3).

Under a view of evolution in which new species arise from adaptations of large populations, it appears that the extinction process will continue as populations of plants and animals dwindle and cannot adapt to the human-imposed environmental conditions. If this leads to the collapse of entire ecosystems, the repercussions for us will be severe—eventually our resources will become very limited as well. If, on the other hand, small isolated populations evolve quickly, then the Earth should rebound quickly with a host of new species. Again, we do not know which direction these evolutionary events may take for plant and animal species; it may be a direction to which the human population will have to adapt. But even if one takes this view of evolution, the current extinction rate may outpace rapid evolution and lead to ecological collapse.

The legacy of our human evolutionary past has been one of unparalleled evolutionary success, due to remarkable behavioral adaptability born of our expanded brains. The legacy we leave for the future will depend on how well we choose to adapt to the predicament we have brought upon this planet.

Glossary

Acheulian handaxe Lower Paleolithic Old World tool type usually associated with *H. erectus*.

adaptation Result of natural selection acting on a variable gene pool to produce a population capable of efficient interaction with the environment.

adaptive radiation Branching out from a basic form to meet diversified ecological niches—basic feature in early evolutionary stages of new forms.

allele Variant of a gene at a particular gene locus.

allometry Referring to the fact that growth in some parts of the body is related to growth in other parts.

amino acid racemization Chronometric dating technique, which has practical range of up to 100,000 years.

anagenesis Evolution of one species from another of the same lineage; phyletic evolution.

analogous structures Functionally similar structures in nonrelated forms, for example, butterfly and bird's wings.

ancestral characteristics Inherited adaptations from a form's ancestors.

Anthropoidea The suborder of Primates, including living and fossil higher primates: the New and Old World monkeys, apes, and hominids. This category excludes the prosimians, which belong to the suborder Prosimii.

apomorphy A unique derived trait of a population or species.

arboreal Tree dwelling.

artifact Cultural remains, often tool remains.

ascending ramus Vertical branch of mandible or lower jaw.

auditory aperture (or meatus) External ear opening.

bicuspid Pertaining to the presence of two cusps; a characteristic of hominid premolar teeth, especially the first lower premolar (P_3), distinguishing it from the unicuspid (sectorial) premolar of monkeys and apes.

bifacial flaking Taking flakes from both sides of a tool.

binomial The official scientific name of an organism.

biodiversity The amount of variation among organisms in an ecosystem; usually measured as number of species.

bipedal Walking erect on the hind legs.

B.P. Abbreviation for "before present." The "present" for all B.P. dates is 1950.

brachiation Locomotor mode referring to swinging beneath branches by the arms; characteristic especially of modern gibbons.

breccia A sedimentary rock with bone and stone fragments, such as found in ancient cave fills.

burin Chisel-edged artifact for incising and cutting bone, wood, ivory, etc. Found in Mousterian, Upper Paleolithic, and later sites.

canine diastema Gap between the mandibular canine and premolar teeth to accommodate the projecting canine from the opposite jaw.

ceboid New World monkey.

cercopithecoid Pertaining to Old World monkeys; Cercopithecoidea is the superfamily of Old World monkeys.

cerebellum Section of the hindbrain that maintains equilibrium, most importantly with learned hand movements.

chopper Crude, heavy, unifacial and bifacial general-purpose stone tool.

chronometric dating Determination of an age, in years, of a specimen or geological formation.

cingulum Enamel ring around part or all of the base of a tooth crown.

clade Group of a species sharing a single common ancestor.

cladogenesis Splitting of one lineage into two.

classification A formal system used to relate organisms to one another and place them into related groups.

clavicle Bone connecting the sternum, or breastbone, with the scapula, or shoulder blade. Functions to keep the shoulders off the chest.

Clovis point Earliest fluted-point tradition in New World.

convergence Dissimilar, unrelated lineages evolving superficially similar structures.

cranial capacity Referring to brain size. The figure is given in cubic centimeters.

cranium Part of the skull enclosing the brain, also referred to as the *braincase*.

cusps Elevations on the crowns of the premolar and molar teeth, the shape, disposition, and number of which are important taxonomic diagnostic traits.

deciduous Refers to the first set, or temporary, teeth.

dental formula Count of the different teeth. In most Old World primates the count is 2-1-2-3: 2 incisors, 1 canine, 2 premolars, and 3 molars on each side of each jaw.

derived character Characteristic resulting from recent adaptations.

directional selection Natural selection toward one end of the range of variation.

disruptive selection Natural selection against the average form, simultaneously toward opposite ends of the range of variation, as in sexual dimorphism.

diurnal Day living vs. nocturnal, or night living.

encephalization quotient A measure of brain size relative to body size, calculated as the ratio of brain size to the expected brain size for an animal of a particular weight.

endocranial cast Cast of the interior of the skull. The cast represents the brain's shape and, to some degree, its surface.

Eocene Second Cenozoic geological epoch.

ethnoarchaeology Use of living populations to reconstruct the past.

femur Upper leg bone.

fibula Smaller of the two lower leg bones.

fission-track dating Method of dating volcanic substances.

Folsom tradition Second fluted-point tradition in the New World.

foramen magnum Skull opening through which the spinal cord passes. The position of the foramen magnum on the skull helps determine whether an animal was quadrupedal or bipedal.

fossil Remains or imprints of plants or animals that once existed.

fossiliferous Containing fossil materials.

frontal bone Bone forming the forehead.

frugivorous Feeding on fruit.

gene flow Hybridization of populations having different gene pools.

gene mutation Change in a gene or chromosome resulting in the spontaneous appearance of a new genetic expression.

generalized Animal or organ not specifically adapted to any given environment or task; the ability to function in a number of ways or in a number of environments.

genetic drift Sampling error changing allele frequencies in small populations.

genus Taxonomic category larger than the species and smaller than the family. A genus may include a number of species; a number of genera form a family.

glaciation The covering of high-latitude landmasses by ice, particularly during "ice ages."

habitat The area in which a species lives.

half-life The length of time during which half the original atoms in a C^{14}-dated sample decay.

handaxe Superficially flaked core tool probably used as one of the first formal implements.

herbivorous Feeding on buds and leaves, vegetable matter only.

heterodontism Differentiation of teeth for different functions.

homeothermy Maintenance of a constant body temperature.

hominid Living or fossil member of the family Hominidae.

hominoid Referring to members of the families Hominidae and Pongidae. Pertains to the taxonomic superfamily of Hominoidea.

homologous structures Structures that indicate a close evolutionary relationship among the forms that share them. The similarities are traceable to common descent.

humerus Upper arm bone.

ilium Uppermost part of the innominate (pelvis).

insectivorous Feeding on insects.

ischial callosities Hairless area about the buttocks found on Old World monkeys and some apes.

ischium Lowermost portion of innominate bone.

knuckle-walking Walking on the knuckles, as do modern chimpanzees and gorillas.

Levallois technique Method of tool manufacture in which a core is percussion flaked to a desired shape, and a large flake of predetermined form is struck from the core.

living floors Areas of intense activity within a hominid fossil site.

macroevolution Evolutionary changes leading to the rise and divergence of genetically related populations.

mandible Lower jaw.

manuports Exotic material carried into a human fossiliferous site; often refers to unworked stones.

masseter muscle Large muscle of the lower jaw that is important for mastication (chewing).

mastoid Referring to the projection from the temporal bone behind the ear.

megaevolution Temporary state of rapid evolutionary change.

Messinian salinity crisis A climatic event beginning about 6 mya and culminating about 5.3 mya when the Mediterranean Sea became isolated from the other oceans and began to dry into a barren land.

microevolution Small changes within a potentially continuous population.

microlith Small blade, an inch or less in length, used alone or with a handle. Becomes abundant in the Mesolithic.

Miocene Fourth geological epoch of the Cenozoic era.

molecular clock The supposition that neutral mutations accumulate at a stochastically regular rate and can be used to date times of taxic divergence.

morphology Referring to structure or form.

mosaic evolution Evolution of different body parts at differing rates over time.

Mousterian Cultural assemblage commonly associated with the Neandertals.

mtDNA The DNA found in the mitochondrion, inherited only from one's mother.

natural selection The theory of Darwin and Wallace that individuals with the greatest fitness (ability to survive and reproduce) will have the greatest chance of passing their genes to the next generation; a fundamental tenet of Darwinian evolution.

niche The role a species plays in an ecological system.

nomenclature Act of assigning names to the groups that are recognized in a classification scheme.

nuchal Pertaining to the back of the skull.

occipital Rearmost part of the skull.

occipital torus Raised portion on the occipital bone.

Oldowan Toolmaking tradition in which pebbles are crudely percussion-flaked to form an irregular cutting edge on one side. The modified tool is a general, all-purpose tool.

olfactory Referring to the sense of smell.

Oligocene Third geological epoch of the Cenozoic era.

omnivorous Method of feeding that includes ingestion of various foodstuffs; a diet not specialized for one food source.

opposable Ability to rotate a digit out of the plane of others, allowing it to be opposed into a grasping movement.

orthognathic Referring to a vertically straight, flat face; opposite of prognathic.

osteodontokeratic culture Dart's claim for a bone, tooth, and antler culture for the australopithecines; this preceded a stone tool culture.

paedomorphism Retention of infantile traits into adulthood.

Paleocene First geological epoch of the Cenozoic era.

paleoecology The study of prehistoric environments and ecological relationships.

paleomagnetic dating One of several forms of relative dating.

palynology Analysis of fossil pollen and spores; very helpful for reconstructing past ecological conditions.

parallelism Related species independently acquire similar lifeways and come to resemble each other in special adaptations.

parietal Two bones on either side of the top of the skull.

pebble tools Crudely worked early stone tools associated with early hominid deposits.

pentadactyly Having five fingers and five toes on each hand and foot.

percussion flaking Use of a stone as a hammer to chip off flakes on one or two sides of another stone.

phenotype Observable characteristics of an organism collectively that result from its heredity and its environment.

phyletic evolution The evolution of one species from another of the same lineage; anagenesis.

phyletic tree Branching diagram representing evolutionary relationships.

phytolith Fossilized wood and plant matter.

placenta In placental mammals, the embryo produces a tissue, the placenta, which permits fluid exchange between a mother and developing infant.

Plano tradition Late Paleo-Indian tradition in the New World.

platycephaly Flattening of top of the skull; characteristic of *Homo erectus*.

Pleistocene Sixth geological epoch of the Cenozoic era.

plesiomorphy An ancestral trait of a population or species, descended from preceding species.

Pliocene Fifth geological epoch of the Cenozoic era.

pluvials Periods of increasing rainfall.

pongid Referring to the apes.

postorbital bar Bone enclosure at the rear of the eye orbit; diagnostic characteristic of most living and fossil primates.

postorbital constriction Constriction of the cranium behind the brow ridges.

potassium-argon (K/Ar) dating Method of chronometric dating of volcanically derived material.

power grip Grip used in wielding an object such as a hammer forcefully; the thumb and forefingers are not opposed.

precision grip Grip used in holding small objects such as a pen by opposing thumb and forefingers.

prepared core Form obtained by removal of small flakes from the entire surface of the rock. This allowed more cutting edge in less time from less stone, as well as manufacture of a more standardized tool.

procumbent Jutting forward of the front teeth, particularly the incisors.

prognathism Forward protrusion of the lower face.

prosimian A member of the taxonomic suborder Prosimii, which includes all fossil and living lemurs, lorises, and galagos.

punctuated equilibrium Model of evolutionary change in which long periods of stasis alternate with briefer periods of rapid evolution stimulated by speciation.

radius Lower arm bone on the thumb side of the arm.

relative dating Dating method that establishes a chronological sequence from oldest to most recent.

sagittal crest Strut of bone across the top of the skull from front to back to which the temporalis muscles attach.

sectorial premolar Unicuspid premolar; characteristic of the lower first premolar of all primates excepting humans. The sectorial premolar accommodates the projecting canine from the opposing jaw.

secular trends Temporal changes in morphology and physiology due to development rather than evolution.

serrate roots A pattern of molar roots in which the mesial (front) roots are longer than the distal (back) roots, and the distal roots are angled in a distal direction.

sexual dimorphism Marked differences in the characteristics of males and females.

sites Locations, often of varying sizes, where traces of occupation or activity are found.

soft-hammer technique Wood, bone, or antler used instead of rock to chip flakes from a core. Allowed more control over length, width, and thickness of flake removed.

specialization Close adaptation of an animal or organ to a way of life or function. It limits evolutionary possibilities.

species Taxonomic category below the genus; theoretically members breed with one another but not with members of another species.

stabilizing selection Natural selection for the average or norm of variation in a population.

stereoscopic (binocular) vision Ability to merge visual images from both eyes; allows three-dimensional or depth perception.

stratigraphy Sequence of geological strata and/or the study of sequence.

subspecies Subdivision of a species, consisting of individuals in a given geographical area, which differs slightly from, but which can interbreed with, other subspecies of the same species.

supraorbital torus Development of heavy bony ridges above the eyes, also referred to as *brow ridges*.

symplesiomorphy Sharing of ancestral traits in common.

synapomorphic features Shared derived features identifying a monophyletic group.

systematics Scientific study of the types and diversity of living organisms and of the relationships among them.

T-complex Dental traits that C. Jolly relates to dietary adaptation.

taphonomy Study of groups of fossils deposited together, as well as the processes of deposition.

taurodontism Referring to an enlarged molar root cavity and perhaps root fusion of the molar teeth.

taxon (pl. taxa) A group containing members that are evolutionarily related.

taxonomy Science of the classification of living forms in a manner best suited to show their relationship to each other.

temporal Lateral skull bones; bones comprising the side of the head.

tibia Larger of the two bones in the lower leg.

tufa A limestone accretion formed by the precipitation of calcium carbonate; caves such as those at Taung may form in tufa.

tuff A rock formed by compaction of volcanic sediments.

turnover-pulse hypothesis The notion that climatic change causes a simultaneous surge in speciation, extinction, immigration, and emigration among many taxa of plants and animals.

type specimen The specimen with which all subsequent finds of that type are compared.

ulna Lower arm bone of the little finger side of the hand.

vertebrate Animal possessing a spinal column.

Villafranchian fauna Faunal assemblage marking the beginning of the Pleistocene; the assemblage includes representatives of modern genera of horses, elephants, and cattle.

viviparous Giving birth to live young rather than laying eggs.

zygomatic arches The bone from which the masseter muscle originates.

zygote A fertilized egg.

Bibliography

CHAPTER 1

AITKEN, M. 1961. *Physics and Archaeology.* New York: Interscience.

ANDREWS, P. 1991. *Owls, Caves and Fossils.* Chicago: University of Chicago Press.

BADA, J., R. SCHROEDER, AND G. CARTER. 1974. New evidence for the antiquity of man in North America deduced from aspartic acid racemization. *Science* 184:791.

BEHRENSMEYER, A. 1984. Taphonomy and the fossil record. *American Scientist* 72:558–567.

BROCK, A., AND G. ISAAC. 1974. Paleomagnetic stratigraphy and chronology of hominid-bearing sediments east of Lake Rudolf, Kenya. *Nature* 247:344.

BROOKS, A. AND OTHERS. 1990. Dating Pleistocene archaeological sites by protein diagenesis in ostrich eggshell. *Science* 248:60–64.

BROTHWELL, D., AND E. HIGGS, EDS. 1970. *Science in Archaeology.* New York: Praeger.

BUTZER, K. 1964. *Environment and Archaeology: An Introduction to Pleistocene Geography.* Chicago: Aldine-Atherton.

COX, A., G. DALRYMPLE, AND R. DOELL. 1967. Reversals of the earth's magnetic field. *Scientific American* 216:44.

DIMBLEBY, G. 1970. Pollen analysis. In *Science in Archaeology*, ed. D. Brothwell and E. Higgs. New York: Praeger.

FLEISCHER, R., L. LEAKEY, P. PRICE, AND R. WALKER. 1965. Fission-track dating of Bed I, Olduvai Gorge. *Current Anthropology* 6:389.

FLEISCHER, R., P. PRICE, AND R. WALKER. 1970. Quaternary dating by the fission track technique. In *Science in Archaeology*, ed. D. Brothwell and E. Higgs, New York: Praeger.

GIBBONS, A. 1992. Following a trail of old ostrich eggshells. *Science* 256:1281–1282.

GIBBONS, A. 1997. Doubts over spectacular dates. *Science* 278:220–222.

GROMME, C., AND R. HAY. 1963. Magnetization of basalt, Bed I, Olduvai Gorge, Tanganyika. *Nature* 200:560.

GROOTES, P. 1978. Carbon-14 time scale extended: Comparison of chronologies. *Science* 200: 11–15.

HIGGS, E. 1970. Fauna. In *Science in Archaeology*, ed. D. Brothwell and E. Higgs. New York: Praeger.

KAPPELMAN, J. 1993. The attraction of paleomagnetism. *Evolutionary Anthropology* 2:89–99.

KOMINZ, M., AND N. PISIAS. 1979. Pleistocene climate: Deterministic or stochastic? *Science* 204:171–173.

LEAKEY, M. 1975. A summary and discussion of the archaeological evidence from Bed I and Bed II, Olduvai Gorge, Tanzania. In *Human Origins: Louis Leakey and the East African Evidence*, ed. G. Isaac and E. McCown: Menlo Park, CA: W.A. Benjamin.

LIBBY, W. 1955. *Radiocarbon Dating.* Chicago: University of Chicago Press.

MARSHALL, E. 1990. Paleoanthropology gets physical. *Science* 247:798–801.

MERRILL, R., AND P. MCFADDEN. 1990. Paleomagnetism and the nature of the geodynamo. *Science* 248:345–350.

MUSSETT, A., T. REILLY, AND P. RAJA. 1965. Paleomagnetism in East Africa. In *East Africa Rift System: Report of the Upper Mantle Committee—UNESCO Seminar*, Nairobi, 1965, Nairobi, University College, part II.

OAKLEY, K. 1953. Dating fossil human remains. In *Anthropology Today*, ed. A. Kroeber. Chicago: Aldine-Atherton.

OAKLEY, K. 1966. *Frameworks for Dating Fossil Man.* Chicago: Aldine-Atherton.

OAKLEY, K. 1970. Analytical methods of dating bones. In *Science in Archaeology*, ed. D. Brothwell and E. Higgs. New York: Praeger.

PARTRIDGE, T., B. WOOD, AND P. DE MENOCAL. 1995. The influence of global climatic change and regional uplift on large-mammalian evolution in East and Southern Africa. In *Paleoclimate and Evolution, with an Emphasis on Human Origins*, ed. E. Vrba, G. Denton, T. Partridge, and L. Burcke. New Haven; Yale University Press.

PETERHAUS, J., R. WRANGHMAN, M. CARTER, AND M. HAUSER. 1993. A contribution to tropical rainforest demography: Retrieval and documentation of chimpanzee remains from Kibale Forest, Uganda. *Journal of Human Evolution* 26:485–514.

PRICE, P., AND R. WALKER. 1963. A simple method of measuring how uranium concentrates in natural crystals. *Applied Physics Letters* 2:23.

RENFREW, C. 1971. Carbon 14 and the prehistory of Europe. Reprinted in *Avenues to Antiquity* (1975), ed. B. Fagan. San Francisco: W.H. Freeman & Co.

SHUEY, R., F. BROWN, AND M. CROSE. 1974. Magnetostratigraphy of the Shungura Formation, Southwestern Ethiopia: Fine structure of the Lower Matuyama Polarity epoch. *Earth and Planetary Science Letters* 23:249–260.

STRUVER, M., C. HEUSSER, AND I. YANG. 1978. North American Glacial History extended to 75,000 years ago. *Science* 200:16–20.

WAGNER, G. 1996. Fisson-track dating in paleoanthropology. *Evolutionary Anthropology* 5:165–171.

WILLIS, E. 1970. Radiocarbon dating. In *Science in Archaeology*, ed. D. Brothwell and E. Higgs. New York: Praeger.

ZEUNER, F. 1958. *Dating the Past.* London: Methuen & Co. Ltd.

CHAPTER 2

ASHLOCK, P. 1974. The uses of cladistics. *Annual Review of Ecology and Systematics* 5:81–99.

BRACE, C.L. 1981. Tales of the phylogenetic woods: The evolution and significance of evolutionary trees. *American Journal of Physical Anthropology* 56:411–429.

CLARK, W.L.G. 1967. *The Fossil Evidence for Human Evolution: An Introduction to the Study of Paleoanthropology.* Chicago: University of Chicago Press.

CRONIN, J., N. BOAZ, C. STRINGER, AND Y. RAK. 1981. Tempo and mode in hominid evolution. *Nature* 292:113–122.

DARLINGTON, P. 1970. A practical criticism of Hennig-Brundin "Phylogenetic Systematics": And Antarctic biogeography. *Systematic Zoology* 19:1–18.

ECKHARDT, R. 1972. Population genetics and human origins. *Scientific American*, January: 94.

ELDREDGE, N., AND I. TATTERSALL. 1982. *The Myths of Human Evolution.* New York: Columbia University Press.

GODFREY, L., AND J. MARKS. 1991. The nature and origins of primate species. *Yearbook of Physical Anthropology* 34:39–68.

GOULD, S. 1974. The evolutionary significance of "bizarre" structures: Antler size and skull size in the "Irish Elk," *Megaloceros giganteus. Evolution* 28:191–220.

GOULD, S. 1984. Smooth curve of evolutionary rate: A psychological and mathematical artifact. *Science* 226:994–995.

GOULD, S. J., AND N. ELDREDGE. 1993. Punctuated equilibrium comes of age. *Nature* 366:223–227.

HARRISON, G., AND J. WEINER. 1963. Some considerations in the formulation of theories of human phylogeny. In *Classification and Human Evolution*, ed. S. Washburn. New York: Viking Fund Publications.

HENNING, W. 1966. *Phylogenetic Systematics.* Urbana: University of Illinois Press.

HUXLEY, J., ED. 1940. *The New Systematics.* London: Oxford University Press.

LEVINGTON, J., AND C. SIMON. 1980. A critique of the punctuated equilibria model and implications for the detection of speciation in the fossil record. *Systematic Zoology* 29:130–142.

LEWIN, R. 1980. Evolutionary theory under fire. *Science* 210:883–887.

LEWIN, R. 1986. Recognizing ancestors is a species problem. *Science* 234:1500.

MAYR, E. 1942. *Systematics and the Origin of Species.* New York: Columbia University Press.

MAYR, E. 1969. *Principles of Systematic Zoology.* Cambridge, MA: Belknap Press.

MAYR, E. 1970. *Populations, Species and Evolution.* Cambridge, MA: Belknap Press.

SCHULTZ, A. 1963. Age changes, sex differences, and variability as factors in the classification of primates. In *Classification and Human Evolution*, ed. S. Washburn. New York: Viking Fund Publications.

SCHWARTZ, J., I. TATTERSALL, AND N. ELDREDGE. 1978. Phylogeny and classification of the primates revisited. *Yearbook of Physical Anthropology* 21:95–133.

SIMPSON, G. 1951. *The Meaning of Evolution.* New York: New American Library.

SIMPSON, G. 1961. *Principles of Animal Taxonomy.* New York: Columbia University Press.

SNEATH, P. AND R. SOKAL. 1973. *Numerical Taxonomy.* San Francisco: W.H. Freeman.

SOKAL, R. AND P. SNEATH. 1963. *Principles of Numerical Taxonomy.* San Francisco: W.H. Freeman.

SPENCER, F. 1990. *Piltdown: A Scientific Forgery.* London: Oxford University Press.

STANLEY, S. 1979. *Macroevolution: Pattern and Process.* San Francisco: W.H. Freeman.

STANLEY, S. 1981. *Fossils, Genes and the Origin of Species.* New York: Basic Books.

STEBBINS, G., AND F. AYALA. 1981. Is a new evolutionary synthesis necessary? *Science* 213:967–971.

TATTERSALL, I. 1986. Species recognition in human paleontology. *Journal of Human Evolution* 15:165–175.

TOBIAS, P. 1992. Piltdown: An appraisal of the case against Sir Arthur Keith. *Current Anthropology* 33:243–293.

TOBIAS, P. 1994. Piltdown unmasked. *The Sciences.* 38–43.

VRBA, E. 1980. Evolution, species and fossils: How does life evolve? *South African Journal of Science* 76:61–84.

WILLIAMS, B.J. 1987. Rates of evolution: Is there a conflict between neo-Darwinian evolutionary theory and the fossil record? *American Journal of Physical Anthropology* 73:99–110.

CHAPTER 3

BRUCE, E., AND F. AYALA. 1978. Humans and apes are genetically very similar. *Nature* 276:264–265.

CLARK, W. LE GROS. 1970. *The Antecedents of Man.* Chicago: Quadrangle Books.

DE RICQLES, A. 1974. Evolution of endothermy: Histological evidence. *Evolutionary Theory* 1:51–58.

DESMOND, A. 1975. Hot-Blooded Dinosaurs: A revolution in Paleontology. New York: Dial Press.

FITCH, W. 1976. Molecular evolutionary clocks. In *Molecular Evolution*, ed. F. Ayala. Sunderlands, MA: Sinauer Associates.

GIBBONS, A. 1990. Our chimp cousins get that much closer. *Science* 250:176.

GOODMAN, M. 1975. Protein sequence and immunological specificity. In *Phylogeny of Primates*, ed. F. Luckett and F. Szalay. New York: Plenum Press.

GOODMAN, M., R. TASHIAN, AND J. TASHIAN, EDS. 1976. Molecular Anthropology: Genes and Proteins in the Evolutionary Ascent of the Primates. New York: Plenum Press.

HU, Y., Y. WANG, Z. LUO, AND C. LI. 1997. A new symmetrodont mammal from China and its implications for mammal evolution. *Nature* 390:137–142.

HUXLEY, T. 1872. *Evidence as to Man's Place in Nature.* New York: Appleton.

JOLLY, A. 1985. The evolution of primate behavior. *American Scientist* 73:230–239.

KEMP, T. 1982. *Mammal-like Reptiles and the Origin of Mammals*, New York: Academic Press.

KERR, R. 1998. Pushing back the origins of mammals. *Science* 279:803–804.

KOHNE, D. 1970. Evolution of higher organism DNA. *Quarterly Review of Biophysics* 3:327.

LAURIN, M., AND R. REISZ. 1990. *Tetraceratops* is the oldest known therapsid. *Nature* 345:249–250.

LEWIN, R. 1984. DNA reveals surprises in human family tree. *Science* 226:1179–1182.

LEWIN, R. 1987. My close cousin the chimpanzee. *Science* 238:273–275.

MAHANEY, M., AND P. SCIULLI. 1983. Hominid-pongid affinities: A multivariate analysis of hominoid odontometrics. *Current Anthropology* 23:382–387.

MARKS, J. 1991. What's old and new in molecular phylogenetics. *American Journal of Physical Anthropology* 85:207–219.

MARKS, J., C. SCHMID, AND V. SARICH. 1988. DNA hybridization as a guide to phylogeny: Relations of the Hominidae. *Journal of Human Evolution* 17:769–786.

McALISTER, A. 1968. *The History of Life*. Englewood Cliffs, NJ: Prentice Hall.

MUJAMOTO, M., J. SLIGHTOM, AND M. GOODMAN. 1987. Phylogenetic relations of humans and African apes from DNA sequences in the ψ η-Globin region. *Science* 238:369–373.

RACLE, F. 1979. *Introduction to Evolution*. Englewood Cliffs, NJ: Prentice Hall.

READ, D., AND P. LESTEL. 1970. Hominid phylogeny and immunology: A critical appraisal. *Science* 168:578.

REISZ, R., AND M. HEATON. 1980. Origin of mammal-like reptiles. *Nature* 288:193.

RICH, A. ET AL. 1997. A tribosphenic mammal from the Mesozoic of Australia. *Science* 278:1438–1442.

ROMER, A. 1970. *The Vertebrate Body*. Philadelphia: Saunders.

SARICH, V. 1971. A molecular approach to the question of human origins. In *Background for Man*, ed. P. Dolhinow and V. Sarich. Boston: Little, Brown.

SCHWARTZ, J. 1984. Hominoid evolution: A reassessment. *Current Anthropology* 25:655–672.

SCHWARTZ, J. 1987. *The Red Ape: Orang-utans and Human Origins*. Boston: Houghton Mifflin.

SEUANEZ, H. 1979. *The Phylogeny of Human Chromosomes*. Berlin: Springer-Verlag.

THOMAS, R., AND E. OLSON, EDS. 1980. *A Cold Look at the Warm-Blooded Dinosaurs*. Boulder, CO: Westview Press.

WASHBURN, S., AND R. MOORE. 1980. *Ape into Human*, 2nd ed. Boston: Little, Brown.

WEISS, M. 1987. Nucleic acid evidence bearing on hominoid relationships. *American Journal of Physical Anthropology* 30:41–73.

WILSON, M., AND A. WILSON 1975. Similar amino acid sequences in *Pan* and *Homo*. *Science* 188:107.

WUETHRICH, B. 1997. Will fossil from down under upend mammal evolution? *Science* 278:1401–1402.

YUNISH, J., AND G. PRAKASH. 1982. The origin of man: A chromosomal pictorial legacy. *Science* 215:1525–1529.

CHAPTER 4

BADRIAN, A., AND N. BADRIAN. 1984. Social organization of *Pan paniscus* in the Lomako Forest, Zaire. In *The Pygmy Chimpanzee: Evolutionary Morphology and Behavior*, ed. R.L. Susman. New York: Plenum Press.

BIRDSELL, J. 1972. *Human Evolution*. Chicago: Rand McNally.

BOESCH-ACHERMANN, H., AND C. BOESCH. 1994. Hominization in the rainforest: The chimpanzee's piece of the puzzle. *Evolutionary Anthropology* 3:9–16.

BOESCH, C., AND H. BOESCH. 1983. Optimization of nutcracking with natural hammers by wild chimpanzees. *Behaviour* 83:265–286.

BOESCH, C., AND H. BOESCH. 1984. Possible causes of sex differences in the use of natural hammers by wild chimpanzees. *Journal of Human Evolution* 13:415–440.

BOESCH, C., AND H. BOESCH. 1989. Hunting behavior of wild chimpanzees in the Tai National Park. *American Journal of Physical Anthropology* 78:547–573.

BOESCH C., AND H. BOESCH-ACHERMANN. 1991. Dim forest, bright chimps. *Natural History*, September: 50–56.

FEDIGAN, L. 1982. Primate Paradigms: Sex Roles and Social Bonds. St. Albans, VT: Eden Press.

FREEMAN, L. 1968. A theoretical framework for interpreting archaeological materials. In *Man the Hunter*, ed. R. Lee and I. DeVore. Chicago: Aldine-Atherton.

GALDIKAS, B. 1996. *Reflections of Eden*. New York: Little, Brown.

GHIGLIERI, M. 1985. The social ecology of chimpanzees. *Scientific American*, June: 102–113.

GIBBONS, A. 1992. Chimps: More diverse than a barrel of monkeys. *Science* 255:287–288.

GIFFORD, D. 1980. Ethnoarchaeological contributions to the taphonomy of human sites. In *Fossils in the Making: Vertebrate Taphonomy and Paleoecology*, ed. A. Behrensmeyer and A. Hill. Chicago: University of Chicago Press.

GOODALL, J. 1964. Tool-using and aimed throwing in a community of free-living chimpanzees. *Nature* 201:1264–1266.

GOODALL, J. 1979. Life and death at Gombe. *National Geographic* 155:592–620.

GOODALL, J. 1986. *The Chimpanzees of Gombe: Patterns of Behavior*. Cambridge: The Belknap Press of Harvard University Press.

GOULD, R. 1968a. Chipping stones in the outback. *Natural History* 68:83.

GOULD, R. 1968b. Living archaeology: The Ngatatjara of western Australia. *Southwestern Journal of Anthropology* 24:210.

GOULD, R. 1969. *Yiwara: Foragers of the Australian Desert*. New York: Charles Scribner's Sons.

HASEGAWA, T., M. HIRAIWA, T. NISHIDA, AND H. TAKASAKI. 1983. New evidence on scavenging behavior in wild chimpanzees. *Current Anthropology* 24:231–232.

INGMANSON, E., AND H. IHOBE. 1992. Predation and meat eating by *Pan paniscus* at Wamba, Zaire. *American Journal of Physical Anthropology*, Suppl. 14:93.

JAY, P. C., ED. 1968. *Primates: Studies in Adaptation and Variability*. New York: Holt, Rinehart & Winston.

JOLLY, C. 1970. The seed-eaters: A new model of hominid differentiation based on a baboon analogy. *Man* 5:5–26.

JONES, C., AND J. SABATER PI. 1969. Sticks used by chimpanzees in Rio Muni, West Africa. *Nature* 223:100.

KANO, T. 1982. The social group of pygmy chimpanzees (*Pan paniscus*) of Yalosidi, Republic of Zaire. *International Journal Primatology* 4:1–31.

KANO, T. 1990. The bonobos peaceable kingdom, *Natural History*, November: 62–70.

KAWABE, M. 1966. One observed case of hunting behavior among wild chimpanzees living in the savanna woodland of Western Tanzania. *Primates* 7:393.

KINZEY, W., ED. 1987a. *The Evolution of Human Behavior: Primate Models*. Albany: SUNY Press.

KINZEY, W. 1987b. Introduction: In *The Evolution of Human Behavior: Primate Models*, ed. W. Kinzey. Albany: SUNY Press.

KORTLANDT, A. 1965. How do chimpanzees use weapons when fighting leopards? Philadelphia: *Yearbook of the American Philosophical Society*, p. 327.

KORTLANDT, A., AND M. KOOJ. 1963. Protohominid behavior of primates. *Symposium of Zoological Society of London* 10:61.

KURODA, S. 1979. Grouping of pygmy chimpanzees. *Primates* 20:161–183.

KURODA, S. 1980. Social behavior of the pygmy chimpanzees. *Primates* 21:181–197.

LEE, R. 1978. *The !Kung San*. New York: Cambridge University Press.

LEE, R., AND I. DeVORE, EDS. 1968. *Man the Hunter*. Chicago: Aldine-Atherton.

LOVEJOY, C.O. 1981. The origin of man. *Science* 211:341–350.

MacKinnon, J. 1974. The behaviour and ecology of wild orang-utans (*Pongo pygmaeus*). *Animal Behavior* 22:3–74.

McGrew, W.C. 1978. Evolutionary implications of sex differences in chimpanzee predation and tool use. In *The Great Apes*, ed. D. Hamburg and E. McCown. Menlo Park, CA: Benjamin/Cummings.

McGrew, W. 1983. Animal foods in the diets of wild chimpanzees (*Pan troglodytes*): Why cross cultural variation? *J. Ethology* 1:46–61.

McGrew, W. 1991. Chimpanzee material culture: What are its limits and why? In *The Origins of Human Behavior*, ed. R. Foley. London: Unwin and Hyman.

McGrew, W. C., C. Tutin, and P. Baldwin. 1979. New data on meat eating by wild chimpanzees. *Current Anthropology* 20:238–239.

Nishida, T. 1968. The social group of wild chimpanzees in the Mahali Mountains. *Primates* 9:167.

Nishida, T., and S. Uehara. 1980. Chimpanzees, tools and termites: An example from Tanzania. *Current Anthropology* 21:671–672.

O'Neill, G. 1994. Cemetery reveals complex aboriginal society. *Science* 264:1403.

Pfeiffer, J. 1985. *The Emergence of Humankind*. New York: Harper and Row.

Poirier, F. 1969. Behavioral flexibility and intertroop variability among Nilgiri langurs of South India. *Folia primatologica* 11:119–183.

Potts, R. 1987. Reconstructions of early hominid socioecology: A critique of primate models. In *The Evolution of Human Behavior: Primate Models*, ed. W. Kinzey. Albany: SUNY Press.

Pusey, A., J. Williams, and J. Goodall. 1997. The influence of dominance rank on the reproductive success of female chimpanzees. *Science* 277:828–831.

Quiatt, D., and M. Huffman. 1993. On home bases, nesting sites, activity centers and new analytic procedures. *Current Anthropology* 34:68–70.

Rodman, P. 1979. Individual activity pattern and the solitary nature of orangutans. In *The Great Apes*, ed. D. Hamburg and E. McCown. Menlo Park, CA: Benjamin/Cummings.

Schaller, G., and G. Lowther. 1969. The relevance of carnivore behavior to the study of early hominids. *Southwestern Journal of Anthropology* 25:307.

Shea, B. 1983. Paedomorphism and neotony in the pygmy chimpanzee. *Science* 222:521–22.

Stanford, C. 1995. To catch a colobus. *Natural History*, January: 48–54.

Stanford, C., and J. Allen. 1991. On strategic storytelling: Current models of human behavioral evolution. *Current Anthropology* 32:58–61.

Susman, R.L. 1987. Chimpanzees: Pygmy chimpanzees and common chimpanzees: Models for the behavioral ecology of the earliest hominids. In *The Evolution of Human Behavior: Primate Models*, ed. W. Kinzey. Albany: SUNY Press.

Takahata, Y., T. Hasegawa, and T. Nishida. 1984. Chimpanzee predation in the Mahale Mountains from August 1979 to May 1982. *International Journal of Primatology* 5:213–233.

Tanner, N. 1981. *On Becoming Human*. New York: Cambridge University Press.

Teleki, G. 1973a. The omnivorous chimpanzee. *Scientific American* 228:33.

Teleki, G. 1973b. *The Predatory Behavior of Wild Chimpanzees*. Lewisburg, PA: Bucknell University Press.

Teleki, G. 1975. Primate subsistence patterns: Collector-predators and gatherer-hunters. *Journal of Human Evolution* 4:125.

Thompson, P. 1975. A cross-species analysis of carnivore, primate, and hominid behavior. *Journal of Human Evolution* 4:113.

Tooby, J., and I. DeVore 1987. The reconstruction of hominid behavioral evolution through strategic modeling. In *The Evolution of Human Behavior: Primate Models*, ed. W. Kinzey. Albany: SUNY Press.

Toshisada, N., S. Uehara, and N. Ramedhani. 1979. Predatory behavior among wild chimpanzees of the Mahale Mountains. *Primates* 20:1–21.

Toth, N. 1987. The first technology. *Scientific American* 256:112–121.

Tuttle, R. 1990. Apes of the world. *American Scientist* March–April: 115–125.

van Lawick, H., and J. van Lawick-Goodall. 1970. *Innocent Killers*. London: Collins.

van Lawick-Goodall, J. 1971. *In the Shadow of Man*. Boston: Houghton Mifflin.

Washburn, S. 1978. What we can't learn about people from apes. *Human Nature* 1:70–75.

Washburn, S., and I. DeVore. 1961. The social life of baboons. *Scientific American* 204:62–71.

Washburn, S., and R. Moore. 1974. *Ape into Man: A Study of Human Evolution*. Boston: Little, Brown.

White, F. 1996. *Pan paniscus* 1973 to 1996: Twenty-three years of field research. *Evolutionary Anthropology* 5:11–17.

Woodruff, D., and P. Morin. 1995. Geneticists out on a limb. *Natural History*, January: 54.

Wrangham, R. 1997. Subtle, secret female chimpanzees. *Science* 277:774–775.

Zimmer, C. 1995. Tooling through the trees. *Discover*, November: 46–47.

CHAPTER 5

Alexander, J. 1992. Alas, poor *Notharctus*. *Natural History* 8:55–58.

Barth, F. 1950. On the relationships of early primates. *American Journal of Physical Anthropology* 8:139–149.

Beard, C. 1990a. Flying lemurs, primates and fossils. *American Journal of Physical Anthropology* 81:192.

Beard, C. 1990b. Gliding behavior and palaeocology of the alleged primate family Paromomyidae (Mammalia, Dermoptera). *Nature* 345:340–342.

Beard, C., M. Dagosto, D. Gebo, and M. Godinot. 1988. Interrelationships among primate higher taxa. *Nature* 331:712–713.

Beecher, W. 1969. Possible motion detection in the vertebrate middle ear. *Bulletin of the Chicago Academy of Science* 2:155.

Broadfield, D. 1992. Dental microwear and diet in nothartine primates. *American Journal of Physical Anthropology*, Suppl. 14:54.

Cachel, S. 1981. Plate tectonics and the problem of anthropoid origins. *Yearbook of Physical Anthropology* 24:139–172.

Cartmill, M. 1972. Arboreal adaptations and the origins of the order Primates. In *The Functional and Evolutionary Biology of Primates*, ed. R. Tuttle, Chicago: Aldine-Atherton.

Cartmill, M. 1974. Rethinking primate origins. *Science* 184:436–443.

CARTMILL, M. 1975a. Primate evolution: Analyses of trends. *Science* 189:129–133.

CARTMILL, M. 1975b. *Primate Origins.* Minneapolis: Burgess.

CLARK, W.L.G. 1969. *History of the Primates.* Chicago: Phoenix Books.

CLARK, W.L.G. 1971. *The Antecedents of Man.* Chicago: Quadrangle Books.

CONROY, G. 1980. Ontogeny, auditory structures, and primate evolution. *American Journal of Physical Anthropology* 52:443–451.

GINGERICH, P. 1972. Molar occlusion and jaw mechanics of the Eocene primate *Adapis. American Journal of Physical Anthropology* 36:359.

GREGORY, W. 1950. On the structure and relation of *Notharctus*, an American Eocene primate. *Memoirs of American Museum of Natural History* 3:49–243.

HAINES, R. 1958. Arboreal or terrestrial ancestry of placental mammals? *Quarterly Review of Biology* 33:1–23.

JONES, F.W. 1916. *Arboreal Man.* London: Arnold.

KAY, R., AND M. CARTMILL. 1977. Cranial morphology and adaptations of *Palaechton naciemienti* and other Paramomyida (Plesiadapoida? Primates), with a description of a new genus and species. *Journal of Human Evolution* 6:19–53.

KAY, R., R. THORINGTON, AND P. HOUDE. 1990. Eocene plesiadapiform shows affinities with flying lemurs not primates. *Nature* 345:342–344.

MACPHEE, R. 1981. Auditory Regions of Primates and Eutherian Insectivores, Morphology, Ontogeny and Character Analysis. *Contributions to Primatology*, Vol. 18. Basel: S. Karger.

MARTIN, R. 1968. Towards a new definition of Primates. *Man* 3:377–401.

MARTIN, R. 1988. Several steps forward for Eocene primates. *Nature* 331:660–661.

MARTIN, R. 1990. Some relatives take a dive. *Nature* 345:291–292.

MARTIN, R. 1991. New fossils and primate origins. *Nature* 349:19–20.

MCKENNA, M. 1960. Fossil mammalia from the early Wasatchian Four Mile fauna, Eocene of northwest Colorado. *University of California, Publications in Geological Science* 37:1–130.

MELDRUM, D.J. 1990. New fossil platyrrhine tali from the early Miocene of Argentina. *American Journal of Physical Anthropology* 83:403–418.

NAPIER, J., AND P. NAPIER. 1970. *A Handbook of Living Primates*, 3rd ed. New York: Academic Press.

ROSE, K. 1996. The earliest primates. *Evolutionary Anthropology* 5:159–172.

ROSE, M., AND A. WALKER. 1985. The skeleton of early Eocene *Cantius*, oldest lemuriform primate. *American Journal of Physical Anthropology* 66:73–89.

SCHWARTZ, J., I. TATTERSALL, AND N. ELDRIDGE. 1978. Phylogeny and classification of primates revisited. *Yearbook of Physical Anthropology* 21:92–133.

SETOGUCHI, T., AND A. ROSENBERGER. 1987. A fossil owl monkey from La Venta, Colombia. *Nature* 326:692–694.

SHAKLEE, A. 1975. Primate evolution: Analyses of trends. *Science* 189:128.

SIMONS, E. 1972. *Primate Evolution: An Introduction to Man's Place in Nature.* New York: Macmillan.

SIMPSON, G. 1940. Studies on the earliest primates. *Bulletin of American Museum of Natural History* 77:185–212.

SMITH, G.E. 1912. Presidential address to the anthropology section (H) of the Eighty-second Annual Meeting, British Association for the Advancement of Science.

SUSSMAN, R. AND P. RAVEN. 1978. Pollination by lemurs and marsupials: An archaic evolutionary system. *Science* 200:731–736.

SZALAY, F. 1968. The beginnings of primates. *Evolution* 22:19–36.

SZALAY, F. 1969. Mixodectidae, Microsyopidae, and the insectivore–primate transition. *Bulletin of American Museum of Natural History* 140:193–330.

SZALAY, F. 1972a. Cranial morphology of the early Tertiary *Phenacolemur* and its bearing on primate phylogeny. *American Journal of Physical Anthropology* 36:59–76.

SZALAY, F. 1972b. Paleobiology of the earliest primates. In *The Functional and Evolutionary Biology of Primates*, ed. R. Tuttle. Chicago: Aldine-Atherton.

SZALAY, F. 1973. A review of some recent advances in paleoprimatology. *Yearbook of Physical Anthropology* 17:39–64.

SZALAY, F., AND E. DELSON. 1978. *Evolutionary History of the Primates.* New York: Academic Press.

SZALAY, F., AND C. LI. 1986. Middle Paleocene euprimate from southern China and the distribution of primates in the Paleogene. *Journal of Human Evolution* 18:387–398.

SZALAY, F., A. ROSENBERGER, AND M. DAGOSTO. 1987. Diagnoses and differentiation of the order Primates. *Yearbook of Physical Anthropology* 30:75–106.

TARLING, D. 1980. The geologic evolution of South America with special reference to the last 200 million years. In *Evolutionary Biology of the New World Monkeys and Continental Drift*, ed. R. Ciochan and A. Chiarelli. New York: Plenum.

VAN VALEN, L. 1965. Tree shrews, primates, and fossils. *Evolution* 19:137–151.

VAN VALEN, L. 1969. A classification of the primates. *American Journal of Physical Anthropology* 30:295–296.

VAN VALEN, L., AND R. SLOAN. 1965. The earliest primates. *Science* 150:743–745.

WILSON, J., ED. 1972. *Continents Adrift.* San Francisco: W. H. Freeman.

CHAPTER 6

ALPAGUT, B., P. ANDREWS, M. FORELIUS, J. KEPPELMAN, I. TEMIZSOY, H. CELBEI, AND W. LINDSAY. 1996. A new specimen of *Ankarapithecus meteai* from the Sinap Formation of central Anatolia. *Nature* 382:349–351.

ANDREWS, P. 1970. Two new fossil primates from the lower Miocene of Kenya. *Nature* 228:537–540.

ANDREWS, P. 1971. *Ramapithecus wickeri* mandible from Fort Ternan, Kenya. *Nature* 231:192–194.

ANDREWS, P. 1981. Hominoid habitats of the Miocene. *Nature* 289:749.

ANDREWS, P. 1992. An ape from the south. *Nature* 356:106.

ANDREWS, P. 1993. Evolution and environment in the Hominidae. *Nature* 360:641–646.

ANDREWS, P., AND J. CRONIN. 1982. The relationship of *Sivapithecus* and *Ramapithecus* and the evolution of the orangutan. *Nature* 297:541–546.

ANDREWS, P., W. HAMILTON, AND P. WHYBROW. 1978. Dryopithecines from the Miocene of Saudi Arabia. *Nature* 274:249–250.

ANDREWS, P., AND H. TOBIEN. 1977. New Miocene locality in Turkey with evidence on the origin of *Ramapithecus* and *Sivapithecus. Nature* 268:699–701.

ANKEL, F. 1972. Vertebrate morphology of fossil and extant primates. In *The Functional and Evolutionary Biology of Primates*, ed. R. Tuttle, Chicago: Aldine-Atherton.

ANKEL-SIMONS, E., J. FLEAGLE, AND P. CHATRATH. 1998. Femoral anatomy of *Aegyptopithecus zeuxis*, an Early Oligocene anthropoid. *American Journal of Physical Anthropology* 106:413–424.

BADGLEY, C. 1984. The palaeoenvironment of South Asian Miocene hominoids. In *The Evolution of the East Asian Environment*, vol. 2, ed. R. O. Whyte. Hong Kong: University of Hong Kong.

BEARD, K., T. QI, M. DAWSON, B. WANG, AND C. LI. 1994. A diverse new primate fauna from middle Miocene fissure-fillings in southeastern China. *Nature* 368:604–609.

BEARD, K., Y. TONG, M. DAWSON, J. WANG, AND X. HUANG. 1996. Earliest complete dentition of an anthropoid primate from the late middle Eocene of Shanxi Province, China. *Science* 272:82–85.

BEGUN, D. 1992. Phyletic diversity and locomotion in primitive European hominoids. *American Journal of Physical Anthropology* 87:311–340.

BEGUN, D. 1994. Observations on the cranial anatomy of *Ouranopithecus*: Taxonomic and phylogenetic implications. *American Journal of Physical Anthropology*, Supplement 18:54.

BEGUN, D., M. TEAFORD, AND A. WALKER. 1994. Comparative and functional anatomy of *Proconsul* phalanges from the Kaswanga Primate Site, Rusinga Island, Kenya. *Journal of Human Evolution* 26:89–166.

BENEFIT, B. 1993. The permanent dentition and phylogenetic position of *Victoriapithecus* from Maboko Island, Kenya. *Journal of Human Evolution* 25:83–172.

BUTZER, K. 1977. Human evolution: Hominoids of the Miocene. *Science* 197:224–246.

CAMERON, D. 1997. A revised systematic scheme for the Eurasian fossil Hominidae. *Journal of Human Evolution* 33:449–477.

CHAIMANEE, Y., V. SUTEETHORN, J. JAEGER, AND S. DUCROCQ. 1997. A new late Eocene anthropoid primate from Thailand. *Nature* 385:429–431.

CLARK, W. L. G. 1967. *The Fossil Evidence for Human Evolution*. Chicago: Chicago University Press.

CLARK, W. L. G., AND L. LEAKEY. 1951. The Miocene Hominoidea of East Africa. *Fossil Mammals of Africa*, no. 1.

CIOCHON, R. 1980. *Amphipithecus* and *Pondaungia* as early anthropoids: The dental evidence. *American Journal of Physical Anthropology* 52:24.

CIOCHON, R. 1984. Asian Miocene hominoid and the phyletic position of *Gigantopithecus*. Paper read at 53rd Annual Meeting of American Association of Physical Anthropologists, Philadelphia.

CIOCHON, R. 1984/1985. Paleoanthropological field research in Vietnam. Newsletter, *The Institute of Human Origins* 4:6–7.

CIOCHON, R. 1991. The ape that was. *Natural History* November: 54–62.

CONROY, G. 1972. Problems in the interpretation of *Ramapithecus*: With special reference to anterior tooth reduction. *American Journal of Physical Anthropology* 37:41–46.

CONROY, G. 1987. Body weight estimates in fossil primates. *International Journal of Primatology* 8:115–138.

CONROY, G. 1990. *Primate Evolution*. New York: W. W. Norton.

CONROY, G., M. PICKFORD, B. SENUT, AND P. MEIN. 1993. Diamonds in the desert: The discovery of *Otavipithecus namibiensis*. *Evolutionary Anthropology* 2:46–52.

CONROY, G., M. PICKFORD, B. SENUT, J. VAN COUVERING, AND P. MEIN. 1992. *Otavipithecus namibiensis*, first Miocene hominoid from southern Africa. *Nature* 356:144–147.

CORRUCCINI, R. 1975. Multivariate analyses of *Gigantopithecus* mandibles. *American Journal of Physical Anthropology* 42:167.

CULLOTA, E. 1995. New finds rekindle debate over anthropoid origins. *Science* 268:1851.

DAEGLING, D., AND F. GRINE. 1987. Tooth wear, gnathodental scaling and diet of *Gigantopithecus blacki*. *American Journal of Physical Anthropology* 72:191–192.

DEBONIS, L., G. BOUVRAIN, D. GERAADS, AND G. KOUFOS. 1990. New hominoid skull material from the later Miocene of Macedonia in northern Greece. *Nature* 345:712–715.

DEBONIS, L., AND G. KOUFOS. 1995. Our ancestor's ancestor: *Ouranopithecus* is a Greek link in human ancestry. *Evolutionary Anthropology* 3:75–83.

ECKHARDT, R. 1972. Population genetics and human origins. *Scientific American*, January: 94.

ECKHARDT, R. 1975. *Gigantopithecus* as a hominid. In *Paleoanthropology, Morphology, and Paleoecology*, ed. R. Tuttle. The Hague: Mouton.

ETLER, D. 1984. The fossil hominoids of Lufeng, Yunnan Province, The People's Republic of China: A series of translations. *Yearbook of Physical Anthropology* 27:1–56.

EVERY, R. 1970. Sharpness of teeth in man and other primates. *Postilla* (Peabody Museum, Yale University) 143: 1–30.

FLEAGLE, J., AND E. SIMONS. 1978. *Micropithecus clarki*, a small ape from the Miocene of Uganda. *American Journal of Physical Anthropology* 49:427–440.

FLEAGLE, J., AND E. SIMONS. 1982. The humerus of *Aegyptopithecus zeuxis*: A primitive anthropoid. *American Journal of Physical Anthropology* 59:175–193.

FLEAGLE, J., E. SIMONS, AND G. CONROY. 1975. Ape limb bone from the Oligocene of Egypt. *Science* 189:135–137.

FLEAGLE, J., T. BROWN, J. OBRADOVICH, AND E. SIMONS. 1986. Age of the earliest African anthropoids. *Science* 234: 1247–1249.

FRAYER, D. 1974. A reappraisal of *Ramapithecus*. *Yearbook of Physical Anthropology* 18:19–30.

GAGNON, M. 1992. Paleoecological changes in the Fayum of Egypt. *American Journal of Physical Anthropology*, Suppl. 14:78.

GEBO, D., L. MACLATCHY, R. KITYO, A. DEINO, J. KINGSTON, AND D. PILBEAM. 1997. A hominoid genus from the early Miocene of Uganda. *Science* 276:401–404.

GEBO, D., AND E. SIMONS. 1987. Morphology and locomotor adaptations of the foot in early Oligocene anthropoids. *American Journal of Physical Anthropology* 74:83–102.

GELVIN, B. 1976. Odontometric affinities of *Ramapithecus* to extinct and extant hominoids. *American Journal of Physical Anthropology* 44:217.

GELVIN, B. 1980. The morphometric affinities of *Gigantopithecus*. *American Journal of Physical Anthropology* 53:541–568.

GIBBONS, A. 1994. Primate origins: New skull fuels debate. *Science* 266:541.

GIBBONS, A., AND E. CULOTTA. 1997. Miocene primates go ape. *Science* 276:355–356.

GODENOT, M., AND M. MAHKOUBI. 1992. Earliest known simian primates found in Algeria. *Nature* 357:324–326.

GREENFIELD, L. 1974. Taxonomic reassessment of two *Ramapithecus* specimens. *Folia primatologica* 22:97–115.

GREENFIELD, L. 1979. On the adaptive pattern of *Ramapithecus*. *American Journal of Physical Anthropology* 50:527–548.

GREENFIELD, L. 1980. A late divergence hypothesis. *American Journal of Physical Anthropology* 52:351–366.

GREENWELL, R., AND F. POIRIER. 1989. Further investigation into the reported Yeren. *Cryptozoology* 8:47–57.

GREGORY, W., M. HELLMAN, AND G. LEWIS. 1938. Fossil anthropoids of the Yale-Cambridge Indian Expedition of 1935. *Carnegie Institute of Washington Publication* 495:1–27.

HAMILTON, W., P. WHYBROW, AND H. MCCLURE. 1978. Fauna of fossil mammals from the Miocene of Saudi Arabia. *Nature* 274:248–249.

HARRISON, T. 1986. Fossil anthropoids from the middle Miocene of East Africa and their bearing on the origin of the Oreopithecidae. *American Journal of Physical Anthropology* 71:265–284.

HARRISON, T. 1998. Evidence of a tail in *Proconsul heseloni*. *American Journal of Physical Anthropology,* Suppl. 26:93–94.

HRDLIČKA, A. 1935. The Yale fossils of anthropoid apes. *American Journal of Science* 229:533–538.

HURZELER, J. 1958. *Oreopithecus bambolii* Gervais: A preliminary report. *Verhandlungen der naturforschenden Gesellschaft* 69:1–48.

JOLLY, C. 1970. The seed-eaters: A new model of hominid differentiation based on a baboon analogy. *Man* 5:5–26.

KAY, R. 1973. Mastication, molar tooth structure, and diet in primates. Ph.D. dissertation. Yale University.

KAY, R. 1977. Post-Oligocene evolution of catarrhine diets. *American Journal of Physical Anthropology* 47:141–142.

KAY, R. 1982. *Sivapithecus simonsi*, a new species of Miocene hominoid, with comments on the phylogenetic status of the Ramapithecine. *International Journal of Primatology* 3:113–174.

KAY, R. 1983. *Ramapithecus* reclaimed. *The Sciences*, Jan./Feb.: 26–27.

KAY, R., J. FLEAGLE, AND E. SIMONS. 1981. A revision of the Oligocene apes of the Fayum Province, Egypt. *American Journal of Physical Anthropology* 55:293–322.

KAY, R., AND E. SIMONS. 1980. The ecology of Oligocene African Anthropoidea. *International Journal of Primatology* 1:31–38.

KOLATA, G. 1977. Human evolution: Hominoids of the Miocene. *Science* 197:244–245.

KOUFOS, G. 1993. Mandible of *Ouranopithecus macedoniensis* (Hominidae, Primates) from a new late Miocene locality of Macedonia (Greece). *American Journal of Physical Anthropology* 91:226–234.

KRETZOI, M. 1975. New ramapithecines and *Pliopithecus* from the lower Pliocene of Rudabanya in north-eastern Hungary. *Nature* 257:578–581.

LANGDON, J. 1986. *Functional Morphology of the Miocene Hominoid Foot.* Basel: S. Karger.

LEAKEY, L. 1967. An early Miocene member of Hominidae. *Nature* 213:155–163.

LEAKEY, L. 1968. An early Miocene member of Hominidae. In *Perspectives on Human Evolution,* ed. S. Washburn and P. Jay. New York: Holt, Rinehart & Winston.

LEAKEY, L. 1969. Ecology of North Indian *Ramapithecus. Nature* 223:1075.

LEAKEY, L. 1970. Newly recognized mandible of *Ramapithecus. Nature* 225:199.

LEAKEY, M., P. LENGAI, AND A. WALKER. 1995. A new genus of large primate from the Late Oligocene of Lothidok, Turkana District, Kenya. *Journal of Human Evolution* 28:519–531.

LEAKEY, R., AND M. LEAKEY. 1986a. A new Miocene hominoid from Kenya. *Nature* 324:143–146.

LEAKEY, R., AND M. LEAKEY. 1986b. A second new Miocene hominoid from Kenya. *Nature* 324:146–148.

LEAKEY, R., AND M. LEAKEY. 1987. A new Miocene small-bodied ape from Kenya. *Journal of Human Evolution* 16:369–387.

LEAKEY, R., M. LEAKEY, AND A. WALKER. 1988a. Morphology of *Turkanopithecus kalokolensis* from Kenya. *American Journal of Physical Anthropology* 76:277–288.

LEAKEY, R., M. LEAKEY, AND A. WALKER. 1988b. Morphology of *Afropithecus turkanensis* from Kenya. *American Journal of Physical Anthropology* 76:289–300.

LEWIS, G. 1934a. Preliminary notice of the new manlike apes from India. *American Journal of Science* 27:161–181.

LEWIS, G. 1934b. Taxonomic syllabus of Siwalik fossil anthropoids. *American Journal of Science Series* 34:139–147.

LI, C. 1978. A Miocene gibbon-like primate from Shihung, Kiangsu Province. *Vertebrata Pal. Asiatica* 16:187–192.

MARTIN, L. 1985. Significance of enamel thickness in hominoid evolution. *Nature* 314:260–263.

MARTIN, L., AND P. ANDREWS. 1982. New ideas on the relationships of the Miocene hominoids. *Primate Eye* 18:4–7.

MARTIN, L., AND P. ANDREWS. 1993. Renaissance of Europe's ape. *Nature* 365:494.

MAW, B., R. CIOCHON, AND D. SAVAGE. 1979. Late Eocene of Burma yields earliest anthropoid primate, *Pondaungia cotteri. Nature* 282:65–67.

MORBECK, M. 1975. *Dryopithecus africanus* forelimb. *Journal of Human Evolution* 4:39–46.

MORRIS, D. 1970. On deflecting wrinkles and the *Dryopithecus* pattern in human mandibular molars. *American Journal of Physical Anthropology* 32:97.

MOYA SOLÁ, S., AND M. KOHLER. 1993. Recent discoveries of *Dryopithecus* shed new light on evolution of great apes. *Nature* 365:643–645.

NAPIER, J., AND P. DAVIS. 1959. The forelimb skeleton and associated remains of *Proconsul africanus. Fossil Mammals of Africa* 16:1–69.

PILBEAM, D. 1967. Man's earliest ancestors. *Scientific Journal* 3:47–53.

PILBEAM, D. 1968. The earliest hominids. *Nature* 219:1335–1338.

PILBEAM, D. 1969. Tertiary Pongidae of East Africa: Evolutionary relationships and taxonomy. *Bulletin 31, Peabody Museum of Natural History, Yale University,* pp. 1–185.

PILBEAM, D. 1970. *Gigantopithecus* and the origins of the Hominidae. *Nature* 225:516–519.

PILBEAM, D. 1972. *The Ascent of Man.* New York: Macmillan.

PILBEAM, D. 1979. Recent finds and interpretations of Miocene hominoids. *Annual Review of Anthropology* 8:333–352.

PILBEAM, D. 1982. New hominoid skull material from the Miocene of Pakistan. *Nature* 295:232–234.

PILBEAM, R. 1983. *Ramapithecus* disowned. *The Sciences,* Jan./Feb.: 24–25.

PILBEAM, D. 1984. Bone of contention. *Natural History,* June: 2–5.

PILBEAM, D., J. BARRY, G. MEYER, AND OTHERS. 1977a. Geology and paleontology of Neogene strata of Pakistan. *Nature* 270:684–689.

PILBEAM, D., G. MEYER, C. BADGLEY, AND OTHERS. 1977b. New hominoid primates from the Siwaliks of Pakistan and their bearing on hominoid evolution. *Nature* 27:689–695.

PILBEAM, D., M. ROSE, C. BADGLEY, AND B. LIPSCHUTZ. 1980. Miocene hominoids from Pakistan. *Postilla* 181:1–94.

PILBEAM, D., AND E. SIMONS. 1971a. A gorilla-sized ape from the Miocene of India. *Science* 173:23.

PILBEAM, D., AND E. SIMONS. 1971b. Humerus of *Dryopithecus* from Saint Gaudens, France. *Nature* 229:408–409.

PILGRIM, G. 1910. Notices of new mammalian genera and species from the tertiaries of India. *Geological Survey of India Records* 40:63–71.

PILGRIM, G. 1915. New Siwalik primates and their bearing on the question of the evolution of man and the Anthropoidea. *Geological Survey of India Records* 45:1–74.

POIRIER, F., H. HU, AND C. CHEN. 1983. The evidence for Wildman in Hubei Province, The People's Republic of China. *Cryptozoology* 2:25–39.

PRASAD, K. 1969. Observations of mid-Tertiary hominids *Sivapithecus* and *Ramapithecus. American Journal of Physical Anthropology* 31:11.

PREUSS, T. 1982. The face of *Sivapithecus indicus*: Description of a new, relatively complete specimen from the Siwaliks of Pakistan. *Folia Primatologica* 20:141–157.

RADINSKY, L. 1973. *Aegyptopithecus* endocasts: Oldest record of a pongid brain. *American Journal of Physical Anthropology* 39:239–248.

RADINSKY, L. 1974. The fossil evidence of anthropoid brain evolution. *American Journal of Physical Anthropology* 41:15–28.

RADINSKY, L. 1977. Early primate brains: Facts and fiction. *Journal of Human Evolution* 6:79–86.

RASMUSSEN, D., AND E. SIMONS. 1992. Paleobiology of the Oligopithecines, the earliest known anthropoid primates. *International Journal of Primatology* 5:477–508.

RETTALACK, G., D. DUGA, AND E. BESTLAND. 1990. Fossil soils and grasses of a Middle Miocene East African grassland. *Science* 247:1325–1327.

ROBINSON, J. 1972. *Early Hominid Posture and Locomotion.* Chicago: University of Chicago Press.

ROSE, K. 1996. The earliest primates. *Evolutionary Anthropology* 5:159–172.

SCHON YBARRA, M. 1984. Locomotion and postures of red howlers in a deciduous forest-savanna interface. *American Journal of Physical Anthropology* 63:65–76.

SCHWARTZ, J. 1984. Phylogeny of humans and orangutans. Paper given at 53rd Annual Meetings of American Association of Physical Anthropologists, Philadelphia.

SIMONS, E. 1960. *Apidium* and *Oreopithecus. Nature* 186:824–826.

SIMONS, E. 1961. The phyletic position of *Ramapithecus. Postilla* 57:1–9.

SIMONS, E. 1962. Two new primate species from the African Oligocene. *Postilla* 64:1–12.

SIMONS, E. 1964. On the mandible of *Ramapithecus. Proceedings of the National Academy of Science* 51:528–535.

SIMONS, E. 1965a. The hunt for Darwin's third ape. *Medical Opinion and Review,* November: 74–81.

SIMONS, E. 1965b. New fossil apes from Egypt and the initial differentiation of Hominoidea. *Nature* 205:135–139.

SIMONS, E. 1967a. The earliest apes. *Scientific American* 217:28–35.

SIMONS, E. 1967b. New evidence on the anatomy of the earliest catarrhine primates. *Neue Ergebnisse der Primatologie* 2:15–18.

SIMONS, E. 1968a. Hunting the "dawn apes" of Africa. *Discovery* 4:19–32.

SIMONS, E. 1968b. A source for dental comparison of *Ramapithecus* and *Australopithecus* and *Homo. South African Journal of Science* 64:92–112.

SIMONS, E. 1969a. Late Miocene hominid from Fort Ternan, Kenya. *Nature* 221:448–451.

SIMONS, E. 1969b. Origin and radiation of the primates. *Annals of New York Academy of Science* 167:319–331.

SIMONS, E. 1972. *Primate Evolution: An Introduction to Man's Place in Nature.* New York: Macmillan.

SIMONS, E. 1976. The nature of the transition in the dental mechanism from pongids to hominids. *Journal of Human Evolution* 5:511–528.

SIMONS, E. 1977. *Ramapithecus. Scientific American* 236:28–35.

SIMONS, E. 1984. Dawn ape of the Fayum. *Natural History,* May: 18–20.

SIMONS, E. 1987. New face of *Aegyptopithecus* from the Oligocene of Egypt. *Journal Human Evolution* 16:273–289.

SIMONS, E. 1990. Discovery of the oldest known anthropoidean skull from the Paleogene of Egypt. *Science* 247:1567–1569.

SIMONS, E. 1993. Egypt's simian spring. *Natural History* 102:58–59.

SIMONS, E. 1995. Skulls and anterior teeth of *Catopithecus* (Primates: Anthropoidea) from the Eocene and anthropoid origins. *Science* 268:1885–1888.

SIMONS, E., AND S. CHOPRA. 1969. A new species of *Gigantopithecus* (Hominadae, Primates) from northern India with some comments on its relationship to earliest hominids. *Postilla* 138:1–18.

SIMONS, E., AND D. PILBEAM. 1965. Preliminary revision of the Dryopithecinae (Pongidae, Anthropoidea). *Folia Primatologica* 3:81–152.

SIMONS, E., AND D. PILBEAM. 1972. Hominoid paleoprimatology. In *The Functional and Evolutionary Biology of Primates,* ed. R. Tuttle. Chicago: Aldine-Atherton.

SIMONS, E., D. RASMUSSEN, AND D. GEBO. 1987. A new species of *Propliopithecus* from the Fayum, Egypt. *American Journal of Physical Anthropology* 73:138–147.

STRAUS, W. 1963. The classification of *Oreopithecus.* In *Classification and Human Evolution,* ed. S. Washburn. Chicago: Aldine-Atherton.

SZALAY, F. 1972. Paleobiology of the earliest primates. In *The Functional and Evolutionary Biology of Primates,* ed. R. Tuttle. Chicago: Aldine-Atherton.

SZALAY, F., AND E. DELSON. 1979. *Evolutionary History of the Primates.* New York: Academic Press.

TATTERSALL, I. 1969a. Ecology of North Indian *Ramapithecus. Nature* 224:451–452.

TATTERSALL, I. 1969b. More on the ecology of North Indian *Ramapithecus. Nature* 224:821–822.

VAN COUVERING, J., AND J. MILLER. 1969. Miocene stratigraphy and age determinations, Rusinga Island, Kenya. *Nature* 221:628–632.

VON KOENIGSWALD, G. 1969. Miocene Cercopithecoidea and Oreopithecoidea from the Miocene of East Africa. *Fossil Vertebrates of Africa* 1:39–52.

VERDCOURT, B. 1963. The Miocene and nonmarine mollusca of Rusinga Island, Lake Victoria, and other localities in Kenya. *Palaeontographica* 121:1.

WALKER, A. 1983. The puzzle of *Proconsul. The Sciences,* Jan./Feb.: 22–23.

WALKER, A., AND M. TEAFORD. 1989. The hunt for *Proconsul. Scientific American,* January: 76–82.

WANG, S. 1980. Discoveries and expectations for the remains of anthropoids and human beings in Hubei Province. *Jiang-Han Archaeology* 2:1–6 (in Chinese).

WHITTEN, P., AND M. NICKLES. 1983. Our forebearers' forebears. *The Sciences,* Jan./Feb.: 20–28.

WOLPOFF, M. 1971. Interstitial wear. *American Journal of Physical Anthropology* 34:205–228.

WOLPOFF, M. 1980. *Paleoanthropology.* New York: Alfred A. Knopf.

WOLPOFF, M. 1982. *Ramapithecus* and hominid origins. *Current Anthropology* 23:501–510.

WOOD, B. 1973. Locomotor affinities of hominoid tali from Kenya. *Nature* 246:45–46.

WU, R. 1984. The crania of *Ramapithecus* and *Sivapithecus* from Lufeng, China. In *The Early Evolution of Man,* ed. P. Andrews and J. L. Franzen. Frankfurt: Senckenberg Museum.

WU, R., X. QINGHUA, AND L. QINGWU. 1986. Relationship between Lufeng *Sivapithecus* and *Ramapithecus* and their phylogenetic position. *Acta Anthropologica Sinica* 4:1–31.

WU, X., AND F. POIRIER. 1995. *Human Evolution in China.* New York: Oxford University Press.

YINYAN, Z. 1982. Variability and evolutionary trends in tooth size of *Gigantopithecus. American Journal of Physical Anthropology* 49:21–32.

ZHANG, X., G. ZHOU, Y. HU, AND Y. LIN. 1981. Stratigraphy of *Ramapithecus* bearing Pliocene beds of Lufeng, Yunna. *Memoirs of Beijing Natural History Museum* 10:1–20.

ZIHLMAN, A., AND J. LOWENSTEIN. 1979. False start of the human parade. *Natural History* 88:86–91.

CHAPTER 7

AIELLO, L. 1994. Thumbs up for our ancestors. *Science* 265:1540–1541.

ARENSBURG, B., L. SCHEPARTZ, A. TILLIER, B. VANDERMEERSCH, AND Y. RAK. 1990. A reappraisal of the anatomical basis for speech in Middle Paleolithic hominids. *American Journal of Physical Anthropology* 83:137–146.

ARENSBURG, B., A. TILLIER, B. VANDERMEERSCH, H. DUDAY, L. SCHEPARTZ, AND Y. RAK. 1989. A Middle Paleolithic human hyoid bone. *Nature* 338:758–760.

AZEN, E., W. LEUTENEGGER, AND E. PETERS. 1978. Evolutionary and dietary aspects of salivary basic (Pb) and Post Pb (PPb) proteins in anthropoid apes. *Nature* 273:775–778.

BLUMENSCHINE, R. 1987. Characteristics of an early hominid scavenging niche. *Current Anthropology* 28:383–408.

BLUMENSCHINE, R. 1989. A landscape taphonomic model of the scale of prehistoric scavenging opportunities. *Journal of Human Evolution* 18:345–372.

BONIN, G. VON. 1963. *The Evolution of the Human Brain.* Chicago: University of Chicago Press.

BRACE, C. L. 1962. Comments on food transport and the origin of human bipedalism. *American Anthropologist* 64:606–607.

CALVIN, W. 1983. A stone's throw and its launch window: Timing precision and its implications for language and hominid brains. *Journal of Theoretical Biology* 104:121–135.

CAMPBELL, B. 1966. *Human Evolution: An Introduction to Man's Adaptation.* Chicago: Aldine-Atherton.

CARTMILL, M. 1975. *Primate Origins.* Minneapolis: Burgess.

CARTMILL, M. 1990. Human uniqueness and theoretical content in paleoanthropology. *International Journal of Primatology* 11:173–192.

CAVALLO, J. 1990. Cat in the human cradle. *Natural History,* February: 53–60.

CAVALLO, J., AND R. BLUMENSCHINE. 1989. Tree-stored leopard kills: Expanding the hominid scavenging niche. *Journal of Human Evolution* 18:393–400.

CHAPLIN, G., N. JABLONSKI, AND N. CABLE. 1994. Physiology, thermoregulation and bipedalism. *Journal of Human Evolution* 27:497–510.

CHENEY, D. 1982. Females as strategists (Review of S. B. Hrdy) *The Women That Never Evolved. Science* 215: 1090–1091.

COON, C. 1971. *The Hunting Peoples.* Boston: Little, Brown.

DARWIN, C. 1871. *The Descent of Man, and Selection in Relation to Sex.* London: John Murray (Publishers) Ltd.

EISENBERG, J. 1973. Mammalian social systems: Are primate social systems unique? In *Precultural Primate Behavior,* ed. E. Menzel. Basel: S. Karger.

FALK, D. 1984. The petrified brain. *Natural History,* September: 36–39.

FALK, D. 1990. Brain evolution in *Homo*: The "radiator" theory. *Behavioral and Brain Sciences* 13:333–381.

FIALKOWSKI, K. 1986. A mechanism for the origin of the human brain: A hypothesis. *Current Anthropology* 27:288–290.

HALLOWELL, A. 1961. The protocultural foundations of human adaptations. In *Social Life of Early Man,* ed. S. Washburn. Chicago: Aldine.

HEIPLE, K., AND C. LOVEJOY. 1971. Femoral anatomy of *Australopithecus. American Journal of Physical Anthropology* 35:75–84.

HEWES, G. 1961. Food transport and the origin of human bipedalism. *American Anthropologist* 63:687–710.

HEWES, G. 1964. Hominid bipedalism: Independent evidence for the food-carrying theory. *Science* 146:416.

HOLLOWAY, R. 1967. Tools and teeth: Some speculations regarding canine reduction. *American Anthropologist* 93: 63–67.

HOLLOWAY, R. 1982. Human brain evolution: A search for units, models and synthesis. In *Human Evolution,* ed. G. Sperber, Edmonton: University of Alberta Press.

HOLLOWAY, R. 1983. Cerebral brain endocast pattern of the *Australopithecus afarensis* hominid. *Nature* 303:420–422.

HUNT, K. 1994. The evolution of human bipedality: Ecology and functional anatomy. *Journal of Human Evolution* 26:183–202.

ISAAC, G. 1978. The food-sharing behavior of protohuman hominids. *Scientific American* 238:90–109.

JOLLY, A. 1985. The evolution of primate behavior. *American Scientist* 73:230–239.

KAY, R. F., M. CARTMILL, AND M. BALOW. 1998. The hypoglossal canal and the origin of human vocal behavior. *Proceedings of the National Academy of Sciences. USA* 95:5417–5419.

KRANTZ, G. 1968. Brain size and hunting ability in earliest man. *Current Anthropology* 11:176.

LAITMAN, J. 1984. The anatomy of human speech. *Natural History* 93:21–27.

LAITMAN, J., J. REIDENBERG, P. GANNON, AND B. JOHANSSON. 1990. The Kebara hyoid: What it tells us about the evolution of the hominid vocal tract. *American Journal of Physical Anthropology* 81:254.

LANCASTER, J. 1971. On the evolution of tool-using behavior. In *Background for Man,* ed. P. Dolhinow and V. Sarich. Boston: Little, Brown.

LANCASTER, J. 1975. *Primate Behavior and the Emergence of Human Culture.* New York: Holt, Rinehart & Winston.

LEE, R. 1968. What hunters do for a living, or how to make out on scarce resources. In *Man the Hunter,* ed. R. Lee and I. DeVore. Chicago: Aldine-Atherton.

LEONARD, W., AND M. ROBERTSON. 1995. Energetic efficiency of human bipedality. *American Journal of Physical Anthropology* 97:335–338.

LEWIN, R. 1982. How did humans evolve big brains? *Science* 216:840–841.

LIEBERMAN, P. 1992. On Neanderthal speech and Neanderthal extinction. *Current Anthropology* 4:409–410.

LOVEJOY, C. O. 1981. The origin of man. *Science* 211:341–350.

LOVEJOY, C. O. 1984. The natural detective. *Natural History,* October: 24–27.

LOVEJOY, C. O. 1988. Evolution of human walking. *Scientific American,* November: 118–125.

MCHENRY, H. 1982. The pattern of human evolution: Studies on bipedalism, mastication, and encephalization. *Annual Review of Anthropology* 11:151–173.

MCHENRY, H. 1991. Petite bodies of the "robust" australopithecines. *American Journal of Physical Anthropology* 86:445–454.

MCHENRY, H., AND L. TEMERIN. 1979. The evolution of hominid bipedalism: Evidence from the fossil record. *Yearbook of Physical Anthropology* 22:105–131.

MILTON, K. 1981. Distribution patterns of tropical plant foods as an evolutionary stimulus to primate mental development. *American Anthropologist* 83:534–548.

NAPIER, J. 1963. The locomotor functions of hominids. In *Classification and Human Evolution,* ed. S. Washburn. Chicago: Aldine-Atherton.

NAPIER, J. 1964. The evolution of bipedal walking in hominids. *Archives de Biologie* 75:673–708.

NAPIER, J. 1967a. The antiquity of human walking. *Scientific American* 216:56–66.

NAPIER, J. 1967b. Evolutionary aspects of primate locomotion. *American Journal of Physical Anthropology* 27:333–342.

POIRIER, F. 1997. What monkeys and apes can and can not tell us about human evolution. Paper presented at conference, Barcelona, Spain.

POIRIER, F., AND K. HUSSEY. 1982. Nonhuman primate learning: The importance of learning in an evolutionary perspective. *Anthropology and Education Quarterly* 12:133–148.

POLYAK, W. 1957. *The Vertebrate Visual System: Its Origin, Structure and Function.* Chicago: University of Chicago Press.

POTTS, R. 1984. Home bases and early hominids. *American Scientist* 72:338–347.

RODMAN, P., AND H. McHENRY. 1980. Bioenergetics and the origin of hominid bipedalism. *American Journal of Physical Anthropology* 52:103–106.

SHIPMAN, P. 1984. Scavenger hunt. *Natural History* 93:20–27.

SHIPMAN, P. AND A. WALKER. 1989. The costs of becoming a predator. *Journal of Human Evolution* 18:373–392.

SIGMON, B. 1971. Bipedal behavior and the emergence of erect posture in man. *American Journal of Physical Anthropology* 34:55.

SINCLAIR, A., M. LEAKEY, AND M. NORTON-GIFFITHS. 1986. Migration and bipedalism. *Nature* 324:307–308.

SMALL, M. 1990. Political animal: Social intelligence and the growth of the primate brain. *The Sciences*, March/April: 36–42.

SPHULER, J. 1957. Somatic paths to culture. *Human Biology* 31:1–13.

STEKELIS, H. 1985. Primate communication, comparative neurology, and the origin of language reexamined. *Journal of Human Evolution* 18:157–173.

STRAUS, W. 1962. Fossil evidence of the evolution of the erect bipedal posture. *Clinical Orthopedics* 25:9–19.

SUSMAN, R. 1994. Fossil evidence for early hominid tool use. *Science* 265:1570–1573.

TANNER, N. 1981. *On Becoming Human.* New York: Cambridge University Press.

TIGER, L., AND R. FOX. 1971. *The Imperial Animal.* New York: Holt, Rinehart & Winston.

TOBIAS, P. 1971. *The Brain in Hominid Evolution.* New York: Columbia University Press.

TOBIAS, P. 1982. Hominid evolution in Africa. In *Human Evolution,* ed. G. Sperber. Edmonton: University of Alberta Press.

TOBIAS, P. 1987. The brain of *Homo habilis*: A new level of organization in cerebral evolution. *Journal of Human Evolution* 16:742–761.

TOBIAS, P. 1994. The craniocerebral interface in early hominids: Cerebral impressions, cranial thickening, paleoneurology, and a new hypothesis on encephalization. In R. Corrucini and R. Ciochan, eds., *Integrative Paths to the Past: Paleoanthropological Advances in Honor of F. Clark Howell.* Englewood Cliffs, NJ: Prentice Hall.

TUNNELL, G. 1973. *Culture and Biology: Becoming Human.* Minneapolis: Burgess.

WASHBURN, S. 1960. Tools and human evolution. *Scientific American* 203:62–75.

WASHBURN, S. 1968. *The Study of Human Evolution.* Eugene: University of Oregon Press.

WASHBURN, S. 1971. The study of human evolution. In *Background for Man,* ed. P. Dolhinow and V. Sarich. Boston: Little, Brown.

WASHBURN, S., AND C. LANCASTER. 1968. The evolution of hunting. In *Man the Hunter,* ed. R. Lee and I. DeVore. Chicago: Aldine-Atherton.

WASHBURN, S., AND R. MOORE. 1980. *Ape into Human,* 2nd ed. Boston: Little, Brown.

WHEELER, P. 1984. The evolution of bipedality and loss of functional body hair in hominids. *Journal of Human Evolution* 13: 91–98.

WHEELER, P. 1994. The foraging times of bipedal and quadrupedal hominids. *Journal of Human Evolution* 27:4.

WILEY, J. 1984. Phenomena, comment and notes. *Smithsonian* 15:38, 40, 42, 44.

WUNDRAM, I. 1986. Cortical motor asymmetry and hominid feeding strategies. *Journal of Human Evolution* 2:183–188.

ZIHLMAN, A. 1967. Human locomotion: A reappraisal of the functional and anatomical evidence. Ph.D. dissertation. Berkeley: University of California.

ZIHLMAN, A., AND L. BRUNKER. 1978. Hominid bipedalism: Then and now. *Yearbook of Physical Anthropology* 22:132–162.

CHAPTER 8

ABITBOL, M. 1987. Evolution of the lumbosacral angle. *American Journal of Physical Anthropology* 72:361–372.

BEHRENSMEYER, A. 1977. The habitat of Plio-Pleistocene hominids in East Africa: Taphonomic and microstratigraphic evidence. In *Early Hominids of Africa,* ed. C. Jolly. New York: St. Martin's Press.

BERG, C. 1994. How did the australopithecines walk? A biomechanical study of the hip and thigh of *Australopithecus afarensis. Journal of Human Evolution* 26:259–273.

BERGER, L. R. 1994. *Functional Morphology of the Hominoid Shoulder, Past and Present.* Ph.D. Thesis, University of the Witwatersrand.

BERGER, L. R., A. KEYSER, AND P. V. TOBIAS. 1993. Brief communication: Gladysvale: First early hominid site discovered in South Africa since 1948. *American Journal of Physical Anthropology* 92:107–111.

BOAZ, N. 1988. Status of *Australopithecus afarensis. Yearbook of Physical Anthropology* 31:85–114.

BRACE, C. 1972. Sexual dimorphism in human evolution. *Yearbook of Physical Anthropology* 16:31–49.

BRAIN, C. 1967a. Bone weathering and the problem of bone pseudo-tools. *South African Journal of Science* 63:97.

BRAIN, C. 1967b. Hottentot food remains and their bearing on the interpretation of fossil bone assemblages. *Scientific Papers Namib Desert Reserve Station* 32:1.

BRAIN, C. 1968. Who killed the Swartkrans ape-man? *South African Museums Association Bulletin* 9:127–139.

BRAIN, C. K. 1970. The south African australopithecine bone accumulations. *Transvaal Museum Memoir* 18.

BRAIN, C. 1974. A hominid skull's revealing holes. *Natural History*, December: 44.

BRAIN, C. 1981. *The Hunters or the Hunted? An Introduction to African Cave Taphonomy.* Chicago: University of Chicago Press.

BROMAGE, T., AND M. DEAN. 1986. Re-evaluation of the age at death of immature fossil hominids. *Nature* 317:525–527.

BROOM, R. 1938. The Pleistocene anthropoid apes of South Africa. *Nature* 142:377–379.

BROOM, R., J. T. ROBINSON, AND G. W. H. SCHEPERS. 1950. *Sterkfontein Ape-Man* Plesianthropus. Transvaal Museum Memoir no. 4.

BRUNET, M., A. BEAUVILAIN, Y. COPPENS, E. HEINTZ, A. H. E. MOUTAYE, AND D. PILBEAM. 1995. The first australopithecine 2,500 kilometres west of the Rift Valley (Chad). *Nature* 378:273–274.

BRUNET, M., A. BEAUVILAIN, Y. COPPENS, E. HEINTZ, A. H. E. MOUTAYE, AND D. PILBEAM. 1996. *Australopithecus bahrelghazali,* a new species of early hominid from Koro Toro region, Chad. *Comptes Rendus de L'Academie des Sciences Serie II Sciences de la Terre et des Planetes* 322:907–913.

BUSH, M. 1980. The thumb of *Australopithecus afarensis. American Journal of Physical Anthropology* 52:210.

CERLING, T.E. 1992. Development of grasslands and savannas in East Africa during the Neogene. *Palaeogeography, Palaeoclimatology, Palaeoecology* 97:241–247.

CLARKE, R. J. 1988. A new *Australopithecus* cranium from Sterkfontein and its bearing on the ancestry of *Paranthropus.* In *Evolutionary History of the "Robust" Australopithecines,* ed. F. E. Grine. New York: Aldine de Gruyter.

CLARKE, R. J. 1994. On some new interpretations of Sterkfontein stratigraphy. *South African Journal of Science* 90:211–214.

CLARKE, R. J., AND P. V. TOBIAS. 1995. Sterkfontein Member 2 foot bones of the oldest South African hominid. *Science* 269:521–524.

CONROY, G., A. KANE, H. SEIDLER, G. WEBER, AND P. V. TOBIAS. 1998. Endocranial capacity of Stw 505 ("Mr. Ples"), a large new hominid cranium from Sterkfontein. *American Journal of Physical Anthropology,* Suppl., 26:69–70.

CONROY, G., AND M. VANNIER. 1991. Dental development in South African australopithecines. Part I: Problems of patterns and chronology. *American Journal of Physical Anthropology* 86:121–136.

CONROY, G., M. VANNIER, AND P. V. TOBIAS. 1990. Endocranial features of *Australopithecus africanus* revealed by 2- and 3-D computed tomography. *Science* 247:838–841.

DART, R. 1925. *Australopithecus africanus:* The man-ape of South Africa *Nature* 115:195–199.

DART, R. 1926. Taungs and its significance. *Natural History* 26:315–327.

DART, R. 1953. The predatory transition from ape to man. *International Anthropological and Linguistic Review* 1:201.

DART, R. 1955. Cultural status of the South African man-apes. *Smithsonian Annual Report* 317:33.

DART, R. 1956. Myth of the bone-accumulating hyaena. *American Anthropologist* 58:40.

DART, R. 1957. The osteodontokeratic culture of *Australopithecus prometheus. Transvaal Museum Memoir* 10.

DART, R. 1971. On the osteodontokeratic culture of the Australopithecinae. *Current Anthropology* 12:333.

DART, R. A., AND D. CRAIG. 1959. *Adventures with the Missing Link.* London: Hamish Hamilton.

DARWIN, C. 1871. *The Descent of Man.* London: John Murray.

DAY, M., AND B. WOOD. 1968. Functional affinities of the Olduvai hominid 8 talus. *Man* 3:440–445.

DEAN, M. 1985. The eruption pattern of the permanent incisors and first permanent molars in *Australopithecus (Paranthropus) robustus. American Journal of Physical Anthropology* 67:251–257.

DENYS, C. 1992. Les analyses multivariees: Une aide a l'interpretation des paleoenvironnements. L'example des rongeurs Plio-Pleistocenes d'Afrique Australe. *Geobios* 14:209–217.

DUNCAN, A., J. KAPPELMAN, AND L. SHAPIRO. 1994. Metatarsophalangeal joint function and positional behavior in *Australopithecus afarensis. American Journal of Physical Anthropology* 93:67–81.

ELLIOT SMITH, G. 1925. The fossil anthropoid ape from Taungs. *Nature* 115:235.

FALK, D., C. HILDEBOLT, AND M. VANNIER. 1989. Reassessment of the Taung early hominid from a neurological perspective. *Journal of Human Evolution* 18:484–492.

GRINE, F. E. 1981. Trophic differences between "gracile" and "robust" australopithecines: A scanning electron microscope analysis of occlusal events. *South African Journal of Science* 77:203–230.

GRINE, F. 1987. On the eruption pattern of the permanent incisors and first permanent teeth in *Paranthropus. American Journal of Physical Anthropology* 72:352–360.

HARTWIG-SCHERER, S., AND R. MARTIN. 1991. Was "Lucy" more human than her "child"? Observations on early hominid postcranial skeletons. *Journal of Human Evolution* 21:439–449.

HAUSLER, M., AND P. SCHMID. 1995. Comparison of the pelves of the STS 14 and AL 288-1: Implications for birth and sexual dimorphism in australopithecines. *Journal of Human Evolution* 29:363–384.

HEIPLE, K., AND C. LOVEJOY. 1971. The distal femoral anatomy of *Australopithecus. American Journal of Physical Anthropology* 35:75.

HILL, A. 1985. Early hominid from Baringo, Kenya. *Nature* 315:222–224.

HILL, A., AND S. WARD. 1988. Origin of the Hominidae. *Yearbook of Physical Anthropology* 31:49–84.

HILL, A., S. WARD, AND B. BROWN. 1992. Anatomy and age of the Lothagam mandible. *Journal of Human Evolution* 22:439–451.

HOLLOWAY, R. 1974. The casts of fossil hominid brains. *Scientific American* 23:106–116.

HOLLOWAY, R. 1975. The role of human social behavior in the evolution of the brain. Forty-third James Arthur lecture on the evolution of the human brain. New York: American Museum of Natural History.

HUNT, K. D. 1994. The evolution of human bipedality: Ecology and functional morphology. *Journal of Human Evolution* 26:183–202.

JOHANSON, D., AND B. EDGAR. 1996. *From Lucy to Language.* New York: Simon & Schuster Editions.

JOHANSON, D., AND T. WHITE. 1979. A systematic assessment of early African hominids. *Science* 203:321–330.

JOHANSON, D. J., AND T. WHITE. 1980. On the status of *Australopithecus afarensis. Science* 207:1104–1105.

JOHANSON, D., T. WHITE, AND Y. COPPENS. 1978. A new species of the genus *Australopithecus* (Primates: Hominidae) from the Pliocene of eastern Africa. *Kirtlandia* 28:1–14.

JUNGERS, W. 1982. Lucy's limbs: Skeletal allometry and locomotion in *Australopithecus afarensis. Nature* 297:676–678.

KEITH, A. 1925. The Taungs Skull. *Nature* 116:462–463.

KIMBEL, W. H., D. C. JOHANSON, AND Y. RAK. 1994. The first skull and other new discoveries of *Australopithecus afarensis* at Hadar, Ethiopia. *Nature* 368:449–451.

KINGSTON, J., B. MARINO, AND A. HILL. 1994. Isotopic evidence for Neogene hominid paleoenvironments in the Kenya Rift Valley. *Science* 264:955–960.

KLEIN, R. G., K. CRUZ-URIBE, AND P. B. BEAUMONT. 1991. Environmental, ecological, and paleoanthropological implications of the Late Pleistocene mammalian fauna from Equus Cave, Northern Cape Prov, SA. *Quaternary Research* 36:94–119.

KUYKENDALL, K. L. 1996. Dental development in chimpanzees *(Pan troglodytes):* The timing of tooth calcification stages. *American Journal of Physical Anthropology* 99:135–158.

LATIMER, B., AND C. O. LOVEJOY. 1990. Hallucal tarsometatarsal joint in *Australopithecus afarensis*. *American Journal of Physical Anthropology* 62:125–134.

LEAKEY, M. G., C. S. FEIBEL, I. McDOUGALL, AND A. WALKER. 1995. New four-million-year-old hominid species from Kanapoi and Allia Bay, Kenya. *Nature* 376:585–571.

LEAKEY, M., R. HAY, G. CURTIS, AND OTHERS. 1976. Fossil hominids from the Laetoli Beds. *Nature* 262:460–466.

LEONARD, W., AND M. HEGMON. 1987. Evolution of morphology in *Australopithecus afarensis*. *American Journal of Physical Anthropology* 73:41–63.

LEWIN, R. 1985. The Taung baby reaches sixty. *Science* 233:720–721.

LOTH, S. R., M. HENNEBERG, J. F. THACKERAY. 1995. Assessment of the sex of Sts 5 and Stw 53: A new consideration of sexual dimorphism in fossil hominids. *American Journal of Physical Anthropology*, Suppl. 20:136–137.

LOVEJOY, C. O. 1973. The gait of australopithecines. *Yearbook of Physical Anthropology* 17:147–161.

LOVEJOY, C. O. 1975. Biomechanical perspectives on the lower limb of early hominids. In *Primate Functional Morphology and Evolution*, ed. R. Tuttle. The Hague: Mouton.

LOVEJOY, C. O. 1988. Evolution of human walking. *Scientific American*, November 118–125.

LOVEJOY, C. O., AND K. G. HEIPLE. 1970. A reconstruction of the femur of *Australopithecus africanus*. *American Journal of Physical Anthropology* 38:757–780.

LOVEJOY, C. O., K. G. HEIPLE, AND A. H. BURSTEIN. 1973. The gait of *Australopithecus*. *American Journal of Physical Anthropology* 38:757–780.

MANN, A. 1968. *The Paleodemography of Australopithecus*. Ph.D. dissertation. University of California, Berkeley.

MANN, A. 1975. *Paleodemographic Aspects of the South African Australopithecines*. Philadelphia: University of Pennsylvania Press.

MARZKE, M. W. 1997. Precision grips, hand morphology, and tools. *American Journal of Physical Anthropology* 102:91–110.

McHENRY, H. 1991a. Early hominid stature. *American Journal of Physical Anthropology* 85:149–158.

McHENRY, H. 1991b. Petite bodies of the "robust" australopithecines. *American Journal of Physical Anthropology* 86:445–454.

McHENRY, H. 1992. Body size and proportions in early hominids. *American Journal of Physical Anthropology* 87:407–431.

McHENRY, H. M. 1994. Tempo and mode in human evolution. *Proceedings of the National Academy of Science* 91:6780–6786.

McHENRY, H. M., AND L. R. BERGER. 1998. Body proportions in *Australopithecus afarensis* and *A. africanus* and the origin of the genus *Homo*. *Journal of Human Evolution* 35:1–22.

McKEE, J. K. 1989. Australopithecine anterior pillars: A reassessment of the functional morphology and phylogenetic significance. *American Journal of Physical Anthropology* 80:1–9.

McKEE, J. K. 1991. Palaeo-ecology of the Sterkfontein hominids: A review and synthesis. *Palaeontologia Africana* 28:41–51.

McKEE, J. K. 1996. Faunal evidence and Sterkfontein Member 2 foot bones of early hominid. *Science* 271:1301–1302.

McKEE, J. K. In press. The autocatalytic nature of hominid evolution in African Plio-Pleistocene environments. In *African Biogeography, Climate Change, and Early Hominid Evolution*, ed. F. Schrenk & T. Bromage. Oxford University Press.

McKEE, J. K., J. F. THACKERAY, AND L. R. BERGER. 1995. Faunal assemblage seriation of southern African Pliocene and Pleistocene fossil deposits. *American Journal of Physical Anthropology* 96:235–250.

PARTRIDGE, T. C., B. A. WOOD, AND P. B. deMENOCAL. 1995. The influence of global climatic change and regional uplift on large-mammalian evolution in East and Southern Africa. In *Paleoclimate and Evolution, with Emphasis on Human Origins*, eds. E. S. Vrba, G. H. Denton, T. C. Partridge, L. H. Burckle. New Haven: Yale University Press.

PETERS, C. 1979. Toward an ecological model of African Plio-Pleistocene hominid adaptations. *American Anthropologist* 81:261–278.

POIRIER, F. E. 1993. *Understanding Human Evolution* 3rd Edition. Englewood Cliffs: Prentice Hall.

RAK, Y. 1985. Australopithecine taxonomy and phylogeny in light of facial morphology. *American Journal of Physical Anthropology* 66:281–288.

RAYNER, R. J., B. P. MOON, AND J. C. MASTERS. 1993. The Makapansgat australopithecine environment. *Journal of Human Evolution* 24:219–231.

REED, K. E. 1997. Early hominid evolution and ecological change through the African Plio-Pleistocene. *Journal of Human Evolution* 32:289–322.

RYAN, A. 1981. Teeth fossils may link Lucy to gorilla and man. *The L.S.B. Leakey Foundation News*, 13.

RYAN, A., AND D. JOHANSON. 1989. Anterior dental microwear in *Australopithecus afarensis*: Comparisons with human and non-human primates. *Journal of Human Evolution* 18:235–268.

ROBINSON, J. 1972. *Early Hominid Posture and Locomotion*. Chicago: University of Chicago Press.

SMITH, B. H. 1986. Dental development in *Australopithecus* and early *Homo*. *Nature* 317:525.

SMITH, B. H. 1991. Dental development and the evolution of life history in Hominidae. *American Journal of Physical Anthropology* 86:157–174.

SPOOR, F., B. WOOD, AND F. ZONNEVELD. 1994. Implications of early hominid labyrinthine morphology for evolution of human bipedal locomotion. *Nature* 369:645–648.

STERN, J., AND R. SUSMAN. 1983. The locomotor anatomy of *Australopithecus afarensis*. *American Journal of Physical Anthropology* 60:279–318.

TOBIAS, P. V. 1971. *The Brain in Hominid Evolution*. New York: Columbia University Press.

TOBIAS, P. V. 1980. "*Australopithecus afarensis*" and *A. africanus*: Critique and an alternative hypothesis. *Palaeontologia Africana* 23:1–17.

TOBIAS, P. V. 1992. New researches at Sterkfontein and Taung with a note on Piltdown and its relevance to the history of palaeo-anthropology. *Transactions of the Royal Society of South Africa* 48(1):1–14.

TOBIAS, P. V. 1994. The craniocerebral interface in early hominids: cerebral impressions, cranial thickening, paleoneurobiology, and a new hypothesis on encephalization. In *Integrative Paths to the Past: Paleoanthropological Advances in Honor of F. Clark Howell*, Eds. R. S. Corrucini & R. L. Ciochon. Englewood Cliffs: Prentice Hall.

TUTTLE, R. 1985. Ape footprints and Laetoli impressions: A response to the SUNY claims. In *Hominid Evolution: Past, Present, and Future*, ed. P. V. Tobias. New York: Alan R. Liss.

WARD, S., AND A. HILL. 1987. Pliocene hominid partial mandible from Tabarin, Baringo, Kenya. *American Journal of Physical Anthropology* 72:21–37.

WHEELER, P. E. 1991. The influence of bipedalism on the energy and water budgets of early hominids. *Journal of Human Evolution* 20:117–136.

WHEELER, P. E. 1993. The influence of stature and body form on hominid energy and water budgets: A comparison of *Australopithecus* and early *Homo* physiques. *Journal of Human Evolution* 24:13–28.

WHITE, T. D., G. SUWA, AND B. ASFAW. 1994. *Australopithecus ramidus,* a new species of early hominid from Aramis, Ethiopia. *Nature* 371:306–312.

WHITE, T. D., G. SUWA, AND B. ASFAW. 1995. *Australopithecus ramidus,* a new species of early hominid from Aramis, Ethiopia. Corrigendum. *Nature* 375:88.

WHITE, T. D., G. SUWA, G., W. K. HART, R. C. WALTER, G. WOLDEGABRIEL, J. DE HEINZELIN, J. D. CLARK, B. ASFAW, AND E. VRBA. 1993. New discoveries of *Australopithecus* at Maka in Ethiopia. *Nature* 366:261–265.

WOLDEGABRIEL, G., T. D. WHITE, G. SUWA, P. RENNE, J. DE HEINZELIN, W. K. HART, AND G. HEIKEN. 1994. Ecological and temporal placement of early Pliocene hominids at Aramis, Ethiopia. *Nature* 371:330–333.

WOOD, B., AND P. QUINNEY. 1996. Assessing the pelvis of AL 288–1. *Journal of Human Evolution* 31:563–568.

ZIHLMAN, A. 1985. *Australopithecus afarensis* two sexes or two species? In *Hominid Evolution: Past, Present and Future,* ed. P. V. Tobias. New York: Alan R. Liss.

ZUCKERMAN, S. 1954a. The australopithecine occiput. *Nature* 174:263.

ZUCKERMAN, S. 1954b. Nuchal crests in the australopithecines. *Nature* 174:1198.

CHAPTER 9

AIELLO, L. C., AND P. WHEELER. 1995. The expensive-tissue hypothesis. *Current Anthropology* 36(2):199–221.

AYALA, F. 1970. Competition, coexistence and evolution. In *Essays in Evolution and Genetics in Honor of Theodosius Dobzhansky,* ed. M. Hecht and W. Steere. New York: Appleton-Century-Crofts.

AYALA, F. 1972. Competition between species. *American Scientist* 60:348–357.

BEHRENSMEYER, A., K. GORDON, AND G. YANAGI. 1986. Trampling as a cause of bone surface damage and pseudo-cutmarks. *Nature* 319:768–771.

BEHRENSMEYER, A. K., N. E. TODD, R. POTTS, AND G. E. MCBRINN. 1997. Late Pliocene faunal turnover in the Turkana Basin, Kenya and Ethiopia. *Science* 278:1589–1594.

BINFORD, L. 1985. Human ancestors: Changing views of their behavior. *Journal of Anthropological Archaeology* 4:292–327.

BINFORD, L. 1987. The hunting hypothesis, archaeological methods, and the past. *Yearbook of Physical Anthropology* 30:1–9.

BRAIN, C. 1981. Hominid evolution and climatic change. *South African Journal of Science* 77:104–105.

BRAIN, C. K., AND J. MEESTER. 1964. Past climatic changes as biological isolating mechanisms in Southern Africa. In *Ecological Studies in Southern Africa,* ed. D. H. S. Davis, pp. 332–340. The Hague: Dr. W. Junk Publishers.

BROOM, R. 1938. The Pleistocene anthropoid apes of South Africa. *Nature* 142:377–379.

BROOM, R., AND J. ROBINSON. 1949. A new type of fossil man. *Nature* 164:332.

BUNN, H. 1981. Archaeological evidence for meat-eating by Plio-Pleistocene hominids from Koobi Fora and Olduvai Gorge. *Nature* 291:574–577.

BUNN, H., AND E. KROLL. 1986. Systematic butchery by Plio/Pleistocene hominids at Olduvai Gorge, Tanzania. *Current Anthropology* 27:431–452.

CERLING, T. E. 1992. Development of grasslands and savannas in East Africa during the Neogene. *Palaeogeography, Palaeoclimatology, Palaeoecology* 97:241–247.

CLARK, J. D. 1976. African origins of man the toolmaker. In *Human Origins,* ed. G. Isaac and E. McCown. Menlo Park, CA: W. A. Benjamin.

CLARK, J. D., J. DE HEINZELIN, K. D. SCHICK, W. K. HART, T. D. WHITE, G. WOLDEGABRIEL, R. C. WALTER, G. SUWA, B. ASFAW, E. VRBA, AND Y.- H. SELASSIE. 1984. African *Homo erectus*: Old radiometric ages and young Oldowan assemblages in the Middle Awash Valley, Ethiopia. *Science* 264:1907–1910.

COLE, S. 1975. *Leakey's Luck.* London: William Collins Sons.

DARWIN, C. 1871. *The Descent of Man.* London: John Murray.

DAY, M., AND J. NAPIER. 1966. A hominid toe bone from Bed I, Olduvai Gorge, Tanzania. *Nature* 211:929.

DAY, M., AND B. WOOD. 1968. Functional affinities of the Olduvai hominid 8 talus. *Man* 3:440–445.

DEMENOCAL, P. B. 1995. Plio-Pleistocene African climate. *Science* 270:53–59.

FOLEY, R. A. 1994. Speciation, extinction and climatic change in hominid evolution. *Journal of Human Evolution* 26:275–289.

GRINE, F., AND R. KAY. 1988. Early hominid diets from quantitative image analysis of dental wear. *Nature* 353:765–768.

HARRIS, J., AND OTHERS. 1987. Late Pliocene hominid occupation in Central Africa: The setting, context and character of the Senga 5A site, Zaire. *Journal of Human Evolution* 16:701–728.

HARTWIG-SCHERER, S., AND R. MARTIN. 1991. Was "Lucy" more human than her child? Observations on early hominid post-cranial skeletons. *Journal of Human Evolution* 21:439–449.

HILL, A. 1986. Tools, teeth and trampling. *Nature* 319: 719–720.

HILL, A., S. WARD, A. DEINO, G. CURTIS, AND R. DRAKE. 1992. Earliest *Homo. Nature* 355:719–722.

ISAAC, G., AND J. HARRIS. 1978. Archaeology. In *Koobi Fora Research Project,* vol. 1, ed. M. Leakey and R. Leakey. Oxford: Clarendon Press.

JOHANSON, D., F. MASO, G. ECK, AND OTHERS. 1987. New partial skeleton of *Homo habilis* from Olduvai Gorge, Tanzania. *Nature* 327:205–209.

JONES, P. 1979. Effects of raw materials on biface manufacture. *Science* 204:835–836.

KEELEY, L., AND N. TOTH. 1981. Microwear polishes on early stone tools from Koobi Fora, Kenya. *Nature* 293:464–465.

KIDD, R., P. O'HIGGINS, P., AND C. OXNARD. 1996. The OH 8 foot: A reappraisal of the functional morphology of the hindfoot utilizing a multivariate analysis. *Journal of Human Evolution* 31:269–291.

KIMBEL, W. H. 1995. Hominid speciation and Pliocene climatic change. In *Paleoclimate and Evolution,* ed. E. Vrba et al. New Haven, CT: Yale University Press.

KIMBEL, W. H., D. C. JOHANSON, AND Y. RAK. 1997. Systematic assessment of a maxilla of *Homo* from Hadar, Ethiopia. *American Journal of Physical Anthropology* 103:235–262.

KIMBEL, W. H., R. C. WALTER, D. C. JOHANSON, K. E. REED, J. L. ARONSON, Z. ASSEFA, C. W. MAREAN, G. G. ECK, R. BOBE, E. HOVERS, Y. RAK, C. VONDRA, T. YEMANE, D. YORK, Y. CHEN, N. M. EVENSEN, AND P. E. SMITH. 1996. Late Pliocene *Homo* and Oldowan tools from the Hadar Formation (Kada Hadar Member), Ethiopia. *Journal of Human Evolution* 31:549–561.

KIMBEL, W., T. WHITE, AND D. JOHANSON. 1988. Implications of KNM-WT 17000 for the evolution of "robust" *Australopithecus.* In *Evolutionary History of the "Robust" Australopithecines,* ed. F. Grine. Hawthorne, NY: Aldine de Gruyter.

KINGSTON, J., B. MARINO, AND A. HILL. 1994. Isotopic evidence for Neogene hominid paleoenvironments in the Kenya Rift Valley. *Science* 264:955–960.

KLEIN, R. 1989. *The Human Career. Human Biological and Cultural Origins.* Chicago: University of Chicago Press.

LEAKEY, L., P. V. TOBIAS, AND J. NAPIER. 1964. A new species of the genus *Homo* from Olduvai Gorge. *Nature* 202:5–7.

LEAKEY, M. 1967. Preliminary survey of the cultural material from Beds I and II, Olduvai Gorge, Tanzania. In *Background to Evolution in Africa,* ed. W. W. Bishop and J. D. Clark. Chicago: University of Chicago Press.

LEAKEY, R. E. F., AND A. WALKER. 1988. New *Australopithecus boisei* specimens from East and West Lake Turkana, Kenya. *American Journal of Physical Anthropology* 71:1–24.

LEE-THORP, J. A., N. J. VAN DER MERWE, AND C. K. BRAIN. 1994. Diet of *Australopithecus robustus* at Swartkrans from stable carbon isotopic analysis. *Journal of Human Evolution* 27:361–372.

LEWIN, R. 1988. A new tool maker in the hominid record? *Science* 240:724–725.

MARZKE, M. W. 1997. Precision grips, hand morphology, and tools. *American Journal of Physical Anthropology* 102:91–110.

MCHENRY, H. 1991a. Early hominid stature. *American Journal of Physical Anthropology* 85:149–158.

MCHENRY, H. 1991b. Petite bodies of the "robust" australopithecines. *American Journal of Physical Anthropology* 86:445–454.

MCHENRY, H. 1992. Body size and proportions in early hominids. *American Journal of Physical Anthropology* 87:407–431.

MCHENRY, H. M. 1994. Tempo and mode in human evolution. *Proceedings of the National Academy of Science* 91:6780–6786.

MCKEE, J. K. 1995. Turnover patterns and species longevity of large mammals from the Late Pliocene and Pleistocene of southern Africa: A comparison of simulated and empirical data. *Journal of Theoretical Biology* 172:141–147.

MCKEE, J. K. 1996. Faunal turnover patterns in the Pliocene and Pleistocene of southern Africa. *South African Journal of Science.* 92:111–113.

MCKEE, J. K. 1997. East African confirmation of constant turnover among Plio-Pleistocene large mammals. *American Journal of Physical Anthropology,* Suppl. 24:167.

MORELL, V. 1986. The unkindest cut. *Science* 867:71–72.

MORSE, D. 1974. Niche breadth as a function of social dominance. *American Naturalist* 108:818–830.

NAPIER, J. 1959. Fossil metacarpals from Swartkrans. *Fossil Mammals of Africa,* No. 17. London: British Museum (Natural History).

NAPIER, J. 1962. Fossil hand bones from Olduvai Gorge. *Nature* 196:409–411.

OXNARD, C., AND P. LISOWSKI. 1980. Functional articulation of some hominoid foot bones: Implications for the Olduvai (Hominid 8) foot. *American Journal of Physical Anthropology.* 52:107–117.

PARTRIDGE, T. C., B. A. WOOD, AND P. B. DEMENOCAL. 1995. The influence of global climatic change and regional uplift on large-mammalian evolution in East and Southern Africa. In *Paleoclimate and Evolution, with Emphasis on Human Origins,* ed. E. S. Vrba, G. H. Denton, T. C. Partridge, and L. H. Burckle. New Haven CT: Yale University Press.

PETERS, C. 1979. Toward an ecological model of African Plio-Pleistocene hominid adaptations. *American Anthropologist* 81:261–278.

POTTS, R. 1984. Home bases and early hominids. *American Scientist* 72:338–347.

POTTS, R. 1988. *Early Hominid Activities at Olduvai.* New York: Aldine de Gruyter.

POTTS, R. 1996a. Evolution and climate variability. *Science* 273:922–923.

POTTS, R. 1996b. *Humanity's Descent—The Consequences of Ecological Instability.* New York: William Morrow.

POTTS, R., AND P. SHIPMAN. 1981. Cutmarks made by stone tools on bones from Olduvai Gorge, Tanzania. *Nature* 291:577–580.

ROBINSON, J. 1962. Australopithecines and artifacts at Sterkfontein. Part I. Sterkfontein stratigraphy and the significance of the extension site. *South African Archaeological Bulletin* 17:87.

ROBINSON, J. 1963. Adaptive radiation in the australopithecines and the origin of man. In *African Ecology and Human Evolution,* ed. F. Howell and F. Bourliere. Chicago: Aldine-Atherton.

ROBINSON, J. 1965. *Homo habilis* and the australopithecines. *Nature* 205:21.

ROBINSON, J. 1972. *Early Hominid Posture and Locomotion.* Chicago: University of Chicago Press.

SCHRENK F., T. G. BROMAGE, C. G. BETZLER, U. RING, AND Y. M. JUWAYEYI. 1993. Oldest *Homo* and Pliocene biogeography of the Malawi Rift. *Nature* 365:833–836.

SEMAW, S., P. RENNE, J. HARRIS, C. FEIBEL, R. BERNOR, N. FESSEHA, AND K. MOWBRAY. 1997. 2.5–million-year-old stone tools from Gona, Ethiopia. *Nature* 385:333–336.

SHACKLETON, N. J. 1995. New data on the evolution of Pliocene climatic variability. In *Paleoclimate and Evolution,* ed. E. Vrba et al. New Haven: Yale University Press.

SHIPMAN, P. 1986. Scavenging or hunting in early hominids: Theoretical framework and tests. *American Anthropologist* 88:27–49.

SILLEN, A. 1992. Strontium-calcium ratios (Sr/Ca) of *Australopithecus robustus* and associated fauna from Swartkrans. *Journal of Human Evolution.* 23:495–516.

SUSMAN, R. 1988. Hand of *Paranthropus robustus* from Member 1, Swartkrans: Fossil evidence for tool behavior. *Science* 240:781–783.

SUSMAN, R., AND J. STERN. 1979. Telemetered electron myography of flexor digitorum profundus and flexor digitorum superficialis in *Pan troglodytes* and implications for interpretation of the OH 7 hand. *American Journal of Physical Anthropology* 50:565–574.

SUWA, G., B. ASFAW, Y. BEYENE, T. D. WHITE, S. KATOH, S. NAGAOKA, H. NAKAYA, K. UZAWA, P. RENNE, AND G. WOLDE-GABRIEL. 1997. The first skull of *Australopithecus boisei. Nature* 389:489–492.

TANNER, N. 1981. *On Becoming Human.* New York: Cambridge University Press.

TOBIAS, P. V. 1987. The brain of *Homo habilis:* A new level of organization in cerebral evolution. *Journal of Human Evolution* 16:741–761.

TOBIAS, P. V. 1991. *Olduvai Gorge,* vol. 4: *The Skulls, Endocasts and Teeth of Homo habilis.* Cambridge: Cambridge University Press.

TOBIAS, P. V. 1994. The craniocerebral interface in early hominids: Cerebral impressions, cranial thickening, paleoneurobiology, and a new hypothesis on encephalization. In *Integrative Paths to the Past: Paleoanthropological Advances in Honor of F. Clark Howell,* ed. R. S. Corrucini and R. L. Ciochon. Englewood Cliffs, NJ: Prentice Hall.

TOTH, N. 1987. The first technology. *Scientific American* 256:122–131.

TRINKAUS E., AND J. LONG. 1990. Species attribution of the Swartkrans Member 1 first metacarpals SK 84 and SKX 5020. *American Journal of Physical Anthropology* 83:419–424.

VRBA, E. S. 1980. Evolution, species and fossils: How does life evolve? *South African Journal of Science* 76:61–84.

VRBA, E. S. 1985a. African bovidae: Evolutionary events since the Miocene. *South African Journal of Science* 81:263–266.

VRBA, E. S. 1985b. Ecological and adaptive changes associated with early hominid evolution. In *Ancestors: The Hard Evidence*, ed. E. Delson. New York: Alan R. Liss.

VRBA, E. S. 1988. Late Pliocene climatic events and hominid evolution. In *Evolutionary History of the "Robust" Australopithecines*, ed. F. E. Grine. New York: Aldine de Gruyter.

VRBA, E. S. 1995a. The fossil record of African antelopes (Mammalia, Bovidae) in relation to human evolution and paleoclimate. In *Paleoclimate and Evolution*, ed. E. Vrba et al. New Haven, CT: Yale University Press.

VRBA, E. S. 1995b. On the connections between paleoclimate and evolution. In *Paleoclimate and Evolution*, ed. E. Vrba et al. New Haven, CT: Yale University Press.

WALKER, A., R. LEAKEY, J. HARRIS, AND F. BROWN. 1986. 2.5 myr *Australopithecus boisei* from west of Lake Turkana, Kenya. *Nature* 322:517–522.

WHITE, T. D. 1988. The comparative biology of "robust" Australopithecus: clues from context. In *Evolutionary History of the "Robust" Australopithecines*, ed. F. E. Grine. New York: Aldine de Gruyter.

WHITE, T. D. 1995. African omnivores: Global climatic change and Plio-Pleistocene hominids and suids. In *Paleoclimate and Evolution*, ed. E. Vrba et al. New Haven, CT: Yale University Press.

WINTERHALDER, B. 1980. Hominid paleoecology: The competitive exclusion principle and determinants of niche relationships. *Yearbook of Physical Anthropology* 23:43–64.

WOOD, B. 1987. Who is the "real" *Homo habilis*? *Nature* 327:187–188.

WOOD, B. 1988. Are "robust" australopithecines a monophyletic group? In *Evolutionary History of the "Robust" Australopithecines*, ed. F. E. Grine. New York: Aldine de Gruyter.

WOOD, B. 1992. Origin and evolution of the genus *Homo*. *Nature* 355:783–790.

WOOD, B. 1997. The oldest whodunnit in the world. *Nature* 385:292–293.

CHAPTER 10

ABDUL NAYEEM, M. 1998. *Qatar: Prehistory and Protohistory from the Most Ancient Times.* Hyderabad: Hyderabad Publishing.

ACKERMAN, S. 1989. European history gets even older. *Science* 246:28–30.

ANDREWS, P. 1984a. An alternative interpretation of the characters used to define *Homo erectus.* In *The Early Evolution of Man*, ed. P. Andrews and J. Frazen, Frankfurt: Senckenberg Museum.

ANDREWS, P. 1984b. On the characters that define *Homo erectus. Courier Forschungsinstitut Senckenberg* 69:167–178.

BARTSTRA, G. 1982. *Homo erectus erectus*: The search for his artifacts. *Current Anthropology* 23:318–320.

BAR-YOSEF, O. 1980. The prehistory of the Levant. *Annual Review of Anthropology*, pp. 101–135.

BEHRENSMEYER, A., AND L. LAPORTE. 1981. Footprints of a Pleistocene hominid in northern Kenya. *Nature* 289:167–169.

BINFORD, L. 1981. *Bones.* New York: Academic Press.

BINFORD, L. 1985. Human ancestors: Changing views of their behavior. *Journal of Anthropological Archaeology* 4:292–327.

BINFORD, L. 1987a. The hunting hypothesis, archaeological methods, and the past. *Yearbook of Physical Anthropology* 30:1–9.

BINFORD, L. 1987b. Were there elephant hunters at Torralba? In *The Evolution of Human Hunting*, ed. M. Nitecki and D. Nitecki. New York: Plenum Press.

BINFORD, L., AND L. TODD. 1982. On arguments for the "butchering" of giant geladas. *Current Anthropology* 23:108–110.

BINFORD, L., AND C. HO. 1985. Taphonomy at a distance: Zhoukoudian, the cave home of Beijing man? *Current Anthropology* 26:413–442.

BINFORD, L., AND N. STONE. 1986. Zhoukoudian: A closer look. *Current Anthropology* 27:453–475.

BLACK, D. 1931. On an adolescent skull of "Sinanthropus pekinensis" in comparison with an adult skull of the same species and with other hominid skulls, recent and fossil. *Paleontologia Sinica*, Series D 7.

BORJA, C., M. GARCIA-PACHECO, F. OLIVARES, G. SCHEUENSTUHL, AND L. LOWENSTEIN. 1997. Immunospecificity of albumin detected in 1.6 million-year-old fossils from Venta Micena in Orce, Granada, Spain. *American Journal of Physical Anthropology* 103:433–441.

BOWER, B. 1997. Ancient roads to Europe. *Science News* 151:12–13.

BRACE, C. 1967. Environment, tooth form and size in the Pleistocene. *Journal of Dental Research* 46:809.

BRAIN, C. K., AND A. SILLEN. 1988. Evidence from the Swartkrans cave for the earliest use of fire. *Nature* 336:464–466.

BRAUER, G., AND M. SCHULTZ. 1996. The morphological affinities of the Plio-Pleistocene mandible from Dmanisi, Georgia. *Journal of Human Evolution* 30:445–481.

BROOM, R. 1949. Another new type of fossil ape-man. *Nature* 163:57.

BROOM, R., AND J. ROBINSON. 1949. A new type of fossil man. *Nature* 164:322.

BROOM, R., AND J. ROBINSON. 1950. Man contemporaneous with the Swartkrans ape-man. *American Journal of Physical Anthropology* 8:151.

BROWN, F., AND C. FEIBEL. 1985. Stratigraphical notes on the Okote Tuff Complex at Koobi Fora, Kenya. *Nature* 316:794–797.

BROWN, F., J. HARRIS, R. LEAKEY, AND A. WALKER. 1985. Early *Homo erectus* skeleton from west Lake Turkana, Kenya. *Nature* 316:788–792.

BUTZER, K., AND G. ISAAC, EDS. 1975. *After the Australopithecines: Stratigraphy, Ecology, and Culture Change in the Middle Pleistocene.* The Hague: Mouton.

BYE, B., F. BROWN, T. CERLING, AND I. McDOUGALL. 1987. Increased age estimate for the Lower Paleolithic hominid site at Olorgesailie, Kenya. *Nature* 329:237–239.

CACHEL, S., AND J. HARRIS. 1995. Ranging patterns, land-use and subsistence in *Homo erectus*, from the perspective of evolutionary ecology. In *Evolution and Ecology of* Homo erectus, ed. J. Bower and S. Sartono. Leiden: DSWO Press.

CARBONELL, E., AND OTHERS. 1995. Lower Pleistocene hominids and artifacts from Atapuerca-TD6 (Spain). *Science* 269:826–830.

CHANG, K. 1962. New evidence on fossil man in China. *Science* 136:749.

CHANG, K. 1973. Radiocarbon dates from China: Some initial interpretations. *Current Anthropology* 14:525.

CHANG, K. C. 1977. Chinese paleoanthropology. *Annual Review of Anthropology* 6:137–159.

CIOCHON, R. 1984/1985. Paleontological field research in Vietnam. *Newsletter, The Institute of Human Origins* 4:7–8.

CIOCHON, R. 1996. The earliest Asians yet. *Natural History* 104:50–55.

CLARK, J. D. 1976. African origins of man the toolmaker. In *Human Origins*, ed. G. Isaac and E. McCown. Menlo Park, CA: W. A. Benjamin.

CLARK, J. D. 1987. Transitions: *Homo erectus* and the Acheulian: The Ethiopian sites of Gadeb and the Middle Awash. *Journal of Human Evolution* 16:809–826.

CLARK, J. D., AND J. KURASHINA. 1979. Hominid occupation of the east-central highlands of Ethiopia in the Plio-Pleistocene. *Nature* 282:33–39.

CLARK, J. D., J. DE HEINZELIN, K. SCHICK, W. HART, T. WHITE, G. WOLDEGABRIEL, R. WALTER, G. SUWA, B. ASFAW, E. VRBA, AND Y.-H. SELASSIE. 1994. African *Homo erectus*: Old radiometric ages and young Oldowan assemblages in the Middle Awash Valley, Ethiopia. *Science* 264:1907–1910.

CLARK, W. L. G. 1967. *The Fossil Evidence for Human Evolution.* Chicago: University of Chicago Press.

COON, C. 1962. *The Origin of Races.* New York: Alfred A. Knopf.

DAVIS, R., V. RANOV, AND A. DODONOV. 1980. Early man in Soviet Central Asia. *Scientific American* 243:130–138.

DAY, M. 1971. Postcranial remains of *Homo erectus* from Bed IV. Olduvai Gorge, Tanzania. *Nature* 232:383.

DAY, M., AND T. MOLLESON. 1973. The Trinil femora. *Journal of Human Evolution* 11:127.

DE CASTRO, J. B., J. ARSUGA, E. CARBONELL, A. ROSASA, I. MARTINEZ, AND M. MOSQUERA. 1997. A hominid from the Lower Pleistocene of Atapuerca, Spain: Possible ancestor to Neandertals and modern humans. *Science* 276:1392–1395.

DELSON, E. 1985. Paleobiology and age of African *Homo erectus*. *Nature.* 316:762–763.

DUBOIS, E. 1896. *Pithecanthropus erectus*: A form from the ancestral stock of mankind. In *The Annual Report for the Smithsonian Institute for the Year Ending June 30, 1898*. Washington, DC: U.S. Government Printing Office.

GABUNIA, L., AND A. VEKUA. 1995. A Plio-Pleistocene hominid from Dmanisi, East Georgia, Caucasus. *Nature* 373:509–512.

GAULD, S. 1996. Allometric patterns of cranial bone thickness in fossil hominids. *American Journal of Physical Anthropology* 100:411–426.

GIBBONS, A. 1990. Paleontology for bulldozer. *Science* 247:1407–1409.

GIBBONS, A. 1992. Jawing with our Georgian ancestors. *Science* 255:401.

GIBBONS, A. 1994. Rewriting—and redating—prehistory. *Science* 263:1087–1088.

GIBBONS, A. 1996. *Homo erectus* in Java: A 250,000-year anachronism. *Science* 274:1841–1842.

GIBBONS, A. 1997a. Doubts over spectacular dates. *Science* 278:220–222.

GIBBONS, A. 1997b. A new face for human ancestors. *Science* 276:1331–1333.

GLEADOW, A. 1980. Fisson track age of the KBS Tuff and associated hominid remains in northern Kenya. *Nature* 284:225–230.

GOULD, S. J. 1990. Men of the thirty-third division. *Natural History* April:12–27.

GOWLETT, J., J. HARRIS, D. WALTON, AND B. WOOD. 1981. Early archaeological sites, hominid remains and traces of fire from Cheswonja, Kenya. Kenya. *Nature* 294:125–129.

GUTIN, J. 1995. Remains in Spain now reign as oldest Europeans. *Science* 269:754–755.

HOLDEN, C. 1994. Old human bones found in Spain. *Science* 265:755.

HOLDEN, C. 1997. Tooling around: dates show early Siberian settlement. *Science* 275:1268.

HOWELL, F. 1960. European and Northwest African Middle Pleistocene hominids. *Current Anthropology* 1:195–232.

HOWELL, F. 1965. *Early Man.* New York: Time-Life Books.

HOWELL, F. 1976. Some views of *Homo erectus* with special reference to its occurrence in Europe. Paper presented at Davidson Black Symposium, Canadian Association of Physical Anthropologists, Toronto.

HOWELLS, W. 1966. *Homo erectus. Scientific American* 215:46–53.

HOWELLS, W. 1973. *Evolution of the Genus* Homo. Reading, MA: Addison-Wesley.

HOWELLS, W. 1980. *Homo erectus*—Who, when and where: A survey. *Yearbook of Physical Anthropology* 23:1–24.

HUANG, W. 1960. Restudy of the Choukoutien *Sinanthropus* deposits. *Vertebrata Paleasiatica* 4:45.

ISAAC, G. 1968. Traces of Pleistocene hunters: An East African example. In *Man the Hunter*, ed. R. Lee and I. DeVore. Chicago: Aldine-Atherton.

ISAAC, G. 1969. Studies of early cultures in East Africa. *World Archaeology* 1:1–28.

ISAAC, G. 1975. Stratigraphy and cultural patterns in East Africa during the middle ranges of Pleistocene time. In *After the Australopithecines*, ed. K. Butzer and G. Isaac. The Hague: Mouton.

ISAAC, G. 1977. *Olorgesailie: Archaeological Studies of a Middle Pleistocene Lake Basin in Kenya.* Chicago: University of Chicago Press.

JACOB, T. 1967. Recent "Pithecanthropus" finds in Indonesia. *Current Anthropology* 8:501.

JACOB, T., R. SOEJONO, L. FREEMAN, AND F. BROWN. 1978. Stone tools from Mid-Pleistocene sediments in Java. *Science* 202:885–887.

JAMES, S. 1989. Hominid use of fire in the lower and middle Pleistocene: A review of the evidence. *Current Anthropology* 30:1–26.

JIA, L. P. 1975. *The Cave Home of Peking Man.* Peking: Foreign Languages Press.

JIA, L. P. 1989. On problems of the Beijing Man site: A critique of new interpretations. *Current Anthropology* 30:200–204.

JIA, L. P., AND W. HUANG. 1990. *The Story of Peking Man.* New York: Oxford University Press.

JING, JUN. 1984. "Apeman" clue to evolution. *China Daily*, November 39, p. 1.

JOLLY, C., AND F. PLOG. 1976. *Physical Anthropology and Archaeology.* New York: Alfred A. Knopf.

KLEIN, R. 1987. Reconstructing how early people exploited animals: Problems and prospects. In *The Evolution of Human Hunting*, ed. M. Nitecki and D. Nitecki. New York: Plenum Press.

KRETZOI, M., AND L. VÉRTES. 1965. Upper Biharian (Intermindel) pebble-industry occupation in western Hungary. *Current Anthropology* 6:74–87.

LEAKEY, L. 1961. New finds at Olduvai Gorge. *Nature* 89:649.

LEAKEY, L. 1966. *Homo habilis, Homo erectus*, and the australopithecines. *Nature* 209:1279–1281.

LEAKEY, L. 1971. Discovery of postcranial remains of *Homo erectus* and associated artifacts in Bed IV at Olduvai Gorge, Tanzania. *Nature* 232:380–383.

LEAKEY, R. 1970a. New hominid remains and early artifacts from northern Kenya: Fauna and artifacts from a new Plio-Pleistocene locality near Lake Rudolf in Kenya. *Nature* 226:223.

LEAKEY, R. 1970b. In search of man's past at Lake Rudolf. *National Geographic* 137:712.

LEIGH, S. 1991. Cranial capacity evolution in *Homo erectus* and early *Homo sapiens*. *American Journal of Physical Anthropology* 87:1–13.

LEWIN, R. 1984. Unexpected anatomy in *Homo erectus*. *Science* 226:529.

LI, Y., AND H. JI. 1981. Environmental change in Peking man's time. *Vertebrata Palasiatica* 19:347 (in Chinese with English summary).

MALLEGNI, F., AND A. RADMILLI. 1988. Human temporal bone from the Lower Paleolithic site of Castel di Guido, near Rome, Italy. *American Journal of Physical Anthropology* 76:175–182.

MANN, A. 1971. *Homo erectus*. In *Background for Man*, ed. P. Dolhinow and V. Sarich. Boston: Little, Brown.

MARSCHACK, A. 1989. Evolution of the human capacity: The symbolic evidence. *Yearbook of Physical Anthropology* 32:1–34.

MCDOUGALL, I., R. MAIER, P. SUTHERLAND-HAWKES, AND A. GLEADOW. 1980. K-Ar age estimate for the KBS Tuff, Lake Turkana. *Nature* 284:230–234.

MCDOUGALL, I., T. DAVIES, R. MAIER, AND R. RUDOWSKI. 1985. Age of the Okote Tuff Complex at Koobi Fora, Kenya. *Nature* 316:792–794.

MORELL, V. 1994. Did early humans reach Siberia 500,000 years ago? *Science* 261:611–612.

MORWOOD, M., P. O'SULLIVAN, F. AZIZ, AND A. RAZA. 1998. Fission-track ages of stone tools and fossils on the east Indonesian island of Flores. *Nature* 392:173–176.

OAKLEY, K. 1955a. Cave-fire. *Science Digest* 73:8.

OAKLEY, K. 1955b. Fire as a Paleolithic tool and weapon. *Proceedings of the Prehistoric Society* 21:36.

OAKLEY, K. 1961. On man's use of fire, with comments on tool-making and hunting. In *Social Life of Early Man*, ed. S. Washburn. Chicago: Aldine-Atherton.

O'BRIEN, E. 1984. What was the Acheulean hand ax? *Natural History* June:20–24.

PARÈS, J., AND A. PEREZ-GONZALEZ. 1995. Paleomagnetic age for hominid fossils at Atapuerca archaeological site, Spain. *Science* 269:830–832.

PFEIFFER, J. 1971. When *Homo erectus* tamed fire, he tamed himself. In *Human Variation*, ed. H. Bleibtreu and J. Downs. Beverly Hills, CA: Glencoe Press.

PFEIFFER, J. 1972. *The Emergence of Man*. New York: Harper & Row.

PILBEAM, D. 1975. Middle Pleistocene hominids. In *After the Australopithecines*, ed. K. Butzer and G. Isaac. The Hague: Mouton.

POPE, G. 1989. Bamboo and human evolution. *Natural History* October:48–56.

POPE, G. 1993. Ancient Asia's cutting edge. *Natural History*, May: 55–58.

PUECH, P. 1983. Tooth wear, diet, and the artifacts of Java Man. *Current Anthropology* 24:381–382.

RIGHTMIRE, G. P. 1979. Cranial remains of *Homo erectus* from Beds II and IV, Olduvai Gorge, Tanzania. *American Journal of Physical Anthropology* 51:99–116.

RIGHTMIRE, G. P. 1983. The Lake Ndutu cranium. *American Journal of Physical Anthropology* 61:245–254.

ROBINSON, J. 1953a. The nature of "Telanthropus capensis." *Nature* 171:33.

ROBINSON, J. 1953b. "Telanthropus" and its phylogenetic significance. *American Journal of Physical Anthropology* 11:445.

ROSAS, A. 1987. Two new mandibular fragments from Atapuerca/Ibeas (SH site). A reassessment of the affinities of the Ibeas mandibles sample. *Journal of Human Evolution* 16:417–422.

ROSAS, A. 1995. Seventeen new mandibular specimens from the Atapuerca/Ibeas Middle Pleistocene hominids sample (1985–1992). *Journal of Human Evolution* 28:533–559.

RUFF, C. 1993. Climatic adaptation and hominid evolution: The thermoregulatory imperative. *Evolutionary Anthropology* 2:53–60.

RUFF, C., AND A. WALKER. 1991. Body size of KNM WT 1500. Paper presented at Sixtieth Annual Meeting of the American Association of Physical Anthropologists, Milwaukee.

SARTONO, S. 1972. Discovery of another hominid skull at Sangiran, central Java. *Current Anthropology* 13:124.

SEÑGE, A., AND A. ASCENZI. 1984. Fontana Ranuccio: Italy's earliest Middle Pleistocene hominid site. *Current Anthropology* 25:230–233.

SHAPIRO, H. 1971. The strange, unfinished saga of Peking man. *Natural History* 80:8, 74.

SHAPIRO, H. 1974. *Peking Man*. New York: Simon & Schuster.

SHIPMAN, P., W. BOSLER, AND K. DAVIS. 1981. Butchering of giant geladas at an Acheulian site. *Current Anthropology* 22:257–268.

SILLEN, A., AND C. BRAIN. 1990. Old flame. *Natural History*, April: 6–11.

SORIANO, M. 1970. The fluoric origin of the bone lesion in the "Pithecanthropus erectus" femur. *American Journal of Physical Anthropology* 32:33.

STRINGER, C. 1984. The definition of *Homo erectus* and the existence of the species in Africa and Europe. In *The Early Evolution of Man*, ed. P. Andrews and J. Franzen. Frankfurt: Senckenberg Museum.

SWISHER, C., III, G. CURTIS, T. JACOB, A. GETTY, A. SUPRIJO, AND WIDIASOMORO. 1994. Age of earliest known hominids in Java, Indonesia. *Science* 263:1118–1121.

SWISHER, C., W. RINK, S. ANTON, H. SCHWARCZ, G. CURTIN, A. SUPRIJO, AND WIDIASOMORO. 1996. Latest *Homo erectus* of Java: Potential contemporaneity with *Homo sapiens* in Southeast Asia. *Science* 274:1870–1874.

TCHERNOV, E. 1987. The age of the 'Ubeidiya Formation, an early Pleistocene hominid site in the Jordan Valley, Israel. *Israel Journal of Earth Science* 36:3–30.

THEUNISSEN, B. 1989. *Eugene Dubois and the Ape-Men from Java*. Amsterdam: Kluwer Academic Publications.

THIEME, H. 1997. Lower Paleolithic hunting spears from Germany. *Nature* 385:807–810.

THOMA, A. 1966. L'occipital de l'homme mindelien de Vértesszöllös, *L'Anthropologie* 70:495.

THOMA, A. 1967. Human teeth from the lower Paleolithic of Hungary. *Zeitschrift fur Morphologie und Anthropologie* 58:152.

THOMA, A. 1969. Biometrische studie uber das occipatale von Vértesszöllös. *Zeitschrift fur Morphologie und Anthropologie* 60:229.

TOBIAS, P. 1971. *The Brain in Hominid Evolution*. New York: Columbia University Press.

VILLA, P. 1990. Torralba and Aridos: Elephant exploitation in Middle Pleistocene Spain. *Journal of Human Evolution* 19:299–309.

WALKER, A. 1993. The origin of the genus *Homo*. In *The Origin and Evolution of Humans and Humanness*, ed. T. Rasmussen. Boston: Jones and Bartless.

WALKER, A., AND R. LEAKEY. 1978. The hominids of East Turkana. *Scientific American* 239:54–66.

WALKER, A., AND R. LEAKEY. 1993. *The Nariokotome Homo erectus Skeleton*. Cambridge, MA: Harvard University Press.

WANGPO, W., R. CIOCHON, G. YUMIN, R. LARICK, F. QIREN, H. SCHWARCZ, C. YONGE, J. DE VOS, AND W. RINK. 1995. Early *Homo* and associated artefacts from Asia. *Nature* 378:275–278.

WANPO, H., F. DUSHE, AND Y. YONGZIANG. 1981. Preliminary observation on a fossil hominid skull found in Longtan cave in Hexian County, Anhui Province. *Kexue Tongbao* 26:1116–1120 (in Chinese).

WATERS, M., S. FORMAN, AND J. PIERSON. 1997. Diring Yuriakh: A Lower Paleolithic site in Central Siberia. *Science* 275:1281–1284.

WATERS, T. 1990. Traveling man. *Discover,* June: 22.

WEIDENREICH, F. 1936. The mandibles of "Sinanthropus pekinensis." *Paleontologia Sinica,* New Series D 1.

WEIDENREICH, F. 1938. The ramification of the middle meningeal artery in fossil hominids and its bearing upon phylogenetic problems. *Paleontologia Sinica,* New Series D 3.

WEIDENREICH, F. 1941. The extremity bones of "Sinanthropus pekinensis." *Paleontologia Sinica,* New Series D 5.

WEIDENREICH, F. 1943. The skull of "Simanthropus pekinensis." *Paleontologia Sinica,* New Series D 10:1–485.

WHALEN, N., W. DAVIS, AND D. PEASE. 1989. Early Pleistocene migrations into Saudi Arabia. *Atlal* 12:59–75.

WHALEN, N., AND D. PEASE. 1990. Variability in Developed Oldowan and Acheulian bifaces in Saudi Arabia. *Atlal* 13:43–48.

WHALEN, N., AND D. PEASE. 1992. Early mankind in Arabia. *Aramco World* 4:16–23.

WHALEN, N., AND K. SCHATTE. 1997. Pleistocene sites in southern Yemen. *Arabian Archaeology and Epigraphy* 8.

WHALEN, N., H. SINDI, G. WAHIDAH, AND J. SIRAJ-ALI. 1982. Excavation of Acheulian sites near Saffqah in al-Dawadmi. *Atlal* 9–21.

WHALEN, N., J. SIRAJ-ALI, AND W. DAVIS. 1984. Excavation of Acheulian sites near Saffaqah, Saudi Arabia, 1403 AH 1983. *Atlal* 8:9–24.

WHALEN, N., J. SIRAJ, H. ALI, AND D. PEASE. 1986. A lower Pleistocene site near Shuwayhitiyh in northern Saudi Arabia. *Atlal* 10.

WHITEHEAD, P. 1982. Hominid discovery in the Awash Valley. *Explorers Journal* 60:123–125.

WOLPOFF, M. 1970. The evidence for multiple hominid taxa at Swartkrans. *American Anthropologist* 72:567.

WOLPOFF, M. 1971. Is Vértesszöllös II an occipital of European *Homo erectus*? *Nature* 232:567.

WOLPOFF, M. 1977. Some notes on the Vértesszöllös occipital. *American Journal of Physical Anthropology* 47:357–364.

WOLPOFF, M. 1980. *Paleoanthropology.* New York: Alfred A. Knopf, Inc.

WOOD, B., AND A. TURNER. 1995. Out of Africa and into Asia. *Nature* 378:239–240.

WOO, JU-KANG. 1964. Mandible of "Sinanthropus lantianensis." *Current Anthropology* 5:98.

WU, M. 1983. *Homo erectus* from Hexian, Anhui, found in 1981. *Acta Anthropologica Sinica* 2:110–116 (in Chinese with English summary).

WU, R., AND X. DONG. 1980. The fossil human teeth from Yunxian, Hubei. *Vertebrata Palasiatica* 17:149 (in Chinese with English summary).

WU, R., AND X. DONG. 1982. Preliminary study of *Homo erectus* remains from Hexian, Anhui. *Acta Anthropologica Sinica* 1:2–13 (in Chinese with English summary).

WU, R., AND J. OLSEN, EDS. 1985. *Paleoanthropology and Paleolithic Archaeology in the People's Republic of China.* Orlando, FL: Academic Press.

WU, X., AND F. E. POIRIER. 1995. *Human Evolution in China: A Metric Description of the Fossils and a Review of the Sites.* New York: Oxford University Press.

WU, X., AND L. WANG. 1985. Chronology in Chinese paleoanthropology. In *Paleoanthropology and Paleolithic Archaeology in the People's Republic of China.* New York: Alan R. Liss.

ZHEN, S. 1983. Micromammals from the Hexian man locality. *Vertebrata Palasiatica* 20:239–240 (in Chinese with English summary).

ZHOU, G. 1987. The first man in China: Yuanmou man, his date and living environment. Unpublished manuscript.

ZIHLMAN, A., AND J. LOWENSTEIN. 1996. A Spanish Olduvai? *Current Anthropology* 37:695–697.

CHAPTER 11

ABBATE, E., ET AL., 1998. A one-million-year old *Homo* cranium from the Danakil (Afar) depression of Eritrea. *Nature* 393:458–460.

ARSUGA, J.-I., J. M. BERMUDEZ DE CASTRO, AND E. CARBONELL, EDS. 1997. The Sima de los Huesos hominid site. *Journal of Human Evolution* 33:105–421.

ARSUGA, J.-I., I. MARTINEZ, A. GARCIA, J.-M. CARRETERO, AND E. CARBONELL. 1993. Three new human skulls from the Sima de los Huesos Middle Pleistocene site in Sierra de Atapuerca, Spain. *Nature* 362:534–537.

BILSBOROUGH, A. 1979. Reply to "Implications of Border cave skeletal remains for later Pleistocene human evolution." *Current Anthropology* 20:27.

BUTZER, K. 1970. Review of H. de Lumley. *American Anthropologist* 762:1172.

CLARK, W. L. G. 1967. *Fossil Evidence for Human Evolution.* Chicago: University of Chicago Press.

COON, C. 1962. *The Origin of Races.* New York: Alfred A. Knopf.

DE LUMLEY, H. 1969. A Paleolithic camp at Nice. *Scientific American* 220:42–50.

DE LUMLEY, H., AND M. DE LUMLEY. 1973. Pre-Neanderthal human remains from Arago cave in southeastern France. *Yearbook of Physical Anthropology* 17:162–168.

DE LUMLEY, H., AND A. SONAKIA. 1985. Contexte stratigraphique et archeologique de l'homme de la Narmada, Hathnora, Madhya Pradesh, Inde. *L'Anthropologie* 89:3–12.

DOROZYNSKI, A. 1993. Possible Neandertal ancestor found. *Science* 262:991.

GRÚN, R., J. BRINK, J. SPOONER, L. TAYLOR, C. STRINGER, R. FRANCISCUS, AND A. MURRAY. 1996. Direct dating of Florisbad hominid. *Nature* 382:500–501.

HARMON, R., J. GLAZEK, AND K. NOWACK. 1980. ^{230}Th/^{234}U dating of travertine from the Bilzingsleben archaeological site. *Nature* 248:132–135.

HEMMER, H. 1972. Notes sur la position phylétique de l'homme de Petralona. *L'Anthropologie* 76:155.

HENNIG, G., W. HERR, E. WEBER, AND X. XIROTIRIS. 1981. ESR-dating of the fossil hominid cranium from Petralona cave, Greece. *Nature* 292:533–536.

HOFFMAN, M. 1991. Handaxe throws light on European prehistory. *Science* 253:515.

HOWELLS, W. 1973. *Evolution of the Genus* Homo. Reading, MA: Addison-Wesley.

HOWELLS, W. 1980. *Homo-erectus*—who, when and where: A survey. *Yearbook of Physical Anthropology* 23:1–24.

KENNEDY, K., A. SONAKIA, K. CHIMENT, AND P. VERMA. 1991. Is the Narmada hominid an Indian *Homo erectus*? *American Journal of Physical Anthropology* 66:475–496.

KLEIN, R. 1973. Geological antiquity of Rhodesian man. *Nature* 244:331.

KURTÉN, B. 1983. The age of Petralona man. *Anthropos* 10:16–17.

LEAKEY, L. 1966. *Homo habilis, Homo erectus* and the australopithecines. *Nature* 209:1279–1281.

LEWIN, R. 1986. Recognizing ancestors is a species problem. *Science* 234:1500.

LU, ZU'ER. 1984. How *Homo erectus* was found. *China Daily*, November 30, p. 5.

MARSCHAK, A. 1972. *The Roots of Civilization.* New York: McGraw-Hill.

MURRILL, R. 1981. *Petralona Man. A Descriptive and Comparative Study, with New Information on Rhodesian Man.* Springfield, IL.: Charles C. Thomas Co.

MURRILL, R. 1983. On the dating of the fossil hominid Petralona skull. *Anthropos* 10:12–15.

OAKLEY, K. 1952. Swanscombe man. *Proceedings of Geological Association of London* 63:271.

OVEY, C., ED. 1964. *The Swanscombe Skull: A Survey of Research on a Pleistocene Site.* London: Royal Anthropological Institute.

PILBEAM, D. 1975. Middle Pleistocene hominids. In *After the Australopithecines,* ed. K. Butzer and G. Isaac. The Hague: Mouton.

RIGHTMIRE, P. 1979. Cranial remains of *Homo erectus* from Beds II and IV, Olduvai Gorge, Tanzania. *American Journal of Physical Anthropology* 51:99–116.

SHREEVE, J. 1994. Infants, cannibals, and the Pit of Bones. *Discover*, January: 39–41.

STRINGER, C. 1993. Secrets of the Pit of the Bones. *Nature* 362:501–502.

TATTERSALL, I. 1986. Species recognition in human paleontology. *Journal of Human Evolution* 15:165.

VELO, J. 1984. Ochre as medicine: A suggestion for the interpretation of the archaeological record. *Current Anthropology* 25:674.

VLČEK, E. 1978. A new discovery of *Homo erectus* in central Europe. *Journal of Human Evolution* 7:239–252.

WHITE, T. 1986. Cut marks on the Bodo cranium: A case of prehistoric defleshing. *American Journal of Physical Anthropology* 69:503–509.

WOLPOFF, M. 1980. *Paleoanthropology.* New York: Alfred A. Knopf.

WU, X., AND F. E. POIRIER. 1995. *Human Evolution in China: A Metric Description of the Fossils and a Review of the Sites.* New York: Oxford University Press.

CHAPTER 12

AKAZAWA, T., S. MUHESEN, Y. DODO, O. KONDON, AND Y. MIZOGUCHI. 1995. Neanderthal infant burial. *Nature* 33:585–686.

ANDERSON, C. 1989. Neanderthal pelves and gestation length: Hypotheses and holism in paleoanthropology. *American Anthropologist* 91:327–340.

BINFORD, L., AND S. BINFORD. 1966. A preliminary analysis of functional variability in the Mousterian of Levallois facies. In *Recent Studies in Paleoanthropology* (*American Anthropologist* special publication).

BINFORD, S. 1968. Early Upper Pleistocene adaptations in the Levant. *American Anthropologist* 70:707.

BORDES, F. 1953. Notules de typologie paleolithique. I. Outils mousteriens a fracture volontaire. *Bulletin de la Société Prehistorique Francaise* 50.

BORDES, F. 1961. Mousterian cultures in France. *Science* 134:803.

BORDES, F. 1972. *A Tale of Two Caves.* New York: Harper & Row.

BOUCHUD, J. 1954. Le renne et le problème des migrations. *L'Anthropologie* 58:79.

BOULE, M. 1912/1913. *L'Homme Fossile de La Chapelle-aux-Saints.* Paris: Masson & Cie.

BOULE, M., AND H. VALLOIS. 1957. *Fossil Man.* New York: Dryden Press.

BRACE, C. 1962a. Cultural factors in the evolution of the human dentition. In *Culture and the Evolution of Man,* ed. A. Montagu. New York: Oxford University Press.

BRACE, C. 1962b. Refocusing on the Neanderthal problem. *American Anthropologist* 64:729–741.

BRACE, C. 1964. The fate of the "classic" Neanderthals: A consideration of hominid catastrophism. *Current Anthropology* 65:3–34.

BRACE, C. 1967. More on the fate of the "classic" Neanderthals. *Current Anthropology* 7:204.

BRACE, C. 1968a. Neanderthal. *Natural History* 77:38.

BRACE, C. 1968b. Ridiculed, rejected, but still our ancestor, Neanderthal. *Natural History* 77:38–42.

BRACE, C. 1971. Digging Shanidar. *Natural History* 80:82.

BRAUER, G. 1984. The "Afro-European *sapiens* hypothesis," and hominid evolution in East Asia during the late Middle and Upper Pleistocene. In *The Early Evolution of Man,* ed. P. Andrews and J. Franzen. Frankfurt: Senckenberg Museum.

BREITINGER, E. 1955. Das schadelfragment vox Swanscombe und das "Praesapiens-problem." *Mitteilungen der Anthropologischen Gesellschaft in Wein* 1:84–85.

BREITINGER, E. 1957. Zur phyletischen evolution von *Homo sapiens. Anthropologischer Anzeiger* 21:62.

BROSE, D., AND M. WOLPOFF. 1971. Early Upper Paleolithic man and late Paleolithic tools. *American Anthropologist* 73:1156–1194.

BROTHWELL, D. 1961. The people of Mount Carmel. *Proceedings of the Prehistoric Society* 37:155.

BUTZER, K. 1971. *Environment and Archaeology: An Ecological Approach to Prehistory,* 2nd ed. Chicago: Aldine-Atherton.

CAMPBELL, B. 1966. *Human Evolution.* Chicago: Aldine-Atherton.

CHASE, P., AND H. DIBBLE. 1987. Middle Paleolithic symbolism: A review of current evidence and interpretations. *Journal of Anthropological Archaeology.* 6:262–296.

CHURCHILL, S., AND E. TRINKAUS. 1990. Neanderthal scapular glenoid morphology. *American Journal of Physical Anthropology* 83:147–160.

CLARK, W. L. G. 1967. *Fossil Evidence for Human Evolution.* Chicago: University of Chicago Press.

COON, C. 1962. *The Origin of Races.* New York: Alfred A. Knopf.

CORNWALL, I. 1968. *Prehistoric Animals and Their Hunters.* New York: Praeger Publishers.

DEMES, B. 1987. Another look at an old face: Biomechanics of the Neandertal facial skeleton reconsidered. *Journal of Human Evolution* 16:297–303.

DENNELL, R. 1983. A new chronology for the Mousterian. *Nature* 301:199–200.

FISCHMAN, J. 1992. Hard evidence. *Discover*, February: 44–51.

FRAYER, D. 1985. Review of E. Trinkaus, *The Shanidar Neanderthals. American Journal of Physical Anthropology* 66:334.

GORJANOVIC-KRAMBERGER, K. 1906. *Der diluviale Mensch von Krapina in Kroatien.* Wiesbaden: W. Kreidels.

GRAVES, P. 1991. New models and metaphors for the Neanderthal debate. *Current Anthropology* 32:513–542.

GREENE, D., AND L. SIBLEY. 1986. Neanderthal pubic morphology and gestation length revisited. *Current Anthropology* 27:517–518.

HENRI-MARTIN, G. 1951. Remarques sur la stratigraphie de Fontéchevade. *L'Anthropologie* 55:242.

HIGGS, E., AND D. BROTHWELL. 1961. North Africa and Mount Carmel: Recent developments. *Man* 61:138.

HOLLIDAY, T. 1997. Cold adaptation in Neandertals. *American Journal of Physical Anthropology* 104:245–258.

HOWELL, F. 1951. The place of Neanderthal man in human evolution. *American Journal of Physical Anthropology* 9:379.

HOWELL, F. 1957. Pleistocene glacial ecology and the evolution of "classical" Neanderthal man. *Quarterly Review of Biology* 32:330.

HOWELL, F. 1960. European and northwestern African Middle Pleistocene hominids. *Current Anthropology* 1:195–232.

HOWELL, F. 1965. *Early Man*. New York: Time-Life Books.

HOWELLS, W. 1967. *Mankind in the Making: The Story of Human Evolution*. Garden City, NY: Doubleday.

HOWELLS, W. 1974a. L'homme de Neanderthal. *La Recherche* 5:634–642.

HOWELLS, W. 1974b. Neanderthals: Names, hypotheses and scientific method. *American Anthropologist* 76:24–38.

HOWELLS, W. 1976. Explaining modern man: Evolutionist versus migrationist. *Journal of Human Evolution* 5:477.

HRDLIČKA, A. 1927. The Neanderthal phase of man, *Journal of the Royal Anthropological Institute of Great Britain and Ireland* 57:249–274.

HUBLIN, J., F. SPOOR, M. BRAUN, F. ZONNEVELD, AND S. CONDEMI. 1996. A late Neanderthal associated with Upper Paleolithic artefacts. *Nature* 381:224–226.

HUBLIN, J., E. TRINKAUS, AND V. STEFAN. 1998. The Mousterian human remains from Zafarray (Andalucia, Spain). *American Journal of Physical Anthropology*, Suppl. 26:122.

JELINEK, J. 1969. Neanderthal man and *Homo sapiens* in central and eastern Europe. *Current Anthropology* 10:475.

JELINEK, J. 1976. A contribution to the origin of *Homo sapiens sapiens*. *Journal of Human Evolution* 5:207.

JOLLY, C., AND F. PLOG. 1976. *Physical Anthropology and Archaeology*. New York: Alfred A. Knopf.

KAHN, P., AND A. GIBBONS. 1997. DNA from an extinct human. *Science* 277:176–178.

KEITH, A. 1925. *The Antiquity of Man*, 2nd ed. London: Williams & Norgate.

KEITH, A., AND T. MCCOWN. 1939. *The Stone Age of Mount Carmel*, vol. 2. Oxford: Clarendon Press.

KENNEDY, K. 1975. *Neanderthal Man*. Minneapolis: Burgess.

KOLATA, G. 1974. The demise of the Neanderthals: Was language a factor? *Science* 186:618–619.

KRINGS, M., A. STONE, R. SCHMITZ, H. KRAINITZI, M. STONEKING, AND S. PÄÄBO. 1997. Neandertal DNA sequences and the origin of modern humans. *Cell* 90:19–30.

KURTÉN, B. 1976. *The Cave Bear Story*. New York: Columbia University Press.

LEMAY, M. 1975. The language capability of Neanderthal man. *American Journal of Physical Anthropology* 42:9.

LEROI-GOURHAN, A. 1975. The flowers found with Shanidar IV, a Neanderthal burial in Iraq. *Science* 190:562.

LEWIN, R. 1986. A new look at an old fossil face. *Science* 234:1326.

LEWIN, R. 1988. Modern human origins under close scrutiny. *Science* 239:1240–1241.

LEWIN, R. 1996. *The Origin of Modern Humans*. New York: W. H. Freeman.

LIEBERMAN, P., AND E. CRELIN. 1971. On the speech of Neanderthal man. *Linguistic Inquiry* 2:203.

LIEBERMAN, P., AND E. CRELIN. 1974. Speech and Neanderthal man: A reply to Carlisle and Siegel. *American Anthropologist* 76:323.

LINDAHL, T. 1997. Facts and artifacts of ancient DNA. *Cell* 90:1–3.

MALEZ M., F. SMITH, F. RADOVCIC, AND D. RUKAVINA. 1980. Upper Pleistocene hominids from Vindija, Croatia, Yugoslavia. *Current Anthropology* 21:365.

MANN, A., AND E. TRINKAUS. 1973. Neanderthal and Neanderthal-like fossils from the Upper Pleistocene. *Yearbook of Physical Anthropology* 17:169–193.

MARSCHACK, A. 1989. Evolution of the human capacity: The symbolic evidence. *Yearbook of Physical Anthropology* 32:1–34.

MCCOWN, T., AND A. KEITH. 1939. *The Stone Age of Mount Carmel*, Vol. 2. *The Fossil Human Remains from the Levalloiso-Mousterian*. Oxford: Clarendon Press.

MELLARS, P. 1986. A new chronology for the French Mousterian period. *Nature* 322:410–411.

MERCIER, N., H. VALLADAS, J-I. REYSS, F. LÉVÊQUE, AND B. VANDERMEERSCH. 1991. Thermoluminescence dating of the late Neanderthal remains from Saint-Césaire. *Nature* 351:737–739.

PATTE, E. 1955. *Les Neanderthaliens*. Paris: Masson & Cie.

PFEIFFER, J. 1969. *The Emergence of Man*. New York: Harper & Row.

PROETZ, A. 1953. *Essays on the Applied Physiology of the Nose*, 2nd ed. St. Louis: Annals.

RAK, Y. 1986. The Neanderthal: A new look at an old face. *Journal of Human Evolution* 15:151–164.

RAK, Y. 1990. On the differences between two pelvises of Mousterian context from the Qafzeh and Kebara Caves, Israel. *American Journal of Physical Anthropology* 81:323–333.

RAK, Y., AND B. ARENSBURG. 1987. Kebara 2 Neanderthal pelvis: First look at a complete inlet. *American Journal of Physical Anthropology* 73:227–231.

ROTHSCHILD, B., AND P. THILLAUD. 1991. Oldest bone disease. *Nature* 349:283.

RUSSELL, M. 1987a. Bone breakage in the Krapina hominid collection. *American Journal of Physical Anthropology* 72:373–379.

RUSSELL, M. 1987b. Mortuary practices at the Krapina Neanderthal site. *American Journal of Physical Anthropology* 72:381–397.

SANTA LUCA, A. 1978. A re-examination of presumed Neanderthal fossils. *Journal of Human Evolution* 7:619–636.

SCHOENINGER, M. 1982. Diet and evolution of modern human form in the Middle East. *American Journal of Physical Anthropology* 58:37–53.

SCHWARCZ, H., R. GRUN, B. VANDERMEERSCH, O. BAR-YOSEF, H. VALLADAS, AND E. TCHERNOV. 1988. ESR dates for the hominid burial site of Qafzeh in Israel. *Journal of Human Evolution* 17:733–737.

SCHWARCZ, H., AND OTHERS. 1991. On the reexamination of Grotta Guattari: Uranium-series and electron-spin-resonance dates. *Current Anthropology* 32:313–316.

SERGI, S. 1967. The Neanderthal Palaeanthropi in Italy. In *Ideas on Human Evolution: Selected Essays*, 1949–61, ed. W. Howells. New York: Atheneum.

SMITH, F. 1976. Dental pathology in fossil hominids: What did Neanderthals do with their teeth? *Current Anthropology* 17:149–150.

SMITH, F. 1982. Upper Pleistocene hominid evolution in south central Europe: A review of the evidence and analysis of trends. *Current Anthropology* 23:667–686.

SOLECKI, R. 1960. Three adult Neanderthal skeletons from Shanidar cave in northern Iraq. *Smithsonian Report*, Publication 4414:603–635.

SOLECKI, R. 1971. *Shanidar: The First Flower People*. New York: Alfred A. Knopf.

SOLECKI, R. 1989. On the evidence for Neanderthal burial. *Current Anthropology* 30:324.

STEEGMANN, A. 1970. Cold adaptation and the human face. *American Journal of Physical Anthropology* 23:243.

STEEGMANN, A. 1972. Cold response, body form, craniofacial shape in two racial groups of Hawaii. *American Journal of Physical Anthropology* 37:193–221.

STEWART, T. 1958a. First views of the restored Shanidar I skull. *Sumer* 14:90.

STEWART, T. 1958b. Restoration and study in Baghdad, Iraq. *Yearbook of the American Philosophical Society*, pp. 274–278.

STEWART, T. 1958c. The restored Shanidar I skull. *Smithsonian Report*, Publication 4369:473–478.

STEWART, T. 1961. The skull of Shanidar II. *Sumer* 17:97.

STEWART, T. 1962. Neanderthal scapulae with special attention to the Shanidar Neanderthals from Iraq. *Anthropos* 57:778.

STEWART, T. 1963. Shanidar skeletons IV and VI. *Sumer* 19:8.

STINER, M. 1991. The faunal remains from Grotta Guattari: A taphonomic perspective. *Current Anthropology* 2:103–117.

STRAUS, W., AND A. CAVE. 1957. Pathology and the posture of Neanderthal man. *Quarterly Review of Biology* 32:340–363.

STRINGER, C. 1984. Fate of the Neanderthal. *Natural History*, December 6–12.

STRINGER, C. 1987. The dates of Eden. *Nature* 331:565–566.

STRINGER, C. 1990. The emergence of modern humans. *Scientific American*, December: 98–104.

STRINGER, C., AND P. ANDREWS. 1988. Genetic and fossil evidence for the origin of modern humans. *Science* 239:1263–1268.

STRINGER, C., AND C. GAMBLE. 1996. *In Search of the Neanderthals: Solving the Puzzle of Human Origins*. New York: Thames and Hudson.

STRINGER, C., AND R. GRÜN. 1991. Time for the last Neanderthals. *Nature* 351:701–702.

STRINGER, C., R. GRÜN, H. SCHWARCZ, AND P. GOLDBERG. 1989. ESR dates for the hominid burial site of Es-Skhūl in Israel. *Nature* 338:756–758.

STRINGER, C., J. HUBLIN, AND B. VANDERMEERSCH. 1984. The origin of anatomically modern humans in Western Europe. In *The Origin of Modern Humans*, ed. F. Smith and F. Spencer. New York: Alan R. Liss.

TAPPEN, N. 1985. The dentition of the "old man" of La Chapelle-aux-Saints and inferences concerning Neanderthal behavior. *American Journal of Physical Anthropology* 67:43–45.

TILLIER, A-M. 1988. Croissance et development chez les Neandertaliens. *Dossiers Historie et Archeologie* 124:34–39.

TRINKAUS, E. 1973. A reconsideration of the Fontéchevade fossils. *American Journal of Physical Anthropology* 39:25.

TRINKAUS, E. 1978. Hard times among the Neanderthals. *Natural History* 87:58–63.

TRINKAUS, E. 1982a. Artificial cranial deformation in the Shanidar 1 and 5 Neanderthals. *Current Anthropology* 23:198–199.

TRINKAUS, E. 1982b. The Shanidar 3 Neanderthal. *American Journal of Physical Anthropology* 57:37–60.

TRINKAUS, E. 1983. *The Shanidar Neanderthals*. New York: Academic Press.

TRINKAUS, E. 1984. Neanderthal pubic morphology and gestation length. *Current Anthropology* 25:509–514.

TRINKAUS, E. 1985a. Pathology and the posture of the La Chapelle-aux-Saints Neanderthal. *American Journal of Physical Anthropology* 67:19–42.

TRINKAUS, E. 1985b. Cannibalism and burial at Krapina. *Journal of Human Evolution* 14:203–216.

TRINKAUS, E. 1986. The Neandertals and modern human origins. *Annual Review of Anthropology* 15:193–218.

TRINKAUS, E. 1987. The Neandertal face: Evolutionary and functional perspective on a recent hominid face. *Journal of Human Evolution* 16:429–443.

TRINKAUS, E., AND M. LeMAY. 1982. Occipital bunning among later Pleistocene hominids. *American Journal of Physical Anthropology* 57:27–35.

TRINKAUS, E., AND M. ZIMMERMAN. 1982. Trauma among the Shanidar Neanderthals. *American Journal of Physical Anthropology* 57:61–76.

VALLADAS, H., J. GENESTE, J. JORON, AND J. CHADELLE. 1986. Thermoluminescence dating of Le Moustier (Dordogne, France). *Nature* 32:452–454.

VALLADAS, H., J. REYSS, J. JORON, G. VALLADAS, AND OTHERS. 1987a. Thermoluminescence dating of Mousterian Proto-Cro-Magnon remains from Israel and the origin of modern man. *Nature* 331:644–646.

VALLADAS, H., J. REYSS, J. JORON, G. VALLADAS, AND OTHERS. 1987b. Thermoluminescence dates for the Neanderthal burial site at Kebara in Israel. *Nature* 330:359–360.

VALLOIS, H. 1949a. The Fontéchevade man. *American Journal of Physical Anthropology* 7:339.

VALLOIS, H. 1949b. L'Origine de l'*Homo sapiens*. *Comptes-rendus Hebdomadaires des Seances de l'Académie des Sciences* (Paris) 228:949.

VALLOIS, H. 1952. Monophyletism and polyphyletism in man. *South African Journal of Science* 49:69.

VALLOIS, H. 1954. Neandertháls and Presapiens. *Journal of the Royal Anthropological Institute* 84:11.

VALLOIS, H. 1958. La Grotte de Fontéchevade: Anthropologie (deuxieme partie). *Archives de l'Institut de Paleontologie Humaine*, Memoire 29:5.

WANG, S. 1980. Discoveries and expectations for the remains of anthropoids and human beings in Hubei Province. *Jiang-Han Archaeology* 2:1–6 (in Chinese).

WARD, R., AND C. STRINGER. 1997. A molecular handle on the Neanderthals. *Nature* 388:225–226.

WHITE, T., AND N. TOTH. 1991. The question of ritual cannibalism at Grotta Guattari. *Current Anthropology* 2:118–124.

WOLPOFF, M. 1968. Climatic influence on the skeletal nasal aperture. *American Journal of Physical Anthropology* 29:405–424.

WOLPOFF, M. 1971a. *Metric Trends in Hominid Dental Evolution*. Cleveland: Case Western Reserve University Studies in Anthropology 2.

WOLPOFF, M. 1971b. Vértesszöllös and the Presapiens theory. *American Journal of Physical Anthropology* 35:209.

WOLPOFF, M. 1979. The Krapina dental remains. *American Journal of Physical Anthropology* 50:67.

WOLPOFF, M. 1980. *Paleoanthropology*. New York: Alfred A. Knopf, Inc.

WONG, K. 1997. Neanderthal notes. *Scientific American*, September: 28–29.

ZILBERMAN, U., M. SKINNER, AND P. SMITH. 1992. Tooth components of mandibular deciduous molars of *Homo sapiens* and *Homo sapiens neanderthalensis*: A radiographic study. *American Journal of Physical Anthropology* 87:255–262.

CHAPTER 13

ADOVASIO, J., AND R. CARLISLE. 1984. An Indian hunter's camp for 20,000 years. *Scientific American* May:130–136.

ADOVASIO, J., AND R. CARLISLE. 1988. The Meadowcroft Rock Shelter. *Science* 239:713–714.

AIGNER, J. 1984. The Asiatic–New World continuum in late Pleistocene times. In *The Evolution of the East Asian Environment*, Vol. 2, ed. R. O. Whyte. Hong Kong: University of Hong Kong.

ALTHEIDE, T., AND M. HAMMER. 1997. Evidence for a possible Asian origin of YAP + Y chromosomes. *American Journal of Human Genetics* 61:462–466.

AMATO, I. 1993. American family tree gets new root. *Science* 260:22.

APPENZELLER, T. 1992. A high five from the first New World settlers? *Science* 255:920–921.

AYALA, F. 1995. The myth of Eve: Molecular biology and human origins. *Science* 270:1930–1936.

BADA, J., AND H. HELFFMAN. 1975. Amino acid racemization dating of fossil bones. *World Archaeology* 7:160.

BADA, J., R. SCHROEDER, AND G. CARTER. 1974. New evidence for the antiquity of man in North America deduced from aspartic acid racemization. *Science* 184:791–793.

BAHN, P. 1985. Ice age drawings on open rock faces in the Pyrenees. *Nature* 313:530–531.

BAHN, P. 1990. Pigments of the imagination. *Nature* 347:426.

BAHN, P. 1996a. Further back down under. *Nature* 383:577–578.

BAHN, P. 1996b. New developments in Pleistocene art. *Evolutionary Anthropology* 4:204–215.

BAILEY, G. 1982. Late Pleistocene life in Tasmania. *Nature* 301:30.

BARBETTI, M., AND H. ALLEN. 1972. Prehistoric man at Lake Mungo, Australia, by 32,000 years B.C. *Nature* 240:46.

BARINAGA, M. 1992. "African Eve" backers beat a retreat. *Science* 255:686–687.

BORDEN, C. 1979. Peopling and early cultures of the Pacific Northwest. *Science* 203:963–971.

BORDES, F. 1958. Le passage du Paléolithique moyen au Paléolithique superieu. In *Neanderthal Centenary*, ed. R. Von Koenigswald. Utrecht: Kemink en Zoon.

BOWLER, J., A. THORNE, AND H. POLACH. 1972. Pleistocene man in Australia: Age and significance of Mungo skeleton. *Nature* 240:48.

BRAÜER, G. 1984a. A craniological approach to the origin of anatomically modern *Homo sapiens* in Africa and implications for the appearance of modern Europeans. In *The Origins of Modern Humans*, ed. F. Smith and F. Spencer. New York: Alan R. Liss, Inc.

BRAÜER, G. 1984b. The Afro-european sapiens hyphothesis and hominid evolution in Asia during the Middle and Upper Pleistocene. In *The Early Evolution of Man*, ed. P. Andrews and G. Franzen. Senckenberg: Courier Forschunginstitut Senckenberg.

BRAÜER, G. 1984c. Presapiens-hypothese oder Afro-europäische Sapiens-hypothese. *Zeitschrift Morpologie Anthropologie.* 75:1–25.

BRAY, W. 1986. Finding the earliest Americans. *Nature* 321:726.

BROOKS, A., AND MULTIPLE COAUTHORS. 1995. Dating and context of three Middle Stone Age sites with bone points in the Upper Semliki Valley, Zaire. *Science* 268:548–553.

BROTHWELL, D. 1961. Upper Pleistocene human skull from Niah caves, Sarawak. *Sarawak Museum Journal* 9:323–349.

BRYAN, A. 1969. Early man in America and the late Pleistocene chronology of western Canada and Alaska. *Current Anthropology* 10:339.

BUSCH, L. 1994a. A glimmer of hope for coastal migration. *Science* 263:1088–1089.

BUSCH, L. 1994b. Alaska sites contend as Native Americans' first stop. *Science* 264:347.

BUSHNELL, G., AND C. MCBURNEY. 1959. New World origins as seen from the Old World. *Antiquity* 33:93.

BUTZER, K. 1964. *Environment and Archeology*. Chicago: Aldine-Atherton.

CANN, R., M. STONEKING, AND A. WILSON. 1987. Mitochondrial DNA and human evolution. *Nature* 325:31–37.

CHARD, C. 1959. New World origins: A reappraisal. *Antiquity* 33:44.

CHARD, C. 1963. The Old World roots: Review and speculations. *Anthropological Papers of the University of Alaska* 10:115.

CHURCHILL, S., O. PERSON, F. GRINE, E. TRINKAUS, AND T. HOLLIDAY. 1996. Morphological affinities of the proximal ulna from Klasies River Main Site: Archaic or modern? *Journal of Human Evolution* 31:213–237.

CIGLIANO, E. 1962. *Le Ampajanguese*. Universidad Nacional del Litorae, Instituto de Anthropologia no. 5.

CLARK, G. 1967. *The Stone Age Hunters*. New York: McGraw-Hill.

CLARK, J. 1960. Human ecology during the Pleistocene and later times in Africa south of the Sahara. *Current Anthropology* 1:307.

CLOTTES, J. 1995. Rhinos and lions and bears (Oh, My!). *Natural History*, May: 30–34.

CONKEY, M. 1981. Altamira: The study of Paleolithic art. *L.S.B. Leakey Foundation Newsletter* 21:16–18.

COOK, H. 1927. New geological and palaeontological evidence bearing on the antiquity of mankind in America. *Natural History* 27:240.

COON, C. 1962. *The Origin of Races*. New York: Alfred A. Knopf.

COSGROVE, R. 1989. Thirty thousand years of human colonization in Tasmania: New Pleistocene dates. *Science* 243:1706–1708.

COSGROVE, R. 1995. The fall and rise of the Tasmanians. *Natural History*, August: 32.

COTTER, J. 1937. The occurrence of flints and extinct animals in pluvial deposits near Clovis, New Mexico, IV. Report on the excavations at the gravel pit in 1936. *Proceedings of the Philadelphia Academy of Natural Sciences* 89:2.

CRESSMAN, L., AND S. BEDWELL. 1968. *Report to the Secretary of the Department of the Interior on archaeological research on public lands in northern Lake County, Oregon*.

DAUGHERTY, R. 1956. Archaeology of the Lind Coulee site, Washington. *Proceedings of the American Philosophical Society* 100:223.

DAY, M. 1969. Omo human skeletal remains. *Nature* 222:1135–1138.

DAY, M. 1971. The Omo human skeletal remains. In *The Origin of Homo sapiens*, ed. F. Bordes. Paris: UNESCO.

DAY, M., M. LEAKEY, AND C. MAGORI. 1980. A new hominid skull (L.H. 18) from the Ngaloba Beds, northern Tanzania. *Nature* 284:55–56.

DEACON, H., AND V. GELEIJINSE. 1988. The stratigraphy and sedimentology of the mainsite sequence, Klasies River, South Africa. *South African Archaeological Bulletin* 43:5–14.

DEGARMO, G. 1970. Big game hunters: An alternative and a hypothesis. Paper presented at the Thirty-fifth Annual Meeting of the Society for American Archaeology, Mexico City.

DENNELL, R. 1986. Needles and spear-throwers. *Natural History*, October: 70–78.

DIAMOND, J. 1987. Who were the first Americans? *Nature* 329:580–581.

DIAMOND, J. 1993. Drowning dogs and the dawn of art. *Natural History* 3:23–29.

DILLEHAY, T. 1989. *Paleoenvironment and Site Context*, Vol. 1 of *Monte Verde: A Late Pleistocene Settlement in Chile*. Washington, DC: Smithsonian.

DILLEHAY, T., ED. 1997. *The Archaeological Context*, Vol. 2 of *Monte Verde: A Late Pleistocene Settlement in Chile*. Washington, DC: Smithsonian.

DRENNAN, M. 1929. An Australoid skull from Cape Flats. *Journal of the Royal Anthropological Institute* 59:417.

DUBOIS, E. 1921. The proto-Australian fossil man of Wadjak, Java. *Proceedings: Koninklijke Nederlandse Akademie van Wetenschappen* 23:1013.

DUNCAN, R. 1972. The Cohise culture. Master's thesis, University of California, Los Angeles.

ECKHARDT, R. 1991. Fish scales for human origins. *Nature* 349:112.

EISELEY, L. 1955. The Paleo-Indians: Their survival and diffusion. In *New Interpretations of Aboriginal American Culture History* (anniversary volume of Anthropological Society of Washington), pp. 1–11.

FENNER, F. 1944. Fossil skull fragments of probable Pleistocene age from Aitape, New Guinea. *Records of the South Australian Museum* 6:335.

FIGGINS, J. 1927. The antiquity of man in America. *Natural History* 27:229.

FISCHMAN, J. 1996. Evidence mounts of our African origins— and alternatives. *Science* 271:1364.

FLADMARK, K. 1979. Routes: Alternative migration corridors for early man in North America. *American Antiquity* 44:55–69.

FLADMARK, K. 1986. Getting one's bearings. *Natural History* 95:8–19.

FORBIS, R., AND J. SPERRY. 1952. An early man site in Montana. *American Antiquity* 18:127.

FREEMAN, L., R. KLEIN, AND J. ECHEGARAY. 1983. A Stone Age sanctuary. *Natural History* 92:47–52.

GIBBONS, A. 1993a. Pleistocene population explosions. *Science* 262:27–28.

GIBBONS, A. 1993b. Geneticists trace the DNA trail of the first Americans. *Science* 259:312–313.

GIBBONS, A. 1995. Old dates for modern behavior. *Science* 268:495–496.

GIBBONS, A. 1997a. Ideas on human origins evolve at anthropology gathering. *Science* 276:535–536.

GIBBONS, A. 1997b. Y chromosome shows Adam was an African. *Science* 278:804–805.

GIBBONS, A. 1998. Calibrating the mitochondrial clock. *Science* 279:28–29.

GREENBERG, J. 1986. *Language in the Americas*. Stanford, CA: Stanford University Press.

GREENMAN, E. 1963. The Upper Paleolithic and the New World. *Current Anthropology* 4:41.

GRIFFIN, J. 1960. Some prehistoric connections between Siberia and America. *Science* 131:801.

GRINE, F., AND R. KLEIN. 1985. Pleistocene and Holocene human remains from Equus Cave, South Africa. *Anthropology* 8:55–98.

GROUBE, L., J. CHAPPELL, J. MUKE, AND D. PRICE. 1986. A 40,000-year-old human occupation site at Huon Peninsula, Papua New Guinea. *Nature* 324:453–455.

GRUHN, R. 1965. Two early radiocarbon dates from the lower levels of Wilson Butte cave, south central Idaho. *Tebiwa* 8:57.

GRÜN, R, N. SHACKELTON, AND H. DEACON. 1990. Electron-spin resonance dating of tooth enamel from Klasies River Mouth Cave. *Current Anthropology* 31:427–432.

GUIDON, N. 1987. Cliff notes. *Natural History* 96:6–12.

GUIDON, N., AND G. DELIORIAS. 1986. Carbon-14 dates point to man in the Americas 32,000 years ago. *Nature* 231:769–771.

GUILDAY, J. 1967. Differential extinction during late Pleistocene and recent times. In *Pleistocene Extinctions: The Search for a Cause*, eds. P. Martin and H. Wright. New Haven, CT: Yale University Press.

HAAG, W. 1962. The Bering Strait land bridge. *Scientific American* 206:112–123.

HABGOOD, P. 1986. A late Pleistocene prehistory of Australia: The skeletal material. *Physical Anthropology News* 5:1–5.

HALLAM, S. 1977. The relevance of Old World archaeology to the first entry of man into the New Worlds: Colonization seen from the Antipodes. *Quaternary Research* 8:128–148.

HAMMER, M. 1995. A recent common ancestry for human Y chromosomes. *Nature* 378:376–378.

HAMMER, M., A. SPURDLE, T. KARAFET, M. BONNER, E. WOOD, A. NOVELLETTO, P. MALASPINA, R. MITCHELL, S. HORAI, T. JENKINS, AND S. ZEGURA. 1997. The geographic distribution of human Y chromosome variation. *Genetics* 145:787–805.

HARRINGTON, M. 1955. Man's oldest date in America. *Natural History* 64:513, 554.

HAURY, E., ET AL. 1950. *The Stratigraphy and Archaeology of Ventana Cave*, Arizona. Albuquerque: University of New Mexico Press.

HAYNES, C. 1964. Fluted projectile points: their age and dispersion. *Science* 145:1408.

HAYNES, C. 1966. Elephant hunting in North America. *Scientific American*, June: 314.

HAYNES, C. 1967. Muestras de C14. de Tlapocoya Estado De México. *Boletín, Instituto Nacional de Antropología y Historia* 29:49.

HAYNES, C. 1969. The earliest Americans. *Science* 166:709.

HEDGES, S. B., S. KUMAR, K. TAMURA, AND M. STONEKING. 1992. Human origins and analysis of mitochondrial DNA sequences. *Science* 255:737–739.

HRDLIČKA, A. 1925. The origin and antiquity of the American Indian. *Annual report of the Board of Regents, Smithsonian Institution*, pp. 481–494.

IRWIN-WILLIAMS, C. 1967. Associations of early man with horse, camel and mastodon of Hueyatlaco, Valsequello (Puebla, Mexico). In *Pleistocene Extinctions: The Search for a Cause*, ed. P. Martin and H. Wright. New Haven, CT: Yale University Press.

JELINEK, J. 1961. Příspěvek k otázce středo-evropských Neandertálců. [Ein Beitrag zur Frage der Mitteleuropäischen Neanderthaler.] *Anthropos* 14(6): 147.

JELINEK, J. 1969. Neanderthal man and *Homo sapiens* in central and eastern Europe. *Current Anthropology* 10:475.

JENNINGS, J. 1978. Origins. In *Ancient Native Americans*, ed. J. Jennings. San Francisco: W. H. Freeman.

JENNINGS, J., AND E. NORBECK, EDS. 1964. *Prehistoric Man in the New World*. Chicago: University of Chicago Press.

KENNEDY, G. 1984. Are the Kow Swamp hominids "archaic"? *American Journal of Physical Anthropology* 65:163–168.

KIERNAN, K., R. JONES, AND D. RANSON. 1982. New evidence from Fraser cave for glacial age of man in South-west Tasmania. *Nature* 301:28–32.

KLEIN, J., N. TAKAHATA, AND F. AYALA. 1993. MHC polymorphism and human origins. *Scientific American*, December: 78–83.

KLEIN, R. 1969. *Man and Culture in the Late Pleistocene*. San Francisco: Chandler.

KLEIN, R., K. CRUZ-URIBE, AND P. BEAUMONT. 1991. Environmental, ecological, and paleoanthropological implications of the Late Pleistocene mammalian fauna from Equus Cave, North Cape Prov., SA. *Quaternary Research* 36:94–119.

KLIMA, B. 1987. A triple burial from the Upper Paleolithic of Dolni Vèstonice, Czechoslovakia. *Journal of Human Evolution* 16:831–835.

KRAMER, A. 1991. Modern human origins in Australasia: Replacement or evolution? *American Journal of Physical Anthropology* 86:455–473.

KUHN, H. 1929. *Kunst und Kultur der Vorzeit Europas: das Paläolithikum*. Berlin: de Gruyter.

KUNZ, M., AND R. REANIER. 1994. Paleoindians in Beringia: Evidence from arctic Alaska. *Science* 263:660–662.

LAHR, M. 1997. History in the bones. *Evolutionary Anthropology* 6:2–6.

LAHR, M., AND R. FOLEY. 1994. Multiple dispersals and modern human origins. *Evolutionary Anthropology* 3:48–60.

LANNING, E., AND T. PATTERSON. 1967. Early man in South America. *Scientific American*, November: 44.

LEAKEY, L. 1935. *The Stone Age Races of Kenya*. London: Oxford University Press.

LEROI-GOURHAN, A. 1965. *Préhistoire de l'art*. Paris: Mazenod.

LEROI-GOURHAN, A. 1967. *Treasures of Prehistoric Art*. New York: Harry N. Abrams.

LEWIN, R. 1986. Myths and methods in Ice Age art. *Science* 234:936–938.

LEWIN, R. 1987. The first Americans are getting younger. *Science* 238:1230–1232.

LI, T., AND D. ETTLER. 1992. New Middle Pleistocene hominid crania from Yunxian in China. *Nature* 357:404–407.

LIBBY, W. 1955. *Radiocarbon Dating*, 2nd ed. Chicago: University of Chicago Press.

LYNCH, T., R. GILLESPIE, J. GOWLETT, AND R. HEDGES. 1985. Chronology of Guitarrero cave, Peru. *Science* 229:864–867.

LYNCH, T., AND K. KENNEDY. 1970. Early human cultural and skeletal remains from Guitarrero cave, northern Peru. *Science* 169:1307.

MACGOWAN, K., AND J. HESTER. 1962. *Early Man in the New World*. New York: Anchor Books.

MACINTOSH, N. 1952. The Cohuna cranium, history and commentary from Nov. 1925 to Nov. 1951. *Mankind* 4:307.

MACINTOSH, N. 1965. The physical aspect of man in Australia. In *Aboriginal Man in Australia*, ed. E. Berndt and C. Berndt. Sydney: Angus & Robertson (U.K.) Ltd.

MACINTOSH, N. 1967. Fossil man in Australia. *Yearbook of Physical Anthropology* 15:39.

MACNEISH, R. 1976. Early man in the New World. *American Scientist* 64:316–327.

MAHONY, D., W. BARAGWANATH, F. W. JONES, AND A. KENYON. 1936. Fossil man in the state of Victoria, Australia. *International Geological Congress*, pp. 1335–1342.

MARTIN, P. 1987. Clovisia the beautiful! *Natural History*, October: 10–13.

MASON, R. 1962. The Paleo-Indian tradition in eastern North America. *Current Anthropology* 3:227.

MELLARS, P. 1973. The character of the Middle-Upper Paleolithic transition in southwest France. In *The Explanation of Culture Change*, ed. C. Renfrew. London: Duckworth.

MELLARS, P. 1989. Major issues in the emergence of modern humans. *Current Anthropology* 30:349–385.

MELTZER, D. 1997. Monte Verde and the Pleistocene peopling of the Americas. *Science* 276:754–756.

MIRAMBELL, L. 1967. Excavaciones en un sitio Pleistocenio de Tlapocoya, México. *Boletin, Instituto de Antropologia y Historia* 29:37.

MORELL, V. 1990. Confusion in earliest America. *Science* 248:439–441.

MORELL, V. 1995. Siberia: Surprising home for early modern humans. *Science* 268:1279.

MOVIUS, H. 1960. Radiocarbon dates and Upper Paleolithic archeology in central and western Europe. *Current Anthropology* 1:335.

MULVANEY, D. 1969. The prehistory of Australia.

PEI, W., AND J. WOO. 1957. *Tzeyang Paleolithic man*. Institute of Vertebrate Paleontology Memoirs 1.

PFEIFFER, J. 1969. *The Emergence of Man*. New York: Harper & Row.

PFEIFFER, J. 1982. *The Creative Explosion: An Inquiry into the Origins of Art and Religion*. New York: Harper & Row.

PFEIFFER, J. 1983. Was Europe's fabulous cave art the start of the Information Age? *Smithsonian*, April: 36–45.

RIGHTMIRE, G. P. 1975. Problems in the study of later Pleistocene man in Africa. *American Anthropologist* 77:28.

RIGHTMIRE, G. P. 1979. Implications of Border cave skeletal remains for later Pleistocene human evolution. *Current Anthropology* 20:23–26.

RIGHTMIRE, G. P., AND H. DEACON. 1991. Comparative studies of Late Pleistocene human remains from Klasies River Mouth, South Africa. *Journal of Human Evolution* 20:131–156.

ROBERTS, F. 1935. A Folsom complex: Preliminary report on investigations at the Lindenmeier site in northern Colorado. *Smithsonian Miscellaneous Collections* 94.

ROBERTS, F. 1936. Additional information on the Folsom complex: Report on the second season's investigations at the Lindenmeier site in northern Colorado. *Smithsonian Miscellaneous Collections* 95, No. 10.

ROBERTS, F. 1937. New World man. *American Antiquity* 11:172.

SAUTER, M-R. 1957. Etude des vestiges osseux humains des grottes préhistoriques de Farincourt (Hauté-Marne, France). *Archives Suisses d'Anthropologie Générale* 22:6.

SIMPSON, R. 1955. Hunting elephants in Nevada. *The Master-key* (Southwest Museum, Los Angeles) 29:114.

SMITH, F. 1976. A fossil hominid frontal from Velika Pécina (Croatia) and a consideration of Upper Pleistocene hominids from Yugoslavia. *American Journal of Physical Anthropology* 44:127–134.

SMITH, F., D. BOYD, AND M. MALEZ. 1985. Additional Upper Pleistocene human remains from Vindija cave, Croatia, Yugoslavia. *American Journal of Physical Anthropology* 68:375–383.

SMITH, F., G. FALSETTI, AND S. DONNELLY. 1990. Modern human origins. *Yearbook of Physical Anthropology* 32:35–68.

SMITH, M. 1987. Pleistocene occupation in arid central Australia. *Nature* 328:710–711.

SMOLLA, G. 1960. Neolithische Kulturerscheinungen: Studien zur Frage ihrer Herausbildungen. *Antiquitas* 3:1.

SPHULER, J. 1988. Evolution of mitochondrial DNA in monkeys, apes and humans. *Yearbook of Physical Anthropology* 31:15–48.

STEWART, T. 1960. A physical anthropologist's view of the peopling of the New World. *Southwestern Journal of Anthropology* 16:259–273.

STEWART, T. 1973. *The People of America*. New York: Charles Scribner's Sons.

STRINGER, C. 1990. Replacement, continuity, and the origin of *Homo sapiens*. In *Continuity or Replacement: Controversies in Homo sapiens*, ed. G. Braüer and F. Smith. Rotterdam: Balkema.

STRINGER, C., AND P. ANDREWS. 1988. Genetic and fossil evidence for the origin of modern humans. *Science* 239:1263–1268.

SUAREZ, B. ET AL. 1985. Genetic variation to North Amerindian populations: The geography of gene frequencies. *American Journal of Physical Anthropology* 67:217–232.

SVOBODA, J. 1987. A new male burial from Dolni Věstonice. *Journal of Human Evolution* 16:827–830.

TAYLOR, A., L. PAYEN, C. PRIOR, P. SLOTA, AND OTHERS. 1985. Major revisions in the Pleistocene age assignments for North American human skeletons by C-14 accelerator mass spectometry! None older than 11,000 C-14 years B.P. *American Antiquity* 50:136–140.

TAYLOR, R. 1996. Radiocarbon dating: The continuing revolution. *Evolutionary Anthropology* 4:169–181.

TEMPLETON, A. 1992. Human origins and analysis of mitochondrial DNA sequences. *Science* 255:737.

THENIUS, E. 1961. Paläozoologie und Prähistorie. *Mitteilungen der Urgeschichte und Anthropologie Gessellschaft* (Vienna) 12:39.

THORNE, A., AND P. MACUMBER. 1972. Discoveries of late Pleistocene man at Kow Swamp, Australia. *Nature* 238:316.

THORNE, A., AND M. WOLPOFF. 1992. The multiregional evolution of humans. *Scientific American*, April: 76–83.

TISHKOFF, S., AND MULTIPLE COAUTHORS. 1996. Global patterns of linkage disequalibrium at the CD4 locus and modern human origins. *Science* 271:1380–1387.

TURNER, C. 1984. Advances in the dental search for Native American origins. *Acta Anthrogenetica* 8:23–78.

TURNER, C. 1986. The Native Americans: The dental evidence. *National Geographic Research* 2:37–46.

TURNMIRE, K. 1990. Pre-Clovis barrier broken in New Mexico? *Mammoth Trumpet* 6:1, 6, 8.

VALLOIS, H. 1961. The social life of early man. The evidence of skeletons. In *Social Life of Early Man*, ed. S. Washburn. Chicago: Aldine-Atherton.

VIGILANT, L., M. STONEKING, H. HARPENDING, K. HAWKES, AND A. WILSON. 1991. African populations and the evolution of human mitochondrial DNA. *Science* 253:1503–1507.

VLČEK, E. 1961a. Die in Pavlov aufgefundenen Menschenreste aus dem Jungpleistozän. *Památky Archaeologické* 52:46.

VLČEK, E. 1961b. Nouvelles trouvailles de l'homme du Pleistocéne du Pavlov (CSSR). *Anthropos* 14:41.

WAINSCOAT, J. 1987. Out of the garden of Eden. *Nature* 325:13.

WEIDENREICH, F. 1938/1939. On the earliest representatives of modern mankind recovered on the soil of East Asia. *Peking Natural History Bulletin* 13:161.

WEIDENREICH, F. 1943. The skull of *Sinanthropus pekinensis*, a comparative study of a primitive hominoid skull. *Paleontologica Sinica* 127:1–184.

WEIDENREICH, F. 1945. Giant early man from Java and South China. *Anthropological Papers of American Museum of Natural History* 40.

WENDORF, F., AND T. TULLY. 1951. Early man sites near Concho, Arizona. *American Antiquity* 17:107.

WHITE, J., AND J. ALLEN. 1980. Melanesian prehistory: Some recent advances. *Science* 207:728–733.

WHITE, P., AND J. O'CONNELL. 1979. Australian prehistory: New aspects of antiquity. *Science* 203:21–28.

WHITE, R. 1982. Rethinking the Middle/Upper Paleolithic transition. *Current Anthropology* 23:169–192.

WOBST, H. 1977. Stylistic behavior and information exchange. *University of Michigan Museum of Anthropology Papers* 61.

WOLKOMIR, R. 1991. Have archaeologists found the oldest digs yet? *Smithsonian* 21:130–144.

WOLPOFF, M. 1980. *Paleoanthropology*. New York: Alfred A. Knopf, Inc.

WOLPOFF, M. 1990. Theories of modern human origins. In *Continuity or Replacement: Controversies in Homo sapiens*, ed. G. Braüer and F. Smith. Rotterdam: Balkema.

WOLPOFF, M., AND R. CASPARI. 1990. On Middle Paleolithic/Middle Stone Age hominid taxonomy. *Current Anthropology* 31:394–395.

WOLPOFF, M., X. WU, AND A. THORNE, 1984. Modern *Homo sapiens* origins: A general theory of hominid evolution involving the fossil evidence from east Asia. In *The Origins of Modern Humans*, ed. F. Smith and F. Spencer. New York: Alan R. Liss.

WOO, J. 1958. Tzeyang Paleolithic man—earliest representative of modern man in China. *American Journal of Physical Anthropology* 16:459.

WOO, J. 1959. Human fossils found in Liukiang, Kwangsi, China. *Vertebrata Palasiatica* 3:109.

WOOD, B. 1994. The problems of our origins. *Journal of Human Evolution* 27: 519–529.

WORMINGTON, H. 1957. Ancient man in North America. *Denver Museum of Natural History*, No. 4.

WU, X., AND F. POIRIER. 1995. *Human Evolution in China*. New York: Oxford University Press.

WUNDERLEY, J. 1943. The Keilor skull, anatomical description. *Memoires of the National Museum of Melbourne* 13:57.

YELLEN, J., A. BROOKS, E. COMELISSEN, M. MEHLMAN, AND K. STEWART. 1995. A Middle Stone Age bone industry from Katanda, Upper Semliki Valley, Zaire. *Science* 268:553–555.

CHAPTER 14

CARTMILL, M. 1990. Human uniqueness and theoretical content in paleoanthropology. *International Journal of Primatology* 11:173–192.

COMFORT, A. 1966. *The Nature of Human Nature*. New York: Harper & Row.

HALLOWELL, A. 1961. The protocultural foundations of human adaptation. In *Social Life of Early Man*, ed. S. Washburn. Chicago: Aldine-Atherton.

HOLLOWAY, R. 1969. Culture: A human domain. *Current Anthropology* 10:395.

HUTCHINSON, G. 1965. *The Ecological Theater and the Evolutionary Play*. New Haven, CT: Yale University Press.

KROGMAN, W. M. 1951. The scars of human evolution. *Scientific American* 185:54–57.

LIEBERMAN, P. 1975. *On the Origins of Language*. New York: Macmillan.

OAKLEY, K. 1961. *Man the Toolmaker*, 5th ed. London: British Museum (Natural History).

OAKLEY, K. 1967. Tools makyth man. In *Ideas on Human Evolution: Selected Essays, 1949–1961*, ed. W. Howells. New York: Atheneum.

POIRIER, F. 1974. Colobine aggression: A review. In *Primate Aggression, Territoriality and Xenophobia*, ed. R. Holloway. New York: Academic Press.

ROE, A. 1963. Psychological definitions of man. In *Classification and Human Evolution*, ed. S. Washburn. New York: Viking Fund Publications.

SIMPSON, G. 1968. The biological nature of man. In *Perspectives on Human Evolution*, ed. S. Washburn and P. Jay. New York: Holt, Rinehart & Winston.

WASHBURN, S. 1959. Speculations on the interrelations of the history of tools and biological evolution. *Human Biology* 31:21–31.

WASHBURN, S. 1960. Tools and human evolution. *Scientific American* 203:63–75.

WASHBURN, S. 1963. Behavior and human evolution. In *Classification and Human Evolution*, ed. S. Washburn. Chicago: Aldine-Atherton.

WASHBURN, S. 1973. Human evolution: Science or game? *Yearbook of Physical Anthropology* 17:67–70.

Index

377